The Blackwell Companion
to the Hebrew Bible

Blackwell Companions to Religion

The *Blackwell Companions to Religion* series presents a collection of the most recent scholarship and knowledge about world religions. Each volume draws together newly commissioned essays by distinguished authors in the field, and is presented in a style which is accessible to undergraduate students, as well as scholars and the interested general reader. These volumes approach the subject in a creative and forward-thinking style, providing a forum in which leading scholars in the field can make their views and research available to a wider audience.

Published

1. *The Blackwell Companion to Judaism*
Edited by Jacob Neusner and Alan J. Avery-Peck

2. *The Blackwell Companion to Sociology of Religion*
Edited by Richard K. Fenn

3. *The Blackwell Companion to the Hebrew Bible*
Edited by Leo G. Perdue

Forthcoming

The Blackwell Companion to Political Theology
Edited by William T. Cavanaugh and Peter Scott

The Blackwell Companion to Hinduism
Edited by Gavin Flood

The Blackwell Companion to Religious Ethics
Edited by Charles Hallisey and William Schweiker

The Blackwell Companion to Postmodern Theology
Edited by Graham Ward

The Blackwell Companion to Theology
Edited by Gareth Jones

The Blackwell Companion to the Study of Religion
Edited by Robert A. Segal

The Blackwell Companion to the Hebrew Bible

Edited by

Leo G. Perdue
Brite Divinity School
Texas Christian University

BLACKWELL
Publishers

First published 2001

2 4 6 8 10 9 7 5 3 1

Blackwell Publishers Ltd
108 Cowley Road
Oxford OX4 1JF
UK

Blackwell Publishers Inc.
350 Main Street
Malden, Massachusetts 02148
USA

British Library Cataloguing in Publication Data

A CIP catalogue record for this book is available from the British Library.

Library of Congress Cataloging-in-Publication Data

The Blackwell companion to the Hebrew Bible / edited by Leo G. Perdue.
     p.   cm. — (Blackwell companions to religion)
   Includes bibliographical references and index.
   ISBN 0–631–21071–7 (hardcover : alk. paper)
  1. Bible. O.T.—Criticism, interpretation, etc.   I. Perdue, Leo G.   II. Series.

  BS1171.3 B53   2001
  221.6—dc21

                                  00–069786

Typeset in 10.5 on 12.5 pt Photina
by Graphicraft Limited, Hong Kong
Printed in Great Britain by T.J. International, Padstow, Cornwall

This book is printed on acid-free paper.

Contents

Contributors

Leo G. Perdue is Professor of Hebrew Bible and President of Brite Divinity School, Texas Christian University, Fort Worth, Texas.

Bruce C. Birch is Dean and Professor of Biblical Theology at Wesley Theological Seminary, Washington, D.C.

Phyllis A. Bird is retired Professor of Old Testament Interpretation at Garrett-Evangelical Theological Seminary, Evanston, Illinois.

Joseph Blenkinsopp is John A. O'Brian Professor Emeritus of Biblical Studies, University of Notre Dame, Notre Dame, Indiana.

Walter Brueggemann is Professor of Old Testament at Columbia Theological Seminary, Decatur, Georgia.

Antony F. Campbell is Professor of Old Testament at Jesuit Theological College, Melbourne, Australia.

Calum Carmichael is Professor of Comparative Literature, Cornell University, Ithaca, New York.

Robert P. Carroll, who died in 2000, was Professor of Hebrew Bible, The Faculty of Divinity, The University of Glasgow, Glasgow, Scotland.

Charles E. Carter is Associate Professor of Religious Studies at Seton Hall University, South Orange, New Jersey.

R. E. Clements is Professor Emeritus of Old Testament Studies at King's College, University of London, England.

John J. Collins is Holmes Professor of Old Testament at Yale Divinity School, New Haven, Connecticut.

James L. Crenshaw is Robert L. Flowers Professor of Old Testament at Duke University, Durham, North Carolina.

Katharine J. Dell is Lecturer in Old Testament at Cambridge University, Cambridge, England.

William G. Dever is Professor of Near Eastern Archaeology and Anthropology at the University of Arizona, Tucson, Arizona.

Erhard S. Gerstenberger is Professor Emeritus of Old Testament, Evangelical Theology, Philipps University Marburg, Marburg, Germany.

Leslie J. Hoppe is Professor of Old Testament Studies at Catholic Theological Union, Chicago, Illinois.

David Jobling is Professor of Hebrew Bible at St. Andrew's College, Saskatoon, Canada.

Ralph W. Klein is Professor of Old Testament at Lutheran School of Theology at Chicago, Chicago, Illinois.

Klaus Koch is Professor Emeritus of Old Testament and History of Ancient Near Eastern Religions, at the University of Hamburg, Hamburg, Germany.

André Lemaire is Professor at École Pratique des Hautes Études, The Sorbonne, Paris, France.

Carol Meyers is Professor of Biblical Studies and Archaeology at Duke University, Durham, North Carolina.

Dennis Pardee is Professor of Northwest Semitic Philology at the University of Chicago, Chicago, Illinois.

Rolf Rendtorff is Professor Emeritus of Old Testament at the University of Heidelberg, Germany.

Henning Graf Reventlow is retired Professor of Old Testament, University of the Ruhr, Bochum, Germany.

Hermann Spieckermann is Professor of Old Testament, Theological Faculty, Georg-August-Universität, Göttingen, Germany.

Preface: The Hebrew Bible in Current Research

This collection of twenty-six essays provides a coherent, up-to-date introduction to the major areas of Old Testament biblical scholarship. The essays, written by leading scholars who hail from six different countries, are placed into eight major parts:

I   The Hebrew Bible in Modern Study
II   Israelite and Early Jewish History
III   Archaeology of Ancient Israel and Early Judaism
IV   The Religious and Social World of Ancient Israel and Early Judaism
V   Old Testament Theology
VI   The Torah
VII   The Prophets
VIII   The Writings.

These essays provide the student of the Hebrew Bible with basic introductions to each of these areas as they have developed in present research. The essays represent both the older methods of historical criticism and newer ones that have developed in more recent times.

The Hebrew Bible in Modern Study

During the past generation, biblical research has experienced the addition of newer approaches, at times even major transformations in regard to methods, discoveries, and insights. The first essay, "Preparatory Issues in Approaching Biblical Texts," written by Antony F. Campbell of Melbourne, Australia, concentrates primarily on the important features of the historical criticism that still dominates most of biblical scholarship. His is a critical overview that points to the strengths and weaknesses of each approach to biblical study. He provides helpful textual examples that illustrate each approach. Campbell submits that the expression "historical-critical method" is itself misleading. "Critical" refers to a "state of intellectual awareness," a "critical spirit" that must be present in the task of interpretation of biblical texts. "Method," by contrast, is an inappropriate term, for it implies a series of steps to take in interpreting texts. For Campbell, one begins by establishing the elusive "boundaries" of the text to be interpreted, not always an easy task, since it is not always clear where a text begins and ends. "Text Criticism" seeks to sort out the various readings of textual witnesses in different languages (especially Hebrew, Greek, Aramaic, Syriac, and Latin) and to determine which is the best reading to follow in a particular instance and the variety of readings that affect the meaning of a text. "Source Criticism," or better, "Origin Criticism," refers to diverse backgrounds, dates, and meanings for various sources and biblical passages. "Form Criticism" refers to an approach in which social settings are thought to give rise to particular genres of writing that contain specific features, how these features may relate to each other, and how they operate in concert to communicate meaning. "Tradition History" refers to the attempt to trace the history of various religious traditions central to Israelite faith and practice. "Editing History" indicates the views of redactors expressed in their editing of various texts. Taken as a whole, these approaches will not yield the same results, depending on the interpreters who use them. Nevertheless, Campbell submits that these approaches will give shape to the different procedures and the common matrix for interpreting the texts present in the Hebrew corpus.

The second essay in this initial selection on modern study is written by David Jobling of Saskatoon, Canada. He focuses on the more recent methods of literary criticism that derive from Departments of English and comparative literature. Jobling distinguishes between traditional and non-traditional advocates of literary criticism. Traditionalists focus on literature understood to be the "classics" of a society and attempt to provide the "correct" meaning of these texts. Non-traditionalists point out that the "classics" or the texts of the "canon" often omit the voices of the marginalized and that their interpreters who practice traditional methodology have largely been white and male. New literary criticism seeks to accomplish two strategies: the expansion of the culture's collection of classics to include marginal writings; and related to this, the reading of texts from contexts that are socially conservative. One effect of new literary criticism is "intertextuality," i.e. reading "texts" that include literature or even a larger social system in ways that bring new understandings to both. However, new literary efforts cannot expand the "canon" of the Hebrew Bible, meaning that they have to be applied to the existing canonical texts. More recent "literary" readings of the biblical texts include structuralism, which compares the ways that people produce texts with how they understand sentences in ordinary language; rhetorical criticism, which examines the close literary reading of a text; poststructuralism and ideological criticism, which attempt to examine the political commitments of the biblical texts and its interpreters; and deconstructionism, which indicates how texts fail to claim to prove what they assert, make arbitrary choices between possibilities that cannot be decided, and assume to exist what they seek to demonstrate. Feminism has also come into play in reading texts as have Afro-American "womanist" criticisms. These last-mentioned discourses engage in "ideological criticism" that seeks to detect and undermine social oppressions that must be sustained by "false consciousness." The oppressor and the oppressed must be convinced that what they believe belongs to the "natural" order of things. While some liberation movements have embraced deconstruction of the other modes of postmodern analysis mentioned above, because they determine the ideologies at work in texts and their interpreters, others reject these new approaches since they appear to deny all meaning, including that which liberationists attempt to construct. More recent contributions of non-traditional or counter-reading approaches include newer developments in feminist criticism, folklore, fantasy literature, and autobiographical criticism that point to how the study of one's own experience shapes one's readings of texts.

Charles E. Carter of South Orange, New Jersey, undertakes to write a comprehensive survey of the "social scientific" study of the Hebrew Bible. He notes that biblical scholarship has made uses of models from cultural anthropology and macrosociology to understand the cultural matrices that gave rise to the Bible. Following a history of the developments of social scientific methodology, the essay turns to examine the basic features of models and methods. Carter notes that all social sciences are at heart comparative. However, perhaps the greatest weakness often noted is that the social data gathered to compare to the biblical cultural reality originate mostly from recent societies and are not applicable to ancient worlds so radically different than modern ones. These methods need to take these differences into account, and they should consider the fact that biblical cultures were in flux, i.e., they themselves often changed and were not monolithic even in a particular time frame. Social science models must examine similar cultures, those of the Bible and those with which the Bible is compared, before any legitimate conclusions may be drawn. Ethnography is now commonly used to focus on premodern cultures to clarify practices and beliefs in dead societies, and to construct controls that set forth similarities in cultures and construct hypotheses that may be tested by research. The critics of social scientific approaches often indicate that they falsely try to present findings as "hard data," attempt to ignore important variables in describing human societies, and illegitimately impose modern models onto the past. Social science methods have been applied to a variety of significant topics in ancient Israel and the Old Testament: the emergence of Israel and state formation, the social locations of Israelite and Judean institutions (prophetism, apocalypticism, and the cultus), social distinctions (due to the rise of the monarchy) and gender differences, the exile and beyond, and the biblical literature as a cultural artifact. Carter concludes that scholars need to become more familiar with social science criticism, that they will have to develop more methodological rigor in its application, and that they must become more interdisciplinary in their work.

Israelite and Early Jewish History

Part II also contains three essays, using a variety of different methods, that cover the periods from premonarchic Israel to the colonial period under Persian rule. Carol Meyers opens this section with a survey of the period of early Israel and the rise of the Israelite monarchy. She notes that earlier scholarly historiography considered the beginning of Israel to have been the exodus from Egypt, the wilderness wandering, the establishment of the covenant, and the conquest of Canaan. The tribal system is then established, followed by the defeat at the hands of the Philistines, and the rise of the monarchy needed to provide the military means to defend against foreign enemies and to establish the Davidic–Solomonic empire, the center of which was the royal city of Jerusalem. The multiple problems with this reconstruction include the contradictory and varied accounts of these "events," including divergent accounts of the taking of the land (peaceful infiltration and conquest). Likewise, Meyers notes that the absence of reference to the exodus and the conquest of Canaan in Near Eastern sources is a major problem. Finally, she indicates archaeological fieldwork and the rise of postmodern scholarship point to the problems of premonarchic Israel as presented in biblical sources.

Meyers begins her assessment of the problems of regarding the Bible as history with the insights provided by archaeology. For example, the conquest model for taking the land has now been repudiated, as has the theory of pastoral nomads. In addition, Meyers notes that there is no archaeological evidence for Israel's sojourn in the desert, since the earliest ruins in the Sinai date from the 10th century BCE. Meyers indicates that viewing the Bible only as a historical document fails to recognize the highly tendentious nature of much of the text. Ideological biases are present in biblical writings, but this does not mean that the text cannot be a source for the writing of history. Biblical sources are not pure fiction, but are a combination of historical memory and fiction. Meyers contends that the writings of the Bible are not historical records, but rather express ideas and values through the telling of a story. Indicators that suggest the Bible contains some history about early Israel and the transition to statehood include some personal names attested elsewhere in the ancient Near East, toponyms that refer to sites identified by archaeology, poetic sections (for example, the Song of Deborah in Judges 5) that are archaic, the existence of examples of charismatic leadership that suggest no centralized authority existed, the uncovering of redactors who put together the early story of Israel through the monarchy (the D School), and the use of extra-biblical sources that include texts and monuments. Archaeology deals with patterns of settlement in early Iron Age Canaan and the increasing number and size of highland sites in the premonarchic period that might be identified as Israelite.

Meyers points to new explanatory models from the social sciences that pull together the biblical narrative and primary data in order to write a biblical history. She is especially attracted to "ethnoarchaeology," a method that combines archaeology with data from current premodern societies that are similar to the biblical society of early Israel. Meyers notes that the turmoil witnessed by the Aegean and eastern Mediterranean worlds at the end of the late Bronze Age led to population shifts that included the migration of stateless individuals, some of whom were those who settled the central highlands during the latter end of the second millennium BCE. Instead of revolution, conquest, or pastoral infiltration, Meyers opts for ruralization, in which new farming villages began to appear at the end of the 13th century BCE that were composed of refugees from existing empires, Canaanite peasants, and pastoralists from the Canaanite pasturelands. Tribes formed to deal with communal exigencies that included military defense, territorial boundaries, and the development of mutual aid. Tribes also bound together to deal with the threats to subsistence farming found in poor and rocky soil, the lack of substantial rainfall during lengthy periods, and hilly terrain. Drawing on ethnoarchaeology, Meyers suggests that what the Bible calls tribes might better be captured by the term "chiefdom", a "territorially based unit of society, in which hierarchies of leadership are based on kinship, not on merit or appointment." "Sub-chiefs" served the dominant chief, though the vying for power often led to struggles resulting in conflicts that are reflected in the archaeological record of the 12th and 11th centuries BCE. Groups that centered around chiefs and sub-chiefs developed a sense of ethnicity and shared identity by means of the concept of "descendants" and the fashioning of a shared history that in Israel came to include the worship of one deity, YHWH, and the tradition of a sacred mountain, coming perhaps from ancient Midianites.

According to archaeological excavations and surveys, the end of the early Iron Age witnessed the emergence of national states. These were necessitated by demographic and territorial expansion and the threat of external enemies, in Israel's case the Philistines. David's defeat of this group, recognition as king, and selection of Jerusalem as his own city led to the establishment of a new national state, Israel. The religious legitimation of David as the "son of YHWH," the "territorial expansions," the increasing wealth, and the additional manpower led to Israel's conquest and rule over neighboring nations and thus the establishment of a small Near Eastern empire. The archaeological data, including monumental architecture, from the early Iron II period points to that expected of a centralized state. The labor force for royal building projects and their costs came not only from Israel but also from these subjugated peoples. The establishment of this new state and its prestige during the reigns of its first two rulers, David and Solomon, led to the creation of a unified kingdom.

The second essay in Part II is written by Leslie J. Hoppe of Chicago, Illinois. "The History of Israel in the Monarchic Period" begins with the failures of Saul's early monarchy and moves into the success of David and his successor Solomon to establish and expand a small empire. Unfortunately, the only written sources to reconstruct this early history are the biblical narrative in 1 Samuel 8 through 1 Kings 2 and a recent stele discovered at Tel Dan that refers to "the house of David." The biblical narratives are largely legendary, save for the possibility that the "Succession Narrative" in 2 Samuel 9–20 and 1 Kings 1–2 may have been written by a member of Solomon's court. Hoppe questions the argument that archaeological excavations have pointed to the existence of a political system in the form of a monarchy in the 10th century BCE. The notion that the Davidic empire was administered from Jerusalem is disputed among archaeologists, and even the datings of monumental structures at Hazor, Megiddo, and Gezer are not necessarily from the time of Solomon.

Hoppe then approaches the characteristic features of the two Israelite states that emerged in Israel to the north and Judah in the south. The two states shared certain common features: language, worship of the same deity, descent from the same ancestors, similar economies, and the appearance of social stratification with substantial disparities between the rich and poor. Two sources exist for reconstructing the history of Israel and Judah during the period of the monarchy: the biblical narratives (Kings and Chronicles, and other sources like Josephus dependent on the Bible) claiming to be based on documents that now no longer exist, and archaeological data. There are internal contradictory problems in the Bible, no clear dating, and sources that represent a Judahite perspective, not an Israelite one, making the Bible a questionable historical source possessing some objectivity. Archaeological data for this period rarely include textual material along with the artifacts uncovered. The only written materials about Saul come from the Bible, those referring to David are the Bible and the Tel Dan inscription, while the non-written data about Solomon coming from excavations are questionable in terms of dating. In reconstructing Northern Israelite history, the biblical narratives and prophetic texts are decidedly pro-Judahite and biased towards the North. While the biblical narratives consider the first five rulers of Northern Israel to be kings, they more than likely were chieftains. Omri (879–869 BCE) was likely the founder of the Kingdom of Israel. Save during the reign of Jeroboam II (788–748), Israel experienced turmoil from without (Amram and Assyria). For most of its history, the Judahite Kingdom was a vassal nation to Israel, then Assyria, then Egypt, and finally Babylon. The South was largely a weak, subjugated country. The prophetic critique against Judah largely was caused because of the inequities of the economic burden imposed on a poor country.

Robert P. Carroll of Glasgow, Scotland, concludes Part II with an essay on "Exile, Restoration, and Colony: Judah in the Persian Empire." Using a more literary approach than Meyers and Hoppe, Carroll emphasizes that the biblical sources reflect the theology, values, and ideologies of those who wrote them as well as those of the communities for whom they were written. In many ways the entire Hebrew Bible is a metanarrative that includes deportation, displacement, diaspora, and the hope for return and restoration. The various biblical accounts of the destruction of Jerusalem and conquest of Judah are characterized by Carroll as "the myth of the empty land." This myth describes a territory devoid of people and celebrations of the Sabbath until a future restoration in a purified land.

Carroll contrasts a conventional view of the history of this period with that of a more mythical reading of the biblical materials. In the conventional view of biblical scholarship, derived from the biblical narratives in Kings and Chronicles,

Jerusalem was sacked by the Babylonians and the citizens of the city were taken into exile. Later, "diaspora novellas" that speak of Jews in exile (Daniel, Esther, Judith, and Tobit) indicate the exiles faired reasonably well, though there is little historical information about the Jews in Babylon. The novellas that speak of thriving Jewish communities in exile may be more mythical in character than historical.

The Persian ruler Cyrus issues a decree that allows the Jews to return to Jerusalem to rebuild the temple (2 Chr 36:22–23). The returns result in Jerusalem and Judah becoming a Persian colony protected by the Persian imperial forces. More contemporary approaches read the exile and return as a biblical myth, which Carroll prefers. He notes that many Jews did not return, including communities in Egypt and Babylonia, a fact that parallels Jewish communities outside of Israel today. Thus, there is ancient literature that indicates the return has occurred, and other texts that indicate it has yet to occur. These two literatures often clash. This newer approach takes a "literary-cultural reading" of exile and return over against that of the "archeological-historical" approach that has been in vogue. What the Bible contains is only one ideological reading of the exile and return, told primarily by the returnees from Babylon. The biblical narrative becomes propaganda for their central role as the temple community enjoying the favor of imperial rule. All other claims to power are rejected. Carroll contends that "The Hebrew Bible is . . . *on one level* the propaganda of the 'deported and returned' occupants of Jerusalem in the post-Babylonian periods." Thus, should we read the biblical texts in the light of archaeology of the period or in reference to our own ideological presuppositions or as a combination of both? Did Ezra come first or Nehemiah? Did Nehemiah come to rebuild the walls of Jerusalem and then Ezra to rebuild the temple? The wise reader of secondary literature will recognize that there are many different views that may be taken in interpreting the Bible.

Carroll continues with the "myth of the exile," questioning whether there ever was one in Jewish history. The myth of the exile, real or imagined for propaganda purposes, indicates the deportees and/or their descendants returned to shape a Persian colony as a new Jerusalem community around the rebuilt temple. However, if this myth is ideological, it may be that it legitimizes the Jerusalem community as the remnant of YHWH. Those who did not participate in the return are taken out of the biblical story and made invisible. Finally, Carroll explains that the returnees from whom developed much of early Judaism and early Christianity have become a root metaphor, a myth, and a metaphysic for many Jews in Israel and the Diaspora and for non-Jewish peoples who have been scattered on the face of the earth.

Archaeology of Ancient Israel and Early Judaism

William G. Dever of Tucson, Arizona, has written two essays dealing with archaeology that point to a more traditional combining of biblical texts with data from excavations. The second, "Biblical and Syro-Palestinian Archaeology," focuses on Palestine (i.e., modern Israel and Jordan) and the period of the Iron Age. Dever traces the development of these related disciplines, while lamenting that no major history has been written on these fields. The two disciplines began to separate in the 1970s, aided in part by divergent understandings of theory and method. New Archaeology, stressing the "scientific testing of universal cultural laws," came to life in the 1970s, but largely disappeared in the 1980s. By 1985 "post-processualism" emerged and rejected the anti-historical thrust of much of the New or processual archaeology, emphasizing a return to historiography as archaeology with an emphasis on the role of ideology in cultural change. However, regrettably little has come of this approach in Syro-Palestinian and biblical archaeology. By the mid-1980s the debate between biblical and Syro-Palestinian archaeology was over, with Syro-Palestinian archaeology developing its own discipline. American biblical archaeology, which used archaeology to correlate with, explain, or even prove the Bible, has long since died, though it has been resurrected as a straw man by "revisionist" biblical scholars to argue against any historicity in the Hebrew Bible.

Larger issues that are among the most critical today include chronology and terminology in the effort to write history from things, not texts (thus attempting to refine prehistoric eras, the different Bronze Ages, and the various Iron Ages), transitional horizons that move from one era to the next, poorly known periods (e.g., Early Bronze I–III and Iron I), and revisionism that challenges the existence of long accepted historical data (e.g., an historical Solomon or a United Monarchy). Dever himself, as an archaeologist, argues against the so-called revisionists. He calls revisionists the "new nihilists" who deny the ability to obtain any secure knowledge of the past. This is a postmodern paradigm wrongly applied to history writing. Revisionists argue ancient biblical texts have been fashioned into a "metanarrative" that supports the claims of those in power, and thus is to be rejected. While arguing against the revisionists, Dever suggests that archaeologists need to develop their own "hermeneutics" that set forth the scientific principles on which the discipline is based.

Dever's first essay, "Archaeology and the History of Israel," indicates that older biblical archaeology attempted to prove the Bible and dealt with issues like the period of the Patriarchs, Moses and monotheism, the exodus and conquest, the early Israelite and Judean states, and the religion of ancient Israel. Archaeology was thought to have been capable of verifying biblical history or making it more precise. These and similar issues have not been resolved, and the results of biblical archaeology in the old style have been questioned and often rejected. However, "biblical archaeology" is still a valid discipline when seen as a dialogue between two disciplines: biblical studies and Syro-Palestinian archaeology. However, this dialogue has not materialized. The larger question has become: "Is it possible to write a truly critical history of ancient Israel?" Certain recent scholars have said no. They have argued that biblical or ancient Israel were projections of Jewish and Christian scholars, while an historical Israel may have existed, but is largely beyond recovery. This nihilist position, contends Dever, has appeared in the writings of numerous current biblical scholars. Dever still contends that a dialogue between biblical historiography and Syro-Palestinian archaeology can and should be carried out. What archaeology can provide includes external, "objective" information about ancient Israel that is devoid of theological biases, evidence that supplements, corroborates, corrects, or even supplants the biblical sources, and a setting for understanding ancient Israel in its ancient Near Eastern context. Yet archaeology cannot prove the Bible either, in terms of confirming what happened or especially what the events meant. Examples include archaeology's discoveries that early Israel consisted more of indigenous groups than those from the outside who engaged in military conquest. This corrects the Book of Joshua's presentation. However, the features of centralization necessary for statehood do appear in the 10th century BCE, thus undermining the "revisionist" position that Israel did not become a state until the 9th century and Judah the 7th century. Another example is archaeology's recovery of "folk" religion that had been largely obscured by the biblical texts. Dever is convinced that this conversation is important for advancing biblical and archaeological studies.

The Religious and Social World of Ancient Israel and Early Judaism

Part IV deals with the religious and social world of ancient Israel and early Judaism. Dennis Pardee of Chicago, Illinois, initiates this section with an overview of the written and archaeological materials from 3000 BCE to the turn of the eras in ancient Syria-Palestine (= Canaan). Written materials surveyed include the Ebla (Tell Mardikh) library in north central Syria in Eblaite, which has affinities with East-Semitic Akkadian (ca. 2400 BCE). About five hundred years later, a series of collections of texts from various sites in Syria were discovered, written in the Old Babylonian dialect of Akkadian, the most important being those from Mari (Tell Hariri on the middle Euphrates river). The earliest important textual data on the Canaan appear in the early part of the 14th century. Written in Akkadian, these texts were sent by vassal princes in Canaan to the Egyptian court (Tell el Amarna). The most important library for Canaan is that of ancient Ugarit (Ras Shamra), dating from the 14th century to the early part of the 12th century BCE. The variety of languages includes Ugaritic, Akkadian, Hurrian, Egyptian, and Hittite. Other Late Bronze Age sources of importance come from Alalakh and Emar. However, very few texts have emerged from 1150 to 1000 BCE. Phoenician inscriptions appeared later, and western Arameans borrowed the Phoenician writing system and began to write in their own language, beginning as early as the 10th century BCE. Aramaic became during the Neo-Assyrian and Neo-Babylonian empires the *lingua franca* of the entire Near East. The speakers of Hebrew adopted the Phoenician alphabet as early as the 10th century BCE. By the 8th century BCE, a scribal tradition is attested in Samaria, and significant Hebrew inscriptions began appearing in

Judah in the 7th century BCE, including the Mesad Hashavyahu inscriptions and the Siloam tunnel. The most important corpus dates to the last decade and a half of the existence of the state of Judah, the Lachish letters and the texts from Arad. The Hebrew Bible is in some sense a Canaanite document in that the Israelites were to an extent Canaanites.

Archaeological sources have been used to fill in the gaps of written sources. Texts come mainly from the upper strata of society and thus reflect their beliefs and practices. A more complete history may be composed only when written and non-written data may be correlated. Even with this wealth of material, it remains unclear what a Canaanite was in the first half of the first millennium BCE. Few would doubt the general outline of the political events in the Hebrew Bible from Omri to the Babylonian exile, due to the corroboration primarily from Assyrian and Babylonian annals, though the validity of details and the religious interpretation is much debated. The small number of Hebrew inscriptions makes it impossible to engage in more than guesswork about the development of Hebrew. The socioeconomic system reconstructed from archaeology is incomplete. Written and archaeological records demonstrate the primary form of government was royal, with a patrimonial pattern. The king was the patriarch of the city or state with the rest of society in a hierarchical system. Interest groups (priests, council of elders), various forms of production (tradesmen, artisans, and farmers), a royal administration funded by taxes and service requirements, urban sites, and non-sedentary or partially sedentary populations in a tribal patrimonial society are attested. Canaanite religion at Ugarit was highly polytheistic (over 200 deities) and also included a sacrificial cult (primarily sheep, goats, and cattle), song and prayer, divination, incantations, and mythological texts.

Joseph Blenkinsopp of South Bend, Indiana, continues this overview of the religious and social world in his survey of "The Household in Ancient Israel and Early Judaism." He begins with the limitations of our knowledge of the household. Archaeologists have focused more on monumental architecture. In addition, there is the lack of iconographical material, there are only a small number of references to the household in the biblical narrative, and the information is largely limited to rural settings. The rural villages comprised more than 90 percent of the population, and these villages engaged in the raising of livestock and growing of crops. The population lived in villages consisting of a cluster of households consisting at most of a few hundred inhabitants engaged in cooperative activities to provide for irrigation, terracing, defense, and sharing a common pastureland. Most houses were a work site for production of textiles and food processing, while households maintained a bare subsistent life. Households were multigenerational and lateral (unmarried brothers, sisters, nephews, in-laws, etc.), while affluent ones would have had slaves and servants. During recent years, archaeologists have collected data on households from the Iron Age and Second Temple period. Houses had normally two to four rooms with a central courtyard in which food preparation, crafts, and socializing occurred. Some had two stories, the second of which was domestic in purpose. Households were generally patrilineal and patrimonial, including not just people but also assets of the families. Adoption, concubinage, and surrogate marriages were practiced, especially when infertility led to the lack of offspring. Women lived private roles, prepared crafts and food, raised and nurtured children, worked in the fields in certain seasons, and lived under the protection of a senior male. Marriage was a contract between households and was seen as promoting the economic welfare of the households and the senior male. Virginity was expected before marriage, while divorce was initiated by the husband. Minors had no rights and lived under the authority of the senior male. Children were nurtured and educated by the mother. Once old enough to work, the male child came under the authority of the father. Religion in the household appears to have included an ancestor cult, household deities, and festivals coinciding with the major harvests. The annual clan sacrifice was designed to reinforce the solidarity of the kinship network. Family values included marriage that was for the economic interest of the husband and the two households, while offenses against women were judged in terms of the interest of the father or husband.

William G. Dever of Tucson, Arizona, contributes to Part IV on the social world of ancient Israel with his essay, "Archaeology, the Israelite Monarchy, and the Solomonic Temple." Dever begins by noting that a group of "revisionist" scholars have recently questioned the literary texts and archaeological data, concluding that the biblical texts are retrojections of the Hellenistic era with no historical value, while the archaeological data is mute in speaking of an ancient "biblical Israel." Focusing on the "Israelite Monarchy" in the 10th–7th centuries BCE, Dever begins with evidence for the existence of a 10th century United Monarchy. He notes that while much of the Deuteronomistic History covering this period is legendary, it is not the case as the "revisionists" maintain that Jerusalem did not become the capital of a state before the mid-7th century BCE or an important city before the 2nd century BCE during the Hasmonean period or that there was no Israelite or Judean monarchy. They erroneously argue that the recently discovered Tel Dan inscription of the mid to late 9th century BCE mentioning the "house of David" and a "king of Israel" must be a modern forgery. By contrast, Dever attempts to show that the narrative themes of the Hebrew Bible come from the Iron Age, beginning with a United Monarchy. Saul fits well the model of the "chiefdom" found in social anthropology. David, says Dever, founded the small state of Israel, and some archaeological evidence (e.g. the stepped-stone terrace of the City of David and "Warren's Shaft" associated with the water conduit by which David took the city) does exist. Increasing urbanization (and monumental entry gates and casemate walls at Gezer, Hazor, and Meggido) suggests a unification of towns and villages from this period for his reign. Red burnished pottery and hand-slipped wares from these and other sites below the destruction level of the Egyptian Shishak's campaign shortly after the death of Solomon contrasts with the wheel-burnished wares above the destruction layers. This suggests a mid-10th century Palestine. Dever has documented some 30 urban sites that date from the 10th century. The synchronisms with Neo-Assyrian and Neo-Babylonian king-lists support the general historical character of 1 and 2 Kings.

The Temple of Solomon is one important feature of the United and Divided Monarchy. "Revisionists" have regarded the Temple of Solomon as mythological or as priestly propaganda. In reality, they contend, there was no "Solomonic Temple." Dever notes, by contrast, that there are 30 or more comparative examples of temples from the Bronze and Iron Ages in Syria-Palestine that date from the 15th to 8th centuries BCE, and not from the later Hasmonean period. Many features of the Solomonic temple mentioned in the biblical narratives parallel elements of these ancient temples, ranging from the "long room" temple plan, to the dressed masonry with interlaced wooden beam construction, to the two columns, to the motifs of the interior decoration of the temple and its furnishings. Archaeology has demonstrated that the stories, events, and features of the early monarchy and the temple originated in the Iron Age and not in the Hellenistic period.

The final essay in Part IV, "Schools and Literacy in Ancient Israel and Early Judaism," is written by André Lemaire of Paris, France. Lemaire provides an overview of epigraphic documentation discovered in excavations in Israel and attempts to reconstruct the spread of writing. His reconstruction results in the following: from 1200 to 800 BCE, alphabetic writing was not unknown, but rather limited. From 800 to 722 BCE the paleo-Hebrew script is present to a significant degree in the royal administration. From 722 to 587 BCE, the ability to read and write paleo-Hebrew is present in all levels of the Judean royal administration. Schools came into existence to transmit knowledge involving reading and writing in ancient Israel for the education and work of royal administrative officials. These schools presumably began as early as Solomon and continued throughout the royal period. These in turn were replaced by schools that trained scribes such as Baruch and Ezra for the written and legal materials necessary for later Judaism. Ben Sira (2nd century BCE) points to a *bēt midraš* that centered on the writing and interpretation of biblical books. The library and excavation of Qumran suggest an idea of what a *bēt midraš* would have been among the Essenes: the center for copying, studying, and interpreting biblical books. Eventually the synagogue developed in the early centuries of the Common Era that included the reading of Jewish texts, especially the Tanak.

Old Testament Theology

A strong renewal of interest in Old Testament Theology has developed in the last decade, with more recent approaches influenced by new developments in biblical interpretation. This topic is addressed by Part V – Old Testament Theology. Henning Graf Reventlow provides a survey of Old Testament Theology, beginning with the 18th century CE and moving into the current period. Reventlow notes that one of the ongoing questions has been the relationship between the approach of the History of Religion and Old Testament Theology. While there is a rebirth of interest in the History of Religion's approach, which seeks to develop the religious ideas of the Old Testament, Old Testament Theology that focuses upon the theological contents of the Bible continues to be a distinctive and important approach. Thus there is a major distinction between the two disciplines. The question of an historical or systematic approach to Old Testament Theology is also investigated by Reventlow with examples and combinations of the two set forth. The systematic approach raises the question of a "center" of the Old Testament, with theologians on both sides of the issue. Some scholars have preferred a dialectic as the center of the Old Testament: blessing and redemption, a social world and the "embrace of pain," and creation and history. More recent developments have shaped the contours of Old Testament Theology. The role of wisdom in this area has become important in recent scholarship, in part due to wisdom's emphasis on creation. Another issue in Old Testament Theology is the question of whether it should be descriptive or confessional. Recent hermeneutics, some of which are grounded in postmodernism, have shown that the claim of historical objectivity is not valid. A confessional approach has gained keen interest in more recent times. This confessional approach has been seen in recent canonical studies, though the issue of plurality has become a major dividing point in this area. Narrative theology has represented a shift from history to literature. However, the question emerges as to whether literature and literary studies are theology or the materials from which theology is developed. Liberation theology, including feminist approaches, also represents new developments. These developments look to the Bible to support existing political movements and their causes or seek to undercut biblical arguments that oppose their efforts. Another new approach derives from recent sociological and materialistic approaches. This approach develops out of the matrix of Israelite and Jewish social life. Much of the work has been a Christian enterprise, though lately some Jews are pointing to the need for a Jewish Biblical Theology. Finally, the issue of doing an entire Biblical Theology has emerged as a major concern, with a variety of ways of proceeding being espoused.

The second essay on Old Testament Theology is written by Walter Brueggemann of Decatur, Georgia, and is entitled, "Symmetry and Extremity in the Images of YHWH." In this essay on God, he notes that there is no single characterization that covers the entire Hebrew Bible. He points to the tension between the faith articulated in the ancient culture and the canonical formulations of Christianity. Brueggemann emphasizes more the canonical, theological claims of the text. To do so he points to important metaphors for God. Brueggemann notes that God is most characteristically represented by political metaphors in the Old Testament: king, judge, and warrior. However, there is no ancient Near Eastern deity who has God's power, nor is there one who identifies, like YHWH, with the marginalized. As governor, YHWH creates and sustains the world order and rehabilitates this order when it is lost. While deeply committed to Israel, YHWH is also the law giver, who demands loyalty from the people of the covenant, and yet must, while punishing, still live with disloyalty. Metaphors of relationship involve familial ones that point to divine pathos, mercy, and covenant. As the God of the marginalized, YHWH enters into solidarity with and leads the slaves out of Egypt and gives them the land of Israel to become the people of God. God becomes the special protector of the weak and poor in Israel. As family member, Israel (son or wife) is the recipient of YHWH's special care and empathy. Yet as the lover or father of Israel, YHWH becomes enraged at the disloyalty of wife or child. Any canonical depiction of YHWH must take into consideration these dichotomies of governance and intimacy, and love and rage.

The third essay in Part V, "Theological Anthropology in the Hebrew Bible," is written by Phyllis Bird of Evanston, Illinois. She notes that the "image of God" (Gen 1:26–28) has played a substantial role only in Christian, but not Jewish, theology. Genesis 1:26–28 in the Priestly account presents the origin of humankind as the final and climactic act of the six days of creation. The human creature who models the divine must do so in the world. The "image" and "likeness" of the human creature plays no role elsewhere in the Hebrew Bible, save in the Priestly texts of Gen 5:1–3 and 9:6. However, humans in Gen 1:26 are to exercise dominion over other creatures and thus contrast with their counterparts in the ancient Near East who were slaves to the gods. While God in the Priestly narrative has no sexuality or gender, humans do. Thus to be made in the image of God involves both human genders who, like the animals, receive the blessing that enables them to "be fruitful and multiply." The view of the exaltation of human creatures is found in Psalm 8. Thus Genesis 1 and Psalm 8 both portray humans as superior to other creatures in the world.

The divine image is not lost in the Fall narrated in Genesis 2–3. The Yahwist's account of creation and the expulsion from the garden is found in Gen 2:4b–3:24. Chapter 3 is the depiction of the conditions under which humans now live, having lost immortality and paradise. Chapter 2 seeks to describe the creation of humans, male and female. He becomes a living breath, having been shaped from the soil, while she is made of his substance as a "help." The institution of marriage is a clear result from this union of the two. The two genders are made for each other. Human life is characterized by interactions with other humans, other creatures, and with God. Social institutions, represented here by marriage, are necessary for survival. Genesis points to the limitations placed on humans, e.g., they may not eat of the tree of wisdom. These boundaries are extended as a result of human sin to include alienation from God, from paradise, from the soil, from other creatures, and from the opposite sex. Furthermore, death is the final punishment and ultimate boundary to human life. When these two accounts (Priestly and Yahwistic) are combined, they envision a different world: one of order proceeding according to divine plan and one of disruption and failure in which humans may live only according to divine grace. The Hebrew Bible's first words about humans set the tone for all subsequent words by emphasizing their relationship to God.

R. E. Clements of London, England, writes the fourth essay in Part V: "The Community of God in the Hebrew Bible." Clements notes that the canon is closely connected to the community of faith, both of the Church and of Judaism. Christians view the Hebrew Bible as the Old Testament and consider it to be a collection that gives testimony to the origin of the Church. For Jews the Hebrew

Bible answers the question of who a Jew is and shows how Jewish historical experience originated. Each modern community shares a spiritual identity with the ancient communities of the Hebrew Bible.

Clements provides the following overview. The historical forms of the Biblical community of Israel begin with a group of tribes. This community of tribes shared a common bond of fellowship much like a large family. The deity was related to the tribes as a kinsman who was worshipped as El in different sanctuaries. The deity was seen as the owner of the land and responsible for its productivity. Worship was directed to achieving the good will of the deity. Eventually, El was identified with the militant warrior deity YHWH who defended the tribes from external threats. This tribal system was followed by the beginning of a nation-state appearing in 1000 BCE. The emphasis on territory took on new importance. Its protection, gain, or loss was thought to reflect divine blessing or anger and punishment. YHWH was now worshipped as the supreme deity of Israel. The divine election of David and his dynasty became central to the religion of the community. Solomon's building of the temple was seen as the construction of a house for YHWH. YHWH's supremacy over other gods began to lead to a monotheising tendency. The kingdom eventually split into the two kingdoms of Israel and Judah. Israel fell to the Assyrians by 722 BCE, and in 587 BCE the state of Judah was taken by the Babylonians. This story of the rise and fall of Israel was related in the Deuteronomistic History in Joshua, Judges, 1 & 2 Samuel, and 1 & 2 Kings. The Book of Deuteronomy and the redaction of Jeremiah complete the trilogy of D texts. They combine together the concepts of election, covenant, and national unity. Yet to be the people of YHWH bore with it a condition of faithfulness. Only obedience to the law (in the form of Deuteronomy) could insure this relationship. The prophetic D redaction in Jeremiah points to the faithlessness that led to the destruction of the nation and to the hope in a future restoration. While building up the importance of the royal tradition of king and temple, the D source also notes the destruction of the nation as the consequence of its sins. With the fall of first Israel and then Judah, the understanding of the community was reshaped. The written Torah was finalized, which led to the view of it as the heart of the canon. This provided the way of life for those in and outside the land. The former and latter prophets became critical in pointing out how past failures could be acknowledged, repentance could be shaped, and the future could be one of restoration from exile. God was to intervene on behalf of a faithful community. The city and temple of Jerusalem no longer had its own territory, was not an independent nation, and lacked a king to rule. This led to a new community called a "congregation" or in Greek a synagogue. A small temple community in 520–516 BCE emerged following the Persians' allowing the return of the Jewish exiles to their homeland. Other Jewish groups lived in the Diaspora and developed their own forms of religious and social life. During this period and later, Judaism began to take shape. The notion of "exile" began to shape both Jewish and Christian religious understanding. Hope in restoration and becoming a faithful people of God formed both developing concepts, Jewish and Christian, of the community.

The final essay in Part V is written by Bruce C. Birch of Washington, D.C. In "Old Testament Ethics" Birch notes that the 1990s witnessed a series of important works on Old Testament ethics. He surveys a variety of different understandings and concludes that the value of the Hebrew canon for Jewish and Christian ethics is not dependent on the reconstruction of ancient Israelite morality. Rather, the value comes from the ongoing discussion of the biblical texts as scripture, which become an important foundation for ethics in Judaism and Christianity. Problems arising in the quest to find the ethical features of the Hebrew Bible include the diversity of the texts and their perspectives. One could simply point to different ethical views. A better way is to regard these texts as multiple voices in a moral dialogue, something the modern communities could learn to do. An additional problem results from the socio-religious world of the Bible as a world totally alien from our own. There are elements that do not require normative behavior intended for unquestioning emulation. Some texts speak of Israel's participation in a social practice that is no longer valued, others tell of Israel's sins including the excesses of nationalism and idolatry, and others present an incomplete understanding of God's will. The Old Testament does not present a coherent view of morality or possess common moral principles. Rather, the Old Testament contains cultural data preserved for testimony to its own varied communities and succeeding generations.

Birch emphasizes the community as the foundation of Old Testament ethics. In addition, the community provides the context for understanding ethics in the Old Testament. There is no private morality in the Hebrew Bible. Ethics in the Old Testament are designed to form community. The various ethical materials are incorporated into Israel's basic story. For example, law codes have been surveyed because of their inclusion in the story. The knowledge of God becomes the condition for Old Testament ethics. God as a God of justice and compassion is known by Israel, and his deeds and revelation in words are actualized in human behavior within the community formed by ethical materials. Moral norms derive not only from the knowledge of God, but also from acknowledging all life as a part of divine creation. Morality consists of imitating the character and activity of God. Obedience to the divine will is critical for Old Testament ethics. Finally, the view of creation in Wisdom literature sees the order of the cosmos as the basis for moral behavior. This "natural law" is combined with the God of salvation history and the divine words uttered by the prophets. The trajectories of Old Testament morality are the Church, which views this first testament as scripture, and Judaism, which also regards the Tanak as scripture.

The Torah

Part VI deals with the Torah. Rolf Rendtorff of the University of Heidelberg examines "Creation and Redemption in the Torah." To do so he uses a canonical method that takes the text in its final form to set forth the two major themes of creation and exodus. While creation may not be the most ancient feature of Israelite faith, the Torah and later texts speak of YHWH as the one God who is the creator of all that is, and this precedes the story of ancient Israel. Creation in Genesis 1 is not *ex nihilo*, but rather out of a formless void. Israel demythologizes the Babylonian story of creation that speaks of a battle of Marduk (creator) against Tiamat (chaos monster). Darkness and the flood both become parts of God's creation. Other de-mythologization happens with the heavenly bodies, no longer gods as is the case in religions of the ancient Near East. The creation of humanity includes both male and female in the enigmatic "in our image, according to our likeness," a phrase subject to many interpretations. This image continues to be transmitted to succeeding human generations. The divine rest occurs on the seventh day, reflected also when God on Mount Sinai gives the Israelites the Ten Commandments. Yet in the Ten Commandments a second version speaks, not of creation, but of the exodus from Egypt where Israel was still in slavery (Deut 5:15; cf. Ps 136:10–12). Thus, the second major theme, after creation, in the Torah is the exodus from Egypt. The struggle occurs mainly between Pharaoh and YHWH. The purpose is not simply the liberation of pre-Israel from Egypt, but also so that the Egyptians will know that YHWH alone is God. This linkage between creation and the exodus is picked up not only in the Torah, but also in later texts, including Isaiah 59:9–11. This prophet goes on to speak about return from exile, so that creation, Egyptian exodus, and return from exile are seen as the great acts of YHWH.

Calum Carmichael of Ithaca, New York, examines the issue of "Law and Narrative in the Pentateuch" in Part VI. He notes that only recently have scholars begun to consider together the legal materials and the narratives in which they are embedded. Carmichael points to the weaknesses in the comparison of ancient Near Eastern suzerainty treaties and Israelite law and covenant. He doubts that Israel simply borrowed this type of treaty from other cultures. Instead, he argues that the relationship between law and narrative in part has to do with the fact that the narratives deal with origins. The laws become the foundation documents for each major episode in the narrative history of Israel. Thus Moses' laws are authoritative because they come from the formative period of the nation's history. Many of the laws refer to the issues arising in the narratives. For example, while the revelation and giving of the law at Sinai provides the foundation of the nation, the event is also a return to creation (Deut 4:32, 33). Thus, there is a rather close relationship between the narrative and the law.

The Prophets

Part VII, "The Prophets," contains three major essays: "Former Prophets: The Deuteronomistic History," "Latter Prophets: The Major Prophets," and "Latter Prophets: The Minor Prophets." Hermann Spieckermann of Göttingen, Germany, initiates the section with an important essay on the Deuteronomistic History. Drawing on the research of tradition history, Spieckermann notes that the Deuteronomistic History ("the former prophets") refers to the Books of Joshua, Judges, 1–2 Samuel, and 1–2 Kings. The term Deuteronomistic History goes back to Martin Noth (1943). These books reflect the language and theology of the Book of Deuteronomy. The unity of these books is based on style and theology. Spieckermann argues that the Deuteronomistic Historian (DtrH) has composed the basic outline of the work that later is redacted by DtrP, that is oriented to the prophets and the fulfillment of the prophetic word, and by DtrN, a legal editing that emphasizes the Deuteronomic law. According to the Deuteronomistic History, Israel is the people elected by YHWH and led by Moses and Joshua regardless of disobedience. The history becomes one of guilt that continues through the kings of Israel, most of the rulers of Judah, and the exile to Babylon.

The essay on the Major Prophets is composed by Klaus Koch of Hamburg, Germany. Koch, using traditional methodology, begins by examining Isaiah. He notes that First Isaiah includes chapters 1–39, while Second Isaiah is found in chapters 40ff. First Isaiah is concerned with Judah in the 8th century BCE, criticizes kings and cult, and warns of an Assyrian invasion. Second Isaiah (40–55) is directed toward the exiles in Babylon and promises a return to Jerusalem. Third Isaiah (56–66) speaks of the poor conditions in post-exilic Palestine and consists of prophecies uttered by several disciples of Second Isaiah. Jeremiah and Ezekiel cover the same main subjects; predictions of disaster for Judah, oracles against the foreign nations, and promises of salvation for Judah. The sequence of Ezekiel is 1–24, 25–32, and 33–48. The old Greek version of Jeremiah contains the same literary sequencing: 1–25, 26–32, 33–42, and 43–51. In First Isaiah the same sequencing may be found: 1–12, 13–23, 24–27, and 36–39. The third part (28–35) combines predictions of salvation and condemnation of Israel. In recent years, some scholars have asserted that few if any texts go back to the historical prophets, whereas other scholars have continued to claim that a core indeed reflects historical personages and their socio-historical periods. The disagreement thus continues over how large the redactional additions are and whether anything goes back to historical figures. Koch follows the more traditional, older path and reconstructs the history of the prophets and their redactions.

The essay on the minor prophets is written by James L. Crenshaw of Durham, North Carolina. Crenshaw notes that twelve brief prophetic books follow the larger major prophets. These are Hosea, Joel, Amos, Obadiah, Jonah, Micah, Nahum, Habakkuk, Zephaniah, Haggai, Zechariah, and Malachi. While the books have been associated with historical prophets, their content speaks of considerable later redaction. This disallows any unitary interpretation of each of the texts. Crenshaw notes that earlier scholarship, based on theological and stylistic features, attempted to distill the various redactions added to a prophetic text. Today, however, postmodernism's issues of gender, ethnicity, sexual preference, and marginalization find in the texts evidence of whatever the ideology may seek. Older questions of authorship, date, and historical setting have been replaced by queries concerning the self-interests of various groups. Crenshaw prefers the older approach with some degree of objectivity and traces the major themes and socio-historical settings of each text. The Minor Prophets issue judgment against Israel or Judah, extend that judgment to the foreign nations, and then offer the hope of salvation to a few survivors. The social roles of the prophets, Crenshaw argues, included the providing of instruction for the king, people, and royal cult. In many ways, the Minor Prophets followed Neo-Assyrian prophecy. Judahite prophets spoke of the revitalization of the Davidic dynasty, proclaimed oracles against the enemies of YHWH and the State of Judah, instructed kings and their subjects, and spoke of hopes for the future. The major theological themes of the Minor Prophets included justice, the purity of worship, the character of God, the identity of the community of God, and its future. Eventually, prophecy fell into disregard when doubts began to be raised about the authenticity of divine oracles proclaimed through spokespersons.

The Writings

Part VIII pertains to the "Writings." These include essays on narrative texts (the Chronicler), the Psalter, Wisdom, and Apocalyptic. Ralph W. Klein of Chicago, Illinois, writes the essay on "Narrative Texts: Chronicles, Ezra, and Nehemiah." These narrative texts tell the story of Israel from the death of Saul to the announcement of the rise of Cyrus who allowed the Jews to return home from Babylonian captivity. Most scholars until recently have seen these four books as a unified "Chronicler's History," beginning with Chronicles and concluding with Nehemiah. Klein argues that Chronicles and Ezra–Nehemiah had separate origins. Chronicles, for example, has two prominent themes almost absent in Ezra–Nehemiah: immediate retribution and prophecy. In addition, Chronicles has a reasonably favorable view of Israel, whereas Ezra–Nehemiah is limited to Judah and Benjamin. Kingship is idealized and emphasized in Chronicles.

Chronicles can be studied by constructing a synoptic parallel with Samuel–Kings. Additions, omissions, and changes in Chronicles thus may be easily identified. Klein points to the differences and notes their significance. This tendency toward change is already present in the supposition that the ancient Greek translation of Samuel–Kings was based on an earlier Hebrew text that varies from the Masoretic Text. In turning to Ezra–Nehemiah, the biggest issue has been who preceded whom, a question not easily answered. The thematic concerns in Ezra–Nehemiah include YHWH's return of the exiles to Jerusalem, the rebuilding of the temple, and the celebration of the Feasts of Tabernacles and Passover. The place of the prominence of the law resides in the background of these two books.

Erhard S. Gerstenberger of Giessen, Germany, composes the essay on "The Psalter." He begins by noting the fact that various exegetical approaches to the

Psalms have been used over the last one hundred years. With Hermann Gunkel in the first part of the 20th century, the Psalter began to be seen in terms of genres and life settings instead of authorship. Today, the interpretation of the Psalms is not uniform. Varied backgrounds of interpreters produce different results. Literary analyses are developing that regard the individual psalms as literature. New literary theories include structuralism, deconstruction, post-modernism, reader-response, and so forth. Psalms are looked at as independent autonomous units, each with its own voice. Other approaches include the psychological, dramatic, musical, and pedagogic.

Gerstenberger views the following fields as the most promising for study of the Psalter. To begin with, there is socio-liturgical research. The Psalter is linked to some kind of worship. Even so, the psalms had their diverse life settings including temple feasts, victory celebrations, household cults, and so forth. Worship from early Israel to the Persian and perhaps even Hellenistic periods should be seen as the background of the psalms. Thus, social and liturgical settings should be examined in terms of each psalm. Feminist interpretation also provides an important area of psalm research. Women's participation in Israelite worship needs to be recovered. Another area of importance for psalm research is worship literature in the ancient Near East along with appropriate iconography. These include hymns, the connection with sacrificial and festival traditions, laments, the New Year's festival, enthronements of kings, and iconography that betrays at times psalmodic metaphors and images. Thus, Old Testament psalms are a part of ancient Near Eastern sacred literature. Psalms also need to be examined by comparative data from anthropological research. Prayer services, rites of worship, and purification from uncleanness present in other cultures provide possible insights into the settings for the various Old Testament psalms. Redaction criticism is a continuing method that helps to uncover collections of psalms beyond individual texts. And even the superscriptions may provide some clues to groupings of psalm sets. Finally, continuing research in the theology of the psalms remains important. This includes basic human conditions of needs and fears, experiences of divine and demonic powers, and the relationship to God in history, creation, and daily life. The emphasis on Zion, faith, and morality reflects the political and social world that is present in a psalm's background.

Katharine J. Dell of Cambridge, England, writes the third essay in Part VIII. Using traditional methodologies, Professor Dell's essay on "Wisdom Literature" explores three Wisdom texts from the Hebrew Bible: Proverbs, Job, and Ecclesiastes. While having many similarities, the three books have differences that indicate a movement from a confident view of world order and justice to one of pessimism. There also is a change from sentence literature to dialogues to autobiographical narrative. In Proverbs, there is a strong affirmation of retribution that is grounded in the justice of God enacted in world order. God is the creator and sustainer of life. This shifts in Job when a righteous person suffers unjustly. Job's real debate is with God. Only God can provide the answer to Job's questions of "Why?" Once more God is the creator, though he does not answer

Job's questions directly. Ecclesiastes offers a mood of resignation and views that often are contradictory. Death is ultimately the fate of all, both good and evil, wise and foolish. God is mysterious, and while he possesses the knowledge of what is to be, humans do not. Thus, in all three books there is an emphasis on the relationship between God and humanity. The social contexts for wisdom are varied ranging from the family to the school. Proverbs is largely pre-exilic, dating from the monarchy, while Job likely comes from the exile, and Ecclesiastes from the late post-exilic period, from the 5th to the 3rd centuries BCE. This dating points to the progression of thought in the three wisdom texts.

The final essay – "Apocalyptic Literature" – in Part VIII, which concludes the volume, is written by John J. Collins of New Haven, Connecticut. In the Hebrew Bible, the genre of apocalyptic literature is represented only by Daniel, but there was a series of apocalyptic Jewish texts not included in the Hebrew canon, some three centuries before the writing of the New Testament Book of Revelation. Using traditional methodologies, Collins points to major features of apocalyptic. These include the point that the revelation of God, mysterious as it is, is usually given indirectly, say in dreams or by an angel. Daniel presents an overview of history, divided into periods of four kingdoms. The four great beasts are four kings arising from the sea. These are usually identified as Babylon, Media, Persia, and Greece. Thus, the literature is often deterministic, since God controls human history. However, predictions, as for example the three and a half years the temple would be defiled and then restored, proved to be unreliable and often in need of reformulation. Judgment is seen as a judgment of the dead, resulting in eternal reward or punishment for individuals. Daniel, like other apocalypses, draws heavily on ancient Near Eastern mythology for images to speak, not of beginnings, but of the end-time. Thus in Daniel the Sea suggests chaos in Ugaritic lore, while the "one like a son of man" riding on the clouds and the white-haired deity recall the Canaanite deities Baal and El. Apocalyptic is usually seen as crisis literature where visionaries dream of salvation beyond this world. For instance, in Daniel the suffering Jews wished to know how long their affliction would continue. Apocalyptic, like Daniel, often speaks of moral dualism, where the world is divided into good and evil. Yet the present world of evil and suffering is passing away, and will be replaced by an enduring Kingdom over which God would reign. This literature, far from being pessimistic, is one of hope in a new reality, though its time is not known.

Conclusion

These essays demonstrate the principal areas of biblical study that are undergoing major investigation. New results in each of these areas have been summarized. However, the varieties of approaches at work in these essays indicate that the interpretation of the Hebrew Bible is witnessing major transition. Scholarship is no longer experiencing unanimity in ways of studying the Bible. This variety of approaches will likely continue for many years to come.

PART I
The Hebrew Bible in Modern Study

CHAPTER 1
Preparatory Issues in Approaching Biblical Texts

Antony F. Campbell, SJ

Interpretation does not happen in a void. Interpretation emerges out of a context and speaks into a context. Interpreters are not disembodied voices. There is an interplay of interests at work, whether social or emotional, cultural or national, academic, financial, or religious. It is tempting to focus exclusively on the insights and achievements of individuals; these are usually accessible in their publications. We need to be aware of the existence of wider influences and interests that surge around individual scholars and shape something of their work.

This contribution to *The Blackwell Companion to the Hebrew Bible* aims at providing those interested with a basic understanding of some of the insights and practices at work in modern scholarship. Fundamentally, this means coming to grips with preparatory questions that may be relevant for modern biblical study and recognizing elements important for the exploration of a biblical text. There is no such beast as "modern biblical scholarship"; there is a multitude of biblical scholars. Observations about what is done must, therefore, remain tentatively sketchy; not all will recognize themselves. On the other hand, what is written here may initiate people into what this practitioner believes are among the central preparatory tasks of biblical interpretation.

This contribution is not a history of modern biblical interpretation. That has been done in German (Kraus, 1969). Something similar has been done in English (Hahn, 1966). John Rogerson has gone into detail for the 19th century in Germany and England (Rogerson, 1984). A study of the Hebrew Bible and its modern interpreters has appeared in the SBL centennial trilogy (Knight and Tucker, eds., 1985). Significant figures and movements have left their mark on modern biblical interpretation; their concerns cannot be ignored. Here, however, respectful mention of our forebears will be subordinated to the attempt to prepare for the task that they have left to us: interpreting the biblical text.

The key element of biblical interpretation in recent centuries can be summed up in the adjective "critical." "Historical-critical" is misleading; it can suggest a concern with history that is not necessarily central. Understood as the opposite of "ahistorical," "historical" describes a state of intellectual awareness; in this acceptation, "historical-critical" is an acceptable descriptor. "Method" is misleading; it can suggest predetermined steps that follow each other in logical sequence instead of the verification of insight and intuition. "Critical" is the element that separates moderns from their predecessors. The interpreters of the past were often great scholars and brilliant minds. But at a certain point in the intellectual history of western Europe a critical spirit emerged and decisively influenced the way that texts have been read ever since. It is this critical spirit that we need to identify and see at work in the task of interpretation.

Some maps of the United States trace a continental divide or watershed from Montana to New Mexico. Mountains obviously mess this up – for example, the Appalachians in the northeast or the San Gabriels in the southwest. The messiness is helpful for the use of the watershed as a literary metaphor. For there is a watershed between the process of a text's coming into being, its growth and development, and the task of interpreting the text that has come into being, that exists. But it is messy. There is no hermetic partition keeping the two aspects apart; they tend to impact on one another. Where biblical text is concerned, most of the issues discussed in this chapter explore aspects of the development of a text, its coming into being. The modern issues relating to the task of interpreting the already existing text are treated in chapter 2.

Beneath the watershed separating development from interpretation lies the massive issue of the nature of the text involved. The issue can be considered from the point of view of the origins of the text: from above or from below – directly divine (few), directly human (few), somewhere in between (most). Considered reflection reveals that origins do not determine nature. Both divine and human texts can claim to impose thought or to invite to it. The nature of the biblical text can only be determined by observation of the text itself. A signpost pointing in a single direction is helpful to the traveler, if the direction is the right one. Several signposts pointing in different directions to the same destination may also be helpful, but not immediately; perhaps they invite to reflection and further exploration. Many readers will find that the Bible often offers conflicting signposts (i.e., competing YHWH faith claims), from extensive issues – such as creation, flood, deliverance at the sea, sojourn in the desert, conquest of the land, emergence of monarchy, and even divine providence – to matters that can be compassed in a verse or two. The biblical text tends not to adjudicate, but to amalgamate. In such cases, readers are invited to thought; the signposts point in differing directions. The decision about what is predominantly the nature of biblical text and how it functions is one that needs to be remade out of the experience of the text by each generation of its readers. Any other way risks dogmatism or superstition. These considerations should not deflect attention from the complementary roles of the biblical text: to arouse feeling, fire imagination, and fuel faith.

It may also be helpful to realize that we approach texts in much the same way as we approach people. Mutual communication requires us to sort out languages and accents; the influence of cultural origins may be important; at some stage we become aware of whether someone has their act together or can, for example, be subject to unexpected emotions; over time, we come to know something of people's early history and later influences. We have people we meet for the first time, where we learn as much of this as we need to for the present; we have old friends, where much of this is well-known to us. Reading a biblical text can involve similar processes, both when we are reading it for the first time and when it is an old favorite.

It is also helpful to be aware of the difference between our meeting people, and doctors, psychiatrists, therapists – health professionals – meeting patients. We listen attentively; they listen attentively too, but differently. They pay attention to things we might not think of: skin color, tension, breathing, energies, conflicts, posture and body language, etc. We are meeting somebody; they are not only meeting somebody but they are also making a diagnosis, correlating symptoms with possible conditions. The enjoyment of friends is not a time for the exercise of professional expertise. Professionals approach a patient differently. The difference between *reading* a text and *studying* a text has a lot in common with the difference between meeting a person and meeting a patient.

What we discuss below are aspects of biblical text that experience has shown – in shifting contexts – to be of lasting value for modern study.

The Developmental Insights and Questions of Modern Study

Text boundaries

Boundaries are important, whether we are talking about acquaintances, friends, or professionals – to say nothing of real estate. Boundaries are also important for texts. Since Aristotle, we have known that a text has a beginning, a middle, and an end. Not all the texts we are called upon to study will form such rounded wholes.

The boundaries of a text – where a passage begins and ends – are not always easily determined. A student needs to be aware of the issue; more may not be readily possible. Hebrew usually repeats subjects and objects sparingly. Prefixes and suffixes, often translated by pronouns etc. in a language like English, can sustain meaning for longish passages of text. Independent passages do not normally begin with a prefix or suffix; subjects and objects are named within such passages. As a rule of thumb, this can be useful; beyond it, a student is often left to reflection and intuition.

Where a text is considered to begin or end may radically alter its interpretation. Often, all that can be asked of an interpreter is awareness of the issue.

Text criticism

With the wealth of texts available to us today, text criticism – i.e., among differing textual witnesses, determining which to rely on in a given passage – is best left to professionals (cf. Tov, 1992).

The reevaluation of subjectivity has correctly crept up on the text critic. Modern discoveries have tended away from simplicity: "the Scriptures were pluriform . . . until at least 70 CE probably until 100, and quite possibly as late as 135 or beyond. Thus we must revise our imaginations and our explanations . . . we can see now more clearly that there were multiple literary editions of many of the biblical books" (Ulrich, 1994, p. 92).

In Gen 1:26, the Hebrew text has "over the cattle, and over all the earth"; the Syriac text has "over the cattle, and over all the wild animals of the earth." Comparison with vv. 24 and 25 leads many moderns to the view that the Syriac is correct; the Greek and Latin, however, follow the Hebrew. In 1 Sam 1:18, the Hebrew text has "and the woman went her way and she ate and she no longer had her [sad] face"; the Greek text has "and the woman went her way and entered her lodging and she ate with her husband and drank and her face was no longer fallen." Explanations are possible; certainty is not. In Isa 2:12, the Hebrew text has "against all that is lifted up and low"; the Greek text has "against all that is high and towering, and they shall be brought low." Translations follow the Hebrew, or emend the Hebrew, or follow the Greek; unanimity is not to be had.

Origin criticism

This section should be headed "source criticism"; why "origin criticism" can be explained a little later. The basic insight from which this approach began was that some biblical passages were made up of material from more than one origin. In 1753, Jean Astruc entitled his book: *Conjectures about the sources which it appears Moses used in the composition of the book of Genesis*. For those who worry about Darwinism, it helps to note Darwin's dates: 1809–82. Critical analysis of the Bible began from the Bible; it was on the scene before Darwin boarded the Beagle (cf. Roberts, 1999). While we can trace the beginnings of this insight back at least to Richard Simon in 1678, the name most deservedly associated with its application is that of Julius Wellhausen (1844–1918). His insight and clarity of expression have left their mark indelibly on modern biblical studies.

Wellhausen was not alone. While for many his name stands as symbolic of critical analysis of the Older Testament, he came toward the end of a long period of passionate engagement with such studies, above all at German universities. Figures such as Herder (1744–1803), Eichhorn (1752–1827), De Wette (1780–1849), Ewald (1803–75), and Vatke (1806–82) are only a few of those who preceded him. Many were to follow, with shifting emphases; among the Germans, there are scholars like Gunkel, Greßmann, Alt, Noth, von Rad, Fohrer. There are others of eminence in other countries; overall, it would be invidious to single out names. For many, the analytical study of biblical origins brought conflict with traditional church teachings or traditional church people. Wellhausen himself wrote to the government minister responsible asking to be transferred from his chair in theology, because he did not consider he was adequately fulfilling his practical task of preparing theology students for their future. While the fact of diverse origins is taken for granted today, the best way of understanding the shape of such origins is vigorously debated. Academics and church people have come to terms with the diversity of origins in biblical text. It may not be unfair to say that many adherents, whether in academic or church circles, have not yet come to terms with how these understandings can be fully used to fire imagination and fuel faith.

Once upon a time, this aspect of biblical study was designated "literary criticism," following the German term *Literarkritik*. With the application of literary study, properly so called, to the realm of biblical literature, "literary criticism" in English at least could only be used for the study of the literary qualities of a text. The old "literary criticism" came to be referred to generally as "source criticism." This would be perfectly suitable, if it were not for the drawback of confusion with pentateuchal sources (e.g., J, E, and P). What is now termed "source criticism" should have a far wider range than the comparatively narrow concern for pentateuchal sources. Source criticism is concerned to ask about the origin of material in a biblical passage. If we think of it as "origin criticism," we will understand the term "source" correctly.

Once the insight has been gained, the question has to be asked: what is the origin of this material? As no less a critic than Martin Noth has argued, the fact that a source division is possible does not mean that it is necessary. The practice of some source criticism, especially in the Pentateuch, has given rise to obsessive fragmentation of texts as well as conditioned refusal to see the obvious. The observation of origins is largely about differences and duplication. Not all duplication and not all differences, however, go back to different origins. So the focus has to be sharpened to differences that cause difficulty and duplication that causes difficulty. When such difficulties arise, the issue of origins needs to be raised and the question has to be asked.

Examples from the Pentateuch, the Deuteronomistic History, and the prophets will shed light on what is meant. The issue here is not primarily how questions are best answered; rather, the issue is primarily what in the text requires that such questions be asked?

In the early chapters of Genesis, two sets of details are found about the flood. One set involves a forty-day block of time – with seven pairs of clean animals and a sacrifice and only one pair of unclean animals, and the floodwaters come from a rainstorm. The other set involves a one hundred and fifty-day block of time – with one pair of all animals and no sacrifice, and with floodwaters that come from above and below. However these signals are accounted for, there are difficulties that need to be considered. Later in Genesis, two stories are told about Hagar. In Genesis 16, harshly treated she takes the initiative and is a survivor; she leaves her brutal mistress and is found at a well on her way home. In Genesis 21, she is deprived of initiative and expects her child to die. Harmonization is possible; the biblical text does it with Gen 16:9. But difficulties are there and need to be considered. Difficulties need to be considered regarding Jacob the deceiving rat of Genesis 27 and Jacob the model son of Gen 28:1–9. Different origins may be helpful in making sense of the difficulties.

In Exodus 13–14, there is the traditionally significant account of Israel's deliverance at the Reed Sea. At the gesture of Moses' hand, the waters are parted to left and right, Israel marches across, followed by the Egyptians who are then swamped. But also, in the same text, there is reference to the pillar of cloud moving from in front of Israel to take up station between Israel and the Egyptians all night (14:19–20*), to God's wind blowing the water away all night (14:21*), and finally to God from the pillar of cloud causing panic among the Egyptians at the end of the night so that they retreated across the dry seabed and were swamped by the returning waters (14:27*) – assuming that God's "all-night" wind stopped with the dawn. Since the Israelites were told to turn back and camp by the sea (14:2), they had already gone past it. Crossing the sea was not the problem; escaping the Egyptian pursuit was. The text has difficulties; they need consideration. Exod 15:1–18 adds to the complexity. Different origins may need to be taken into account.

In the Deuteronomistic History, similar difficulties can be encountered and appeal to different origins may be involved in a solution. In 1 Samuel 7–12, for example, chs. 7–8 have the prophet Samuel subdue the Philistines for a generation and agree to setting up a king for Israel (cf. 7:13; 8:22) before chapter 9 gives God the initiative of bringing Saul to Samuel to be anointed by Samuel as ruler and to save Israel from the Philistines, since Israel's cry has reached God (cf. 9:15–17). Furthermore, Saul is acclaimed king in 10:24 and made king again in 11:15. Harmonization is attempted in 1 Samuel 12, but not very successfully. According to 8:1–5, the request for a king resulted from the unjust behavior of Samuel's sons; in ch. 11 the crowning of Saul as king followed his stunning victory over the Ammonite Nahash. According to 12:12, it was the threat posed by Nahash that triggered the demand for a king. Some modern harmonizations have done better, but Noth's comment remains: "it was not without obvious effort and contrivance that Dtr. supplemented the old account which dealt favorably with the institution of the monarchy by adding long passages reflecting his disapproval of the institution" (Noth, 1991, pp. 83–4). Appeal to different origins may help interpret a difficult text. Other examples may be found in 1 Samuel 17–18 and 1 Kings 8 (see Campbell and O'Brien, 2000).

In the prophets, assessment of the origin of material often comes under the rubric of "editing history" (see below). However, there are cases where the assumed combination of prophetic collections of sayings is not unlike the combination of traditions assumed for the Pentateuch. A case in point may be found in Isaiah 5–10. Isaiah 6 witnesses to Isaiah's call (or at least a commission to the prophet). Isa 7:1–8:15 follows with traditions relating to the Syro-Ephraimite war, including the famous Immanuel oracle. With Isa 8:16–22, Isaiah's activity appears to have reached closure. Finally, Isa 9:1–7 (NRSV) has a strong prophecy of salvation for those now in gloom and darkness. In short, all the components of a prophetic collection are encompassed: commission, ministry, closure, and future hope.

Surrounding this collection, however, there may be another. Isa 5:1–7 is the Song of the Vineyard. It ends with the powerful poetry of v. 7:

> he expected justice (*mišpāṭ*),
> but saw bloodshed (*miśpāḥ*);
> righteousness (*ṣĕdāqâ*)
> but heard a cry (*ṣĕ'āqâ*)!

A series of "woe" sayings (in the NRSV: "Ah, you") follow (5:8–24), illustrating the absence of justice and righteousness and exemplifying the bloodshed and outrage. There are seven sayings in the series, but the seventh is in 10:1–4. After the joyous ending of 9:7 comes a series of sayings against Israel, each ending with a refrain: "For all this his anger has not turned away; his hand is stretched out still." The refrain occurs in 9:12, 17, 21; 10:4, but also in 5:25. That a collection should be put together exemplifying and illustrating a poem as powerful as the Song of the Vineyard is not surprising. That the series of woe sayings and the series with the refrain should both be represented on either side of the apparent collection in Isa 6:1–9:7 is surprising. These are difficulties that need explanation. A difference of origins may contribute to better understanding.

The issue of origins in the Pentateuch is a special case. Over more than a couple of centuries of analytical study, it was observed that relatively coherent texts could be built up from extensive passages attributed to a Yahwist (using the personal name of Israel's God, YHWH), or to an Elohist (using the common noun for God, *elohim*), or to a Priestly writer (initially using the common noun for God, *elohim*). To these was added the book of Deuteronomy, thus giving four so-called sources, J, E, P, D. Debate raged over the nature of these texts, their relationship to the law codes (Ex 20:22–23:33; Lev 1–16 and 17–26; Deut 12–26), the order and dating of their composition, and the manner of their combination to form the present text. Further subdivisions and variants were proposed; various ways of combination or supplementation were put forward. When consensus seemed achieved, consensus fell apart (cf., Campbell and O'Brien, 1993). Since the collapse of consensus, there is agreement that the Pentateuch is made up of materials of widely differing origins; there is agreement on precious little else. For the present, a fresh consensus seems unlikely.

Form criticism

Form criticism may be the most elusive of the creatures in the garden of Older Testament scholarship. The association of form with setting promised histories of Israel's literature, and its religion; such promises were not fulfilled. The psalms would seem an ideal field for form-critical research. Assured results have been meager: a distinction between individual and communal, between psalms of complaint and lament and psalms of praise and thanksgiving, and royal psalms; the leftovers are left over. After Westermann, we have grown familiar with the form-critical structure of the prophetic oracle: accusation, messenger formula, and announcement (Westermann, 1967). The most rigorous attempt to put form-critical study on a thoroughly scientific basis had the unexpected effect of making clear that this is not a fruitful way to go (Richter, 1971). For all its elusiveness, form criticism embodies one of the central gains of modern biblical study.

Form criticism is based on the insight that significant features of certain works of literature derive from something quintessential to those works, often associated with the social settings that generated the literature. Form criticism appeals to a modern concern for the whole, the gestalt. It seeks to answer the question, "What sort of text are we dealing with?" and to address the issue of the interrelationship of the parts within the whole.

Viewed generally, form criticism is as automatic as breathing; it is something we do regularly, for example, when we distinguish reporting from comment from humor from advertising in our newspapers. Few of us, confronted with "Dear Sir or Madam" and "My darling beloved", would hesitate as to which was the business letter and which the love letter. From another point of view, it may not be easy to distinguish convincingly between a story being told and a report being given of what happened. In theory, reports follow the sequence of events and stories move through plot from the creation of tension to its resolution. In practice, such distinctions may not be easy to make. Is the text about Samuel's beginnings (1 Samuel 1) a story or a report? Does it matter? The text about the first couple in the garden (Genesis 2–3) is one thing if it is a story and another if it is a report. As a rule, report is uninterpreted; story begins the task of interpretation – or may have been created to address what needs interpretation.

From one standpoint, form criticism is a liberation from the obsession with history. The so-called "historical books" (i.e., Joshua, Judges, Samuel, Kings) may well be more theological than historical, more concerned with the meaning of Israel's destiny than with reporting its past. To ask the question "What is the literary form of this text?" is to open the way to what may be a more adequate understanding of a text's meaning.

What robs form criticism of the capacity for tidy classification is an essential quality of literature and art: there needs to be a fundamental model of expectation in relation to which the individual work can situate itself. It was the hope of form criticism to be able to work back toward the understanding of such matrixes. It is the sorrow of form criticism that we are usually left contemplating the individual achievement, without the matrix. Nevertheless, despite the uncertainty of the answers, the form-critical questions are essential for the interpreter.

The first question is: what is the literary form of this text? The answer may be simplistically easy. Apodictic law is quite different from casuistic law. A psalm of praise is quite different from a psalm of lament. The answer may not be easy at all, relying on the observation and intuition of the interpreter. The second question is more complex: what are the basic components of this text and how do they relate to each other? It is relatively easy to talk about features in a text; it is more challenging to talk about their interrelationship. If a passage is only a part of a larger text, then we need to ask what sort of a part it is, how it relates to its context, and what is the literary form of the larger text to which it belongs? Similarly, we can address this question to the larger blocks forming a text or to the elements that go to forming one of the blocks. The third question is: how does the interrelationship of the text's components function to communicate its meaning?

Two trends particularly militate against the successful application of form criticism. One is the security given by a focus on detail; outreach to the whole is dangerous. The other is the difficulty of putting persuasive words on the perceptions that underlie an intuitive conviction. Up till now, there has been no adequate codification of the body of experience and observation that takes form criticism beyond the relatively obvious and easy. It may be that no such codification is possible; the equivalent to a diagnostic manual may never be achieved. Just as anxieties about air quality should not stop us breathing, anxieties about form-critical uncertainty should not stop us from attempting to articulate what is intuitively assumed.

Some examples will help. Early in Genesis, it is relatively simple to realize that Genesis 2–3 (the garden) and Genesis 4 (Cain and Abel) are stories and that Genesis 5 and 10–11 are genealogies. It takes closer observation to notice the differences between Priestly and Yahwist (10:8–30) genealogies. The different origins of the material in the flood text (Gen 6:5–9:17) have been noted above; the structural interrelationships of the present text are noteworthy. The decision to destroy is first made in God's heart (6:5–8), then communicated to Noah (6:9–22); after the flood, the decision never again to destroy is first made in God's heart (8:21–22) and then communicated to Noah (9:1–17). The significance of this second decision is theologically huge: despite human sinfulness, God's commitment is unshakable.

The sacrifice of Isaac (Genesis 22; in Jewish tradition, the binding of Isaac) is a story; it begins with the announcement of a test and the whole hangs on its outcome. The story form reaches its conclusion in v. 14, with the naming "The LORD will provide," closed off with Abraham's return to Beer-sheba in v. 19. It is possible to see the highly enigmatic story as one of basic trust – "The LORD will provide." The angel's second intervention (vv. 15–18) has a different focus (blessing) and a different interpretation (obedience, v. 18b). The variant has been skillfully introduced between vv. 14 and 19.

In the Deuteronomistic History, the text on the loss of the ark is instructive (1 Samuel 4). The structure is simple. There is a battle report; Israel lost (vv. 1b–2). There is an inquiry into the loss and a decision to bring the ark from Shiloh (vv. 3–9). There is a second battle report; Israel lost more heavily and lost the ark (vv. 10–11). Appended to this are two anecdotes, emphasizing the significance of the loss: Eli died when he heard of it (vv. 12–18); his daughter-in-law, dying in labor, gave her child a name meaning "the glory has departed from Israel" (vv. 19–22). The form-critical question is whether all this is a matter of report or a matter of storytelling.

If it is a matter of report, then the question of the elders in v. 3 is reported because the elders asked it before anything else happened. If it is a story, then the storyteller has the question asked knowing full well what the outcome is going to be in vv. 10–11. The question is: "Why has the LORD put us to rout today before the Philistines?" (v. 3a). In a report of what happened, one might surmise that the elders answered their question with the thought that they may have lost because they did not have the ark with them. In a story, where vv. 10–11 are known as the outcome, the answer to the elders' question has to be to the effect that it was the LORD's will to do so. The absence of the names of any military leaders and the emphasis on Philistines, Israel, and elders may be a pointer to a story rather than a report. The reaction credited to the Philistines (vv. 6–9) heightens the likelihood of the text being a story; it heightens the tension. If it is a report, the potential is there for theological reflection to be distilled from the event; if it is a story, the process of theological distilling has been begun. Israel's storytellers were often theologians.

In 1 Kgs 4:1–19, there is an account of Solomon's officials and those responsible for the provisions of his court. The text is regarded as deriving from authentic records of the royal court. In Numbers 2, there is an account of the marching order of Israel for the journey from Sinai to the promised land. The slightest familiarity with the tortuous terrain of the Sinai peninsula dismisses its authenticity as a record; it can then be recognized as a programmatic document, with interest for the priorities of the tribes. These are form-critical decisions. They are made in the light of our knowledge today, building on what we know of the Bible and the Ancient Near East.

In 2 Kgs 6:8–24, there is a fascinating text about Elisha supplying intelligence to the king of Israel, the Aramean king getting upset about it, and Elisha blinding the commandos sent to arrest him, leading them through the city of Samaria, and providing them with a banquet before sending them home. Plausibility is not the issue. As a report, it would tell of a remarkable event – whether fact or fiction. As a story, the interpretation of the event has been begun: prophetic knowledge is praised, Aramean folly laughed at, and the power of God's prophet celebrated. Report or story? Asking the question is sometimes easier than ascertaining the answer.

In the book of the prophet Amos, form-critical observation of Amos 1–2 and 7–9 shows how strongly patterned both collections are and how different they are from each other and from Amos 3–6. Both collections, however, portray Israel's situation as beyond appeal, beyond intercession. Close observation of form-critical aspects of a small passage such as Amos 3:3–8 is also revealing. In vv. 3–6, questions are asked, each assuming a statement or state of affairs. "Do two walk together unless they have made an appointment?" In v. 8, however, two statements are made, each followed by a question. Clearly, v. 8 is the formal climax of the passage.

Verses 3–5 constitute a five-line series, each line containing one example and each beginning with the Hebrew interrogative particle (hă-). The examples are drawn from natural observation; if the effect can be observed, then the cause may be assumed. Verse 6 consists of two lines, each beginning with the Hebrew "if." A literal translation is:

> If a trumpet is blown in the city, surely (Heb. "and") the people are afraid?
> If disaster befalls a city, surely (Heb. "and") the LORD has done it?

The first is a natural observation; given the cause, the effect follows – when the alarm is sounded, people are afraid. The second is a theological observation, a faith claim; if an effect can be observed (destruction), then the cause (the LORD) may be assumed. The final pair of lines in v. 8 builds on all this. The cause is stated: "the lion has roared . . . the LORD God has spoken"; the effect necessarily follows: "who will not fear? . . . who can but prophesy?" A further step is needed to articulate the full interpretation of the passage, but the use of form in the service of meaning is clear.

Tradition history

The insight that lies behind the traditio-historical question is the realization that often aspects of tradition can be identified – whether by language, faith, concern, or other particulars – so that a text can be situated within the sweep of Israel's traditions, highlighting the earlier contributions it draws on and the contribution of its own that it makes. Sometimes a distinction has been attempted between oral and written tradition; it is complex and difficult at best – and dubious where it seeks to blend orality with antiquity and antiquity with God. The capacity to trace Israel's traditions, allowed us by Israel's reverence for its past, permits us precious access to the unfolding of Israel's thinking. The intensive pursuit of such insights can have wide ramifications (e.g., von Rad, Noth); in other situations, the observations remain within a more restricted realm.

Examples may be taken from the Pentateuch, the Deuteronomistic History, and the prophets. The scope is wide; the examples only a tiny fraction of the totality available. So, for example, it is possible that Gen 17:1–2 echoes an older tradition of God's commitment to Abraham, earlier expressed in Gen 12:1–3 (or equivalent). The promise that through Abraham blessing will be mediated to all the families of the earth is expressed in identical terms in Gen 12:3b and 28:14, in slightly different terms in Gen 18:18b, and with a further difference again in the deuteronomistic passages Gen 22:18 and 26:4b. The implication of tracing this tradition through these five occurrences is the possibility of its theological claim having existed in Israel at least from the Yahwist to the Deuteronomist (perhaps beyond; cf. Isa 19:24–25 and Gal 3:8).

In 1 Kings 8, in Solomon's prayer of dedication (vv. 14–21), there is a strong appeal to God's promise to David in 2 Samuel 7. It is a good example of how two texts, presumably of interest to the same deuteronomistic circles, can formulate the same tradition with notable differences. For all its reverence for the past, there are places where Israel's theologians appear remarkably free of any obsession with verbal accuracy.

At the end of the Deuteronomistic History (in 2 Kgs 25:27–30), there is a notice of King Jehoiachin, the last reigning survivor of David's line, being released into a form of house arrest at the Babylonian court. The passage can be read as echoing favorable actions of God in Israel's past; it can also be read as echoing the fate of Mephibosheth and the end of Saul's line (2 Sam 9:1–13; also 2 Sam 19:28 and 21:7). Whatever the implications of the passage, it plays on the traditions of Israel (cf. Granowski, 1992).

In Hosea 12, we find a wide range of references to Jacob, among them: trying to supplant his brother in the womb, wrestling with God, the encounter with God at Bethel, his service in Syria for a wife and his shepherding there. Much of the pentateuchal tradition associated with the patriarch Jacob can here be the subject of discussion in the 8th century prophet (cf. de Pury, 1989).

Editing history

The insight that leads to asking questions about editing is the realization that Israel's editors often allowed their interventions to be visible – inviting reflection. In English, the terms "redaction criticism" and "redaction history" are widely used. These reflect transpositions of the German "Redaktion" and the French "rédaction," both terms that refer to matters in English called "editorial." The English word is preferred here, not on chauvinistic grounds, but to avoid potential mystification arising from the use of foreign terms. "Editing" is appropriate to the partial or total reworking of a text; it can be operative at any stage in a document's history, from early to middle to late – but it presumes the existence of a text. Editors can piece together components to form extensive documents (so the editors termed R^{JE} and R^{JEP} in the Pentateuch or the editors of prophetic collections and prophetic books); naturally, they can also do smaller editing jobs. Some study of a text's editing history (as for its tradition history) might be described in terms of intertextuality. There is scope for overlap between origin criticism and editing history.

From the Pentateuch, for example, Ex 19:3b–9a is of a different origin from its surroundings; it could owe its place in the text to editorial activity. The difference of origin is evident: 19:5 already has a covenant in view, before the one that lies well ahead in the present text. In v. 9a, the passage has its own preparations for God's self-disclosure. Two aspects may have attracted an editor's attention. It is an unusual covenantal text, in that the outcome is explicitly conditional: "if you obey my voice and keep my covenant." On the other hand, at stake is more than bare relationship. Israel does not become simply God's people, but God's "treasured possession," "a priestly kingdom and a holy nation." The last two are unheard of elsewhere in the Hebrew Bible; the first is rare (cf. Deut 7:6; 14:2; 26:18). The passage does not appear to belong in one of the pentateuchal sources; an editor may well have felt the need to preserve the tradition.

In the Deuteronomistic History, 1 Kgs 9:6–9 offers an example. In vv. 3–5, God has answered Solomon's prayer, consecrated the temple Solomon has built, and has put there for all time God's name and God's eyes and heart. Solomon's dynastic rule over Israel is assured, on condition of Solomon's fidelity (v. 4). All this is expressed in second person *singular* address to Solomon. With the exile of Judah in 587, the Davidic/Solomonic dynastic rule came to an effective end; with the Babylonian sack of Jerusalem, God's consecrated temple was destroyed. So in vv. 6–9, God's words are expanded in a second person *plural* address that has to include the people and that deals with the possibility of infidelity and apostasy. The tension is acute and difficult. One solution is to see vv. 6–9 as an editorial expansion, bringing an earlier theology into line with a later reality. Similar editorial comments on this issue are to be found in 1 Kgs 11:32–33*, 39.

Toward the end of the Deuteronomistic History, King Josiah and Judah made a covenant before YHWH. Details of the participants are given in 2 Kgs 23:2. The final statement is: "all the people joined in the covenant" (23:3). A few verses earlier, these same people are written off as hopeless apostates who have incurred God's unquenchable wrath (see 22:16–17). The context does not allow for repentance; editorial adjustment is an appealing possibility. If the hypothesis of a Josianic Deuteronomistic History is envisaged, Josiah's death and the abandonment of his reform required an extensive editorial undertaking, bringing a different vision to bear on seven books of biblical text (see Campbell and O'Brien, 2000).

Among the prophets, Amos has a couple of chapters in which God's judgment is pronounced over Israel's neighbors and, finally, over Israel itself (Amos 1–2). The pronouncements are structured on a remarkable pattern. There is an introduction ("Thus says the LORD"), a proverbial opening ("for three . . . and for four"), a denial of appeal ("I will not cause it to return"), a reference to the crime, a reference to the punishment, and in all but three cases a concluding phrase ("says the LORD"). There are eight such sayings: against Damascus, Gaza, Tyre, Edom, Ammon, Moab, Judah, and Israel. In seven of them, the crime is a matter of social justice, usually related to excessive violence in war. In the case of Judah, however, the crime is in a totally different sphere: "they have rejected the law of the LORD, and have not kept his statutes, but they have been led astray by the same lies after which their ancestors walked" (2:4). Of course, prophets are entitled to an exception or two. On the other hand, the combination of factors may suggest later editorial activity here.

While with Amos we might note 3:7, passed over earlier. Its interruption of the tight sequence of vv. 3–6 and v. 8 creates a difficulty. Its reference to the prophets as God's servants suggests deuteronomistic origin. The combination of the two makes an editorial comment from deuteronomistic circles a distinct possibility.

Conclusion

How recent and how radical the discovery of the Ancient Near East has been regularly comes as a surprise. The staples of early exploration were languages and archaeology.

Among the major languages, Egyptian was deciphered in 1822 (thanks to the Rosetta Stone, a tri-lingual inscription we owe to Napoleon's troops in 1799). Of the Mesopotamian languages, Sumerian was not translated until 1907; the translation of Assyrian and Babylonian was recognized by 1857 (thanks to the Behistun inscription, again a tri-lingual carved on a mighty rockface). Fledgling studies of Hittite civilization culminated in excavations at Boghazköy, begun in 1907; decipherment of the language had to wait for the discovery of the bilingual Karatepe inscription in 1947. The discovery of Ugarit (also known by its modern name of Ras Shamra) began in 1928; decipherment of the language, in an alphabetic cuneiform script, was agreed on by 1932.

Archaeology is a recent science, especially when distinguished from the adult version of a glorified treasure hunt. Excavation in Mesopotamia led the way, but did not begin until 1843 (Khorsabad, 1843; Nimrud, 1845; Warka, 1850; Ur and Eridu, begun in 1854–55). In 1871, Schliemann began digging at Hissarlik in western Turkey and found Homer's city of Troy. In 1877, de Sarzec, a French consul, began digging at Telloh and found the Sumerian civilization. In 1899, Sir Arthur Evans began digging at Knossos in Crete and discovered the Minoan civilization. Where Palestine is concerned, tunneling began in Jerusalem in 1864–67, the Palestine Exploration Fund was founded in 1865, and in 1890 Sir Flinders Petrie undertook the first stratigraphical excavation in Palestine at Tell Hesi (cf. generally, Daniel, 1968).

There are many more; others take up the story. In recent years, much has been learned; in the years ahead, we may assume there will be much more to learn.

What was said early in this essay may be recalled: the approaches discussed here are related to insights and questions about the nature of Older Testament text and its development; they are not methods, to be applied in much the same way that sausage-making processes are applied to minced meat and the rest.

As insights, these approaches have been validated over a long period of time. The phenomena discussed are to be found in some biblical texts, not in all. Not all are equally important for understanding a text where they might be found. As questions, they need to be asked of texts. Not all interpreters will give the same answers. Not all interpreters will give their answers the same significance. Nevertheless, the awareness flowing from these insights and questions will in varying ways shape part of the context within which any interpretation of biblical text proceeds.

Further Reading

Method and "how to" books are often problematic. Some leave nothing out and cover too many good things; others leave too much out and do not cover enough good things. The inexperienced risk being confused, misled, or overwhelmed; the experienced, who ought not need them, can find them insightful and stimulating. Rather like reading the

Bible, it is a matter of knowing what to make one's own and what to leave alone; an experienced guide can be most helpful. If that caution can be taken to heart, the English-language books listed below may be useful in varying ways.

Barton, J., *Reading the Old Testament: Method in Biblical Study* (London: Darton Longman and Todd, 1984).

Hayes, J. and C. Holladay, *Biblical Exegesis: A Beginner's Handbook* (Atlanta: John Knox, 1982).

Haynes, S. and S. McKenzie (eds.), *To Each Its Own Meaning: An Introduction to Biblical Criticisms and Their Application* (Louisville: Westminster/John Knox, 1993).

Kaiser, O. and W. Kümmel, *Exegetical Method: A Student's Handbook* (New York: Seabury. German copyright: 1963; translator's copyright: 1967).

Morgan, R. with J. Barton, *Biblical Interpretation* (Oxford: Oxford University Press, 1988).

Steck, O., *Old Testament Exegesis: A Guide to the Methodology* (translated from the 13th German edition by J. D. Nogalski. Second edition. SBLRBS 39. Atlanta: Scholars Press, 1998). German versions have been in use for over 25 years.

Stuart, D., *Old Testament Exegesis: A Primer for Students and Pastors* (2nd edn. Philadelphia: Westminster, 1984).

The series of booklets, *Guides to Biblical Scholarship*, with an Old Testament series and a New Testament series, published by Fortress Press.

Bibliography

Campbell, A. and M. O'Brien, *Sources of the Pentateuch: Texts, Introductions, Annotations* (Minneapolis: Fortress Press, 1993).

——, *Unfolding the Deuteronomistic History: Origins, Upgrades, Present Text* (Minneapolis: Fortress Press, 2000).

Daniel, G., *The First Civilizations: The Archaeology of their Origins* (London: Thames and Hudson, 1968).

Granowski, J., "Jehoiachin at the King's Table: A Reading of the Ending of the Second Book of Kings," in D. Fewell, ed., *Reading Between Texts: Intertextuality and the Hebrew Bible* (Louisville: Westminster/John Knox, 1992), 173–90.

Hahn, H., *The Old Testament in Modern Research* (Philadelphia: Fortress Press, 1966).

Knight, D. and G. Tucker, eds., *The Hebrew Bible and Its Modern Interpreters* (The Bible and Its Modern Interpreters. Philadelphia: Fortress Press, 1985).

Kraus, H., *Geschichte der historisch-kritischen Erforschung des Alten Testaments*, 2nd edn., (Neukirchen: Neukirchener Verlag, 1969).

Noth, M., *The Deuteronomistic History*, JSOTSup 15, 2nd edn. (Sheffield: JSOT, 1991; German original, 1943).

Pury, A. de, "La tradition patriarchale en Genèse 12–35," in A. de Pury, ed., *Le Pentateuque en question: Les origines et la composition des cinq premiers livres de la Bible à la lumière des recherches récentes*, MDB (Geneva: Labor et Fides, 1989), 259–70.

Richter, W., *Exegese als Literaturwissenschaft: Entwurf einer alttestamentlichen Literaturtheorie und Methodologie* (Göttingen: Vandenhoeck & Ruprecht, 1971).

Roberts, M., "Not Literalist After All: A Response to Paul Badham," *Expository Times*, 111 (1999), 17–18.

Rogerson, J., *Old Testament Criticism in the Nineteenth Century: England and Germany* (London: SPCK, 1984).

Tov, E., *Textual Criticism of the Hebrew Bible* (Minneapolis: Fortress Press, 1992).

Ulrich, E., "The Bible in the Making: The Scriptures at Qumran," in E. Ulrich and J. VanderKam, eds., *The Community of the Renewed Covenant: The Notre Dame Symposium on the Dead Sea Scrolls* (Notre Dame: University of Notre Dame, 1994), 77–93.

Westermann, C., *Basic Forms of Prophetic Speech* (Philadelphia: Westminster, 1967).

CHAPTER 2

Methods of Modern Literary Criticism

David Jobling

The work surveyed in this chapter is the outcome of meetings between biblical studies and the discipline of "literary criticism" – the critical study of world literature focused in departments of English and other languages, or of comparative literature.

Biblical Criticism and Literary Criticism

Over the last thirty years, which is the scope of this survey, literary criticism has been riven, perhaps more than any other discipline, by "culture wars." The conflict is basically between a traditional and a resistant understanding of what literature is and how it should be studied, or, though the terminology is imprecise and much disputed, between a "modern" and a "postmodern" approach to literature (on postmodernism, see Bible and Culture Collective, 1995, pp. 1–19). Traditionalists concentrate their work on literature which they regard as being of supreme quality, sometimes referred to as the "canon of great books," or the "classics," the ones which everyone needs to know in order to be an educated member of society. Explicitly or implicitly, they claim for their work a high degree of objectivity; that their methods are the best available, able to be learned and practiced equally by everyone, and that they produce correct understandings of the literature to which they are applied. Those who resist this tradition point to the many things that it excludes. The "canon" leaves out, for the most part, literary work by people at the margins of privileged society, whether this be women, members of racially repressed groups, peasant cultures whose "literary" productivity consists of oral folktales, or others. The resisters note also that the academic guild of literary critics has grossly underrepresented these same marginal groups, that it has been overwhelmingly male, white, etc.

These critics, it is further said, utilize only a fraction of the methods available, and, in defense of the autonomy of literature, tend to be suspicious of interdisciplinary approaches.

Those who seek to redefine literary criticism pursue two strategies (not at all mutually exclusive). On the one hand, they introduce new works to the "canon" (or simply get rid of the notion of canon). Introductions to literature cease to be parades of "great books," and begin to include works by marginal writers which often have been repressed and almost forgotten. On the other hand, they reread the books of the "canon" from previously marginalized social locations and using new methodological tools. They often suggest that the "great books" themselves have reinforced social practices which limit women, denigrate people of color, and so on. For the most part these resistant critics do not suggest that the classics should no longer be read, or even that they should be no longer regarded as great literature, but that they should be read with new eyes, giving a voice to groups of people whose experiences and interests they do not represent and using approaches apt for this task. To this new kind of reading the name "deconstruction" is often applied in a general and inexact way. We will later give a more precise meaning to this very important word.

One major effect of this explosion of new methods of literary criticism is that the very term "literary" has ceased to have a clear definition. What happens, some recent critics ask, when we read "as literature" – using the methods of literary criticism – writings which have not normally been included in that category: works of history or science, for example, or even products of popular culture like horoscopes? One way of expressing this shift is to see the object of criticism not as "literature" in the accepted sense but as "texts" in a much broader sense. Once this move is made, the object of attention quickly ceases to be confined even to written texts, and comes to include the "text" of a film, a social system, even the human genome. One typical postmodern move is to read "texts" of very different kinds in unexpected combinations, to discover ways in which they may illuminate each other; this is called "intertextuality."

Already in the early 1980s, the literary critic Terry Eagleton invited literary criticism to put itself out of business and redirect its efforts into contributing to a general critique of culture (p. 204). This typically postmodern agenda is by now both enthusiastically embraced and fiercely resisted within departments of "literature."

Up to a point, the work on the Bible here surveyed can be seen in analogous terms. In the recent literary study of the Bible we can discern a relatively orthodox stream with old antecedents and a resistant movement which, at least in its present extent and the variety of forms it takes, is quite new. The situation of resistant biblical critics differs in one major respect, however, from that of their colleagues in general literary studies. They cannot do much to change the "canon." The Bible is "canon" in a much more precise and exclusive sense than any "canon of great books" could be (in fact the very term "canon" is borrowed from the religious tradition). Aside from a certain amount of renewed attention to non-canonical texts from the biblical period, resistant reading of the Bible consists of new kinds of critical attention to the canonical text itself. The developments we will review have tended to follow, after some lapse of time, similar developments in general literary criticism. But Eagleton's process of the merging of literary approaches into a general cultural criticism is now well advanced even in biblical studies. We will seek to give reasonably specific senses to the word "literary," but the reader should be warned that hard and fast definition of this term will not help us to understand what is now going on. New methods emerge, combine and recombine in bewildering ways. For the decade of the 1990s it is really not possible to "survey" all the things that have emerged under the general heading of "literary approaches" to the Bible. We can only direct the reader's attention to some that seem particularly important.

One more introductory point is in order. Recent contributions to the literary study of the Bible have come, to an extent unmatched in any other area of biblical studies, from scholars who do not belong to the "guild," who do not define themselves as scholars or teachers of the Bible. We will be constantly referring to, and will include in the Key Readings for this chapter, works by specialists in English or other literary disciplines. For example, the figures who have done most to create a main current in the literary study of the Hebrew Bible, Robert Alter and Meir Sternberg, fall in this category. So do many postmodern readers of the Bible, whose work has in many cases been virtually unknown to specialist biblical scholars (but now see the collection by Jobling, Pippin, and Schleifer). In this situation, it is not surprising that specialists on both the biblical and the literary side sometimes belittle each other's work on the grounds of ignorance of each other's discipline. Much of this is just self-interested sniping – in the current interdisciplinary climate we all make use of work in fields not our own and can only do our best to do so responsibly. We will not in what follows press distinctions between the work of biblical and literary specialists.

The Bible as a Literary Classic

As late as the 1960s (as the present writer can personally attest from having studied at that time) "the Bible as literature" was simply excluded from academic biblical studies. Biblical studies was a historical discipline. It existed in an unclearly defined relationship to theology and practices of religious faith, but neither history nor faith was perceived to have any interest in the Bible's quality as literature or its accessibility by the methods of literary criticism. This sorry situation has now been utterly transformed. When we identify a mainstream approach in the literary study of the Bible, against which many scholars now feel the need to rebel, we should not lose sight of the fact that *any* kind of literary study of the Bible represents a revolution in the field, against the unjustified dominance of historical criticism (which itself, if we go far enough back, was a revolution against ecclesiastical control over the reading of the Bible!).

The literary revolution has been accomplished over a remarkably brief period, and the credit for it is shared by literary readers of the Bible of all stripes.

Nor does what we are calling the mainstream consist of one narrowly defined school. Rather, it is made up in a loose way of the work of scholars who, for a variety of reasons, want to preserve for the Bible a place of some centrality and authority. This may be for religious reasons, but it may also arise, with no overt religious motive, within a conservative approach to literature in general (see above), as some critics seek to demonstrate and preserve the Bible's *literary* importance within western culture, sometimes even its centrality in the canon of great books. It is as *both* the religious and the cultural effects of the Bible have begun to be questioned, as people have asked whether its centrality in church and society has been a good thing, that the resistant methods have emerged. But no one should deny the immense accomplishments within the mainstream or try to flatten their great variety. Those who reach out in new directions frequently acknowledge their debt to more orthodox readers and realize that the lines of demarcation are never clear.

As we consider the antecedents of the new literary trend, we need to recognize that some of the great pioneers of historical methods (see chapter 1) brought to their work a large measure of literary skill. For example, the founder of form criticism, Hermann Gunkel, was a highly sensitive literary critic whose work paved the way for recent developments. James Muilenburg, one of the few major scholars to resist the historical captivity of biblical studies in the 1960s, deeply appreciated Gunkel's literary accomplishment and sought to extend it to the Bible's larger literary units by a method he called "rhetorical criticism." The 1960s also saw important contributions from Luis Alonso Schökel, Edwin Good, and others to what by 1970 was an emerging – though still not an established – literary trend (for this paragraph and much else on antecedents, see Morgan with Barton, 1988, pp. 205–24).

During the 1970s, literary approaches gained in sophistication. One trend in America arose out of the literary "New Criticism," which subordinated historical issues to consideration of the literary text as a work of art. Representative here is the first of the volumes edited by Kenneth R. R. Gros Louis (1974). It is uneven, though James Ackerman's reading of the Moses birth story is notable. By the time of the second volume (1982) the methods are much more varied and the readings less predictable. In 1978 David Gunn published an impressive book-length treatment of King David which affirmed the literary autonomy of the text while remaining in touch with historical criticism. But the most remarkable – and uncompromising – assertion in the 1970s of the necessity of a close literary reading of the biblical text was J. P. Fokkelman's reading of parts of Genesis (1991). Fokkelman tries to determine in objective fashion the literary organization of biblical narratives, from the micro-level of words to the macro-level of large groups of chapters. The full development of his method is not to be seen until his later four-volume work on Samuel and Kings (1981–93), but the Genesis book provides a less daunting introduction to his unique approach.

The next stage is the one that can be summarized under the names of "Alter and Sternberg." Robert Alter is an American literary critic who demonstrates in biblical texts a literary skill and imagination no less than (though different from) what we seek in great novels and poetry. In *The Art of Biblical Narrative* he examines the Bible according to both general literary-critical categories – like character, dialogue, and repetition – and its own special conventions, such as the "type-scene" (scenes like "the woman at the well" which reappear in varied forms). Throughout he shows a deep sensitivity to the Bible's techniques of narration (1981; cf., 1985, where he applies literary insights to biblical poetry; further on poetry, see Kugel). Students whose experience of academic biblical studies has been confined to a survey course frequently report how a reading of Alter opens up a new biblical world for them, making them dwell on the detail, showing them the compositional skill. Meir Sternberg is an Israeli critic who approaches the biblical text with an eye to features of its literary *form* (his background is in Russian Jewry, and he is influenced by the Soviet school of "formalist" literary criticism founded by Mikhail Bakhtin). Sternberg is harder to read than Alter. The text-based chapters of his seminal work (1985) are long and extremely detailed, but richly rewarding. They show the Bible's immense literary power, to be discovered when we respect its autonomy and listen without imposing our categories and questions upon it. Sternberg's lengthy arguments at the beginning of the book for the Bible's uniqueness and literary preeminence are less rewarding.

A considerable group of other scholars, both Israeli and American, mostly but not exclusively Jewish, work with assumptions generally similar to those of Alter and Sternberg. Among the most prominent are Shimon Bar-Efrat, Adele Berlin, Lyle Eslinger, Herbert Marks, Robert Polzin, Joel Rosenberg, and George Savran. The work of these and other like-minded scholars represents in sum a vast contribution to the new literary reading of the Bible. An inexperienced reader might begin with Alter (1981) and Berlin (who gives particular attention to women characters), and then move to some of the chapters of Sternberg and to Polzin's work on 1 or 2 Samuel (1989, 1993).

By the mid-1990s, there were signs that this general approach had achieved a considerable degree of dominance in the literary study of the Hebrew Bible. It staked its most powerful claim through the 1987 publication of *The Literary Guide to the Bible*, edited by Alter and Frank Kermode. This physically imposing volume brings together a notable list of contributors who provide literary readings of all the books (or sections) of both testaments (along with some general essays). It exudes great confidence that "this is the way to do it."

Yet from the perspective of the year 2000, this intended summation of the field seems to have missed the boat. The fundamental problem is that it takes a view of the literary study of the Bible which, already in 1987, was much too narrow. The narrow methodological scope is the editors' deliberate choice – in their Introduction they give reasons why they have excluded a variety of approaches, including Marxist, psychoanalytic, deconstructive, and feminist. And the list of authors, despite their individual credentials, is grotesquely white male. Some excellent things in the book, particularly by authors who refused to respect the "Keep Out" signs posted in the Introduction (James Ackerman, David Gunn, Francis Landy, Gabriel Josipovici), fail to offset the sense of anachronism which a reader feels now. The dominance of the approach spearheaded by Alter and Sternberg has already receded (for critiques, see Bal, 1987, pp. 59–72; Long).

Counter-reading 1: The Beginnings

We turn now to the explosively varied trends in the recent "literary" reading of the Bible, beginning with some antecedents. In 1969, the English anthropologist Edmund Leach published his *Genesis as Myth and Other Essays*. Though few realized it, this marked a major turning point, and it is emblematic of the complexity of the field that it came from one who was *neither* a biblical *nor* a literary specialist. Leach's work introduced "structuralism" into biblical studies. Structuralism is a major twentieth-century current of thought derived from pioneering work in many disciplines, including Ferdinand de Saussure in linguistics, Vladimir Propp in folklore studies, and Claude Lévi-Strauss – on whom Leach directly depended – in anthropology. Structuralists posit that humans find intelligibility in the world of experience through largely unconscious processes whereby they organize experience in terms of "binary oppositions" (up–down, light–dark, male–female, and so on). Humans manipulate the many different oppositions into structures of sufficient complexity to explain the world to their satisfaction.

It was in France that structuralism was first adapted by literary specialists (such as A. J. Greimas and Gérard Genette) into methods for reading literature, and eventually for reading the Bible (see Bible and Culture Collective, 1995, pp. 70–118; Jobling, 1995). Structural analysis is very different from, in fact almost directly opposite to, close reading in the manner of Alter and Sternberg. It looks not for conscious literary art, but for evidence of literary *structuring*, which is likely to be mostly unconscious. In this view, people produce and understand stories in a way analogous to how they produce and understand sentences in ordinary language – by applying internalized rules for what constitutes a well-formed utterance. Structuralism works better for large collections of literature (whole biblical books or even the whole of scripture) than for single stories. Its impact has been greater on New Testament (especially through the many works of Daniel Patte) than on Hebrew Bible studies. The present author has explored the possibilities of reading narrative texts of the Hebrew Bible in ways based on Lévi-Strauss and Greimas, with emphasis more on exegetical and theological pay-off than on the technical apparatus of structuralism (Jobling 1986a, 1986b; see also *Semeia* 18 and, following a different structuralist track, Polzin, 1980).

Meanwhile, still in the 1970s, a quite different but equally momentous turn was occurring in the literary study of the Bible, this time in America. As the women's movement extended its impact through many aspects of American culture, women and some men began to develop new ways of looking at the

Bible. Few of these worked in consciously literary ways. The most important of those who did was Phyllis Trible. A student of Muilenburg, she heeded his call for a new "rhetorical criticism," and analyzed through close literary reading the Bible's presentation of women characters and their stories, as well as female images of God. Trible's early work (1978), at once impassioned and meticulous, had a unique impact, as much on laywomen and men in church settings as in the academy. It remains essential reading.

Counter-reading 2: Poststructuralism and Ideological Criticism

Trible's book not only made a unique contribution to the development of biblical feminism, it also established a link between literary reading of the Bible and reading from a position of political commitment. (It was not quite the first such link; in an astonishing book first published as early as 1974 Fernando Belo had adapted a form of structuralism to the reading of the Bible in the context of Latin American liberation theology.) The establishment of this link has done much to give to the postmodern reading of the Bible in the last two decades its particular form. To use a rather precarious metaphor, the feminism and the structuralism which in the 1970s existed in isolation from each other both bred offspring in the 1980s, and their offspring have interbred prolifically.

Structuralism, first of all in France, gave rise to a whole range of "post-structural" trends in philosophy (Jacques Derrida), psychoanalysis (Jacques Lacan, Julia Kristeva), cultural history (Michel Foucault), and other disciplines. These trends had a variety of impacts on the reading of literature, but perhaps the most direct impact was that of Derrida's method of "deconstruction." Derrida's philosophical program is to reread the entire history of western philosophy as establishing certain values or "truths" by the suppression of their opposites. Starting from Lévi-Strauss's work on binary oppositions in human consciousness, Derrida suggests that key oppositions, such as male–female, light–darkness, reason–emotion, have been put in hierarchical relationship. The first term of each pair is valued above the second, and this superiority is presented as belonging to the natural order of things. This order in due course becomes self-evident, and questioning it becomes in effect impossible within the categories that the philosophical tradition makes available. The "naturalness" of this state of things has been asserted or just assumed in the classics of philosophy from Plato onward. The method of deconstruction is a way of reading texts (especially, in Derrida himself, the texts of this western philosophical tradition) to show how they fail to prove what they claim to prove, how they make arbitrary choices between "undecidable" possibilities, how they must always at some point *assume* what they exist to demonstrate.

The "offspring" of early feminism consists not only of the new forms feminism has taken since the 1970s, but also of other liberation movements in the areas of gender, race, and class. This is not to say that the others are somehow logically dependent on feminism, but rather that feminism's establishment of itself as a powerful counter-discourse in American and other cultures came first and created space for the others. To some degree, these counter-discourses have entered into relationship with each other; for example "womanist" criticism exists in a complex relationship to feminist and Afro-American criticisms.

One way of naming the cumulative cultural critique exercised by these counter-discourses is "ideological criticism." According to the Marxist theory out of which this term originates, social oppression of any kind must always be sustained by the creation of "false consciousness." Class-divided societies generate structures of thought that justify and perpetuate the preeminence of a dominant class. The same analysis can be extended to ideologies which justify the dominance of one sex or race. For such dominance to be comfortably sustained, the *dominated* group, as well as the dominant, must be brought under the umbrella of false consciousness – the oppressed must accept their oppression as "natural." Ideological criticism examines such structures of false consciousness, in a way that reveals the interconnectedness of different forms of oppression. False consciousness tends to "divide and conquer." Different forms of dominance, according to class, sex and race, generally coexist in the same ideology, but the ideology obscures these links, trying to set the oppressed against each other. Ideological criticism reveals the links, showing, for example, how the denial of full rationality to both women and blacks is part of a single system of oppression. (The New Testament critic Elisabeth Schüssler Fiorenza has helpfully given to this complex system of dominations the name "kyriarchy.")

The relationships over the last two decades between what we are calling ideological criticism and poststructuralism (including particularly deconstruction) have been profound, but also extremely complex and conflictual. Some people engaged in liberation struggle have rejected deconstruction and other modes of postmodern analysis on the grounds that they undermine all meaning and leave liberation struggle no ground on which to stand. But others have perceived an almost total convergence between deconstruction and ideological criticism, since both are trying to undermine dominant systems of thought and practice. Leading intellectual figures within postmodernism have responded to political liberation movements with everything from full participation to hostility or indifference (see Jobling, 1990).

For postmodernism and deconstruction the Bible seems to represent an obvious target. In the development of western culture it has been one of the foundational documents, claiming to give a comprehensive account of all experience. It is just such foundations and comprehensive accounts (often called "metanarratives") that postmodernism subverts. The fundamental oppositions which the Bible seems to establish – between God and humanity, humanity and the non-human world, law and grace, spirit and letter, etc. – eminently invite deconstruction.

In fact, this agenda has not been much pursued by biblical scholars. The most skillful appropriation of Derrida (and Foucault) for biblical studies has been by

Stephen Moore, a New Testament critic (1994). Perhaps the best early examples of a straightforwardly deconstructive reading of Hebrew Bible narrative, without any obvious political agenda, are two books by Peter Miscall (1983, 1986). Miscall stresses the ambiguity or "undecidability" of the biblical narrative, over many issues, as an intrinsic feature to be exploited in interpretation, rather than as a problem to be solved.

Some scholars (see Handelman, and cf. also Harold Bloom) hypothesize a special link between the rise of postmodernism and Judaism, including specific-ally the Jewish tradition of biblical interpretation. Jewish intellectuals (including among many others, Derrida himself) have been prominent in the establishment of the postmodern climate. Why should this be? Judaism, we might say, is the part of itself which the dominant Christian West has had to repress in order to create its own specific identity, and eventually, as Freud would way, the repressed will return (Freud himself speculated that only a Jew could have invented psychoanalysis). Postmodernism is a turning inside-out of the Christian west-ern tradition. But, beyond these general historical considerations, some see the Jewish tradition of midrashic biblical interpretation as having entered into the texture of postmodern literary theory in a more specific way. In contrast to most Christian commentary, where an individual authoritative voice presents the latest "truth" about the text, the work of midrash is communal and open-ended, a conversation between different rabbinic authorities in which minority views are preserved for further consideration by future generations.

The essays in the excellent collection edited by Hartman and Budick explore the link between Judaism and postmodernism through the reading of various biblical texts. But the reader might do even better to turn to Emmanuel Levinas's "talmudic readings" (1990). Levinas is a French philosopher who has been largely credited with the turn in postmodern discourse towards philosophical ethics. He expounds portions of the Talmud, which is itself the deposit of the vast work of rabbinic interpretation of the Bible in the first centuries of the Common Era, and finds there – both in the contents and in the communal method of interpretation – the basis for dialogue between the Bible and the postmodern world.

Some readers, notably Bloom and Sternberg, compare the Hebrew Bible with the New Testament in point of literary merit, to the extreme disadvantage of the latter. At their worst, such comparisons show little care for the religious sensibil-ities involved. Nonetheless, a critical literary reading can open up fundamental differences between the different scriptures in a way which encourages rather than stifles dialogue. This is superbly done in a book that ought to be better known, Gabriel Josipovici's *The Book of God*. Josipovici brings to his reading of the Bible the skills of a novelist as well as a literary critic. He concentrates most of his attention on the Hebrew Bible, showing the fundamental rhythm, the interplay of repetition and novelty, by which it establishes its view of the world. He looks at its presentation of memory, dialogue, character, and so on with a literary finesse not inferior to Alter's, and more engaging because it is so resolutely "personal." Later he turns to the New Testament, first contrasting it sharply with the Hebrew Bible, but then softening the contrast. By its very juxtaposition with the Hebrew Bible, the New Testament takes on a literary character utterly different from and better than any other early Christian writings, and wins itself a place as permanent religious literature. It is the present writer's experience that Josipovici, better than any other book, enables beginning (especially Christian) students to discern and reflect on their most fundamental assumptions about scripture.

A literary assessment of ideological criticism of the Bible, readings of the Bible done in conscious relation to movements for liberation, is made more difficult by the fact that many liberation writers do not define their methods as "literary" or look for connections with general literary criticism. Some certainly do – the feminist writings, for example, of Claudia Camp, Cheryl Exum, or Danna Fewell and David Gunn have always been deliberate and skilled in their employment of the categories of literary criticism. But in the mid-1980s a catalyst was needed for a more profound linking of liberation and postmodern readings of the Bible (on this need, see Jobling, 1990). The catalyst came in the form of a trilogy of books on the Bible by Mieke Bal (1987, 1988a, 1988b), in which she brought biblical texts into critical conversation with an unprecedented range of other disciplines. The field was ready to explode in this way; if Bal had not come along, we would have had to invent her. But her particular combination of skills had a definite shaping effect.

Bringing long experience of a European feminism that was theoretically powerful but politically without a very clear location, Bal entered a North American scene (initially via a major Protestant theological seminary) where the women's movement had made political gains but was thirsty for new and more fundamental ways of critiquing the dominant culture. The resources Bal brought were, first of all, those of a "critical narratology" (the French subtitle of the book partially translated as *Lethal Love* was "The Old Testament at risk from a critical narratology"!). This theory of narrative emerged from the literary structuralist approach of Genette. In Bal, Genette's ideas are exposed to all the critical, political, postmodern currents of Europe in the 1970s and early 1980s; his meticulous and probing analysis of the ways literature works becomes in her hands a tool for analyzing how literature works as a dominant, conservative cultural system. The central literary monuments of western culture, not least the Bible, are certainly "at risk" from such an approach. The chapter of *Lethal Love* on Genesis 38 (the story of Tamar and Judah), for example, shows how some interesting analysis by Genette of how literature organizes time (by flashbacks, simultaneous action, and so on) can be turned into a means of questioning the Bible's fundamental notions of time and history.

Lethal Love is the best point of entry into Bal; its five biblical readings touch on most of the issues which she develops elsewhere. *Murder and Difference* is more for specialists in biblical studies – here Bal examines, using the specific example of Judges 4–5, the assumptions underlying the whole range of methods of biblical interpretation. Judges is also the topic of the last of the trilogy, *Death and Dissymmetry*. This is the best but also the most challenging of the books. In a series of chapters, Bal brings all of her particular interests, notably psychoanalysis, anthropology, and the theory of graphic art and film, to bear in turn on the question of just what the book of Judges is, what it achieves in its position in the Bible. Her answer is that it provides literary justification for what probably was a historical process in Israel, the transition, resulting in significant loss of power for women, from one form of marriage to another.

Counter-reading 3: Recent Contributions

Since Bal's trilogy the floodgates have been open to an extraordinary variety of literary reading of the Bible. We shall review some contributions from the 1990s, trying to discern a certain order, but conscious that many of these contributions (which are only a fraction of the body of work we might have alluded to) deliberately cross disciplinary boundaries and transgress any narrow limit to the "literary." Like Hamlet's players, our authors offer us "tragedy, comedy, history, pastoral, pastoral-comical, historical-pastoral, tragical-historical, tragical-comical-historical-pastoral" (*Hamlet* II ii) – for which read "feminist–deconstructive–psychoanalytic– . . ." Though often playful, they are engaged in very serious play, applying a range of reading methods that they find appropriate to the particular cultural issues which they wish to address. The authors here mentioned are in almost every case biblical specialists, though they often use methods that they have learned from literary critics.

One problem the general reader faces is that it has been relatively rare for biblical critics to pursue these issues at book length. A large proportion of the books in question are edited collections of essays, since it is at essay-length that the pioneering work is often done. Helpful collections (in addition to others mentioned below) are Black, Boer, and Runions; Exum and Clines; Schwartz (1990). Important essays also regularly appear in journals, notably *Biblical Interpretation, Journal for the Study of the Old Testament*, and *Semeia*.

Two books which are helpful in giving the reader a sense of the large territory here covered are those by Adam, though he stresses New Testament, and The Bible and Culture Collective. Also useful is Gunn and Fewell (1993).

In the wake of Bal, perhaps the most pervasive influence in the postmodern literary reading of the Bible continues to be feminism. Cheryl Exum's recent work shows a revealing progression. First, an exemplary treatment of tragedy in the Hebrew Bible (1992) which carries on a conversation with the classical literary tradition of the West while bringing feminism to bear as a secondary theme; next (1993), a powerfully feminist reading of the stories of mistreated biblical women, using cultural stereotypes of women (virgin, mother, whore) as an analytic tool; more recently (1996) an extension of this stereotype-analysis beyond the bounds of literature and into painting and film (see also Exum and Moore, a collection of essays which extends the search for traces of the Bible's presence into the broadest areas of historical and contemporary culture). There are other important critiques of the Bible's cultural influence which have been shaped by feminism. In *The Curse of Cain*, Regina Schwartz demonstrates how monotheism itself, the unquestioned bedrock of the Bible's view of reality, has shaped and been shaped by a nexus of exclusionary human practices, including the marginalization of the female. The role of the Bible in forming unequal human – especially gender – identities is likewise explored, using a great variety of literary methods, in the volume edited by Beal and Gunn.

Among the most accessible of the major contributions to feminist study of the Bible is Danna Fewell and David Gunn's *Gender, Power, and Promise.* They write at a level reminiscent of the widely read works of Phyllis Trible, though with different assumptions. They offer a reading of the long narrative beginning of the Bible (Genesis to Kings) which foregrounds the stories of women. They proceed *as if* women were the theme of the story, or rather – turning the text inside out – they make the very suppression of women into the "theme." Other feminist readings move in a specifically deconstructive direction. David Rutledge (1996) develops a theory of *marginal* reading – reading from places (such as women's places) from which the Bible does *not* invite us to read it – in explicit repudiation of Alter and Kermode's narrow definition of permissible reading. He applies his approach to the beginning of Genesis. Yvonne Sherwood (1996) brings the resources of Derrida to the reading of Hosea's enforced marriage to (perhaps) a prostitute (Hosea 1–3); no less valuable than the reading itself is her superb introduction to Derrida and literary deconstruction. A reader of Sherwood would do well to place alongside it Francis Landy's commentary on Hosea. Landy is hard to define methodologically, but out of a profound knowledge of both traditional and postmodern approaches he creates a scintillating reading of the biblical text.

For a broad overview of what has been happening in feminist reading of the Bible one should consult by far the most extensive of the many collections of essays, namely Athalya Brenner's multi-volume *Feminist Companion to the Bible* (including the methodological volume edited by Brenner and Carole Fontaine). This series is eclectic in the most positive sense, looking for the best material available regardless of its particular feminist style.

Black reading of the Bible has not engaged the academic field of literary criticism to anything like the extent that feminist reading has – no doubt because blacks have been even more excluded from that field than women – though some readers, such as Randall Bailey and Renita Weems, always show deep literary sensitivity. Here the question of what counts as "literary" becomes particularly pressing. Black writing on the Bible draws on traditions, such as preaching, spirituals, or the blues, which have not usually been called literature. Yet they are uses of language as fully developed as novels or sonnets, and postmodernism includes them in its decentered view of literature. (For explorations in these areas, see a number of the essays in Felder, 1991, and *Semeia* 47.)

A very powerful current in literary criticism which has still not made its full impact in biblical studies is the Marxist tradition. This is potentially fertile ground for any kind of ideological criticism, but it seems nearly invisible to biblical critics, especially in America. The English Marxist critic Terry Eagleton has been directly used by Norman Gottwald (*Semeia* 59, pp. 43–78) and has himself contributed a short reading of Jonah (in Schwartz, 1990, pp. 231–6). But the

Marxist critic whose work holds most promise for biblical studies is the American, Fredric Jameson. His book *The Political Unconscious* sets out a precise method for reading literature as symptomatic of the socio-political conditions of its creation, and he includes in his purview ancient and folk literatures, as well as the modern novel. His procedure has been used by the present writer (*Semeia* 59, pp. 95–127) and much more substantially by Roland Boer (1996). Boer's is a difficult book, but its exegetical chapters, with their combination of exact detail and breadth of philosophical implication, repay careful examination, and the long opening chapter is not only an introduction to Jameson but also a superb primer in Marxist criticism.

Just as the Jewish Bible (unlike the Christian one) lacks a "sense of an ending" and ends in a miscellany of different voices (the Writings), so we end by simply mentioning a number of good books which cover the whole methodological map. A fairly narrowly-defined form of the structuralist approach continues to generate impressive exegetical results in van Wolde (1994). Susan Niditch, in a series of books (of which 1993 is the best introduction), explores the origin of much biblical narrative in folklore, and sets the Bible in a rich transhistorical and cross-cultural context. A compelling and very funny style of feminist-psychoanalytic reading is invented by Ilona Rashkow (1993) as she sets the classic texts of Genesis and of Freud over against each other. The theory of fantasy literature, which has recently been developed in general cultural criticism, is used as a framework for reading biblical texts (including a number from the Hebrew Bible) in two books edited by George Aichele and Tina Pippin (1997, 1998). Religious readers may baulk at the idea of the Bible as fantasy, but it is clear that prophets and apocalyptic writers, for example, often address their own real world by creating worlds entirely outside human experience. "Autobiographical criticism," the critical study of how one's own experience shapes how one reads texts (and even decides what texts one reads), is presented in many guises in Kitzberger (1999; see also *Semeia* 72). Boer even turns the history of biblical criticism into fictional literature, "novelizes" it (1997).

Finally, several recent books attempt to continue the program that Bal consistently practices, of keeping texts and methods in immediate dialogue. As one reads texts, one keeps a constant eye on why one is reading them that way, and as one discusses methods, one keeps oneself honest by trying them on real texts. Such books can seem slow going, not offering quick exegetical results, as they try to accord full respect both to the Bible and to the postmodern context in which we now read it. But they afford the reader an excellent insight into the current practice of the literary study of the Bible. Books that adopt this style are Beal (1997) on Esther, Jobling (1998) on 1 Samuel, and Pyper on 2 Samuel.

Bibliography

Adam, A., *What is Postmodern Biblical Criticism?* Guides to Biblical Scholarship: New Testament Series (Minneapolis: Fortress Press, 1995).

32   DAVID JOBLING

Aichele, G. and T. Pippin, eds., *The Monstrous and the Unspeakable: The Bible as Fantastic Literature*, Playing the Texts 1 (Sheffield: Sheffield Academic Press, 1997).
——, *Violence, Utopia and the Kingdom of God: Fantasy and Ideology in the Bible* (London and New York: Routledge, 1998).
Alter, R., *The Art of Biblical Narrative* (London: Allen & Unwin, 1981).
——, *The Art of Biblical Poetry* (New York: Basic Books, 1985).
Alter, R. and F. Kermode, eds., *The Literary Guide to the Bible* (Cambridge, MA: Harvard University Press, 1987).
Bal, M., *Lethal Love: Feminist Literary Readings of Biblical Love Stories* (Bloomington: Indiana University Press, 1987).
——, *Death and Dissymmetry: The Politics of Coherence in the Book of Judges* (Chicago: University of Chicago Press, 1988a).
——, *Murder and Difference: Gender, Genre and Scholarship on Sisera's Death*, trans. Matthew Gumpert (Bloomington: Indiana University Press, 1988b).
——, *On Story-Telling: Essays in Narratology*, ed. David Jobling (Sonoma, CA: Polebridge Press, 1991).
Beal, T., *The Book of Hiding: Gender, Ethnicity, Annihilation, and Esther*, Biblical Limits (London and New York: Routledge, 1997).
Beal, T. and D. Gunn, eds., *Reading Bibles: Writing Bodies: Identity and the Book* (London and New York: Routledge, 1997).
Belo, F., *A Materialist Reading of the Gospel of Mark*, trans. Matthew J. O'Connell. (Maryknoll, NY: Orbis, 1981, orig. 1974).
Berlin, A., *Poetics and Interpretation of Biblical Narrative*, Bible and Literature Series 9 (Sheffield: Almond, 1983).
Bible and Culture Collective, The, *The Postmodern Bible* (New Haven: Yale University Press, 1995).
Black, F., R. Boer, and E. Runions, eds., *The Labour of Reading: Desire, Alienation, and Biblical Interpretation*, Semeia Studies 36 (Atlanta: Scholars Press, 1999).
Boer, Roland, *Jameson and Jeroboam*, Semeia Studies (Atlanta: Scholars Press, 1996).
——, *Novel Histories: The Fiction of Biblical Criticism*, Playing the Texts 2 (Sheffield: Sheffield Academic Press, 1997).
Brenner, A., ed., *The Feminist Companion to the Bible* (A series of volumes on different sections of the Bible) (Sheffield: Sheffield Academic Press, 1993–).
Brenner, A. and C. Fontaine, eds., *A Feminist Companion to Reading the Bible: Approaches, Methods and Strategies* (Sheffield: Sheffield Academic Press, 1997).
Eagleton, T., *Literary Theory: An Introduction* (Oxford: Blackwell, 1983).
Exum, J., *Tragedy and Biblical Narrative: Arrows of the Almighty* (Cambridge: Cambridge University Press, 1992).
——, *Fragmented Women: Feminist (Sub)versions of Biblical Narratives*. JSOTSup 163 (Sheffield: JSOT, 1993).
——, *Plotted, Shot, and Painted: Cultural Representations of Biblical Women*, JSOTSup 215 (Sheffield: JSOT, 1996).
Exum, J. and D. Clines, eds., *The New Literary Criticism and the Hebrew Bible*, JSOTSup 143 (Sheffield: JSOT, 1993).
Exum, J. and D. Moore, eds., *Biblical Studies/Cultural Studies: The Third Sheffield Colloquium*, Gender, Culture, Theory 7 (Sheffield: Sheffield Academic Press, 1998).
Felder, C., ed., *Stony the Road We Trod: African American Biblical Interpretation* (Minneapolis: Fortress Press, 1991).

Fewell, D. and D. Gunn, *Gender, Power, and Promise: The Subject of the Bible's First Story* (Nashville: Abingdon, 1993).

Fokkelman, J., *Narrative Art and Poetry in the Books of Samuel*, 4 vols. (Assen: Van Gorcum, 1981–1993).

——, *Narrative Art in Genesis: Specimens of Stylistic and Structural Analysis*, 2nd edn. (The Biblical Seminar 12 (Sheffield: JSOT, 1991, orig. 1975).

Gros Louis, K., with J. Ackerman and T. Warshaw, *Literary Interpretations of Biblical Narratives* (Nashville: Abingdon, 1974).

Gros Louis, K., with J. Ackerman, *Literary Interpretations of Biblical Narratives*, vol. 2 (Nashville: Abingdon, 1982).

Gunn, D., *The Story of King David: Genre and Interpretation*, JSOTSup 6 (Sheffield: JSOT, 1978).

Gunn, D. and D. Fewell, *Narrative in the Hebrew Bible* (New York: Oxford University Press, 1993).

Handelman, S., *The Slayers of Moses: The Emergence of Rabbinic Interpretation in Modern Literary Theory* (Albany: State University of New York Press, 1982).

Hartman, G. and S. Budick, eds., *Midrash and Literature* (New Haven and London: Yale University Press, 1986).

Jobling, D., *The Sense of Biblical Narrative: Structural Analyses in the Hebrew Bible 1*, 2nd edn., JSOTSup 7 (Sheffield: JSOT, 1986a).

——, *The Sense of Biblical Narrative: Structural Analyses in the Hebrew Bible 2*, JSOT Supplement Series 39 (Sheffield: JSOT, 1986b).

——, "Writing the Wrongs of the World: The Deconstruction of the Biblical Text in the Context of Liberation Theologies," *Semeia* 51 (1990), 81–118.

——, "Structuralist Criticism: The Text's World of Meaning," in G. Yee, ed., *Judges and Method* (Minneapolis: Fortress Press, 1995), 91–118.

——, *1 Samuel. Berit Olam* (Collegeville, MN: Liturgical, 1998).

Jobling, D., T. Pippin and R. Schleifer, eds., *The Postmodern Bible Reader* (Oxford: Blackwell, 2001).

Josipovici, G., *The Book of God: A Response to the Bible* (New Haven and London: Yale University Press, 1988).

Kitzberger, I., ed., *The Personal Voice in Biblical Interpretation* (London and New York: Routledge, 1999).

Kugel, J., *The Idea of Biblical Poetry: Parallelism and Its History* (New Haven and London: Yale University Press, 1981).

Landy, F., *Hosea*, Readings: A New Biblical Commentary (Sheffield: Sheffield Academic Press, 1995).

Leach, E., *Genesis as Myth and Other Essays* (London: Jonathan Cape, 1969).

Levinas, E., *Nine Talmudic Readings*, trans. with an Introduction by Annette Aronowicz (Bloomington and Indianapolis: Indiana University Press, 1990).

Long, B., "The 'New' Biblical Poetics of Alter and Sternberg," *Journal for the Study of the Old Testament* 51 (1991), 71–84.

Miscall, Peter D., *The Workings of Old Testament Narrative* (Philadelphia: Fortress, and Chico, CA: Scholars Press, 1983).

——, *1 Samuel: A Literary Reading* (Bloomington: Indiana University Press, 1986).

Moore, S., *Poststructuralism and the New Testament: Derrida and Foucault at the Foot of the Cross* (Minneapolis: Fortress Press, 1994).

Morgan, R., with J. Barton, *Biblical Interpretation*, The Oxford Bible Series (Oxford and New York: Oxford University Press, 1988).

Niditch, S., *Folklore and the Hebrew Bible*, Guides to Biblical Scholarship: Old Testament Series (Minneapolis: Fortress Press, 1993).

Polzin, R., *Moses and the Deuteronomist: A Literary Study of the Deuteronomic History. Part One: Deuteronomy, Joshua, Judges* (New York: Seabury, 1980).

——, *Samuel and the Deuteronomist: A Literary Study of the Deuteronomic History. Part Two: 1 Samuel* (San Francisco: Harper & Row, 1989).

——, *David and the Deuteronomist: A Literary Study of the Deuteronomic History. Part Three: 2 Samuel*, Indiana Studies in Biblical Literature (Bloomington: Indiana University Press, 1993).

Pyper, H., *David as Reader: 2 Samuel 12:1–15 and the Poetics of Fatherhood*, Biblical Interpretation Series 23 (Leiden: E. J. Brill, 1996).

Rashkow, I., *The Phallacy of Genesis: A Feminist-Psychoanalytic Approach*, Literary Currents in Biblical Interpretation (Louisville: Westminster/John Knox), 1993.

Rutledge, D., *Reading Marginally: Feminism, Deconstruction and the Bible*, Biblical Interpretation Series 21 (Leiden: E. J. Brill, 1996).

Schwartz, R., *The Curse of Cain: The Violent Legacy of Monotheism* (Chicago and London: University of Chicago Press, 1977).

——, ed., *The Book and the Text: The Bible and Literary Theory* (Oxford: Blackwell, 1990).

Sherwood, Y., *The Prostitute and the Prophet: Hosea's Marriage in Literary-Theoretical Perspective*, Gender, Culture, Theory 2 (Sheffield: Sheffield Academic Press, 1996).

Sternberg, M., *The Poetics of Biblical Narrative: Ideological Literature and the Drama of Reading* (Bloomington: Indiana University Press, 1985).

Trible, P., *God and the Rhetoric of Sexuality*, Overtures to Biblical Theology (Philadelphia: Fortress Press, 1978).

van Wolde, E., *Words Become Worlds: Semantic Studies of Genesis 1–11*, Biblical Interpretation Series 6 (Leiden: E. J. Brill, 1994).

Key Readings

Alter, Robert. 1981. *The Art of Biblical Narrative*. London: Allen & Unwin.

Bal, Mieke. 1988. *Death and Dissymmetry: The Politics of Coherence in the Book of Judges*. Chicago: University of Chicago Press.

Bible and Culture Collective, The. 1995. *The Postmodern Bible*. New Haven: Yale University Press.

Brenner, Athalya, ed. 1993. *The Feminist Companion to the Bible*. (A series of volumes on different sections of the Bible.) Sheffield: Sheffield Academic Press.

Exum, J. Cheryl. 1992. *Tragedy and Biblical Narrative: Arrows of the Almighty*. Cambridge: Cambridge University Press.

Fewell, Danna Nolan, and David Miller Gunn. 1993. *Gender, Power, and Promise: The Subject of the Bible's First Story*. Nashville: Abingdon.

Fokkelman, J. P. 1991. *Narrative Art in Genesis: Specimens of Stylistic and Structural Analysis*. 2nd edn. The Biblical Seminar 12. Sheffield: JSOT. (Orig. 1975.)

Jobling, David. 1998. *1 Samuel*. Berit Olam. Collegeville, MN: Liturgical.

Josipovici, Gabriel. 1988. *The Book of God: A Response to the Bible*. New Haven and London: Yale University Press.

Levinas, Emmanuel. 1990. *Nine Talmudic Readings*. Trans. with an Introduction by Annette Aronowicz. Bloomington and Indianapolis: Indiana University Press.

Miscall, Peter D. 1986. *1 Samuel: A Literary Reading*. Bloomington: Indiana University Press.

Sherwood, Yvonne. 1996. *The Prostitute and the Prophet: Hosea's Marriage in Literary-Theoretical Perspective*. Gender, Culture, Theory 2. Sheffield: Sheffield Academic Press.

Sternberg, Meir. 1985. *The Poetics of Biblical Narrative: Ideological Literature and the Drama of Reading*. Bloomington: Indiana University Press.

Trible, Phyllis. 1978. *God and the Rhetoric of Sexuality*. Overtures to Biblical Theology. Philadelphia: Fortress Press.

CHAPTER 3
Social Scientific Approaches

Charles E. Carter

The last four decades of the twentieth century saw the emergence of a new form of biblical criticism, one that gradually took its place alongside the more traditional types of analysis that had dominated scholarship since the middle of the nineteenth century. Social science criticism (Gottwald, 1992) developed from more modest uses of the social sciences to examine various aspects and functions of biblical cultures. It became its own form of analysis as biblical scholars studied and applied insights and models from cultural anthropology and macrosociology to the study of the Hebrew Bible in a holistic manner. Scholars took the same care in analyzing cultural traditions and developments as they previously had in the study of literary forms and biblical historiography. What they discovered as they applied the social sciences to the biblical worlds was that just as words and texts must be interpreted within literary contexts, cultures and traditions must be interpreted within social contexts. Thus, what began with two seminal articles by George Mendenhall, (1962) and Norman Gottwald (1974), brought a revolutionary shift in the discipline of Hebrew Bible studies. Now, many scholars are practicing and experimenting with social science criticism and Philip Davies has hailed literary and social science analyses of biblical texts as the primary methods of inquiry most likely to promote new understanding of scripture (Davies 1992, 1994). This chapter will examine briefly the events that led to the formation of this new discipline, discuss its context within the social sciences themselves, propose a set of guidelines for its appropriate use, and identify some contributions of social science criticism to First Testament studies.

Historical and Methodological Contexts

While the acceptance of social science criticism alongside its more traditional forms of analysis is rather recent, several significant studies laid its foundation and made it possible. If one broadly defines social sciences as observations about one's social and cultural setting, one can point to several "proto-sociological" observations about biblical Israel in the Hebrew Bible itself, in Classical Greek sources, in early works within Rabbinic Judaism (Carter, 1996, 1999b); (Wilson, 1984), and in Islamic historiography (Carter, 1999a, pp. 60–1). Similarly, some early biblical scholars conducted important studies of the flora, fauna, geography, archaeology, and climate of Syria–Palestine as a result of their pilgrimages to the "Holy Land" as early as the 17th century (Benjamin, 1994).

This was followed in the 19th century by explorations of Syria–Palestine and then by early scientific surveys such as those conducted by Edward R. Robinson (1856) and the later surveys of Conder and Kitchener (1883). These explorations and surveys continue to prove useful for analyses of the geographic, archaeological, geological and topographical context of the territory. These works are not typically included in the history of social science criticism of the Hebrew Bible, but have in fact helped set the context for sociological and anthropological understandings of antiquity. Societies are directly affected by their environment and develop technologies and social structures that allow them to adapt to their surroundings. Their physical surroundings may influence subsistence strategies, site distribution, and population, all of which have sociopolitical and socioeconomic ramifications that, if neglected, may decrease the accuracy of one's understanding of past cultures.

One of the first studies to apply the social sciences directly to Israelite culture was John Fenton's *Early Hebrew Life: A Study in Sociology* (1880). Fenton's brief work is important not only for its pioneering entry into sociology, but also because he maintained that one must distinguish between the literary form and social realities of texts. Acknowledging that many biblical traditions are not "historically accurate," he held that they could still reveal something valuable about the social world(s) behind them.

Scottish theologian and biblical scholar W. Robertson Smith is generally considered the founder of cultural anthropology (Douglas, 1966, p. 14). Smith is best known for two studies of social and cultural structures. His first major work, *Kinship and Marriage in Early Arabia* (1885), is still considered a classic on acephalous social groups. *Lectures on the Religion of the Semites: The First Series* (1889) presents Smith's analysis of the religious traditions and structures in different periods of Israel's history. He suggests that there was a movement from spontaneous worship to a more rigid ritual tradition. In the former, tribal cultures considered sacrifice to be an opportunity for the direct contact between people and the deity; in the latter, a more highly developed sense of moral responsibility and "payment" for sin developed. Smith's broad knowledge encompassed numerous semitic traditions and cultures and sought to draw parallels between Bedouin culture and ancient Israelite culture and society. Smith was not content to study Arab and Bedouin culture from texts alone but traveled to Syria–Palestine four times, conducting what could be seen as a precursor of ethnographic fieldwork. In 1991, John Day discovered the second and third series of lectures in the W. Robertson Smith library in Cambridge.

These analyzed social and religious traditions in Mesopotamia and Syria and sought to treat these cultures in a more sympathetic way. He wrote after the initial discoveries of some of the major Akkadian texts, but before the Ugaritic materials were unearthed. Despite the fact that some of Smith's conclusions have been discarded in the century since his lectures were delivered, his many studies remain important for any who would use the social sciences in biblical interpretation.

Although it is common to root the origins of sociology in the studies of August Comte, two fundamental ways of viewing social order are rooted in the work of Ferdinand Tönnies. Tönnies, a historian, suggested that European society had evolved from a community (*Gemeinschaft*) to a society (*Gesellschaft*), phases that he believed constituted "ideal types" that could be profitably applied to other societies (Mayes, 1989, pp. 7–8). This concept was developed, though in distinct ways, in the later studies of Durkheim, Marx, and Weber. These three thinkers in turn laid the foundations for three of the major currents within sociology. The work of Weber is more closely related to *conflict theory*, an approach that examines the ways in which societies and social groups respond to the variety of sociopolitical and socioeconomic pressures that inevitably develop (Malina, 1982, pp. 233–4). It asserts that the interests of different groups are often competing and that these competing interests often ultimately lead to one group being more central, the other more marginalized.

Emil Durkheim is considered the founder of the structural–functional approach, one that suggests not that groups never have competing interests, but that the tension that exists among various groups can often lead to a cultural consensus (Malina, 1982, p. 234). This approach is generally considered to be a response to an evolutionary and deterministic bias that had developed within the emergent social sciences of the late 19th and early 20th centuries. It focuses primarily on the structure and function of social groups, institutions, and ideologies within societies. While it emerged within European sociology and anthropology it has been a major form of social science theory in both Europe and the United States since the 1950s (Lenski, Lenski, and Nolan, 1991).

Karl Marx's thought focused more on the material aspects of cultural development, and gave rise to what has now become known as cultural materialism (Harris, 1980). In his view, all cultural developments, such as art, literature, music, religion, ideology and so forth – commonly referred to as the "superstructure" – are embedded directly in the social and economic realities in which those developments take shape – often called the "base." In this "base-superstructure" model, changes in the economic realm ("base") influence the developments within the cultural realm ("superstructure"). This suggests that ideas and ideologies are influenced, if not determined, by changes in the socioeconomic structure of societies. This approach, which is gaining popularity in biblical applications of the social sciences, stands in direct tension to the more common sociological theory that sees ideas as primary movers in the development of societies and their social, political, and economic orders.

Of Models and Methods

All social sciences are at their heart comparative in nature. This comparison of societies and cultures allows social scientists to make observations in one culture that may apply to another culture, though distant in time and perhaps place. The use of models might involve, for example, examining the role and function of shamans in tribal and/or agrarian societies to draw conclusions about the nature of mediation. These conclusions might, in turn, be applied to the role and function of the prophet in Israelite society (Wilson, 1980, 1984; Overholt, 1974, 1982, 1996).

One of the critiques that more traditional exegetes have levied against social science criticism is that it applies these types of external models onto biblical cultures. Further, much post-World War II western sociology focuses on the "microsociological" – the component parts of societies. It typically gathers social data about specific issues such as gender, racism and race relations, class structure, families, and political and economic settings. These approaches are less applicable to ancient cultures and social groups because the methods that they employ are dependent on gathering contemporary, representative data of the type that cannot be easily recovered from antiquity.

This is precisely why one must apply a macrosociological perspective to the biblical texts in order to understand the cultural patterns that they sometimes hide. Macrosociology is historical in nature, concerned with the development of cultures rather than their instance in one particular point in time. It is also comparative, recognizing that cultures dating to different eras may have common features, particularly if they exist in similar environmental settings or subsistence strategies (Lenski, Lenski, and Nolan, 1991). Finally, the developmental concern of macrosociology allows it to contribute to the biblical cultures, which were not in a state of constancy, but rather in a state of flux. That flux included movements from relative simplicity to complexity, from an independent monarchy to a vassal state, from a vassal state to a colonial province.

It is also important to note that modeling is a major part of traditional interpretive methodology, though it is more often transparent to the interpreter than is sociological modeling. When one examines suzerainty–vassal treaties to see how Deuteronomy functioned in biblical Israel, one is comparing genres based on the model of an "ideal type" of this form of Ancient Near Eastern treaty. The same is true of the study of Hebrew itself. If a scholar is studying a particularly rare Hebrew root, it is not uncommon to seek linguistic cognates from other Semitic languages or even to search for non-Semitic loanwords. Literary and linguistic models form the foundation upon which we build and revise our understanding of the biblical literature. Social science modeling is similarly comparative and seeks cultural cognates for particular biblical practices or institutions. However, while this type of modeling can lead to important breakthroughs in our understanding of ancient cultures, biblical scholars must be careful to observe appropriate controls when comparing premodern cultures to biblical ones, lest the scholars' own history color his or her interpretation of particular texts and the ensuing social reconstruction (Sasson, 1981; Herion, 1986).

The need for precision in modeling goes beyond its application to biblical worlds. Indeed, any social science discipline that engages in reconstructions of past societies must take special care to construct its models carefully and to govern the application of these data to the cultures in question. It is common-place within archaeology to apply social models to ancient cultures in an attempt to look beyond the narrow interpretation of specific artifacts and sites to the place within society that these sites and their remains held. Some have used the interpretive model of Ferdinand Braudel and analyzed the material culture of sites and even site distribution from the perspective of *la longue durée*. Thomas Levy and Suzanne Richard have employed social science models and patterns – such as sedentarism, nomadism, cultural adaptation, and chiefdoms – better to understand the transitional phases of the Chalcolithic period (Levy, 1986) and the Early Bronze Age (Richard, 1987). The chiefdom model has also proven valuable in interpreting textual and archaeological data concerning Israel in the transitional period between that of the "judges" and the early monarchy (Frick, 1985; Flanagan, 1981, 1988).

Ethnography and ethnoarchaeology are being increasingly used within biblical studies to shed light on the ancient past. Ethnographic studies are typically conducted among premodern cultures in order to clarify practices and beliefs in non-living cultures (Carter, 1997, pp. 280–1). The data gained from carefully conducted fieldwork may be applied to ancient cultures by "analogy" or "analogical reasoning" – the use of practices, material objects, and ideologies from observable cultures to help understand past cultures. Although ethnoarchaeology was initially used to clarify issues concerning prehistoric hunting and gathering societies, archaeologists gradually began to conduct studies to answer questions that emerged from research on historical societies. The population of ancient cultures could be more carefully estimated on the basis of ethnographic studies of the population density of premodern villages. The social function of potters and other craft specialists could be better reconstructed when the role and place of similar specialists was clarified through modern ethnographic research.

While most scholars would apply some controls on the use of ethnographic data in social reconstructions, a minority would eschew the use of these data altogether. Controls might range from a rather loose expectation of similarities in cultural types and environmental setting to the construction of a series of hypotheses to be tested through the ethnographic research. Some biblical scholars and social scientists are uncomfortable with the construction of these hypothetical models and believe that they lead to a false sense of "objectivity" and are an attempt simply to mimic the "hard sciences." They point out that numerous variables exist when one discusses human societies – the most unpredictable is humankind itself – and therefore that society does not lend itself to this type of testing (Lemche, 1990, pp. 82, 87). In this view, to use macrosociological and general social science models to reconstruct ancient societies is to obscure rather than to clarify those cultures, and to impose modern models onto the past.

If addressed carefully these critiques have the potential of sharpening the focus and improving the results of social science study of scripture. They present those who would apply ethnographic, cultural anthropological, archaeological, or macrosociological models to the biblical world with a challenge to do so with care and precision. Indeed, the methodology within each of these subfields of the social sciences is constantly maturing, adding an additional responsibility to biblical scholars who would employ them. Only as biblical scholars remain aware of newer developments in sociological and anthropological theory can they continue to further the understanding of biblical cultures. Otherwise, scholars will find themselves either trying to "unscramble omelettes" – seeking to untangle complicated literary histories – or "collecting butterflies" – i.e., categorizing social practices without understanding them (McNutt, 1999, pp. 1–32). As McNutt points out, an approach that uses multiple sources and models, one that examines social settings to provide not a "definitive word" but a working hypothesis, provides the best hope for understanding the complex nature of Israelite society in any point of its history.

Social science analysis of biblical cultures: early examples

The attempts to apply the fledgling social sciences to biblical cultures continued after W. Robertson Smith's early influential works. Two of the immediate uses concerned the role of magic in society, and cultural evolution. Both of these concerns are evident from an anthropological perspective in Smith's writings, but were taken in a different, more literary, direction by those who followed him. Once his protégé – and always claiming to be applying his methodology – Sir James Frazer led the social sciences into counterproductive territory (Douglas, 1966, pp. 17–28; Anderson, 1987, pp. 4–7). He focused on the role of magic within society and considered it to be the primary phase of societal or intellectual development. Following the magical stage, societies tended to adopt a "religious" character, and finally developed modern, "scientific" worldviews. Lucien Lévy-Bruhl likewise posited a gradual movement within cultures from what he called a "collective mentality," to one he referred to as "empirical–logical," and ultimately to a "logical" mentality that led to the rise of individual consciousness (Kimbrough, 1972, pp. 198–202).

Most of the early sociological and anthropological studies relating to the Hebrew Bible were conducted by Europeans. The work of Louis Wallis (1907, 1912) marks an exception to this trend. Wallis was one of the first scholars to distinguish between theological and social science approaches, a distinction that has been developed in the last two decades in the work of Philip Davies (1992) and Robert Oden (1987). Wallis suggested that scholars view biblical culture and ideology from the standpoint of its common features with other

Ancient Near Eastern traditions and proposed that a sociological reading of the text could add significantly to one's understanding of those texts. American biblical scholarship later came to be dominated by the work of W. F. Albright and his students; their interests were more theological than anthropological. Albright himself viewed the social sciences with suspicion and considered their application to the biblical worlds to be positivist (Kimbrough, 1972, pp. 199, 202). On the Continent two major works appeared that significantly impacted critical scholarship. French biblical scholar Antonin Causse applied a structural–functional methodology to his study of scripture, but was overly influenced by the flawed perspectives of Lucien Lévy-Bruhl delineated above. Causse's analysis of Israelite culture was insightful at points, and was certainly exhaustive. His major studies focused on the treatment of the poor, on the evolution of Israelite society, on the mission of the prophets, and on the emergence of Judaism from the Israelite and Judean traditions (Causse, 1922, 1937).

Without question the study that most impacted subsequent biblical scholarship is Max Weber's *Ancient Judaism* (1952), a sociologist's sortie into the world of Hebrew Bible studies and emergent Judaism. While some cross-disciplinary forays into new territory are marked by poor methodology, a lack of understanding of the field, or both, Weber's study serves as a model for interdisciplinary study. He availed himself of the best of biblical and Ancient Near Eastern scholarship and applied his insightful mind to material ranging from Mesopotamian mythic traditions to the Amarna correspondence, from the tribal structure to Second Temple period Judaism, from covenantal and legal traditions to Israelite concepts of the divine. His work and methodology remain influential in modern biblical studies (Carter, 1996, 1999) even if critical foundations upon which he based his understanding of biblical studies have shifted and some of his conclusions have been eclipsed. Not until the studies of Norman Gottwald was biblical scholarship to receive such a thoroughgoing infusion of social science perspectives and broadly-based challenge.

Albrecht Alt (Alt, 1929) and Martin Noth (1930, 1960) continued to apply some insights from the social sciences to their study of biblical texts. Although both were working directly from what Gottwald has identified as a "humanities" approach to the Hebrew Bible, their attention to the social settings of texts is nonetheless notable. Alt's methodology was influenced deeply by the models of both Wellhausen and Robertson Smith, and he frequently made uncritical comparisons of Bedouin culture to "tribal" Israel. Having said this, his erudition, his careful use of archaeological data, his sensitivity to the traditions and their literary contexts, make his work exemplary. Indeed, it was not until Mendenhall's study of tribalism and his call for more careful methodology that biblical scholars began to differentiate between premodern Bedouin culture and that of biblical tribal settings. Likewise, Noth applied cultural parallels from Greek culture to his analysis of the premonarchic social setting, viewing the tribal "league" as an amphictyony. While this model (from ancient Greece) held sway for several decades, it has since been shown to be inexact. Nevertheless, his work contributed to a comparative approach to Israelite and Judean history.

After Alt and Noth, very little substantive application of the social sciences to the Hebrew Bible occurred until the late 1960s and early 1970s. This may be in part because of a shift within western sociology away from macrosociological methodology with its historical and comparative approaches and toward more culturally-specific questions. Another reason for this drop-off in the use of the social sciences may be traced to the antipathy of Albright to the social sciences, and to an increased focus on "biblical theology." It is ironic that Albright rejected sociological and anthropological perspectives, given his contributions to emergent "biblical archaeology." His scholarship and methodology, tied as it was to a traditional historical-critical and theological reading of scripture, dominated an entire generation of scholarship.

Revolutionary perspectives: the renaissance of the social sciences in biblical studies

The theory of cultural revolution was at the heart of the next application of the social sciences to Israelite culture. In 1962, George Mendenhall published a short but immensely influential essay entitled "The Hebrew Conquest of Palestine" (Mendenhall, 1962). Mendenhall asserted that too often underlying assumptions are uncritically accepted; he challenged the scholarly establishment to attain a higher degree of methodological rigor. He used the then prevailing theories of Israelite origins proposed by W. F. Albright/G. Ernest Wright (the "conquest" model) and Albrecht Alt/Martin Noth (the "peaceful infiltration" model) as a test case. Like Albright/Wright and Alt/Noth before him, he made careful use of both archaeological and biblical data, but added to them a sociological dimension that both scholars had lacked. He proposed that the use of the term "tribe" was imprecise at best and misleading at worst. Because biblical scholars do not understand the social conventions that characterize tribal cultures and because they look to an idealized model of Bedouin culture as their starting point, these prevailing models are flawed.

Mendenhall claimed that the theory that emergent Israel is best understood as an example of nomadic or semi-nomadic cultures "is entirely in the face of both biblical and extra-biblical evidence" (1962, p. 67). A tribal setting is not the same, he suggests, as a nomadic lifestyle, though the two had become roughly synonymous within biblical scholarship. Nor was there any evidence that the people who would become Israel must have entered the land from the outside. Instead, Mendenhall proposed that the Hebrews should be understood in the light of the *Hab/piru* known from the Amarna letters and other Akkadian sources. The *Hab/piru*, he argued, had withdrawn from and/or rebelled against the stratified Canaanite culture that had for long oppressed them. They ultimately joined with the group of slaves liberated by Moses, who did enter from the Transjordan region. The two groups – the disaffected Canaanites and newly freed slaves from Egypt – were united by the story of a liberating God, YHWH.

This focus on methodology, on the uncritical acceptance of theoretical models, and on a new understanding of the emergence and character of earliest Israel, became the focus of a series of studies by Norman K. Gottwald. Gottwald's first contribution was in an article entitled "Domain Assumptions and Societal Models in the Study of Pre-Monarchic Israel." Here Gottwald, like Mendenhall, delineated what he considered to be predominant theoretical models of the emergence of Israel, and after showing their inadequacy, proposed alternative models based in the social sciences. These "domain assumptions" presume that: (1) Social change is a result of population displacement; (2) the desert regions play a "creative" role in promoting social change within sedentary cultures; and (3) social change is often idiosyncratic and arbitrary (Gottwald, 1974, pp. 90–1). All three assumptions are reflected in the conquest and peaceful infiltration models of Israel's emergence, but none adequately explain the social reasons for or impact of the changes that occurred in Syria–Palestine in the 13th century BCE. Instead, Gottwald suggests that three new assumptions should be applied to the study of Israel's growth: (1) Social change normally comes from inner social pressures and/or conflicts; (2) the desert has a secondary, rather than primary influence in social change; and (3) social change is a result of numerous, interconnected, multileveled factors (Gottwald, 1974, 92).

Gottwald's most influential work remains *The Tribes of Yahweh: A Sociology of the Religion of Liberated Israel, 1250–1050 BCE* (Gottwald, 1979). The book has been compared to Wellhausen's *Prolegomena to the History of Israel* (Wellhausen, 1885) and Albright's *From the Stone Age to Christianity* (Albright, 1957) in both scope and substance (Bruggemann, 1980). Signaling its importance, Sheffield Academic Press has just reissued *Tribes* and a special session of the Ideological Criticism Section of the 1999 annual meeting of the Society of Biblical Literature was convened to honor the twentieth anniversary of its publication.

Contrary to Rainey's biting critique, this is not a work that can "safely and profitably be ignored" (Rainey, 1987). Gottwald carefully expands the boundaries of interpretation from one that is dominated by a humanities perspective to one that analyzes social setting and the nature of social systems. He argues not for doing away with traditional means of interpretation but for an approach that is more inclusive and more broadly based. As such, he employs traditional literary, theological, traditions-history, and linguistic criticisms – while going beyond their narrow application. Texts and traditions are produced by social groups and by individuals within (or outside of) those groups. Without addressing the social contexts one may miss the significance of the texts even if their literary and historical contexts are considered.

Using this broader methodology, Gottwald examines the origins and social context for earliest Israel. As part of this analysis, he combines a careful reading of biblical texts with an assessment of then prevailing theories such as Noth's amphictyony model, Alt's peaceful infiltration model, Albright's conquest model, and Mendenhall's peasant revolt model. In addition, he carefully considers issues such as tribalism, transhumant pastoralism, social backgrounds of the *Hab/piru* and the *Shasu* Bedouin, and cultural materialist approaches to relgion.

Gottwald's *Tribes* is somewhat eclectic in its use and application of social models. Gottwald employs insights from social scientists such as Max Weber, Emile Durkheim, Karl Marx, Talcott Parsons, and Marvin Harris. The two prevailing models of sociology/anthropology he applies are structural–functional and cultural materialism. The latter is one for which he has been criticized, sometimes stridently, since this approach often subjugates the ideological developments to their material context (Mendenhall, 1983). While some cultural materialists are deterministic – suggesting that changes in the material setting of a society are responsible for any ideological change – Gottwald's application of this methodology is more nuanced. Still, one of his central tenets is that "only as the full *materiality* of ancient Israel is more securely grasped will we be able to make proper sense of its *spirituality*" (Gottwald, 1979, p. xxv). This approach sets Gottwald apart from Mendenhall, whose commitment is to a more idealistic (or ideological) understanding of biblical Israel, and who saw Yahwism as a prime mover in the emergence of Israel. Gottwald likewise seeks to account for the development of Yahwism, but sees it as part of Israel's broader social world and context, some of which is rooted in its "materiality."

At the same time that Mendenhall and Gottwald were breaking new ground as biblical scholars, two prominent anthropologists were addressing the biblical narratives from the standpoint of ideological and cultural materialist approaches. Mary Douglas's *Purity and Danger* appeared in 1966 and continues to influence scholarly understandings of the purity legislation in the Hebrew Bible. Douglas analyzes the laws concerning ritual and dietary purity from a broader anthropological context and suggests that they serve to establish and protect social boundaries. Marvin Harris addresses the same legislation and suggests that the idea for dietary boundaries emerged from competing needs for natural resources. From economic and resource-management standpoints, pig husbandry was not viable; this material reality gave rise to the taboo on eating pig-flesh. The difference in perspectives and methodology between Douglas and Harris may explain their relative usage by biblical scholars. More scholars make use of Douglas's explanation, perhaps because it is ideologically oriented. That the materialist perspectives of Harris have gained less support within the study of the Hebrew Bible may reflect a general discomfort of biblical scholarship with material rather than "spiritual" approaches.

Enhanced Understandings of Biblical Cultures

Gottwald issues a challenge in *Tribes* for scholars to apply his broader, social science approach to specific problems and questions within the Biblical traditions. The proliferation of such studies and the wide variety of social science theories and perspectives that have been applied to the biblical record in the last twenty years is impressive, and stands as evidence that Gottwald's massive work has had an equally substantial impact on the field. Social science studies of Hebrew scripture focused initially on two major areas: the emergence of Israel and the social location of prophetism. As social science criticism became a subdiscipline within Hebrew Bible studies, more and more areas of Israelite and Judean society in every historical period have been studied from these perspectives. These newer areas include: gender, the social location of Israelite and Judean institutions, sacrifice as a socioeconomic system, social differentiation, the social setting of the Babylonian exile and of Persian period Yehud, and the social function of biblical literatures. Most recently, full-length studies have appeared proposing a social history of Israel and Judah from their emergence through the end of the Persian period (McNutt, 1999) or Yehud during the Persian period (Berquist, 1995). These studies apply a wide variety of social science methodologies but share a common interest in uncovering and contextualizing the social worlds of biblical cultures.

The emergence of Israel and state formation

Although much of the current focus on the contribution of the social sciences to biblical studies came from issues surrounding Israel's emergence, the interest in this complex subject has not abated. Some would claim that the archaeological picture has disproved the models of conquest and peasant revolt in favor of a neo-Altian peaceful infiltration model (Finkelstein, 1988). Others would seek a broader understanding of the socioeconomic, cultural, and political contexts of Late Bronze Age Palestine (Coote and Whitelam, 1986; Chaney, 1983). A series of important questions must be answered, including: what were some of the socioeconomic pressures at the end of the second millennium that may have allowed a new social entity to inhabit the previously undersettled central hill country? Were the "Israelites" indigenous Canaanites or were they indeed, as the biblical record seems to indicate, a distinct group that entered the central hills from the outside? What, if any, is the relationship of the Amarna letters and the notorious *Hab/piru* to the Hebrews and to emergent "Israel"? How likely is it that a peasant revolt of the type proposed by Mendenhall and Gottwald would succeed and lead to the emergence of a new people? Would a "frontier" model more likely account for early Israel and its trajectory from a (re)tribal setting, toward a petty-state? How are we to use both text and artifact to understand social worlds. What models and cultural parallels might help us in our quest better to understand Israel's emergence?

These questions continue to give rise to a robust debate and no genuine consensus appears to be likely without new interpretive strategies or new forms of material data. However, some lines of agreement about the nature of earliest Israelite society and the general approach to it do seem to be emerging. Israelite beginnings must be examined not in isolation, but as part of broader social contexts, what Ferdinand Braudel referred to as *la longue durée*. While the exact character of Israelite cultures in this formative period is open to debate, it is clear from the material remains that it was a relatively "rustic" society, with little social differentiation and a relatively egalitarian (or non-heirarchical) setting.

What of state formation? Similar care must be exercised in reconstructing this phase of the social evolution of Israel. The "judges" functioned as "charismatic heroes," an ideal type of leader that Weber identified as one of the phases in the routinization of authority (Malamat, 1976). Using the model of the phases of social development of Elman Service (Service, 1962, 1975), Flanagan identified this period of Israelite development as a chiefdom, a phase that generally precedes monarchies and petty statehood (Flanagan, 1981). Similarly, Frick proposed that a series of social pressures were responsible for the development of the state, rather than the prime mover being the Philistine threat (which the biblical narratives presume). These included adaptations of specific technologies to the central hill country and its environment, population pressures and increases in productive capabilities (Frick, 1985).

Two other studies analyze the early monarchy and its social context by examining the symbolic function of ancient and modern technologies. Flanagan uses the analogy of a hologram to provide an interpretive framework for the David narratives (Flanagan, 1988). Just as a hologram presents different images when viewed from a variety of angles, so the early monarchy must be approached from a multiplicity of perspectives. Each one adds to the depth and richness of the portrait of Iron Age Israel in the early phase of state formation. Paula McNutt (1990) examines the relationship of technology to culture, seeking to understand figurative as well as technological function of iron working. Using ethnographic data from African societies, she shows that iron technology is often used to symbolize both social and ritual relationships. In the First Testament, iron and its forging are used to represent strength, durability, power, Israelite slavery in Egypt (or any form of oppression), and God's transformation of the people of Israel.

Social locations of Israelite and Judean institutions

Three major institutions and/or movements of Israel and Judah have been the subject of intense study from a social science standpoint: prophetism, apocalypticism, and the cultus. Those working on the prophetic traditions and their social setting have turned to comparative studies of mediation and spirit possession from the perspectives of cultural anthropology and social psychology. The first scholars to employ a thoroughgoing social science methodology to the prophetic tradition were Thomas Overholt and Robert Wilson. Overholt has examined the role of the prophet and the nature of prophetic authority in light of native American religious groups and holy men (Overholt, 1974, 1982). Wilson has compared prophetism with shamanism and spirit mediation and proposed a framework for understanding prophetic speech and action from the standpoint of location in and relationship to other social institutions (Wilson, 1980). Prophets typically performed either a central role in support of the state and/or ruling structure, or functioned peripherally to that ruling group, often resisting its policies. Both central and peripheral mediation often required and relied upon complex forms of social maintenance.

The development of the apocalyptic tradition has benefited from social science understandings, particularly the perspectives of deprivation theory and millennialism. The pioneering work of both Plöger (1968) and Hanson (1979) set apocalypticism in the context of social deprivation theory. Hanson, for example, proposes that this movement arose from a conflict between priestly "hierocrats" and apocalyptic "visionaries," both of whom had radically different views of the status quo and distinct views of the future. More recently, Berquist (1995) has proposed that the apocalyptic tradition emerged from a group of disenfranchised, "middle-management," scribes. The scribes, frustrated by their lack of access to power and the true elite, sought to uproot and overturn that social class. A more helpful theory of the emergence of apocalyptic has been that of S. Cook, who places it in a framework of millenarian movements. Cook points out that millennial apocalyptic groups have at times been in positions of power. He further maintains that the tenor of the "proto-apocalyptic" texts of Ezekiel 38–39, Joel, and Zechariah 1–8, reflect a central location in the priesthood rather than a peripheral "visionary" viewpoint. What makes his position superior to those of Plöger, Hanson, and Berquist is his sensitivity to a broad variety of social models and contexts. He thus avoids the methodological pitfall of reductionism that occurs when an overly narrow orientation is applied to a particular biblical setting.

The cult has often been approached from a narrowly religious standpoint. Parallels were often drawn from other Ancient Near Eastern cultures, but tended to bring attention to the ostensible uniqueness of the Israelite tradition and practice compared with that of its neighbors. Several fruitful lines of inquiry emerged in the last two decades, ones that examine Israelite and Judean cultic practices from the perspective of their socioeconomic and socioreligious standpoints. These studies have in common an understanding that highlights the commonality of beliefs and practices with those of Israel and Judah's cultural and geographic neighbors. As Gary Anderson points out, the Israelites and Judeans, like all peoples in the Levant, appealed to deities for fertility and believed that sacrifices provided food for their deities. Likewise sacrifice in Israel and Judah had socioeconomic functions, such as supporting the temple system and providing a system of redistribution of resources (Anderson, 1987).

Carol Meyers and Frank Frick have turned to ethnoarchaeology to uncover aspects of the sacrificial and cultic system. Meyers examines the sacrifice made by Hannah by first placing it in its environmental context (Meyers, 1995). The three-year-old bull Hannah brings as a sacrificial animal and the fact that grain and wine, but not oil, are offered, all point to a setting in the foothills of Ephraim where the ecological context mandates a mixed animal husbandry and agricultural regimen. Further, the absence of oil from the sacrificial regimen would support this interpretation, as cultivation of grains and wine, but not olive trees, is more typical of this region. Thus, subsistence patterns and ritual acts function together in a symbiotic fashion; one, the pastoral and agricultural "infrastructure" of village life, supports the ritual "superstructure" of the emergent Israelite culture. Frick examines the religion of Israel from a multidisciplinary perspective, examining it through the frameworks of processual archaeology, the "new" archaeology, environmental contexts, and sociopolitical theory (Frick, 1979). He suggests that the religious structures and rituals of Israelite culture are but one of many social elements and claims that "the religion of early Israel is rather the expression (albeit a very important one) of a particular cultural identity rather than its sole foundation" (Frick, 1979, p. 234). Further, ritual functioned in Israelite society as it does in many others, in a way that tends to support stability through both belief and practice, and often regulates both social and environmental systems.

Social distinction and gender differentiation

As the social complexity of Israel and Judah grew, so changes in social distinction and differentiation of both roles and equity followed. Whatever social model best describes the earliest period of ancient "Israel," it is clear from the archaeological record that the villages in the central highlands were marked by a subsistence-level economy, one fraught with high risk and poverty (Hopkins, 1985, 1987). This relatively egalitarian or non-hierarchical setting placed most families in a similar social setting with little differentiation. As the chiefdom and ultimately the monarchy emerged, many of these tribal and familial institutions were undermined, often as a result of a conscious effort on the part of the ruling structure to assert its central authority. Land tenure policies shifted in favor of the emergent upper classes, and a tributary mode of production emerged (Gottwald, 1992). Resources of the peasantry were extracted in favor of the state, the official cult, and the elite. This differentiation is confirmed in both textual traditions and the archaeological record. The biblical ideal of providing for the weak, oppressed and marginalized is enshrined in both legal and prophetic texts, and excavations in many Iron II sites, such as Samaria, show the existence of great extremes of wealth and poverty. The domestic tributary mode of production shifted to an imperial tributary mode of production with the onset of the Neo-Babylonian and Persian periods. Here, the method of extraction of resources remained the same, but the surplus went to the elite and their imperial overlords.

The emergence of feminist criticism has led to a clearer understanding of the male-dominated nature of scripture and its interpretive history and of the role and place of women in Israel, Judah, and Yehud. Perhaps the first work of substance from a "modern" viewpoint was Elizabeth Cady Stanton's The Woman's Bible (Stanton, 1895–8). Her work had limited immediate impact on the religious world, and Stanton herself is more often remembered for her contributions to the suffrage and abolitionist movements (Schottroff, 1998). Beginning in the 1970s, a generation of feminist scholars questioned traditional social structures that had largely excluded women and marginalized their contributions. Mary Daly's now famous sermon and later book of the same title, "Beyond God the Father" (1973), and the early interpretations of Rosemary Radford Ruether (1974), Phyllis Bird (1974), Carol Meyers (1983, 1988), Claudia Camp (1985) and Phyllis Trible (1978, 1984), challenged traditional interpretations of the Hebrew Bible and, in varying degrees, contemporary patriarchal religion. Feminist interpretation of scripture is often more literary than social science in orientation, but when these interpretive approaches are used in tandem it is possible to uncover the often obscured position of women in antiquity.

One of the most common assumptions scholars have brought to the interpretation of the Israelite and Judean cultus is that women were totally excluded from any public function. What is closer to the truth is that women's roles were limited in official religious institutions, but that significant positions of power were open to them in the more popular but suppressed "folk-religions." In the official cultic sphere, women's roles included serving as leaders of worship and song, preparing clothing and other textiles, as unspecified attendants, and more rarely, as prophets (Huldah and the unnamed wife of Isaiah). Within the suppressed religious spheres, women functioned as prophets, as "cult-prostitutes," and as mediums and "spirit manipulators" (Bird, 1987).

Understanding the role and place of women is now further enhanced by two very recent works. The *Women's Bible Commentary* (Newsom, 1998) presents feminist interpretations of the Hebrew Bible, Apocrypha, and New Testament. It includes lengthy introductions to the social and historical contexts of ancient Israel and early Christianity as well as commentary on the canonical texts. *Women in Scripture* (Meyers, 2000) is a one-volume dictionary that includes entries on named and unnamed women in the Hebrew Bible, Deuterocanonical works, and the New Testament. In addition to the attempt to shed light on biblical texts and cultures, feminist critics continue to try to come to terms with the legacy of biblical interpretation, women's historical roles in church and synagogue, and current religious practice. These include *Women and Redemption: A Theological History* (Ruether, 1998), *Rhetoric and Ethic: The Politics of Biblical Studies* (Schüssler Fiorenza, 1999), *Standing Again at Sinai: Judaism from a Feminist Perspective* (Plaskow, 1990), and *Feminist Interpretation: The Bible in Women's Perspective* (Schottroff, 1998).

The exile and beyond

After decades of being an afterthought for scholars of the First and Second Testaments, the Neo-Babylonian and Persian periods have become the subject of renewed scrutiny. The nature and the extent of the exile at the end of the Judean monarchy in 586 BCE and the return to Jerusalem and its surroundings at the beginning of the Persian period remain hotly contested issues. Some prefer the term "deportation" to "exile," noting that the latter term is more of a theological construct than a historical reality (Davies, Grabbe). Others are content to employ the terminology of the biblical writers, recognizing it as a theological concept that arose from the crisis of the destruction of the social fabric of the monarchy. All agree, however, that significant social and cultural changes occurred in this tumultuous period.

Daniel Smith has proposed a series of social models for analyzing the social context of the Babylonian exile. He suggests that the exilic community can be examined in the light of other societies that have undergone similar levels of upheaval and identifies four major social coping strategies: structural adaptation, competition for leadership, developing new boundaries and rituals, and the production of a literature of resistance (Smith, 1989). The population, demography, and social setting of Yehud have also been the subject of recent studies. Most influential, perhaps, has been the proposal of Joel Weinberg that Yehud is an example of a *Büger-Tempel-Gemeinde* (a Citizen-Temple-Community). This type of community, centered around a temple economy, provides Weinberg with a model for the *gōlâ* community. The returnees, he argues, were a distinct community from those who had remained in the land, and their economy and leadership were initially separate from the ruling structure of Yehud. This gradually changed as more people joined the Temple Community and the latter took over both political and religious control of Yehud.

This model has several weaknesses including misuse of epigraphic data, a misreading of some key biblical texts, and a lack of reliable population data (Carter, 1999a, pp. 294–307). Recent population estimates made on the basis of archaeological excavations and surveys suggest a population ranging between 13,000 and 21,000 for Yehud in the Persian period. These estimates point toward a province that was relatively small in size and site distribution, poor, and subject to the whims of Persian imperial policy. It is this type of social context that best explains the emphasis on purity and distinction that Ezra–Nehemiah reflects and accounts for the rise of apocalyptic traditions.

Biblical literature as a cultural artifact

One of the issues that has complicated both archaeological and social science reconstructions of the biblical worlds is the nature of the Bible itself. W. F. Albright and G. Ernest Wright both operated with a methodology in which the biblical record was given pride of place. Excavations were conducted on sites that figured prominently in biblical and extra-biblical sources, but most often in order to clarify if not prove the veracity of the biblical history. The views of Wright are telling in this regard; he claimed that biblical archaeologists' "central and absorbing task is the understanding and exposition of the Scriptures" (Meyers and Meyers, 1989, p. 143*). A distinctly different viewpoint prevails in the current academic climate, which is far more cautious – often skeptical – in its approach to the traditions central to the Hebrew Bible. Indeed, some are claiming that only a history written *without* use of scripture can approach objectivity. In the former view, because scripture is privileged it is the source of questions about the biblical world and its cultures; it therefore dominates all forms of interpretation, including social science and archaeological endeavors. In the latter view, because the Bible is by nature biased and because it has been privileged in interpretive endeavors, it has little or no value for creating reconstructions of the past of Syria–Palestine.

If both extremes are problematic, is a mediating position possible? I propose treating the Hebrew Bible and its traditions as a cultural artifact, one that, like material remains, can shed light on socioeconomic, sociopolitical, and socioreligious realities of the past. In fact, if one does not use the biblical traditions at all, one is ignoring a significant product of some of the peoples and perspectives of Syria–Palestine in the Late Bronze Age through early Hellenistic period. Certainly the beliefs and practices of the dominant classes and religious groups are given pride of place in the anthology of Israelite and Jewish literature we call the Hebrew Bible. But those narratives, beliefs, and practices contribute to a full view of that past and the groups that inhabited it. While one must keep in mind that the biblical records are biased, even so, they do reveal what the people who lived through the events or reflected upon them thought they meant (Dever, 1993). Even if, as the current consensus holds, the bulk of the Hebrew Bible had reached its final form – some would claim was invented or composed – during the Persian and Hellenistic periods, it is an important cultural artifact of that world.

Future Directions: Prospects and Potential

The contributions of the social sciences to the study of the Hebrew Bible have already been substantial. As scholars include social science criticism as one of the many forms of analysis in the interpretive process, these contributions will be more widely disseminated and better understood. To continue to grow, however, social science criticism will have to reach certain benchmarks. Scholars will have to become more versed in various sociological and anthropological theories and methods, they will need to promote a greater level of methodological rigor, and their work will need to become more broadly interdisciplinary.

The first two of these benchmarks require no small commitment – equivalent, perhaps, of mastering the full range of Semitic languages or the subtleties of postmodern literary theory. There are numerous subfields within the social sciences, and no one person can become an expert in all of them. Yet, it is only as scholars become proficient in anthropological and macrosociological theory that they can cogently apply these fields to the biblical record. This commitment, then, will require that a new generation of scholars receive some training in social science criticism just as they are exposed to historical or literary criticism. The example of Max Weber is one to follow; just as his work has been used by biblical scholars, so the conclusions of those who engage in social science criticism should meet the standards of sociologists and anthropologists. This call for rigor resounds through the social sciences themselves. Indeed, Gerhard Lenski has proposed the use of carefully delineated social models, of creating multi-layered theories, and of forming and testing falsifiable hypotheses. His appeal can function as yet another guideline for the use of the social sciences in Hebrew Bible studies: we must continue to critique, develop, and refine the theory and application of a social science methodology. In the so-called "hard sciences," theory is "continually being refined and improved. Theories stimulate research, and research leads to theoretical advances" (Lenski, 1988, p. 165).

The final benchmark is one that has been part of the study of the Hebrew Bible for some time but that needs to continue to expand nonetheless: interdisciplinary and multidisciplinary study. The studies that I have discussed above that are the strongest are those that have been characterized by going beyond the confines of one particular approach. One could argue that so-called "biblical archaeology" is interdisciplinary in nature, in that it combines traditional biblical studies and archaeological artifacts. While this would be true in some respects, what characterized most early biblical archaeology was a commitment, perhaps subjugation, to scripture and theology. Only as archaeological research began to be governed by a broader set of questions and presuppositions did it begin to make contributions to the worlds behind the texts, i.e., the social world of Syria–Palestine as a whole. The same is true of all forms of social science study of the First Testament: when they seek to clarify social systems, cultural development, popular and official ritual and beliefs, socioeconomic relationships and so forth, and when they employ a broad range of disciplinary approaches, they make the most substantive contributions to the field. As these multiple forms of inquiry are used to complement one another and to supplement the textual traditions, we become better able to arrive at a multifaceted and deeply enriched understanding of the multiple social worlds of Israel, Judah, and Yehud.

Bibliography

Albright, W., *From the Stone Age to Christianity: Monotheism and the Historical Process*, 2nd edn. (Garden City, NY: Doubleday, 1957).

Alt, A., *Der Gott Der Väter: Ein Beitrag Zur Vorgeschichte Der Israelitischen Religion, Beitrage Zur Wissenschaftt von Alten und Neuen Testament* (Stuttgart: Kohlhammer, 1929).

Anderson, G., *Sacrifices and Offerings in Ancient Israel: Studies in Their Social and Political Significance* (Atlanta: Scholars Press, 1987).

Beidelman, T., *W. Robertson Smith and the Sociological Study of Religion* (Chicago: University of Chicago Press, 1974).

Benjamin, D. and V. Matthews, "Social Sciences and Biblical Studies," *Semeia* 68 (1994), 7–21.

Berquist, J., *Judaism in Persia's Shadow: A Social and Historical Approach* (Minneapolis: Fortress Press, 1995).

Bird, P., "Images of Women in the Old Testament," in R. R. Ruether, ed., *Religion and Sexism: Images of Women in the Jewish and Christian Traditions* (New York: Simon and Schuster, 1974), 44–88.

——, "The Place of Women in the Israelite Cultus," in P. Miller, P. Hanson and S. McBride, *Ancient Israelite Religion: Essays in Honor of Frank Moore Cross* (Philadelphia: Fortress Press, 1987), 397–419.

——, *Missing Persons and Mistaken Identities: Women and Gender in Ancient Israel* (Minneapolis: Fortress Press, 1997).

Bruggemann, W., "The Tribes of Yahweh: An Essay Review," *Journal of the American Academy of Religion* 48 (1980), 441–51.

Camp, C., *Wisdom and the Feminine in the Book of Proverbs*, Bible and Literature 11 (Decatur, GA: Almond Press, 1985).

Carter, Charles E., "A Discipline in Transition: The Contributions of the Social Sciences to the Study of the Hebrew Bible," in C. Carter and C. Meyers, *Community, Identity, and Ideology: Social Science Approaches to the Hebrew Bible* (Winona Lake, IN: Eisenbrauns, 1996), 3–36.

——, "Ethnoarchaeology," in E. Meyers, *The Oxford Encyclopedia of Archaeology in the Near East*, ed. E. M. Meyers, vol. 2 (New York: Oxford University Press, 1997), 280–4.

——, *The Emergence of Yehud in the Persian Period: A Social and Demographic Study*, JSOTSup (Sheffield: Sheffield Academic Press, 1999a).

——, "Opening Windows onto Biblical Worlds: Applying the Social Sciences to Hebrew Scripture," ed. D. Baker and B. Baker, *The Face of Old Testament Studies: A Survey of Contemporary Approaches* (Grand Rapids, MN: Baker Books, 1999b), 421–51.

Causse, A., *Les "Pauvres" d'Israël: Prophètes, Psalmistes, Messianistes* (Strasbourg: Librairie Istra, 1922).

——, *Du Group Ethnique à la Communauté Religieuse: Le Problème Sociologique de la Religion d'Israël*, Études d'histoire et de Philosophie Religieuses 33 (Paris: Alcan, 1937).

Chaney, M., "Ancient Palestinian Peasant Movements and the Formation of Pre-Monarchic Israel," in D. Freedman and D. Graf, *Palestine in Transition: The Emergence of Ancient Israel* (Sheffield: Almond Press, 1983), 30–90.

Conder, C. and H. Kitchener, *The Survey of Western Palestine: Memoirs of the Topography, Orography, Hydrography, and Archaeology*, vol. 3 (London: Palestine Exploration Fund, 1883).

Cook, S., *Prophecy and Apocalypticism: The Postexilic Social Setting* (Minneapolis: Augsburg Fortress, 1995).

Coote, R. and K. Whitelam, "The Emergence of Israel: Social Transformation and State Formation Following the Decline in Late Bronze Age Trade," *Semeia* 37 (1986), 107–47.

Daly, M., *Beyond God the Father: Toward a Philosophy of Women's Liberation* (Boston: Beacon Press, 1973).

Davies, P., "How Not to Do Archaeology: The Story of Qumran," *Biblical Archaeologist* 51 (1988), 203–7.

——, *In Search of "Ancient Israel*,*"* JSOTSup (Sheffield: Sheffield Academic Press, 1992).

——, "The Society of Biblical Israel," in T. Eskenazi and K. Richards, eds., *Second Temple Studies 2. Temple and Community in the Persian Period* (Sheffield: Sheffield Academic Press, 1994), pp. 22–33.

Dever, W., "Biblical Archaeology: Death or Rebirth?" in J. Aviram and A. Biran, eds., *Biblical Archaeology Today: Proceedings of the Second International Congress on Biblical Archaeology* (Jerusalem: Israel Exploration Society, 1993), 706–22.

Douglas, M., *Purity and Danger: An Analysis of the Concepts of Pollution and Taboo* (London: Routledge and Kegan Paul, 1966).

Fenton, J., *Early Hebrew Life: A Study in Sociology* (London: Trubner & Co., 1880).

Finkelstein, I., *The Archaeology of the Israelite Settlement* (Jerusalem: Israel Exploration Society, 1988).

——, "The Emergence of the Monarchy in Israel: The Environmental and Socio-Economic Aspects," *Journal for the Study of the Old Testament* 44 (1989), 43–74.

Flanagan, J., "Chiefs in Israel," *Journal for the Study of the Old Testament* 20 (1981), 47–73.

——, *David's Social Drama: A Hologram of Israel's Early Iron Age*, Social World of Biblical Antiquity (Sheffield: Almond Press, 1988).

Frick, F., "Religion and Socio-Political Structure in Early Israel: An Ethno-Archaeological Approach," in P. Achtemeier, ed., *Society of Biblical Literature, 1979: Seminar Papers* (Missoula, MT: Scholars Press, 1979), 233–53.

——, *The Formation of the State in Ancient Israel: A Survey of Models and Theories*, Social World of Biblical Antiquity Series (Decatur, GA: Almond Press, 1985).

Gottwald, N. K., "Domain Assumptions and Societal Models in the Study of Pre-Monarchic Israel," *Supplements to Vetus Testamentum* 28, Congress Volume Edinburgh (Leiden: E. J. Brill, 1974), 89–100.

——, "Sociology of Ancient Israel," *Anchor Bible Dictionary* 6 (1992), 79–89.

——, "Reconstructing the Social History of Early Israel," *Eretz-Israel* 24, Malamat Volume (1993), 77*–82*.

——, *The Tribes of Yahweh: A Sociology of the Religion of Liberated Israel, 1250–1050 BCE* (Maryknoll, NY: Orbis, 1979).

Hanson, P. D., *The Dawn of Apocalyptic: The Historical and Sociological Roots of Jewish Apocalyptic Eschatology*, revised edn. (Philadelphia: Fortress Press, 1979).

Harris, M., *The Rise of Anthropological Theory: A History of the Theories of Culture* (New York: Columbia University Press), 1968.

——, *Cultural Materialism: The Struggle for a Science of Culture* (New York: Vintage, 1980).

Herion, G., "The Impact of Modern and Social Science Assumptions on the Reconstruction of Israelite History," *Journal for the Study of the Old Testament* 34 (1986), 3–33.

Hopkins, D., *The Highlands of Canaan: Agricultural Life in the Early Iron Age* (Decatur, GA: Almond Press, 1985).

——, "Life on the Land: The Subsistence Struggles of Early Israel," *Biblical Archaeologist* 50 (1987), 178–91.

Kimbrough, S., "A Non-Weberian Sociological Approach to Israelite Religion," *Journal of Near Eastern Studies* 31 (1972), 197–202.

Lemche, N. P., "On the Use of 'System Theory,' 'Macro Theories,' and 'Evolutionistic Thinking' in Modern Old Testament Research and Biblical Archaeology," *Scandinavian Journal of the Old Testament* 2 (1990), 73–88.

Lenski, G., "Review of Norman K. Gottwald's the Tribes of Yahweh," *Religious Studies Review* 6 (1980), 275–8.

——, "Rethinking Macrosociological Theory," *American Sociological Review* 53 (1988), 163–71.

Lenski, G., J. Lenski and P. Nolan, *Introduction to Human Societies: A Macro-Sociological Approach*, 6th edn. (New York: McGraw-Hill, 1991).

Levy, T., "The Chalcolithic Period in Palestine," *Biblical Archaeologist* 49 (1986), 82–108.

Malamat, Abraham, "Charismatic Leadership in the Book of Judges," in F. Cross, W. Lemke and P. Miller, eds., *Magnelia Dei – the Mighty Acts of God: Essays on the Bible and Archaeology in Memory of G. Ernest Wright* (New York: Doubleday, 1976), 152–68.

Malina, B., "The Social Sciences and Biblical Interpretation," *Interpretation* 37 (1982), 229–42.

Mayes, A. D. H., *The Old Testament in Sociological Perspective* (London: Pickering, 1989).

McNutt, P., *The Forging of Israel: Iron Technology, Symbolism, and Tradition in Ancient Society*, The Social World of Biblical Antiquity Series 8 (Sheffield: Almond Press, 1990).

——, *Reconstructing the Society of Ancient Israel* (Louisville, KY: Westminster/John Knox Press, 1999).

Mendenhall, G., "The Hebrew Conquest of Palestine," *Biblical Archaeologist* 25 (1962), 66–87.

——, "Ancient Israel's Hyphenated History," in D. Freedman and D. Graf, *Palestine in Transition: The Emergence of Ancient Israel* (Sheffield: Almond Press, 1983), 91–103.

Meyers, C. L., "Procreation, Production, and Protection: Male–Female Balance in Early Israel," *Journal of the American Academy of Religion* 51 (1983), 569–73.

——, *Discovering Eve: Ancient Israelite Women in Context* (New York: Oxford University Press, 1988).

——, "An Ethnoarchaeological Analysis of Hannah's Sacrifice," in D. Wright, D. Freedman and A. Hurvitz, *Pomegranates and Golden Bells: Studies in Biblical, Jewish, and Near Eastern Ritual, Law, and Literature in Honor of Jacob Milgrom* (Winona Lake, IN: Eisenbrauns, 1995), 77–91.

Meyers, C. L. and E. M. Meyers, "Expanding the Frontiers of Biblical Archaeology," *Eretz Israel* 20 (1989), 140*–47*.

Meyers, C. L., T. Craven, and R. Kramer, eds., *Women in Scripture: A Dictionary of Named and Unnamed Women in the Hebrew Bible, the Apocryphal/Deuterocanonical Books, and the New Testament* (Boston: Houghton Mifflin Company, 2000).

Newsom, C. and S. Ringe, eds., *Women's Bible Commentary*, expanded edn. (Louisville, KY: Westminster/John Knox Press, 1998).

Noth, M., *Das System Der Zwölf Stämme Israels*, Beitrage Zur Wissenschaft Vom Alten und Neuen Testament 4 (Stuttgart: Kohlhammer, 1930).

——, *The History of Israel*, 2nd edn. (London: Black, 1960).

Oden, R., *The Bible without Theology: The Theological Tradition and Alternatives to It* (San Francisco: Harper & Row, 1987).

Overholt, T., "The Ghost Dance of 1890 and the Nature of the Prophetic Process," *Ethnohistory* 21 (1974), 37–63.

——, "Prophecy: The Problem of Cross-Cultural Comparison," *Semeia* 21 (1982), 55–78.

——, *Cultural Anthropology and the Old Testament* (Minneapolis: Fortress Press, 1996).

Plaskow, J., *Standing Again at Sinai: Judaism from a Feminist Perspective* (San Francisco: Harper & Row, 1990).

Plöger, O., *Theocracy and Eschatology*, trans. S. Rudman (Richmond, VA: John Knox Press, 1968).

Rainey, A., "Review of the Tribes of Yahweh: Sociology of the Religion of Liberated Israel," *Journal of the American Oriental Society* 107 (1987), 541–3.

Richard, S., "The Early Bronze Age: The Rise and Collapse of Urbanism," *Biblical Archaeologist* 50 (1987), 22–43.

Robinson, E., *Biblical Researches in Palestine, Mount Sinai and Arabian Petraea* (London: J. Murray, 1856).

Ruether, R. R., *Religion and Sexism: Images of Women in the Jewish and Christian Traditions* (New York: Simon and Schuster, 1974).

——, *Women and Redemption: A Theological History* (Minneapolis: Fortress Press, 1998).

Sasson, J., "On Choosing Models for Recreating Israelite Pre-Monarchic History," *Journal for the Study of the Old Testament* 21 (1981), 3–24.

Schottroff, L., S. Schroer and M.-T. Wacker, *Feminist Interpretation: The Bible in Women's Perspective* (Minneapolis: Fortress Press, 1998).

Schüssler Fiorenza, E., *Rhetoric and Ethic: The Politics of Biblical Studies* (Minneapolis: Fortress Press, 1999).

Service, E., *Primitive Social Organization*, 2nd edn. (New York: Random House, 1962).

——, *Origins of the State and Civilization* (New York: Norton, 1975).

Smith, D., *The Religion of the Landless: A Sociology of the Babylonian Exile* (Bloomington: Meyer-Stone, 1989).

Stanton, E. C., *The Woman's Bible* (New York: European Publishing Co., 1895–8).

Trible, P., *God and the Rhetoric of Sexuality*, Overtures to Biblical Theology (Philadelphia: Fortress Press, 1978).

——, *Texts of Terror: Literary-Feminist Readings of Biblical Texts*, vol. 13, Overtures to Biblical Theology (Philadelphia: Fortress Press, 1984).

Wallis, Louis, "Sociological Significance of the Bible," *American Journal of Sociology* 12 (1907), 532–52.

——, *Sociological Study of the Bible* (Chicago: University of Chicago Press, 1912).

Weber, M., *Ancient Judaism*, trans. H. Gerth and D. Martindale (Glencoe, IL: Free Press, 1952).

Wellhausen, J., *Prolegomena to the History of Israel*, trans. J. S. Black and A. Mensies (Edinburgh: A. & C. Black, 1885).

Wilson, R., *Prophecy and Society in Ancient Israel* (Philadelphia: Fortress Press, 1980).

——, *Sociological Approaches to the Old Testament* (Philadelphia: Fortress Press, 1984).

PART II
Israelite and Early Jewish History

CHAPTER 4

Early Israel and the Rise of the Israelite Monarchy

Carol Meyers

The Biblical Story

A generation ago, an overview of early Israel, from its beginnings in its land through the rise of the monarchy several centuries later, would have relied heavily on the information contained in the Hebrew Bible. Most scholars wrote Israelite history as "biblical history"; they followed quite closely the basic frame-work and also many of the details that are presented in the grand narrative of Israel's formation as presented in the book of Exodus, in parts of other penta-teuchal books, and in the books of Joshua and Judges and of 1 and 2 Samuel. They recognized the folkloristic quality of some of these materials; and they also acknowledged that those biblical books took their present shape many centur-ies, if not half a millennium or more, after the events they purport to describe. Nonetheless, they treated the biblical sources, whatever their embellishments, nationalist functions, or religious programs, as historiography (history-writing) that preserved a reliable account of the formation and early development of ancient Israel. The ancestor narratives of Genesis were understood as highly fictionalized or legendary accounts, but the national story beginning in Exodus was seen as an historical record.

The broad outlines of that story are well known to most people living in the West, where Jewish and Christian tradition has permeated general cultural forms and values. The story opens with the dramatic account of the exodus, in which a group of people laboring on the Pharaoh's building projects miraculously escape from Egyptian oppression. A god known as YHWH is ultimately responsible for this move towards freedom, but human leaders – Moses, Miriam, and Aaron – carry out the divine will. For some forty years, the people traverse the Sinai wilderness, where they experience a theophany (appearance of God) of unpre-cedented national scope. This event bonds them as a people with a formal con-stitution, the covenant, and gives them a destiny to inhabit a land said to have been promised to their ancestors. They then travel across the Sinai peninsula and the Negev desert to the plateau east of the Jordan River, avoiding or over-coming hostile groups along the way. Next they invade the promised land en masse, violently destroying first the seemingly impregnable city of Jericho, and then proceeding to annihilate the city of Ai and its inhabitants. In short order – less than five years – the rest of the land falls to the onslaught of Joshua (Moses' successor) and his warriors.

Having established their presence throughout the promised land, this people – known as the Israelites because of their common descent from the ancestor Jacob = Israel – settle in their allotted territories, tribe by tribe. For several centuries, these tribes survive in the land, despite periodic military threats from neighboring peoples and the internal negative effects of adding local Canaanite religious practices to the worship of their one God. Time and again, as related in the vivid detail of the narratives in Judges, military heroes rise to the occasion, rallying militias from their own tribes and even others, to conquer their enemies despite great odds that often call for miraculous divine intervention.

The leadership provided by those heroes, called judges (a word that sometimes denotes military leadership rather than judicial authority), ultimately proves unable to cope with the growing military threat of a people known as Philistines, who had migrated from the Aegean and lived in five cities (pentapolis) along the southern coast of the land – Palestine – that ultimately came to bear their name (Palestine being a Latinized Greek form, "Palestina," of the name of Philistine territory). The people of Israel realize that their ad hoc pattern of occasional supra-tribal leadership could not deal with the expanding Philistine power. Consequently, they cry out to Samuel, a priest and a prophet as well as the last major judge, to appoint a king so that they would be like the other nations and have a standing army to withstand the assaults of Philistines and others. Despite Samuel's opposition – he insists that only YHWH should be ruler and that a human king would mean the burden of taxes and the conscription of Israelites to be soldiers and laborers for the crown – Saul is installed as king.

Saul begins the defense against the Philistines, but true and lasting victory comes only at the hands of his successor David, founder of a dynasty that would rule in Jerusalem for nearly half a millennium. David conquers the Philistines, subdues a number of other enemies, and unites all the tribes in a monarchic government headquartered in Jerusalem, which he captures from the Jebusites. With the ark of God, the symbol of divine presence and the repository of YHWH's covenant with Israel, brought into the new capital, David extends his power base over extensive regions of Transjordan and Syria. His son Solomon more or less retains these holdings while building a lavish palace for himself and an elaborate temple for YHWH, both buildings befitting an imperial power.

Assessments of the Story

The narrative of exodus, of settlement of the land, and of the establishment of the monarchy is replete with accounts of the perpetration of violence against innocent people – from the first-born Egyptian children killed in the last of ten plagues God visits upon the Egyptians in order to shake loose the Pharaoh's reluctance to release the Hebrews, to the populations of the towns annihilated by Joshua and his men, to the enemy troops slaughtered by Saul and David. The existence of such accounts of death and slaughter, which would seem to depict ungodly behavior, might itself lead to skepticism about the reliability of the master biblical narrative of Israel's beginning as a people and a nation. Even more difficult to accept is the Bible's justification for such acts – that the violence was part of God's scheme for redemption of the Hebrews from Egypt and for assuring their acquisition of land meant for them, and their eventual establishment of a sovereign state in that territory.

The moral problems inherent in these narratives are not the only difficulties that emerge from critical assessments. Another chink in the armor of historical reliability lies in the self-contradictions that appear in the biblical story. Perhaps the most striking example is that of the portrayal of the Israelite tribes taking possession of their territories. Many episodes in the book of Judges, as well as the introductory passages in Judges 1–2, depict the acquisition of the land as being quite different from the unified, godly, rapid, and complete taking of "the whole land" that the book of Joshua describes in vivid and compelling prose. According to Judges, even after the tribal settlement in the land, Canaanites and other peoples continued to occupy major urban centers along the coast and in some of the larger inland valleys; and they persisted in attacking and harassing the newcomers. Some biblical scholarship has tried valiantly to harmonize the divergent traditions, but most scholars understand the contradictions as signaling the unreliability of at least some of the narratives of settlement.

Another difficulty is posed by the contrast between the earth-shaking nature of the events described in the biblical accounts of the origins of the people and the state and the virtual absence of information about these events in the records of other peoples of the ancient biblical world. Indeed, no mention of anything like the exodus of a significant group from Egypt, the sweeping battles to establish control of the promised land, or the formation of the first territorial state in the history of the land of Canaan appears in the extra-biblical records that date from the time period involved, namely, the end of the Late Bronze Age (13th century BCE) and the beginning of the Iron Age (12th to 10th centuries BCE). This argument from silence may not be truly significant, if the events that loom large in the Bible turn out to be less consequential in international terms and perhaps not worthy of mention by Israel's neighbors. Yet this argument too has tended to erode biblical credibility.

Despite these problems, the biblical account of early Israel, as a people and then a nation-state, endured as a largely reliable witness of ancient Israel for modern historiography until the advent of two major developments – one now decades old, the other more recent – in biblical study. The first is the extensive archaeological work carried out in the land of the Bible; excavations and surveys began in the mid-19th century but only in the mid-20th century did they become instrumental in undermining perceptions of biblical historicity. The second is the postmodern questioning, at the end of the 20th century, of the very project of writing history and of using sources that were never intended as accurate factual accounts.

Archaeology and the Problem of Using the Bible as History

In its earliest efforts (and in many projects carried out to this very day), archaeology of the land of the Bible had as a goal, implicitly and sometimes quite explicitly, the verification of scripture as well as the illumination of material conditions reflected in the Bible. Ironically, instead of being an instrument of scriptural validation, archaeology has undermined the scholars' reliance on the biblical stories of Israelite origins, as a people and a state, as somewhat embellished but basically accurate sources.

The biblical presentations of Joshua's conquest of Jericho is a case in point. The Jericho tale occupies a major role – in length (six chapters), detail, and drama – in the book of Joshua and thus in the story of Israelite occupation of the land. Excavations at the ruins of Jericho began in the first decade of the 20th century, when a German team initiated work there. Further excavations were carried out in the 1930s by a British archaeologist, John Garstang, who traced the city's history back to the Stone Age. He uncovered a thick layer of destruction debris, nearly two feet deep in places, which he identified as evidence of the great conflagration that took place as the result of the Israelite assault on the city. After all, he reasoned, according to Josh 6:24, Joshua and his men "burned down the city, and everything in it."

Garstang's interpretation of the archaeological evidence was contested as the result of another British dig at Jericho, carried out in the 1950s by Dame Kathleen Kenyon. She used Carbon 14 dating as well as meticulous stratigraphic analysis of the occupation layers that comprise the ruins of Jericho; and she concluded that the ashy destruction debris that had been identified as evidence of Joshua's deadly assault on the city was several centuries older than the period of Israelite beginnings in the land. Furthermore, she established that Jericho was virtually uninhabited in the late 13th century, the period to which most scholars assign Israelite settlement. An American field project at Ai, the only other site, in addition to Jericho, singled out by the narrator of the book of Joshua for extensive treatment (two chapters), yielded similar results. Ai was also supposed to have been completely torched by the Israelites – indeed, its very name means "the ruin." Yet careful excavations revealed that the city had in fact already lain in ruins for nearly a thousand years by the end of the 13th century BCE.

The book of Joshua reports on the violent conquest of twenty-nine other cities, twenty-one of which have been identified with reasonable certainty. Excavation or careful survey of most of them indicates that only Bethel, and perhaps Hazor, show evidence of massive destruction at the end of the Late Bronze Age followed by a small unwalled settlement that would have been home to victorious Israelites. But even for these two sites, evidence of destruction at the time of

Israelite beginnings is not evidence that a group known as Israelites caused the destruction. Archaeology may confidently confirm that a city was destroyed at a particular time, but it cannot identify the perpetrators of such a calamity. Because of the general political instability at the end of the Late Bronze Age, a destructive conflagration could just as well have been the result of intercity warfare.

Many of the cities in Transjordan reported in the book of Numbers (21:21–31) to have been taken by the Israelites in their advance from Egypt to Canaan have also been excavated with similar results. At Heshbon and Dibon, for example, no evidence for a Late Bronze Age occupation was uncovered. Indeed, Transjordan was largely unoccupied at the time of the supposed Israelite passage.

In short, archaeology has demolished the depiction, in the book of Joshua, of the virtually synchronous conquest of all the major Canaanite cities as well as Transjordanian ones by an invading group. In so doing, it has overturned a theory of Israelite emergence in Canaan that dominated biblical studies, especially in America and Israel, for decades. In the late 1930s, the great American archaeologist and biblical scholar W. F. Albright, formulated what became known as the "conquest" hypothesis. Followers of this model for Israelite beginnings were convinced of the essential reliability of the Joshua and Judges narratives in reporting a unified military conquest in the late 13th century BCE by invaders from the east. Archaeological work early in the 20th century seemed to bear out this hypothesis, and it is only the results of the more sophisticated fieldwork and of the systematic surveys of mid-century and later that have undermined that regnant hypothesis.

Serious flaws in another major theory about the emergence of Israel have also become visible as the result of archaeological data. That theory, known as the "pastoral nomad" hypothesis, accepts as historically reliable the biblical insistence that the Israelite newcomers represented a movement of people from the east. The proponents of this theory saw the invasion as a gradual and largely peaceful migration rather than a swift and violent invasion. The brilliant German scholar Albrecht Alt first articulated this theory in the 1920s. Working without the use of archaeological data, he had carefully compared the territorial configurations of Canaan known from Egyptian sources with those claimed by the Bible for early Israel. He concluded, drawing on early 20th century notions of the progress of civilization from nomadic pastoralism to peasant agriculture to urbanism, that the early Israelites were sheep and goat herders who gradually moved into the sparsely settled highlands of Canaan and became farmers, where they lived mostly in peace, among their urban Canaanite neighbors, for generations. These pastoralists have sometimes been identified with groups of tent-dwellers, originating in northern Arabia and southern Transjordan and known as Shasu in Egyptian texts of the Late Bronze Age. The pastoral nomadic theory dominated German biblical studies for generations and also found its way into some Israeli scholarship.

Archaeological data, however, have made the basic features of the nomadic hypothesis untenable. The archaeological investigation of new settlements of the early Iron Age (12th and 11th centuries BCE), associated by most scholars with early Israel, has revealed that the "Israelite" material culture is essentially a continuation of Canaanite culture. This continuity is most evident in pottery forms, which are in direct development from Late Bronze Canaanite ceramic traditions. A group of people invading en masse from the outside would have been expected to bring their own cultural forms, as did the Philistines. Arriving in Canaan slightly later than the Israelites, the Philistines brought with them distinctive ceramic traditions that persisted in their cities for generations.

Recent anthropological research has likewise revealed flaws in the nomadic hypothesis. The concept of nomads, as groups subsisting largely on herd animals and their byproducts and living in isolation from settled peoples, is no longer considered valid, nor is the related concept of semi-nomads. Both socioeconomic constructs are part of the now outmoded notion of an evolutionary transition of social forms, from nomad to farmer to city-dweller. Archaeological analysis has shown that various subsistence strategies operated simultaneously among premodern groups in the Near East. To put it simply, there is no evidence for pure pastoralists nor for pure farmers. The raising of crops was combined, in various proportions, by Bronze and Iron Age inhabitants of the Levant to maximize survival in a risky environment.

Another questionable aspect of the biblical presentation of an invasion of people, whether nomads or farmers, whether peaceful or warlike, is the strong tradition that the invaders exited from Egypt and spent significant periods of time at various sites in the Sinai peninsula, including the elusive Mount Sinai. For generations archaeologists have been scouring the Sinai wilderness in vain, looking for traces of such a movement; and biblical geographers have been trying without success to determine, on the basis of known sites in relation to places mentioned in the biblical text, the route of the trans-Sinai migration and the identity of the mountain of divine revelation. Indeed, excavations at Kadesh Barnea, the large oasis in northern Sinai at which the Israelites are reported to have encamped for a considerable length of time, have revealed that the earliest ruins at the site date to the 10th century BCE – several centuries later than the purported date of the exodus.

Historiography and the Problem of Using the Bible as History

Using the biblical text as a reliable witness to the emergence of Israel, as a people and then a nation, is also problematic from the perspective of the very concept of history-writing. The reliance on the biblical narrative as a source for information about early Israel is predicated upon the notion that, whatever its literary embellishments and folkloristic features, it constitutes a form of history-writing. Jewish and Christian tradition have certainly taken it as such, as have the 19th and most of the 20th century writers of Israel's early history. Because those writers were, for the most part, members of theological faculties in Europe and the United States, even the most liberal among them had a stake in the authenticity of the scriptural word. Thus, although they could accept the ancestral narratives of Genesis as legendary, their writing of Israelite history from the exodus on was little more than the biblical stories retold.

Recent attention to the nature of history-writing has shown that ideological biases are inherent in the very project of history-writing. It has also made clear that biblical sources from which we might attempt to write history were never intended to be eyewitness accounts or even general summaries of events. Rather they are highly selective and imaginatively expanded accounts of the meaning and nature of past times. That is, the texts themselves have strong ideological biases that distort or mask events and characters. Thus, some scholars today question the very notion that a history of the eastern Mediterranean in the Late Bronze and Iron Ages can ever be written. They suggest that to produce such an account would have to be done without relying at all on information in the Hebrew Bible. They insist that all the biblical materials were formed centuries after the events they describe and that they are literary productions with little or no reliability as witness to events or persons. The most extreme among such critics, heavily influenced by postmodernism, particularly as it has affected the study of literature, question the validity or possibility of writing Israelite history or any history.

Most scholars, however, believe it is reductionist to look at biblical literature as if it is "pure" literature, created only as aesthetic expression. Being literary does not preclude being referential to historical context and event; and it certainly does not preclude the composition of deliberate acts of communication. Thus, the basically anti-historic stance of a few has not made serious inroads into biblical studies, although it has, rightfully, made biblical scholars aware of literary features of their sources. Few today would claim that the books and chapters of the Hebrew Bible that set forth the story of the beginnings of Israel as a people and a nation represent an historiographical enterprise. Yet those materials are not pure fiction, freely invented. Rather, they can be viewed as a mixture of fictional imagination and historical memory brought together for ideological purposes. They were not written as an historical record but rather as an expression of ideas and values using the vehicle of story.

Despite this literary and ideological crafting, several kinds of evidence, contained in the biblical text itself, indicate that the Hebrew Bible can be used as a source that has a modicum of historical authenticity. One kind of evidence is represented by the Bible's onomastican, that is, by the repertoire of personal names contained in various sections of the Bible. The names of the twelve non-Israelites mentioned in Joshua are of particular interest because those names can be compared with the personal names found in non-Israelite written sources from the biblical period. The results are striking. All twelve of the names are attested in extra-biblical sources. This means that the author or redactor of the book of Joshua did not make up names but rather drew upon authentic traditions about the kinds of names non-Israelites, such as the prostitute Rahab of the Jericho tale (Joshua 2, 6), and the Eglonite king Debir (Josh 10:3), possessed.

Even more striking is the fact that the extra-biblical evidence for the use of those names, in eleven of the twelve cases, comes from a specific time period, namely, the Late Bronze Age – precisely the era in which the Joshua narratives are set. This congruence implies strongly that at least some of the traditions preserved in the Joshua materials originated in the Late Bronze Age. This authenticity of names does not necessarily mean that the narratives in which they are found are equally ancient and authentic; but it does indicate the preservation in ancient Israel of traditions that date from the period, the 13th century BCE, of its emergence in the highlands of Canaan.

Another feature of the biblical materials depicting early Israel likewise attests to a measure of authenticity. Embedded in the prose narrative that presents the early "history" of Israel from the exodus to the monarchy are a number of poetic sections. Prominent among them are the Song of the Sea in Exodus 15 and the Song of Deborah in Judges 5. Both poems contain information that also appears in the accompanying prose accounts, a fact that implies that other parts of the narrative, for which a poetic version is not preserved, may likewise be drawing on authentic traditions dating to the early Iron Age. The poetry in Judges 5 is archaic, and virtually all scholars maintain that it dates to the 12th century BCE. The information it contains about the Israelite tribes – their relationships, their economy, their beliefs – is, then, important for reconstructing early Israel as well as for establishing the possibility that even the much later narrative accounts draw from authentic and archaic traditions.

One other kind of evidence points to a measure of reliability. Many of the toponyms (place names) in the books of Judges and 1 Samuel correspond to sites that can be identified in the archaeological record. Furthermore, those places that remained in enemy hands according to the biblical narrative turn out, as excavations have shown, to survive as non-Israelite cities until the monarchy. Many reliable traditions about political control have apparently survived in the saga of settlement and, eventually, of statehood.

Acknowledging that the master narrative of early Israel may draw upon and preserve early traditions does not solve the problem of judging which aspects of the narrative are authentic and which are literary expansions. There is no single or fool-proof way to extract reliable data from the artfully crafted tales. The stories are so masterfully crafted that the boundaries between historical event and literary expression have been blurred forever. But certain aspects of the tales themselves, rather than specific details, tend to support the notion that, at least for the account in the book of Judges of the premonarchic existence of Israelites in the highlands, the overall outlines of that era and its social and political features are authentic. For example, the tales of heroes (the so-called "major" judges: Othniel, Ehud, Deborah, Gideon, Jephthah, Samson), who are unlikely leaders ruling through their own charisma, make sense only for a period of little or no central authority. Literary analysis may identify the folkloristic and thus fictive nature of the tales, but the pattern of charismatic leadership seems to be a constant and reliable feature of that era.

Similarly, the narratives of the Hebrew Bible dealing with state formation and the early ("United") monarchy are replete with the mark of the redactors who compiled the story of Israel from its beginnings through most of the monarchy. The dramatic tales of the first three monarchic rulers (Saul, David, and Solomon), as well as of the premonarchic leaders (Moses, Joshua, and the judges), are embedded in the so-called Deuteronomic History (DH). A "school" or group of traditionalists, probably beginning at the time of King Josiah (7th century BCE) as part of the resurgence of nationalism during his reign, formed a coherent narrative of Israel's existence as a people. That narrative contains speeches and prayers, introductions and summaries, all of which put an unmistakable spin on the events recounted: the deeds of the people and their leaders are evaluated in terms of their compliance with the Torah of Moses. At the same time, as literary analysis has shown, the DH redaction incorporated highly legendary and folkloristic, if not novelistic, segments. Such segments are signaled by the presence of dialogue in private settings that preclude eyewitness records, the use of type-scenes of military chivalry, and the focus on tensions and conflicts in the personal lives of the rulers. Scholars have attempted to identify and calculate the amount of authentic materials, drawn from annalistic sources such as court records or from popular stories, oral or written, about battles and intrigues, that survive in the DH narrative. It has been suggested that less than 5 percent of the Saul stories, about 8 percent of the David accounts, and as much as 45 percent of the Solomonic coverage is reliable.

Although the biblical record does preserve authentic traditions about the emergence of a people called Israel and the transformation of that people to a political state, the difficulties in identifying the reliable aspects of the master narrative make the use of other materials essential. Just what are those extra-biblical sources? Broadly speaking, they are all archaeological – that is, they are aspects of the material culture of the biblical world. More specifically, the archaeological remains consist of two kinds of data: ancient written (epigraphic) and iconographic depictions of events and peoples that may shed light on the Israelites; and the dwellings and settlements of the Israelites themselves as recovered through excavation and survey.

Extra-biblical Sources: Texts and Monuments

Although an extensive corpus of written materials and artistic monuments has been recovered from the ancient Near Eastern world of the biblical period, very few such remains come from the settlements of the ancient Israelites themselves. Rather, they come largely from the lands of the superpowers – Egypt, the various large political states in Mesopotamia (especially Babylonia and Assyria), the Hittites of Anatolia and, to a lesser extent, the large Canaanite city-states (such as Ugarit and Byblos) on the northern Levantine coast. Not surprisingly, the epigraphic and iconographic legacies of those cultures provide little information about Israel and the Israelites, especially from the period of Israelite beginnings. With a few exceptions, "Israel" or Israelites are not mentioned outside the Bible until the 9th century BCE.

This "silence" in the texts and monuments of the people surrounding Israel is taken by a minority of scholars to indicate that the "Israel" of the late 13th century through the 10th century is a fictive biblical retrojection of a people and then a nation-state in order to legitimate a much later Israelite or Judean entity. Yet the few extra-biblical written and artistic sources that have survived constitute evidence that cannot be turned aside; they provide important witnesses to a pre-9th century Israel. The lack of attention to early Israel in Near Eastern sources can and must be explained in other ways – such as the fact that Israel was rather unimportant on the social, political, and economic map of the ancient Near East, or that the superpowers themselves were weak in the 13th to 10th centuries – than by claiming that Israel/Israelites did not exist.

Perhaps the most important source for establishing the existence of early Israel as well as for providing some clues as to its location and its character comes from ancient Egypt. About a century ago, the brilliant English archaeologist and Egyptologist, Sir Flinders Petrie, discovered a large black granite slab, or stele, in his excavations at Thebes in Upper Egypt. Dating to the reign of the pharaoh Merneptah (1213–1203 BCE), it bears a series of inscriptions, in prose and poetry, that celebrate Egyptian military triumphs. At the end of the poetic sections, these words appear:

> Canaan has been plundered into every sort of woe;
>   Ashkelon has been overcome,
>   Gezer has been captured,
>   Yanoam was made nonexistent;
> Israel is laid waste, its seed is not;
> Hurru is become a widow because of Egypt . . .
> All lands together – they are pacified.

The mention of Israel is a stunning piece of evidence, not simply because it is the only mention of Israel in an Egyptian text. The way Israel is signified in the inscription is another important feature. The inscription uses a hieroglyphic sign, or determinative, for a fortified city-state in its listing of the three Canaanite city-states (Ashkelon, Gezer, and Yanoam). But the word for Israel is the only proper name in this inscription that is written with the determinative indicating a people rather than a place. The Egyptians considered Israel a polity that differed from the Canaanite kingdoms of the late 13th century.

Several other aspects of early Israel can be gleaned from this inscription. The "people" determinative is a masculine collective, in contrast to the treatment in Egyptian of cities and countries as feminine, and may signify that Israel was regarded as a people bearing the name of an eponymous male ancestor. Also, the use of the term *seed*, denoting seeds for planting and not seed as offspring, denotes an agrarian people. This adds to the sense that early Israel was a rural collective entity rather than an urban-based kingdom; "Israel" in the inscription likely refers to tribal, largely agrarian, rural groups. Finally, the appearance of "Israel" alongside the names of major political entities of the Late Bronze

Age (Canaanites and Hurrians) in a context of military victory implies that Israel, like the others, was regarded as having sufficient military resources to constitute a threat to the Egyptian attempt to control the east Mediterranean trade routes.

The stele is thus solid evidence that the Egyptians were aware of a sociopolitical entity called Israel and that Merneptah took this people seriously enough to brag that he had annihilated them. That he actually wiped them out, as he claimed, is unlikely: first because pharaohs tended to exaggerate their accomplishments in commemorative inscriptions; and second, because Israel survived for some 600 years after the time of Merneptah.

Another extra-biblical source for early Israel is an iconographic one, a battle relief from Karnak, now also dated to Merneptah, which depicts a group of Israelites. Shown together with Canaanites, they look like Canaanites, having the same clothing and hairstyles. This visual as well as textual linkage of Israelites and Canaanites helps to dispel the notion that Israelites were a discrete entity originating outside the land of Canaan. It also poses the possibility that they participated with the Canaanites and others in activities that the Egyptians considered rebellious and felt constrained to quell.

With one exception – the possible appearance of a place called "the Highlands of David" in a 10th century BCE hieroglyphic list of places conquered by Pharaoh Sheshonk I (or Shishak, as in 1 Kgs 14:25) – no epigraphic references to Israel or any Israelite appear again until the 9th century BCE. The 1993 excavations at the northern site of Tel Dan uncovered a victory stele with an Aramaic inscription apparently celebrating the defeat, in about 840 BCE, of Israel and Judah by an Aramean king. The inscription mentions the "house of David." A Moabite stele, also of the mid-9th century, may likewise refer to the Davidic dynasty. Although all these readings have been contested by a few skeptics, they seem to point quite clearly to the existence of a dynastic state ruling over Israelites by the 10th century BCE. The date fits the chronology, based on biblical as well as extra-biblical evidence, that assigns the rise of the monarchy to the end of the 11th and beginning of the 10th centuries BCE.

Extra-biblical Sources: Archaeology

This textual and visual evidence for early Israel and the beginnings of the monarchy is accompanied by striking information provided by archaeology. For early Israel, the archaeological data are of two major kinds: (1) the patterns of settlement in the land of Canaan in the early Iron Age, especially as provided by systematic surveys; and (2) the nature of the highland sites located in the areas that might be identified as Israelite on the basis of the Merneptah inscription as well as biblical texts. The value of both kinds of evidence involves comparisons. In what ways do the size and location of the Iron Age I settlements differ from those of the previous Late Bronze Age and of the succeeding Iron IIA period?

And what are the salient features of the buildings and layout of the Iron I sites in comparison with earlier and later ones?

For virtually all of the Bronze Age – that is, for nearly two millennia of settled life in the land of Canaan and even before – settlements were located mainly along the coastal plain, in the rift and Jezreel Valley, and in the larger valleys in the central highlands and Galilee. In contrast, the hill country of Judea and Samaria as well as that of Upper and Lower Galilee was sparsely settled, with good reason – the scarcity of perennial water sources along with the rocky, forested, hilly terrain made cultivation, and therefore survival, difficult. Throughout the Bronze Age, albeit with ebbs and flows, the seacoast and valleys saw periods of intense urbanization and international trade while the highlands remained isolated, remote, and largely unpopulated.

Extensive survey work has shown a vastly different pattern in the Iron I period. For example, in the highland areas shown to be within the territories ultimately associated with the tribes of Judah, Benjamin, Ephraim, and Manasseh – tribes that would be the core of monarchic Israel – the number of settlements jumps nearly ninefold, from 36 to 319. And most of the settlements are new ones – small, unwalled villages built on previously unoccupied sites. There can be no doubt that, by the 12th century BCE, the highlands of Canaan are populated to an extent that had never before been the case. Furthermore, population in most of these areas continued to expand into the Iron II, or monarchic era.

The dramatic increase in the number of settlements located in the highlands of Canaan in the period associated with the emergence of Israel is accompanied by a marked change in the nature of the settlements. In the Late Bronze Age, most of the sites were walled settlements that archaeologists call "cities," in conformation with terminology in ancient literary sources. Those cities bear little resemblance, however, to the sprawling urban centers – some as large as 400 hectares (nearly 1000 acres) – in Egypt or Mesopotamia. Rather, with a few exceptions, the major Canaanite cities were ten to twenty hectares (twenty-five to forty-five acres) in size, with a population calculated to be about 100 people per acre. A strategically located Late Bronze Age center such as Megiddo was about ten hectares and would have had a population of about 2500 people. In contrast, the new, unfortified settlements were only one to two acres in size and supported populations of 100 to 200 people.

This dramatic change in the settlement landscape is not the only kind of information that surveys and excavations have provided. The configuration of settlements with respect to each other is also significant, as is the nature of the settlements themselves.

A detailed study of the highland area north of Jerusalem provides a good example of the settlement patterns of the 12th–11th centuries. The settlements there can be classified into four groups according to size, some as small as one acre with only a half dozen or so dwellings, others – the largest ones – being two acres in extent; in between are sites one to one-and-a-half acres in size and those one-and-a-half to two acres in size. In addition, a few sites verge on being towns, rather than hamlets or villages; such sites are five to ten acres in size and were home to some four hundred people. In the area north of Jerusalem, five or six of those towns can be identified, with a number of smaller sites stretching out in a line from them in decreasing size, like spokes in a wheel. This pattern suggests that the hundreds of new sites dotting the highland landscape are not random or isolated settlements. Rather, there are clear centers with smaller sites, in a hierarchy by size, surrounding them.

The sites are all agricultural settlements, surviving on a mixed economy of grain crops, horticulture (grapes and olives), and small animals (mostly sheep and goats). The environmental niches in the highlands are extremely diverse, even short distances apart; and the proportions of the various main crops and supplementary ones varied from village to village. Most sites consisted of groups of houses situated on hilltops, with no surrounding enclosure or defense walls. The small dwellings of three or four rooms, which probably held living and working quarters for nuclear families of four or five people (two adults plus the two to three children that survived past infancy) as well as stabling areas for the animals, were often clustered around a beaten-earth courtyard. These clusters probably represented an extended family – brothers and their wives and children, plus their surviving parents. The smaller villages were largely self-sufficient. But the environmental risk factors (drought, pestilence, and the like) were often great; and the pooling of resources and labor within and across villages would have been likely.

The four categories of small villages showed little variation among the houses; but in the towns several larger dwellings, with more rooms and perhaps paved courtyards, along with some few luxury goods, give testimony of local elites. None of the settlements contained anything near the palatial dwellings, temple precincts, extensive storage facilities, quantities of imported ceramics, and other luxury goods that were characteristic, along with city walls, of the Canaanite cities of the Late Bronze Age as well as those associated in Judges 1 with non-Israelites and that continued into the Iron Age. The highland towns of the Iron Age indicate the existence of ruling families of elders that received some small amounts of support, in terms of goods and probably also labor, from the villages extending out from them on all sides. The hierarchy in size correlates with slight economic hierarchies, also visible archaeologically. Together, these differentials suggest small, localized social and political hierarchies.

However the relatively minor hierarchies are to be understood, the overall picture is one of small farming villages dotting the landscapes in locations removed from the coastal and lowland urban Canaanite cities but yet representing a continuation of many aspects of the material culture of those cities. The presence of both similarities and differences led to the formation of another theory about Israelite beginnings. First proposed by George Mendenhall in the early 1960s as the "peasant revolt" hypothesis and then expanded and refined by Norman Gottwald in the 1970s, this theory sees early Israelites as Canaanite peasants who could no longer tolerate the economic and social tyranny of the ruling urban elites. They withdrew from the city-states and the villages around them, where they had been servants in elite households or sharecroppers or tenant farmers supplying the ruling class. This movement of propertyless peasants and laborers to the largely uninhabited countryside was perhaps motivated by a new faith, as Mendenhall proposed; or it was the resistance of those people to Canaanite exploitation, and the establishment of a village culture that led to a revolutionary concept of YHWH as the true and only ruler, as Gottwald suggested. In either case, a "Yahwistic revolution" was a possible concomitant of the peasants' revolt.

This theory represents a great improvement upon the older conquest and peaceful infiltration models. Yet it too has its shortcomings. Similar small farming villages appear in the Iron I period outside the boundaries of early Israel, even according to the most generous estimates of its extent. Also, features of the material culture of early Iron Age highland farming villages of the highlands – a kind of dwelling called the "four-room house," and a distinctive kind of storage vessel called a "collar-rim jar" – also extend, chronologically as well as geographically, beyond those generous borders of the highland "Israelite"settlements. The peasants' revolt theory to account for the highland settlements has now lost much of its explanatory power.

However one is to understand its social, religious, and political aspects, the increase of highland villages over the two centuries associated with premonarchic Israel is evidence of an increasing population. With an emphasis on enlarging family size, probably preserved in the biblical ancestor legends and perhaps also in the notion of being fruitful and multiplying (Gen 1:28; 9:1), the highland farming households were able to meet the labor demands of their challenging environment. As the first villages grew beyond the size that could be sustained by the surrounding ecological niches, new villages were established. In the area in the Judean hills east of Jerusalem, the thirty-four sites of the Iron IIA period represented an almost 90 percent increase over the Iron I periods.

Ultimately, during the Iron IIA period (the beginning of the monarchy), a number of prominent sites, many of them now walled and somewhat larger than the few towns of the Iron I period, emerge in strategic locations. However, these "cities," as towns with walls are called, are significantly different in character from the Bronze Age city-states. For one thing, they are smaller than their Late Bronze precursors. They are also less complex; that is, they do not have the full range of buildings that are found in Bronze Age urban centers and that served the economic, political, regal, military, religious, and residential functions of a tiny independent kingdom, or city-state. Furthermore, many of the Iron IIA cities are more similar to each other in layout and architecture than were the Bronze Age ones. This is especially true of the cities, three of which (Gezer, Hazor, and Megiddo) have been identified and excavated, that are reported in the Bible to have become strategic regional centers serving a central political, economic, and military power (1 Kgs 9:15–20). Finally, a series of fortresses, with domestic structures and animal pens in the vicinity, were built in the northwest Negev, an area never before settled so extensively. These fortresses date from the late 11th to late 10th centuries BCE.

Other features of the material record of the Iron IIA period also indicate changes from the previous centuries. The repertoire of ceramic forms increases

significantly, and the pottery forms exhibit considerable homogeneity throughout the land. The distinct local traditions discernible in the preceding Iron I
and also the succeeding Iron IIB periods are not nearly so visible in the 10th
century. In addition, imported wares, evidence of international trade, begin to
appear in quantity, especially at the larger sites. And iron objects, also indicative of international exchange, also appear in significant numbers for the first
time in this period.

Overall, the change in the character of the settlement landscape and of the
nature of the material culture from the Iron I period to that of Iron IIA (10th
century BCE), while not quite so dramatic as the one marking the transition
from Late Bronze II to Iron I, likewise represents a significant shift. In both
cases, the changes in settlement location and size, along with changes in the
nature of buildings and artifacts, must be related to developments in political
and social structures. Because the biblical evidence is of limited historiographic
value, the use of models from the social sciences is invaluable in efforts to
understand Israel's emergence as a people and then as a national state.

Explanatory Models

Doing a "critical" history of early Israel, instead of taking the biblical narrative
at face value, involves more than examining the primary data (extra-biblical
textual, graphic, and archaeological materials). Those data are extremely important, as is also the biblical story. Still, for most scholars who use the Bible critically
along with these other sources, the prospect of writing Israel's early history
does involve probabilities and guesses. It is difficult to be absolutely sure about
recent occurrences – even with the aid of eyewitness accounts, videotapes, and
newspaper reports; so much greater is the challenge to establish what happened
three or more millennia ago.

Yet the prospects for writing a history that may have a reasonable approxima-
tion to past events, a history that is a likely reconstruction of developments
visible in the primary data and referenced in the biblical narrative, are promising because of the models available from social science research. Studies of
human societies and institutions are central to various disciplines, including
anthropology, sociology, economics, political science, and social psychology.
Sociological and anthropological theory in particular have been influential in
biblical studies for more than a century, although historical-critical approaches,
involving philological and comparative Ancient Near East studies, dominated
biblical study for most of the twentieth century.

In the last few decades, however, as the reliance on the Bible as straightforward history became untenable, biblical scholars have drawn increasingly
on models from the social sciences. They have used knowledge about how premodern societies develop and change, how their institutions function, and how
their human constituents live their lives in order to reconstruct the formation

of Israel as a people and its transformation to a national state. Just as literary approaches can identify the non-historiographic nature of many parts of the Bible, social science approaches can fill the interpretive gaps between archaeological realities and biblical texts that were never intended to preserve a factual record of Israelite experience. Indeed, the analytical possibilities provided by the social sciences may even enable us to see and understand aspects of ancient Israel that those who actually lived in the highlands of the early Iron Age might not themselves have discerned.

Social science perspectives are especially helpful in looking at major cultural transitions, such as those described above, that are observable in the archaeological record of the biblical period. More specifically, an ethnoarchaeological approach allows researchers to utilize data collected by ethnographers – data from living, premodern societies that are similar in environmental settings and cultural character to the society one wishes to study – in order to interpret both material and textual sources for ancient Israel. In this respect, ethnoarchaeology is particularly helpful in understanding such aspects of society as tribal organization and leadership, ethnicity with its material and ideological components, the nature of chiefdoms, and the dynamics of state formation. Drawing on social science models, a narrative first of early Israel and then of the beginnings of monarchic rule can be offered. This reconstruction will diverge from the master biblical narrative but will nonetheless echo some of the historical moments textualized in the Bible by centuries of transmission of both oral and written folklore.

The Emergence of "Israel"

For reasons that scholars are still trying to understand – perhaps rooted in subtle but significant climatic changes – the end of the Late Bronze Age saw widespread unrest and turmoil in the Aegean and east Mediterranean worlds. Shortages of labor and even of the basic commodities in the city-states that dominated the political landscape of the land of Canaan, partly because of the extra demands placed on those cities by Egyptian domination in the 13th century BCE, led to dramatic population shifts. Some agricultural workers serving the urban centers probably left the intolerable economic situation in those polities. In addition, groups of pastoralists who perhaps specialized in supplying the cities with meat and usable animal byproducts (skin, hair, bone) found those markets and the trade routes that maintained them disrupted by Late Bronze Age unrest. The verse (Judg 5:8) in the 12th century BCE Song of Deborah that mentions the cessation of "caravans" and the difficulty of travel depicts such disruption. Under such conditions, pastoralists would have augmented, or even replaced, part of their livelihood as stock-breeders by settling in agricultural villages and turning to farming. Finally, "newcomers" to the highlands could have included refugees from the state systems – Anatolia, Syria, and especially Egypt – that were experiencing various degrees of instability and collapse toward the end of the Late Bronze Age. Such stateless individuals, fleeing or cast out from urban contexts, are attested especially for the late 2nd millennium BCE in Ancient Near Eastern written sources.

This last possible group of people moving into the highlands of Canaan in the late 13th century BCE may be the ones both reflected in and giving rise to the biblical exodus traditions. Although those narratives are notoriously resistant to attempts to identify authentic historical or even topographic data, they nonetheless do contain a pattern of non-Egyptians entering Egypt, sojourning there as laborers, and later departing, that can be discerned in Egyptian records. Foreigners frequently entered Egypt, either willingly as traders or craftspeople, or against their will as prisoners-of-war or as conscripted pastoralists taken from the margins of the Nile Valley. Such unwilling immigrants were time and again exploited by the Egyptian rulers as agricultural laborers or as construction workers. Egyptian texts attest to many examples of such entry into Egypt along with a sojourn of difficult work.

Egyptian records of the departure of workers are less numerous, as might be expected. That is, loss of laborers might be viewed in the same way as loss of battles, which Egyptian texts rarely admit. Nonetheless, there are occasional references to people leaving Egypt and their onerous tasks. Although no emigration from Egypt can be linked specifically to the end of the Late Bronze Age, such out-migrations did exist. The exodus traditions of the Bible are so powerful that their origin in a small migration of Semitic construction workers back to the east Mediterranean lands of their ancestors is a reasonable hypothesis. It fits our understanding of the movements of people in and out of Egypt during the New Kingdom (1550–1069 BCE); and it accounts for the strength of the biblical proposition, otherwise unlikely, that Israel's national origins are linked to an experience of servitude. It may also, in conjunction with another aspect of the exodus tradition, account for an ideological (theological) feature of emerging Israel, to be discussed below.

The entrance of various groups, all of whom might be considered West Semitic or Canaanite, to the largely vacant highlands of Canaan (as well as to the plateaus of Transjordan) in the late 13th century can be described as a process of ruralization – not revolution, or conquest, or infiltration. The peoples moving to the highland "frontier" areas included refugees from Egypt and/or other imperial powers, disaffected Canaanite peasants, and pastoralists from the Canaanite hinterlands. This mixture (cf. Ex 12:38, "mixed company") formed the population of the new farming villages dramatically appearing, mostly for the first time, in the "safe" areas beyond the control of the small Canaanite kingdoms or the Egyptian imperial power. The relative political safety of the remote highlands enabled the farming families to live in unwalled hilltop villages.

Yet the dangers of political and economic exploitation or hardship that they may have escaped by settling the highland core of Canaan were replaced by other difficulties – uneven terrain, poor soils, and frequent years without rainfall. Life-sustaining crop yields were uncertain, and groups of settlements had to connect with each other as sources of mutual aid and survival. At this point the word "tribe" and the concept of "tribalism" become relevant. The Bible is replete with the use of a term translated "tribe" in reference to subdivisions, usually twelve in number, of the entity called "Israel." Although it is unlikely that the development of all tribes, however many there may have been, followed the same trajectories of formation, territorial identity, and survival or demise, it is clear that Israelite literature associated its premonarchic existence with the tribe as a unit of social and political organization that comprised dozens of settlements.

Biblical scholars have long tried to associate the term "tribe" with anthropological studies of premodern social units called "tribes." Unfortunately, most of those tribes were rather primitive, acephalous groups without any permanent hierarchy of leadership and without evidence that such groups could become (as the Israelite tribes did) part of state polities. More recent analysis of the kinds of political organization documented by ethnography indicate that what the Bible calls "tribes" might better be understood by the term "chiefdom". A chiefdom is a territorially based unit of society, in which hierarchies of leadership are based on kinship, not on merit or appointment. (In a dynastic state, the ruling family clearly has heredity as its determinant, but not so for its bureaucracy.) This does not rule out, however, exceptional – or charismatic – leadership, in response to military threats from external groups, as portrayed in the book of Judges. Chiefdoms typically construct genealogies, partly authentic and partly fictive, to account for the connectedness of the groups subsumed by a tribal name. An Israelite "tribe" thus consisted of the population of towns and villages in a circumscribed area; and the menfolk in these settlements traced their lineage to a common, eponymous ancestor.

An Israelite chiefdom (biblical tribe) can be considered a unit, comprised of one or more towns surrounded by villages, formed by the ruralization of the highlands. It was a flexible system of political organization that allowed small groups of farmers in neighboring settlements to cooperate with each other to offset the risks of an uncertain natural environment. At the same time, the farm families provided some surpluses or "tribute" as well as occasional labor to sub-chiefs (perhaps biblical "elders," as Judg 2:7) as well as chiefs, who in return provided religious as well as political leadership and may also have redistributed some of the tribute as a form of economic aid.

Such chiefdom systems have limits to their stability, with sub-chiefs often vying with each other for the tribute of the villagers or sometimes even attempting to depose the main chief. Such localized strife apparently is reflected in the archaeological record, which shows the destruction of some of the larger towns at various points during the 12th and 11th centuries, as well as in the biblical narrative. Shiloh, apparently an important center of early Israel (see Joshua 18–19, 22), is a case in point. The usual practice of the sacral chief Eli was to redistribute tribute (i.e., sacrificial foods) brought to Shiloh; but his sons keep all those resources, thus angering the people (1 Sam 2:14–17). That anger perhaps erupted into armed attack, for the Iron Age I settlement was destroyed in the mid-11th century (a memory of this may be preserved in Jer 7:12, 14 and 26:6). A similar convergence of archaeological and biblical records of strife among competing chiefs and sub-chiefs can be found for other hill-country sites. At Shechem, for example, Abimelech is made a "super" chief (biblical "king," Judg 9:6). Yet there was opposition to his rule, and the destruction of Shechem in ca. 1125 BCE can probably be related to this squabbling among local rulers.

This sketch of the chiefdoms, which may be consonant with the biblical concept of the premonarchic tribe, is based largely on archaeological data from the central highlands. It is difficult to know whether the population of all the Iron I villages of Canaan, in other parts of what would later be monarchic Israel, were similarly organized. In Galilee, for example, the excavation of several small villages indicates that they were not newly established in Iron I and that they were the country estates of elite Canaanites rather than settlements of twenty to thirty agrarian families. Those villages were eventually incorporated into a nation-state called Israel by the 10th century, but prior to that time it is doubtful that they were either parts of chiefdoms or considered themselves Israelite.

The question of what constituted "Israelite" identity in the premonarchic era is one that involves more than territorial location. The concept of ethnicity and of what constitutes the identity of a discrete people, both in their eyes and in the view of others, plays a role in understanding the emergence of Israel. The use of the name "Israel" by the Egyptians in the late 13th century BCE indicates that outsiders viewed the population of at least some parts of the highlands of Canaan as a people. But how did the Israelites perceive themselves? And what features allowed them to draw boundaries between themselves and others living among them or nearby?

Social scientists concerned with ethnicity have failed to find agreement about what constitutes and characterizes an ethnic group. They have compiled various lists of features that ethnicities exhibit, including: a common name, the myth (or reality) of shared ancestry, memories (real or constructed) of a common history, elements of material culture (such as food, clothing, language) in common, link to territory understood to be an ancestral land, and a sense of solidarity. This is not the only such list, but it does provide a group of features that may reflect the way Israel as a people constructed its self-identity. None of these features alone necessarily accounts for ethnicity; Israelite farmers, for example, apparently wore much the same clothing and hairstyles, lived in similar dwellings, and used identical pottery as did Canaanite or Transjordanian farmers of the early Iron Age. Food habits, however, may be more likely indicators of Iron Age ethnicities. Pigs were apparently part of the dietary regime of coastal, lowland, and Transjordanian sites in the Bronze and early Iron Ages; yet they are virtually non-existent in the faunal assemblages from hill-country sites associated with early Israel. Much more analysis of faunal remains from Iron I sites as well as from those of the Late Bronze and Iron II periods needs to be done before pig avoidance, as a possible Israelite ethnic marker visible in the material culture, can be established. Yet initial studies are promising.

Meanwhile, it is important to consider features of ethnicity that are not visible in the material culture but that are suggested by ethnography and are present in biblical tradition. The notion of common ancestry and history is one such feature. Whether through biological or fictive processes, or some combination thereof, people living in villages participating in a larger system led by chiefs and sub-chiefs characteristically consider themselves linked by descent. Furthermore, the noteworthy experiences of some of the ancestors, transmitted as folklore by their "descendants," become the shared history of all. The biblical narratives of exodus, of settlement, and of the "tribal" life of the premonarchic period are best understood as traditions, some historical and some highly legendary, that spread to village populations that identified with each other, and thus became accepted as the "history" of all.

This reconstruction of early Israel as a people, however, must also recognize that ideological factors, invisible in the archaeological record but prominent in the textual one, also were critical. What, after all, motivated village populations to support their elders and chiefs? What led them to feel kinship with other villagers? And, ultimately, what might have led to a sense of solidarity or of expected solidarity, such as is preserved in the book of Judges, that transcended the allegiances of tribe/chieftaincy? The Deborah episode in particular involves the banding together of militias that crossed tribal/chiefdom boundaries, and the "tribes" that failed to contribute to the military effort are criticized (Judg 4:6, 10; 5:13–18).

At this point, the powerful biblical traditions of Yahwism – allegiance to a deity, said to have become the God of Israel just before the time of the immigration of various people to hill-country sites (Ex 3:13–15; 6:3–7) – become relevant. Where might the YHWH traditions have originated? The answer may lie in the connection of the Moses saga with a people called the Midianites, who lived east of the Gulf of Aqaba in the northwestern sector of the Arabian peninsula. Good relations as well as cultural contacts between Midianites and Israelites would have had to predate the Midianite wars of the 11th century BCE (see Judges 6), at which time the presence of distinctive Midianite pottery along the fringes of Israelite territories also diminishes. In pentateuchal traditions, the Midianites are considered the kin of Israelite ancestors. Their special role (especially of the priest Jethro and his daughter Zipporah, whom Moses marries) in the Moses materials suggests that Yahwism, as the ideological or religious component cementing Israelite solidarity, may have originated in Midian. The name YAHWEH and the sacred mountain associated with theophanies to Moses seem to be imbedded in authentic memories of a connection to Midian among the leaders of a group departing from Egypt and ultimately merging with other disaffected groups settling in the highlands.

The nascent Israelite groups apparently rallied around a single deity, brought to the highlands by emigrés from Egypt, who had interacted with Midianites. Their allegiance to YHWH contributed to the supra-tribal/chiefdom identity of the farmers occupying the rural highland sites. That self-identity of the inhabitants of the central highlands, as the people of YHWH, probably did not extend to the entire area claimed for premonarchic Israel in the tribal allotments of the Bible. It remained for the next major transition – from complex chiefdom to state – to bring about the use of the term "Israel" for an expanded territory controlled by a dynastic political regime, the house of David.

The Early Monarchy in Israel

Over the two centuries or so of premonarchic existence, the highland villages that were inhabited by people known as Israelites increased in number until the marginal agricultural lands could no longer support relatively self-sufficient villages and small towns. Ways to share resources, by trade and exchange across longer and longer distances, were needed. Similarly, population increases meant more lands had to be tilled; and the need for iron implements, available only through international trade, increased. Finally, the demographic expansion often created heirs in each family group for which there was not enough land, nor were there new frontiers with adequately productive soils available; those offspring needed, and were available for, employment in bureaucracies and the military. Developments visible in the archaeological record of the end of the early Iron Age are ones that ethnographers identify as factors leading to the formation of centralized governments, or national states.

These developments were not the only ones, however, that propelled the Israelite highlanders toward statehood. They are mentioned first here in order to emphasize their significance. But the biblical account of state formation, which is consonant with archaeological discoveries, provides evidence of another powerful motivation for monarchic rule. That is, the threat of an external enemy – the Philistines – in combination with internal demographic and territorial expansion made the establishment of centralized rule essential.

Like other Aegean peoples, the Philistines left their European homelands in the wake of the general disruption of life in the east Mediterranean at the end of the Late Bronze Age. They settled on the southern coast of Canaan at the beginning of the 12th century (ca. 1180 BCE), destroying many Canaanite or Egypto-Canaanite cities and establishing their own five city-states. In the subsequent century and a half, they expanded northward, at least as far as the Jezreel Valley and southward toward Egypt, in the process of gaining control of the "Way of the Sea," one of the major arteries of international trade. At the same time, as their economy prospered and their population grew, the Philistines sought to expand their control eastward, into the Shephelah, where they eventually ran smack into the expanding Israelite groups occupying the highlands and expanding westward.

The inevitable conflict between Israelites and Philistines provides most of the material for the biblical account of state formation. The Philistines are depicted as terrorists raiding Israelite settlements, ruthlessly destroying their quasi-administrative towns, and capturing the ark, the symbol of God's presence among the people. In the face of this threat and because of internal developments, a Benjamite chieftain named Saul and then a charismatic leader from

Judah named David were able to rally support from increasingly large numbers of highland dwellers – sons without lands to farm – to oppose the better equipped professional Philistine warriors.

The Philistines were eventually driven back. David, appointed leader of his local tribal group and then formally anointed king over all those identified as Israelites (2 Sam 5:1–5) after Saul's death in battle, succeeded in overcoming the Philistines and in taking some lands away from them. Also, by consolidating his base of support among the highland Israelites, he was able to extend Israelite control over extensive lowland and Galilean areas formerly held by Canaanites. From his new capital in Jerusalem, a neutral site not identified with any Israelite subgroup, he was able to overcome, for the first and only time until the mid-20th century CE, the fragmentation that characterized local political structures in Canaan. Although this area of the east Mediterranean has often been controlled by superpowers, from the ancient Egyptians to the modern Turks, a territorial state under local leadership had never before existed.

The new nation-state was called Israel, probably because the initial and dominant core of preexisting groups were known by that name. Thus the highland people designated Israelites were transformed into citizens of a territorial state that included lowlands and valleys and that stretched "from Dan to Beersheba." Like all political states of the Ancient Near East, Israel's national identity was intertwined with what we would call a religious dimension. That is, there was a sacral component to royal rule. The king was perceived as appointed by the Israelite god YHWH, and thus all inhabitants of territorial Israel came under the sovereignty of YHWH and were brought into the community of those who saw themselves as descendants (biblical "children") of Israel and as the people of YHWH. The king was considered the "son of YHWH" (2 Sam 7:14; cf. Pss 2:7; 89:26–27), a status that contributed to the notion that his rule had legitimating divine sanction.

David's success did not stop with the territorial borders of the twelve "tribes." The new "tribal" manpower available for his army and the economic support and bureaucratic personnel supplied by his expanded territorial base perhaps enabled David to dominate neighboring peoples such as the Moabites, Arameans, Ammonites, Amalekites, and Edomites (2 Sam 8:2–13; 12:26–31) as well as Philistines. The tribute and forced labor provided by the polities that succumbed to Israelite military power meant that, for a brief period during the end of David's reign and during that of his son and successor Solomon, Israel may have had minor imperial domain.

Most of the archaeological materials associated with the early monarchy come from the end of that period, the time when Solomon would have ruled (ca. 965–925 BCE). The material features of the late Iron IIA period are precisely those which social scientists have identified as correlates of a centralized nation-state regime. Regional centers with a uniformity of architecture, a relatively homogeneous repertoire of pottery, and evidence of increased international trade are all features of a complex central government with a bureaucracy in the capital and with appointed officials at strategic spots throughout a realm organized into administrative districts. Furthermore, the establishment of fort-resses in the northern Negev contributed to the safety of trade with Arabia as well as protection from the Philistines.

Other evidence for the formation of a state, especially in its brief period of imperial control, lies in the biblical description of the capital city Jerusalem. Archaeological remains from Iron IIA are discouragingly scanty, as would be expected for a city that became so strategically, politically, and religiously sig-nificant that it was destroyed, razed, and rebuilt countless times in the three millennia after it became Israel's capital. The discrepancy between the few ma-terial remains and the rich biblical record of a temple–palace precinct should not be used to discredit the latter. The description in 1 Kings 5–7 of monumental architecture in Jerusalem may not be literally accurate, but it is hardly fictitious. The biblical details of the palace and the temple built in the "City of David" can be tested against what is known about architectural styles, construction tech-niques, and artistic motifs of the 10th century BCE. All those aspects of the public buildings in Jerusalem have parallels in artifacts and structures known from contemporary Syrian, Phoenician, Canaanite, Hittite, Assyrian, and Egyp-tian sites.

The workforce necessary to carry out monumental building projects in the capital as well as in the regional centers would have been substantial. It is likely that Israelites who left the farms to work in the military or bureaucracy did not constitute a large enough labor pool for all those projects. Similarly, the cost of materials could not have been borne only by Israelites. The labor and materials needed for those projects required additional resources – precisely what the imperial control over non-Israelites in the 10th century would have provided. Military conquest beyond Israel's borders brought spoils of war (1 Sam 15:9; 27:9; 2 Sam 8:7–12; 12:30) as well as prisoners-of-war (2 Sam 8:2, 6, 14; 12:31; 1 Kgs 9:20). The massive public works of the 10th century could hardly have been designed and constructed without the resources provided by spoils, tribute, and enforced labor.

The construction of an elaborate palace and a richly appointed temple – residences for the king and the deity – would have served as visual propaganda for the new national state. They announced to the emissaries of the state's regional components (1 Kgs 4:7–19, 27–28) and also of its tributary peoples that the Jerusalem regime was legitimate and powerful. The resources provided by conquest would also have secured the loyalty of the new bureaucracy and military establishment (as 1 Kgs 7:22), whose members shared some of the wealth accruing to the dynastic head (see 1 Sam 22:7; 30:21–30; cf. 1 Sam 17:25). Both David and Solomon are reported to have established cabinets, which were at the top of a hierarchy of government officials overseeing the army, the temple, the mercenary forces, domestic policy, the palace's business, and the conscripted or captured labor force (2 Sam 8:16–18; 20:23–26; 1 Kgs 4:1–6). At the same time, the old units ("tribes" or chiefdoms) organized by kinship probably continued as the basic social units, above the family level, for most of the population.

It is doubtful that the Israelite village communities that existed in the premonarchic period would have survived the external military threat and the instability caused by demographic increase without the protective and integrative functions of a centralized state. The emergence of a monarchy, apparently through the brilliant military strategies of David and the astute organizational and diplomatic skills of Solomon, meant the creation of a national identity, both political and religious in nature. At least in its early stages, in the 10th century BCE, the residents of larger territorial Israel would have been well served by the security, stability, and economic prosperity accompanying centralized royal government. It is no wonder that this golden age became elaborated in the legendary accounts of the first two members of the Davidic dynasty. The need for myths or traditions of origin and for culture heroes is characteristic of every national culture. The uncertainties and insecurities of the early stages of a new system of rule inevitably mean that the new rulers become surrounded by a folklore relating their valorous deeds.

But that Israelite folklore of valor also contains tales of palace intrigues, royal misdeeds, and rebellious activities. Such literary productions reflect the downside of monarchic rule – the coercive use of power and the jealousy that groups with little or no power feel toward the privileges of the rulers and their officials. Ultimately, by the end of Solomon's reign, the overseer (Jereboam, son of Nabat) of building projects north of Jerusalem led a movement that disrupted the continuity of the Davidic dynasty and split the nation into two separate kingdoms.

Bibliography

Albright, W., "The Israelite Conquest in the Light of Archaeology," *Bulletin of the American Schools of Oriental Research* 74 (1939), 11–22.

Alt, A., "The Settlement of the Israelites in Palestine," trans. R. Wilson, *Essays on Old Testament History and Religion* (Garden City, NY: Doubleday, 1968), 177–221.

Ben-Tor, A., ed., *The Archaeology of Ancient Israel*, trans. R. Greenberg (New Haven: Yale University Press, 1997).

Biran, A. and J. Naveh, "An Aramaic Stele Fragment from Tel Dan," *Israel Exploration Journal* 43 (1993), 881–98.

Callaway, J., "The Settlement in Canaan: The Period of the Judges," in H. Shanks, ed., *Ancient Israel: A Short History from Abraham to the Roman Destruction of the Temple* (Englewood Cliffs, NJ: Prentice-Hall, 1988), 53–84.

Carter, C., "A Discipline in Transition: The Contributions of the Social Sciences to the Study of the Hebrew Bible," in C. Carter and C. Meyers, eds., *Community, Identity, and Ideology: Social Science Approaches to the Hebrew Bible*, Sources for Biblical and Theological Study 6 (Winona Lake, IN: Eisenbrauns, 1996), 3–36.

Cross, F., "Reuben, First-Born of Jacob," chapter 3 in *From Epic to Canon: Essays in the History and Literature of Ancient Israel* (Baltimore: Johns Hopkins University Press, 1998), 53–70.

Dever, W., "Ceramics, Ethnicity, and the Question of Israel's Origins," *Biblical Archaeologist* 58 (1995), 200–13.

─────, "Archaeology, Ideology, and the Quest for an 'Ancient' or 'Biblical' Israel," *Near East Archaeology* 61 (1998), 39–52.

Edelman, D., *King Saul and the Historiography of Judah*, JSOTSup 121 (Sheffield: Sheffield Academic Press, 1991).

Finkelstein, I., "Pots and Peoples Revisited: Ethnic Boundaries in the Iron Age," in N. Silberman and D. Small, eds., *The Archaeology of Israel: Constructing the Past, Interpreting the Present*, JSOTSup 237 (Sheffield: Sheffield Academic Press, 1997), 216–37.

─────, *The Archaeology of the Israelite Settlement* (Jerusalem: Israel Exploration Society, 1988).

─────, "The Emergence of the Monarchy in Israel and the Environmental and Socio-Economic Aspects, *Journal for the Study of the Old Testament* 44 (1989), 43–74.

Finkelstein, I. and N. Na'aman, eds., *From Nomadism to Monarchy: Archaeological and Historical Aspects of Early Israel* (Jerusalem: Yad Izhak Ben-Zvi, 1994).

Flanagan, J., *David's Social Drama: A Hologram of Israel's Early Iron Age*, The Social World of Biblical Antiquity Series 7; and JSOTSup 73 (Sheffield: Almond Press, 1988).

Frerichs, E. and L. Lesko, eds., *Exodus: The Egyptian Evidence* (Winona Lake, IN: Eisenbrauns, 1997).

Frick, F., *The Formation of the State in Ancient Israel*, The Social World of Biblical Antiquity Series 4 (Sheffield: Almond Press, 1985).

Fritz, V. and P. Davies, eds., *The Origin of the Ancient Israelite States*, JSOTSup 228 (Sheffield: Sheffield Academic Press, 1996).

Gottwald, N., *The Tribes of Yahweh: A Sociology of Liberated Israel, 1250–1050* BCE (Maryknoll, NY: Orbis, 1979).

─────, "Monarchy – Israel's Counter-revolutionary Establishment," in *The Hebrew Bible: A Socio-Literary Introduction* (Philadelphia: Fortress Press, 1986), 293–404.

─────, *The Politics of Ancient Israel*, Library of Ancient Israel (Louisuille, KY: Westminster/ John Knox Press, 2001).

─────, ed., *Social Scientific Criticism of the Hebrew Bible and Its Social World*, Semeia 37 (1986).

Grabbe, L., ed., *Can a "History of Israel" be Written?*, JSOTSup 245 (Sheffield: Sheffield Academic Press, 1997).

Hackett, J., " 'There Was No King in Israel': Era of the Judges," in M. Coogan, ed., *The Oxford History of the Biblical World* (New York, Oxford: Oxford University Press, 1998), 177–218.

Halpern, B., *The Constitution of the Monarchy in Israel*, HSM 25 (Chico, CA: Scholars Press, 1981).

─────, "The Exodus and the Israelite Historians," *Eretz-Israel* 24 (1993), 89*–96*.

Hasel, M., "*Israel* in the Merneptah Stela," *Bulletin of the American Schools of Oriental Research* 296 (1994), 45–61.

Hess, R., "Non-Israelite Personal Names in the Book of Joshua," *Catholic Biblical Quarterly* 58 (1996), 205–14.

Hesse, Brian and Paula Wapnish, "Can Pig Remains be Used for Ethnic Diagnosis in the Ancient Near East?" in N. Silberman and D. Small, eds., *The Archaeology of Israel: Constructing the Past, Interpreting the Present*, JSOTSup 237 (Sheffield: Sheffield Academic Press, 1997), 238–70.

Hopkins, D., *The Highlands of Canaan: Agricultural Life in the Early Iron Age*, The Social World of Biblical Antiquity Series 3 (Sheffield: Sheffield Academic Press, 1985).

Hutchinson, J. and A. Smith, eds., *Ethnicity* (Oxford, New York: Oxford University Press, 1996).

Ishida, T., ed., *Studies in the Period of David and Solomon and Other Essays* (Tokyo: Yamakawa-Shuppansha, 1987).

Kitchen, K., "A Possible Mention of David in the Late Tenth Century BCE, and Deity Dod as Dead as the Dodo?" *Journal for the Study of the Old Testament* 76 (1997), 29–44.

Lemaire, A., "'House of David' Restored in Moabite Inscription," *Biblical Archaeology Review* 20 (1994), 30–7.

Levy, T., ed., *The Archaeology of Society in the Holy Land* (New York: Facts on File, Inc., 1995).

Machinist, P., "Outsiders or Insiders: The Biblical View of Emergent Israel and Its Contexts," in *The Other in Jewish Thought and History: Construction of Jewish Culture and Identity*, in L. Silberstein and R. Cohn, eds. (New York: New York University Press, 1994), 35–60.

Mazar, A., *Archaeology of the Land of the Bible 10,000–586 B.C.E.* (New York: Doubleday, 1990).

McNutt, Paula, Reconstructing the Society of Ancient Israel, *Library of Ancient Israel* (Louisville, KY: Westminster/John Knox Press, 1999).

Mendenhall, G., "The Hebrew Conquest of Palestine," *Biblical Archaeologist* 25 (1962), 66–87.

Meyers, C., "Kinship and Kingship: The Early Monarchy," in M. Coogan, ed., *The Oxford History of the Biblical World* (New York, Oxford: Oxford University Press, 1998), 220–71.

——, "David as Temple Builder," in P. Miller, Jr., P. Hanson and S. McBride, eds., *Ancient Israelite Religion: Essays in Honor of Frank Moore Cross* (Winona Lake, IN: Eisenbrauns, 1987), 357–76.

——, "The Israelite Empire: In Defense of King Solomon," in D. Freedman and M. O'Connor, eds., *Backgrounds for the Bible* (Winona Lake, IN: Eisenbrauns, 1987), 181–98.

——, "Demythologizing Israelite Origins," *Humanistic Judaism* 26 (1998), 9–16.

Miller, R., II, *A Social History of Highland Israel in the 12th and 11th Centuries BCE*, Ph.D. dissertation (University of Michigan), 1998.

Shanks, H., W. Dever, B. Halpern and P. McCarter, Jr., *The Rise of Ancient Israel* (Washington, D.C.: Biblical Archaeology Society, 1992).

Stager, L., "The Archaeology of the Family in Ancient Israel," *Bulletin of the American Schools of Oriental Research* 260 (1985), 1–35.

——, "Forging an Identity: The Emergence of Ancient Israel," in M. Coogan, ed., *The Oxford History of the Biblical World* (New York, Oxford: Oxford University Press, 1998), 123–75.

Yurco, F., "Merneptah's Canaan Campaign," *Journal of the American Research Center in Egypt* 23 (1986), 189–215.

CHAPTER 5

The History of Israel in the Monarchic Period

Leslie J. Hoppe

The two ancient Israelite states were able to come into existence because of the absence of any imperial powers that could effectively prevent the development of the smaller states in the Levant. By the end of the Late Bronze Age, Egypt and Hatti wore themselves out in contending for hegemony in the region. Assyria would not become seriously aggressive in the region until the 8th century. During the 400 years from the 12th to the 8th centuries BCE, then, the peoples in the settled territories between Egypt and Mesopotamia were developing ever more complex economic and political systems.

At first, the people of Canaan's central highlands favored a decentralized polity. Clan elders ruled by consensus according to traditional norms. The various central highland groups banded together occasionally for self-defense when threatened by raiders. When the Philistines began expanding beyond their footholds along the southern end of the coastal plain, the people in the central highlands were no longer coping with raiders but with an aggressive and expansionist threat. It is likely that this threat led to the move toward monarchy with a standing, professional army.

The Bible describes the establishment of a single monarchy and unified national state, first unsuccessfully by Saul and then very successfully by David, as a response to that threat. It tells the story of a division of that unified national state following the death of Solomon into two kingdoms: Israel and Judah. The historical reliability of the biblical narratives about Saul, David and Solomon is open to question. Were these individuals responsible for the establishment of the Israelite monarchy or was the idea of a single, national state a projection of ideologically driven biblical writers to justify an attempted Judahite expansion into the territory of the former Northern Kingdom during the period of Assyrian decline? If Saul, David and Solomon were historical figures, were they anything more than chieftains whose story belongs to the prehistory of the monarchy in Israel and Judah?

The only source we have for reconstructing the "history" of Saul, David, and Solomon is the Bible, although a recently discovered stele does mention "the house of David."[1] Most of the narratives connected with these three appear to have a legendary character, describing a "golden age," though at one time the story of Solomon's succession (in 2 Samuel 9–20; 1 Kings 1–2) was described as written by a member of Solomon's court.[2] Excavation has not been able to resolve the issue. In fact, archaeologists dispute with one another about whether excavations have uncovered evidence of the type of settlements in Israel and Judah during the 10th century that is consonant with the existence of a complex political system like monarchy. There is little undisputed archaeological evidence consonant with a Davidic empire administered from Jerusalem. The dating of monumental structures at Hazor, Megiddo, and Gezer to the "Solomonic period" is being reconsidered. While a history of Israel during the monarchic period needs to take the biblical material into account, the data about the so-called united monarchy do not allow for firm *historical* conclusions to be drawn. This essay will focus, then, on the history of the two Israelite states that did emerge in the central highlands: Israel in the north and Judah in the south.

Though the central highland groups shared the same language, worshiped the same deity, and believed that they were descended from the same ancestors, their decentralized political traditions were so entrenched that they grouped themselves into two states: Israel and Judah. The relations between the two were sometimes cordial and cooperative but usually they were tense and competitive. The economies of both states were based on agriculture and trade. At first, most farmers tilled small, family farms that operated on the subsistence level, but eventually larger estates developed that made more efficient farming methods possible. This, in turn, led to the export of olive oil and wine. Because these exports made the large landowners wealthy, more land was devoted to the cultivation of grapes and olives and less land was available for grain production, driving up the price of grain. Many of the small farmers could not compete with the estate farms. The result was that there developed a serious socioeconomic cleavage in both kingdoms. There was a serious disparity between rich and poor in both societies, causing internal divisions that seriously weakened each.

Compounding these internal political problems was the rise of the Neo-Assyrian Empire. Under Tiglath-pileser III, Assyria began making tentative military incursions into territories of the states in the eastern Mediterranean region. At first, the goal was simply tribute, but soon the Assyrians wanted territory as well. The real object of the Assyrian expansion was, of course, Egypt. Still, the Assyrians had to neutralize any potential interference before they could mount a serious campaign against a military power like Egypt. Once Assyria began the path of its aggressive expansion, the survival of both Israel and Judah as independent states was doubtful. Assyria began to dominate both the economies and politics of both states with consequences for their ancestral religious traditions as well. Though Israel was the stronger of the two economically and militarily, it was more vulnerable because of its geography. In a series of military campaigns, the Assyrians ended the political existence of the Kingdom of

Israel, incorporating its territory directly into the Assyrian provincial system. Judah retained the veneer of independence though it was reduced to vassalage.

The Assyrian Empire itself fell toward the end of the 7th century for several reasons, the most serious of which was a succession of incompetent rulers. The Babylonians took control of the former Assyrian Empire. The Kingdom of Israel had no opportunity to reconstitute itself. The Kingdom of Judah remained in vassalage though nationalist elements took every opportunity to urge rebellion against Babylonian hegemony. The Babylonians put down one Judahite rebellion, allowing Judah to continue the pretense of political independence. A second rebellion ended even that pretense. The Kingdom of Judah ceased to exist.

There are two principal sources for reconstructing the history of Israel during the monarchy. Each has its value but each has serious problems connected with it. Until recently, the only source of Israelite and Judahite history has been the Bible and other ancient written sources like Josephus that are dependent on it. The advantage of this source is that the Bible is a continuous narrative of ancient Israel's history during the period of the monarchy. While it is not as complete as it could have been, it is coherent and, by its admission, dependent on now lost ancient documents: the Book of Yashar, e.g., 2 Sam 1:18, and the Annals of the Kings of Israel and Judah, e.g., 2 Kgs 14:18; 15:6. Even those who consider the Bible a reliable source for the reconstruction of history have problems with the data it provides. For example, the chronological information provided in the Books of Kings is problematic and sometimes contradictory, and no system for dating the Israelite and Judahite kings has achieved universal acceptance.[3] Also, the principal aim of the biblical narratives is theological, and different theological concerns gave rise to the different narratives in the Deuteronomistic and Chronicler's histories, although both are written from a Judahite perspective. No history written from a perspective of sympathy toward the Northern Kingdom has survived. These ideological considerations caution against taking the biblical narratives at face value.

A second source is the archaeology of ancient Israel and the Ancient Near East. The value of archaeology is that it often provides a needed supplement of literary sources. It can help reconstruct ancient culture more thoroughly. The problem with the archaeology of sites in the eastern Mediterranean area is that they are silent – for the most part. Very little textual material has been uncovered along with the artifacts, leaving the excavators to offer hypotheses regarding the interpretation of artifactual data. A second problem is the chance nature of archaeological discovery. It is scientifically inadvisable and economically prohibitive to excavate an entire site so what is recovered in excavations at individual sites is a matter of chance. Only when there is an attempt at integrating the interpretation of artifacts found at several sites with similar occupational histories can more firm conclusions be drawn. Third, conclusions drawn by archaeologists forty years ago about sites from the monarchic period are being reexamined on the basis of new excavations and more sophisticated analysis of artifacts. Fourth, the ideological concerns of the excavators have influenced their interpretation of the material they uncovered.

In contrast to the archaeology in the territories of the former Israelite kingdoms, excavations in Egypt and Mesopotamia have uncovered a wealth of textual material. Some of it is particularly germane to the reconstruction of ancient Israelite history. While these texts can be very helpful, it is important to remember that they were not written as historical documents. Like the biblical narratives, Ancient Near Eastern texts are ideologically driven and, as archaeological discoveries, they are accidental finds. What remains to be discovered, if anything, may require a reassessment of any historical reconstruction.

Precursors of the Israelite and Judahite Kingdoms

The only written data about Saul comes from the Bible. No material remains have been linked directly to him. What we do know about Saul is his role in biblical tradition, which presented him as a tragic figure unable to fulfill his destiny as king. Haunted by his failures, he committed suicide after the Philistines defeated his army on Mt. Gilboa (1 Sam 31). The Saul whose memory is the basis for the biblical narrative was likely the king of the city-state of Gibeon. From this base he expanded his rule into the central highlands and into the Transjordan. His expanded territory took the name "Israel" (2 Sam 1:24). The economic base for Saul's realm was agriculture and trade. His competitors were the Philistines from the coastal plain and the states in the Transjordan. He died trying to expand his territory north into the Jezreel and Beth Shean valleys.

As is the case with Saul, available data about David is limited to the Bible, except for an Aramaic inscription found at Tel Dan (see above, p. 88). The Bible tells the story of David in a thematic rather than a chronological way. Also, the nature, purpose, and date of these stories are still a matter of sustained study. They tell the story of one who began, like Saul, as the king of a city-state, though David's city was in Hebron toward the southern end of the central highlands. As he began expanding his territory, he had much more success at checking the Philistines than Saul did (1 Sam 18:7). After becoming king of all Israel, David transferred his capital to Jerusalem (2 Sam 5:6–10) and from there led victorious campaigns against the Philistines, Arameans, and the Transjordanians. To consolidate the support for these campaigns from the Israelites, he proposed building a national shrine for the God of Israel in Jerusalem and moved the Ark, a battle palladium used by the Israelites, there (2 Samuel 4–7). Though there was some resistance to David's rule (2 Sam 15:7–19; 16:9–14; 20:1–3), he was able to maintain his position and pass on the monarchy to his son Solomon.

The Bible asserts that though David handed on his throne to his son Solomon (1 Kings 1–2), the kingdom that David established began crumbling and fell apart completely following Solomon's death (1 Kgs 12). Some finds point to archaeological evidence of urbanization at sites such as Hazor, Megiddo, and Gezer as support for the existence of Solomon's rule though there is some dispute about dating this evidence. Others use sociological models to interpret the data in First Kings as reflecting the centralized government, social stratification, and surplus economy that supposedly characterized Solomon's kingdom. As is the case with Saul and David, the reality behind the biblical portrait has yet to be determined with assurance.

The Israelite Kingdom

Although the Bible is the principal source for reconstructing the history of both the Israelite and Judahite kingdoms, it is important to note that both the narrative sources (1–2 Kings and 1–2 Chronicles) and the relevant prophetic material reflect a bias against the Israelite kingdom. This is to be expected since the Scriptures took their present shape in Judah. Also, the Scriptures are not historical sources in the contemporary sense. They were written long after the events they narrate took place and their ideological goals are primary.

Even the biblical account of the Northern Kingdom is imprecise. The Hebrew and Greek versions of the Bible preserve somewhat conflicting accounts of the events leading up to the rise of Jeroboam I (927–906) as the first monarch of the Israelite kingdom. He was an Ephraimite "strong man" (1 Kgs 11:26, 28), who was probably successful in conflicts with groups like the Philistines, Arameans and Judahites, contestants for the limited resources of the region. He fortified the towns of Shechem and Penuel (1 Kgs 12:25) and engaged in continuing wars with Judah over the borders (2 Chr 12:15; 13:2–20). He was not able, however, to defend the central highlands against the raid of Pharaoh Shishak (ca. 918). The biblical narratives condemn Jeroboam and all his successors for departing from ancestral liturgical traditions. The practices condemned, however, were likely to be simple variations in the worship of the God that both Israel and Judah regarded as their patron. Jeroboam was succeeded by his son Nadab (905–904) who was assassinated while fighting the Philistines (1 Kgs 15:27).

Nadab's assassin, Baasha (903–882), led Israel in a continuing war with Judah. This led Judah to bribe Ben Hadad, the king of Aram, to begin a series of raids into Israel's territory. These raids occupied Israel's army and relieved the pressure on Judah. Baasha's son, Elah (881–880), ruled less than two years before being assassinated by Zimri, an officer in the Israelite army – probably because Elah proved to be a less than capable leader (1 Kgs 16:9–10). Although Zimri (880) no doubt saw himself as the leader that Israel needed, Omri, a more popular military commander, moved against him. Zimri committed suicide when he saw support for him crumbling (2 Kgs 16:18).

While the Bible considers the first five rulers of Israel to be kings, they were more likely military chieftains who owed their position to their ability to lead Israelite forces in their conflicts with other groups contending for dominance in

the region. Omri (879–869), whose success drove Zimri to suicide, was probably the real founder of the Kingdom of Israel. Almost two hundred years later
the Assyrians would call Israel "the land of Omri" (*ANET*, 280–1, 284–5). He
founded a dynasty that produced four kings over three generations. Under Omri,
the border wars with Judah ended – most likely because the Judahites thought
better of challenging Israel's military superiority. Omri turned his attention to
the Transjordan, defeated Moab and annexed its territory (*ANET*, 320), though
he was unsuccessful in his conflict with the Arameans (1 Kgs 20:34). Omri also
chose diplomacy as a way to secure Israel's future, making an alliance with
Phoenicia and sealing it by the marriage of his son Ahab with Jezebel, a princess
of Sidon (1 Kgs 16:31). This outward thrust of his foreign policy was reflected
in his choice of a capital. He built a new city on the top of a hill. On a clear day,
standing on the top of that hill in Omri's Samaria, one can see the Mediterranean
as well as the Israelite heartland.

Aram, Israel's neighbor to the north, occupied the attention of Ahab (868–
854), Omri's son and successor. Both states were vying for territory and, more
importantly, for commercial supremacy in the region. After one battle, Ahab
spared the life of Ben Hadad of Aram for trade concessions in Damascus (1 Kgs
20:26–30). Judah was a compliant ally to Israel in this conflict (1 Kgs 22:1–4).
Another measure of Ahab's dominance over Judah was the marriage of his
daughter Athaliah to Jehoram of Judah (2 Kgs 8:18). Moab took the opportunity afforded by Ahab's continuing conflict with Aram to assert its independence (*ANET*, 320). Though Aram and Israel were bitter rivals, they joined forces
to oppose Assyria's attempt to enter the region. Ahab was the first Israelite king
to engage the Assyrians, who grudgingly noted the size of Ahab's army at the
battle of Qarqar (*ANET*, 278–281). Though usually successful in his conflicts
with the Arameans, Ahab died fighting them for control of Ramoth-gilead (1
Kgs 22:36–37). The Bible devotes considerable attention to the religious consequences of Ahab's marriage to Jezebel. The main purposes of this marriage
were political and economic. Still, the Scriptures note how Jezebel's influence
led Ahab to flout the norms of traditional Israelite morality (1 Kings 21) and
to introduce Israel to the worship of Baal (1 Kgs 16:32). These policies bred
resentment among some segments of Israelite society, which eventually led to
a violent revolution.

Azariah's short reign (853–852) was not marked by the military success
enjoyed by his father. He lost control of most of Israel's territories in the
Transjordan (2 Kgs 1:1; 2 Chr 20:1). Like his father Ahab, Azariah encouraged
the worship of the god that his Sidonian mother honored (1 Kgs 22:53–54).
Azariah died unexpectedly following an accidental fall (2 Kgs 1:2–18). Because
he had no male heir, his brother Jehoram (851–840) succeeded him. Jehoram
tried to hold on to the gains made by his father Ahab, but he was not successful.
He did win a decisive but ultimately inconclusive victory over Moab (2 Kgs
3:4–27). Still, Israel could not longer consider Moab one of its vassals. The
alliance that Ahab forged with Aram unraveled after the death of Ben Hadad.
Hazael, the new Aramean king, was determined to chart an independent course.

Old battles were renewed and in the course of another conflict over the Ramoth-gilead, Jehoram was severely wounded.

Jehoram's political and military failures served to heighten the dissatisfaction with the royal house – dissatisfaction that was brewing since Ahab's reign. At the urging of religious traditionalists like the prophet Elisha, a revolution against Jehoram broke out while the king was convalescing from his battle wounds. The revolutionaries were not content with eliminating Jehoram (2 Kgs 9:22–26). They also killed Ahaziah of Judah, Jezebel, the entire Israelite royal family, the royals visiting from Judah, and the priests of Baal (2 Kgs 9:27–10:14, 18–27). It was a bloody affair whose ferocity was still remembered and condemned by Hosea one hundred years later (Hos 1:4).

Jehu (839–822), the commander of Jehoram's army and the leader of the revolution, became the new king. Five generations of his descendants ruled Israel over a period of almost one hundred years. His actions against Jezebel and her retinue no doubt ended Israel's commercial alliance with the Phoenicians but consolidated support of the more conservative elements in Israelite society for the monarchy – support that the Omride dynasty did not enjoy. The Arameans took advantage of the chaos brought on by Jehu's revolution to reassert their territorial claims in Gilead. Jehu knew that he did not have the military might to defeat the Arameans so he negotiated an alliance with the Assyrians. Under Shalmaneser III, they made several raids into Hazael's territory. When the raids were over, Hazael still had enough force to take all of Gilead from Jehu (2 Kgs 10:32–33). Jehu has the distinction of being the only Israelite or Judahite king for whom we have a contemporary portrait. Shalmaneser's Black Obelisk (*ANEP*, 120, pl. 351) depicts Jehu kneeling in obeisance to the Assyrian king, who calls him "the son of Omri," an ironic title to give the man who killed every member of Omri's family.

Jehoahaz (821–805) was no more successful than his father Jehu in checking the Arameans. His decimated army (2 Kgs 13:7) was no match for that of Hazael and Ben Hadad II. Relief finally came in the person of the Assyrian king Adad-nirari who defeated the Arameans in 802. The beneficiary of the Assyrian victory was Jehoash (804–789), who was able to recover much of the Israelite territory lost to Aram since the time of Jehu (2 Kgs 13:25). Judah challenged Israel to battle following raids by Israelite mercenaries on Judahite cities. The army of Jehoahaz thoroughly humiliated Judah (2 Kgs 14:8–14; 2 Chr 25:6–13).

The most successful king of Israel was Jeroboam II (788–748). His long reign witnessed a resurgence of the Israelite kingdom after the exhausting campaigns against Aram. After devastating Israel's northern antagonist, the Assyrians had to withdraw from the region because of internal political problems. This left Jeroboam with a free hand to reclaim lands, including the Transjordan, that had once been part of the Kingdom of Israel (2 Kgs 14:25–28). These new lands were given to the king's retainers, who became owners of large estates. The small subsistence farmers who formed the bulk of Israel's population could not compete with the great landowners and soon the "prosperity" that was the fruit of peace created a class of servants and slaves. Excavation at Samaria reveals the wealth of

Jeroboam's Israel – a wealth not shared by all. The Book of Amos condemns the economy of Jeroboam's Israel – an economy that created poverty in the kingdom.

The rest of the Northern Kingdom's history is dominated by the Neo-Assyrian Empire. Under Tiglath-pileser III, Assyria became an aggressively expansionist power. It was no longer content to make the states of the eastern Mediterranean vassals, required to pay tribute. The Assyrians were interested in territory. The specter of an Assyrian invasion engendered political anarchy in Israel. Its first victim was Zechariah (748), the last king of Jehu's dynasty. He was assassinated after ruling for just three months. Shallum (748), his assassin and replacement, had even less luck. He survived only one month before being killed by Menahem (746–737). Menahem survived because he became a compliant vassal of the Assyrians (*ANET*, 283), taxing the wealthy to pay the required tribute (2 Kgs 15:19–20). Of course, his policies toward the Assyrians engendered resentment, though Menahem was able to hold on to power. Pekahiah, his son (736–735), was not so fortunate. He was assassinated by Pekah. Menahem was the last Israelite king to pass the throne to his son.

Pekah's (734–731) assassination of Pekahiah brought an end to a policy of subservience to the Assyrians, thus relieving the wealthy. Pekah embarked on his anti-Assyrian policy by allying himself with Rezin of Aram. Tyre and Philistia joined the coalition but Judah resisted, in part because it was occupied in the south with Edom. Pekah invaded Judah with the intention of deposing Ahaz and installing "the son of Tabeel" who, of course, would bring Judah into the anti-Assyrian coalition (2 Kgs 16:5; Isa 7:4–6). Tiglath-pileser III took action against the coalition with a series of campaigns from 734 to 732. He neutralized Aram and incorporated the Galilee into his empire as the Province of Magiddu. He also stripped Israel of its Transjordanian territory.

No king could sustain such defeats and still hold on to power. In 731, Pekah fell to an assassin: Hoshea (730–722), who could take the throne only with the consent of Assyria. Tiglath-pileser claims that he made Hoshea king (*ANET*, 284). When Tiglath-pileser died, Hoshea decided to take advantage of the disorder that frequently accompanied an interregnum in the ancient Near East. He not only withheld tribute, but he negotiated with Egypt for support against Assyria (2 Kgs 17:3). When Shalmaneser VI ascended Assyria's throne, he responded to Hoshea's disloyalty by imprisoning him (2 Kgs 17:4). Apparently Shalmaneser did not want to deal with such an unreliable vassal so he decided to end Israel's political existence and incorporate its remaining territory into a new Assyrian province: Samarenu. The Bible implies that Shalmaneser took Samaria though actually it was his successor Sargon II. The fate of Hoshea is unknown.

The Kingdom of Israel did not know much peace except for the forty-year reign of Jeroboam II. It had good agricultural resources such as the fertile Jezreel Valley. It enjoyed commercial contacts with Phoenicia and controlled trade that passed through its territory. Unfortunately, Israel never had the opportunity to exploit the opportunities that its resources afforded it. It was in an almost continuous conflict with Aram over territory. It had its conflicts with Judah, but these were merely a minor irritant. Still, this nearly continuous state of war did not make for political stability nor foster economic prosperity. Of its nineteen kings, seven ruled for two years or less and seven were assassinated. When Assyria made its appearance in the region, the Kingdom of Israel quickly collapsed – its political existence ended and its territory was incorporated into the Assyrian Empire. The Assyrians exiled the kingdom's leadership class and brought in foreigners to repopulate the region in accordance with their policies of pacification (2 Kgs 17:5–6).

The Judahite Kingdom

The beginnings of the Judahite kingdom were marked with almost continuous border wars with the Israelite kingdom. These wars occupied the attention of Judah's first three kings: Rehoboam, Abijam (Abijah), and Asa (1 Kgs 12:21–24; 14:30; 1 Kgs 15:6, 22). Continuing conflicts with Israel put Judah's economy under a severe strain and left it vulnerable to attack from the south. Rehoboam (926–910) built a string of sixteen fortresses spaced three miles apart to protect his southwestern flank from the Philistines. This defensive line did not take in the coastal plain nor did it protect access to the Mediterranean Sea. Judah, then, did not control the lucrative trade route known as the Way of the Sea that went along the coast from Egypt to the north. Both the biblical narrative and Egyptian sources describe a raid by Pharaoh Shishak into Judahite territory. The purpose of this incursion apparently was not to reestablish an Egyptian presence in the eastern Mediterranean but it was simply for booty. Shishak left an account of this raid inscribed on a wall of Amun's Temple in Karnak. The inscription asserts that the pharaoh defeated 156 cities in the region. The Bible notes that the Egyptians looted the treasury of the Jerusalem Temple (1 Kgs 14:25–28) though the Egyptian account does not mention Jerusalem by name.

The border wars with Israel continued during the reign of Abijam (909–907) as both kingdoms were trying to claim as much territory as possible (1 Kgs 15:6). The conflict with the Israelite kingdom became so serious that Asa (906–878) of Judah found it necessary to conclude a treaty with Ben Hadad of Aram. While the latter kept Israel's forces busy in the Galilee, Judah experienced some relief. Asa was able to build forts at Gebah and Mizpah to guard the border Judah shared with Israel. Still, as the 9th century began, Judah was a virtual vassal state of Israel. Its territory was mostly a desert, it had no access to the sea or the principal north–south commercial routes, its treasury was looted by raids and impoverished by military expenditures, and many of its cities and towns were ruined by the Egyptians. The Judahite kings had little choice but to ally themselves with the more powerful and prosperous Israelite kingdom.

Jehoshapat (877–853) was a subordinate ally to Israel's Ahab in the latter's conflict with Moab (1 Kgs 22:1–4). To seal his alliance with Ahab, Jehoshapat accepted Ahab's daughter Athaliah as wife for his son Jehoram. Jehoshapat continued his alliance with Israel by supporting Jehoram of Israel (the brothers-in-law had the same name), Abah's successor, in the continuing conflict with Moab (2 Kgs 3:4–27). Judah's support for Israel left it vulnerable to attack from the south. Edom and Libnah regained their independence from Judah during Jehoram's reign (852–841; 2 Kgs 8:22). The presence of an Israelite princess as Jehoram's queen insured that he would do nothing contrary to the interests of Israel. Ahaziah (840; 2 Chr 21:17) succeeded his father Jehoram and continued his policy of subservience to Israel's interests. In furtherance of that policy, Ahaziah joined his uncle Jehoram in a war with Hazael of Aram to recover Israelite territory. Jehoram was severely wounded in that war and while he was recuperating in Jezreel, Ahaziah paid him a visit. The visit took place as Jehu began his revolution. Besides assassinating Jehoram, Jehu also had Ahaziah murdered (2 Kgs 9:27–29), probably because the two kings were relatives and the Judahite king was a loyal vassal to his uncle. Ahaziah ruled Judah for less than a year.

When Athaliah heard that her son was dead, she decided to take Judah's throne for herself. She had all other claimants for the throne murdered. Jehoash, one of her grandsons, was hidden during the purge and escaped. Undoubtedly during her six-year reign (839–833), Judah continued its vassalage to Israel. Of course, there was serious opposition to her policies. This led to Athaliah's assassination. Jehoash, the child who escaped her purge of the Judahite royal family, was enthroned by the priest Jehoiada who enlisted the army in overthrowing Athaliah and the purging of the pro-Israel elements in the government (2 Kgs 11:4–20). After years of humiliation at the hands of Israel, the army's commanders needed little encouragement to depose an Israelite princess sitting on the throne of Judah. Taking advantage of the strained relationships between Israel and Judah, Hazael of Aram attacked Israel and threatened Jerusalem, forcing Jehoash to empty the Temple's treasury to pay Hazael not to destroy the city (2 Kgs 12:18–19). Though Jehoash enjoyed a long reign (832–803), his administration was marked by military humiliation, economic corruption (2 Kgs 12:10–17) and the murder of political opponents (2 Chr 24:20–22). Like his father and mother, he too was assassinated (2 Kgs 12:21–22).

Amaziah (802–786) had his father's assassins executed but took no further vengeance. He turned his attention to retaking Edom, which had gained its independence from Judah while the Judahite kings were doing the bidding of Israel (2 Kgs 8:20–22; 14:7). Making too much of his victory over the Edomites, Amaziah attacked Israel and was soundly defeated. He was taken prisoner, the Temple was plundered, and Judah again was reduced to vassalage (2 Kgs 14:8–20). These failures, no doubt, contributed to his becoming the fourth Judahite monarch in succession to be assassinated. This may have led Isaiah to condemn Jerusalem as a city of assassins (Isa 1:21).

Uzziah (Azariah; 785–760) succeeded his father Amaziah. His forty-year reign (781–740) saw Judah's fortunes change for the better. Israel was preoccupied with other matters, leaving Judah free to pursue its own interests. This freedom spawned economic prosperity but the prophets Isaiah and Micah testify that

Judahite society was actually becoming two societies: one made up of people of means – royal officials, wealthy traders, and owners of large estates – the other of the poor, who paid the price for Judah's prosperity with their labor and lost land. Uzziah was successful in his military adventures against the Philistines and Arab tribes both of which populated areas along his southwestern borders, which he extended to the edge of Egyptian territory (2 Chr 26:6–8). He strengthened Jerusalem's defenses, but also paid attention to the agricultural basis of the Judahite economy (2 Chr 26:9–15). Uzziah also trained and equipped an army and, according to Assyrian sources, used it in a battle with Tiglath-pileser III in 743 (*ANET*, 282–3). Toward the end of his reign, Uzziah suffered from a skin disease that made it impossible for him to participate in Temple rituals. He probably was forced to abdicate in favor of his son Jotham.

Uzziah's battle with Assyria was a harbinger of what lay ahead for Judah. Tiglath-pileser III began turning Assyria into an imperial power that came to dominate Judahite politics for the next one hundred and fifty years. Jotham (759–744) continued his father's policies, which combined public works projects at home and carefully chosen military adventures abroad (2 Chr 27:3–6). Unfortunately, Judah was no longer in control of its own destiny because of the stirring of the Assyrian army. Two former rivals in the north, Aram and Israel, joined forces to oppose any Assyrian incursions into the eastern Mediterranean region and sought to enlist Judah in their coalition. When Jotham resisted, they determined to depose him and force Judah to join them. Jotham died before this could happen.

Ahaz (743–728) was twenty years old when he succeeded his father. Jerusalem was under siege and he had to do something to deal with the threats that Pekah of Israel and Rezin of Aram made to replace him with an Aramean named Tabeel. Ahaz considered Isaiah's advice to do nothing but trust in God unrealistic (Isa 7:7–9). The prophet probably realized that Assyria would deal with Aram and Israel in a short time, thus ending their siege of Jerusalem. Ahaz, however, did not feel that he could wait. He asked Assyria to make Judah one of its protectorates. This made the king extremely unpopular with religious nationalists, who thought that Judah should be free to choose its destiny. At the same time, the cleavage between the rich and poor in Judahite society was becoming steadily greater. Unfortunately, Judah did not have the freedom to deal with this serious internal problem. At the beginning of the 8th century, the Neo-Assyrian Empire reached the height of its power. Its rulers were not content with raids to bring in tribute. They wanted to acquire permanent control of the trade that made its way between Egypt and Mesopotamia with the ultimate goal of conquering Egypt itself. Between Assyria and its goals stood the two Israelite kingdoms.

When Hezekiah (727–699) succeeded his father Ahaz, Assyria had already stripped Israel of its territory in the Transjordan and the Galilee. In 722, Assyria ended the existence of the Kingdom of Israel as a political entity. Judah, while it had the veneer of political independence, was completely subservient to Assyria. Still, there was pressure on Hezekiah to assert Judahite independence – pressure that he did not resist. Hezekiah took measures to prepare for a siege. He built a strong defensive wall around Jerusalem and took measures to protect its water supply. The Babylonians, whose imperial aspirations conflicted with those of Assyria, sent an ambassador to Hezekiah to enlist him in their plots against the Assyrians (2 Kgs 20:12–13). The death of Sargon II of Assyria in 705 BCE gave Hezekiah what he thought was the perfect opportunity to revolt against the empire – while it was without an effective ruler. He began his revolution by attacking Assyrian allies along the coastal plain, believing he had Egyptian support. The people of Judah had to sustain Hezekiah's military moves with financial and personnel support. This put a considerable strain on Judah's economy, seriously eroding the ability of small farmers to survive. Sennacherib, Sargon's successor, mounted a serious campaign that began by taking the Phoenician and Philistine cities that were also in revolt. Then he turned his attention to the cities of Judah, taking them one by one until only Jerusalem remained. Hezekiah surrendered and had to pay a heavy indemnity (2 Kgs 18:14–16). Sennacherib stripped Judah of much of its territory and gave it to the coastal city-states that remained loyal, leaving Hezekiah as king of Jerusalem and its environs (ANET, 287–8). Hezekiah and Judah survived but barely. While Hezekiah's policies brought Judah to the brink of political extinction, the Bible presents him as an ideal monarch because of his supposed concern for the worship of YHWH alone (2 Kgs 18:1–8).

Manasseh (698–644) learned well from the example of his father's futile revolt against Assyria, which was at the height of its power. The Assyrian Empire extended from the Nile to the Taurus Mountains and east to the Iranian plateau. Manasseh determined that Judah would be Assyria's loyal vassal. Besides paying regular tribute, he sent Judahite laborers to help build the royal palace in Nineveh and Judahite soldiers to fight alongside the Assyrians in Egypt. According to 2 Chronicles, the Assyrians imprisoned him for disloyalty (33:11–13). Perhaps they misinterpreted his work on Jerusalem's fortifications (2 Chr 33:14) and were wary following Esarhaddon's death. But Manasseh was a survivor, reigning for forty-five years – the longest of any Judahite king. Of course, someone had to pay the price for Manasseh's collaboration with the Assyrians. While all sectors of the Judahite economy were likely to have been adversely affected, the people with the fewest economic resources had to bear the heaviest burden. Commercial contacts with the peoples of the Assyrian Empire probably led to the religious innovations decried by the Bible (2 Kgs 21:3–9). There was resistance to Manasseh's policies, but he put down all opposition ruthlessly and quickly (2 Kgs 21:16). Ammon (643–642) decided to continue his father's policies but was not as successful in controlling those who opposed his pro-Assyrian stance. His own courtiers assassinated him (2 Kgs 21:23).

Josiah (641–610) came to the throne at the age of eight and those who actually ruled had little choice but to continue Judah's subservience to Assyria. But that great empire was in decline. A succession of incompetent rulers and the internal problems that this spawned plus the rise of the Neo-Babylonian empire did not bode well for continued Assyrian hegemony. When Josiah reached the age of majority, he began a cultural revolution by promoting attempts at reinstating the place of Judah's ancestral religious traditions in national life (2 Kgs 22:3–23:27). He also took steps not only to take control of what once was Judahite territory in the southwest but he tried to extend his authority into areas that were once part of the former Israelite kingdom (2 Kgs 23:19; 2 Chr 34:6). The impotence of the Assyrians allowed him to do this, but apparently Josiah wanted to take a more active role in shaping the post-Assyrian world and this was his undoing.

Egypt, once Assyria's most powerful enemy, intended sending an expeditionary force to Nineveh to assist the Assyrians in fending off a Babylonian invasion force. The Egyptians preferred a weak Assyria to a strong Babylon. To get to Nineveh, the Egyptians had to pass through territory controlled by Judah. Josiah may have wanted to show the Babylonians that he could be a powerful ally as they attempted to wrest control of Assyria's empire so Josiah tried to halt the Egyptian column at Megiddo. He died in battle and with him the Judahite resurgence. With Josiah's defeat, Judah became a vassal of Egypt. To express their sovereignty over Judah the Egyptians deposed Jehoahaz (609), who was the popular choice to succeed Josiah, and required Judah to pay a heavy indemnity for its interference with Egypt's plans. They took the unfortunate Jehoahaz as a hostage to Egypt after just a three-month rule. The Egyptians installed another of Josiah's sons, Eliakim, as king of Judah, changing his name to Jehoiakim (608–598). Of course, the circumstances of his enthronement did not endear him to the people of Judah; neither did the policies he had to follow. Jehoiakim had to pay the Egyptians a heavy tribute and he raised the funds by taxation (2 Kgs 23:33–34). He also engaged in costly building projects requiring additional taxes and forced labor (Jer 22:13–17). All opposition was immediately and ruthlessly suppressed (Jer 26:20–21; 36:20–23; 2 Kgs 24:4).

When the Babylonians under Nebuchadrezzar defeated the Egyptians at the battle of Carchemish in 605, Judah's economic and political problems remained since Judah simply changed masters: Babylon for Egypt. When Egypt dealt some reverses to the Babylonian juggernaut three years later, Jehoiakim took the opportunity to revolt against Babylonian rule. Nebuchadrezzar was preoccupied with other matters so he simply encouraged raids into Judahite territory by its neighbors eager for booty (2 Kgs 24:2). Eventually the Babylonians did come and lay siege to Jerusalem. Jehoiakim died during the siege on December 6, 598. It was left to his son and successor to answer to the Babylonians.

Jehoiachin (Joiachin, Jeconiah, Coniah) was just eighteen when his father died. After reigning for only three months, he and the entire royal court surrendered to the Babylonians on March 16, 597. Judah had to pay the price for its rebellion. The temple was looted and the country's administrators and craftsmen were taken to Babylon (2 Kgs 24:14). Jehoiachin's quick capitulation probably saved his life since he too was taken to Babylon rather than executed. He remained there until his death although Amel-Marduk (Evil-merodach), Nebuchadrezzar's successor, raised him to the status of a royal retainer (2 Kgs 25:27–30).

The Babylonians replaced Jehoiachin with the third son of Josiah to rule as king of Judah: Mattaniah. Nebuchadrezzar gave him the throne name of Zedekiah (596–586). Despite Judah's military and political impotence, there were the extreme nationalists who kept urging Zedekiah to revolt against Babylon, though a minority like Jeremiah counseled submission. The king even went to Babylon to assert his loyalty, but in the end he was not able to withstand the pressure brought to bear by the nationalists. Encouraged by Egypt (Jer 44:30), Zedekiah took an opportunity brought about by internal problems in Babylon, to assert Judah's independence. Nebuchadrezzar invaded Judah and besieged Jerusalem in 587. Though the siege was lifted briefly so that the Babylonian army could neutralize an Egyptian force that was threatening its flank (Jer 37:5). This afforded Judah only a short respite from its fate. Jerusalem's wall was breached in July 587. Zedekiah and his family tried to escape. They were caught near Jericho. The last thing that Zedekiah saw before the Babylonians blinded him was the execution of his children (2 Kgs 25:4–7). He was taken to Babylon in chains as a prisoner-of-war. The temple was looted and then destroyed, and more Judahites were taken as hostages to Babylon.

To rule over those Judahites left behind, the Babylonians appointed Gedaliah (585–582; 2 Kgs 25:22). The text does not specify the office Gedaliah had, but it is likely that the Babylonians made him king though he did not belong to the Judahite royal family. A member of that family assassinated Gedaliah and his supporters (2 Kgs 25:25), bringing to an end the Kingdom of Judah.

From its inception and through most of its history, the Kingdom of Judah was a vassal state with little real freedom of action. It was subject first to Israel, then to Assyria, Egypt and finally Babylon. Though a single dynasty did rule over the Kingdom of Judah throughout its history except for the six years of Athaliah's reign, the vaunted stability of the Judahite dynasty is an illusion. Of the twenty monarchs who ruled from Rehoboam to Zedekiah, five were assassinated, three were taken into exile, three died during sieges, one died in battle. Five ruled for periods less than three years. Most ruled by the favor of imperial powers – at least two were placed on the throne by such powers. Those who did manage to maintain a modicum of stability were roundly condemned in the biblical narratives precisely for the accommodations with the dominant culture that made political and economic stability possible. What is evident is not a stable state but a very weak one, one whose continued existence depended on expending vast amounts for tribute and defense and the maintenance of a subservient posture toward the reigning military power. The economy of the Judahite state was thus crippled by its political impotence. Though the royal family and their retinue were able to prosper, most people had a very difficult time. Many farmers could not sustain themselves and their families even on the subsistence level. The condemnation of Judah's social structure and economic system by Isaiah, Jeremiah, and Micah testify to the inequities caused by the economic burden that Judah had to bear. Its people not only had to support Judah's court and army, but they also had an extra burden of taxation to cover the tribute expected by imperial powers. Though some Judahites hoped for a restoration of their state and their native dynasty, no such restoration took place. The story of the two Israelite kingdoms is a tragic one indeed.

Notes

1   A. Biran, "An Aramaic Stele Fragment from Tel Dan," *Israel Exploration Journal* 43 (1993), 81–98.
2   L. Rost, *The Succession to the Throne of David*, W. D. Rutter and D. M. Gunn (trs.) (Sheffield: Almond Press, 1982), 105–6.
3   The dates used in this essay are those found in John H. Hayes and Paul K. Hooker, *A New Chronology for the Kings of Israel and Judah* (Atlanta: John Knox Press, 1988).

Bibliography

Ahlström, G., *The History of Ancient Palestine* (Minneapolis: Fortress Press, 1993), chs. 11–19, 455–783.
Conner, H., "The Separate States of Israel and Judah," in J. Hayes and J. Miller, eds., *Israelite and Judaean History* (Philadelphia: Westminster, 1977), 381–434.
Malamat, A., ed., *The Age of the Monarchies: Political History* (Jerusalem: Massada, 1979).
Miller, J. and J. Hayes, *A History of Ancient Israel and Judah* (Philadelphia: Westminster Press, 1986), chs. 4–12, 120–415.
Tadmor, H., "The Period of the First Temple, the Babylonian Exile and the Restoration," in H. Ben-Sasson, ed., *History of the Jewish People* (Cambridge, MA: Harvard University Press, 1976), 91–182.

Further Reading

Aharoni, Y., *The Land of the Bible: An Historical Geography* (Philadelphia: Westminster Press, 1979).
Becking, B., *The Fall of Samaria* (Leiden: E. J. Brill, 1992).
Bright, J., *A History of Israel*, 3rd edn. (Philadelphia: Westminster Press, 1981).
Castel, F., *The History of Israel in Old Testament Times* (New York: Paulist, 1985).
Grant, M., *The History of Ancient Israel* (Phoenix: Phoenix Press, 1997).
Horn, S., "The Divided Monarchy," in H. Shanks, ed., *Ancient Israel* (Washington, D.C.: Biblical Archaeological Society, 1988), 109–49.
Jagersma, H., *A History of Israel in the Old Testament Period* (Philadelphia: Fortress Press, 1983).
Noth, M., *The History of Israel* (New York: Harper, 1958).
Soggin, J., "The Davidic Solomonic Kingdom," in *Israelite and Judaean History*, pp. 332–80.
——, *A History of Ancient Israel* (Philadelphia: Westminster Press, 1985).
Whitelam, K., *The Invention of Ancient Israel* (London: Routledge, 1997).

CHAPTER 6

Exile, Restoration, and Colony: Judah in the Persian Empire

Robert P. Carroll

> *There is a tale that Spinoza found the onions of Amsterdam particularly tasteless*
> *and accepted their insipidity as part of the price one pays for exile, for being able*
> *to live as he pleased. But he discovered one day that all along he had been eating*
> *tulip bulbs, not onions.*
>
> (Davenport, 1984, p. 130)
>
> *. . . exile is a metaphysical condition.*
>
> (Brodsky, 1995, p. 25)

At the end of the 20th century it is plain for all to see that the century has been one of the most appalling centuries ever of wars of destruction, devastation, death camps, deportation, displacement of peoples, and the creation of huge refugee problems all across the world. In a sense the social life of human communities has always had such dimensions to it, but the century just ended has had more than its fair share of such disrupted and deported displacement of peoples and families. So many groups of people now live in exile from their homelands and so many other peoples live elsewhere permanently, with no possibility of returning to lands which have long ceased to be their homelands. There are, of course, many kinds of exiles, whether economic, political or being among forcibly deported peoples, so a spectrum of diaspora experiences would need to be constructed which allowed for properly nuanced terms of description. But reading across that spectrum would provide ample evidence for the claim that exile, deportation, and displacement constitute *one* of the basic forms of communal existence among human societies (cf. Chaliand and Rageau, 1997). It is therefore hardly surprising that a collection of cultural literature such as is constituted by the Hebrew Bible itself also should bear such ample testimony to the common human experience of expulsion, exile, deportation, and displacement and should represent these human experiences from its beginnings with the book of Genesis to its endings in the book of Chronicles. As with all culturally produced literature, the Bible reflects the experiences, values, languages, and ideologies both of the writers who produced it and of the communities for which it was produced. So we may include the Bible as part of the description of the human condition in this scrutiny of the phenomena of expulsion, deportation, displacement, and hopes for return to the homeland. In so many different ways the whole Bible reflects and represents the discourses and narratives of deportation, displacement, and diaspora. The grand narratives, even the metanarrative itself, of the Bible are about deportations, little and large, real and symbolic, and the constant hope of return, of restoration, of homecoming. From Abraham to Cyrus and Ezra, diaspora is the context of biblical Jews; the whole Bible itself may well be regarded as the production of such diasporic experiences (including reactions to the destruction of the city Jerusalem).

Biblical Narratives of Expulsion and Deportation

There are a considerable number of deportations recorded in the Hebrew Bible, so the phenomenon is well known to the biblical writers. They may be noted here so as to provide comparative and contrastive material for analyzing the main biblical focus on the Babylonian deportation and the emergence of Judah as a colony in the Persian province. The paradigmatic biblical stories may easily be summarized: the expulsion of Adam and Eve from the Garden of Eden, from which we may argue the case that the whole Bible takes exile as its clue to the normal condition of human existence; the stories of the movement of Abram's family, driven out (commanded) by God, from Babylonia to the land of Canaan, Jacob's self-imposed exile from his homeland for crimes against his brother Esau, and his son Joseph's deportation by his brothers (Jacob's other sons) from homeland to Egypt, followed by the consequent movement of all the sons of Jacob, and Jacob himself, to Egypt and then their descendants' expulsion from Egypt (back) to the land of Canaan. All these stories may be taken as biblical paradigm narratives of social movement and also as a template for what follows in the edited construction of the various metanarratives and canons of the Bible. Reflection on the experience of deportation and the "exilic" condition of so many of the Jewish communities in Babylonia and Egypt provided the biblical writers with the context and inspiration for writing the stories of the nation/community's passage through time and space.

Thus we may read the Hebrew Bible from beginning to end as a series of narratives, tales, and depictions of deportation and displacement (the pattern continues in the post-Torah literature in the stories of David and Saul in 1 Samuel). Within such a dominant series of stories, the set of tales which has the most bearing on the topic of this chapter is to be found in the book of Kings, with parallel material in the relevant prophetic books (see Isaiah, Jeremiah, Ezekiel; also the Book of Lamentations and the relevant psalms in the Book of

Psalms [e.g. Psalm 137]). These stories represent various deportations of Israel and Judah under the hegemonic rules of Assyria and Babylon, thus providing the narrative pattern and data for the construction of the topic of "exile and restoration" in a context of foreign imperial rule. All the other biblical stories may use the pattern of exile (with or without return) but are not presented as representations of the imperial displacement of the people, thus disrupting their occupancy of the land (Palestinian, promised, or however described). The pattern of social movement seems fairly fixed in the biblical narratives, but only the material in Kings and the Prophets contributes to the more focused imperial deportation pattern of invasive overthrow, followed by deportation, with the potential for return and restoration to an imagined original state (*šûb šebût*) of the displaced peoples (cf. Bracke, 1985). Yet Adam does not return to Eden, Abram does not return to Babylonia nor Moses to Egypt, so the stories of expulsion and displacement in Kings have a different sense and purport to be the tales of deportation and (potential) return – even if the Moses story of the exodus from Egypt does provide the Deuteronomistic writers with the negative theme of the possibility of return to Egypt as an ever-present threat arising from the expulsion of the people from the land of Palestine (on the currently vexed issue in contemporary biblical scholarship of whether there were or were not Deuteronomistic writers involved in writing parts of the Hebrew Bible – see the discussions in Schearing and McKenzie, 1999).

The biblical metanarrative as represented by the book of Kings includes various accounts of the demise of the Kingdom of Israel, in the late 8th century BCE, due to Assyrian invasion and destruction of cities and land, and the destruction of Jerusalem and Judah (cities and land), at the beginning of the 6th century BCE at the hands of the Neo-Babylonian empire, with various deportations of the leading citizens of the city (2 Kings 17–25). The story of the fall of Israel, with the subsequent deportation of its people, is represented in the Bible in quite a different way from the various tales of Judean deportations by the Babylonians. It is told in a much more polemical fashion in 2 Kings 17, a representation of the events surrounding the deportation of Israelite citizens and ruling classes designed to denigrate the northern kingdom in favour of the different treatment of the Judean southern kingdom. The land of Israel is represented as having been repopulated, after the deportation of the people of Israel, with foreign nations from different areas of the Assyrian empire, nations given over to the worship of alien gods and graven images (2 Kgs 17:24–41). Thus the Samaritans (v. 29) are here represented as being both polytheistic and syncretistic in their religion and this pejorative representation may well function as an aetiology for the polemical disputes between the Judeans (Jews) and Samaritans in the literature of Ezra–Nehemiah, reflecting ideological tensions in the (so-called) Second Temple period. So many ideological issues are raised by 2 Kings 17, especially the ones surrounding such a derogatory and dismissive term as "polytheism" (see the fine discussion of the "pathologies of monotheism" in Hare, 1999, pp. 160–9, 190–200, 228–32), that I shall have to ignore them in this chapter while advising readers to be on their guard against simplistic readings of biblical texts and the imagined values contained therein. A critical approach to reading the Bible is an absolute *sine qua non* in these matters.

The destruction of Jerusalem and the deportation of its leading citizens and ruling classes to Babylon are represented by a number of somewhat different narratives in Kings (2 Kings 24–25; cf. 2 Chronicles 36) and in the parallel stories in the Book of Jeremiah (Jeremiah 39–40). The event of the destruction of the city of Jerusalem itself is hardly focused on in any concentrated or systematic fashion. The eighteen-month siege of the city is mentioned in passing as background to the breach of the city's wall and the seizing of the king and his retinue (2 Kgs 25:1–7, 8–12). A little more detail is given in Jer 39:3–10, but the details of the actual taking of Jerusalem is not the subject or focus of any major biblical narrative. More attention is paid to the themes of the invading Babylonian forces, the sieges of Jerusalem and the Babylonian practice of deporting people. In point of fact biblical material provides accounts of *three* such sieges and deportations: according to Dan 1:1–7 there was a siege and breach of Jerusalem by Nebuchadrezzar in 605 BCE, followed by the ransacking of the temple and the deportation of members of the royal family and the nobility; then in 597 BCE, Nebuchadrezzar came up against Jerusalem again and laid siege to it, deporting *all Jerusalem* (2 Kgs 24:14), that is royalty, the army, all the guilds and skilled workers, as well as the treasures of the temple and the royal palaces; and then in 587 BCE, Nebuchadrezzar made his third invasion of the Judean territory, laying siege to Jerusalem for eighteen months, taking it and deporting royalty and all the leading citizens and skilled workers, as well as ransacking the treasures of temple and palace *yet again* and burning the temple and the palaces (2 Kgs 25:9, 13–21). Within the context of those three accounts of different and distinctive invasions, sieges of Jerusalem, ransackings, and deportations, are to be found the setting for many biblical stories (cf. Jeremiah 39–44; Daniel 1–5). A briefer version of the three invasion and deportation stories appears in 2 Chr 36:1–21.

Piecing together the various stories from a wide range of different sources in the Bible it is possible to construct a rather less than complete account of how things were with Judah and Jerusalem in the sixth century. Apart from the people who were slaughtered during the Babylonian invasions and the many who died of wounds, starvation, pestilence and/or disease during the sieges and breaches of Jerusalem, there were those who survived the onslaughts and fled from the city or who left the land and either went to Egypt voluntarily (cf. Jeremiah 44) or were deported to Babylon. It is said that a few poor people were left in charge of the land (2 Kgs 25:12; Jer 39:10), but apart from these unidentified poor people the land and city were effectively drained and deprived of people. This state of affairs (or its lack, as it were) may be characterized as *the myth of the empty land* or, as the Chronicler constructs the matter rhetorically, in terms of a prophetic activity and sabbath cessation of activity to fulfill the word of YHWH by the mouth of Jeremiah until the land had enjoyed its sabbaths: "All the days that it lay desolate it kept sabbath, to fulfil seventy years" (2 Chronicles 36:21). This trope or myth of *the empty land* is used to imagine a territory emptied of people and desolate, keeping its sabbaths until the time of restoration of a (purified) people to a purified land, in keeping with prophecy (cf. Barstad, 1996; Carroll, 1992a; Carroll, 1997a, pp. 308–15). As the last book in the Jewish "canon" of the Bible the Chronicler's focus on the sabbath motif makes a fitting (literary) closure for a collection of literature which began with the book of Genesis and its stories of creation, where the first story of creation ends with *the sabbath rest of God* (Gen 2:1–3). The "empty land" notion also makes connections with the theme of the conquered land which Joshua and his army had emptied of alien people, in the story of the conquest of the land of Canaan. The rest is history and a history which depends entirely on who is constructing it and for what purposes.

The Conventional View of the Biblical Exile

When it comes to biblical scholarship at the end of the 20th century it must be said that as far as the Bible is concerned surface image and depth analysis are currently at loggerheads among scholars and historians. The reading of the Bible by scholars has very much become bifurcated into the retailing of conventional scholarly points of view and the rethinking of the coventional categories used by scholars in order to clear away the centuries of misrepresentation and misinterpreted texts and to move to better informed and more acutely discerned accounts of the matter. So I will start with a brief account of the conventional way of treating the biblical exile as it appears in the dominant textbooks and then move on to provide what I would hope may yet turn out to be the account of how things are moving in the field as we enter the 21st century. From this emergent account will come, in my judgment, the standard treatment of the period in the immediate future of scholarship and in the textbooks of the 21st century, even though it must be recognized that due to the inevitable prevailing ecclesiastical hegemonies in biblical scholarship *the paraphrasing of scripture* will also remain an alternative and perhaps even more dominant mode of "historical" reconstruction in biblical "scholarship" too. As for the biblical picture itself, that inevitably and invariably is a matter of interpretation which must be construed and constructed by scholars for themselves. There is no one picture in the Bible because there are so many different and differing accounts and stories included in the Bible on any and all topics. That point has already been made in the emphasis put on the fact that there are *three separate and distinct* accounts of *three* Babylonian invasions, *three* besiegings of Jerusalem, *three* breachings and takings of the city, *three* ransackings of temple and palaces, *three* deportations of the leadership and citizens. *The Bible does things by threes!*

Piecing together the various narrative strands and stories might yield a conventional story along the lines of the following account. After the third breach, destruction, ransacking and deportation of citizens from Jerusalem, the deported people were taken to Babylon where the king (and his immediate family?) were imprisoned and the deported people distributed around the Babylonian territory to live and work. According to the stories known as "diaspora novellas" (that is, stories set among the deported Jews in exile), such as Daniel, Esther, Judith and Tobit, individual Jews did very well under these circumstances (cf. the story of Joseph in Egypt in Gen 37–50), though always liable to suffer from occasional outbreaks of violence against the Jews (e.g., Haman's plot in the Book of Esther or Nebuchadrezzar's megalomania in the Book of Daniel). Perhaps psalmic phrases such as "by the waters of Babylon there we sat and wept, when we remembered Zion. On the willows (poplars) there we hung our lyres" (Pss 137:1–2 RSV) may give some indication of life along the irrigation canals of Babylonia, but otherwise there is not much in the biblical literature that affords a keen insight to how life was lived among the deportees. The diaspora novellas represent communities thriving among the nations, and deported Jews becoming invaluable citizens contributing to the gross national product and to the gaiety of nations, but these stories may be more reflective of mythic thinking than of the common experience of ordinary people (e.g. Daniel or Esther).

At the very end of the Jewish Bible the Persian emperor Cyrus is represented by the Chronicler as issuing a decree which permitted the deported Jews to return to Jerusalem and there to *rebuild* the temple of YHWH (2 Chr 36:22–23). In the books of Ezra and Nehemiah, as well as in the prophetic books associated with Haggai and Zechariah, the people are reported as having returned to Palestine under the leadership of Sheshbazzar and to the ruined city of Jerusalem in order to rebuild it and its ruined temple of YHWH (Ezra 1–6). The literature represents the return as a highly structured procession back across the desert to the ruined, empty land (now filled with rogues, vagabonds, and enemies of the people) and, after various struggles, stoppages and crises, the temple is rebuilt in grand style. "They finished their building by command of the God of Israel and by decree of Cyrus and Darius and Artaxerxes king of Persia" (Ezra 6:14). Such overwhelming and surplus authorization of the temple project – one deity and *three* imperial Persian emperors – suggests either grandiosity on a magnificent scale or (equally) a fearful anxiety about the need for official recognition (or a combination of both). The many questions which arise about the historical accuracy and generic nature of the Ezra–Nehemiah literature must be sidestepped here because space does not permit the complex and complicated investigation required to analyze all the problems and their many possible solutions (see the standard history books, commentaries and especially Eskenazi, 1988; Garbini, 1988; Smith, 1987). Once the city had been rebuilt and its temple reconstructed, normal life was restored for the deportees who had returned (the *benê haggōlâ*, "people of the deportation" as the biblical text has it) and the Babylonian deportation/ exile may be said to have ended. The "empty land" motif used in the Chronicler's mythological depiction of the land resting a sabbath rest from its polluted times (an anthropomorphism) may reflect an historical trace of a land emptied by the depredations of the invaders, that is a genuinely empty land – the archaeological evidence for the state of Jerusalem during the 6th century BCE is always difficult to read, especially given the fact that much of Jerusalem (around the temple area) is today prohibited to archaeological investigation – or it may just be the implication of this kind of metaphysical discourse. After the return and the rebuilding projects of the reconstruction period, Jerusalem and the people of Judah settled down to live in a Persian colony under the blessing and protection of the imperial forces and functioning as an outpost of empire in the province known as "Beyond the River" (see Grabbe, 1992, pp. 1–145). That, in a nutshell, is more or less the conventional view of the "deportation, exile and return" themes and topoi in the Bible as they are currently read my mainstream biblical scholarship.

Contemporary Approaches to Reading Exile and Return as a Biblical Myth

I want to turn from the kind of conventional reading which can be derived from certain rearrangements of the biblical text as illustrated in the section above to a more sophisticated and, I think, a better way – or at least a more modern approach – of investigating the text in the light of current rethinking going on in biblical studies. This approach really begins from the premise that although the Bible appears to represent the Babylonian exile as coming to an end with the return of Sheshbazzar and the people, thus bringing the exile to a symmetrical conclusion – having lasted the fabled *seventy years* of Jeremiah (Jer 25:12; 29:10; cf. 27:7; Zech 1:12) – life also goes on among the Jewish deportees in Babylonia and the Jewish refugees in Egypt *as if* nothing had come to an end. In the long centuries of the Persian, Greek, Roman and Christian empires, Jewish communities flourished in Babylonia and Egypt (and elsewhere throughout the civilized western world), so in no real sense could the so-called exile be said to have come to an end. On the contrary, life in the diaspora continued for millennia to this very day, and even now at the beginning of the 21st century (third millennium CE) more Jews belong to the diaspora than are ever likely to live (or have lived) in Palestine or, since 1948, the Land of Israel (*Eretz Yisrael*). This fact, *and fact it is*, has to be factored into any realistic, scholarly, knowledgeable, and historical account of the matter. It has to be recognized that the kind of literature incorporated into the Bible tends to favor the "end of exile" approach to ancient history and probably represents the propaganda literature of the temple community in Jerusalem as opposed to other ancient literature which represents Diaspora communities for whom there has been no end to exile (see in particular the Dead Sea Scrolls). So we must make allowance for two different literatures, different that is in focus and emphasis: literature which maintains the end to exile and literature which knows no such ending (cf. Knibb, 1976; Carroll, 1992a). The very many, different Jewish communities scattered across the empires of Persia, Egypt, Greece and Rome (Graeco-Roman) should not be categorized by the straitjacket of one specific approach derived from a limited selection of biblical tropes, nor should modern scholarship take as its task *the mimicry of ancient partisan voices* – even if the voices are imagined to be in the Bible.

Throughout this chapter the approach taken is that of a literary–cultural reading of the biblical texts bearing on the twin motifs of "exile and return" rather than an archaeological–historical approach favored by many biblical scholars (cf. Albertz, 1994, pp. 369–436; Carter, 1999; Grabbe, 1992; Grabbe, 1998). That is, in the judgment of this writer what we possess in the Hebrew Bible is the ideological construction of only *one* of the ancient Jewish parties (cf. Morton Smith's notion of "the YHWH-alone party") representing their own story of Israel–Judah's past, both before and after the Babylonian crisis. Taking as their center the temple-city of Jerusalem in the Persian, Greek, and Roman periods (or Graeco-Roman era) as constituted by the "returned exiles" of the Babylonian captivity, the story of the Bible then reads as propaganda for their claims and position as a kind of citizens-temple community, to use Joel Weinberg's designation (see Weinberg, 1992), flourishing as YHWH's people in the midst of imperial domination. Such an ideology would necessarily combat and exclude all other claims to power, position and representation, so the different communities in the diaspora would be marginalized simply by being outside "the holy land" or simply outside the sacred enclave of the temple community-territory. While there may be counter-claims and competing ideologies at work in the Bible and even detectible in it, the metanarrative as represented from Genesis to Chronicles – that is, the grand narrative of the canonical scriptures – seems to be that of a single story (no matter how many ruptures and deviations may be detected in the narratives) of departure from Babylonia by Abram and his family *in the prehistory of the nation* (Genesis) and the return of Abram's deported family from Babylonia in order to rebuild the temple in Jerusalem *at the end of the nation's story* (Chronicles). Of course that is only *one* reading of the biblical text as put together at some point in the past by the text's canonizers and currently available to us as a *canonical* text. It may in no way represent how things were before the collection of all the scrolls into a single canonical text. Reading the extra-biblical literature, including the Dead Sea Scrolls from Qumran, provides rather different pictures and competing claims of a much more complex and complicated past.

The Hebrew Bible is, among many other things, *on one level* the propaganda of the "deported and returned" occupants of Jerusalem in the post-Babylonian periods. Communities which continued to live and thrive in the diaspora have no place in or purchase on this particular myth of a return under Sheshbazzar. In the millennia that followed, the Persian period Diaspora has proved to have been the homeland of Jewish communities much more than the Palestinian homeland ever was, even though it would be fair to say that notions of permanent exile (diaspora) do not necessarily fit well with the ideological claims of the Bible or of modern Zionist points of view (see Wheatcroft, 1996, for a discussion of modern Zionism). Be that as it may, we do need the Persian Empire to factor into any account of the matter the idea and practice of *the permanency of exile* which is constituted by actual Diaspora existence. Then we need to allow that fact to undermine the alternative myth of *exile and return* in the Bible or at least

compete dialectically with the biblical myth as an alternative way of reading
the Bible.

Leaving aside the Diaspora novellas which represent life lived in the territory of Palestine, where the Jerusalem *gōlâ*-community is represented as being
in conflict with the local population (or people who were never deported), we
still face uncertain sources and their representations of the rebuilding of that
"new" community (Haggai–Zechariah, Ezra–Nehemiah). As a Persian colony
this Jerusalem community is difficult to describe adequately, lacking as we do
sufficiently reliable sources. According to the biblical sources city and temple
were rebuilt and the land, repopulated with the returnees, began to flourish
under the leadership of the Persian governor Nehemiah in spite of the fierce
opposition of the local inhabitants. Yet in point of fact, the province of Yehud,
as it is known in contemporary scholarship (cf. Carter, 1999), of which Jerusalem
may be said to have been the center, is *only dimly discernible in obscure texts.*
Reconstructing its existence and dimensions from biblical texts and whatever
archaeological remains may be deemed to be pertinent to the discussion (excellent discussion in Carter, 1999, pp. 114–248; see also Stern, 1982) will invariably produce many and much disputed accounts of the matter. *Nothing about
the Bible is simple, least of all its interpretation.* However, when interpretation of
the Bible is combined with interpretation of highly disputed (as to their interpretation) archaeological remains, then the net result is one of even more highly
disputed interpretations. Difficulties in one area of scrutiny are not resolvable
by difficulties in a different area of scrutiny, and the defects of the biblical texts
cannot be made good by imaginative manipulations of non-biblical data. We
are here up against some of the most fundamental and intractable issues in
current biblical hermeneutics – how are we to interpret these texts? Should we
be reading them in the light of the archaeology of the period or should we be
reading them against our own ideological presuppositions or a combination of
both, or in very different ways? This chapter is not the place for a discussion of
fundamental issues in hermeneutics, and yet without engaging in such a discussion *in the first place* it is difficult to see how the problems may be posed, let alone
resolved – if resolvable they are in the first place – to the satisfaction of serious
readers of the Bible. The problems of interpretation are alluded to here because
they are of the essence in the whole discussion about such topics as the exile,
the restoration and the Persian colony of Judah (excellent discussion in Carter,
1999, pp. 249–324; see also Davies, 1995; Grabbe, 1998; Hoglund, 1992).

As an example of the problematical nature of the biblical material consider
the vexed question of the Ezra–Nehemiah texts. Did Ezra's visit to Jerusalem
precede Nehemiah's or come after it, or did Ezra visit Jerusalem twice with
Nehemiah's visit taking place in-between those two visits? Is it reasonable to
reconstruct the biblical texts along rational lines and claim that Nehemiah visited *first* in order to help to rebuild the wall(s) of Jerusalem and *then* Ezra visited
in order to get the temple built and install in that rebuilt shrine the Torah? Or is
it much more complicated than such a rational reading? And what about Ezra?
Was he a historical figure or the invention of the Chronicler or some other

writer (cf. Garbini, 1988, pp. 151–69)? What about the Ezra–Nehemiah literature? Does it have a common author (the Chronicler?) or are they two independent pieces of writing, with different authors? So many questions must be debated
and resolved before the texts can be brought into play in the discussion about
the Persian colony in Jerusalem. The sensible way of handling such enigmas
may be to dismiss them as illegitimate readings of texts not designed to answer
such conundra in the first place. But sense is not necessarily a dominant quality
much in evidence in the history of biblical interpretation. Readers who wish to
find answers to all these questions are invited to read a large stock of secondary
literature on Ezra–Nehemiah (e.g. Ackroyd, 1968; Blenkinsopp, 1988; Carroll,
1998; Eskenazi, 1988; Garbini, 1988, pp. 151–69; Torrey, 1910; Williamson,
1987). Of course different writers will answer these difficult questions in their
own way and then proceed to interpret the texts accordingly, providing distinctive accounts of the matter as they bear on the larger issues of exile, restoration
and the Jerusalem colony in the Persian era. Thus there will be no one view of
the matter – *there can be no one view* – only the different perspectives taken by
different writers who have decided for themselves how best to handle the intractable problems raised by the texts in relation to the Persian and subsequent
periods. In my judgment we are currently in a period when there are many
competing points of view jostling for territorial gain in this area and wise readers
will allow for diversity of opinion, uncertainty and agnosticism, and will therefore
recognize the lack of any consensus in the treatment of this topic. The approach
of this chapter may be assigned to one, and only one, possible interpretive reading
of the matter and should not be confused with being a statement of how things
really were or should be.

The Myth of the Exile

Given the problematics of reading the biblical texts and interpreting the archaeological "evidence" (if evidence it be) bearing on the topic of exile, restoration
and Persian colony, one might ask the larger question "was there ever an exile?"
or, in slightly different form, "should the exile be read as if it had been the great
watershed in Judah's history?" I ask these questions because Charles Torrey
raised them at the beginning of the 20th century and they have come back into
biblical scholarship at the end of the 20th century (see Grabbe, 1998; cf. Noth,
1960, pp. 289–99). It all depends upon how terms are defined, texts interpreted
and traditions questioned. Torrey was of the opinion that there is "no trust-
worthy evidence that any numerous company returned from Babylonia, nor is
it intrinsically likely that such a return took place" (Torrey, 1910, p. 288). He
was also of the opinion that the scholarly emphasis on and highlighting of the
exile was "a thoroughly mistaken theory." Mistaken theory it may well have
been, but biblical scholars can at least claim that they had been misled by
reading the Bible. It is the biblical writers who *represent* the story of Judah as

one punctuated or ruptured by the Babylonian exile, but of course the scholars then compounded their reading of the relevant texts by insisting that somehow things had been much better before the exile and much worse after it. That further egregious error was entirely their own doing and reflected their own fundamentally anti-Semitic Christian ideological positions. One need not follow Torrey's point of view in order to avoid becoming contaminated by Christian supersessionistic points of view. That there were many deportations by foreign imperial powers need not be denied or disputed, yet there need not have been an exile *as understood by the biblical writers* because that representation may be more myth than history and more ideology than reality. That is, the deported people may have ceased to play any significant part in the life of the people left behind in Jerusalem and Palestine, and whatever "return" there might have been – its extent and dimensions are much debated and hotly disputed by historians – was not in itself anything like as significant as the writers of Ezra–Nehemiah make it out to have been (cf. Noth, 1960, pp. 289–99). That is *the myth of the exile*: those who were deported returned, or their descendants returned, and these returnees were the ones who shaped and constructed the new Jerusalem community around the rebuilt temple, thus producing the Persian colony of Jerusalem. If these biblical representations are disputed or rejected as ideologically constructed distortions of whatever was the reality of those times, then the notion of the exile ceases to be a watershed or important moment in the life of Jerusalem and the biblical account is greatly reduced in importance as a witness to what may have happened in the Persian period.

The new historians writing on the Bible (e.g. Lemche, 1998, pp. 86–132; Thompson, 1999; cf. Whitelam, 1996) would tend to read the "exile" as mythic in this sense. Not that it did not happen but because so many deportations happened exile becomes more myth, metaphor, and metaphysic than historically significant event. There are just too many stories in the Bible about the deportations of peoples – too many exiles as it were – but only one exilic event seems to be singled out for the focus of the biblical writers, and this one particular event of deportation – *three such events* in the Book of Kings but *only one* is singled out in the Book of Jeremiah (Jer 24) – tends to conceal from us the extraordinary ordinariness of such events and to privilege just one group in history. Thus we must think in terms of *a myth of exile and return*, which has been used by the writers to construct their myth of origination and legitimation in the Bible. As Thompson writes:

> What we have in the Bible's stories of deportation, exile and return are not accounts of a past at all but a perfect example of how literature plays with the metaphors that experience has created for us. It is to this literary play, to the myth of exile, that we should now turn in asking about the quality of this biblical tradition which is so firmly and unquestionably "anchored in history". (Thompson, 1998, pp. 110–11; cf. Thompson, 1999, pp. 217–25)

The end result of this ideological myth of *an exile* during the Babylonian period *and of a return* of such deportees (or their descendants) during the Persian period is the privileging of the Jerusalem community centered on the rebuilt city and temple. Such a myth helps to render invisible or "written out of history" – whether literally or effectively is a moot point – peoples and communities who do not participate in the myth and its chosen community. Similar ideological moves will take place later in history as supersessionistic Christian communities will write out of history or write off all Jewish communities who refuse to recognize the Christian messiah and attach themselves to the churches associated with the crucified messiah. I think something similar may be going on in the Hebrew Bible in the material in Haggai–Zechariah, Ezra–Nehemiah and Chronicles. It is not easy to be sure here because the Diaspora novellas (Daniel, Esther, Judith etc.) seem to presuppose a pre-return situation and yet may also reflect *the non-return dimension* of the deported communities in exile. Perhaps it is only the readers of the Bible who have misread the texts and, I think, the canonizers who wish to provide this specific reading of the tradition *as if* only the Jerusalem temple community (whether of a Weinbergian nature or otherwise) could be counted as the continuation of the history of the people of Israel temporarily ruptured by the Babylonian deportations.

Exile as Metaphor, Myth, and Metaphysic

The literature and sociocultural influences of the Persian period (and afterwards) are such major dynamic influences in the creation and production of the Bible (cf. Grabbe, 2000) that an adequate account of them would provide the subject-matter for a whole book (cf. Berquist, 1995; Cook, 1995). To that period (in its largest sense of Persian plus Graeco-Roman) we may attribute the beginnings of the foundations and roots of what would many centuries later become the Jewish matrix out of which came the early Christian communities and the formation of various Judaisms. It was also the great era of writing: Torah was written and produced, prophetic texts emerged also as combative counter-traditions (accidental literature), and the Wisdom literature also appeared during the centuries of and after the Persian imperial influences. The Persian contribution to the origins of apocalyptic writings also should not be ignored (cf. Cohn, 1993; Berquist, 1995, pp. 177–192; Cook, 1995, pp. 19–84). Indeed, one might read the production of so many writings, of what was to become so much biblical literature, in the centuries after the emergence of the Jerusalem community in the Persian era as a consequence of deportation and exile, that is, of Diaspora living. What eventually came to stand for land, temple, and people in the absence of all these things were the writings which proved to be independent of time and space in that they could be carried *wherever* necessary and rewritten *whenever* necessary (see the story in Jeremiah 36 as an analogy and a parable). George Steiner has expressed the matter rather well:

> Heine's phrase is exactly right: *das aufgeschriebene Vaterland*. The "land of his fathers", the *patrimoine*, is the script. In its doomed immanence, in its attempt to immobilize the text in a substantive, architectural space, the Davidic and Solomonic

Temple may have been an erratum, a misreading of the transcendent mobility of the text.

   At the same time, doubtless, the centrality of the book does coincide with and enact the condition of exile. There are radical senses in which even the Torah is a place of privileged banishment from the tautological immediacy of Adamic speech, of God's direct, unwritten address to man. Reading, textual exegesis, are an exile from action, from the existential innocence of praxis, even where the text is aiming at practical and political consequence. The reader is one who (day and night) is absent from action. The "textuality" of the Jewish condition, from the destruction of the Temple to the foundation of the modern state of Israel, can be seen, has been seen by Zionism, as one of tragic impotence. The text was the instrument of exilic survival; that survival came within a breath of annihilation. To endure at all, the "people of the Book" had, once again, to be a nation. (Steiner, 1996, p. 305)

Steiner's metaphors work well for the topic of exile because Jews have lived through time better and for much longer *in their texts than in their land*. The emergence of the modern state of Israel has not changed the Diaspora dimensions of Jewish existence, only offered Jews an alternative program of "returning" – the sense in which people who have never lived in the land can *return* to it raises all the complex issues involved in metaphysical notions of people, land, exile, and return – whereby Jews throughout the world now have options and choices they may make in relation to where they choose to live if they so wish. But exile has become a root metaphor, a myth, and a metaphysic of existence not only for Jews (cf. Scott, 1997), but for many peoples scattered around the surface of the earth. Even those who live in their own homeland may entertain themselves by using *the discourse of exile* to describe their well-appointed places in society (see contemporary American biblical theologians), whereas many of us know all too well *from personal experience* how it is to live in exile (the writer is Irish but lives in a foreign land as an economic exile). But more especially for Jews, deportation and diaspora have been very live realities and nowhere more dominatingly than in the 20th century when the death camps of Nazi Germany added further deportations to a Diaspora-existence and inscribed death across European Jewry. Yet exile, Diaspora and hopes of return have always been part and parcel, warp and woof, of Jewish existence. As Jacob Neusner has expressed it: "The paradigm of exile and return contains all Judaisms over all times, to the present" (Neusner, 1997, 221; cf. Neusner, 1987; Scott, 1997).

Bibliography

Ackroyd, P., *Exile and Restoration: A Study of Hebrew Thought in the Sixth Century* BC, OTL (London: SCM Press, 1968).

Albertz, R. 1994, *A History of Israelite Religion in the Old Testament: 2. From the Exile to the Maccabees* (London: SCM Press, 1994).

Barstad, H., *The Myth of the Empty Land: A Study in the History and Archaeology of Judah During the "Exilic" Period*, Symbolae Osloenses Fasc. Suppl. XXVIII (Oslo: Scandinavian Press), 1996.

Berquist, J., *Judaism in Persia's Shadow: A Social and Historical Approach* (Minneapolis: Fortress Press, 1995).

Blenkinsopp, J., *Ezra–Nehemiah: A Commentary*, OTL (Philadelphia: Westminster Press, 1988).

Bracke, J., "šûb šebût: A Reappraisal," *ZAW* 97 (1985), 233–44.

Brodsky, J., "The Condition We Call Exile," in J. Brodsky, ed., *On Grief and Reason: Essays* (Harmondsworth: Penguin Books, 1995), 22–34.

Carroll, R. P., "Israel, History of (Post-Monarchic period)," *The Anchor Bible Dictionary*, vol. 3 (New York: Doubleday, 1992a), 567–76.

——, "The Myth of the Empty Land," in D. Jobling and T. Pippin, eds., *Ideological Criticism of Biblical Texts*, Semeia 59 (Atlanta: Scholars Press, 1992b), 79–93.

——, "Clio and Canons: In Search of a Cultural Poetics of the Hebrew Bible," in S. Moore, *The New Historicism*, Biblical Interpretation 5 (1997a), 300–23.

——, "Deportation and Diasporic Discourses in the Prophetic Literature," in J. Scott, ed., *Exile: Old Testament, Jewish, and Christian Conceptions*, SJSJ 56 (Leiden: E. J. Brill, 1997b), 63–85.

——, "Exile! What Exile? Deportation and the Discourses of Diaspora," in L. Grabbe, ed., *Leading Captivity Captive: "The Exile" as History and Ideology*, JSOTSupp 278/ESHM 2 (Sheffield: Sheffield Academic Press, 1998), 62–79.

Carter, C., *The Emergence of Yehud in the Persian Period: A Social and Demographic Study*, JSOTSup 294 (Sheffield: Sheffield Academic Press, 1999).

Chaliand, G. and J-P. Rageau, *The Penguin Atlas of Diasporas*, trans. A. M. Berrett [French original] (Harmondsworth: Penguin Books, 1997).

Cohn, N., *Cosmos, Chaos and the World to Come: The Ancient Roots of Apocalyptic Faith* (New Haven and London: Yale University Press, 1993).

Cook, S., *Prophecy and Apocalypticism: The Postexilic Setting* (Minneapolis: Fortress Press, 1995).

Davenport, G., "Spinoza's Tulips," in G. Davenport, ed., *The Geography of the Imagination: Forty Essays* (London: Picador, 1984), 123–30.

Davies, P., *In Search of "Ancient Israel,"* JSOTSupp 148, 2nd edn. (Sheffield: Sheffield Academic Press, 1995).

Eskenazi, T., *In An Age of Prose: A Literary-Approach to Ezra–Nehemiah*, SBL Monograph series 36 (Atlanta, GA: Scholars Press, 1988).

Garbini, G., *History and Ideology in Ancient Israel* (London: SCM Press, 1988).

Grabbe, L., *Judaism from Cyrus to Hadrian* (London: SCM Press, 1992).

Grabbe, L., ed., *Leading Captivity Captive: "The Exile" as History and Ideology*, JSOTSupp 278/ESHM 2 (Sheffield: Sheffield Academic Press, 1998), 62–79.

Grabbe, L., *Did Moses Speak Attic?*, ESHM 3 (Sheffield: Sheffield Academic Press, 2000).

Hare, T., *Remembering Osiris: Number, Gender, and the Word in Ancient Egyptian Representational Systems* (Stanford, CA: Stanford University Press, 1999).

Hoglund, K., *Achaemenid Imperial Administration in Syria-Palestine and the Missions of Ezra and Nehemiah* (Atlanta, GA: Scholars Press, 1992).

Knibb, M., "The Exile in the Literature of the Intertestamental Period," *Heythrop Journal* 17 (1976), 253–72.

Lemche, N., *The Israelites in History and Tradition*, Library of Ancient Israel (London and Louisville, KY: SPCK and Westminster/John Knox Press, 1998).

Neusner, J., *Self-Fulfilling Prophecy: Exile and Return in the History of Judaism* (Boston: Beacon Press, 1987).

Neusner, J., "Exile and Return as the History of Judaism," in J. Scott, ed., *Exile: Old Testament, Jewish, and Christian Conceptions*, SJSJ 56 (Leiden: E. J. Brill, 1997), 221–37.

Noth, M., *The History of Israel* (London: Adam & Charles Black, 1960).

Schearing, L. S. and S. L. McKenzie, eds., *Those Elusive Deuteronomists: The Phenomenon of Pan-Deuteronomism*, JSOTSupp 268 (Sheffield: Sheffield Academic Press, 1999).

Scott, J. M., ed., *Exile: Old Testament, Jewish, and Christian Conceptions*, SJSJ 56 (Leiden: E. J. Brill, 1997).

Smith, M., *Palestinian Parties and Politics that Shaped the Old Testament* (London: SCM Press, 1987).

Steiner, G. 1996, "Our Homeland, the Text," in G. Steiner, *No Passion Spent: Essays 1978–1996* (London and Boston: Faber & Faber, 1996), 304–27.

Stern, E., *Material Culture of the Land of the Bible in the Persian Period 538–332* BC (Warminster, England: Aris & Phillips, 1982).

Thompson, T., "The Exile in History and Myth: A Response to Hans Barstad," in L. Grabbe, ed., *Leading Captivity Captive: "The Exile" as History and Ideology*, JSOTSupp 278/ESHM 2 (Sheffield: Sheffield Academic Press, 1998), 101–18.

——, *The Bible in History: How Writers Create a Past* (London: Jonathan Cape, 1999).

Torrey, C., *Ezra Studies* (Chicago: University of Chicago Press, 1910).

Weinberg, J., *The Citizen-Temple Community*, JSOTSupp 151 (Sheffield: Sheffield Academic Press, 1992).

Wheatcroft, G., *The Controversy of Zion or How Zionism tried to resolve the Jewish Question* (London: Sinclair-Stevenson, 1996).

Whitelam, K., *The Invention of Ancient Israel: The Silencing of Palestinian History* (London: Routledge, 1996).

Williamson, H., *Ezra, Nehemiah*, WBC 16 (Waco, TX: Word Books, 1987).

PART III
Archaeology of Ancient Israel and Early Judaism

CHAPTER 7

Archaeology and the History of Israel

William G. Dever

The archaeology of ancient Palestine, widely regarded as the "Holy Land," has inevitably been intertwined in many ways with biblical studies ever since the first explorations and discoveries in the mid-19th century CE. Particularly in America, Palestinian archaeology as it developed in the 1920s–1950s was dominated by the "biblical archaeology" movement of the legendary W. F. Albright and his followers. The major agenda of this school was to elucidate such issues in Israelite history as: (1) the Age of the Patriarchs; (2) Moses and Monotheism; (3) the Exodus and Conquest; (4) the early Israelite and Judean states; and (5) the religion of ancient Israel. Today the "assured results of scholarship" in *all* these areas are questioned, if not rejected altogether (Dever, 1977, 1997a, 1997b, 1997c).

"Biblical Archaeology": A Failed Dialogue

"Biblical archaeology" of the classic style is now defunct, at least as an academic and professional discipline, and its obituary has been written (Dever, 1985). Yet "biblical archaeology" still persists as a legitimate field of inquiry for both scholars and laypeople – a dialogue between *two* disciplines, biblical studies and what is now widely called "Syro-Palestinian" archaeology, now a largely secular discipline.

For those of us who helped to foster Palestinian archaeology's "coming of age" as an autonomous discipline in the 1970s–1990s, the trauma of our discipline's separation from its venerable parents – biblical and theological studies – was compensated for by what we saw as greatly expanded possibilities for an honest, searching, critical dialogue. And one of the joint objectives was, of course, to write new, better balanced, and more satisfying histories of ancient Israel, using both texts and archaeological data as our sources (Dever, 1996).

It must be admitted candidly, however, that the dialogue we confidently envisioned a generation ago has not materialized. In fact, it appears that the fields of archaeology and biblical studies are further apart than ever as *scholarly* enterprises, even though the public sometimes perceives the two to be virtually one (see below). Thus the popular view, especially in sensational reporting in the media, is that with each new discovery archaeology "proves the Bible" again. Yet most biblical scholars currently writing either abuse the archaeological evidence in producing "pseudo-histories" of ancient Israel, or else ignore archaeology altogether as though it were irrelevant to their inquiry. How did we get to this impasse; and can we break out of it?

Toward a New Agenda for the Archaeology and History of Ancient Israel

In the last decade or so, the focus of biblical scholarship has turned away from the analysis of specific eras and issues in the history of ancient Israel to larger, fundamental questions of historiography. That is to say, what methods and sources of data are most appropriate to a historical inquiry? Putting the issue that way, and thus questioning all approaches, has led to an even more fundamental question: Is it still *possible* to write a truly critical history of ancient Israel?

A brief review of recent literature will illustrate the trend just noted. Basic works on Israelite and modern biblical historiography had been published by John van Seters (1983) and Baruch Halpern (1988). And several modern full-scale histories of ancient Israel had been produced in the same era, notably those of Hermann (1975); Soggin (1984); and Hayes and Miller (1986).

All of these modern histories of Israel accepted Syro-Palestinian archaeology's potential contribution, but in practice they cited archaeological data only sparingly (especially Hermann). To be sure, the major handbooks available today had not yet been published, such as those of Helga Weippert (1988); Amihai Mazar (1990); Amnon Ben-Tor (1991); and Thomas E. Levy (1995).

In 1992 Phillip Davies, of Sheffield University, published a work that cast doubt upon the whole historical enterprise, *In Search of "Ancient Israel"* (1992). Davies distinguished three "Israels": (1) "biblical" Israel; (2) "ancient" Israel; and (3) "historical" Israel. The first two, he asserted, were simply "constructs" of Jewish and Christian theologians (i.e., invented); and the third, or "historical," Israel may have actually existed in the Iron Age (ca. 1200–600 BCE), but is largely beyond recovery. This is because the Hebrew Bible as it now stands was written only in the Persian–Hellenistic period and is mostly late Jewish propaganda; and archaeology, although theoretically a source of contemporary information, is mostly "mute."

Davies was soon joined by other "revisionist" historians, as they came to be known, chiefly Thomas L. Thompson and Niels Peter Lemche of the University of Copenhagen, and Keith W. Whitelam of Stirling University in Scotland (Davies,

1992; Lemche and Thompson, 1994; Thompson, 1992, 1999; Whitelam, 1996; cf. critique in Dever, 1998). Thompson had produced a massive volume, *The Early History of the Israelite People from the Written and the Archaeological Sources* (1992). By 1994, however, he began to argue that few if any of the Hebrew Bible's "stories" were historical at all. As he put it, "The Bible is not history, and only very recently has anyone ever wanted it to be" (Lemche and Thompson, 1994, p. 18). And by 1999, Thompson's book *The Mythic Past: Biblical Archaeology and the Myth of Ancient Israel* made his essentially nihilist position clear (1999; cf. Dever, 1998).

Even more explicit was Whitelam's work, *The Invention of Ancient Israel: The Silencing of Palestinian History* (1996; cf. Dever, 1998). Whitelam argues that not only had Jewish and Christian scholars (particularly Americans and Israelis) "invented" their Israel, but in the process they had deliberately disenfranchised the *Palestinian* peoples. Here was exposed not only the postmodern stance of the "revisionists" (there *is* no objective past to be known), but also something of their political ideology and their rhetorical style. Yet the theme – "the history of Palestine, not biblical Israel" – had already been taken up by at least one fairly mainstream biblical scholar, Gösta Ahlström, in his work *The History of Ancient Palestine from the Paleolithic Period to Alexander's Conquest* (1993).

Meanwhile, skeptical voices grew, as heard for instance in the volume edited by L. L. Grabbe, *Can a "History of Israel" Be Written?* (1997). Most of the authors, members of the "European Seminar in Historical Methodology" – 21 biblical scholars, but no archaeologists – came up with essentially negative answers to the question; and all either ignored or caricatured "biblical archaeology" (included were Davies, Lemche, and Thompson).

By now, the essential question was not only whether a history of ancient Israel *could* be written, but also by implication other questions, such as these. (1) What do we *mean* by "history"? (2) What are our *sources* for history-writing, and what constitutes "primary" and "secondary" sources? (3) What role, if any, may be accorded to *archaeology*, and how can we critically *evaluate* archaeological data? (4) Is a *dialogue* between textual and artifactual specialists desirable and possible? (Dever, 1996). Extremists on both sides, of course, refused even to acknowledge these as issues. That would include biblical scholars who are increasingly preoccupied with *literary* analyses, ever more faddish; and many American and Israeli archaeologists, who were competent technicians but were often uninterested in the larger intellectual issues of either historiography or biblical studies, dismissing them as "philosophical."

Some Reflections on Archaeology, Biblical Studies, and History-Writing

Any productive discussion of a dialogue between archaeology and biblical history would have to begin with a definition of the terms involved. (1) By "biblical studies," we refer here to the attempt to recover the history of ancient Israel in the period of the Hebrew Bible (i.e., in the Iron Age, Persian, and Hellenistic eras), based largely on texts, separating "history of events," however, from theologically-derived "salvation-history," ancient or modern. (2) By "archaeology," we refer here to the modern secular, inter-disciplinary field or inquiry usually called "Syro-Palestinian archaeology," which attempts to reconstruct a picture of the past using both material culture remains and any written evidence brought to light through excavation and survey. (3) By "history," we mean a systematic, narrative account of past events, based as far as possible on established facts, which attempts to explain the cause and meaning of these events. Ideally, this history would include: (a) an environmental or "natural" history; (b) long-term settlement history; (c) a history of technology; (d) socioeconomic history; (e) political history; (f) a history of ideas; and (g) cultural history in the broadest sense. To be sure no *one* of the disciplines noted above can produce or control all of the varied and complex data needed to write such a comprehensive history – thus the need for dialogue. After all, archaeology is uniquely capable of producing the "external," or independent, data that are needed to complete and perhaps to corroborate the biblical texts, which will always be limited because of their selectivity, their idealistic character, and their theological biases. Furthermore, the Hebrew Bible is a fixed *corpus* of literature, a closed "canon" that can never be expanded, while archaeology is theoretically unlimited in the vast new information that it can bring to light. Yet archaeology in general, and Syro-Palestinian archaeology in particular, has only recently begun to appreciate its unparalleled potential for history-writing.

During the impact of the "New Archaeology" of the 1960s–1980s, archaeology eschewed old-fashioned objectives of particularistic history in favor of general *science*, or the testing of "universal laws of the cultural process." For this school, ideology – that is, religion and culture – were "mere epiphenomena" in explaining cultural change. Culture, in fact, and therefore history, was for the most part simply adaptation to the natural environment and its challenges (see essays in Whitley, 1998).

In recent years, "processual" archaeology has been severely criticized for its reductionist, determinist, and "pseudo-scientific" views of culture and culture change. Thus the prevailing archaeological theory of the 1990s sees itself as "post-processual," "interpretive," and "cognitive." And history-writing is very much back in vogue (Whitley, 1998). These trends in worldwide archaeology bode well for the archaeology of ancient Israel and the biblical world; but few in our discipline have yet grasped the opportunity (but see Dever, 1993).

Given the prevailing skepticism among biblical scholars regarding the historicity of the texts of the Hebrew Bible, it might well be that archaeology in future will come to constitute our *primary* data for writing new histories of ancient Israel. Yet one must ask in that case precisely what it is that archaeology contributes and texts do not. In short, as a previous generation of scholars asked: What is it that archaeology can – and cannot – do?

I would suggest that today's sophisticated archaeology can often provide (1) external, "objective" information about ancient Israel, valuable precisely because it is independent of the often tendentious biblical texts. (2) Archaeology can also provide evidence that supplements that derived from the Hebrew Bible, limited as it is in perspective – in some cases perhaps corroborating the biblical version of events, in others correcting or even supplanting it. (3) Finally, archaeology provides a context for understanding ancient Israel in the much larger world of the ancient Near East, bringing to light long-lost neighboring places, peoples, and cultures that make the Bible more "credible" by making it more human. Archaeology brings a fresh and dramatic perspective on the biblical world, and thus it fosters understanding and appreciation of the Bible and ancient Israel.

On the other hand, archaeology cannot, and must not presume to, "prove the Bible" – either in terms of confirming what actually happened in history, much less in indicating what the biblical writers claimed that the presumed events *meant*. In short, the historical and theological quests must be kept strictly separate. Archaeology can answer such questions as Who, What, Where, When, and How? But it cannot answer the ultimate question: Why?

Some "Case-studies" in Archaeology and History

Of all the eras of Israelite history that archaeology today might illuminate, we can only deal with a few here. (1) Since there is little or nothing that we can say archaeologically about a "Patriarchal Age" (Dever, 1977), the earliest era upon which we can realistically focus is that of Israelite origins in the 13th–12th centuries BCE. Here archaeological surveys and excavations in the past twenty years have brought to light some 300 small, unfortified hilltop villages of the early Iron I period, the 12th–11th centuries BCE. These villages are mostly founded *de novo*, not on the remains of destroyed Late Bronze Age Canaanite cities. They represent in all likelihood the "colonization" of the relatively underpopulated hill-country frontier by displaced elements of the local Canaanite population. These newcomers would then represent the group of people designated "Israel" in the well-known "Victory Stela" of Pharaoh Merneptah dated ca. 1210 BCE. If so, the "Proto-Israelites" would be the direct ancestors of later "biblical Israel" during the Monarchy.

The scholarly consensus today, based largely on the new *archaeological* data, is thus one of "indigenous origins" for much of early Israel, not "military conquest." That picture does not fit easily with the Joshua narratives; but it brilliantly illuminates Judges' depiction of a protracted life-or-death *cultural* conflict with other elements of the Canaanite population in the "period of the judges" (12th–11th centuries, BCE). Archaeology has thus revolutionized our understanding of early Israel, forcing a reevaluation of the biblical texts, to be sure, but in the process bringing us much closer to an account of "what actually happened."

The *theological* implications of that, however, have yet to be worked out (cf. Finkelstein, 1988; Dever, 1997a).

(2) A second "case-study" of archaeology's recent contribution to the history of Israel would be the rise of the Monarchy. The "revisionist" historians noted above have denied that Israel (the Northern Kingdom) attained statehood before the 9th century, BCE, Judah before the late 7th century, BCE. Thus "Solomon," for instance, was no more an actual historical figure than King Arthur, to quote Thompson. Yet archaeology in the past 30 to 40 years has brought to light a vast body of evidence that Israel and Judah in the 10th century, BCE had a population of ca. 100,000, were highly urbanized, and were characterized by an emergent homogeneous "national" material culture. More significantly, district administrative centers actually mentioned in the Bible, such as Hazor, Megiddo, and Gezer (1 Kgs 9:15–17), have been excavated and have produced nearly *identical* four-entryway city gates and casemate (or double) city walls. Such city-planning is clear evidence of the *centralization* that is universally acknowledged as the principal criterion for defining the emergence of a "state." The archaeological evidence is ignored or disputed, of course, by the "revisionists"; but it is overwhelming to the unbiased observer (Dever, 1997b). If not "Solomon," then there was a similar king by another name.

(3) A final area in which archaeology has illuminated ancient Israelite life and times is the recent recovery of the popular or "folk" religion that the orthodox texts of the Hebrew Bible had blurred or almost totally obscured. Archaeology has brought to light in the past generation or so a wealth of information on non-Yahwistic or syncretistic cults of the 12th–7th centuries, BCE. The evidence includes: (1) nearly a dozen Canaanite-style temples, "high places," altars, and shrines; (2) hundreds of cult-stands, model temples, female figurines, amulets, depictions of iconography on seals, and other cult paraphernalia either proscribed or ignored in the Hebrew Bible; and (3) at least two Hebrew inscriptions actually mentioning the old Canaanite Mother Goddess "Asherah" in connection with YHWH, ostensibly the only (and male) deity in the canonical tradition. The new evidence again forces us to rethink "Israelite monotheism," which now appears to have been a minority tradition until after the exile. Disturbing as that is to some, it gives us a new understanding and appreciation of the prophetic protest against the prevalent popular cults. Archaeology shows that the prophets were realistic; they knew what they were up against (Dever, 1990, 1997c).

Conclusion

The "case-studies" above represent only the tip of the iceberg concerning archaeology's vast and proven potential for illuminating the history, religion, and culture of ancient Israel. Excavation, research, and publication in Israel and Jordan are moving at a faster pace than ever, and many more dramatic new discoveries can be expected in future. It is no exaggeration to say, as Albright did fifty years ago, that archaeology is a "revolutionary tool" for illuminating the world of the Bible.

Bibliography

Ahlström, G., *The History of Ancient Palestine from the Paleolithic Period to Alexander's Conquest* (Sheffield: JSOT Press, 1993).

Ben-Tor, A., ed., *The Archaeology of Ancient Israel* (New Haven: Yale University Press, 1991).

Davies, P., *In Search of "Ancient Israel"* (Sheffield: JSOT Press, 1992).

Dever, W., "Palestine in the Second Millennium B.C.E.: The Archaeological Picture," in J. H. Hayes and J. Miller, eds., *Israelite and Judean History* (Philadelphia: Fortress Press, 1977), 70–120.

——, "Syro-Palestinian and Biblical Archaeology," in D. Knight and G. Tucker, eds., *The Hebrew Bible and Its Modern Interpreters* (Philadelphia: Fortress Press, 1985), 31–74.

——, *Recent Archaeological Discoveries and Biblical Research* (Seattle: University of Washington Press, 1990).

——, " 'Biblical Archaeology' – Death and Rebirth?" in A. Biran and J. Aviram, eds., *Biblical Archaeology Today, 1990, Proceedings of the Second International Congress on Biblical Archaeology, Jerusalem, June 1990* (Jerusalem: Israel Exploration Society, 1993), 706–22.

——, "Philology, Theology, and Archaeology. What Kind of History Do We Want and What is Possible?" in N. Silberman and D. Small, eds., *The Archaeology of Israel: Constructing the Past, Interpreting the Present* (Sheffield: Sheffield Academic Press, 1996), 290–310.

——, "New Archaeological Data and Hypotheses on the Origins of Ancient Israel," in J. R. Barlett, ed., *Archaeology and Biblical Interpretation* (London: Routledge, 1997a), 20–50.

——, "Archaeology and the 'Age of Solomon': A Case Study in Archaeology and Historiography," in L. K. Handy, ed., *The Age of Solomon: Scholarship at the Turn of the Millennium* (Leiden: E. J. Brill, 1997b), 217–51.

——, "Folk Religion in Early Israel: Did Yahweh Have a Consort?" in H. Shanks, ed., *Aspects of Monotheism: How God Is One* (Washington: Biblical Archaeology Society, 1997c), 27–56.

——, "Archaeology, Ideology, and the Quest for an 'Ancient' or 'Biblical' Israel," *Near Eastern Archaeology* 61 (1998), 39–52.

Finkelstein, I., *The Archaeology of the Israelite Settlement* (Jerusalem: Israel Exploration Society, 1988).

Grabbe, L. L., ed., *Can a "History of Israel" Be Written?* (Sheffield: Sheffield Academic Press, 1997).

Halpern, B., *The First Historians: The Hebrew Bible and History* (San Francisco: Harper & Row, 1988).

Hayes, J. and J. Miller, eds., *Israelite and Judaean History* (London: SCM Press, 1986).

Hermann, S., *A History of Israel in Old Testament Times* (London: SCM Press, 1975).

Lemche, N. and T. Thompson, "Did Biran Kill David? The Bible in the Light of Archaeology," *Journal for the Study of the Old Testament* 64 (1994), 3–22.

Levy, T., ed., *The Archaeology of Society in the Holy Land* (Leicester: University of Leicester Press, 1995).

Mazar, A., *The Archaeology of the Land of the Bible, 10,000–586 BCE* (New York: Doubleday, 1990).

Pritchard, James, B., *The Ancient Near East in Pictures* (ANEP; Princeton: Princeton University Press, 1954).

Soggin, J., *A History of Israel: From the Beginning to the Bar Kochba Revolt, AD135* (London: SCM Press, 1984).

Thompson, T., *The Early History of the Israelite People from the Written and the Archaeological Sources* (Leiden: E. J. Brill, 1992).

——, *The Mythic Past: Biblical Archaeology and the Myth of Ancient Israel* (London: Jonathan Cape, 1999).

Van Seters, J., *In Search of History: Historiography in the Ancient World and the Origins of Biblical History* (New Haven: Yale University Press, 1983).

Weippert, H., *Palästina in vorhellenischter Zeit* (Munich: C. H. Beck, 1988).

Whitelam, K., *The Invention of Ancient Israel: The Silencing of Palestinian History* (London: Routledge, 1996).

Whitley, D., ed., *Reader in Archaeological Theory: Post-Processual and Cognitive Approaches* (London: Routledge, 1998).

CHAPTER 8

Biblical and Syro-Palestinian Archaeology

William G. Dever

Syro-Palestinian archaeology, as well as "biblical" archaeology (if the latter can be said still to exist), has progressed so far toward independent and highly specialized professional status in the last two decades or so that the non-specialist finds it almost impossible to keep up. This state-of-the-art assessment, covering the period of ca. 1975–2000, is intended as a user-friendly end of the millennium guide, especially for biblical scholars who may still envision a dialogue between the two pertinent disciplines. For reasons that will become apparent, our treatment will focus largely on Palestine (i.e., modern Israel and Jordan) and on the period of ancient Israel and the Hebrew Bible, or the Iron Age.

The History of the Discipline(s)

Periodic assessments of Syro-Palestinian and "biblical" archaeology have appeared from time to time, especially early on when a single scholar like Albright or Wright could still comprehend the field as a whole (see for example Albright, 1969; Wright, 1969). Yet no full-scale history of our branches of archaeology has ever been written, such as Willey and Sabloff's *A History of American Archaeology* (1980), or for that matter histories of other branches of Near Eastern archaeology.[1] The closest might be that of the Ashmolean Museum's P. R. S. Moorey, *A Century of Biblical Archaeology* (1991); but Moorey is not a specialist in the field, and furthermore his work is intended largely as a critique of a particular and no longer typical movement within the field. Elsewhere I have offered my own prolegomenon to a broader history, although still

Originally published in *Currents in Research: Biblical Studies*, vol. 8, 2000, pp. 91–116, as "Biblical and Syro-Palestinian Archaeology: A State-of-the-Art Assessment at the Turn of the Millennium."

from an admittedly Americanist perspective, in several shorter works (especially 1974; 1985; 1992a). Israeli archaeologists are not much inclined to self-reflection, but several essays give some insights into the way they view their own now dominant position in the field.[2] The few other "national schools," now peripheral (below), are represented by scant literature.[3]

Theory and Method

As the two branches of archaeology under review here began to diverge in the 1970s, discussions of theory and method, long neglected, began to emerge – particularly in attempts of a few to redefine the older-style "biblical archaeology," now under attack (Dever, 1974; 1981; 1988; 1992a; 1993a; and cf. Toombs, 1987; Meyers and Meyers, 1989; Bunimovitz, 1995). Meanwhile, the radical "New Archaeology" of the 1970s–1980s in America and Europe had come and gone, largely unnoticed in the scant theoretical literature in our field (Dever, 1981), and reflected in Israel only in certain pragmatic adaptations in fieldwork and analysis of materials (see below).

As early as 1985, "post-processualism" had already begun to supplant the New Archaeology in the broader discipline, but in our field there was scarcely a notice of this potentially revolutionary trend. "Post-processual" archaeology, pioneered as early as the mid-1980s by Ian Hodder of Cambridge and others, rejected the functionalist, determinist, and excessively anti-historical thrust of much of the New or processual archaeology and advocated a return to history-writing as a primary goal. Its emphasis on *cognition* – on the role of ideology in cultural change – should be especially congenial to many archaeologists in our field, as well as to biblical scholars.[4]

In summary, most advances in our field, although impressive, were and still are largely pragmatic, i.e., seen in more and better excavated data, and especially in a flood of improved publications (see below).

Keeping up with the Field

A generation or two ago there were only two handbooks in our field, Albright's classic *Archaeology of Palestine* (1949; only slight revisions in later editions); and Kenyon's semi-popular *Archaeology of the Holy Land* (1960; revised slightly in 1965, 1970). Scattered preliminary reports of excavations appeared in a few journals, but these were descriptive and impressionistic, often highly esoteric. There were brief but largely uncritical summaries of excavated sites in some biblical dictionaries. Yet overall the biblical historian, or for instance the archaeologist in another field, scarcely had access to the basic data, much less to informed interpretive and synthetic discussions in the literature.

Today the situation has changed, dramatically so in the past decade. Comprehensive and up-to-date handbooks now exist in such works as Helga Weippert's *Palästina in vorhellenistischer Zeit* (1988); Amihai Mazar's *Archaeology of the Land of the Bible, 10,000–586 BCE* (1990); the volume edited by Amnon Ben-Tor, *The Archaeology of Ancient Israel* (1992); and especially the superb collection of essays edited by Thomas E. Levy, *Archaeology of Society in the Holy Land* (1995). Other handbooks, more specialized, are Kempinski and Reich (1992); and older but still useful works such as Ruth Amiran's *Ancient Pottery of the Holy Land* (1970).

A goldmine of detailed site reports exists now in the four-volume *New Encyclopedia of Archaeological Excavations in the Holy Land*, edited by Ephraim Stern (1993; replacing the edition of 1975). Recent biblical dictionaries, such as those published by Harpers (Achtemeier, 1996), Mercer (Mills, 1990), or Eerdmans (Freedman, 2000), have employed archaeologists as consulting editors and thus contain many useful entries, on both sites and specific topics. Particularly noteworthy are the six-volume *Anchor Bible Dictionary*, edited by David Noel Freedman (1992); and the more specialized four-volume *Oxford Encyclopedia of Archaeology in the Near East* (1996), edited by Eric M. Meyers and others.

Older mainstream journals continue, especially the *Bulletin of the American Schools of Oriental Research* (1921–); the *Israel Exploration Journal* (1950–); and, of lesser importance, the *Zeitschrift des Deutschen Palästina-vereins* (1984–), and the *Revue Biblique* (1897–). The Israeli journal *Tel Aviv*, begun in 1974, has become a major reference work. Appearing annually in English, *Excavations and Surveys in Israel* (1982–) gives brief preliminary reports of most excavation projects; this is supplemented by the *Annual of the Department of Antiquities in Jordan* (1955–). In 1998 the venerable semi-popular *Biblical Archaeologist* (1938–) became *Near Eastern Archaeology*, with a broader and more professional appeal. Finally, one must mention the magazine *Biblical Archaeology Review* (1974–), which despite its sometimes sensationalist reporting contains many accessible and beautifully illustrated articles by leading American, Israeli, and other archaeologists.

A separate category of synthetic works consists of *Festschriften*, and especially the publication of international conference and symposia volumes. Particularly valuable *Festschriften* include those for D. Glenn Rose (Perdue, Toombs, and Johnson, 1987); and for J. A. Callaway (Drinkard, Mattingly, and Miller, 1988).

Especially noteworthy symposia volumes are the two volumes of the proceedings of the "First" and "Second International Congress on Biblical Archaeology in Jerusalem" (Amitai, 1985; Biran and Aviram, 1993). More recent symposia volumes of broad interest include *The Archaeology of Israel: Constructing the Past, Interpreting the Present* (Silberman and Small, 1997); and *Mediterranean Peoples in Transition: Thirteenth to Tenth Centuries BCE* (Gitin, Mazar, and Stern, 1998; the Trude Dothan *Festschrift*). The first "International Symposium on Near Eastern Archaeology," held in Rome in June of 1998, has a volume in press; and future symposia (Copenhagen, 2000; Paris, 2002) will publish their proceedings as well, including substantial sections on Syria–Palestine.

Recent and Current Trends

Earlier discussions of trends, in the 1970s–1980s, which dealt largely with the belated and minimal impact of the "New Archaeology" on our field, have been noted above. A few more recent treatments have attempted to update the discussion, but they have not necessarily outlined specific overall trends.[5] It may be useful to do so here.

Beyond "biblical archaeology"

By the mid-1980s the heated controversy over "biblical" vs. "Syro-Palestinian" archaeology had abated. It was now widely conceded that Syro-Palestinian archaeology had emerged as a full-fledged, highly specialized professional discipline, with its own aims and methods, independent of (though related to) biblical studies. Such an outcome could have been predicted; but it was assured by the somewhat later ascendancy of the Israeli and Jordanian "national schools." These had never been much influenced by the traditional European and American approaches, characterized as they were by a preoccupation with certain *theological* issues arising from the biblical texts.

Today, the "secularization" of archaeology being carried out by all parties in Israel, Jordan, and Syria is taken for granted. This is true despite recent attempts of a few European "revisionist" biblical scholars such as Davies, Lemche, Thompson, and Whitelam to revive the ghost of "biblical archaeology" as their whipping-boy in a radical attack on any historicity in the Hebrew Bible.[6]

"Biblical archaeology" is long since dead; its obituary has been written; and few mourn its passing. The term "biblical archaeology" itself is currently used by mainstream scholars only as a sort of popular shorthand for the dialogue *between* the two disciplines of Syro-Palestinian archaeology and biblical studies.[7] If the discussion about terminology were to be revived now, it would revolve around the question of whether Albright's original term "Syro-Palestinian" is really suitable after all for the larger discipline, as I had argued forcibly in the 1980s. Current political sensibilities in the Middle East have prompted younger American (and some European) archaeologists to speak rather of "the archaeology of the Southern Levant." Most Israelis, however, still use the term "Palestine" when writing about the past in English, despite growing uneasiness.[8]

A "paradigm shift"?

Although the belated impact of the "New Archaeology" on our field did not in itself produce a radical "paradigm shift" in the sense of Thomas Kuhn's well known *The Structure of Scientific Revolutions* (1970), it did bring lasting and beneficial changes. In particular, there has been a near-universal adoption of such familiar features of new or "processual" archaeology as: (1) the necessity for research design, or "problem-solving" archaeology; (2) an ecological orientation, or the study of sites in their larger environmental and cultural setting; (3) a growing emphasis on comprehensive regional surveys and the investigation of more small, rural, one-period sites; (4) the employment of multi-disciplinary methods in fieldwork, as well as in analysis and presentation (see below); (5) the desirability for moving beyond description to "explanations" of the cultural and historical processes, using appropriate socio-anthropological theory and cross-cultural comparisons; and (6) the increasing production of full, final published reports incorporating the vastly expanded data from modern stratigraphic and multidisciplinary methods, as well as their more sophisticated interpretation. By no means do all current projects in Israel or Jordan exhibit *all* of these desirable features, but an increasing number do; and European and American projects are expected to conform as well, if not to set the standards any longer.

Field and analytical methods

Any modern excavation in the Middle East will by now have adopted the three-dimensional stratigraphic methods introduced by British and American archaeologists in the 1960s–1970s, including the use of measured section-drawings. In some cases, however, the old "baulk-debris layer" method, employing a rigid 5 meter grid system, is being supplanted by "open-field" techniques employing a rolling-baulk. Other practical innovations include the use of various forms of aerial mapping; laser-beam transits; digital photography; ground-penetrating radar; and other scientific devices. In the laboratory, older C_{14} analysis is now supplemented by many other forms of analysis of botanical, zoological, skeletal, mineralogical, metallurgical, and other remains. And, of course, in all aspects of field recording, analysis, workup, graphics, and publication, computers have become basic and indispensable tools.

The maturation of the Middle Eastern "National Schools"

Until sometime in the 1970s, it might have appeared that the foreign schools in Israel and Jordan still dominated the scene, as they had done throughout the earlier 20th century. That is no longer true in Israel, or even in Jordan. In Jerusalem, the German school, the *Deutsche Evangelische Institut für Altertums-wissenschaft des Heiligen Landes*, has not carried out excavations for many years, and in fact closed in 1998 apart from maintaining a visiting scholar. The Dominican *L'École Pratique d'Études Bibliques* in Jerusalem, founded in 1902, now excavates only in Arab territories such as Gaza, and in Jordan. The British School of Archaeology in Jerusalem, founded in 1919, plans to close by 2002. Of the foreign institutions in Israel, only the two American schools – the older

W. F. Albright Institute of Archaeological Research (1900–), and the Nelson Glueck School of the Hebrew Union College–Jewish Institute of Religion (1963–) – maintain vigorous programs of archaeological fieldwork, research, and publication.[9] Similarly, the British and German schools in Jordan have very limited programs, but the American Center of Oriental Research (1968–) is a large and thriving institute, sponsoring much fieldwork and publication.

While the fortunes of most of the foreign schools have declined dramatically in the last twenty years, the local schools in Israel and Jordan have flourished by any criteria, and largely on their own initiative. The colonial era, where the burgeoning local schools were under the tutelage of foreign mentors, is long over. Elsewhere I have characterized the Israeli school specifically (Dever, 1985, 1989a). Here I would note simply that perhaps 90 percent of fieldwork and publication in Israel is Israeli-sponsored. There exist a large government agency, the Israel Antiquities Authority (the old Department of Antiquities); several dozen archaeological museums; four flourishing university departments or institutes of archaeology (Jerusalem, Tel Aviv, Beersheva, and Haifa); numerous publication series in Hebrew and English; dozens and dozens of excavations annually; and as many as 200 working professional people with graduate degrees in archaeology. In Jordan, the numbers are somewhat more modest, but the national school there is enjoying unprecedented growth – so much so that no one any longer can dismiss Jordan as the neglected "other half of the Holy Land." The Jordanians sponsor their own international symposia every few years, the papers published sumptuously in the series *Studies in the History and Archaeology of Jordan*.[10]

The national schools in the Middle East have, however, experienced some "growing pains" recently despite their overall success, perhaps even due in part to this success. (1) As developing countries (although hardly "Third World"), both Israel and Jordan have limited resources to devote to archaeology, never adequate. In Jordan, there is not yet the highly developed sense of archaeology as a national historical and cultural resource that one sees in Israel, so public and government support are sometimes difficult to justify. There is not yet, for instance, a Jordanian university that offers a Ph.D. in archaeology. Even in Israel, where public interest in archaeology approaches levels probably not found anywhere else in the world (sometimes a mania), the Antiquities Authority recently cut its full-time staff by more than one-third; and university budgets for archaeology are currently frozen or are even being reduced. It is candidly admitted by most Israeli archaeologists that without large American endowments their institutes of archaeology could not survive; and that their summer excavations are staffed and funded almost entirely by American student volunteers. Thus archaeology in both Israel and Jordan has grown so exponentially that it cannot support itself without foreign subsidies.

The irony, indeed the injustice, is that while American money goes to support Israeli and Jordanian archaeology, academic positions at home are disappearing; research funds are drying up; and, as I have recently argued (Dever, 1995a), the *discipline* is dying while popular interest continues unabated.

Archaeology and nationalism

The very ideological cohesiveness, concentration of resources, and pursuit of deliberate goals may pose risks for any national archaeological school, and those in the Middle East are no exception. In this particular case, *nationalism* poses the greatest danger. That is because Israel and Jordan (as well as the Palestinians) are in contention over the very same land whose history and culture archaeologists are confidently reconstructing on the basis of supposedly "objective" archaeological evidence. Archaeology can therefore all too easily be subverted to foster artificial notions of ethnicity; to legitimate exclusive claims to the land; and even to create racist notions of cultural superiority. Couple the Bible with such archaeologically-bolstered ideologies, and one has a truly volatile mixture.

Such excesses are never encountered, however, in either Israel or Jordan among professional archaeologists, and are rarely seen even in popular circles, although the temptation is ever present. Indeed a number of prominent Israeli writers have called attention to the problem, among them the Israeli historian Shavit (1997) and the well-known novelist Amos Elon (1997). They have suggested that for many secular Israelis, passion for the archaeology of "Eretz-Israel" (the Land) has become a sort of surrogate for religion – a nostalgia for a long-lost past, one that would offer security and fulfillment. Nationalism and a long sense of historical destiny in Jordan are somewhat less pronounced, for many reasons; and there is no "Bible" with which to make a direct connection (however imagined), so the problem may seem less acute. Nevertheless, one can imagine Jordanians being accused of focusing on Islamic sites to the exclusion of sites of other periods – as Israelis have been accused of giving priority to Iron Age (Israelite) sites.

The fact is that neither charge would be true. With rare exceptions, Israeli archaeologists have devoted themselves equally to every period, from the Lower Paleolithic to the Turkish period (cf. for instance the articles in Levy, 1995). If anything, Israelis until recently have neglected synagogue sites, which would seem to be of critical importance.[11] And Israel Finkelstein, the principal investigator of Iron I or "early Israelite" sites in the central hill country, has argued vociferously that *no* ethnic identification whatsoever can be made on the basis of the archaeological evidence – that in effect there *was* no recognizable "early Israel" (see below). Similarly, in Jordan, where Islamic archaeology might be thought to prevail, this period has been neglected in favor of others. One might ask: *What* "nationalistic archaeology"?

Archaeology and religious ideology

One aspect of the possible relationships between archaeology, religion, and nationalism is peculiar to Israel, namely the *hostility* between archaeology and the religious Establishment. As is well known, the *haredim*, or ultra-Orthodox

Jews, are so adamantly opposed to archaeology that they have sent mobs to physically threaten archaeologists in the field. They have destroyed archaeological sites and materials, and they have even tried to pass a law in the Knesset that would ban all excavations. The ostensible reason is that archaeologists "desecrate Jewish graves." Not only is this charge false, but I would suggest that the real reason is that the Orthodox (at least the extremists among them) simply fear any scientific investigation of their tradition. (And, of course, they are by and large "Messianists," not nationalists, so the combination of archaeology and national self-identity, would seem an especially unholy alliance to them.)[12]

General Trends

Several related trends in the archaeology of Israel and Jordan may be lumped together under the rubric of the question: "Who *owns* the past?" One aspect of the issue of the uses of the past is the reconstruction of archaeological sites by government agencies to promote tourism. While a certain amount of conservation, along with efforts to educate the public on the appreciation of archaeological sites, is commendable, some sites are in danger of becoming Disney World-like "theme-parks," designed for mass tourism. At first this may seem amusing or harmless, but there are inherent dangers. (1) The archaeological integrity of sites may be violated by commercial developers who care little about authenticity as long as the reconstruction is eye-catching. (2) Modern monumental reconstruction often uses methods that are in fact destructive, because they are non-reversible. (3) The choice of sites for development and areas for emphasis may encourage the nationalist and religious biases that we have noted above; sites like Massada have even become national "shrines." (4) In the mad rush to attract the public, uninformed government policy may supersede the judgment of the archaeologists excavating the sites, even dictating what can be dug, removed, or left. (5) Even under the best of supervision, mass tourism degrades and often permanently damages archaeological sites, which by definition constitute unique and irreplaceable cultural resources.

As examples of dangerous trends, I note the "development" of Tel Dan in Israel by the National Parks Authority. Visits are now so rigorously programmed, and so subject to biblicist propaganda in the site labels, that serious archaeological students will be offended. While less offensive, a number of sites in Jerusalem are so popularized and commercialized that they are frustrating to visit. In Jordan, sites like Jerash and Petra are so overcrowded that they are often unpleasant to tour; and the ever-present Tourist Police actually forbid any but licensed local tour guides. (Petra gets up to 3,000 tourists a day in the high season.)

Museums can also become tools of nationalist or other ideologies, as is increasingly recognized.[13] Yet here I see little or no abuse in Israel or Jordan thus far. The officials in charge seem very well aware of the problem, even with small private museums like the "Burnt House" museum in Jerusalem, which might easily lend itself to propaganda regarding the Roman destruction of Jerusalem in CE 70. The Israel Museum, the national repository, surely ranks among the best archaeological museums in the world; and it is hoped that the planned national museum in Amman will be of equally high standard.

The Larger Issues: Some "Case-Studies"

Many of the issues that we have discussed thus far have to do largely with the technique and trappings – even the politics – of archaeology. The larger issues, however, must be *intellectual* if archaeology is to be anything more than antiquarianism.

Here the challenges are immense, and many are urgent given the precarious situations that we have already noted. Here I can only highlight a few of the more critical current issues.

Chronology and terminology

If archaeology is simply a branch of history – writing "history from things," rather than from texts – then chronology provides the essential framework, and terminology scarcely less so.

In the last two decades, chronological and related terminological problems have been much debated, although primarily in terms of refining the traditional schemes set forth by Albright and others in the 1920s–1930s. For the prehistoric eras – Paleolithic–Chalcolithic – C_{14} dates continue to be our principal means of dating, and mounting evidence has clarified most phases. For the Bronze Age, we are now debating issues regarding a century or so, usually much less, and dependent as always largely on synchronisms with astronomically-fixed Egyptian chronology.[14] The major controversy has to do with "high," "middle," and "low" dates for the Middle Bronze Age in Palestine. Manfred Bietak, who is excavating the "Hyksos" capital of Avaris at Tell ed-Dab'a in the Egyptian Delta, opts for the "low" chronology, while almost all Palestinian archaeologists favor the "middle" chronology.[15] Both the chronological and terminological changes can be seen in table 8.1.

Table 8.1

Albright/traditional	Current consensus	Egyptian Dynasties
MB I – 2100–1900 BCE	EB IV – 2300–2000 BCE	6–11
MB IIA – 1900–1750 BCE	MB I – 2000–1750 BCE	12
MB IIB – 1750–1650 BCE	MB II – 1750–1650 BCE	13, 14
MB IIC – 1650–1550 BCE	MB II – 1650–1550/1500 BCE	15–17

Table 8.2

Phase	Approximate dates	Ancient Israel
Iron I	1200–1000 BCE	Period of Judges
Iron IIA	1000–900 BCE	United Monarchy
Iron IIB	900–700 BCE	Early Divided Monarchy
Iron IIC	700–586 BCE	Late Divided Monarchy
Iron III (Persian)	586–539 BCE	Exile

The Late Bronze Age poses problems only for its beginning and, especially, for its end (see below). The destruction of Late Bronze IIB sites can be dated anywhere from ca. 1250 to 1150 BCE. New C_{14} dates may place the fall of Hazor as early as 1250 BCE, with implications for the "Israelite conquest"; while Lachish was destroyed not before the time of Ramses VI, ca. 1140 BCE (Dever, 1992b).

The chronology of the Iron Age remains fixed within rather narrow margins by Egyptian and Mesopotamian synchronisms, together with biblical data. There are, however, still some uncertainties, especially when attempts are made to correlate archaeological phases with supposed events in biblical history, such as the accession of Solomon (ca. 960 or 970 BCE); or the date of the so-called "Solomonic defenses" (10th or 9th century BCE, see below). For the strictly archaeological phases, the scheme as detailed in table 8.2 is almost universally adopted (with biblical correlations).[16] The most pressing issue is the "10th–9th century BCE" controversy (below).

"Transitional Horizons"

With the enormous increase in the quantity and precision of our archaeo-chronometric data, transitional horizons, some newly defined, now emerge as the most fascinating yet intransigent phases. Among these are the Epipaleolithic/Mesolithic (ca. 12,000–8,500 BCE); the Late Chalcolithic/Proto-Urban/Early Bronze I (ca. 3500–3100 BCE); the Early Bronze IV (ca. 2400/2300–2000/1900 BCE); the Middle Bronze III/Late Bronze IA (ca. 1550–1450 BCE); and the Late Bronze IIB/Iron IA (ca. 1250–1150 BCE). In some senses, the remaining differences of opinion are not as great as they may seem. Many have to do with how one assesses elements of continuity/discontinuity, where there will always be legitimate differences; and many terminological disputes are merely semantic, i.e., matters of preference. The point is that we have *working* chronological and terminological formulae – a point that many biblical scholars, especially the "revisionists" (below) do not grasp. The notion that because leading archaeologists may differ on certain points, "they cannot date anything," is absurd and can only impede the dialogue that we need. (We can certainly date our artifacts much more closely than biblical scholars can date their texts.)

Poorly known periods

Despite the cumulative growth in the last two decades in our knowledge of the archaeology of ancient Palestine overall, a few periods have been neglected or else remain poorly illuminated despite our best efforts. If one compares the state of our knowledge just 20 years ago, however, with the situation now, it is evident that certain periods have witnessed spectacular discoveries, and persuasive syntheses are now beginning to appear. These include the Neolithic; the Chalcolithic; Early Bronze I–III; Early Bronze IV ("Intermediate Bronze"); Middle Bronze I–III; and Iron I (the 12th–11th centuries BCE, covering both the "Proto-Israelite" and the Sea Peoples/Philistine horizons).

The Late Bronze Age (ca. 1500–1200 BCE) is reasonably well known, but it has not been a particularly "hot topic" in the past generation. The Iron II period (ca. 900–600 BCE) has seen a steady increase in reliable information on a wide variety of topics, much of it bearing directly on possible reconstructions of the history and religions of ancient Israel (despite the "revisionists" ignoring this data). The Persian period, however (ca. 586–539 BCE), remains poorly known, partly because the ideal "type-sites" have not been located or else not extensively excavated.[17] The Hellenistic and Roman periods begin to be illuminated rather dramatically, particularly the latter, but this has not resulted in the emergence of a *discipline* of "New Testament archaeology" (or the "Archaeology of Late Antiquity"), comparable to the long and complex history of "Biblical/Old Testament" archaeology.[18]

The challenge of "revisionism"

In the last decade or so, *historiographical* issues have come to the fore in both archaeology and biblical studies. This development was long overdue, and it can only be beneficial, since history-writing is fundamental to both disciplines. Yet fierce controversies have raged over this issue, particularly in the 1990s. Indeed, it may be argued that this is the most critical issue confronting archaeology in relation to biblical studies today.

"Revisionism" began on the archaeological front in the early 1980s, when several archaeologists of the Tel Aviv University set out to lower the conventional 10th century date of the distinctive four-entryway city gates and casemate (or double) walls at Hazor, Megiddo, and Gezer to the early–mid-9th century BCE. This initially harmless move precipitated a critical historiographical crisis, because these monumental constructions had traditionally been not only dated confidently to the mid-10th century BCE – on stratigraphic and ceramic typological grounds, I would insist – but had also been taken by leading authorities as "confirmation" of the footnote in 1 Kgs 9:15–17 mentioning that Solomon had "built" or built-up/fortified four cities: Jerusalem, Hazor, Megiddo, and Gezer. The Tel Aviv group's idiosyncratic "low chronology," however, was not accepted by the Jerusalem school, or by any European or American archaeologist (it still is not widely accepted, even by all Tel Aviv archaeologists).[19] The "low chronology" was not only arguable archaeologically, but it would obviously have robbed the supposed "Solomonic kingdom" of much of its architectural basis (Holladay, 1995; Dever, 1997a).

By the early 1990s, a small but vocal group of European biblical scholars were beginning to argue that there *was* no "historical Solomon," no "United Monarchy" – indeed no Israelite state before the 9th century BCE, and no Judean state before the late 7th century BCE (if then). The brouhaha began with Sheffield's Philip R. Davies and his *In Search of "Ancient Israel"* (1992). For Davies, "biblical" and "ancient" Israel were simply modern "social constructs," reflecting the theological biases and quests of Jewish and Christian scholars, ancient and modern. A "historical" Israel was a remote possibility, but largely unknowable because of the limitations of archaeology, the only possible source of information (see below).

Later, even more radical works in this vein were produced throughout the 1990s by Keith W. Whitelam of the University of Stirling (Scotland) and by Niels Peter Lemche and Thomas L. Thompson of Copenhagen.[20] In the end, the Hebrew Bible contained no reliable history of *any* "Israel" in the Iron Age of Palestine, but was simply the original Zionist myth. Archaeology might in theory illuminate some "historical" Israel; but since archaeological data were largely "mute," the task should be given up. Instead, both Biblicists and archaeologists should be writing the history of the *Palestinian* people.

The literature on "revisionism" has burgeoned in the last decade, and the discussion by now has become exceedingly rancorous, leading scholars on the one hand being dismissed as "minimalists" or "nihilists," on the other as "maximalists," "credulists," or even "crypto-Fundamentalists." Since as an archaeologist I have written extensively on one side of this debate (Dever, 1995b; 1995c; 1997d; 1999a) I will confine myself here to a few methodological observations.

First, few archaeologists except myself have bothered to respond to the "revisionists'" efforts to write ancient Israel out of the history of Palestine, probably because it is self-evident to us that such an Israel *did* exist in the Iron Age. It is not *our* Israel that has been "invented" (to use Whitelam's phrase), but *theirs*. Nevertheless, I have argued that the "revisionists'" ignorance or deliberate abuse of archaeology must not be allowed to go unchallenged – not because it poses any real threat to our discipline, or to the histories of ancient Israel that will still be written, but for methodological reasons: it precludes any dialogue between two disciplines that are, after all, complementary. ("Revisionism" also raises serious theological problems, but I leave those to others; cf., Dever, 1997c).

Second, the Tel Aviv "low chronology," now less persuasive than ever, has been seized upon by the biblical "revisionists" to justify their denial of any Israelite state in the 10th century BCE. All the purported evidence of monumental architecture – and therefore of *centralized administration* – is 9th century BCE, rather than 10th century BCE. Unfortunately, Israel Finkelstein, who has now emerged as the leading (indeed the only well-published) proponent of archaeological revisionism, has been coopted by the Sheffield and Copenhagen group, even though he does not deny some small state-like entity in the 9th century BCE (Finkelstein, 1995, 362).

Of course, Finkelstein rarely calls this entity "Israel," any more than he will now concede that his own dozens of 12th–11th century BCE hill-country sites can be labeled "Israelite," even using my cautious term "Proto-Israelite." For Finkelstein, we cannot recognize "ethnicity" in the archaeological remains; but his appears to be a minority view.[21] Most archaeologists would hold that if we can distinguish Egyptians, Canaanites, Philistines, Aramaeans, Phoenicians, Ammonites, Moabites, and Edomites in the archaeological (and textual) record, why not "Israelites"? In that sense, mainstream Palestinian archaeologists remain overwhelmingly positivist: there was an "early Israel" in the 12th–11th centuries BCE; and an Israelite "state" by the 10th century BCE, however modest.

Epistemology

Implied in our brief discussion of historiography is a related issue, one even more fundamental than whether we can any longer write a satisfactory history of ancient Israel: Can we know *anything at all* with certainty about the past? The "revisionists" are inclined to say "No," which is why I have dubbed them the "new nihilists" (recalling the Albright/Bright/Wright vs. Alt/Noth controversy of the 1950s, but with far more negative results). They simply echo Nietzsche a century ago: "There are no facts, only interpretations."

Lurking behind the "revisionists'" loss of confidence in our ability to attain any secure knowledge of the past, I would argue, is a typical, although rarely acknowledged, adaptation of the "postmodern" paradigm that has plagued so many of the social sciences in the past two decades. Postmodernism holds that all claims to knowledge are merely "social constructs." Ancient texts – especially biblical texts – have become a "metanarrative" designed to privilege the Establishment, so they must be resisted, ultimately rejected. Furthermore, since such texts have no intrinsic meaning, are inherently contradictory, we can supply any "meaning" that we choose. In the end, everything becomes an issue of *politics*: race, class, gender, power. I would argue that postmodernism, revisionism, and deconstruction are all theories of knowledge according to which there *is* no knowledge. Obviously biblical historians and archaeologists who consider themselves historians in any sense cannot ignore such a challenge.[22]

"Revisionists," in particular, are fond of declaring that "archaeology is mute." My reply is "No; but some historians are deaf." Archaeology today speaks *volumes* about the reality of an ancient Israel in the Iron Age of Palestine; but the "revisionists" typically ignore or discredit the abundant data. Together, basic archaeological handbooks like those of Weippert, Mazar, Ben-Tor, and Levy have a total of some 1,000 pages of detailed, well documented archaeological information on the Iron Age, or Israelite period. Yet *nowhere* do the "revisionists" confront this body of data, not even to refute it. Even inscriptional data, which they might appreciate, are dismissed. The 9th century BCE Tel Dan inscription, which refers to "the House of David" and a "King of Israel" who must be Jehoram (ca. 849–842 BCE), has been declared by the "revisionists" a "forgery." The growing *corpus* of 8th–7th century BCE *bullae*, or seal-impressions, contains many modern "fakes." The Hezekiah tunnel inscription, securely dated paleographically to the campaign of Sennacherib in 701 BCE, has been declared a Hasmonean text of the 2nd century BCE, in effect another forgery as used by epigraphers.[23]

The overall skepticism of the "revisionists" and some other biblical scholars is scarcely justified, nor would it even be expressed if biblical scholars were better informed. Yet archaeologists themselves bear some responsibility for the absence of dialogue, partly because they have too often failed to publish their data in accessible form, but also because "archaeological hermeneutics" are less well developed than biblical hermeneutics. In fact, there is scarcely *any* theoretical literature on the subject, only discussions of specific controversies where differing principles of interpretation may be alluded to in passing. Such methodological naïveté (or simply confusion) is easily seen, for instance, in the "10th–9th century statehood" controversy treated above. It is not the "facts" that are usually in dispute (contrary to postmodernists, there are some), but their *interpretation* and, moreover, the principles on which any interpretation might rest. Archaeological "arguments" typically are *assertions*, based implicitly or explicitly on unpublished data, often merely disjointed information that has not yet been converted into real data by reference to pertinent questions; or based on appeal to various "authorities" whose opinions cannot be questioned. The irony here is that the two fundamental principles of modern archaeology – stratigraphy and comparative ceramic typology – can easily be defended on *empirical* grounds that would be considered definitive in any of the "real sciences".

What is lacking in our branch of archaeology is a body of appropriate theory and a fully articulated hermeneutic, both of which must be developed with specific reference to archaeological data (Dever, 1994) – in short, a way of "reading" *material culture remains* that is similar to that of reading texts. Elsewhere, I have attempted to outline hermeneutical principles for material culture data and textual data that would be similar, if not identical. That is because both artifacts and texts are symbols – "encoded messages" that seek to communicate a hidden reality. To read either, we need to know the language, grammar, syntax, and vocabulary.[24] Again, archaeology is *not* "mute." As Ernst Axel Knauf notes, the Hebrew Bible is mute for one who does not know Hebrew (Knauf, 1991, p. 41).

The survival of the discipline

We have noted above a number of both theoretical and practical difficulties that plague Syro-Palestinian archaeology. Nevertheless, this field of inquiry is now well developed as a specialized professional discipline, one with growing methodological sophistication, a rapidly expanding database, and in theory an almost limitless potential for generating exciting new knowledge of the past. But what of the *future?*

It seems clear that the national schools in the Middle East will continue to thrive, despite varying difficulties, although much depends upon the volatile political situation. What is not clear is whether the field that I have called here Syro-Palestinian archaeology will survive *outside* the Middle East as a professional and academic discipline. In Israel and Jordan, the few foreign schools will continue to have a place, and perhaps play a minor role; and some foreign excavations, especially American, will still be in the field in future. But unless we can soon train a new generation of students, place them in secure academic positions, and support their research and fieldwork, Syro-Palestinian archaeology will not survive *as a discipline* (Dever, 1995a).

Conclusion

There will always be popular support for this kind of archaeology, especially in Jewish and Christian circles in Europe and America where the Bible is still taken seriously. But amateur archaeology, even in the best sense, cannot sustain a professional discipline. Simply put, we will no longer be able to compete with the national schools in the Middle East. Already the Europeans have largely given up (see above); and American archaeologists are in danger of becoming marginalized.

This may sound alarmist, or even chauvinistic, but it is not. It only recognizes that the archaeology of the Holy Land belongs to all who are a part of the Western cultural tradition in any sense; and that archaeology is not an "armchair" discipline, but one that requires first-hand mastery of the data, in this case excavated remains. And if Syro-Palestinian archaeology – one partner in the hoped-for dialogue between archaeology and biblical studies – does not survive, "biblical archaeology" becomes a monologue, increasingly without authority or relevance, finally sterile.

Notes

1   Cf. Willey and Sabloff, 1980; Wilson, 1964; Lloyd, 1955; and for worldwide archaeology, see Lamberg-Karlovsky, 1989, and Trigger, 1989, both, however, with little specific reference to Near Eastern, much less to Syro-Palestinian archaeology.
2   Cf. Bar-yosef and Mazar, 1982; Mazar, 1988; Stern 1987; Bunimovitz, 1995, the latter the only explicitly theoretical approach. For an "outsider's" view of Israeli archaeology, see Dever, 1989a, with extensive literature.
3   For the British approach, see Davies, 1988; for the French school, Benoit, 1988; and for the German school, Weippert and Weippert, 1988.
4   For orientation to the burgeoning literature on "post-processualism," see Hodder, 1986; Preucel, 1991; Whitely, 1998; and for the only notice of "post-processualism" and its potential implications for Syro-Palestinian and biblical archaeology, see Dever, 1993a.

5   See generally the works cited in nn. 1–3 above; and for more current overviews, cf. Meyers and Meyers, 1989; Dever, 1992a; and Bunimovitz, 1995.

6   "Revisionist" literature is much too cumbersome to cite here; but for full references until ca. 1999 and a critique from an archaeological perspective, see Dever, 1995b; 1995c; 1998; 1999; and Stager, forthcoming. For the belated impact of "revision-ism" on specific archaeological controversies such as the question of the rise of the Israelite and Judean states, see below and nn. 19–25.

7   In retrospect, the pivotal statement seems to be that of mine in 1985 (Dever, 1985). Unfortunately, the presumed dialogue between the two new separate disciplines has not materialized, and it may even be more remote than ever, due largely to the historiographical and epistemological crises discussed below.

8   In Hebrew, of course, the preferred term is "the archaeology of Eretz–Israel." Israelis use the term "biblical archaeology" largely for popular English-speaking audiences, but it *never* carries the theological or even religious connotations of American-style "biblical archaeology"; cf. Dever, 1989b; Ben-Tor and Doron, 1998.

9   For a history of the Albright Institute and its parent, the American Schools of Oriental Research, see King, 1983. These institutions, of course, perpetuate much of the legacy of their mentor Albright, although much of his overarching concep-tion of the field is dated today; cf. Dever, 1993b. The Hebrew Union College–Jewish Institute of Religion in Jerusalem is now largely an American Reform Rabbinical school, although the affiliated "Nelson Glueck School of Biblical Archaeology" is Israeli-directed.

10 This series, published by the Department of Antiquities in Jordan, has now reached volume 6 (1982–). The *Annual of the Department of Antiquities in Jordan* has been mentioned above. For recent synthetic surveys of archaeology in Jordan, see Dornemann, 1983; Geraty and Herr, 1986; Bienkowski, 1992; Edelman, 1995.

11 See the valuable survey of "the archaeology of Late Antiquity" by Eric Meyers in *Currents* (1994), including bibliography on synagogue sites. On the dangers of nationalism in general in archaeology, see Marcus and Fischer, 1986; Shanks and Tilley, 1987; Meskell, 1998 (especially the chapter by Neil Silberman on Palestin-ian archaeology).

12 See the perceptive comments of Elon, 1997; Shavit, 1997.

13 On museums as purveyors of ideology, often nationalistic, see for instance Shanks and Tilley, 1987, pp. 68–99.

14 The chronology of Syria–Palestine from earliest periods (Paleolithic) through the Early Bronze Age (ca. 2000 BCE) is masterfully surveyed in Ehrich, 1992. For the Middle Bronze–Late Bronze–Iron I sequence (to ca. 1000 BCE), see Dever, 1992b. For the Iron II period (to ca. 600 BCE), see Galil, 1996, although mostly for events as narrated in the Hebrew Bible.

15 Cf. Dever, 1992b, with full references to Bietak's excavations at Tell ed-Dabʻa; and add now Bietak, 1996.

16 For syntheses on the Iron Age, including terminology and dates, cf. Weippert, 1988, pp. 354–681; Mazar, 1990, pp. 295–530; Ben-Tor, 1992, pp. 302–73; Levy, 1995, pp. 368–431.

17 Although now outdated, see Stern 1982, and also his forthcoming volume in the Anchor Bible Reference Volume series; see also Meyers, 1994.

18 Practically speaking, "biblical" has always meant the Old Testament, not New, in archaeology, possibly because both the historiographical and theological issues of

Ancient Israel/the Iron Age were regarded as more pertinent to archaeological investigation. For example, one could query the Exodus–Conquest tradition archaeologically; but what could one say archaeologically of the Virgin Birth or the Resurrection? See further Meyers, 1994.

19   For orientation, see Dever, 1990; 1997a; Finkelstein, 1995; 1996a; 1998; Mazar, 1997; Ben-Tor and Ben-Ami, 1998. All American archaeologists, all of the Jerusalem school, and many of the Tel Aviv group as well, still uphold the conventional (neither "high" nor "low") chronology.

20   See references in n. 6 above.

21   Cf. Dever, 1995b; 1995c; 1997b; 1999; Finkelstein, 1988; 1996b.

22   For devastating critiques of "post-modernism," see the comments of Barton, 1996, pp. 234–5; and especially Gress, 1998. I have demonstrated that the biblical "revisionists" are indeed "post-modernists" in Dever, 1999a; 1999b.

23   Cf. Lemche and Thompson, 1995; Davies and Rogerson, 1996; Carroll, 1997.

24   See Dever, 1997c, for an expansion on the idea of similar hermeneutics for the two classes of data. "Reading material culture as text" is a very common theme of "post-processualist" archaeology; cf. Hodder, 1986; Tilley, 1990; Kingery, 1996.

Bibliography

Achtemeier, P., ed., *The Harper Collins Bible Dictionary*, revised edn. (San Francisco: HarperSanFrancisco, 1996).

Albright, W., "The Impact of Archaeology on Biblical Research – 1996," in D. Freedman and J. Greenfield, eds., *New Directions in Biblical Archaeology* (Garden City: Doubleday, 1969), 1–14.

Amiran, R., *Ancient Pottery of the Holy Land* (New Brunswick: Rutgers University Press, 1970).

Amitai, J., ed., *Biblical Archaeology Today, 1983. Proceedings of the First International Congress on Biblical Archaeology, Jerusalem, June 1983* (Jerusalem: Israel Exploration Society, 1985).

Barton, J., *Reading the Old Testament: Method in Biblical Studies* (London: Darton, Longman, and Todd, 1996).

Bar-yosef, O. and A. Mazar, "Israeli Archaeology," *World Archaeology* 13 (1982), 310–25.

Benoit, P., "French Archaeologists," in J. Drinkard, G. Mattingly and J. Miller, eds., *Benchmarks in Time and Culture: Essays in Honor of Joseph A. Callaway* (Atlanta: Scholars Press, 1988), 63–86.

Ben-Tor, A., ed., *The Archaeology of Ancient Israel* (New Haven: Yale University Press, 1992).

Ben-Tor, A. and B.-A. Doron, "Hazor and the Archaeology of the Tenth Century BCE," *Israel Exploration Journal* 48 (1998), 1–37.

Bienkowski, P., ed., *Early Edom and Moab: The Beginning of the Iron Age in Southern Transjordan* (Sheffield: J. R. Collins, 1992).

Bietak, M., *Avaris, The Capital of the Hyksos: Recent Excavations at Tell el-Dabʿa* (London: British Museum Press, 1996).

Biran, A. and J. Aviram, eds., *Biblical Archaeology Today, 1993. Proceedings of the Second International Congress on Biblical Archaeology, Jerusalem, June 1990* (Jerusalem: Israel Exploration Society, 1993).

Bunimovitz, S., "How Mute Stones Speak Up: Interpreting What We Dig Up," *Biblical Archaeology Review* 21 (1995), 58–67, 96.

Carroll, R., "Madonna of Silences: Clio and the Bible," in L. Grabbe, ed., *Can a "History of Israel" Be Written?* (Sheffield: Sheffield Academic Press, 1997), 84–103.

Davies, G., "British Archaeologists," in J. Drinkard, G. Mattingly and J. Miller, eds., *Benchmarks in Time and Culture: Essays in Honor of Joseph A. Callaway* (Atlanta: Scholars Press, 1988), 37–62.

Davies, P. R., *In Search of "Ancient Israel"* (Sheffield: Sheffield Academic Press, 1992).

Davies, P. and J. Rogerson, "Was the Siloam Tunnel Built by Hezekiah?" *Biblical Archaeologist* 59/3 (1996), 138–49.

Dever, W., *Archaeology and Biblical Studies: Retrospects and Prospects* (Evanston: Seabury-Western Theological Seminary, 1974).

——, "The Impact of the 'New Archaeology' on Syro-Palestinian Archaeology," *BASOR* 242 (1981), 15–29.

——, "Syro-Palestinian and Biblical Archaeology," in D. Knight and G. Tucker, eds., *The Hebrew Bible and Its Modern Interpreters* (Philadelphia: Fortress Press, 1985), 31–74.

——, "Impact of the 'New Archaeology,'" in J. Drinkard, G. Mattingly and J. Miller, eds., *Benchmarks in Time and Culture: Introduction to Palestinian Archaeology* (Atlanta: Scholars Press, 1988), 337–52.

——, "Archaeology in Israel Today: A Summation and Critique," in S. Gitin and W. Dever, eds., *Recent Excavations in Israel: Studies in Iron Age Archaeology* (Winona Lake: American Schools of Oriental Research, 1989a), 143–52.

——, "Yigael Yadin: Prototypical Biblical Archaeologist," *Eretz-Israel* 20 (1989b), 44*–51*.

——, "Of Myths and Methods," *BASOR* 277/278 (1990), 121–30.

——, "Archaeology, Syro-Palestinian and Biblical," in D. Freedman, ed., *The Anchor Bible Dictionary* (New York: Doubleday, 1992a), 354–67.

——, "The Chronology of Syria–Palestine in the Second Millennium BC: A Review of Current Issues," *BASOR* 288 (1992b), 1–25.

——, "Biblical Archaeology: Death and Rebirth?" in A. Biran and J. Aviram, eds., *Biblical Archaeology Today, 1990. Proceedings of the Second International Congress on Biblical Archaeology, Jerusalem 1990* (Jerusalem: Israel Exploration Society, 1993a), 706–22.

——, "What Remains of the House that Albright Built?" *Biblical Archaeologist* 56 (1993b), 25–35.

——, "Archaeology, Texts, and History – Toward an Epistemology," in M. Hopfe, ed., *Uncovering Ancient Stones: Essays in Memory of H. Neil Richardson* (Winona Lake, IN: Eisenbrauns, 1994), 105–17.

——, "The Death of a Discipline?" *Biblical Archaeology Review* 21 (1995a), 50–5, 70.

——, "The Identity of Early Israel: A Rejoinder to Keith W. Whitelam," *JSOT* 72 (1995b), 3–24.

——, "Will the Real Israel Please Stand Up? Archaeology and Israelite Historiography: Part I," *BASOR* 297 (1995c), 61–80.

——, "New Archaeological Data and Hypothesis on the Origins of Ancient Israel," in J. Bartlett, ed., *Archaeology and Biblical Interpretation* (London: Routledge, 1997a), 25–50.

——, "Archaeology and the 'Age of Solomon': A Case Study in Archaeology and Historiography," in L. Handy, ed., *The Age of Solomon: Scholarship at the Turn of the Millennium* (Leiden: E. J. Brill, 1997b), 217–51.

——, "On Listening to the Text – and the Artifacts," in W. Dever and J. Wright, eds., *Echoes of Many Texts: Reflections on Jewish and Christian Traditions. Essays in Honor of Lou H. Silberman* (Atlanta: Scholars Press, 1997c), 1–23.

——, "Revisionist Israel Revisited: A Rejoinder to Niels Peter Lemche," *Currents in Research: Biblical Studies* 4 (1997d), 35–50.

——, "Archaeology, Ideology, and the Quest for an 'Ancient' or 'Biblical' Israel," *Near Eastern Archaeology* 61 (1998), 39–52.

——, "Histories and Nonhistories of Ancient Israel: A Review Article," *BASOR* 316 (1999), 39–52.

Dornemann, R., *The Archaeology of the Transjordan in the Bronze and Iron Ages* (Milwaukee: Milwaukee Public Museum, 1983).

Drinkard, J., G. Mattingly and J. Miller, eds., *Benchmarks in Time and Culture: Essays in Honor of Joseph A. Callaway* (Atlanta: Scholars Press, 1988).

Edelman, D., ed., *You Shall Not Abhor an Edomite for He Is Your Brother: Edom and Seir in History and Tradition* (Atlanta: Scholars Press, 1995).

Ehrich, R., ed., *Chronologies in Old World Archaeology*, 3rd revised edn. (Chicago: University of Chicago Press, 1992).

Elon, A., "Politics and Archaeology," in N. Silberman and D. Small, eds., *The Archaeology of Israel: Constructing the Past/Interpreting the Present* (Sheffield: Sheffield Academic Press, 1997), 34–47.

Finkelstein, I., *The Archaeology of the Israelite Settlement* (Jerusalem: Israel Exploration Society, 1988).

——, "The Great Transformation: The 'Conquest' of the Highlands Frontiers and the Rise of the Territorial States," in T. Levy, ed., *The Archaeology of Society in the Holy Land* (London: Leicester University Press, 1995), 349–65.

——, "The Archaeology of the United Kingdom: An Alternative View," *Levant* 28 (1996a), 177–87.

——, "Ethnicity and Origin of the Iron I Settlers in the Highlands of Canaan. Can the Real Israel Stand Up?" *BA* 59 (1996b), 198–212.

——, "Pots and Peoples Revisited: Ethnic Boundaries in the Iron Age," in N. Silberman and D. Small, eds., *The Archaeology of Israel: Constructing the Past, Interpreting the Present* (Sheffield: Sheffield Academic Press, 1996c), 216–37.

——, "Bible Archaeology or Archaeology of Palestine in the Iron Age?" *Levant* 30 (1998), 167–74.

Freedman, D., ed., *The Anchor Bible Dictionary* (New York: Doubleday, 1992).

——, *Eerdmans Bible Dictionary* (Grand Rapids: Eerdmans, 2000).

Galil, G., *The Chronology of the Kings of Israel and Judah* (Leiden: E. J. Brill, 1996).

Geraty, L. and L. Herr, eds., *The Archaeology of Jordan and Other Studies* (Berrien Springs, MI: Andrew University, 1986).

Gitin, S., A. Mazar and E. Stern, eds., *Mediterranean Peoples in Transition: Thirteenth to Tenth Centuries BCE* (Jerusalem: Israel Exploration Society, 1998).

Grabbe, L., ed., *Can a "History of Israel" Be Written?* (Sheffield: Sheffield Academic Press, 1997).

Gress, D., *From Plato to Nato: The Idea of the West and Its Opponents* (New York: The Free Press, 1998).

Hodder, I., *Reading the Past: Current Approaches to Interpretation in Archaeology* (Cambridge: Cambridge University Press, 1986).

Holladay, J., "The Kingdoms of Israel and Judah: Political and Economic Centralization in the Iron IIA–B (ca. 1000–750 BCE)," in T. Levy, ed., *The Archaeology of Society in the Holy Land* (London: Leicester University Press, 1995), 368–98.

Kempinski, A. and R. Reich, eds., *The Architecture of Ancient Israel from the Prehistoric to the Persian Period* (Jerusalem: Israel Exploration Society, 1992).

King, P., *American Archaeology in the Mideast: A History of the American Schools of Oriental Research* (Philadelphia: American Schools of Oriental Research, 1983).

Kingery, D., ed., *Learning from Things: Method and Theory of Material Culture Studies* (Washington: Smithsonian Institution, 1996).

Knauf, E., "From History to Interpretation," in D. Edelman, ed., *The Fabric of History: Text, Artifact and Israel's Past* (Sheffield: Almond Press, 1991), 26–64.

Kuhn, T., *The Structure of Scientific Revolutions*, 2nd edn. (Chicago: University of Chicago, 1970).

Lamberg-Karlovsky, C., ed., *Archaeological Thought in America* (Cambridge: Cambridge University Press, 1989).

Lemche, N. and T. Thompson, "Did Biran Kill David? The Bible in the Light of Archaeology," *JSOT* 64 (1995), 3–22.

Levy, T., ed., *The Archaeology of Society in the Holy Land* (London: Leicester University Press, 1995).

Lloyd, S., *Foundations in the Dust: The Story of Exploration in Mesopotamia and the Great Archaeological Discoveries Made There* (Harmondsworth: Penguin Books, 1955).

Marcus, G. and M. Fischer, *Archaeology as Cultural Critique: An Experimental Moment in the Human Sciences* (Chicago: University of Chicago, 1986).

Mazar, A., "Israeli Archaeologists," in J. Drinkard, G. Mattingly and J. Miller, eds., *Benchmarks in Time and Culture: Essays in Honor of Joseph A. Callaway* (Atlanta: Scholars Press, 1988), 109–28.

——, *Archaeology of the Land of the Bible, 10,000–586 BCE* (New York: Doubleday, 1990).

——, "Iron Age Chronology: A Reply to I. Finkelstein," *Levant* 29 (1997), 155–65.

Meskell, L., ed., *Archaeology Under Fire* (London: Routledge, 1998).

Meyers, E., "Second Temple Studies in the Light of Recent Archaeology, Part I: Persian and Hellenistic Periods," *Currents in Research: Biblical Studies* 2 (1994), 25–42.

Meyers, E., ed., *The Oxford Encyclopedia of Archaeology in the Near East* (New York: Oxford University Press, 1996).

Meyers, E. and C. Meyers, "Expanding the Frontiers of Biblical Archaeology," *Eretz-Israel* 20 (1989), 140*–47.*

Mills, W., ed., *Mercer Dictionary of the Bible* (Macon: Mercer University Press, 1990).

Moorey, R., *A Century of Biblical Archaeology* (Louisville: Westminster/Knox, 1991).

Perdue, L., L. Toombs and G. Johnson, eds., *Archaeology and Biblical Interpretation* (Atlanta: John Knox Press, 1987).

Preucel, R., ed., *Processual and Postprocessual Archaeologies: Multiple Ways of Knowing the Past* (Carbondale: Southern Illinois University, 1991).

Shanks, M. and C. Tilley, *Re-Constructing Archaeology: Theory and Practice* (Cambridge: Cambridge University Press, 1987).

Shavit, Y., "Archaeology, Political Culture, and Culture in Israel," in N. Silberman and D. Small, eds., *The Archaeology of Israel: Constructing the Past, Interpreting the Present* (Sheffield: Sheffield Academic Press, 1997), 48–61.

Silberman, N. and D. Small, eds., *The Archaeology of Israel: Constructing the Past, Interpreting the Present* (Sheffield: Sheffield Academic Press, 1997).

Stager, L. E., "Archaeology and Revisionism," forthcoming.

Stern, E., *The Material Culture of the Land of the Bible in the Persian Period* (Warminster: Aris and Phillips, 1982).

——, "The Bible and Israeli Archaeology," in L. Perdue, L. Toombs and G. Johnson, eds., *Archaeology and Biblical Interpretation* (Atlanta: John Knox Press, 1987), 31–40.

Stern, E., ed., *The New Encyclopedia of Archaeological Excavations in the Holy Land* (Jerusalem: Massada Press, 1993).

Tilley, C., ed., *Reading Material Culture: Structuralism, Hermeneutics and Post-Structuralism* (Oxford: Basil Blackwell, 1990).

Toombs, L., "A Perspective on the New Archaeology," in L., Perdue, L. Toombs and G. Johnson, eds., *Archaeology and Biblical Interpretation* (Atlanta: John Knox, 1987), 41–52.

Trigger, B., *A History of Archaeological Thought* (Cambridge: Cambridge University Press, 1989).

Weippert, H., *Palästina in vorhellenistischer Zeit* (Wiesbaden: C. H. Beck, 1988).

Weippert, M. and H. Weippert, "German Archaeologists," in J. Drinkard, G. Mattingly and J. Miller, eds., *Benchmarks in Time and Culture: Essays in Honor of Joseph A. Callaway* (Atlanta: Scholars Press, 1988), 87–107.

Whitely, D., *Reader in Architectural Theory: Post-processual and Cognitive Approaches* (London: Routledge, 1998).

Willey, G. and J. Sabloff, *A History of American Archaeology*, 2nd edn. (San Francisco: Freeman, 1980).

Wilson, J., *Signs and Wonders upon Pharaoh* (Chicago: University of Chicago, 1964).

Wright, G., "Biblical Archaeology Today," in D. Freedman and J. Greenfield, eds., *New Directions in Biblical Archaeology* (Garden City: Doubleday, 1969), 149–65.

PART IV

The Religious and Social World of Ancient Israel and Early Judaism

CHAPTER 9
Canaan

Dennis Pardee

A great deal of discussion has been devoted to the proper definition of Canaan, in historical, geographical, and literary terms. In the present context, the title of this chapter is to be understood as a conventional abbreviation for the various cultures of Palestine and Syria previous to and contemporary with the Hebrew Bible. Even more specifically, this chapter will deal primarily with the written sources, and its purview will therefore extend from the invention of writing in ca. 3000 BCE to roughly the turn of the eras.

As regards the narrow sense of the term Canaan, two bodies of texts attest to the use of the term (Kinahnu), first in the Middle Bronze Age, then in the Late Bronze Age. In the 18th century texts from Mari, the term designated at least the Beka valley (Durand, 1997, p. 49; 1999, p. 157), while in the 14th century it was used to designate the area controlled by Egypt on the Asiatic continent and thus included the Lebanese coast, Palestine, and the Transjordan (Rainey, 1996b; Na'aman, 1999). Because the purview of the former body of texts rarely extends into Palestine, one may extrapolate backwards from the later texts and surmise that the area designated by the term may have in the 18th century extended further south than the area actually mentioned in the texts.

The term Amurru is attested earlier, for it occurs in some of the earliest Mesopotamian sources to designate the west and westerners (usually written logographically as MAR.TU). In the 18th century, the term designated an area north of Canaan that touched the sea; it was, however, in all probability a vaster area, for it is known to have had at least four kings, though their cities are unfortunately not named (Durand, 1999, p. 156). In the 14th–12th centuries, a small kingdom situated in the same area, that is, in the Homs Gap between Canaan and Ugarit, bore the name Amurru. Until the names of the Amurrite cities of the 18th century are known, it is fruitless to speculate on the extent of the area specifically known by that name (cf. Durand, 1997, p. 49). The term Amorite (i.e., Amurrite), however, following Mesopotamian usage, is also used to designate all the westerners who penetrated Mesopotamia in the late third millennium – and there is no reason to doubt that many of them came from the area that would then have been known as Amurru, perhaps more extensive than what is specifically attested in the 18th century sources and perhaps in part non-urban. The term is used to cover a multitude of sub-groups (usually designated in the literature as tribes or clans) who probably spoke a number of West-Semitic dialects. No Amorite literature has yet been discovered, and their language is known only from the names they bore and from a few of their own words that crept into the texts they wrote in Akkadian (Malamat, 1989). These westerners were depicted in the Mesopotamian literature as uncultured, but they infiltrated the area, became urbanized, adopted Mesopotamian culture, and eventually assumed political control. In the Amorite heyday, known by various groups of texts dating to the 18th–17th centuries, groups definable by their names as Amorites controlled most of the so-called Fertile Crescent, certainly from Hazor to Babylon (the famous Hammurabi is an Amorite name, *Ammurapi*), at least as far north as Aleppo, as far northwest as Ugarit and Alalakh.

It appears clear that, until (and, for that matter, contemporaneous with) the shrinkage of Amurru to a small state in the Late Bronze Age, both terms were regional in scope. This is reflected in the facts that each would have had kings, rather than a king, and that the name of the capital of the Late Bronze kingdom of Amurru was a city called Ṣumur, not Amurru.

In the Hebrew Bible, the terms Canaanite and Amorite have lost specific geographical value, though remnants of the previous situation may remain: the Canaanites are said to have lived primarily in the coastal plains, the Amorites in the mountains and to the east of the Jordan (specifically the kingdoms of Heshbon and Bashan). One may hypothesize that the 14th century extension of Canaan into Transjordan was a reflection of Egyptian administration and that Amurru may originally have extended south of Damascus.

In modern linguistic usage, the Canaanite languages are those that share a group of features that may be traced at least in part as far back as the 14th century (Hackett, 1997; Pardee, forthcoming a). Primary among these is the so-called Canaanite shift, that of /ā/ to /ō/. Languages sharing these features, primarily Hebrew and Phoenician, are later attested in the area known as Canaan in the 14th century, i.e., Phoenicia, Palestine, and southern Transjordan. The relatively few second-millennium data on the Amorite language/dialects show that they did not share the Canaanite features. For example, the word corresponding to later Hebrew *gōy*, ethnic group, was pronounced *gāy(um)* by 18th century Amorites. Because of these differences and in spite of the dearth of details for Amorite, it is generally regarded as a second major linguistic entity over against Canaanite. Finally, in the first millennium, a major new linguistic entity appears, Aramaic, which also differs from the Canaanite languages of the period. Because the western Aramaeans, at least (as opposed to the Chaldaeans of eastern Mesopotamia), appear in an area that was once Amorite (namely, eastern Syria), it is not impossible that Aramaic represents a first-millennium development of one of the Amorite languages/dialects. Both Canaanite, in its Hebrew guise, and Aramaic, in several forms (Jewish Aramaic, Syriac, Mandaean, and various other dialects), have endured to this day, in both literary and spoken forms.

The inclusion of Amurru in this introduction was necessary because by far the most extensive extra-biblical source of data on the Canaanites comes from ancient Ugarit, a site on the north coast of Syria with impeccable Amorite connections (Pardee, 1997j) and whose inhabitants considered Canaanites to be in some sense foreign (Rainey, 1996b). Indeed, the similarity of Canaanite and Amorite personal names, both in grammatical formation and in theological content (many personal names incorporate a divine name, known as the theophoric element), indicates a similar linguistic and cultural heritage. This is true to the point that the division into Canaanites and Amorites reflects subdivisions, proper to the periods under discussion, of an older ethno-linguistic entity corresponding to older common West Semitic. (The precise filiation of the various West Semitic languages is still very much a subject of debate: see, for example, Tropper, 1994; Huehnergard, 1995; Pardee, 1997i.)

Literary Sources

Writing emerged near the end of the fourth millennium BCE, probably in Mesopotamia for the purpose of writing Sumerian and it was borrowed shortly thereafter by the Egyptians (Daniels, 1997; Civil, 1997; Loprieno, 1997), though there are proponents of an Egyptian invention. The alphabetic form of writing was invented over a millennium later, is first attested in a series of brief inscriptions from Sinai and southern Canaan of which the present state of decipherment must be judged unsatisfactory, and came to current use in Syria–Palestine during the second half of the second millennium BCE (Pardee, 1997a, f, g), though the only well-attested West-Semitic language from the period is Ugaritic (see below).

The first important body of inscriptions from Syria–Palestine dates to ca. 2400 and is thus entirely in cuneiform. These texts were discovered at Tell Mardikh (ancient Ebla) in north-central Syria in the 1970s and constitute one of the most important textual discoveries of the second half of that century, for they illustrate a very early use of writing outside of Mesopotamia proper. The texts are for the most part administrative in nature, though there are some ritual and incantational texts. The language in which they are written has been a subject of discussion, though there is general agreement that it is an archaic form of Semitic, closer to East Semitic (Akkadian) than to West Semitic. At this very early stage in the use of the Sumerian writing system for writing a different language, the convention observed is almost wholly logographic, that is, the texts are written as a sequence of Sumerian words, but with an occasional local word or morpheme spelled syllabically, an indication that the entire text was probably read in the local language. The international team responsible for publishing the texts has bit by bit teased out many features of the local language. It shows more similarities with the East-Semitic Akkadian written at this period in Mesopotamia than with West Semitic, though the latter is only attested later, and there presently exists, therefore, no direct point of comparison. Because divine names appear in so many types of texts (administrative, ritual, incantations; in personal names and in place names . . .), the Eblaite pantheon is probably the best-known aspect of central-Syrian religion of the time. It proves to be heavily influenced by Mesopotamian culture, but also to include many local deities as well as a good proportion of deities attested in the more abundant texts of the second and first millennia, e.g., Rashap, an important deity at Ugarit, or Gamish, generally admitted to be an early form of Kemosh, also known from Ugarit and the patron deity of Moab in the first millennium. (A handy recent bibliography on all aspects of Eblaite studies is available in Guardata, Baldacci, and Pomponio, 1997.)

No significant body of texts appears in Syria for another half-millennium. (To keep the chronological track straight: we are descending to about the time when the first attested Proto-Sinaitic and Proto-Canaanite were written – see above.) A series of corpora are attested from various sites in Syria written in the Old-Babylonian dialect of Akkadian, the most important of which is that of Mari (Tell Hariri on the Middle Euphrates), where upwards of 20,000 texts have been unearthed, with much smaller but important groups of texts from the same general area (e.g., Tell Leilan, Tell Rimah) or from further west (e.g., Alalakh, capital of ancient Mukish, later Antioch, near the mouth of the Orontes). By this time, the Sumerian writing system had been fully adapted for writing Akkadian syllabically, and the texts are in a fairly pure form of Babylonian Akkadian, permitting a reasonably straightforward process of decipherment and interpretation. As was the case at Ebla, most of the texts are basically administrative in nature, though the Mari archives contained many more letters, which reveal more events and more of the thought-processes associated with events than do simple lists. It is from these texts that we learn most of what we know about the Amorites who had taken over much of Babylonia and Assyria by the 18th century. Because they had adopted the Babylonian form of expression, however, there are virtually no texts in the Amorite language, and our knowledge of the language is, therefore, derived from the proper names and the odd local word that slips into an Akkadian text (one illustration is provided above, see p. 152). As at Ebla, the pantheon is a combination of Mesopotamian and local deities, though a higher percentage of the latter are now identifiable with West-Semitic deities known from the later texts. For example, one meets here both the single Mesopotamian deity Ishtar and the West-Semitic Ashtarat, the female equivalent of male Ashtar (at Ugarit, both Ashtar and Ashtarat are well attested). The potential contributions of even mundane administrative texts is illustrated by the mention in one of a rite that reflects the later Ugaritic myth of Baal's conflict with the Sea (Durand, 1993; Bordreuil and Pardee, 1993). If not simply the borrowing of a proto-Ugaritic myth, this rite would illustrate that the Amorite group to whom it was important once dwelt by the sea. The Amorites of north and northeast Syria had contacts with western Syria/Lebanon and even with northern Palestine, for the city of Hazor is mentioned several times (Bonechi, 1991). The city of Ugarit apparently held great attraction for these Amorites of the east, for one of the kings of Mari, Zimri-Lim, personally made the journey, passing through Yamhad (Aleppo) on the way, well over a thousand kilometers round trip. The contacts with the central-Syrian cities were regular, in particular with Aleppo, tied to the Mari court by matrimonial bonds (Zimri-Lim married the daughter of the king of Aleppo), and with Qatna. (The bibliography on Mari is immense; for handy introductions, see Margueron, 1997, and Guichard, 1997; for the trip to Ugarit, Villard 1986. The texts from Tell Leilan, discovered more recently, have just begun to appear: see the overview in Weiss 1997. On Tell Rimah, see Dalley, 1997. The Alalakh texts have not yet appeared in final form; for a summary, see Stein, 1997; Greenstein, 1997.)

The first abundant data on Canaan per se appear some four centuries later, on tablets written in the first part of the 14th century. These were actually discovered at Tell el-Amarna in Egypt but represent correspondence of the Egyptian court with vassal states in the province of Canaan. (In virtually all cases, of course, the texts actually discovered were those sent to Egypt, so we essentially have only one side of a dialogue.) These texts also were written in Akkadian, but in a much less pure form than was the case at Mari: here the Akkadian learned by the scribes was strongly influenced by the local language, and there are significant variations from one scribal school to another. This makes the task of decipherment/interpretation more difficult, but, on the other hand, it supplies a larger window on the local language that underlay the jargonized Akkadian: not only are specific glosses more frequent, but the linguistic variations from standard Akkadian allow a partial reconstruction of the underlying language (important summary in Rainey, 1996a). Because the texts are almost entirely epistolary and addressed to a foreign sovereign, there is much less information regarding local society, culture, and religion than was the case with the Mari texts. For this reason, these texts have been exploited primarily for political history and for reconstructing the Canaanite language of the time; occasional references to other matters and the presence of many theophoric names does, however, permit some reconstruction of Canaanite society and religion of the early 14th century. (See Isre'el, 1997, for a general introduction; authoritative translations, French and English, by Moran, 1987 and 1992; on the contributions of the proper names, Hess, 1993.)

The single most varied source of data for Canaan in the broader sense is furnished by the texts from Ras Shamra (ancient Ugarit), located on the north coast of Syria. This variety of data is owing to the following factors: (1) there is a large number of inscriptions (upwards of 4,000 [Bordreuil and Pardee 1989]); (2) these texts cover a period of over a century and a half (from the first half of the 14th century until the destruction of the site in ca. 1185 BCE); (3) they are written in a variety of languages and scripts, of which the most important are Akkadian, Ugaritic (the local West-Semitic language for the writing of which a cuneiform script was invented), Hurrian (a non-Semitic language), and in much smaller numbers, Egyptian and Hittite; (4) a variety of literary genres are attested: in Ugaritic, the main types are mythological, ritual, epistolary, legal, and administrative; in Akkadian, epistolary, administrative, and legal. This variety and the sheer number of texts permit a reasonably complete reconstruction of the political history of the city-state (they make, moreover, a major contribution to our knowledge of the political history of the entire region, from Hatti to Egypt) as well as of many aspects of society and religion. It is from these texts that we learn most of what we know about the background of many of the deities mentioned in the first-millennium sources and about that of many of the cultic practices mentioned in the first-millennium texts. Though the Ugaritic language differs in important respects from the Canaanite revealed by the Amarna texts, the similarities are sufficient to allow us to say that they certainly have a common ancestor, while the similarities between the pantheons and cultic practices also indicate a common background with independent local developments. (A recent handy overview of many aspects of Ugaritic studies may be found in Watson, Wyatt, eds., 1999; recent translations of the major mythological texts by Pardee, 1997h; Parker, ed., 1997; Wyatt, 1998; for the archaeology of Ras Shamra, see Yon, 1997; for that of the neighboring site of Ras Ibn Hani, which has also furnished texts, see Bounni, Lagarce, and Lagarce, 1998.)

Other important Late Bronze Age sources that bear special attention are those from Alalakh (which thus has furnished texts from both Middle and Late Bronze – see above) and Emar. The latter is a site on the Middle Euphrates where some eight hundred texts, mostly in Akkadian, were discovered during excavations in the 1970s (Arnaud, 1985–7), and the number is even larger when texts from illegal digging are included in the count. They date from roughly the same period as the texts from Ugarit and appear in a similar variety of literary genres, but differ in that none is written in the local language, about which we thus know relatively little. The ritual texts here were written in Akkadian (all the Ugaritic ones are in the local language) and show significant differences of content from the Ugaritic examples: not only do they include many more details on any given rite (the Ugaritic texts tend to be very laconic) but the rites themselves tend to be very different from the ones mentioned in the Ugaritic ritual texts. For example, one of the best-known texts is a very detailed prescription for the installation of the high priestess of the weather deity (Fleming, 1992). These differences may reflect the accidents of discovery or a significantly different set of cultic practices among the east-Syrian Amorites as compared with their distant cousins to the west, but without texts from Emar in the local language that is difficult to determine. Certainly in other areas, such as the general pantheon or so mundane an area as an epistolary formula (Pardee, forthcoming b), there are remarkable similarities.

A sort of dark age occurred after the disappearance of much of the Late Bronze culture, and very few texts have been discovered between ca. 1150 and 1000 BCE. The configuration of the new sources has, moreover, changed considerably: (1) The texts tend now to appear in smaller groups, rather than in large archives such as those of Mari, Ugarit, or Emar; (2) most of the texts are now in the local language and in linear (i.e., non-cuneiform script – gone are the large archives in Akkadian, though a few Akkadian texts have been found); (3) most texts were probably written on papyrus and have disappeared, so that the few remaining are for the most part either ostraca (potsherds inscribed with pen and ink) or inscribed stone (ranging in size from monumental building inscriptions or tomb inscriptions to tiny seals). Because of the disparate nature of these sources, they are usually treated according to language affiliation, with the exception of seals, of which the language of the bearer and/or inscriber is some-times difficult to determine (Bordreuil, 1986; Avigad and Sass, 1997).

Mainland Phoenician inscriptions are for the most part monumental – very few Phoenician ostraca are known to date. They provide data on the circum-stances for which they were erected and on the deities to which they were dedi-cated, but little information on everyday life and practice, whether political, social, or religious. The Phoenician language was for a time the prestige language all along the east-Mediterranean coast as well as up into Cilicia (as is illustrated by the 8th century Phoenician–Luwian bilingual from Karatepe [Bron, 1997] and the 7th century Phoenician inscription from Cebel Ires Dagi [Mosca and Russel, 1987]). Owing in no small part to their geographical situation, a narrow strip of arable land on the Mediterranean coast, the Phoenicians were always traders, and Phoenician inscriptions begin appearing in the western Mediterra-nean area as early as the 9th century, first in Cyprus then as far afield as Spain. With the establishment of colonies in North Africa, of which the most famous was Carthage (perhaps as early as the traditional date in the late 9th century), the Phoenician language and script in time took on forms distinguishable from mainland usage. This transplanted Phoenician is known as Punic and the greatest number of Phoenician texts, on the order of 6,000, are actually in Punic (Amadasi Guzzo, 1997). Unfortunately, these texts are mostly votive in nature and highly repetitive in content; moreover, some of the key terms relating to cultic practice are still poorly understood. One of the more important Punic texts, known as the Marseilles Tariff because it was discovered in that French port city, was once fixed on the wall of the temple of Baal-Saphon in Carthage, where its function was "to regulate distributions among priests and offerers of the items presented to the sanctuary, as well as to set the fees that were attached to certain offerings" (Pardee 1997h, p. 305). (A handy collection of the most important Phoenician texts is available in Gibson, 1982; Donner and Röllig, 1966–9, includes Punic inscriptions; extensive data in Lipiński, ed., 1992; Krings, ed., 1995.)

Some time as early as the 10th century, the western Aramaeans (those who were situated in the area corresponding to southeastern Turkey and northern Syria) borrowed the Phoenician writing system and began writing texts in their own language. (The texts from one of the most famous sites, Senjirli, appear in three forms: Phoenician, an archaic dialect of Aramaic, and a more standard form of Aramaic [Tropper, 1993].) It is clear that the alphabet was borrowed from the Phoenicians because the letter forms are identical to the Phoenician forms and because the graphic inventory at first corresponded rather poorly to the Aramaic phonetic inventory; the letter forms are only identifiable as Aramaic after a long period of usage while the orthographic traditions for representing Aramaic sounds developed even more slowly over time (Cook, 1997). The types of early-Aramaic inscriptions are similar to those of Phoenician and give the same general types of information. The big difference is that Aramaic became, during the time of the Neo-Assyrian empire and on into the Neo-Babylonian and Persian empires, the lingua franca of the entire Near East, with the result that Aramaic inscriptions have been found from Afghanistan to Egypt. Huehnergard (1995) argues that this lingua franca served to standardize Aramaic usage throughout its extent and that the later dialects have for the most part descended from this standardized form of the language. One of our largest bodies of information on West Semites in the 5th through 3rd centuries BCE comes, again, from Egypt, but this time in Aramaic. Hundreds of papyri have been found, primarily at Elephantine, but also at sites such as Hermopolis and Saqqara, for the most part legal and epistolary in nature, but with not a few texts of at least a tangentially religious nature, such as an ostracon that mentions Passover (Porten, ed., 1996; Porten, 1997; Porten and Yardeni, 1986–99).

A large body of ostraca inscribed in Aramaic has recently appeared on the antiquities market; these were almost certainly unearthed in the northern Negev (Idumaea). They date to the 4th century and are largely economic in nature (Eph'al and Naveh, 1996; Lemaire, 1996). Another corpus, discovered further north, in a cave in the Wadi ed-Daliyeh, represents documents of Samaritans who had fled Macedonian repression in the late 4th century (Dever, 1997b; Cross, 1985). Because Aramaic was the principal Semitic language in use in Syria–Palestine at the time of the Hellenistic conquest, it was retained throughout the Hellenistic period (with Greek functioning as the prestige language) and on through the Roman period and into the Byzantine, only to be replaced (partially!) by Arabic at the time of the Islamic conquest. An important corpus of Aramaic inscriptions from around the turn of the eras that shows a heavy Hellenistic influence comes from Palmyra in the Syrian desert (Hillers and Cussini, 1996) and another, witnessing a civilization of Arab origin, known as Nabataean, comes from the original center in Edom and from a much larger area to the north, west, and south that it came to control (Graf, 1997). Because of this status as the most common Semitic language in Syria–Palestine at the turn of the eras, Aramaic was used by both Jews and Christians and became the vehicle of much Jewish and Christian literature (the latter known as Syriac).

Various modern dialects are still spoken today in Malula outside Damascus, in a band along the northern border of Syria and Iraq, and in southern Iraq by the Mandaeans – as well, of course, as in various diaspora communities throughout the world. Aramaic, in spite of its long history and the wealth of the various literatures of which it has been the language of expression, has never enjoyed the prestige of Hebrew, Greek, and Latin and has thus never occupied the place in academia that it deserves. (The primary and secondary sources on the Aramaeans as one of the peoples of Canaan are of course less extensive than if one attempted to learn everything in and about Aramaic as a language, but they are nevertheless extensive; for a start, see Cook, 1997; Dion, 1997; and Pitard, 1997.)

Like the Aramaeans, the speakers of Hebrew adopted the Phoenician alphabet, probably as early as the 10th century. Certainly by the 9th century writing traditions existed in the northern and southern kingdoms that were characteristic and distinguishable (attested side by side at Kuntillet 'Ajrud [Briquel-Chatonnet, 1992; Meshel, 1997]). By early in the 8th century a scribal tradition is well attested in texts discovered in Samaria (Israel, 1986, 1989; Kaufman, 1997), and significant Hebrew inscriptions began appearing in Judah in the course of the 7th century, for example, the Mesad Hashavyahu inscriptions (Pardee, 1997d), the Siloam Tunnel inscription (Parker, 1997, pp. 36–9), or two unprovenenced inscriptions (Bordreuil, Israel, and Pardee, 1996, 1998). The most important corpora of Hebrew inscriptions date to roughly the last decade and a half of the existence of the state of Judah: those from Lachish (the famous Lachish letters discovered in the 1930s and to which other texts have been added since for a total of thirty-six [Pardee, 1997c]) and from Arad (well over a hundred Hebrew texts, nearly a hundred Aramaic texts [Lemaire, 1997]). These inscriptions reveal that slightly different dialects were spoken in the north and the south and they leave no doubt that what we know as biblical Hebrew was not a late scribal construct but a linear descendant, with only minor developments, from the language spoken and written in Judah shortly before the exile. To the extent that so few documents of a non-literary nature can bear such a weight of proof, they also show general agreement with the picture of Judaean–Israelite religion and culture as presented in the Hebrew Bible, e.g., the only divine name mentioned is that of YHWH. This does not mean, of course, that every detail of the biblical text is historically accurate, simply that the broad picture painted in these texts that were certainly redacted in the post-exilic period – whatever their origins may have been – reflects reasonably accurately what was going on in the immediate pre-exilic period. To the extent, therefore, that the Hebrews/Israelites were Canaanites, the transformation into a distinct religious and cultural entity had occurred well before the Babylonian exile. (The most extensive recent collection of Hebrew inscriptions is Renz, 1995.)

It must be observed that, also to the extent that the Israelites were Canaanites, a much-debated topic (see references cited in the following sections), the Hebrew Bible is in some sense a Canaanite document. What historians attempt to determine, of course, is to what extent the biblical claims of Israelite distinctiveness from the groups known in the Bible as Canaanites, Amorites, etc. are admissible. The classification of Hebrew as a Canaanite language is of little relevance in answering this question, for extensive socioreligious developments can occur within a given segment of a larger culture. (Few scholars would accept today that the Hebrew language represents only the local language adopted by invading non-Canaanites.) As remarked above, the extra-biblical textual data certainly do not contradict the biblical claims, but texts in significant numbers and of sufficient length to provide extensive data regarding such questions are known only from the last century or so of the history of Judah.

One of the earliest of the West-Semitic textual discoveries was of the so-called Mesha Stone or Moabite Stone (Pardee, 1997e; Parker, 1997, pp. 43–75), but the textual discoveries in the Transjordanian area have not continued on this plane. Texts identifiable as Ammonite (Israel, 1997), Edomite (Israel, 1987b; Israel, 1992; Beit-Arieh and Cresson, 1991), and Moabite (Israel, 1987a, 1992) have been discovered, but their small number makes it difficult to define precisely the linguistic distinctions between these languages/dialects (Bordreuil and Pardee, 1990). One of the most important of the Transjordanian texts for biblical studies in spite of its very fragmentary condition, the famous Balaam text from Tell Deir Alla, is in what appears to be an archaic dialect of Aramaic, though not all agree with this linguistic classification (Hoftijzer and van der Kooij, eds., 1991).

Only the very earliest of the texts known as the Dead Sea Scrolls (discovered in the 1940s–1960s in both regular and unsupervised excavations in various caves near Khirbet Qumran) can have been contemporaneous with the very latest of the biblical texts, but such an overview of the extra-biblical literary sources cannot fail at least to mention them. For not only do they provide the oldest manuscripts available of the Hebrew Bible itself, but also many original compositions expressing the beliefs of several groups of Jews who see themselves as continuing the line of the biblical faithful. Though these documents are in many respects derivative of the Hebrew Bible, in other respects they provide a separate line of tradition, some elements of which (e.g., aspects of the Enochic traditions) have their own origins in the older Canaanite world. The importance of Aramaic in this period is reflected in the fact that many of the non-biblical texts from this corpus are in that language. (Again the bibliography is immense; for a recent brief overview see Wise, 1997.)

Finally, it should be noted that this overview has concentrated on documents written by the local inhabitants of the areas covered, on Canaanite documents, as defined above. But this area was the object of interest and was indeed coveted by its neighbors to the north, the east, and the south, and a not inconsiderable part of what we know about the Canaanites comes from documents that provide the perspective of Egyptians, Mesopotamians (Sumerians, Akkadians, Assyrians, and Babylonians), and Anatolians (most of the known documents are from the Hittites or the post-Hittite states in southern Turkey and northern Syria). It is the function of collections such as Pritchard, ed., 1969, and Hallo and Younger, eds., 1997, to make available in authoritative English translations not only the Canaanite texts but the relevant texts of their neighbors as well.

Archaeological Sources

The above overview only makes the more obvious the enormous lacunae that exist in the written sources for reconstructing the history of the area covered. These lacunae, until new texts appear, may only be filled by non-inscribed archaeological material – and even those written sources that do exist must, of course, be used in conjunction with such material whenever possible (Dever, 1997c; Halpern, 1997; Pardee, 1997b). An overview of the archaeological sources for Canaan will not be offered here because the author is not qualified to do it, and because such an overview would perforce be either very superficial or enormously long (see Meyers, 1997, and Stern, 1993). Of interest for the question of Canaan, however, is the discussion that has become particularly warm over the past decade regarding the interrelationship of textual and archaeological data for the questions of the origins and early history of Israel. (For a quick overview, see Dever, 1996; for a case-study, Dever, 1997a; for an extensive attempt to correlate the two types of data, Ahlström, 1993.) Texts, even in so brief a form as the personal name, do provide elements for determining ethnicity and the specifics of religious belief. These very basic features are, however, very difficult to determine on the basis of non-inscribed archaeological materials (the famous "pots and people" debate) though they must be considered crucial for questions such as determining when an Israelite was distinguishable from a Canaanite. (For the general question, which has much occupied archaeologists in recent years, see Hesse and Wapnish, 1997.)

Because the texts come almost exclusively from the upper strata of society, they tend to reflect primarily the beliefs and practices of those strata (the one exception is that of personal names, for names of underlings can appear in the written sources and the theophorous elements of such names can provide some clues about popular religion: Tigay, 1986; Pardee, 1988). A well-conducted archaeological excavation will delve into the non-palatial areas of a site and unearth data on the lower strata of society. (For the example of the interpretation of the figurines that are commonly found in Judaean/Israelite sites, see Ahlström, 1984.) Agreement is general, however, that a more complete history can be achieved when written and non-written sources may be correlated. Thus the discovery of inscriptions is an important event in even the best-run archaeological excavation (for example, the case of the recently discovered Ekron inscription: Gitin, Dothan, and Naveh, 1997).

Canaanite History, Society, and Religion

It should be obvious that, particularly with Canaan defined as broadly as has been done above, no single description of Canaanite history, society, and religion is possible. Developments may occur across both time and space, and may occur quickly or slowly, across greater or lesser reaches of space. Each of the Phoenician cities appears, for example, to have had a particular tutelary deity, usually a pair of consorts, and these deities varied from one city to another. Thus the functions of deities bearing the same name must have varied from one Phoenician city to another. We can expect every variation on conservatism and innovation to have occurred and may not assume anything without explicit data.

To reconstruct political history in any detail, written records are necessary. From the above survey, it should be clear that the only period in the second millennium for which Canaanite records in the narrow sense of the term are available is the Amarna age, that very brief slice of time for which we have several hundred cuneiform documents that originated in Canaanite cities. In the broader sense of the term Canaan adopted for this overview, we may add the documents from the Amorite floruit in the Middle Bronze Age and those from Alalakh, Ugarit, and Emar in the Late Bronze Age, and these may be fleshed out considerably by documents from Mesopotamia, Anatolia, and Egypt. In spite of these multiple sources, however, the political history of the levantine area in the Middle and Late Bronze Ages is reconstructable in fits and starts, with long periods and large areas going through what are for us dark ages. Local documentation, Phoenician, Aramaic, Hebrew, Moabite, Ammonite, and Edomite, becomes more widespread in the first millennium, but few of these documents provide much in the way of detail. The historian for the period must, therefore, work primarily at correlating these few data with (1) the textual material from the surrounding areas, much more abundant, (2) the archaeological data, and (3) the biblical accounts (with all the attendant difficulties). From the introduction, it should be clear that no consensus has yet been reached on such pivotal questions as precisely what a Canaanite was in the first half of the first millennium or when and how Israel or Judah arose as definable political entities. Because of corroboration primarily by Assyrian and Babylonian sources, few today doubt the general outline of political events indicated in the Hebrew Bible from Omri to the Babylonian exile, though the validity of many details and, particularly, of the religious interpretation put on them in the Bible is hotly debated. Local written sources dry up again at the time of the exile, and the historian of the post-exilic period is even more dependent on outside sources than was the case for the last century and a half of the pre-exilic period. For example, the dearth of Hebrew inscriptions makes the development of that language – and hence such questions as those regarding the society of post-exilic Palestine and the redaction of the Hebrew Bible – objects of speculation. Even the Dead Sea Scrolls, because the themes of these documents are largely theological, do little to relieve this situation, and historians of the Hellenistic and Roman periods rely heavily, therefore, on sources in the classical languages.

More elements of a socioeconomic system are reconstructable from archaeology than are the purely political ones, and one might for that reason expect a more complete description of these elements of Canaanite culture to be available. This is true to a certain extent (e.g., the extensive archaeological surveys done in Israel have resulted in a reasonably comprehensive map of settlement and habitation patterns), but the picture is far from complete. This is owing to two primary factors: (1) in order to know the complete archaeological history of a site, the entire site would have to be excavated, but this is only done in the cases of very small single-period sites; (2) only comparatively recently, say since the late 1960s, has a reasonably solid interest in the archaeology of commoners been evinced (i.e., what they ate and drank, how they lived, what their occupations were, etc.). The texts, also, tend not to provide details in such matters, since they issue from the higher strata of society and reflect primarily those interests. The written and archaeological records show clearly, however, that the primary form of government was royal, organized on a patrimonial pattern, with the king seen as the patriarch of the city, city-state, or regional state, situated at the peak of this societal pyramid, with the rest of society organized in interlocking horizontal and vertical combinations down to the humblest servant. When an outside power conquered a larger region, this structure was usually maintained (at least down to the Neo-Assyrian period), to the extent that the local kings were willing to pay tribute and refrain from revolution. Within this three-dimensional grid are also to be located various interest groups (for example, the sanctuary personnel or the local council of elders/citizens) and the various forms of production, with multiple interlocking combinations patterned on the social bonds (e.g., tradesmen, artisans, farmers). The larger kingdoms would certainly have had, as is illustrated by Ugarit as well as by the biblical accounts of the rise of the Israelite and Judaean kingdoms, an administration, with favorites of the king in the most important positions and multiple categories of service, both permanent and temporary. This royal government was funded by taxes and by service requirements, though many of the permanent administrators would have had their own incomes, from trade or from a family-owned agricultural base or from both. Alongside this urban society and varying in importance according to the fortunes of the kingdoms, there must have existed at all periods – down to the present day – a non-sedentary or partially sedentary population of which the primary economic base was the raising of sheep and goats, rounded out in many cases by seasonal agricultural pursuits; the social organization of these groups would have been of a tribal–patrimonial type. (On the Weberian analysis of Levantine society just presented, see Schloen, 1995 and forthcoming.)

Because of the religious nature of the Hebrew Bible and its enduring value as such, the most hotly debated topics are those of Canaanite religion and the origins of Israelite religion as the background to the better documented Jewish, Christian, and Islamic religions. The resolution of such questions is largely dependent on textual data, and what we know about Canaanite religion is to a considerable extent, therefore, a reflection of the textual sources outlined above. This is not meant as a denigration of the non-literary sources, but as a recognition of the fact that it is often difficult to put a name on a figurine that does not bear one, to count the number of deities to whom sacrifices were offered on an altar, or to know whether an incense burner had a religious or a simple fumigatory function. We are fortunate that the written sources have so dramatically increased over the past century – the vast majority of the sources outlined above were discovered during the twentieth century – but it is nonetheless true that the religious history of the Levantine area, like the political history, may only be described in fits and starts. Many indications allow one to believe, however, that the religious history evolved in a much more linear fashion than did the political one, that a change of dynasty did not significantly change religious practices and that even a major new ethno-political overlay only slowly changed the underlying practices of the common people. Once again, it is Ugarit that provides, because of its wide range of documentation and the relatively extensive excavation that has taken place there, the most complete picture of how Canaanite religion was practiced. This can, of course, only be a snapshot of one area and period, but the many points of comparability with other snapshots, from Mari to the Phoenicians, and even with the more extensively redacted and theologically oriented biblical data, show to the satisfaction of many that the picture is not atypical. Very briefly: the religion of Ugarit was highly polytheistic (well over two hundred deities are attested) and its primary form was that of a sacrificial cult (the ritual texts refer to several types of sacrifice to the deities, primarily of sheep, goats, cattle, and to less numerous offerings of vegetal products, garments, and precious metals). Though poorly attested by the texts preserved, song and prayer were a part of the cult. Several forms of divination were practiced, at least to a certain extent within a cultic context (the term sacrifice appears in some divination texts [Pardee, 2000 and forthcoming c]). Important literary witnesses to religious belief are also attested, from the relatively rare incantations to the famous mythological texts. Texts of the first category definitely reflect daily practice, for they are prepared for a specific person and situation (Pardee, 1997h, pp. 327–8), and the mention of deities in some leaves no doubt about their religious connections (Pardee, 1993, pp. 211–13). The place of the myths in belief and practice is more problematic. Some have depicted them as virtual librettos for ritual (Gaster, 1950), but very few of the texts bear any trace of such usage (a recent translation of one that does is in Pardee, 1997h, pp. 274–83), while none of the prose ritual texts shows any trace of influence from the myths as we know them (Pardee, 2000, p. 933). If most of the myths were written down only very late in the history of the city, their precise place in the thought and practice of the average Ugaritian becomes even more difficult to determine. As for comparisons with the Hebrew Bible, the terminology and practice of the rites show strong similarities (e.g., Ugaritic *dbḥ* = Hebr. *zābaḥ*, to sacrifice; Ugaritic *šlmm* = Hebr. *šalāmîm*, communion sacrifice), while the poetic myths provide the background for many of the formulations used in biblical poetry as well as elements of a history of the deities that are either alluded to or condemned in the biblical text. We find there stories of El, Baal, Ashera, Ashtoret, Dagan, Horon, and a host of others – a century ago these were only names, whether in the biblical text or in the then rare extra-biblical sources.

Bibliography

Ahlström, G., "An Archaeological Picture of Iron Age Religions in Ancient Palestine," *Studia Orientalia* 55 (1984), 3–31.

——, *The History of Ancient Palestine from the Paleolithic Period to Alexander's Conquest*, JSOTSup 146 (Sheffield: Sheffield Academic Press, 1993).

Amadasi Guzzo, M-G., "Phoenician-Punic," *EANE* 4 (1997), 317–24.

Arnaud, D., *Recherches au pays d'Ashtata*, Emar 6 (Paris: Éditions Recherche sur les Civilisations, 1985–7).

Avigad, N. and B. Sass, *Corpus of West Semitic Stamp Seals* (Jerusalem: The Israel Academy of Sciences and Humanities; The Israel Exploration Society; The Institute of Archaeology, the Hebrew University of Jerusalem, 1997).

Beit-Arieh, I. and B. Cresson, "Horvat 'Uza, a Fortified Outpost on the Eastern Negev Border," *BA* 54 (1991), 126–35.

Bonechi, M., "Relations amicales syro-palestiniennes: Mari et Hasor au XVIIIᵉ siècle av. J.C.," in J.-M. Durand, ed., *Recueil d'études en l'honneur de Michel Fleury*, ed. Jean-Marie Durand, Mémoires de N.A.B.U., Florilegium marianum 1 (Paris: SEPOA, 1991), 9–22.

Bordreuil, P., *Catalogue des sceaux ouest-sémitiques inscrits de la Bibliothèque Nationale, du Musée du Louvre et du Musée biblique de Bible et Terre Sainte* (Paris: Bibliothèque Nationale, 1986).

Bordreuil, P., F. Israel and D. Pardee, "Deux ostraca paléo-hébreux de la collection Sh. Moussaïeff: 1) Contribution financière obligatoire pour le temple de yhwh, 2) Réclamation d'une veuve auprès d'un fonctionnaire," *Semitica* 46 (1996), 49–76, pls. 7–8.

——, "King's Command and Widow's Plea: Two New Hebrew Ostraca of the Biblical Period," *Near Eastern Archaeology* 61 (1998), 2–13.

Bordreuil, P. and D. Pardee, *La trouvaille épigraphique de l'Ougarit*. Ras Shamra-Ougarit 5 (Paris: Éditions Recherche sur les Civilisations, 1989).

——, "Le papyrus du marzeah," *Semitica* 38, *Hommages à Maurice Sznycer* 1 (1990), 4, 9–68.

——, "Le combat de *Ba'lu* avec *Yammu* d'après les textes ougaritiques," *MARI* 7 (1993), 63–70.

Bounni, A., J. Lagarce and E. Lagarce, *Ras Ibn Hani, I. Le palais nord du Bronze récent, fouilles 1979–1995, synthèse préliminaire*, Bibliothèque Archéologique et Historique 151 (Beirut: Institut Français d'Archéologie du Proche-Orient, 1998).

Briquel-Chatonnet, F., "Hébreu du nord et phénicien: étude comparée de deux dialectes cananéens," *Orientalia Lovaniensia Periodica* 23 (1992), 89–126.

Bron, F., "Karatepe Phoenician Inscriptions," *EANE* 3 (1997), 268–9.

Civil, M., "Sumerian," *EANE* 5 (1997), 92–6.

Cook, E., "Aramaic Language and Literature," *EANE* 1 (1997), 178–84.

Cross, F., "Samaria Papyrus 1: An Aramaic Slave Conveyance of 335 BCE Found in the Wâdi ed-Dâliyeh," *Eretz-Israel* 18 (1985), 7*–17*.

Dalley, S., "Tell er-Rimah," *EANE* 4 (1997), 428–30.

Daniels, P., "Writing and Writing Systems," *EANE* 5 (1997), 352–8.

Dever, W., "Archaeology and the Religions of Israel," *BASOR* 301 (1996), 83–90.

——, "Archaeology and the 'Age of Solomon': A Case-Study in Archaeology and Historiography," in L. Handy, ed., *The Age of Solomon. Scholarship at the Turn of the Millennium*, Studies in the History and Culture of the Ancient Near East, vol. 11 (Leiden: E. J. Brill, 1997a), 217–51.

——, "Wadi ed-Daliyeh," *EANE* 2 (1997b), 101–2.

——, "Philology, Theology, and Archaeology: What Kind of History of Israel Do We Want and What is Possible?" in A. Silberman and D. Small, eds., *The Archaeology of Israel. Constructing the Past, Interpreting the Present*, JSOTSup 237 (Sheffield: Sheffield Academic Press, 1997c), 290–310.

Dion, P.-R., *Les Araméens à l'âge du Fer: histoire politique et structures sociales*, Études Bibliques, nouvelle série, no. 34 (Paris: Gabalda, 1997).

Donner, H. and W. Röllig, *Kanaanäische und aramäische Inschriften*, 3 vols. (Wiesbaden: Harrassowitz, 1966–9).

Durand, J.-M., "Le mythologème du combat entre le dieu de l'orage et la mer en Mésopotamie," *MARI* (1993), 41–61.

——, *Documents épistolaires du palais de Mari*, vol. 1, Littératures Anciennes du Proche-Orient 16 (Paris: Le Cerf, 1997).

——, "La façade occidentale du Proche-Orient d'après les textes de Mari," in A. Caubet, ed., *L'acrobate au taureau. Les découvertes de Tell el-Dab'a (Égypte) et l'archéologie de la Méditerranée orientale (1800–1400 av. J.-C.). Actes du colloque organisé au musée du Louvre par le Service culturel le 3 décembre 1994* (Paris: La documentation Française, Musée du Louvre, 1999), 149–64.

Eph'al, I. and J. Naveh, *Aramaic Ostraca of the Fourth Century* BC *From Idumaea* (Jerusalem: Magnes, 1996).

Fleming, D., *The Installation of the Baal's High Priestess at Emar: A Window on Ancient Syrian Religion*, HSS 42 (Atlanta: Scholars Press, 1992).

Gaster, T., *Thespis. Ritual Myth and Drama in the Ancient Near East* (New York: Schuman, 1950).

Gibson, J., *Textbook of Syrian Semitic Inscriptions*, vol. 3, *Phoenician Inscriptions Including Inscriptions in the Mixed Dialect of Arslan Tash* (Oxford: Clarendon Press, 1982).

Gitin, S., T. Dothan and J. Naveh, "A Royal Dedicatory Inscription from Ekron," *IEJ* 47 (1997), 1–16.

Graf, D., "Nabateans," *EANE* 4 (1997), 82–5.

Greenstein, E., "Alalakh Texts," *EANE* 1 (1997), 59–61.

Guardata, F., M. Baldacci, and F. Pomponio, "Eblaite Bibliography IV," *SEL* 14 (1997), 109–24.

Guichard, M., "Mari Texts," *EANE* 3 (1997), 419–21.

Hackett, J., "Canaanites," *EANE* 1 (1997), 409–14.

Hallo, W. and K. L. Younger, Jr., eds., *The Context of Scripture*, vol. 1, *Canonical Compositions from the Biblical World* (Leiden: E. J. Brill, 1997).

Halpern, B., "Text and Artifact: Two Monologues?" in N. Silberman and D. Small, eds., *The Archaeology of Israel. Constructing the Past, Interpreting the Present*, JSOTSup 237 (Sheffield: Sheffield Academic Press, 1997), 311–14.

Hess, R., *Amarna Personal Names*, American School of Oriental Research Dissertation Series 9 (Winona Lake: Eisenbrauns, 1993).

Hesse, B. and P. Wapnish, "Can Pig Remains Be Used for Ethnic Diagnosis in the Ancient Near East?" in N. Silberman and D. Small, eds., *The Archaeology of Israel. Constructing the Past, Interpreting the Present*, JSOTSup 237 (Sheffield: Sheffield Academic Press, 1997), 238–70.

Hillers, D. and E. Cussini, *Palmyrene Aramaic Texts*, Publications of the Comprehensive Aramaic Lexicon Project 3 (Baltimore: Johns Hopkins, 1996).

Hoftijzer, F. and G. van der Kooij, eds., *The Balaam Text from Deir 'Alla Re-evaluated. Proceedings of the International Symposium Held at Leiden 21–24 August 1989* (Leiden: E. J. Brill, 1991).

Huehnergard, J., "What is Aramaic?" *Aram* 7 (1995), 261–82.

Israel, F., "Études sur le lexique paléohébraïque: les ostraca de Samarie et l'hébreu du nord," *Journal Asiatique* 274 (1986), 478–9.

——, "Studi Moabiti I: Rassegna di Epigrafia Moabita e i sigilli," G. Bernini and V. Brugnatelle, eds., *Acti della 4a giornata di Studi Camito-Semitici e Indeuropei*. Quaderni della Collana Linguistica Storica et Descrittiva (Milan: Unicopli, 1987a), 101–38.

——, "Supplementum Idumeum I," *Revista Biblica* 35 (1987b), 337–56.

——, "Studi di lessico ebraico epigrafica I: I materiali del nord," *Langues Orientales Anciennes, Philologie et Linguistique* 2 (1989), 37–67.

——, "Note di onomastica semitica 7/2: Rassegna critico-bibliografica ed epigrafica su alcune onomastiche palestinesi: la Transgiordania," *SEL* 9 (1992), 95–114.

——, "Ammonite Inscriptions," *EANE* 1 (1997), 105–7.

Isre'el, S., "Amarna Tablets," *EANE* 1 (1997), 86–7.

Kaufman, I., "Samaria Ostraca," *EANE* 4 (1997), 468–9.

Krings, V., ed., *La civilisation phénicienne et punique. Manuel de recherche*. Handbuch der Orientalistik, Erste Abteilung: Der Nahe und Mittlere Osten, Band 20 (Leiden: E. J. Brill, 1995).

Lemaire, A., *Nouvelles inscriptions araméennes d'Idumée au Musée d'Israël*. Transeuphratène Supplément 3 (Paris: Gabalda, 1996).

——, "Arad Inscriptions," *EANE* 1 (1997), 176–7.

Lipiński, E., ed., *Dictionnaire de la civilisation phénicienne et punique* (Turnhout: Brépols, 1992).

Loprieno, A., "Egyptian," *EANE* 2 (1997), 208–13.

Malamat, A., *Mari and the Early Israelite Experience*, The Schweich Lectures of the British Academy 1984 (Oxford: Oxford University Press, 1989).

Margueron, J.-C., "Mari," *EANE* 3 (1997), 413–17.

Meshel, Z., "Kuntillet 'Ajrud," *EANE* 3 (1997), 310–12.

Meyers, E., ed., *Encyclopedia of Archaeology in the Near East* (New York: Oxford University Press, 1997).

Moran, W., *Les Lettres d'el-Amarna. Correspondance diplomatique du pharaon*. Littératures Anciennes du Proche-Orient 13 (Paris: Le Cerf, 1987).

——, *The Amarna Letters* (Baltimore: Johns Hopkins, 1992).

Mosca, P. and J. Russel, "A Phoenician Inscription from Cebel Ires Dagi in Rough Cilicia," *Epigraphica Anatolica* 9 (1987), 1–27.

Na'aman, N., "Four Notes on the Size of Late Bronze Age Canaan," *BASOR* 313 (1999), 31–7.

Pardee, D., "An Evaluation of the Proper Names from Ebla from a West Semitic Perspective: Pantheon Distribution According to Genre," in A. Archi, ed., *Eblaite Personal Names and Semitic Name-Giving. Papers of a Symposium Held in Rome July 15–17, 1985*, Reali di Ebla, Studi, vol. 1 (Rome: Missione Archeologica Italiana in Siria, 1988), 119–51.

——, "Poetry in Ugaritic Ritual Texts," in J. Moor and W. Watson, *Verse in Ancient Near Eastern Prose*, Alter Orient und Altes Testament 42 (Neukirchen-Vluyn: Neukirchener Verlag, 1993), 207–18.

——, "Alphabet," *EANE* 1 (1997a), 75–9.

——, "Ancient Inscriptions," *EANE* 3 (1997b), 158–62.

——, "Lachish Inscriptions," *EANE* 3 (1997c), 3323–4.

——, "Mesad Hashavyahu Texts," *EANE* 3 (1997d), 475.

——, "Moabite Stone," *EANE* 5 (1997e), 39–41.

——, "Proto-Canaanite," *EANE* 4 (1997f), 352–4.

——, "Proto-Sinaitic," *EANE* 4 (1997g), 354–5.

——, Various annotated translations in Hallo and Younger, eds. (1997h).

——, Review, *JAOS* 117 (1997i), 375–8.

——, "Ugaritic," *EANE* 5 (1997j), 262–4.

——, "Canaanite," in R. Woodard, *Encyclopedia of the World's Ancient Languages* (Cambridge: Cambridge University Press, forthcoming a).

——, "Une formule épistolaire en ougaritique et accadien" (forthcoming b).

——, "Ugaritic Science," *The World of the Aramaeans: Biblical, Historical and Cultural Studies in Honour of Paul.-E. Dion* (forthcoming).

——, *Les textes rituels*, Ras-Shamra – Ugarit XII (Paris: Éditions Recherche sur les Civilisations, 2000).

Parker, S., *Stories in Scripture and Inscriptions. Comparative Studies on Narratives in Northwest Semitic Inscriptions and the Hebrew Bible* (New York: Oxford University Press, 1997).

Parker, S., ed., *Ugaritic Narrative Poetry*, SBL Writings from the Ancient World Series 9 (Atlanta: Scholars Press, 1997).

Pitard, W., "Arameans," *EANE* 1 (1997), 184–7.

Porten, Bezalel, ed., *The Elephantine Papyri in English* (Leiden: E. J. Brill, 1996).

Porten, B., "Egyptian Aramaic Texts," *EANE* 2 (1997), 212–19.

Porten, B. and A. Yardeni, *Textbook of Aramaic Documents from Ancient Egypt*, 4 vols. (Jerusalem: Hebrew University, 1986–99).

Pritchard, J., ed., *Ancient Near Eastern Texts Relating to the Old Testament*, 3rd edn. (Princeton: Princeton University Press, 1969).

Rainey, A., *Canaanite in the Amarna Tablets: A Linguistic Analysis of the Mixed Dialect Used by the Scribes from Canaan*, Handbuch der Orientalistik Erste Abteilung: Der Nahe und Mittlere Osten 25 (Leiden: E. J. Brill, 1996a).

——, "Who is a Canaanite? A Review of the Textual Evidence," *BASOR* 304 (1996b), 1–15.

Renz, J., *Handbuch der Althebräischen Epigraphik*, 3 vols. (Darmstadt: Wissenschaftliche Buchgesellschaft, 1995).

Schloen, J., *The Patrimonial Household in the Kingdom of Ugarit: A Weberian Analysis of Ancient Near Eastern Society*, Dissertation (Harvard University, 1995).

——, *The House of the Father in Canaan and Israel* (forthcoming).

Stein, D., "Alalakh," *EANE* 1 (1997), 55–9.

Stern, E., ed., *The New Encyclopedia of Archaeological Excavations in the Holy Land* (Jerusalem: Israel Exploration Society and Carta, 1993).

Tigay, J., *You Shall Have No Other Gods: Israelite Religion in the Light of Holy Inscriptions*, HSS 31 (Atlanta: Scholars Press, 1986).

Tropper, J., *Die Inschriften von Zincirli. Neue Edition und vergleichende Grammatik des phönizischen, sam'alischen und aramäischen Textkorpus*, Abhandlungen zur Literatur Alt-Syrien-Palästinas 6 (Münster: UGARIT-Verlag, 1993).

——, "Is Ugaritic a Canaanite Language?" in G. Brooke, A. Curtis and J. Healey, *Ugarit and the Bible. Proceedings of the International Symposium on Ugarit and the Bible, Manchester, September 1992*, in *Ugaritisch-Biblische Literatur* 11 (Münster: Ugarit-Verlag, 1994), 343–53.

Villard, P., "Un roi de Mari à Ugarit," *UF* 18 (1986), 387–412.

Watson, W. and N. Wyatt, eds., *Handbook of Ugaritic Studies*, Handbuch der Orientalistik, Erste Abteilung: Der Nahe und Mittlere Osten, Band 39 (Leiden: E. J. Brill, 1999).

Weiss, H., "Tell Leilan," *EANE* 3 (1997), 341–7.

Wise, M. O., "Dead Sea Scrolls," *EANE* 2 (1997), 118–27.

Wyatt, N., *Religious Texts from Ugarit. The Words of Ilimilku and his Colleagues*, The Biblical Seminar, vol. 53 (Sheffield: Sheffield Academic Press, 1998).

Yon, M., *La cité d'Ougarit sur le tell de Ras Shamra*, Guides Archéologiques de l'Institut Français d'Archéologie du Proche-Orient 2 (Paris: Éditions Recherche sur les Civilisations, 1997).

CHAPTER 10

The Household in Ancient Israel and Early Judaism

Joseph Blenkinsopp

The Limitations of our Knowledge

The household was the basic unit of everyday social life in ancient Israel. Together with the institutions, practices, customs, and rituals that sustained it, the household belongs to the study of the private sphere, until recently much neglected by historians in general and historians of ancient Israel in particular. A history of the Israelite household, if we could write it, would be history from the bottom up rather than from the top down. It would deal less with high profile individuals, the usual stock-in-trade of historians, constituting no more than about one percent of the population, and more with social infrastructure, the transactions, interactions and trade-offs of everyday life among the mass of the population. Its agenda would be birth, marriage, and death, together with the rituals accompanying these turning points of the life-cycle, and it would be concerned with available living space, the nurture of children, gender roles, the relations between spouses and between parents and children, to mention only some of the more obvious items. These can be observed only over extended periods of time, over the *longue durée*, and they call for a different attitude of mind and a different approach, and also for different kinds of source material.

Unfortunately, however, the source material at our disposal for writing this kind of social history is not abundant for ancient Israel, and what is available is not user-friendly. Archaeologists working on Iron Age Palestinian sites were from the beginning fixated on monumental architecture, and only quite recently some of them have begun to look out for information of broad cultural interest and develop the ethnoarchaeological skills and techniques required to retrieve this kind of information. Sadly, by the time they became aware of this different approach, much data essential for the social historian had been destroyed. There is also a notable lack of iconographical material from ancient Israel, the kind used to such good effect by Paul Veyne in his reconstruction of the Roman family in antiquity (1987). The flow of information on such matters as life expectancy, infant mortality, health and disease, never more than a trickle, has more or less completely dried up as a result of religious opposition in the State of Israel to the analysis of human remains (Blenkinsopp, 1997a). The relatively few inscriptions extant from Iron Age Israel rarely afford a glimpse of life in the Israelite household, there are no epitaphs of the kind available to the historian of Greek and Roman antiquity, and no contracts, bills of sale, lawsuits or judicial depositions illustrating different aspects of social interchange, as are abundantly available for ancient Mesopotamia.

We do not need to labor the point, either, that the biblical texts were not written to provide information of use to the social historian. Potentially most relevant are the laws, though it is not always clear that they directly reflect judicial practice, and the major compilations (Exodus 20–23 and Deuteronomy 12–26) are in no sense comprehensive. There are, for example, no laws governing divorce or adoption. Beginning in the 8th century BCE, prophetic diatribe occasionally refers to aspects of the living conditions of the peasant population on whose behalf the prophet in question is protesting, whether it be indentured service as a result of insolvency, the confiscation of land on which the household depended for its survival, or the economically marginal state of widows and orphans. The didactic literature (proverbs, instructions and the like) is for the most part addressed to the sons of well-to-do families aspiring to enter public service, and therefore reflects the rather sclerotic ethos and moral code of one social class, and one making up only a small minority of the total population.

A critical reading of the biblical texts as potential source material also calls for a willingness to imagine our way out of our own cultural confines, since the conditions in which social interaction took place within the individual household and between different households at that time and in that place were quite different from those of contemporary society. In the first place *the couple* was not then, as it generally is now, the point of departure and the emotional focus of life in the household. That is to say, our idea of a man and a woman coming together, falling in love, and deciding to "have a family," with or without parental approval, would have been foreign to the experience of Palestinians of the biblical period. The normal situation was that a woman was brought into a household from outside to bear children for the male heir, the choice of a bride and arrangements for the marriage, including the marriage price, being made by the *'āb*, the patriarch and male head of the *bêt'āb* (household). It would also be safe to assume that romantic love, and even the usual manifestations of affection, would have been inhibited by the lack of adequate private space, something most of us tend to take for granted. We recall how Abimelech saw Isaac fondling his wife Rebekah (Gen 26:8) and how David on the palace roof caught sight of Bathsheba taking a bath (2 Sam 11:2). While both of these incidents may be fictional, and while explanations other than lack of private space are in any case possible (e.g., that Bathsheba wanted to be seen from the palace), we may assume that the narrators would have intended to describe *plausible* situations. In general, emotional bonds would probably have been more diffuse, with a greater attachment of the married couple to the family of origin than is normal in our societies. An example: when pestered by his wife to explain his riddle, Samson replies, "Look, I haven't told my father and mother; why should I tell you?" (Judg 14:16).

A further problem for the modern reader is that our information is restricted almost entirely to *rural* households. We know practically nothing about households in the cities, that is, in settlements of upward of about 1,000 people. For example Tell en-Naṣbeh (generally identified with Benjamite Mizpah), a medium-sized town, had a population during Iron II of 800–1,000, according to the careful calculations of J. R. Zorn (1994). Calculations of population density in towns are, however, often skewed by space occupied by administrative buildings and palaces. There was a close symbiosis between these rural settlements and the towns, which depended for their subsistence on produce from the country. The sixty-three inscribed potsherds discovered at Samaria in 1910, dated to the 8th century BCE, record shipments of oil and wine from surrounding rural centers destined for the royal household and its dependants. See J. C. L. Gibson (1971, pp. 5–20, 71–83) for the texts and a brief commentary. Throughout the entire biblical period more than 90 percent of the population was engaged in the typical Mediterranean-rim economy of raising livestock, mostly sheep and goats, and growing crops. They lived in villages consisting of a cluster of households – a pattern which is attested archaeologically from the earliest period of Israel's existence (Iron I) (see Finkelstein, 1988). By necessity these small settlements, with at most a few hundred inhabitants, formed economically interdependent, self-help societies, since the cooperative effort of several households was needed for such operations as irrigation, deforestation, terracing, guarding against intruders and rustlers, and monitoring common pastureland. Furthermore, the idea of the house as the work site and of the household as producing as well as consuming is practically unknown in our post-industrial societies. The great majority of these households would have operated at the subsistence level, which does not mean that under normal conditions they did not live reasonably well. The consequent need to continually replenish the labor force meant that children, especially male children, were considered economically advantageous, not to say indispensable, rather than (as with us) a financial liability, even if gladly accepted. And of course many children did not survive the first five dangerous years.

As a residential unit, a household was not restricted to members of the same biological subgroup. It would therefore rarely be limited to what we would recognize today as a typical family unit. Depending on available economic resources, most households would have been multigenerational including some or all of the following: aged parents or grandparents, married sons with their wives and children, a divorced daughter who had returned to her household of origin, adopted children, cousins, nephews and in-laws, and in the more affluent households retainers and slaves. As in ancient Rome, the very wealthy households would have had clients and retainers in considerable numbers. We read of three hundred and eighteen of these born in Abraham's household (*yĕlîdê bêtô*, Gen 14:14) and his son Isaac was also the head of a "great house-hold" (*'abūddâ*, meaning a body of retainers, Gen 26:14). The household of Ephraimite Micah whose story is told toward the end of the Book of Judges (chapters 17–18) included his widowed mother, his sons, perhaps also their families, and a Levite who acted as a private chaplain and had his own house (18:15). Other dependants lived elsewhere in the compound (18:14–22). The household was therefore by no means necessarily confined to a single dwelling but might, exceptionally, take in an entire settlement.

Over the last few years archaeologists have begun to generate data on private dwellings in Israel during the Iron Age and the late Second Temple period (Shiloh, 1980, pp. 25–35; Stager, 1985, pp. 1–35; and Holladay, 1992, pp. 308–18). Houses usually had between two and four rooms arranged around a courtyard divided off by a row of pillars or in some instances a well – a pattern dictated by climate and more or less identical in lands around the Mediterranean. The courtyard was the shared common space and served for cooking, household crafts, and socializing in general. During the months of inclement weather the members of the unit shared their accommodation with domestic animals, a situation which helped to heat the premises but would hardly have improved the quality of the air. In addition, a fair percentage of the available space was used for storage of seed, animal feed, farming gear and the like. The houses of the more prosperous would have had a second story reserved for domestic quarters, and practically every house would have had a flat roof reached by an outside stairway. As in the Middle East today, this would have been the preferred location for passing the night during the hot season.

In assessing these data it is well to bear in mind that only the foundations of houses have survived in Israel from the Iron Age to the Roman period, and among them only those more sturdily built and therefore belonging to the rel-atively prosperous. For the Hellenistic and Roman periods the documentation is better but still not abundant. Some of the best-preserved dwellings from the Roman period in southern Palestine are the large, complex Nabataean mansions in Mampsis (Kurnub) in the central Negev about twenty-five miles southeast of Beersheba. See especially the plan of Building XII at Mampsis (Negev, 1990, p. 178).

Forefathers and Foremothers

The ancestors of Israel whose life-stories are related in Genesis 12–50 were wealthy as well as pious and God-fearing, and therefore hardly typical of the average anonymous Israelite family. Though these stories are paradigmatic rather than strictly historical, their descriptions of household management and the pattern of relationships within households are not implausible. As to the social and cultural model existing at the time of writing on which the authors may have drawn for background material we can only speculate. The households of Abraham and his descendants are certainly rural, their wealth – like that of Job – consists primarily in livestock, and there is quite a lot of moving about. Many of the incidents are set in the Judaean Negev, which seems to have been the original goal of Abraham's peregrinations (see especially Gen 12:9). Perhaps, then, the social organization and lifestyle of the partially sedentarized and mixed population of the Negev at the time when these stories were put together – no earlier than the 6th century BCE – may have contributed to the rich and varied account of the lifestyle of the Abrahamic household and those of his immediate descendants.

Abraham belonged to the household of Terah in Northern Mesopotamia. He left that land, his extended kinship network (*môledet*), and the paternal household (*bēt 'āb*, Gen 12:1–3) and established his own household with Sarah the half-sister whom he had made his wife, his nephew Lot, an unspecified number of dependants, but as yet no children. The choice of marriage partner was obviously the crucial element in the formation of a new household. The ideal seems to have been a union which was as closely consanguineal as possible without being incestuous. The rationale for marriage in a patrilineal kinship system was the self-perpetuation of the household by means of male descent. Since the woman was always in a sense an outsider in the household of destination, it was important to introduce one who was not too much an outsider, and who therefore would be familiar with and amenable to the ethos of the household into which she had been introduced. So Abraham says to his retainer, "Go to my country and my kin and get a wife for my son Isaac" (Gen 24:4, 38). This matrimonial strategy sometimes resulted in unions which would be prohibited by the levitical rules of affinity and consanguinity. We do not, of course, assume that the levitical rules were in force throughout the entire biblical period (see Tamar and Absalom in 2 Sam 13:13). Abraham's own marriage was of this kind (Gen 11:29; 20:12; cf. Lev 18:9; 20:17), his brother Nahor married his niece (Gen 11:29), and Isaac, Jacob, and Esau married cousins (Gen 24:15, 24; 28:2, 5, 9; 29:9–10). Jacob married Leah and Rachel, sisters, and at a later point in time Amram, Moses' father, married Jochebed his aunt, both cases prohibited by levitical law (Lev 18:12–14, 18; 20:19–20). Cross-cousin marriage appears to have been the ideal in the society depicted in these stories, as it is in many traditional societies to this day. For marriage customs in Genesis, see M. E. Donaldson, 1981; R. A. Oden, 1983; and N. Steinberg, 1993.

As the Hebrew term *bēt 'āb* (father's house, paternal household) suggests, this basic kinship unit functioned by patrilineal descent, the eldest male offspring taking over as head of the household. Carol Meyers has drawn attention to the expression *bêt 'ēm* (mother's house) in Gen 24:28, Ruth 1:8, and Cant 3:4, 8:2. In Genesis 24, however, it is tolerably clear, and generally acknowledged, that Bethuel, the head of the household, was not present and presumed dead (the name is added in v. 50). Futhermore, Orpah and Ruth were Moabites, and in the Canticle *ḥeder* (room, chamber, women's quarters) is in parallelism with *bēt 'ēm*. In any case, none of these occurrences provides grounds for positing an alternative matrilineal or matriarchal form of social organization (Meyers, 1991).

The term *bêt 'ab*, paternal household, should be understood in a broad sense to encompass not just the individuals but the material assets of the unit including livestock, access to water and grazing land, and above all patrimonial domain – the plot of land (*naḥalâ, âḥūzzâ*) on which the economic survival of the household depended. Hence the close association in these stories between the promise of an heir and the promise of land. In theory land was inalienable. All real estate in Israel belonged to the national deity (Lev 25:23), a theological postulate which finds expression in the offering of the first fruits, tithing, the sabbatical year and the jubilee year (von Rad, 1966; and Wright, 1990). Once the state began to encroach on a traditional way of life, however, *raison d'état* had no trouble finding ways to circumvent theology. The confiscation of Naboth's vineyard by Ahab at the prompting of Jezebel (1 Kgs 21:1–19) illustrates a development which was to become increasingly common, leading eventually to the formation of latifundia and the great estates of the Persian and Hellenistic periods. The process is alluded to indirectly here and there in biblical texts, beginning with prophetic diatribe in the 8th century BCE, e.g., Isa 5:8; Mic 2:2; 1 Chr 27:25–31; and 2 Chr 26:10, 32:28–29, and more directly in the Ptolemaic period in the Zeno papyri and Josephus, *passim*.

To return once again to the ancestors: in the case of Abraham the perpetuation of the Abrahamic household, and therefore of the line, was complicated by the infertility of his wife. Some commentators have been tempted to think that chronic female infertility in the ancestral line (Gen 11:30; 25:21; 29:31) was due to closely consanguineal marriage, but the infertility of the matriarchs is clearly a literary motif introduced to allow for a providential reading of events, and in any case the condition was temporary. The initially close relation between Abraham and his nephew Lot suggests that the latter started out as the designated heir (Gen 11:27, 31; 12:4–5; 13:1), but by choosing land outside of Canaan, and thereby severing the connection between land and patriliny, he had to be eliminated from consideration (13:8–13). There followed the proposal to adopt a household retainer (Gen 15:1–3), a fall-back practice which must have been common due to the high rate of infant mortality. On adoption in the Near East inclusive of Israel, see Van Seters, 1975, 69–74, 78–91; and Knobloch, 1992. The practice is alluded to in 1 Chr 2:34–35; Prov 17:2; and Esther 2:7. See Goody (1969, 55–78) for the cultural context. After this option had also been ruled out, Sarah gave her servant Hagar to Abraham as a proxy wife with the understanding that eventual male issue would be the legal heir of Abraham and Sarah (16:1–4; see Van Seters, 1975, pp. 68–71, 87–95). The outcome of this arrangement with respect to Ishmael reminds us that it was not a winner-take-all situation; provision was also made for younger sons. The legal formulation in Deut 21:17 suggests that a younger son would normally receive one-third of the property (cf. 2 Kgs 2:9 and Zech 13:8), and that some such arrangement continued into the Roman period is illustrated by the gospel parable of the Prodigal Son (Luke 15:11–32). Legal provision was also eventually made for daughters to inherit, though with clearly stipulated conditions attached. Daughters inherited when there were no surviving males, and they had to marry within the tribe in order to avoid the risk of alienating the patrimonial domain. For the daughters of Zelophehad (Num 27:1–11; 36:1–12; and Josh 17:3–6), see Ben-Barak, 1980; and Sakenfeld, 1988. But there must have been families unable to support younger sons who would then have had to fend for themselves by day labor, military employment, brigandage, or something of the sort.

Roles Within the Household: Women

Far from being a uniquely Israelite and biblical phenomenon, gender-specific role performance is characteristic of all ancient and traditional societies. Adam delves and Eve spins or, as Samuel put it in his description of the burden of monarchy, men drive chariots, ride horses, fight and plough, while women do the cooking and make or apply perfume (1 Sam 8:10–13). Women belonged to the private sphere and therefore did not have the advantages of mobility; we therefore hear of itinerant "men of God" but not "women of God." The local well or spring – an important point for the reception and transmission of information and gossip – would be as far as most women ventured (e.g., Gen 24:11–27; 29:4–12). Abraham greeted and conversed with his three guests alone while Sarah stayed in the tent, prepared the food, and was embarrassed when caught eavesdropping (Gen 18:1–15). Even in the very different society of ancient Rome women did not accompany their husbands to dinner parties. Women were responsible for the raising, nurture, and education of children; they prepared food and wove clothes; at certain seasons they worked in the fields alongside the men, as women still do in Mediterranean countries. From birth until marriage, usually in the teenage years, they were under the protection of a father or senior male in the household. Outside of this (from our perspective) limiting ambient, women had few options. A woman who did not find a husband, or was divorced by her husband, or left him, might remain in, or return to, the household of origin if it was able and willing to support her. The only other options about which we hear are prostitution, prophecy, witchcraft (like the woman from Endor who carried on a black market in mediumistic consultation [1 Sam 28], midwifery, or running a kind of counseling agency like the "wise women" of Tekoa and Abel Beth-maacah (2 Sam 14:1–20; 20:14–22). As in other cultures, these last two may have gone together (cf. the French *sage femme* for midwife).

In Israel of the biblical period the situation was not improved by the apparent absence of legal provision for widows to inherit. Widows therefore had to depend on public charity inclusive of the triennial tithe, a kind of social security system (Deut 14:29; 26:12–13). The levirate law was meant to ensure their legal rights and keep the property in the family, though we can think of many reasons why it would have been more honored in the breach than the observance and, in any case, it was not mandatory (Deut 25:5–10). Widows also enjoyed some minimal protection from creditors (Deut 24:17) and such minor concessions as gleaning rights (Deut 24:19–21). But we really have no idea to what extent these legal provisions were honored and implemented. Prophetic diatribe on behalf of widows and their surviving children (e.g., Isa 1:27, 23; 10:2; Jer 7:6; Ezek 22:7), taken up in the same terms much later by Jesus (Luke 20:47), suggest that they may have had little impact. Some widows survived and even prospered by using their native wits: Abigail, widow of Nabal (nicknamed The Brute), ended up by marrying David (1 Sam 25:18–42); the woman of Shunam, who appears to have lost her husband, had to relocate due to famine but managed to get an audience with the king who restored her property to her (2 Kgs 4:8–37; 8:1–6); Tamar tricked her father-in-law Judah into playing the part of the *levir* (Gen 38:12–30); helped by her mother, Ruth exploited the institution of the levirate to her own advantage and won a husband. Others, like the widow of Zarephath (1 Kgs 17:8–24) and the wife of the ecstatic prophet, who was about to lose her son to creditors (2 Kgs 4:1–7), were not so fortunate.

In trying to form an idea of how women lived in that kind of society we have to look behind the attitudes and prejudices of the writers and cultures from which our sources derive for aspects of role performance and the social expectations which created the roles. Recent biblical-feminist writers have tended to concentrate on the latter to the neglect of the former. That women are so often represented as reacting rather than acting cannot be due entirely to authorial bias. In the thrice-told and much-exegeted story of the endangered ancestress (Gen 12:10–20; 20:1–18; 26:6–11) the woman (Sarah, Rebekah) is silent and passive, and it is Abraham who, after jeopardizing his wife's honor and virtue, receives compensation from the sexual aggressor (Gen 20:14–16). But we also hear of women fighting back to improve their situation and affirm their rights (defined as food, clothing, and marital relations in Ex 21:10), or even moving outside of their assigned roles, sometimes in remarkable ways. After escaping the gang rape to which their father had exposed them and losing their prospective husbands, Lot's daughters ensure the survival of their line by getting him drunk and having intercourse with him (Gen 19:8, 30–38). Tamar adopts a somewhat similar strategy with her father-in-law who had failed to provide a husband for her (Gen 38:1–30). Rebekah teams up with her favorite son to secure the rights of inheritance for him, in the process risking the curse of her ostensibly dying husband (Gen 27:1–45; he was still alive twenty years later, Gen 35:27–29). Leah and Rachel connive with Jacob to get back at their skinflint father, and Rachel in addition relieves him of his household gods (Gen 31:14–16, 19–21, 32–35).

While several officially sanctioned variations of the male–female bond in Israel of the biblical period are attested, including concubinage, surrogate childbearing and polygamy – this last permitted also in rabbinic law (m.Ketuvim 10:5; m.Ker. 3:7) – the standard marital union was essentially a transaction between households resulting in one household giving away one of its women in exchange for a substantial payment. The much discussed text of Gen 2:24 ("therefore a man leaves his father and his mother and cleaves to his wife so that they become one flesh") does not presuppose the practice of uxorilocal postmarital residence, much less matriarchy. The repetition of the key words *'îš* (man), *'iššâ* (woman), and *bāśār* (flesh) clearly identifies it as a comment or gloss on the previous verse, the exclamation of the Man after the newly formed Woman is brought to him (2:23). That the man does the leaving is therefore not indicative of a particular social organization. In keeping with the context, a man and a woman are to form a new unit distinct from the primary consanguineal bond; they are to reconstitute the unity of bone and flesh that existed before the separation of woman from man (cf. Laban to Jacob his kinsman, "you are my bone and my flesh," Gen 29:14). Not surprisingly, therefore, the laws governing marriage and inheritance are dictated by the economic interests of the household of destination and its male head. This is clearly the whole point of the levirate law (Deut 25:5–10), as also of the law governing the exceptional case of a daughter inheriting property (Num 27:1–11; 36:1–12; and Josh 17:3–6). No less so is it the case with the laws governing sexual mores. A man who rapes a woman either married or engaged to be married (the law makes no difference between the two states) is subject to the death penalty, but the rape of a woman neither married nor engaged results in a fine of fifty shekels payable to the father of the victim (Deut 22:22–29). In no case does the victim herself receive compensation for the violence visited upon her. The payment of a marriage price (*mōhar*) and the threat of losing the use or usufruct of the woman's dowry (*zebed*, Gen 30:20; *šillūḥîm*, 1 Kings 9:16) also constituted a powerful disincentive to divorce. The strange law about the new husband who fails to find the "tokens of virginity" (Deut 22:13–21) is transparently a case of a man looking for a pretext to divorce his newly-wed wife and at the same time recover the marriage fee and keep the dowry (Phillips, 1981). On the discussion as to whether the "tokens" consisted in a cloth stained with either hymenal or menstrual blood, see Pressler, 1993. Rape and adultery are therefore considered more as injuries inflicted on the father or husband rather than on the woman herself – in effect, a form of theft, an equation explicitly made in the didactic literature (e.g., Prov 6:29–35) and much later in Epictetus. On the laws governing these matters, see McKeating, 1979; Gordis, 1984; Westbrook, 1990; and Stulman, 1992.

We have no direct information on the legal aspects of divorce in Israel of the biblical period – who may initiate it, under what circumstances, and with what consequences. Due to a misreading of the text in Jerome's *editio vulgata* the Western Church took Deut 24:1–4 to be a law permitting divorce, and rabbinic authorities have drawn conclusions about marriage and divorce from it, but it simply forbids the remarriage of a divorced woman to her first husband after she has become the wife of another. On this issue of palingamy, see the contrasting views of Yaron, 1966; Wenham, 1979; and Laney, 1992. The text does, however, mention a *sēper kerîtūt* (later known as the *ketūbbâ*) to be given to the woman, presumably a document specifying conditions including the return of the *mōhar* and provision for children. Where divorce is referred to either realistically or metaphorically, it is invariably initiated by the male partner, from which it has been concluded that women could not initiate divorce proceedings. This may be so, but it may also mean no more than that the precarious economic situation of most women practically ruled out divorce as an option.

The first positive evidence for divorce initiated by the female partner comes from the Jewish military colony on the island of Jeb at the first cataract of the Nile in the Persian period, but this may be due to local Egyptian or even Persian influence. Josephus alludes to Salome and Herodias divorcing their husbands, and he himself was divorced twice; but needless to say neither the Herodians nor Josephus can be regarded as typical Jews of the Greco-Roman period. It therefore seems likely that, while divorce was normal and accepted practice during the time of the Second Temple, divorce by the woman remained quite exceptional (Collins, 1997).

Roles Within the Household: Children and Young Adults

Philippe Ariès' thesis that childhood as a distinct life phase only emerged in the early modern period (1962) might draw some support from the relative lack of data about children from Israel and other ancient Near Eastern and Levantine societies. No provision is made in Israelite law for the protection of minors and it would be quite anachronistic to speak of them as the subject of rights. Children were under the absolute authority of the *paterfamilias* as long as they remained in the household, though state encroachment eventually set limits to the exercise of arbitrary judicial and punitive power by the head of the household. A case in point is the law concerning the ungovernable son (Deut 21:18–21), meaning a young adult member of the household. As a last resort both parents bring him before the city elders, presumably to allow for some investigative process that could end with the son being executed. The law is set out in too succinct and abbreviated a form to allow us to see how it might have been implemented; for example, it makes no allowance for refutation of the charges brought by the parents or for appeal. This law may serve to make the point that the household provided security for children but at considerable cost to the latter. So, for example, throughout the entire period inclusive of early Judaism, children could be and no doubt often were sold into indentured service in order to amortize debts (Ex 21:7; 2 Kgs 4:1–7; Neh 5:1–5). Cursing or striking a parent was subject to the death penalty (Ex 21:15,17; Lev 20:9; Deut 27:16), as opposed to mutilation of a hand in the Code of Hammurapi (#195). The decalogic command to honor and obey parents is also one of the most frequently recurring themes in the didactic literature (e.g., Prov 20:20; 30:11,17; Sir 3:1–16), and the precept is reinforced by strict discipline including physical punishment; "beat them," the sage says, "they won't die" (Prov 23:13–14; cf. 13:24; 29:17–18). Of great importance was the duty to see that the parent was buried on the ancestral land and his or her memory perpetuated. In one of the Late Bronze Age texts discovered at Ras Shamra (Ugarit) a king laments the lack of a son who would not only perform services for him during his (the king's) lifetime, such as taking care of him and cleaning him up when he is drunk, but would see to the wellbeing of his spirit after death (Aqhat A I 22–35, trans. Pritchard,

1968, *ANET*, 150; and Coogan, 1978. See Healey, 1979). Such services were considered essential for the continuity and integrity of the household as a totality including both its living and dead members. Failure to honor parents in this way brought on the negligent son the most frightful of curses (cf. Prov 20:20; 30:17).

A ritual act seems to have been carried out at the birth of a child by which the father acknowledged paternity, perhaps by accepting the child on his knees (Job 3:12; cf. Gen 30:3; 50:23). An analogous practice in ancient Babylonia was the simple pronouncement of the phrase "my child" (Hammurapi ##170–1), and much later in Rome the infant was laid on the ground to be picked up by the father. It seems that in Israel the naming could be by either parent (Gen 16:15–16; 21:3; 29:32–30:13; 1 Sam 1:20; 4:21). The exposure or killing of unwanted children, especially female children, common in many ancient societies (e.g., Roman law in the fourth of the Twelve Tablets, ca. 450 BCE; and a letter among the Oxyrhynchus papyri, 1 BCE, quoted by Leftkowitz and Fant, 1982, p. 111), is (unsurprisingly) not referred to in the biblical texts, though the much maligned allegory of the female child cast out in the open field and rescued by YHWH in Ezekiel 16 suggests that the exposure of female children was not unknown. Throughout most of the period we are covering, abortion was not a problem since children were a valuable resource and infant mortality was high. The point may be illustrated by the law requiring monetary restitution for injury to a pregnant woman leading to miscarriage (Ex 21:22–23). The injury is assumed to be directed exclusively at the married couple, but the rewording of the law in the Septuagint, which distinguishes between an unformed fetus and a fully formed child (*'exeikonísmenon* [*paídion*]), shows how abortion had become a problematic issue by the Greco-Roman period (Blenkinsopp, 1992, pp. 202–3; and 1997b, pp. 69–70; and for Roman law, Biale, 1984, pp. 219–38). While abortion was certainly practiced at that time, especially among the upper classes, it was condemned by philosophers and moralists, and the condemnation passed over into early Christianity (e.g., in the *Didache* or *Teaching of the Twelve Apostles*).

Infants would be either breastfed by the mother or handed over to a wet nurse (cf. Ex 2:7; Num 11:12). They would be weaned usually around the age of three (cf. 1 Sam 1:24 LXX; 2 Macc 7:27), a practice which continued for centuries. (We recall how in *Romeo and Juliet* the Nurse reminisces about weaning Juliet at the age of three.) During that period, and for some time thereafter, the nurture and education of the child was the responsibility of the mother. In this context "education" involved nothing more than acculturating the child to the ethos of the household, teaching elementary skills, telling stories, and no doubt also instilling some basic religious ideas. Hence the solicitude shown in the choice of a wife for the eldest son and the (male) anxiety about the "outsider woman" evident throughout the biblical literature. The texts which have drawn the most attention in recent years are those in which the ancestors look for wives from their own kinship network (Genesis 24; 27:46–28:5), Ezra's campaign aimed at dissolving marriages with local women (Ezra 9–10), and the warnings and fulminations against the "outsider woman" ('iššâ zārâ/'iššâ nŏkrîyyâ) in Proverbs 1–9. Once the male child was old enough to take part in the daily tasks of the household he came directly under the authority of the father, a passage which one imagines could have been quite traumatic. Apart from specialist groups engaged in crafts, scribal and cultic activity or the politics of the court, no formal education was necessary and none was available. Literacy was therefore confined to these classes, which constituted a very small percentage of the total, predominantly agrarian, population. The case for widespread literacy in Israel has been argued strenuously by A. Millard (1985). One should compare the more realistic estimates of I. M. Young (1988) and W. V. Harris (1989) who concludes that even in Periclean Athens literacy did not exceed 10 percent. We have no evidence for schools in anything like our understanding of the term before the later Second Temple period when – in the early years of the 2nd century BCE – we hear Ben Sira advertising for students for his "house of instruction" (bêt midrāš, 51:23).

The Religion of the Household

The biblical sources are particularly uncooperative in the matter of religious practice in the private sphere of the household. This is not only because they deal primarily with the public sphere and official religious ideas and practice, but they also tend either to represent people as thinking, speaking, and acting according to these ideas or to condemn them for not doing so. Where available, archaeological data speak more directly, though their interpretation can also be problematic (Dever, 1983; and van der Toorn, 1996). An example of our problem with sources, and one of immediate relevance to the household, is that of mortuary practices accompanying the passing of the paterfamilias, and the veneration of ancestors in general. Mortuary rites, cult offered to ancestors, and any form of commerce with the dead, were condemned in the laws as pagan aberrations (e.g., Deut 14:1–2; 18:9–14; 26:14; Lev 19:27–28; 21:5), but there is enough evidence to show that they were practiced in Israel as they were everywhere else in the Near East. The shades of dead ancestors (rĕpā'îm; Smith, 1992) were thought in some way to have entered the sphere of the divine and therefore required attention and propitiation by the living members of the household. In the way of thinking of ordinary people, the boundary between the human and the divine was permeable, and it is likely that ancestors were thought of as a first layer or level of the sphere of the divine as it impinged on human affairs. At any rate, ancestors are referred to occasionally as 'ĕlohîm, divine beings (Num 25:2; Ps 106:28; 1 Sam 28:12; 2 Sam 14:26; and Isa 8:19–20). This idea was common in the Near East (Bayliss, 1973; Pope, 1981; and Huenergard, 1985). The occasional discovery of cult objects in private dwellings suggests the practice of cult addressed to representations of familial deities known as tĕrāpîm, similar to the Roman lares et penates (cf. Gen 31:19, 34–35).

The authors of the Deuteronomic law code condemned such practices and aimed to impose the worship of YHWH as the one national deity, but success came slowly. That the cult of the goddess Asherah alongside YHWH was part of the official liturgy for long periods is implicitly acknowledged in prohibitions under the Deuteronomic law (Deut 16:21) and explicitly attested in the official history of the two kingdoms (1 Kings 15:13; 18:19; 2 Kings 21:7; 23:4–7). It is also affirmed as something well known by the opponents of Jeremiah in Egypt after the fall of Jerusalem, who remind him that their ancestors, princes, and rulers had long benefited by venerating "the Queen of Heaven" (Jer 44:15–19).

The worship of YHWH alone became the *de facto* official religion of Israel only after a long struggle continuing down into the Second Temple period, and remnants of older practice can be detected even later. A similar situation is attested in the process by which Christianity became the official religion of western European countries. The discovery of numerous figurines of the goddess and inscriptions in which Asherah is closely associated with YHWH confirm the situation which a close reading of the biblical texts insinuates (Mazar, 1990; Day, 1992; and the graffiti at Kuntillet ʿAjrud in the Sinai which contain blessings in the name of YHWH and his Asherah, Meshel, 1992). This is no more than we would expect from the average peasant household concerned as it was with the fertility of the fields, livestock, and womenfolk, and relief from disease, drought, and taxation. Moreover, help would be sought near at hand, from whatever manifestation of YHWH, El, Baal, or Asherah had come to be associated with a local holy place. One interpretation of the opening verse of the *shemaʿ* (*YHWH ʾĕlōhēnû YHWH ʾeḥād*, Deut 6:4), which can be read "YHWH our God is one YHWH," takes it as polemicizing against different local manifestations of YHWH (Miller et al., 1987). At all times religious sentiment has been most closely associated with a sense of and attachment to place, one's own land and familiar surroundings.

The festivals corresponding to the key events of the agrarian year – the barley harvest in the spring (*maṣṣôt-pesaḥ*), the wheat harvest about seven weeks later (*šavuôt*), and the harvesting of grapes, olives, and figs in the late summer (*sukkôt*) – would have been celebrated at one or other of the local sanctuaries known in our texts as "high places" (*bāmôt*), against which the proponents of the state cult polemicized so long and with such limited success. Though their early history is obscure, sabbath and new moon also served to break up the routine of agrarian life. The annual clan sacrifice (*zebaḥ hayyāmîm*), which all adult male members were expected to attend, was an essential means of preserving and reinforcing the identity and solidarity of the larger kinship network (1 Sam 1:3; 20:5–6, 28–29). Sacrifice was the most important way of verifying and controlling membership in the phratry (*mišpāḥâ*), of social bonding, and of sanctioning an order based on patriliny (cf. the Roman *sacra gentilicia*). Inevitably it too came under attack with the increasing encroachment of the state on the traditional kinship nexus and its various manifestations. The centralization of a sacrificial cult in Jerusalem and the requirement that adult males present themselves at the state sanctuary three times a year (Deut 12:5–28; 16:16) would seem to be one strategy for transferring allegiance from the clan or phratry to the state.

Beyond Family Values

In view of the frequent and often contentious discussions of the family and family values going on today it may be useful to conclude with one or two considerations arising out of our survey which caution against absolutizing or canonizing any one understanding of family or a particular set of values and ideals that have come to be associated with the family. The first is the decisive role of the economic factor in maintaining the bond within the household. This is true in the first place of marriage as essentially a system of exchange bringing economic rewards to the household of origination (the marriage price) and destination (the dowry), but only indirectly if at all to the bride. This was the price she had to pay for a measure of security within the household. It is interesting and even amusing to observe how, in the negotiations leading to the espousal of Rebekah to Isaac, things begin to get serious when Laban, her brother and ward, catches sight of the expensive jewelry Abraham's servant dangles before his eyes (Gen 24:30–33). Only then does he affirm enthusiastically that "the thing comes from YHWH" (v. 50). We have noted too how penalties for offenses against women are graded according to the damage to the interest of father or husband. Marriage arrangements were, however, only one aspect of the arbitrary power of the *paterfamilias*. Our own sad familiarity with spouse abuse and child abuse suggests that the encroachment of state jurisdiction on the traditional household was in important respects a positive development.

Throughout the biblical period the household served as a structural model for the formation of alternative "familial" communities the presence of which in some respects provided a counterbalance to the traditional household. The ecstatic–prophetic conventicles known as "sons of the prophets" (*běnê hannebi'îm*), for example, were self-regulating groups of adherents living communally and apart from society under a "father" (*'āb*, 1 Sam 10:12; 2 Kgs 2:12; 13:14). They were poor and not generally held in high esteem. Some of them were married (see, e.g., 2 Kgs 4:1–7), others no doubt single. Artisan and scribal guilds in the later period also seem to have been organized in a quasi-familial way, and in fact were known as families (*mišpāḥôt*, 1 Chr 2:55; 4:21). The sects that emerged in the later Second Temple period must have given at least some of their members the economic and emotional security which the traditional household existed to provide. The same can be said for the other numerous voluntarist organizations attested from late antiquity – cults, funerary societies and the like, especially those frequented by women – as well as religious orders in the history of the Christian church. They also offered alternative models by breaking the monopoly of status, honor, and prestige claimed by kinship and household, or redefining the values associated with the family. In this respect the notable indifference of the Jesus of the gospels to what are usually called family values (e.g., Mark 10:28–31; Luke 12:51–53; 14:25–27), and his sayings directed against the urge to acquire and maintain possessions and exercise control over the lives of others (e.g., Mark 10:17–22, 42–45; Luke 12:25), both well developed tendencies within the traditional household, have not always received due attention. Throughout the biblical period the household was the fundamental social form of life, but no less than other institutions it could serve to diminish as well as to amplify the scope of human living.

Bibliography

Ariès, P., *Centuries of Childhood. A Social History of Family Life*, trans. R. Baldick (London: Jonathan Cape, 1962).

Bayliss, M., "The Cult of the Dead Kin in Assyria and in Babylonia," *Iraq* 35 (1973), 115–25.

Ben-Barak, Z., "Inheritance by Daughters in the Ancient Near East," *JSS* 25 (1980), 22–33.

Biale, R., *Women and Jewish Law* (New York: Schocken Books, 1984).

Blenkinsopp, J., *The Pentateuch* (New York: Doubleday, 1992).

———, "Life Expectancy in Ancient Palestine," *Scandinavian Journal of the Old Testament* 11 (1997a), 44–55.

———, *Families in Ancient Israel* (Louisville: Westminster/John Knox Press, 1997b), 69–70.

Collins, J., "Marriage, Divorce and Family in Second Temple Judaism," in L. Perdue et al., *Families in Ancient Israel* (Louisville: Westminster/John Knox Press, 1997), 104–62.

Coogan, M., *Stories from Ancient Canaan* (Philadelphia: Westminster Press, 1978), 32–47.

Day, J., "Asherah," *ABD* 1 (1992), 483–7.

Dever, W. G., "Material Remains and the Cult in Ancient Israel: An Essay in Archaeological Systematics," in C. Meyers and M. O'Connor, eds., *The Word Shall Go Forth: Essays in Honor of David Noel Freedman in Celebration of his Sixtieth Birthday* (Winona Lake: Eisenbrauns, 1983), 571–87.

Donaldson, M. E., "Kinship Theory in the Patriarchal Narratives: The Case of the Barren Wife," *JAAR* 49 (1981), 77–87.

Finkelstein, I., *The Archaeology of the Israelite Settlement* (Jerusalem: Israel Exploration Society, 1988).

Gibson, J. C. L., *Textbook of Syrian Semitic Inscriptions. Volume I: Hebrew and Moabite Inscriptions* (Oxford: Clarendon Press, 1971), 5–20, 71–83.

Goody, J., "Adoption in Cross-cultural Perspective," *Comparative Studies in Society and History* 11 (1969), 55–78.

Gordis, R., "On Adultery in Biblical and Babylonian Law – a note," *Judaism* 33 (1984), 210–11.

Harris, W. V., *Ancient Literacy* (Cambridge, MA: Harvard University Press, 1989).

Healey, J., "The *Pietas* of an Ideal Son in Ugarit," *Ugarit-Forschungen* 11 (1979), 353–6.

Holladay, Jr., J., "House, Israelite," *Anchor Bible Dictionary* 3 (New York: Doubleday, 1992), 308–18.

Huenergard, J., "Biblical Notes on Some New Akkadian Texts from Emar," *CBQ* 47 (1985), 428–34.

Knobloch, F., "Adoption," *ABD* 1 (1992), 76–9.

Laney, J., "Deut 24:1–4 and the Issue of Divorce," *Bibliotheca Sacra* 149 (1992), 3–15.

Leftkowitz, M. and M. Fant, *Women's Life in Greece and Rome* (Baltimore: The Johns Hopkins University Press, 1982).

McCarter, Jr., P., "Aspects of the Religion of the Israelite Monarchy: Biblical and Epigraphic Data," in P. Miller, et al., eds., *Ancient Israelite Religion* (Philadelphia: Fortress Press, 1987), 137–55.

McKeating, H., "Sanctions against adultery in ancient Israelite society with some reflections on methodology in the study of Old Testament ethics," *JSOT* 11 (1979), 57–72.

Mazar, A., *Archaeology of the Land of the Bible 10,000–586 BCE* (New York and London: Doubleday, 1990), 501–2.

Meshel, Z., "Kuntillet 'Ajrud," *ABD* 4 (1992), 103–9.

Meyers, C., "To Her Mother's House. Considering a Counterpart to the Israelite *Bet 'ab*," in D. Jobling, et al., eds., *The Bible and the Politics of Exegesis* (Cleveland: Pilgrim Press, 1991), 39–51.

Millard, A., "An Assessment of the Evidence for Writing in Ancient Israel," in A. Biran, *Biblical Archaeology Today* (Jerusalem, 1985), 301–12.

Miller, Jr., P. D., et al., *Ancient Israelite Religion* (Philadelphia: Fortress Press, 1987).

Negev, A., *The Archaeological Encyclopedia of the Holy Land*, 3rd edn. (New York and London: Prentice-Hall, 1990), 178.

Oden, R. A., "Jacob as Father, Husband and Nephew: Kinship Studies and Patriarchal Narratives," *JBL* 102 (1983), 189–205.

Phillips, A., "Another Look at Adultery," *JSOT* 20 (1981), 3–25.

Pope, M., "The Cult of the Dead at Ugarit," in G. Young, *Ugarit in Retrospect* (Winona Lake: Eisenbrauns, 1981), 159–79.

Pressler, C., *The View of Women Found in the Deuteronomic Family Laws* (Berlin and New York: Walter de Gruyter, 1993), 22–31.

Pritchard, J., ed., *Ancient Near Eastern Texts*, 3rd edn. (Princeton: Princeton University Press, 1968).

Sakenfeld, K. D., "Zelophehad's Daughters," *Perspectives in Religious Studies* 15 (1988), 37–47.

Shiloh, Y., "The Population of Iron Age Palestine in the Light of a Sample Analysis of Urban Plans, Areas, and Population Density," *BASOR* 239 (1980), 25–35.

Smith, M., "Rephaim," *ABD* 5 (1992), 674–6.

Stager, L., "The Archaeology of the Family in Ancient Israel," *BASOR* 260 (1985), 1–35.

Steinberg, N., *Kinship and Marriage in Genesis: A Household Economics Perspective* (Minneapolis: Fortress Press, 1993).

Stulman, L., "Sex and Familiar Crimes in the D Code: a witness to mores in transition," *JSOT* 53 (1992), 47–64.

van der Toorn, K., *Family Religion in Babylonia, Syria and Israel: Continuity and Change in the Forms of Religious Life* (Leiden: E. J. Brill, 1996).

Van Seters, J., *Abraham in History and Tradition* (New Haven: Yale University Press, 1975).

Veyne, P., *A History of Private Life from Pagan Rome to Byzantium* (Cambridge, MA: The Belknap Press of Harvard University Press, 1987), 1–233.

von Rad, G., "The Promised Land and Yahweh's Land in the Hexateuch," *The Problem of the Hexateuch and Other Essays* (Edinburgh and London: Oliver & Boyd, 1966), 79–93.

Wenham, G., "The Restoration of Marriage Reconsidered," *JJS* 30 (1979), 36–40.

Westbrook, R., "Adultery in Ancient Near Eastern Law," *RB* 97 (1990), 542–80.

Wright, C., *God's People in God's Land* (Grand Rapids: Eerdmans, 1990).

Yaron, R., "The Restoration of Marriage," *JJS* 17 (1966), 1–11.

Young, I. M., "Israelite Literacy: Interpreting the Evidence. Part 1," *VT* 48 (1988), 239–53.

Zorn, J., "Estimating the Population Size of Ancient Settlements: Methods, Problems, Solutions, and a Case Study," *BASOR* 295 (1994), 31–48.

CHAPTER 11

Archaeology, the Israelite Monarchy, and the Solomonic Temple

William G. Dever

No major history of ancient Israel has appeared in nearly fifteen years; and a recent collection of essays raises the question of whether a "history of ancient Israel" can any longer be written (Grabbe, 1997). The fundamental question is one of *sources*, both textual and archaeological. The historiographical malaise is most clearly reflected in the works of a small but vocal group of European biblical scholars in the last decade styling themselves as "revisionists," who question the historical validity of both texts and artifacts. The biblical texts are all "stories" of the Hellenistic era, projected back upon an imaginary "ancient Israel," of no historical value, in effect "pious forgeries." And the archaeological evidence, while potentially illustrative for the Iron Age, is thus far largely "mute," even with regard to an ancient "Palestine," much less "Biblical Israel."[1]

Elsewhere I have reviewed in detail the "revisionist" challenge to biblical historiography and to Syro-Palestinian archaeology.[2] Here I shall confine our treatment largely to what has become the crux of the discussion: Was there an "Israelite Monarchy" in the 10th–7th centuries BCE, as portrayed by the biblical writers?

The Israelite Monarchy and the Iron II Period in General

The United Monarchy in the 10th century BCE

The biblical data in archaeological context.   It is obvious that the school of Deuteronomistic historians (DTR) who produced the narrative that we now have in the Books of Samuel and Kings of the reigns of Saul, David, and Solomon were not writing "history" in our sense. Not only did they have their own later theological biases, but they also embellished and exaggerated greatly in drawing upon whatever oral traditions and written sources that they may have had. Thus modern critical historians may reasonably doubt that Saul was miraculously and universally acclaimed a king, or that he was anything more than a sort of "chieftain"; that David was the serial killer that he is portrayed as having been; or that Solomon had an empire that was gold-plated and extended from the Mediterranean to the Euphrates.

The "revisionists" are thus hardly innovative in pointing out that much of the story of the "United Monarchy" as it now stands is so admittedly filled with legends and so overlain with theocratic agendas that its overall character is largely "mythical." Nevertheless, that scarcely justifies the rejection of the entire tradition as historically *worthless*, as Lemche and Thompson do. They state:

> In the history of Palestine that we have presented, there is no room for a historical United Monarchy, for such kings as those presented in the biblical stories of Saul, David or Solomon. The early period in which the traditions have set their narratives is an imaginary world of long ago that never existed as such. (Lemche and Thompson, 1994, p. 19)

Lemche and Thompson go on to argue that Jerusalem was not the "capital" of *any* polity before the mid-7th century BCE, and not really an important political center until the 2nd century BCE, i.e., in the Hasmonean era. Thus there was no Israelite or Judean "monarchy," only some entity known to the 9th century and later Neo-Assyrian texts as the "province of Samarina," with its center at Samaria in the north.[3]

When confronted by the recently discovered Tel Dan inscription of the mid–late 9th century BCE, mentioning the "house (i.e., dynasty) of David" and a "king of Israel" who must be Jehoram of Israel (ca. 849–842 BCE), the "revisionists" simply dismiss the inscription as a modern forgery.[4] Similarly, other "revisionists" like Davies cavalierly discount the massive archaeological and epigraphic data that enable us to reconstruct an Israelite national culture in the Iron Age, or the 10th–7th centuries BCE, as "irrelevant" because it does not reflect *their* "biblical world" in the Hellenistic era.[5] Yet, nowhere, as far as I can see, have the "revisionists" made a convincing case that the Hebrew Bible is really a product of the Hellenistic era; that would require them to demonstrate that the Bible's "stories" have their *Sitz im Leben* (or "real-life setting") only then, and not earlier, in the Iron Age or era of "ancient Israel" as envisioned by the biblical writers – and, indeed, as assumed by mainstream biblical scholarship today, despite some skeptical voices.

Presently I shall show that archaeology demonstrates that the only believable context for the major narrative themes of the Hebrew Bible lies in the Iron Age. Meanwhile, if we assume that there is a "historical core" within the literary tradition – some reliable history of ancient Israel – of what does such a historical "core" or outline consist, thinking at this point only of the United Monarchy?

I would argue that the "core" of the narrative in Kings, stripped of the obvious fantastic elements and later theological editorializing, is inherently credible.

(1)   For the Saulide era, the portrait of a charismatic, larger-than-life, Saul-like figure around whom a nucleus of power develops fits almost precisely the "chiefdom" model for nascent states that is widespread in social anthropology.[6] Thus Saul's reign "makes sense" as depicted in its essential elements: reputed divine calling; popular acclaim; the raising of a militia; protracted campaigns against military rivals and neighboring peoples; the struggle to achieve ethnic unity; the lack of the traditional trappings of a state; and, after brief success, dramatic downfall and confusion over his successor.

What about external corroboration? Admittedly there are no extra-biblical textual references to Saul, as the "revisionists" point out. But none are to be expected, since the Neo-Assyrian annals – the only possible source in the late 11th/early 10th centuries BCE – have not yet encountered any of the petty states-in-the-making in the west (see below). The archaeological evidence for this period (ca. 1020–1000 BCE) is understandably meager, due to its brevity and dearth of monumental remains. But it is important to note that there is nothing in the archaeological record as it is known thus far that *contradicts* the essentials of the Deuteronomistic narrative of Saul's rise. Archaeologically, the late 11th–early 10th century BCE represents a "proto-urban" era that would provide a suitable context.[7]

(2)   David (ca. 1000–960 BCE) is portrayed by the Deuteronomists as becoming a truly king-like figure also because of charismatic gifts, but largely through political cunning and undisguised ruthlessness. Thus David is the real founder of a sort of "petty-state," held together by shaky alliances but increasingly marked by centralization of power in the hands of a small ruling elite. The fledgling state can even claim a capital in Jerusalem.[8] David, like Saul, has remained without extra-biblical textual documentation, at least until the discovery of the Tel Dan inscription (see above). The archaeological evidence is again slight, although not non-existent as the "revisionists" claim.[9] Jerusalem as a "capital" in the 10th century BCE is the crux; and while the evidence is scant and difficult to interpret, a number of archaeologists and biblical historians have come down on the positive side. The affirmative conclusions of Nadav Na'aman, a well-respected historian whom some would associate with the "minimalist" school, are particularly significant. Na'aman, like many archaeologists, points out that the claimed "lack of any evidence" in Shiloh's City of David, Str. 14, means very little, since the appropriate levels were scarcely reached. He goes on to point out that few if any LB II remains were found either (14th century BCE); yet we *know* from the Amarna letters written by Canaanite princes to the Egyptian court that Jerusalem was already the capital of a kingdom, with kings whose personal names are well attested (Na'aman, 1997). Finally, it should be noted that the massive stepped-stone terrace of the City of David was likely either built or rebuilt by David and Solomon and is probably the *millo*, or "filling," mentioned in 2 Sam 5:9 and 1 Kgs 9:15. In addition, "Warren's Shaft," recleared by Shiloh and his team, can plausibly be connected with the biblical *tsinnor*, or "water conduit," by means of which David took the city (2 Sam 5:8).[10] Elsewhere in the country, a number of sites

show evidence of increasing urbanization and unification, and possibly even some destruction levels that could be associated with David's campaigns against the Philistines.[11]

(3) *Solomon*. It is the "legendary Solomon" who has recently come under the heaviest fire from the "revisionists."[12] However, discounting the obvious legends and fables in the biblical story as it now stands, what we have left is again perfectly reasonable. The essential elements are: a king in reality, who inherits by dynastic succession; a long, stable, and prosperous reign that is marked principally by the centralization of power, prestige, and administration in a royal capital and cultus; and the cultivation of international relations.

The above are *precisely* the elements that constitute a "state" as defined in the voluminous cross-cultural literature in anthropology and archaeology – especially the element of *centralization*. Thus Service, a noted authority, says that the state is "bureaucratic governance by legal force" (1962, p. 175); or Sahlins, equally noted, observes that "the State is a society in which there is a set of offices of the society at large, conferring governance over the society at large" (1968, p. 6).

The "revisionists" unanimously reject the notion of a "Solomonic state" (above); yet nowhere in their voluminous writings on the subject do we encounter even a minimal working definition of "state," much less a knowledge of what would be called the archaeological correlates of "state-formation processes." Nor do the "revisionists" cite the considerable data that we now have from Palestine in the 10th and 9th centuries BCE (below). Once again, we are bombarded by cavalier, minimalist assertions that fly in the face of all the archaeological evidence.[13]

In the anthropological literature on state-formation processes, one should also note that *size* alone is never a criterion for defining statehood, as Lemche and Thompson suppose in claiming that 10th century BCE Israel was "too small" to constitute a state (really their only argument). Compare their "few dozen villages in all the Judean highlands" (Lemche and Thompson 1994, p. 19) with archaeologists' documentation of as many as a dozen fairly large cities and a population estimate of ca. 100,000 in the 10th century BCE.[14] To these and other archaeological data we now turn, examining the evidence entirely *independently* of the biblical narrative, however credible.

Other archaeological evidence. If centralization, usually (although not necessarily) accompanied by increasing urbanization, is the hallmark of a developing state, as argued above, what is the archaeological evidence for 10th century BCE Palestine, where a biblical "United Monarchy" would have to be situated? Until recently some of the primary evidence was thought to be the existence of nearly identical monumental three-entryway city gates and casemate or double walls, sometimes with adjoining palaces, at provincial administrative centers such as Hazor (Str. X), Megiddo (Str VA/IVB), and Gezer (Str. VIII). These were dated confidently by archaeological consensus to the mid–late 10th century BCE

– i.e., "Solomonic" in date – on both stratigraphic and ceramic grounds, *not*, I would stress, on any presumed biblical witness.[15]

The stratigraphic argument rests largely on the fact that most of these gates, certainly that at Gezer, were constructed some time before a fiery destruction. That destruction was most likely due to the 22nd Dynasty Egyptian Pharaoh Sheshonq, whose campaign list of ca. 925 BCE mentions some 175 sites in Palestine, including Megiddo, and in all likelihood Gezer.[16] By coincidence (?), this same Sheshonq (as "Shishak") is mentioned in 1 Kgs 14:25–28 and 2 Chr 12:2–4, and his raid is correlated with the fifth year after Solomon's death. This yields an invaluable *archaeological* synchronism, i.e., one dependent not upon biblical data, but upon stratigraphic sequences fixed by Egyptian astronomical dates. (Coincidentally, how could the biblical editors have *known* about the Shishak synchronism if their account was composed only in the Hellenistic era, some 700 years later?)

The ceramic argument for a 10th century BCE date rests upon the fact that all three of the above sites – as well as some twenty other sites now excavated and mentioned in the Shishak list – are characterized by distinctive red-burnished and *hand*-slipped wares below and in the destruction layers, but *wheel*-burnished wares above. Thus hand-burnishing, pre-Shishak in date, appears to be "diagnostic" for the mid-10th century BCE in Palestine at all sites.[17]

Needless to say, both the stratigraphic and the ceramic arguments are ignored by the "revisionists"; nor would they be competent to assess such archaeological data. They also discount another archaeological correlation with biblical texts, the well-known reference in 1 Kgs 9:15–17 to Solomon's building activities at the specific three sites discussed above: Hazor, Megiddo, and Gezer (plus, of course, Jerusalem).

Before bringing the discussion up to date, we should note that Hazor, Megiddo, and Gezer do not stand alone. Elsewhere I have documented no fewer than thirty 10th century BCE sites in Palestine, a dozen or so of them true cities judged by any of the usual criteria. What is more significant is the fact that these thirty sites fall into the "three-tier" hierarchical arrangement that is widely held to define urban or "highly complex" societies. And together the eleven "tier 1" cities may represent some 20,000 people, or 20 percent of the estimated 10th century population of 100,000.[18] This is further archaeological confirmation of an Israelite "state" at this time, again ignored by the "revisionists": both adequate size and centralization to constitute a true state (see table 11.1).

Despite the apparently fixed date of a number of sites in the 10th century BCE, many yielding evidence of urbanization and centralization and therefore of early statehood, the conventional date has recently been challenged by the "low chronology" proposed by Israel Finkelstein and a few of his colleagues at Tel Aviv University. They argue, for instance, that Hazor X, Megiddo VA/IVB, and Gezer VIII must all be down-dated to the early–mid 9th century BCE, which would obviously rob us of significant data for the United Monarchy.[19] The biblical "revisionists," of course, have seized upon the "low chronology" as support for their denial of any early monarchy, even though it should be noted that

Table 11.1   "Three-tier" hierarchy of major 10th century BCE sites in Palestine with population estimates. Some coastal and Jordan Valley sites are eliminated since they are probably "non-Israelite."

Rank	Sites, 10th cent. BCE	Size (ac.)	Population	9th cent. BCE	Source
"Tier 1"	Dan IV	50	5,000	III	
Cities	Hazor X–XI	15	1,500	VIII–VII	
(22,350	Megiddo VA/IVB*	13.5 (15–25)	1,300 (500)	IVA	YS
total	Ta'anach IIA–B	16	1,600	III	
population)	Beth-shan Upper	10	1,000	IV	
	Tell el-Far'ah N. VIIb	15 (?)	1,500	VIIc–d	
	Shechem X	13	1,300	IX	
	Aphek X_8	15	1,500	X_7	
	Gezer IX–VIII	33	3,300	VII	
	Jerusalem 14	32	2,500	13	YS
	Lachish V	18 (38)	1,800 (500)	IV	YS; H
"Tier 2"	Tel Kinrot V–IV	1.25	1,250	III	
Towns	Tel Amal III	0.75	75		
	Yoqneam XVI–XIV	10	1,000	XIII	
	Tel Qiri VIIA	2.5	2,500	VIIB–C	
	Dothan 4 (?)*	10 (15)	1,000		YS
	Tel Mevorakh VIII–VII	1.5	150		
	Tell Michal XIV–XIII	0.3	30		
	Tell Qasile IX–VIII	4	400	VII	
	Azekah	14 (?)	1,400 (?)		
	Tel Batash IV	6.5	650	III	
	Beth-Shemesh IIa	10	1,000	IIb	
	Tell el-Ful II		?	?	
	Tell Hama		1	100	
	Tell Mazar XII	?	?		
	Tell Beit Mirsim B_3*	7.5	750 (1,300)	A_2	H
	Tel Halif VII		300	VIA	
	Tel Ser'a VII		500	VI	
	Beersheba VI (V?)*	2.5	250 (600)	(?V) IV	H
	Arad XII		?	XI–X	
"Tier 3"	Tell el-Kheleifeh I			II?	
Villages,	Qadesh-Barnea 1			2	
hamlets,	Negev forts				
camps, etc.					

Note: YS = Yigal Shiloh's in parenthesis; H = Ze'ev Herzog.

Finkelstein himself still maintains that there was a 10th century Israelite "territorial state," however small and short-lived (Finkelstein, 1995, p. 362; cf. 1998b, pp. 33, 34). The ceramic arguments on which the "low chronology" rests are too complex and esoteric to be discussed here (cf. Mazar, 1999a). Suffice it to say, however, that thus far no leading archaeologist except Finkelstein has ventured into print to defend the "low chronology"; and the evidence is mounting that it will soon be discredited by excavations in progress and by restudy of the pertinent material.[20] Meanwhile, biblicists should be wary of assuming that this chronology favors a minimalist or even negative view of the United Monarchy.

On the problem of "sources" for the United Monarchy.   Biblical scholarship has traditionally regarded the Deuteronomistic history in which the narratives concerning the United Monarchy are now embedded as having been compiled not earlier than the mid–late 7th century BCE, probably during the Josianic and prophetic reform movements at the end of Judah's history. It is usually assumed, however, that the redactors of the literary tradition possessed older sources. Some of these may have been written close to, and even contemporary with, the original events, such as the long "Court History of David," or the often-mentioned "Chronicle of the Kings of Israel." Yet an early date for any sources, oral or written, is now questioned by the "revisionists." For them, not only the final editing, but the *composition*, of the Deuteronomistic history is to be placed in the Hellenistic era, so that this work is entirely fictional, the product of Judaism's identity crisis long after the "real history" of ancient Israel, if any.[21]

Can archaeology comment on the problem of "sources," possibly serving to date various strands of the literary tradition by providing a credible context? In short, can we use archaeological data to answer the question: "What did the biblical writers know, and when did they know it?" Are there clues in the final redaction to earlier sources, now lost to us? I have already suggested that there are, in noting clear biblical references to such things as the *millo* and *tsinnor* in 10th century Jerusalem or the reference in Kings and Chronicles to the raid of Shishak, correlating it with Solomon's death five years earlier.

We can add other indications, however, of the biblical editor's knowledge of actual conditions in the 10th century, even though remote from their own day. For instance, the well-known list of twelve district administrative centers of Solomon's reign in 1 Kgs. 4 has often been regarded as a later fiction. Yet today one can state confidently that ten of the twelve cities listed can be positively identified with known archaeological sites. All ten have been excavated to some degree and indeed have 10th century levels. And at least five (Tirzah, Hazor, Megiddo, Gezer, and Beth-shemesh) have urban installations, monumental architecture, and other elements that would be consistent with the functions of a district capital in a highly centralized administrative system like that attributed by the biblical writers to Solomon.[22]

Is the biblical editors' mention of such centers a literary invention, the fact that they actually existed three centuries earlier a mere coincidence? Perhaps; but it is hardly likely. Again these are not, as the "revisionists" claim, stories made up in the Hellenistic age, but rather *real* stories from the early Iron Age, resulting from factual knowledge that the biblical writers or editors had in some form. (Incidentally, most of the above sites had long since been abandoned by the Hellenistic era and thus could scarcely have been known to writers living then.)

The Divided Monarchy, 9th–7th Centuries BCE

If the existence of a "United Monarchy," with its seemingly legendary, larger-than-life kings, appears shadowy, the Divided Monarchy finds us upon much solider historical ground. For one thing, the king-lists of the Deuteronomistic history in 1–2 Kings – which provide a detailed chronological framework for at least a "political history" of Israel and Judah – are securely anchored by synchronisms with Neo-Assyrian and Neo-Babylonian king-lists, the latter astronomically fixed within a margin of ten years and often much less. The major synchronisms are illustrated in table 11.2.[23]

The "revisionists" grudgingly accept the bare outline of the biblical king-lists, because they must. The kings of the *Divided* Monarchy can hardly have been made up by the biblical writers, because the major kings are attested by impeccable extra-biblical witnesses. And the main events of their reigns, as narrated in the biblical texts, can be correlated with events in ancient Near Eastern history that are well known to us from other sources. These broader events – an actual *historical context* for the Divided Monarchy – would include, at minimum, (1) the rise of the rival Aramaean kingdoms to the north in the 9th century BCE; (2) the resurgence of Canaanite traditions in the Phoenician culture along the Levantine coast, beginning in the 11th–10th century BCE; (3) the emergence of the "tribal-states" of Ammon, Moab, and Edom in Transjordan, beginning by the 9th century BCE, or perhaps even earlier; (4) the survival of Philistia along the southern coast as a rival of Judah, now well attested; and (5) the destruction of all these petty states in the course of the Neo-Assyrian campaigns in the 8th–7th century BCE and the Neo-Babylonian campaigns of the early, 7th century BCE.[24]

Table 11.2   Kings of Israel and Judah

Israel	Judah	Mesopotamia
Omri, 876–869 BC		Asshur-nasir-pal II, 883–859 BC
Ahab, 869–850 BC		
Jehoram, 849–842 BC		Shalmaneser III, 859–824 BC
Jehu, 842–815 BC		
Menahem, 745–738 BC		Tiglath-pileser III, 745–727 BC
Pekah, 737–732 BC		Shalmaneser V, 727–722 BC
Hoshea, 732–724 BC		Sargon II, 722–705 BC
(fall of Samaria, 722/721 BC)		
	Hezekiah, 715–680 BC	Sennacherib, 705–681 BC
	Josiah, 640–609 BC	Nebuchadrezzar, 605–562 BC
	Jehoiakin, 598 – (died in exile)	

It is precisely these events of world history in the Iron Age, too well documented to require further discussion here, that constitute the backdrop against which the biblical writers played out their drama of political (and religious) history in the 9th–6th centuries BCE. How could *later* writers have "invented" this complex world, long after all these entities had disappeared from the pages of history, not to be rediscovered until modern day archaeology? It is precisely this question that the "revisionists" never seem willing to confront.

It is true that the biblical writers, because of their overriding theocratic framework, usually provide us with little more than a bare outline of the actual course of events in Israel and Judah in any particular period. For many kings, the information is cryptic and formulaic. All that is given is the name of the king; his father's name; his co-regent in the north or south; how old he was when he began to reign; how long he ruled; a few of his principal deeds, almost always condemned as evil; and a notice of his death.

The chief reason for the individual king's inclusion in the Deuteronomistic king-lists, apart from the sake of completeness, is of course to denounce him: "X, who made Israel to sin." The modern historian need not share that doctrinaire theological judgment, may indeed reject it as blatant propaganda. But the point here is that the basic information given, while limited, is not necessarily *false*. And if we can "read between the lines" a bit, the biblical texts may yield in spite of themselves considerable reliable information – especially when corrected or supplemented by new and independent information provided by archaeology.

As a single example, Ahab is acknowledged by the biblical writers as an ambitious and powerful king, but then almost totally discredited as an apostate. Be that as it may, the Assyrian annals record that at the Battle of Qarqar in 853 BCE Ahab of Israel mustered 2,000 chariots and 10,000 troops – more than any other king in the western coalition. And Omri, Ahab's father, dismissed by the biblical writers in nine verses, was in fact so prominent that for nearly 150 years the Neo-Assyrian annals refer to the Kingdom of Israel as "the house (dynasty) of Omri." Are the biblical writers' "stories" then mere fiction, invented centuries later? Obviously not; but the writers are highly selective, as well as highly judgmental, in what they have chosen from their sources to tell us. In short, these writers were not charlatans, but simply typical ancient historians, often more sophisticated than we give them credit for being.

Because of their deliberate selectivity, resulting from a peculiar theological bias, the biblical writers have produced in the final version of the literary tradition what has often been called political or "theocratic" history. I would argue that this narrative history-of-events is not so much wrong, however, as it is simply limited in what it can tell us. What we moderns want, and legitimately so, is a multi-faced environmental or "natural" history; a technological history; a socioeconomic and cultural history; and an intellectual history, or history of ideas, including those of a religious nature. Yet it should be clear that only *archaeology*, in the broad sense of today's multidisciplinary inquiry, can produce the data required for writing such a history (Dever, 1999).

In short, the biblical accounts of the Divided Monarchy, with all their faults, may provide the historian with the basic framework, but continued archaeological investigation will be necessary to fill in most of the details. And that will be especially true of the daily life of *ordinary* folk in Israel and Judah in the Iron Age, in which the elitist biblical writers are scarcely interested, even if they were well informed (as I should argue they were). Archaeology gives back to those anonymous folk who "sleep in the dust" (Dan 12:2) their long-lost voice.

What then do we actually know about what may be called the "secular" history of the Iron Age – the real World of the Bible to which the "revisionists" are simply oblivious? We know a great deal indeed; and now we know *what the biblical writers knew*. The standard recent handbooks on the archaeology of Palestine (almost never cited by the "revisionists") document and illustrate the Divided Monarchy or Iron II period in lavish detail, totaling hundreds of pages.[25] Here I can only note that we have copious and accurate archaeological information on such things as environmental context; soil, water, and other natural resources; settlement types and patterns; demography; technology; economic systems, including agriculture, industry, and trade; social organization; political structure and institutions; town-planning and defense; domestic architecture; commercial activities; recreation; official as well as "popular" religion; dozens of vocations; warfare; diet, disease, and death; and a host of other subjects. Some of the above is hinted at in the Hebrew Bible, often casually; but for most of what we know in any detail and with any assurance we will continue to be dependent upon archaeology. And in future we are certain to know much more from this source. In short, it is neither our Israel nor the Israel of the biblical writers that has been "invented," but that of the "revisionists." *Our* Israel really did exist.

The Temple of Solomon

We turn now to one specific aspect of the United and Divided Monarchy, the Solomonic Temple. It is well known that no physical evidence of such a structure survives. Nor is any evidence ever likely to be found, since the Temple Mount where it presumably once stood is off-limits for many reasons and almost certainly will never be investigated in detail by archaeologists. On the basis of the lack of direct archaeological witness, plus a growing skepticism about the historicity of the biblical texts among "revisionist" biblicists and others, many scholars have come to regard the biblical stories of Solomon's Temple in Jerusalem as little more than myths. This is simply royalist and priestly propaganda, much of it dating not to the Iron Age but to the Persian or even the Hellenistic era, when the Hebrew Bible is alleged by the "revisionists" to have been composed. There was no "Solomonic Temple."[26]

Yet I would argue that no historian who knows even the rudiments of Syro-Palestinian archaeology can any longer dismiss the accounts in 1 Kings 6–9 as entirely fanciful (although they are, of course, somewhat exaggerated). We now possess a mass of archaeological data that provide a *Sitz im Leben* (not merely a *Sitz im Literatur*), that is, a *real*-life context in which virtually every detail of the biblical description, despite linguistic difficulties, can be illuminated, indeed explained. And it is instructive that the thirty or more comparative examples of archaeologically attested Bronze and Iron Age temples in Syria–Palestine date almost exclusively to the 15th–8th centuries BCE, *not* later, when the biblical writers are supposed to have "invented" the stories.

The salient features of the Solomonic Temple, based at this point solely on the biblical accounts, are represented in table 11.3. Here I can only mention in passing the wealth of archaeological corroboration that we now possess for the Solomonic Temple (listed here in reference to the features as numbered in table 11.3).

Table 11.3   Features of the Solomon Temple according to Biblical texts

No.	Features or characteristics	References in 1 Kings, 2 Chronicles
1	Tripartite plan, with three successive rooms along a single axis	Kgs 6:3; Chr 3:3–9
2	Construction in Phoenician style	Kgs 7:13, 18; Chr 2:1–16
3	Overall dimensions of ca. 30 by 90 feet, 45 feet high; vestibule and inner sanctum 20 by 20 feet, nave 50 by 20 feet	Kgs 6:2, 16, 17; 7:9, 10; Chr 3:3, 4
4	Foundation walls ca. 8 feet thick	Kgs 6:2
5	Construction of fitted, quarry-dressed foundation stones; reinforcing wood beams inserted every three courses in superstructure; inner walls lined with decorated cedar panels; cedar roof beams	Kgs 6:6–18, 36; 7:12
6	Two bronze columns with capitals flanking entrance of vestibule, elaborately decorated (pomegranates, lilies)	Kgs 7:15–22; Chr 3:15–17
7	Interior decoration of wooden panels carved with gourds, palm trees, cherubs, open flowers, and chains, some overlaid with gold leaf	Kgs 6:15–32; Chr 3:5–17
8	Two carved olivewood, gold-overlaid cherubs in the inner sanctum, 15 feet high and 15 feet from wingtip to wingtip	Kgs 6:23–28; Chr 3:10–14
9	Furnishings of building and forecourt include cast bronze paneled and spoke-wheeled braziers, some with open top, ca. 4 feet high; decorated with wreaths, lions, oxen, cherubs, and palm trees.	Kgs 7:27–37; Chr 4:1–10
10	Pots, shovels, basins, firepans, and snuffers for offerings.	Kgs 8:48–50; Chr 4:11–22fv

(1)   The supposedly enigmatic tripartite or "long room" temple plan is the standard Late Bronze and early Iron Age temple plan throughout Syria and Palestine, with many examples now archaeologically attested. Even the dimensions, proportions, and details fit the norm. The "Phoenician" derivation in Kings and Chronicles thus turns out to be quite plausible; there was no native tradition of monumental architecture in Israel's earliest phases of urbanization in Iron IIA, so models had to be borrowed from neighboring peoples in the centuries-old Canaanite tradition.

(2)   The dressed masonry with interlaced wooden beam construction seems odd at first glance; but we now know that it was typical of Middle–Late Bronze Age construction in monumental buildings throughout Canaan, with particularly close parallels coming from palatial buildings at Alalakh and Ugarit, as well as at Late Bronze Age Hazor in northern Palestine. Such construction was apparently a practical device for protecting heavy masonry walls from earthquakes with a flexible "break-joint," as in modern construction. As for the biblical description of "sawn" or chisel-dressed masonry blocks, produced in finished form at the quarries and fitted together at the site "without the sound of a hammer," that also seems unusual. So it is, unless one happens to know that *precisely* such dressed, prefitted masonry – known as "ashlar" to archaeologists – has been found to characterize monumental or "royal" construction in Israel in and only in the 10th–9th centuries BCE. The finest examples of such ashlar masonry come from Dan, Hazor, Megiddo, Samaria, and Gezer, all of which were probably administrative centers in some sense in the 10th–9th centuries BCE, and thus under royal administration (above). The introduction of such ashlar masonry into Israel is now thought by some to have been due to the "Sea Peoples," Philistines and others, who brought with them, or at least were acquainted with, Mycenaean-style ashlar masonry in Cyprus in the late 13th century BCE, and thence it came to the Phoenician coast where it was probably adopted locally. Once again, the Hebrew Bible's references to "Phoenician" artisans and craftsmen in stone makes perfect sense; and the 10th century BCE date is just what we would expect for early Phoenician–Israelite contacts. As for the implication of an unusual style of prefitting the stones at the quarry, one must cite ashlar blocks discovered at Megiddo and Gezer precisely in 10th century BCE contexts in monumental buildings and city gates, which exhibit identical geometric masons' marks and even traces of red chalk-lines that are evidence of advance quarry fitting (as Yigal Shiloh long ago pointed out).

(3)   The biblical description of lower courses of masonry combined with upper courses overlaid with wooden panels remained mysterious, unparalleled until modern archaeological discoveries provided the answer. At Middle Bronze Age Ebla and at Late Bronze Age Alalakh in Syria, as well as at Late Bronze Age Hazor in northern Palestine, we now have examples of monumental architecture featuring lower dadoes of black basalt (volcanic) stone orthostats, with regularly-spaced drilled holes on the upper sides that are obviously mortises for tenons on the end of wooden panels that were once attached to the

orthostats. Once again, the biblical descriptions, though thought to be later, are uncannily accurate for the late Late Bronze–early Iron Age.

(6)   The two columns with elaborate capitals at the entrance of the Solomonic temple, so prominent that they received the names "Boaz" and "Jachin" in the Hebrew Bible, are also not unique. The standard Middle Bronze, Late Bronze, and Iron Age bipartite and tripartite temples now known throughout Canaan exhibit just such columns, as revealed by two typical surviving column bases flanking the entrance at the vestibule or entrance-porch (the "temple-in-antis" plan that is well known even down to Classical times). The description of the elaborate decoration of the capitals is not entirely clear, but the motifs fit with the rest of the decor. Elsewhere, in simpler 10th–9th century BCE royal constructions, the carved "palmette" capital (previously called "proto-Aeolic"), usually not free-standing but engaged, is typical; it almost certainly represents the stylized "tree-of-life" that goes back to common Late Bronze Age Canaanite motifs (below).

(7)   All the motifs of the interior decoration of the temple and its furnishings, formerly subject only to speculation, are now well attested in Canaanite art and iconography of the Late Bronze and Iron Ages. The reference to "chains" is not entirely clear, but it recalls the familiar Late Bronze Age Minoan *guilloche* design, featuring a running row of spirals turning back upon themselves, as for instance on a basalt offering basin from the Area H temple at Hazor. "Open flowers" almost certainly refers to lilies or papyrus blossoms, both of which are exceedingly common motifs in the Late Bronze Age. They are also well represented on numerous Iron Age ivories, such as those from 9th–8th century BCE Samaria; on many seals; and on the painted storejars from the 8th century BCE sanctuary at Kuntillet 'Ajrud in the Sinai. "Pomegranates," commonly associated with fertility in the Ancient Near East, have Late Bronze–Iron Age parallels in pendants on bronze braziers (see below); on a cultic bowl from Lahav; and on many seals. They also appear on ivory priests' wands from several sites, including the now famous 8th century one from chance finds in Jerusalem, bearing the Hebrew inscription "Set apart for the priests of the Temple of _____h" (restore "YHWH"), which in all probability comes from the Temple of Solomon.

(8)   The term "cherub" now presents no problem whatsoever, although long misunderstood as some sort of chubby winged creature shooting darts into lovers. The biblical "cherub" is simply a "mixed creature" of the sort widely known from the 3rd millennium BCE onward in the Ancient Near East, usually with the body of a lion, a human head, and wings. From early times the cherub is one of the principal iconographic representations of deities and kings, often occurring in pairs bearing on their backs the king seated on his throne. Such "lion-thrones" occur in Palestine on a well-known 12th century BCE ivory panel from Megiddo, showing a Canaanite king receiving a procession. Later Iron Age examples of cherubs include those on one register of the 10th century BCE terracotta cult stand from Ta'anach; on one of the painted storejars from Kuntillet 'Ajrud (a seated female figure, in my judgment

Asherah); on the Samarian and other ivories; and on numerous seals. The symbolism of a *pair* of cherubs, a supposedly "pagan" motif, in the inner sanctum of the Jerusalem temple is now clear. Israel's national god YHWH sat enthroned on a lion-throne just like all the other deities of the Ancient Near East, except that he was invisible – an exceptionally powerful statement of his spiritual presence in his "house."

(9)   The references to "lions," of course, overlap with references to cherubs, but the lion often appears in its own right in the Late Bronze Age, often carrying a nude female deity riding on its back, almost certainly Asherah. This goddess is widely known in ancient texts as the "Lion Lady" and is much favored in iconography from Egypt all the way to Mesopotamia. Palestinian Iron Age examples of the lion motif would include a 12th century BCE ivory box from Megiddo; both 10th century BCE cult stands from Ta'anach; the storejars at Kuntillet 'Ajrud; several Samarian ivories; and many seals, especially the well-known Megiddo seal of "the servant of Jeroboam." "Oxen" may refer to bulls or bull calves. The bull was commonly associated in the Levant with the preeminent Canaanite male deity El, whose titles and imagery were borrowed in early Israel and associated with the new national god YHWH, as Cross and others have shown. One recalls the famous "golden calf" set up at Mt. Sinai, and again at Bethel when the northern kingdom seceded. Actual Iron Age examples of bulls in cultic context in Palestine include a beautiful bronze bull from a 12th century BCE Israelite open cult-place (the biblical "high place"; see below) in the territory of Mannaseh; on one of the Ta'anach stands, carrying a winged sun-disk on his back (some think it a horse); and on many examples of 8th–6th century BCE seals.

Finally, the reference to "palm trees" is clear, as we have seen in discussing the temple's columns and capitals above. Following the late Yigal Shiloh's work on "palmette" capitals, as well as that of Ruth Hestrin and others, the meaning of the familiar "tree" imagery is now beyond doubt. We finally understand the frequent prohibition in the prophetic and Deuteronomistic literature of trees ('ăšerîm) and the denunciation of Asherah and her hilltop "groves," vividly expressed in the descriptions of Israel's fornication with strange gods "under every green tree and on every high hill" (Isa 53:3–13). Given the capitals that depict the drooping fronds of the palm tree's crown, the columns themselves are clearly stylized palm trees. Indeed we have several Iron Age *naoi*, or terracotta temple models, that have just such a pair of tree-columns flanking the entrance, complete with palmette capitals. One comes from 10th century BCE levels at Tell el-Far'ah North, Biblical Tirzah, which for a time in the 9th century BCE served as the capital of the northern kingdom. Others are known from Transjordan. All have other related temple motifs as well, especially the dove, associated with Asherah/Tanit in the Phoenician world; or the "stars of the Pleiades," again an Asherah symbol. A clear example of a Phoenician *naos* is the one from Idalion in Cyprus, probably late 6th century BCE, which has two fully-represented palm-capitals flanking the doorway and a nude female standing in the doorway, no doubt Asherah (known as "Astarte" in Cyprus and associated with "Adonis," Semitic *'ādōn*, "lord," or the equivalent of Canaanite–Israelite Ba'al).

I have presented here a relatively small sampling of archaeological examples of the individual motifs of the Solomonic temple enumerated in Kings and Chronicles, but we have a number of more or less complete Iron Age temples that may provide even more instructive comparisons. The one usually cited (but of course ignored by the "revisionists") is the small 9th–8th century BCE temple at Tell Tayinat in northern Syria, excavated by the University of Chicago in the 1930s and long since fully published. It is a tripartite building, similar to the biblical description in both plan and size, exhibiting two columns with lion-bases at the portico. The inner sanctum (the biblical *dĕbîr*, or "Holy of Holies") has a podium on the rear wall for a representation of the deity. The excavators presented ample evidence for ashlar construction, as those in some reconstructions. Other examples of Syrian temples from the 9th–8th centuries BCE include the recently-discovered 9th–8th century BCE acropolis temple at the Aramaic capital of 'Ain Der'a, in northern Syria near the Turkish border. Few archaeologists or biblical scholars are aware of this temple, but I have visited it many times. It is of tripartite style, decorated in and out with carved basalt orthostats featuring lions and cherubs. The most stunning feature is the giant footprints carved into the threshold and then into the entrance to the two inner chambers – first two feet, then higher up another foot in a great stride, and finally one foot on the threshold (Monson, 2000). God is manifestly present in the temple, his "house." The Temple of Solomon in Jerusalem was different from the 'Ain Der'a and other tripartite temples of Syria–Palestine in the Iron Age in only one respect: Israel's god was invisible, his footprints present only in his people's history.

Conclusion

This brief résumé has sought to demonstrate that archaeology helps to recover a "history behind the history" in the literary tradition now enshrined in the Hebrew Bible. Thus, using both sources critically, and at first independently, we may arrive at a tentative outline of actual historical events. And these will be events and stories about them, in the *Iron Age*, not in the Hellenistic era as the "revisionists" assert.

We must, however, grant that the overall character of the Hebrew Bible as it has come down to us takes the form of "propaganda" in the true sense, that is, special pleading for the religious and political causes of the ultra-orthodox, nationalist parties who edited the materials into their final form in the post-exilic period. My point is simply that these final redactors had much older *sources*, both oral and written, which they often incorporated into their narratives with little or no editorial changes. Modern archaeology is a powerful tool that can help the historian to separate out genuine historical information that may survive in the biblical texts, material that along with archaeological data can become part of the proper sources for writing history: ecofacts, artifacts, and textual facts.[27]

Notes

1   The "revisionist" literature is now too extensive to cite fully, but for principal works see Davies, 1992; Lemche and Thompson, 1994; Thompson 1995a; 1999; Whitelam, 1996; and Lemche, 1998.

2   Extensive archaeological critique and references to "revisionist" literature will be found in Dever, 1995; 1996a; 1996b; 1998; 2001. For critiques from a biblical perspective, see Japhet, 1996; Hurvitz, 1997; Machinist, forthcoming.

3   These themes run through all the revisionist literature cited in n. 1 above. For the most recent reiteration, see Lemche, 1998; Thompson, 1999.

4   Cf. Lemche and Thompson, 1994; Davies (1994) dismisses the reading "House of David." For the inscription itself, critique, and references in earlier literature, see most conveniently Knoppers, 1997, pp. 36–40.

5   Davies, 1992, p. 24; this is the *only* reference to Mazar's basic handbook, which has 255 pages on the Iron Age (1990, pp. 295–550). Davies dismisses Mazar since he does not deal with the *Persian-Hellenistic* "biblical world." Davies does not cite another basic handbook, Weippert, with similar copious archaeological data (cf. 1988, pp. 344–681).

6   On Saul as a putative king, see most recently Edelmen, 1996, who despite her "revisionist" leanings allows that he may indeed have been the first "king" of Israel. For an earlier "chiefdom model," see Frick, 1985, pp. 71–97, but cf. the critique in Dever 1997, pp. 247–9; and for a critique of the model itself, cf. Yoffee, 1989.

7   Cf. Mazar, 1990, pp. 371–5; Fritz, 1996; Herr, 1997, pp. 120–9.

8   On Jerusalem as a capital, see further below and n. 10.

9   See, for instance, Lemche and Thompson, 1994, p. 18; Thompson, 1997, pp. 34–6. See further n. 10 below (i.e., Steiner, 1998).

10 For the most recent discussions, see Na'aman, 1997; 1998; Cahill, 1998; Steiner, 1998.

11 Cf. Mazar, 1990, pp. 371–5. For the era of David generally, cf. Halpern, 1996; Na'aman, 1996.

12 Thus Lemche and Thompson, 1994: but see positively Fritz, 1996. On the "Age of Solomon" generally, see now the many essays in the magisterial work edited by Handy (1997), with my own 50-page chapter on the archaeological data (Dever, 1997). Knoppers, 1997, provides a useful and well-balanced introduction to the whole "Solomonic state" controversy; also Fritz, 1996.

13 Thus in the essays in the pivotal discussion of Fritz and Davies, 1996, only Schäfer-Lichtenberger treats theories of the state; and she cites *none* of the archaeological data from ancient Palestine. Elsewhere in the voluminous "revisionist" literature the topic does not even come up. By contrast, see the discussion of archaeologists like Holladay (1995) and, most extensively, Dever (1997).

14 Cf. also Thompson (1997, p. 35), who claims that these few dozen villages had a total population of "2,200," a figure he claims he got from Finkelstein, 1996. What Finkelstein actually says, however, is that this figure refers only to the villages around Jerusalem; the *whole* of Judah is estimated at ca. 42,000, and Israel (the north) at ca. 44,000, yielding a *total* 10th century BCE population of ca. 86,000

(Finkelstein, 1996, pp. 184, 185). Elsewhere, Finkelstein's (and others') population estimate for Israel (i.e., Israel and Judah) in the 10th century BCE is ca. 100,000 – easily in excess of the figure of ca. 50,000 often used by social anthropologists as the threshold of true state-formation (Dever, 1997, pp. 219–51; Ofer, 1994, pp. 102–5; Na'aman, 1996; 1998). Thompson does not cite correctly the basic archaeological data.

15   As recently asserted, without any evidence, by Thompson (1996, pp. 29–33). Similarly, Finkelstein – the only archaeologist to side with the "revisionists'" minimalist position – has now charged his Israeli colleague Amihai Mazar with being a "Bible archeologist" on the issue of early Israelite statehood, even though Finkelstein himself still maintains that there was an Israeli state, even if only a sort of small "territorial state," with Jerusalem as its "stronghold" (1998a, pp. 172–3; cf. 1995, pp. 362–3). Most recently, however, Finkelstein (1998b, p. 33) has argued that a *true* Judean state, presumably with its capital in Jerusalem, did not emerge until about the 8th century BCE. See further below.

16   See Dever, 1997, pp. 239–2; Aharoni, 1979, pp. 323–30; Kitchen, 1986; Na'aman, 1992; Currid, 1997, pp. 172–202.

17   The information that as many as two dozen excavated sites on Shishak's list have now produced 10th century BCE destruction layers with hand-burnished pottery is an oral communication from Amihai Mazar; see provisionally Mazar, 1999b, pp. 37–42. On the significance of wheel-burnish as a dating criterion, see Holladay, 1995, pp. 377–8; Dever, 1997, pp. 237–9, and literature there.

18   See Dever, 1997, pp. 219–21. The most recent survey (Herr, 1997, p. 121) raises my 30 10th century BCE sites to more than 40. Cf. also references in n. 10 above.

19   Cf. Holladay, 1995; Finkelstein, 1996; 1998a; Mazar, 1999a; 1999b; Dever, 1997; Ben-Tor and Ben-Ami, 1998. The "10th–9th century" controversy, especially as Hazor, Megiddo, and Gezer are involved, actually dates back to the early 1980s; see Dever 1990 and references there; and add now Knoppers, 1997.

20   The most significant studies, all opposed to Finkelstein's "low chronology," are those of Zarzeki-Peleg, 1997; Ben-Tor and Ben-Ami, 1998; and Mazar, 1999a. The latter's C_{14} dates for two 10th–9th century BCE destruction layers (now being processed at the University of Arizona) are likely to be definitive.

21   Cf. references in nn. 1, 2 above. Thompson calls it all "survival literature" (1999, p. 31). Lemche's latest work (1998) virtually dismisses the literary tradition in the Hebrew Bible as nothing more than the original (although Hellenistic) "Zionist myth" (Hendel, 1999). For an exhaustive résumé of literature on the Deuteronomistic history, see now Eynikel, 1996, who, however, deals only with the question of *literary* composition and date, not the fundamental question here of historical credibility.

22   These and dozens of other "convergences" between artifact and text are elaborated in my book *What Did the Biblical Writers Know, and When Did They Know It? What Archaeology and the Bible can tell us about Ancient Israel* (2001).

23   The basic textual data will be found in Pritchard, 1955, pp. 276–308; for the latest works on the chronology of the Divided Monarchy from a biblical perspective, cf. Barnes, 1991; Galil, 1996.

24   General bibliography is much too extensive to list; but for the archaeological data, see conveniently Weippert, 1988, pp. 344–681; Mazar, 1990, pp. 295–550; Ben-Tor, 1992, pp. 325–72; Herr, 1997.

25   Cf. nn. 5, 24 above.

26 References to the literature are too extensive to cite fully, but details will be found in forthcoming a. Meanwhile, on the Solomonic Temple generally, see Fritz, 1987; Meyers, 1992; Bloch-Smith, 1994.
27 After this essay was completed, I saw the very helpful discussion of Meyers, 1998, courtesy of the author. Our views are completely independent, but highly complementary.

Bibliography

Aharoni, Y., *The Land of the Bible: A Historical Geography* (Philadelphia: Westminster Press, 1979).

Barnes, W. H., *Studies in the Chronology of the Divided Monarchy of Israel* (Cambridge, MA: Harvard University Press, 1991).

Barkay, G., "The Iron Age II–III," in A. Ben-Tor, ed., *The Archaeology of Ancient Israel* (New Haven: Yale University Press, 1992), 302–73.

Ben-Tor, A., ed., *The Archaeology of Ancient Israel* (New Haven: Yale University Press, 1992).

Ben-Tor, A. and Ben-Ami, D., "Hazor and the Archeology of the 10th Century BCE: The Iron II Strata in Area A4," *Israel Exploration Journal* 48 (1998), 1–37.

Bloch-Smith, E., "Who is the King of Glory?" in M. Coogan, J. Exum and L. Stager, eds., *Scripture and Other Artifacts: Essays on the Bible and Archaeology in Honor of Philip J. King* (Louisville: Westminster/John Knox Press, 1994), 18–31.

Cahill, J., "It Is There: The Archaeological Evidence Proves It," *Biblical Archaeology Review* 24 (1998), 4–41, 63.

Currid, J., *Ancient Egypt and the Old Testament* (Grand Rapids: Baker Books, 1997).

Davies, P., *In Search of "Ancient Israel"* (Sheffield: Sheffield Academic Press, 1992).

——, "House of David Built on Sand," *Biblical Archaeology Review* 20 (1994), 54–5.

Dever, W., "Of Myths and Methods," *Bulletin of the American Schools of Oriental Research* 277/278 (1990), 121–30.

——, "Will the Real Israel Please Stand Up? Archaeology and Israelite Historiography: Part I," *Bulletin of the American Schools of Oriental Research* 279 (1995), 61–80.

——, "The Identity of Early Israel: A Rejoinder to Keith W. Whitelam," *Journal for the Study of the Old Testament* 72 (1996a), 3–24.

——, "Revisionist Israel Revisited: A Rejoinder to Niels Peter Lemche," *Currents in Research: Biblical Studies* 4 (1996b).

——, "Archaeology and the 'Age of Solomon': A Case-Study in Archaeology and Historiography," in L. K. Handy, *The Age of Solomon: Scholarship of the Turn of the Millennium* (Leiden: E. J. Brill, 1997), 217–51.

——, "Archaeology, Ideology, and the Quest for an 'Ancient' or 'Biblical Israel,'" *Near Eastern Archaeology* 61 (1998), 39–52.

——, "Histories and Nonhistories of Ancient Israel," *Bulletin of the American Schools of Oriental Research* 316 (1999), 89–105.

——, *What Did the Biblical Writers Know, and When Did They Know It? What Archaeology and the Bible can tell us about Ancient Israel* (2001).

——, "Were There Temples in Ancient Israel? The Archaeological Evidence," in T. Lewis, *Text, Artifact, and Image: Revealing Ancient Israelite Religion* (New Haven: Yale University Press, forthcoming a).

Edelman, D., "Saul, ben-Kish in History and Tradition," in V. Fritz and P. Davies, eds., *The Origins of the Ancient Israelite States* (Sheffield: Sheffield Academic Press, 1996), 142–59.

Eynikel, E., *The Reform of King Josiah and the Composition of the Deuteronomistic History* (Leiden: E. J. Brill, 1996).

Finkelstein, I., *The Archaeology of the Israelite Settlement* (Jerusalem: Israel Exploration Society, 1988).

——, "The Great Transformation: The 'Conquest' of the Highlands Frontiers and the Rise of the Territorial States," in T. Levy, ed., *The Archaeology of Society in the Holy Land* (London: Leicester University Press, 1995), 349–65.

——, "The Archaeology of the United Monarchy: An Alternative View," *Levant* 28 (1996), 177–87.

——, "Bible Archaeology or Archaeology of Palestine in the Iron Age? A Rejoinder," *Levant* 3 (1998a), 167–74.

——, "The Rise of Early Israel: Archaeology and Long-Term History," in S. Ahituv and E. Oren, eds., *The Origin of Early Israel – Current Debate: Biblical, Historical and Archaeological Perspectives* (Beer-Sheva: Ben-Gurion University of the Negev, 1998b), 7–39.

Frick, F., *The Formation of the State in Ancient Israel: A Survey of Models and Theories* (Sheffield: Almond Press, 1985).

Fritz, V., "Temple Architecture – What Can Archaeology Tell Us about Solomon's Temple?" *Biblical Archaeology Review* 13 (1987), 38–49.

——, "Monarchy and Reurbanization: A New Look at Solomon's Kingdom," in V. Fritz and P. Davies, eds., *The Origins of the Ancient Israelite States* (Sheffield: Sheffield Academic Press, 1996), pp. 187–95.

Galil, G., *The Chronology of the Kings of Israel and Judah* (Leiden: E. J. Brill, 1996).

Grabbe, L., ed., *Can a "History of Israel" Be Written?* (Sheffield: Sheffield Academic Press, 1997).

Halpern, B., "The Construction of the Davidic State: An Exercise in Historiography," in V. Fritz and P. Davies, ed., *The Origins of the Ancient Israelite States* (Sheffield: Sheffield Academic Press, 1996), 44–75.

Handy, L., ed., *The Age of Solomon: Scholarship at the Turn of the Millennium* (Leiden: E. J. Brill, 1997).

Hendel, R., Review of N. P. Lemche, *The Israelites in History and Tradition* (Louisville: Westminster/John Knox Press, 1998). *Bible Archaeology Review* 25 (1999), 59, 60.

Herr, L. G., "Iron II Palestine: Emerging Nations," *Biblical Archaeologist* 60 (1997), 114–83.

Holladay, Jr., J., "The Kingdoms of Israel and Judah: Political and Economic Centralization in the Iron IIA–B (ca. 1000–750 BCE)," in T. Levy, ed., *The Archaeology of Society in the Holy Land* (Leicester University Press, 1995).

Hurvitz, A., "The Historical Quest for 'Ancient Israel' and the Linguistic Evidence for the Hebrew Bible: Some Methodological Observations," *Vetus Testamentum* 47 (1997), 301–15.

Japhet, S., "In Search of Ancient Israel: Revisionism at All Costs," in D. Meyers and D. Rudman, *The Jewish Past Revisited: Reflections on Modern Jewish Historians* (New Haven: Yale University Press, 1996), 212–33.

Kitchen, K., *The Third Intermediate Period in Egypt (1,100–650 BC)*, 2nd edn. (Warminster: Aris and Phillips, 1986).

Knoppers, G., "The Vanishing Solomon: The Disappearance of the United Monarchy from Recent Histories of Ancient Israel," *Journal of Biblical Literature* 116 (1997), 19–44.

Lemche, N., *The Israelites in History and Tradition* (Louisville: Westminster/John Knox Press, 1998).

Lemche, N. and T. Thompson, "Did Biran Kill David? The Bible in the Light of Archaeology," *Journal for the Study of the Old Testament* 64 (1994), 3–22.

Machinist, P. M., *The Crisis of History in the Study of the Hebrew Bible* (forthcoming).

Mazar, A., *Archaeology of the Land of the Bible, 10,000–586 BCE* (New York: Doubleday, 1990).

——, "Iron Age Chronology: A Reply to I. Finkelstein," *Levant* 29 (1999a), 157–67.

——, "The 1997–1998 Excavations at Tel Rehov: Preliminary Report," *Israel Exploration Journal* 49 (1999b), 1–42.

Meyers, C., "Temple, Jerusalem," *Anchor Bible Dictionary* 6 (New York: Doubleday, 1992), 350–69.

——, "Kinship and Kingship: The Early Monarchy," in M. Coogan, ed., The Oxford History of the Biblical World (New York: Oxford University Press, 1998), 221–71.

Monson, J. "The New 'Ain Data Temple: Closest Solomonic Comparison," *Biblical Archaeology Review* 26 (2000), 20–36, 67.

Na'aman, N., "Israel, Edom and Egypt in the 10th Century BCE," *Tel Aviv* 19 (1992), 71–93.

——, "The Contribution of the Amarna Letters to the Debate on Jerusalem's Political Position in the Tenth Century BCE," *Bulletin of the American Schools of Oriental Research* 304 (1996), 17–27.

——, "Cow Town or Royal Capital? Evidence for Iron Age Jerusalem," *Biblical Archaeology Review* 23 (1997), 43–7, 67.

——, "Shishak's Raid to the Land of Israel in Light of the Egyptian Inscriptions, the Bible and the Archaeological Data," *Zion* 63 (1998), 247–76 (Hebrew).

Ofer, A., "'All the Hill Country of Judah': From a Settlement Fringe to a Prosperous Monarchy," in I. Finkelstein and N. Na'aman, eds., *From Nomadism to Monarchy: Archaeological and Historical Aspects of Early Israel* (Jerusalem: Israel Exploration Society, 1994), 92–121.

Pritchard, J., ed., *Ancient Near Eastern Texts Relating to the Old Testament* (Princeton: Princeton University Press, 1955).

Sahlins, M. D., *Tribesmen* (Englewood Cliffs, NJ: Prentice-Hall, 1968).

Schäfer-Lichtenberger, C., in V. Fritz and P. Davies, eds., "Sociological and Biblical Views of the Early State," *The Origins of the Ancient Israelite States* (Sheffield: Sheffield Academic Press, 1996), 78–105.

Service, E., *Primitive Social Organization: An Evolutionary Perspective* (New York: Random House, 1962).

Steiner, M., "It's Not There: Archaeology Proves a Negative," *Biblical Archaeology Review* 24 (1998), 26–33, 62.

Thompson, T., "A Neo-Albrightian School in History and Biblical Scholarship?" *Journal of Biblical Literature* 114 (1995a), 683–98.

——, "The Intellectual Matrix of Early Biblical Narrative: Inclusive Monotheism in Persian Period Palestine," in D. Edelman, ed., *The Triumph of Elohim: From Yahwisms to Judaisms* (Grand Rapids: Eerdmanns Publishing Company, 1995b), 107–24.

——, "Historiography of Ancient Palestine and Jewish Historiography: W. G. Dever and the Not So New Biblical Archaeology," in V. Fritz and P. Davis, *The Origins of the Ancient Israelite States* (Sheffield: Sheffield Academic Press, 1996), 26–43.

——, "Remarks Face to Face: Biblical Minimalists Meet Their Accusers," *Biblical Archaeology Review* 23 (1997), 26–42, 66.

——, *The Mythic Past: Biblical Archaeology and the Myth of Israel* (London: Basic Books, 1999).

Weippert, H., *Palästina in vorhellenistischer Zeit* (Munich: C. H. Beck, 1988).

Whitelam, K., *The Invention of Ancient Israel: The Silencing of Palestinian History* (London: Routledge, 1996).

Yoffee, N., "Too Many Chiefs? (or Safe Texts for the '90s)," in N. Yoffee and A. Sharett, eds., *Archaeological Theory: Who Sets the Agenda?* (Cambridge: Cambridge University Press, 1989), 60–78.

Zarzeki-Peleg, A., "Hazor, Jokneam and Megiddo in the 10th Century BCE," *Tel Aviv* 24 (1997), 258–88.

CHAPTER 12

Schools and Literacy in Ancient Israel and Early Judaism

André Lemaire
Translated by Aliou Niang

As a literary corpus, the birth and the transmission of the Hebrew Bible are directly linked to the use and the spread of writing among the people from whom it is born. The study of the role of writing, as well as that of the function and training of scribes in the society of ancient Israel, are thus necessary for understanding the concrete conditions out of which different biblical books were written and transmitted to us.

For the ancient epoch, such an inquiry, in particular, can rest on very diversified types of research:

1   The contemporary research constituted by paleo-Hebraic inscriptions and, in a more general fashion, Palestinian, that has come down to us thanks to archaeological digs and accidental discoveries;
2   The indications contained in the biblical texts themselves whenever they are placed into writing, or, in a more general way, the role of writing in the society which they evoke;
3   The data pertaining to this problem in Israel's neighboring countries, in Egypt and in Mesopotamia in particular, whose civilizations have often dominated Palestine, politically and culturally.

We shall emphasize, however, that the usage of the first two types of research encountered serious difficulties: on the one hand, the information of the biblical books is occasional and elusive and often difficult to date; on the other hand, Israelite or Judean scribes customarily wrote on papyrus or on animal skin (leather), material that is not well preserved in the relatively humid Palestinian climate. Actually, only one papyrus of the royal era came down to us: the papyrus of Wadi Murabbat found in a cave of the Judean desert. This disappearance of the greatest part of epigraphic documentation will always make the historian extremely prudent in the possible use of the argument "from silence."

Therefore, we should pay more attention to the usage of some fragments that came down to us.

Many scarabs, some hieratic ostraca and some stele of the Late Bronze Age show that Egyptian writing was not an unknown phenomenon in Palestine, particularly in the Late Bronze Age. Much more, some fragments of cuneiform tablets found at Hazor, Shechem, Gezer, and Hebron show that the Akkadian cuneiform writing was already used in Palestine in the Middle Bronze Age, whereas the continuation of this scribal tradition down to the Late Bronze Age is confirmed by other fragments and, above all, by the cuneiform tablets of El-Amarna, which reveal that the mayors/petty kings of Canaan had scribes capable of writing their official letters to the pharaoh in cuneiform script. This international scribal culture is confirmed, for example, for the site of Aphek in the 13th century with the discovery of Egyptian, Hittite, and Akkadian documents, and of a fragment of a cuneiform trilingual dictionary (Sumerian, Akkadian, Canaanite). Concurrently, from ca. 1600, some short linear alphabetical inscriptions appeared at Lachish, Gezer, Shechem, and Tell Nagilah.

In Iron I (ca. 1200–1000), this latter type of inscription seems practically the only one to be maintained as the ostracon of Beth-Shemesh, the inscriptions on the vase of Raddana and of Qubur el-Walaydah (near to the south of Tell el-Far'ah), the shards of Manahat (close to Jerusalem) and of Khirbet Tannin (south of Jenin), and the ostracon of Izbet Sartah (to the east of Aphek) and, perhaps, the inscribed arrow-heads said to have come from El-Khadr, near Bethlehem have shown. With the exception of the tablet of Gezer, which could be linked to Philistia, the inscriptions of the 10th century remain all too rare with the short inscriptions of Tell 'Amal, Beth-Shemesh, Tell Batash and, perhaps, Es-Semu'a. The same goes for the 9th century with the inscription of El-Hamme, and probably the oldest ostraca of Arad (no. 76 in particular) (Renz, 1995, pp. 29–66). However, we also can link to the second half of the 9th century the Aramean incisions on a vase found at Ein-Gev and Tel Dan (Gibson, 1975, pp. 5–6) and above all, the fragments of the Aramean stele of Hazael discovered at Tel Dan (Lemaire, 1998).

From ca. 800, the epigraphic documentation has become plainly more prolific with, it seems, the predominance of inscriptions linked to the Samarian kingdom up to its fall around 722. The two groups of Samarian ostraca and the inscriptions of Kuntillet 'Ajrud, relay station for the caravans between Qadesh-Barnea and the Red Sea, constitute the most important evidence, and more than fifty Israelite inscribed seals, the most often illustrated. Yet, since that era, inscriptions of Khirbet el-Qom, some inscriptions of Lachish, and many ostraca of Arad, as well as seals of the royal servants of Uzziah and Ahaz, show that the use of writing had also experienced a significant development in the Kingdom of Judah.

After the fall of Samaria, the epigraphic documentation of neo-Assyrian provinces of the ancient territory of Israel disappeared almost totally. Although the paleo-Hebraic script continued in some milieux, the Neo-Assyrian, Babylonian, and finally Persian administration favored the use of the Akkadian and Aramean scripts. As a matter of fact, epigraphic evidences became somewhat important only from the 4th century on (see below).

On the contrary, since the end of the 8th century under the rule of King Hezekiah, paleo-Hebraic epigraphic evidence tends to multiply. Beyond the famous inscription of Siloam, a fragment of monumental inscriptions, the funeral inscriptions of Silwam, several ostraca and inscriptions of Arad and of Beersheba, and the inscriptions of Khirbet Beit-Lei could be linked to the period that saw also the development of stamps on jars with over 1200 royal stamps and an important number of diversified stamps said to be "private" (Vaughn, 1999, pp. 43–64). Probably, however, as a matter of fact, the latter refer to royal officials. These stamps, as well as the seals and bullae of that period, are more and more without icons, allowing but one inscription arranged generally in one to two lines. This layout supposes that those who used them could only recognize them by reading them. Implicitly, they bear witness to an important use of writing in the royal administration.

The end of the royal era (ca. 630–587) seems to reveal a new extension of the use of writing, if we believe the evidence of the numerous ostraca of Mezad Hashavyahu, Lachish, Arad, Qadesh Barnea, Horvat 'Uza, and Jerusalem, and several hundreds of inscribed seals and bullae that we can link to that period. The great majority are without icons or virtually without icons (Avigad and Sass, 1997, pp. 45–6). In that epoch, both the formula found on three ostraca of Lachish, lines 8–13 (Lemaire, 1977, pp. 100–3) and the content of an inscription on the jar of Horva 'Uza (Beit-Arieh, 1993b) make known that in the Judean army every chief of a station, or a kind of corporal leading four or five men, should know how to read and write.

The fall of Jerusalem in 587 and the transformation of Judea into a Neo-Babylonian and then Persian province caused the disappearance of the Hebrew ostraca directly linked to the Judean royal administration. Even if we could suppose the maintenance of a certain scribal paleo-Hebraic tradition, it is the Aramaic tradition that then becomes the administrative language, as some seals, bullae, and stamps of that period, in particular the stamps of "Mozah" (Zorn et al., 1994) and "Yehud," appear to have attested.

In the 4th century, before the arrival of Alexander, coins of Judean currency were generally engraved in Aramean, even if, at the end of that period, some of them ("Yohanan the priest" and "Hizqiyahu the governor") were written again in paleo-Hebrew (Meshorer, 1982, pp. 13–20, 115–17; 1990, pp. 104–5). In the same epoch, a similar situation is found in the abundant coinage of Samaria where the legends were generally Aramean. Nearly contemporary, the papyri found in a cave of Wadi Daliyeh (sales of slave contracts, title deeds), but originating from Samaria (Cross, 1985, 1988), were all written in Aramean, but the bullae serving to ratify them, like the one of the son of "Sinuballit/Sanballat governor of Samaria," might have been written in paleo-Hebrew. In the 4th century, but continuing up to the beginning of the Hellenistic age (ca. 363–312), the hundreds of Aramean ostraca of Idumea evince clearly the running of a very precise, well kept, and nearly daily bookkeeping by scribes linked probably to the management of a royal store (Lemaire, 1996; Eph'al and Naveh, 1996; Lozachmeur and Lemaire, 1996).

During the 3rd century BCE, some Aramean ostraca, of which there is one bilingual from Khirbet el-Qom, testify to the contemporary use of Aramaic and Greek. This bilingualism is confirmed for Maresha in the 2nd century where rough copies of Aramean marriage contracts on the ostraca (Eshel and Kloner, 1996) sit alongside many Greek funeral inscriptions (Oren and Rappaport, 1984). Further north, recent digs at the temple of Mount Garizim, destroyed ca. 112 BCE, brought to light numerous inscriptions on rock, some in Aramean, essentially dedications, others in paleo-Hebrew of the Samaritan tradition. These latter ones mentioned priests and seem to relate to the cult celebrated in the sanctuary.

Toward the turn of our era, this mixture of Hebrew, Aramaic and, eventually, Greek, is found in Jerusalem and in its surroundings in diverse funeral inscriptions and on ossuaries. However, the most striking evidence of the use of writing in that age comes from the site of Qumran, and some 800 manuscripts made up of the remains of a library constituted more than a fourth of the books that were found later in the canon of the Hebrew Bible. The manuscripts were written in six different languages: plain Hebrew or Judeo-Aramean, clearly in the majority, paleo-Hebrew, Nabatean, cryptics A and B, and Greek. The exact interpretation of the site of Qumran and the function of that library remain debated. Yet, rather than seeing it as a monastery or a publishing house, somewhat anachronistic interpretations, it appears more natural to consider Qumran as a place of instruction, a kind of *bēt-midraš* apparently linked to the interpretive course of the Essenes (Lemaire, 1986; 1997, pp. 134–49).

This rapid evoking of epigraphic evidence reveals that the use of writing, more especially of alphabetic writing, has apparently known many phases. In the ancient epoch, one may schematically distinguish that:

- From ca. 1200 to ca. 800 alphabetical writing was not unknown, but its use was limited enough.
- From ca. 800 to ca. 722, the use of paleo-Hebraic script is strongly developed within the royal administration. This development is evident for the Kingdom of Samaria as clearly attested by the bookkeeping revealed by the ostraca of Samaria and the existence of paleo-Hebraic inscriptions linked to the Kingdom of Samaria in the relay of caravans of Kuntillet 'Ajrud. That seems also true in the Kingdom of Judah, as the inscriptions of Khirbet el-Qom and several ostraca of Arad attest.
- From 722 to 587, the ability to read and write in paleo-Hebrew seems to play a premier role at all the levels of the Judean royal administration, both in the civil administration and in the army (and not only in the higher administration as Young proposes; 1998, pp. 419–20). The latter milieu may reveal a more general diffusion. In fact, according to 2 Kgs 25:19, at least towards the end of the royal epoch, the government seemed to have practiced a certain form of draft. Even if it is difficult to specify the spreading

of writing among peasants and artisans, who could be either totally illiterate, or more occasionally scribes (cf. the graffiti and inscriptions on a vase?), it appears that for that epoch, we could conclude with A. R. Millard (1985, p. 307): "few ancient Israelites were out of reach of the written word, a situation certainly facilitated by the simplicity of the alphabet" (cf. also Demsky and Bar-Ilan, 1988, p. 15: "a literate society").

Still, as S. Warner (1980) has well underlined, the easiness of the alphabetical writing is but one of the factors, though probably not the most important, of the spread of that writing. Actually, the West Semitic linear alphabet, invented towards the 17th century BCE, experienced an important diffusion only about 800. Some political factors, like the development of administrative needs, or cultural, including the wish to develop a certain national or religious identity, were able to play a decisive role. C. Schams (1998, p. 308) has remarked: "Sociological studies of literacy indicate that strong social, political, economical or ideological forces and effective measures to increase literacy are necessary to change the level of literacy of a population."

Among these "effective measures," the existence of places of organized transmission of knowledge must be mentioned. This means the existence of "schools." Such an institution for the transmission of knowledge is generally accepted in Egypt and in Mesopotamia from ancient times. A. Klostermann (1908), L. Dürr (1932), H. J. Hermisson (1968, pp. 96–136), B. Lang (1979), A. Lemaire (1981; 1984; 1992), J. L. Crenshaw (1985), N. Shupak (1987; 1993), E. Puech (1988), and G. I. Davies (1995), have, with diverse nuances, proposed the existence of schools in Israel in the pre-exilic age. However, this thesis has been questioned by F. Golka (1983), M. Haran (1988), and D. W. Jamieson-Drake (1991).

It is true that the word "school" seems not to be mentioned in the Hebrew Bible and that the one occurrence of the *bēt-midraš* designates a particular form of school or, rather of a "college," based on the study of biblical literature (Ben Sira: Greek Prologue). This appears only in the Hebrew of Ben Sira 51:23. According to the Rabbinic tradition, it is Joshua ben Gamla, a high priest, towards 63–65, who "decides that some teachers (*mlmdy tynwqwt*) may have been established in each province and in every village and that some children from six or seven years of age may have been introduced to them" (Babylonian Talmud, *Baba Batra* 21a). However, that decision could, in fact, reach back to Joshua ben Perahyah, ca. 130 BCE (Hengel, 1974, p. 82). It was not until the second half of the 2nd century that Yehuda ben Tema would specify the steps of the Jewish traditional education: "At five years old [one is fit] for the Scripture, at ten years for the Mishnah, at thirteen for [the fulfilling of] the commandments, at fifteen for the Talmud, and at eighteen for the bride-chamber" (Mishnah *Abot* 5, 21).

It is clear that the possible training ascribed to the royal era did not correspond to the subsequent diagram. Much more, it is not necessary to represent the "schools" of the ancient Near East according to what we know today. The "schools" existed wherever a teacher taught his knowledge to some students seated around him, in a room, under a tree, or in the corner of a court. Lastly, one has often objected to the existence of schools due to the fact that the profession of scribe was generally practiced by the father and passed on to the son. Therefore, the teaching of knowledge was essentially transmitted from father to son. Yet such a plan cannot explain the spread of writing from ca. 800. This is well explained only by school institutions, even if the connection with the initiative of the king of Judah (Jehoshaphat?) reported in 2 Chronicles 17:7–9, remains uncertain (Lemaire, 1981, pp. 40–1, 48).

In fact, a certain number of paleo-Hebraic inscriptions, in particular of ostraca, found at Kuntillet 'Ajrud, Qadesh-Barnea, Aroer, Khirbet 'Uza, and Lachish, appeared to have been exercises of apprentices in writing (spelling books, formulae for beginning letters, lists of proper nouns . . .), in accounting (table of scales and measures of Qadesh-Barnea) or in drawing (Kuntillet 'Ajrud, Lachish) (Lemaire, 1981, pp. 7–33). Two ostraca (Arad 88 and Horvat 'Uza: Beit-Arieh, 1993a) could even be copies of literary texts. Even if these ostraca may not be as comprehensive as the manual *Kemyt* in use in Egypt for a thousand years in specifying the steps for the writing apprentice and the scribal formula to use, they probably reveal the classic steps of the writing apprentice and the useful literary genres, in particular, for all royal administrative officials. At the highest level, that instruction comprises probably a moral and philosophical aspect, a study of historical tradition, national judicial laws, and the geography of the country. It is in this context that one can understand the birth and the development of not only sapiential literature (Shupak, 1993, pp. 349–51) but also the largest part of biblical literature (Pentateuch, historical books, and prophetic books), the diverse successive redactions of which were able to serve as "classics" in the instruction (Lemaire, 1981, pp. 72–85).

In fact, in the neighboring civilizations (Egypt, Mesopotamia, and Ugarit), schools appeared to have been linked to the development of governmental bureaucracy. It is also probably in the same context that one may presume a first organization of paleo-Hebraic instruction in the era of Solomon. In fact, according to the ancient Solomonic historiography, this king was celebrated for his political wisdom, leading to the organization of an effective central provincial administration (cf. above all, 1 Kings 4). It is probable that the Egyptian model has influenced largely this first organization of the scribal formation and the ideology inculcated in some passages of the book of Proverbs (Williams, 1975; Shupak, 1993).

•   This expansion (growth) of written Hebraic culture was stopped by the "schism, between North and South," the Egyptian invasion of Shishak and the boundary war between Israel and Judah. It is possible that a new beginning was given to it during the dynasty of Omri (881–841), but this probable revival stopped during the coup d'état of Jehu in 841, consistent with the submission of Shalmaneser III, the Aramean wars, and the domination of King Hazael of Damascus (Lemaire, 1991). Yet, if we believe the epigraphic attestations, the real development of the use of writing dates from ca. 800, that means during the revival of Israel under the kings Jehoash (ca. 805/3–790) and Jeroboam II (ca. 790–750). It is later strengthened in the Kingdom of Judah during the reforms of Hezekiah and Josiah.

Two biblical literary facts seem to confirm this evolution:

- The appearance of the "writing prophets" in the 8th century with Amos and Hosea. The development of the use of writing among the disciples of the prophets led to the formation of written collections of their oracles. In fact, these oracles could have been recorded at first on tablets of wax, diptych or polyptych, well attested on the low relief of the 8th century, before being properly recopied on a role of papyrus or of leather (Lemaire, 1985).
- The insistence on instruction and writing in Deuteronomy was probably promulgated, at least in a primitive form, in 622 (2 Kings 22–23). Also, not only should the king copy the instruction, the "law," and read it all the days of his life (Deut 17:18–19), but also every householder was also supposed to be capable of writing excerpts from it and teaching them to their sons (Deut 6:6–9, cf. 11:18–20).

This large diffusion of writing, at least among all members of the royal administration and notables, did not discontinue the usefulness of professional scribes. Also the king was to have at his disposition a certain number of royal scribes (Lipinski, 1988) among whom a "scribe/secretary" was one of the three leading members of his royal staff (2 Sam 8:17; 20:25; 1 Kings 4:3; 2 Kings 12:11; 18:18–37; 19:2; and 22:3). The Aramean low relief of the king of Zencirli Barrakib (ca. 732–720), represents him sitting on his throne giving his orders to his royal secretary standing before him.

The usefulness of professional scribes is, after all, apparent to us in the book of Jeremiah. We can be virtually certain that the prophet Jeremiah not only knew how to read and write but also had received an advanced scribal education. In fact, he was of a priestly family, protected by the Shaphan family (Jeremiah 26:24), one of the major families of high officials of that period that had numerous relationships to the court. Besides, he himself writes out a bill of purchase for a field of his cousin (Jeremiah 32:10). Yet he afterwards entrusts that bill to Baruch son of Neriah for it to be preserved for a long time according to the customary judicial procedure (Jeremiah 32:12–14). This means that the scribe Baruch, from whom we now have two bullae (Avigad and Sas, 1997; #417), plays here the role of a "notary/archivist." What is more, the same Jeremiah twice asks the same scribe Baruch to write and to put in good form the scroll containing his oracles (Jeremiah 36). Baruch plays here in some way the role of an "editor" of a book that will serve as a reference, later to be recognized as a classic, and then to become a canonical writing. These examples are enough to shed light on some of the functions of professional scribes to people who were far from being entirely illiterate: the presence of professional scribes does not allow us to prejudge the illiteracy of the rest of the society.

This remark is all the more legitimate for the period of the Second Temple where scribes could have very diverse functions as well as those of secretary, bookkeeper, administrator of jurists, and intellectual or savant. We cannot specify the function of "Jeremiah the scribe" that appeared in the bulla of the beginning of the Persian era (Avigad, 1976, p. 7). However, Aramean papyri of Elephantine in Upper Egypt mentioned "some scribes of the province" (*spry mdynt'*: Porten and Yardeni, 1986: A6:1,6), and some scribes of the treasury (*spry 'wsr*: Porten and Yardeni, 1989: B4.4, 14)." In fact, contracts of papyri sale from Wadi Daliyeh, sometimes written in the presence of the governor of Samaria, were probably written by the first category, to which belonged also very likely "Shimshai the Scribe" (Ezra 4:8.17.17.23). "Zadok the scribe" of Nehemiah 13:13 belonged rather to the second category, that of "scribes of the treasury" of the province of Judea.

However, the most famous biblical scribe of that epoch is incontestably Ezra whose precise function and historic mission has been much discussed (Schams, 1998, pp. 50–7). His title of "expert scribe (*sofer mahir*)" corresponds to that given to Ahikar in the Aramean romance of Ahikar "a wise and skillful scribe (*spr ḥkym wmhyr*)" (Porten and Yardeni, 1993: c.1.1.,1) and appears more or less to be the equivalent of a "scholar." Nevertheless, his specific domain is the instruction/law of Moses (Ezra 7:6), and he is precisely the "scribe of the Law of the God of Heaven" (Ezra 7:21). Even if one discusses it again somewhat, it seems better to accept this title as an official reference of the Jewish and Samaritan jurisprudence, the synthesis of which is contained in the five first books of the Bible, the Torah. It inaugurates then a new period, the one in which the text of the Torah is the official reference of the Jewish tradition. Beyond the ordinary sense of the term, the epithet of "scribe" hereafter designates in particular the expert in juridical and religious interpretation of the text of the Torah, an expert who will have also often as a task that interpretation shown in the example of Ezra who "had applied his heart to the study of the instruction/ Law of Yahweh (*lidrôš 'et tōrâ yhwh*), to put it into practice and to teach (*lalamaed*) in Israel law and jurisprudence" (Fishbane, 1990, p. 441).

Towards the turn of our era, the synagogue plays a fundamental role in the spread of the written, mainly biblical, Hebraic culture, even if "children were taught to read from the Bible, but not necessarily to write" (Demsky and Bar-Ilan, 1988, p. 22). This role of the synagogue of the first centuries is also evoked in the Jerusalem Talmud, Megilla 3:1: "There were 480 synagogues in Jerusalem and each had a *bet-sefer* and a *bet-talmud*, the former for the Scripture, the latter for the Mishnah." The association of synagogue and instruction is moreover confirmed by Jerusalemite Greek inscriptions of "Theodotos son of Ouettenos, priest and chief of the synagogue" who "has constructed the synagogue for the reading of the law and the teaching of the commandments (*eis anagnôsin nomou kai eis didachèn entolon*).

In the upper level, the *bet-midraš* centered on the writing and interpretation of biblical books, and addressed youths linked to a certain religious and political "elite." Here the emphasis was on problems of jurisprudence (*halakhah*) and of the interpretation of the Jewish law. The training of Saul of Tarsus, at the feet of the Pharisee teacher, Gamaliel, the former (Acts 22:3) member of the Sanhedrin

(Acts 5:34–39), is characteristic of this superior level of Jewish education in the Jerusalem of the first century, while the manuscripts of the library of Qumran allow one to have an idea of the content of the instruction of a *bet-midraš* linked to the Essenes, essentially centered on the study and interpretation of biblical books.

Bibliography

Avigad, N., *Bullae and Seals from a Post-Exilic Judean Archive*, Qedem 4 (Jerusalem: The Institute of Archaeology, Hebrew University, 1976).

Avigad, N. and B. Sass, *Corpus of West Semitic Stamp Seals* (Jerusalem: The Israel Academy of Sciences and Humanities, The Israel Exploration Society, The Institute of Archaeology, The Hebrew University of Jerusalem, 1997).

Beit-Arieh, I., "A Literary Ostracon from Horvat 'Uza," *Tel Aviv* 20 (1993a), 55–65.

——, "An Inscribed Jar from Horvat 'Uza," in S. Ahituk and B. Levine, eds., *Avraham Malamat* Volume, *Eretz-Israel* 24 (1993b), 34–40.

Crenshaw, J., "Education in Ancient Israel," *JBL* 104 (1985), 601–15.

——, *Education in Ancient Israel: Across the Deadening Silence* (New York: Doubleday, 1998).

Cross, F., "Samaria Papyrus 1: An Aramaic Slave Conveyance of 335 BCE Found in the Wadi ed-Daliyeh," in *N. Avigad Volume*, *Eretz-Israel* 18 (1985), 7–17.

——, "A Report on the Samaria Papyri," in J. A. Emerton, ed., *Congress Volume, Jerusalem 1986*, SVT 40 (1988), 17–26.

Davies, G. I. "Were There Schools in Ancient Israel?" in J. Day, et al., eds., *Wisdom in Ancient Israel, Essays in Honour of J. A. Emerton* (Cambridge: Cambridge University Press, 1995).

Demsky, A. and M. Bar-Ilan, "Writing in Ancient Israel and Early Judaism," in M. Mulder, ed., *Mikra* (Philadelphia, 1988), 1–38.

Dürr, L., *Das Erziehungswesen im Alten Testament und im Antiken Orient*, Mitteilungen der vorderasiatisch-ägyptischen Gesellschaft 36 (Leipzig: Hinrich, 1932).

Eph'al, I and J. Naveh, *Aramaic Ostraca of the Fourth Century BC from Idumaea* (Jerusalem: The Magnes Press, 1996).

Eshel, E. and A. Kloner, "An Aramaic Ostracon of an Edomite Marriage Contract from Maresha, dated 176 BCE," *IEJ* 46 (1996), 1–22.

Fishbane, M., "From Scribalism to Rabbinism: Perspectives on the Emergence of Classical Judaism," in J. Gammie and L. Perdue, eds., *The Sage in Israel and the Ancient Near East* (Winona Lake, IN, 1990), 439–56.

Gibson, J., *Textbook of Syrian Semitic Inscriptions II, Aramaic Inscriptions* (Oxford: Clarendon Press, 1975).

Golka, F., "Die Israelitische Weisheitsschule oder des Kaisers neue Kleider," *VT* 33 (1983), 257–70.

Haran, M., "On the Diffusion of Schools and Literacy," in J. Emerton, ed., *Congress Volume, Jerusalem 1986*, SVT 40 (1988), 81–95.

Hengel, M., *Judaism and Hellenism* I (Philadelphia: Fortress, 1974).

Hermisson, H., *Studien zur israelitischen Spruchweisheit* (Neukirchen: Neukirchener Verlag, 1968).

Jamieson-Drake, D., *Scribes and Schools in Monarchic Judah: A Socio-Archaeological Approach*, JSOTS 109 (Sheffield: JSOT, 1991).

Klostermann, A., "Schulwesen im alten Israel," in *Theologische Studien Th. Zahn* (Leipzig: A. Deichert [Georg Böhme], 1908), 193–232.

Lang, B., "Schule und Unterricht im alten Israel," in M. Gilbert, ed., *La sagesse de l'Ancien Testament* (Louvain: Peters, 1979), 186–201.

Lemaire, A., *Inscriptions hébraïques I, Les ostraca*, Littératures anciennes du Proche-Orient 9 (Paris: Éditions du Cerf, 1977).

——, *Les Écoles et la formation de la Bible dans l'ancien Israël*, OBO 39 (Göttingen: Vandenhoeck und Ruprecht, 1981).

——, "Sagesse et écoles," *VT* 34 (1984), 270–81.

——, "Vom Ostrakon zur Schriftrolle," in W. Röllig, *XXII. Deutscher Orientalistentag*, ZDMGSup 6 (Stuttgart: F. Steiner, 1985), 110–23.

——, "L'enseignement essénien et l'école de Qumran," in A. Caquot, et al., eds., *Hellenica et Judaica, Hommage V. Nikiprovetzky* (Paris: Peeters, 1986), 191–203.

——, "The Sage in School and Temple," in J. Gammie and L. Perdue, eds., *The Sage in Israel and the Ancient Near East* (Winona Lake, IN, 1990), 165–81.

——, "Hazaël de Damas, roi d'Aram," in D. Charpin, and F. Joannès, eds., *Marchands, diplomates et empereurs, études sur la civilisation mésopotamienne offertes à P. Garelli* (Paris: Éditions Recherche sur les Civilisations, 1991), 91–108.

——, "Education, Ancient Israel," in *ABD* 2 (1992), 305–12.

——, *Nouvelles inscriptions araméennes d'Idumée au musée d'Israël*, Supplément à Transeuphratène 3 (Paris: Gabalda, 1996).

——, "Qoumran: sa fonction et ses manuscrits," in E. Laperrousaz, ed., *Qoumran et les manuscrits de la Mer Morte, un cinquantenaire* (Paris, 1997), 117–49.

——, "The Tel Dan Stela as a Piece of Royal Historiography," *JSOT* 81 (1998), 3–14.

Lipinski, E., "Royal and State Scribes in Ancient Jerusalem," in J. Emerton, ed., *Congress Volume, Jerusalem 1986*, SVT 40 (1988), 189–203.

Lozachmeur, H. and A. Lemaire, "Nouveaux ostraca araméens d'Idumée (Collection Sh. Moussaïeff)," *Semitica* 46 (1996), 123–52.

Meshorer, Y., *Ancient Jewish Coinage I, Persian through Hasmoneans* (Dix Hills, New York: Amphora, 1982).

——, "Ancient Jewish Coinage. Addendum I," *Israel Numismatic Journal* 11 (1990), 104–32.

Meshorer, Y. and S. Qedar, *The Coinage of Samaria in the Fourth Century BCE* (Jerusalem: The Israel Numismatic Society, 1991).

Millard, A. R., "An Assessment of the Evidence for Writing in Ancient Israel," in J. Amitai, ed., *Biblical Archaeology Today, Proceedings of the International Congress on Biblical Archaeology, Jerusalem, April 1984* (Jerusalem: The Israel Academy of Sciences and Humanities in cooperation with the American School of Oriental Research, 1985), 301–12.

——, "The Knowledge of Writing in Iron Age Palestine," in K-D. Schunck and M. Augustin, eds., *"Lasset uns Brücken bauen . . ." Collected Communications to the XVth Congress of the IOSOT, Cambridge 1995* (Frankfurt: Peter Lang, 1998), 33–9.

Oren, E. and U. Rappaport, "The Necropolis of Maresha-Beth Govrin," *IEJ* 34 (1984), 114–53.

Porten, B. and A. Yardeni, *Textbook of Aramaic Documents from Ancient Egypt I, Letters* (Jerusalem: The Hebrew University, 1986).

——, *Textbook of Aramaic Documents from Ancient Egypt II, Contracts* (Jerusalem: The Hebrew University, 1989).

——, *Textbook of Aramaic Documents from Ancient Egypt III, Literature, Accounts, Lists* (Jerusalem: The Hebrew University, 1993).

——, *Textbook of Aramaic Documents from Ancient Egypt IV, Ostraca and Assorted Inscriptions* (Jerusalem: The Hebrew University, 1999).

Puech, E., "Les Écoles dans l'Israël préexilique: données épigraphiques," in J. Emerton, ed., *Congress Volume, Jerusalem 1986*, SVT 40 (1988), 189–203.

Renz, J., *Die althebräischen Inschriften*, Handbuch der althebräischen Epigraphik I (Darmstadt: Wissenschaftliche Buchgesellschaft, 1995).

Schams, C., *Jewish Scribes in the Second-Temple Period*, JSOTS 291 (Sheffield: Sheffield Academic Press, 1998).

Shupak, N., "The 'Sitz im Leben' of Proverbs in the Light of a Comparison of Biblical and Egyptian Wisdom Literature," *RB* 94 (1987), 98–119.

——, *Where Can Wisdom be Found? The Sage's Language in the Bible and Ancient Egyptian Literature*, OBO 130 (Göttingen: Vandenhoeck und Ruprecht, 1993).

Vaughn, A., "Palaeographic Dating of Judean Seals and Its Significance for Biblical Research," *BASOR* 313 (1999), 43–64.

Warner, S., "The Alphabet – An Innovation and its Diffusion," *VT* 30 (1980), 81–90.

Williams, R., "'A People Come out of Egypt.' An Egyptologist Looks at the Old Testament," in *Congress Volume, Edinburgh 1974*, SVT 28 (1975), 231–52.

Young, I. M., "Israelite Literacy: Interpreting the Evidence," *VT* 48 (1998), 239–53, 408–22.

Zorn, J., J. Yellin and J. Hayes, "The *m(w)ṣh* Stamp Impressions and the Neo-Babylonian Period," *IEJ* (1994), 161–83.

PART V
Old Testament Theology

CHAPTER 13

Modern Approaches to Old Testament Theology

Henning Graf Reventlow

Background and Definition

Are there modern approaches to Old Testament Theology? The history of Biblical Theology as an independent discipline is connected with Johann Philipp Gabler (1753–1826) and his famous Altdorf inaugural lecture (Gabler, 1787). According to the title, Gabler's main intention was to distinguish between the religious views of the writers of Sacred Scripture and the systems of contemporary dogmatic theologians, who were still accustomed to exploit the Bible for *dicta probantia*, scriptural proof-texts for their preconceived dogma. As a Lutheran theologian, Gabler intended to secure the independence of a Bible-bound theology. But according to the rising historical interest of his period, what the holy writers thought about religion, should be found out by historical exegesis. But as a second step religious ideas of universal value should be extracted from the Bible (starting with the New Testament) and collected for the later use by systematic theology (cf., recently, Knierim, 1995b). In the intellectual climate of the 19th century Gabler's thesis was taken as meaning that biblical theology should be a descriptive, historical-critical discipline. Very soon the trend led to the separation of a Theology of the Old Testament and a Theology of the New Testament (first with Bauer, 1796–1802). Until recently, there was a consensus that "Biblical (Old or New Testament) Theology" was a strictly defined discipline in the cosmos of exegetic theology, following a restricted number of differing models. Thus, one could ask if it is at all justified to speak about "modern approaches" to Old Testament Theology.

Apparently, this depends on a narrow or wide definition of the term. Perdue (1994a) indicates a recent development – which seems to have started first in the USA – to take the term in a widened sense. "Approach" then can be defined as a special access to the Bible (the Old Testament) from a certain premise, which opens specific, perhaps new perspectives and viewpoints. The meaning of "biblical theology" and "hermeneutics" would then nearly coincide. Though such a definition is not without problems, in this overview tentatively the whole circuit of modern approaches to the Old Testament will be considered. It remains to be asked what each of them might contribute to Old Testament Theology in a stricter sense.

History of Religion or Old Testament Theology

Soon in the 19th century, in the vein of historicism and "objectivity," the works which still appeared under the cover of a "Theology of the Old Testament" became more and more the genetic account of the religion of Israel in biblical times. Davidson (1910, p. 11) declared openly: "Though we speak of Old Testament *theology*, all that we can attempt is to present the religion or the religious ideas of the Old Testament." Against this development, after the First World War a growing number of scholars, initially in Germany – though not denying the importance of histories of Israelite religion – stressed the systematic task of a genuine Old Testament theology. Dialectic theology contributed to a revival of the debate on the theological importance of the Old Testament and the publication of works on its theology. However, books on Israelite religion continued to appear. Recently Albertz' *History* (Albertz, 1994), especially his claim that this form of representation is more meaningful and even more theological than an Old Testament Theology, instigated a lively discussion (cf. esp. *JBTh* 10 [1995]; Barr, 1999, pp. 100–39). Gunneweg's posthumous work moves in a similar direction (Gunneweg, 1993). Obviously the rebirth of interest in religious history is the result of an altered theological climate (cf. also Miller, 1985). But Biblical (Old Testament) Theology focusing upon the theological contents of the Bible retains its importance.

Historical or Systematic Exposition

A well-known example for a systematic exposition is Koehler's *Theology* (Koehler, 1957). The structure of the book was still marked by a system at home in dogmatic theology. Cf. even recently Ralph L. Smith's scheme "God, Man, Eschatology" (Smith, 1993). Eichrodt (Eichrodt, 1961–7), instead, for his *Theology* chose a structure taken from the Old Testament itself. It is not unusual that most recent Old Testament theologies display theological concepts of the Bible in a systematic arrangement (i.e., Preuss, 1995–6; Kaiser, 1998. For the system, cf. Knierim, 1995b, pp. 475–86). A mixture of historic and systematic order can be found in Childs, 1993.

The Center of Old Testament Theology

The next step in a systematic approach is searching for a "center" of the Old Testament, a term or idea that would allow an overview of the whole testament from a single perspective (for the older discussion cf. Smend, 1986; Hasel, 1974; Hasel, 1991, pp. 139–71; Reventlow, 1985, pp. 125–33). The term *Mitte* (center) was stamped by Zimmerli (1963, p. 105) in a review article of von Rad's "Theology" (von Rad, 1962–5); but the question is older. Eichrodt chose "covenant" as a heading for the whole Old Testament. For Zimmerli (1978) the "name" of YHWH is the real center of the Old Testament. Similar attempts can be observed in recent works: Preuss takes "election" as the central term. Kaiser declares first (1993, pp. 329–53) the Torah as the center of the whole Scripture. Later (1998) he chooses "YHWH, the god of Israel" as the organizing principle for his exposition. Brueggemann (1997, p. 117) selects "speech about God" (Israel's testimony) as the "proper subject" for his work. But shortly before, he suggests "that we might cease to ask about a center for Old Testament theology" (1997, p. 114). Already von Rad denied that the Old Testament could have a "center" (1965, vol. 2, p. 362). It was also proposed that we should, confronted with the diversity in the Bible, renounce a unifying structure and seek a center "in the dynamics of a living relationship with God" (Bornemann, 1991, p. 121). But somehow we need a "center" for a theological judgment about the Bible: a "canon within the canon" for grasping the essence of the whole. Even if not clearly articulated, there always was a leading viewpoint for the arrangement of the material. This is seen in recent handbooks on Old Testament Theology.

Two-pole Dialectics

Some authors prefer a two-pole dialectics as the "center" of the Old Testament. Eichrodt had already structured his work into three main themes (taken over from his teacher O. Procksch, cf. Procksch, 1950): "God and People," "God and World," "God and Man." Smend proposed Wellhausen's so-called "covenant-formula," "YHWH the God of Israel, Israel the people of YHWH" as the "center" (Smend, 1986, pp. 64f, cf. *Die Bundesformel* [1963], ibid., pp. 11–39). Westermann, 1978 (cf. 1982) detects a bipolarity in the Bible (especially the Old Testament) between blessing and redemption. There are other well-known examples. Recently, Brueggemann (1992, pp. 1–44) opposed the "common theology" of the Old Testament as part of the common theology of the ancient Near East, based on a world- and social-order, to the "embrace of pain," the other side of the Bible. Special to the Old Testament is its reflection of polarity in God himself: besides the God who is the enforcer of structures there is the patient God, yearning for relationship with the disobedient Israel, his partner. "Old Testament theology must be bipolar" (1992, p. 25).

Creation and Wisdom

In the period in which history was the prevailing theme of Old Testament Theology, the topic of creation was nearly forgotten. Von Rad (1962) regarded the creation narratives as pre-structure to salvation history. The Yahwist used creation in his work as a sort of preface. This position found many followers. Westermann first introduced the bipolarity between blessing and redemption (see above). He and his students Albertz (1974) and Doll (1985) distinguished between the creation of humankind and that of the world. The first is especially at home in the Psalms (originally in the lament) and in Deutero-Isaiah. The Canaanite (specifically Jerusalemite) origin of the topic became more and more obvious. In seeing the world order, with the equivalents justice and peace, as basic for Old Testament Theology (cf. Schmid 1968 and the articles in Schmid, 1974), H.-H. Schmid turned the earlier position upside down. Similarly, Knierim regards "the universal dominion of Yahweh in justice and righteousness" as the hinge for Old Testament Theology (1995a, p. 15). This is no isolated voice. Cf. also Anderson, 1984c.

Also Wisdom is now recognized as an important branch of Old Testament witness, reflecting on creation, its orders and gifts. Perdue (1994b, pp. 129ff) lists four major approaches in Wisdom theology: "anthropology, world order, theodicy, and the dialectic of anthropology and cosmology." The earlier position that wisdom is just an instruction on how to master human life (i.e., Brueggemann, 1972) has been dropped nearly completely. Wisdom is always theological. Experience is the basis for the teaching of the sages who develop a sort of "natural theology" (cf. Barr, 1991) in which God's order in the world is reflected in its consequences for human acting. Perdue published a complete theology of wisdom (1994b). Cf. also Clements, 1992; Day, 1995c. However, it should not be forgotten that Wisdom thinking entered into a crisis in post-exilic times. The skeptical (Qoheleth) or believing (Job) provide the insight that God's being free and incomprehensible in his acting is the limit of any natural theology. (For an actual application in the post-holocaust situation, cf. Levenson, 1988.)

Descriptive or Confessional

In his article "Biblical Theology, Contemporary" (Stendahl, 1962) Krister Stendahl gives the classical liberal definition of biblical theology as descriptive, as objective as possible, historical, telling what was theologically thought in biblical times, what it "meant" instead of what it "means." Another representative of historical positivism was George E. Wright. In *God Who Acts* (Wright, 1952) he speaks of divine acts as historical facts reported in the Old Testament and to be confirmed by archaeological evidence. As a member of the Albright school, he had a large impact upon the so-called "Biblical Theology Movement." Recent hermeneutics (Gadamer; Ricoeur, cf. below), however, has shown that the claim of historical objectivity is not tenable. Already Stendahl remarks that a careful hermeneutics connected with faith should afterwards (in the frame of the canon) find out the meaning of the Bible for the present community. When reading a text, everybody understands it against the background of his own presuppositions, marked by the *Zeitgeist* of his age and by personal inclinations. Also the encounter with the Bible becomes a dialogue between reader and text, in which both partners do not remain unaltered. A special problem exists when a text – the Bible – is regarded as an extraordinary authority for a community, as Holy Scripture (cf. Hauerwas, 1993). In recent years, the discussion has become more intense, whether Biblical (Old Testament) Theology should have a confessional (Christian) character. Works of the preceding generation of Old Testament scholars cope with the problem in different ways. Thus, in volume I of his *Theology* (von Rad, 1962) according to his traditio-historical approach, von Rad intends nothing else but to re-tell Israel's "historical traditions" (believed history, not a critical reconstruction of historical events). The kerygmatic theology of the period stands in the background. In repeating the "historical credo" of Israel the modern theologian in a way identifies himself with its "witness." But this intention remains a bit unclear with von Rad. The relation to the "factual" history of YHWH-belief, which he premised, was the subject of a lively discussion.

A special problem with von Rad is the position of the third part of vol. II in his *Theology*. Here von Rad approaches the relationship between the testaments, between the Old Testament worldview and the belief in Christ, salvation history in the Old Testament and fulfillment in the New. A connection to the earlier parts of the work cannot be detected. Other Old Testament theologies show a similar impasse. Already Procksch (1950) begins his work with remarks about the Christian character of his task: "The Old Testament has Christ as its goal" (7ff). "All theology is Christology" (1). But in the following descriptive account nothing can be seen of a christological approach. Similarly, Vriezen (1970), starts with a chapter on "The Christian Church and the Old Testament" (11–21), later, however, leaving this aspect totally aside. Hartmut Gese's consequent traditio-historical solution postulating a tradition leading directly from the Old to the New Testament (i.e., Gese, 1977, 1981) was also unconvincing.

Among recent publications, some show an expressed confessional character. Watson (1994, 1997) stresses the hermeneutical role of canon and church and regards "Old Testament Theology as a Christian Theological Enterprise" (1997, p. 179 [title]). Kaiser sees the task of a Christian Theology of the Old Testament as a Lutheran theologian: Evangelical theology is a theology of the word of God. The Bible can be regarded as both the "word of God," and "the witness of God's acting in human beings, in Israel and the peoples" (1993, p. 79). The dialectics between Law and Gospel is basic for a Christian interpretation of both testaments. Therefore, in describing the witness of the Old Testament (the first step is a descriptive task!), "the relation between Law and Gospel comes automatically into view, because it structures theologically the Torah and lastly the Old Testament as a whole" (1993, p. 88). Kaiser sketches an existentialist interpretation for the understanding of *theologumena*: "It intends to comprehend the understanding of existence and the world that is expressed in them" (ibid.). Kaiser seeks to combine a descriptive method with a believing interpretation stamped by a marked confessional tradition. (On C. R. Seitz, see below.)

W. Brueggemann (1992, p. 116) admonishes his readers to take the Old Testament more theologically, i.e., to take in earnest "the theological claims and affirmations of this text." A bit veiled, this says that the hearer (reader) of the Bible must regain the consciousness of being addressed in this text (cf., earlier, Zimmerli, 1956). This shift obviously is connected with an altered intellectual climate: Whereas until recently the positivist worldview of modern science was omnipotent, in postmodernism the shakiness of its presuppositions has become more and more visible. Faith and confession have received a new chance in a pluralistic, though secularized world (cf. Taylor, 1984; Burnham, 1989; H. Smith, 1990).

Canonical Approaches

The canonical approaches also belong to the confessional type. They can be characterized as one of the recent efforts to direct the attention to the text instead of to a history behind the text. If this text is the Bible, the quest for its authority leads to the subsequent quest for the canon. This is the way in which Brevard S. Childs has tried to go, for many years with a large number of publications (on Childs, cf. Brett, 1991). Also the canon has a history behind it. Childs knows about this history and the intricate problems connected with the formation of the canon (cf. Childs, 1979, pp. 62ff). But in view of the scarceness of reliable information, he decides to start from the final text as a basis for exegesis and theological reflections (ibid., pp. 75–7). After first having treated both testaments separately (i.e., Childs, 1985; for a fuller bibliography see Perdue, 1994b, p. 155, n. 4), he recently approached the whole canon of both testaments (Childs, 1993). Most important for Childs is the relation of the canon to the believing community, the church. The Bible is normative for the church. It contains texts which transmit the word of God to future generations in the church. As such it fixed the results of theological reflections. The "canonical process" continues to be an actualizing of the tripartite canon, in which the theologian uses "intertextuality" to interpret Scripture by Scripture. We are reminded of the pre-critical aspect of *analogia fidei*. But Childs does not deny the usefulness of historical criticism as a first step in understanding the meaning of a text.

A major criticism leveled against Childs' enterprise has been that it neglects the importance of historical particularity. The voice of sources or older texts in the whole of a testament in its original situation and theological speciality will not be heard. Does the Bible, especially the Old Testament, not contain a plurality of voices? To hear a symphony of the whole might remain an illusion. However, others claim that it is impossible to break through the final form of the canon to earlier levels of revelation by critical exegesis and give them the same authority (cf. Seitz, "We Are Not Prophets or Apostles," in Seitz, 1998, pp. 102–9).

An attempt at curing this weakness at least partially is J. A. Sanders' *Torah and Canon* (Sanders, 1972), who investigated the function of the canon and its role in the course of the history of its influence. This leads to a different evaluation of the parts of the canon: The Torah comes first, as a nucleus of crystallization, then the prophetic canon and the writings (cf. Sanders, 1987a,b).

Rolf Rendtorff recently submitted his own "canonical approach" (Rendtorff, 1999). He declares that he is thereby following his teacher von Rad, whose project had been already canonical, in pursuing the order of the main sections of the Hebrew Bible (dedicating to the Pentateuch and then to the Prophets a separate part of his work). But he would go one step further on the way of tradition to its end, leading to the final text. On this he would focus his special attention (Rendtorff, 1999, p. 1).

Similar to von Rad, the structure of volume 1 resembles an introduction, going through the sections and the books of the Old Testament. The provisional plan of the projected volume 2 follows a thematic order that resembles partly the older systematic models. But we must wait upon its publication for a final evaluation.

Narrative Theology

The rise of a "narrative theology" is connected with the recent shift of interest from history to literature. Also in this field, a secular movement gave the first impetus. Wellek and Warren, *Theory of Literature* (Wellek and Warren, 1942), were especially influential in this direction. Scholes and Kellogg defined narrative in the broadest possible way: "By narrative we mean all those literary works which are distinguished by two characteristics: the presence of a story and a story-teller" (Scholes and Kellogg, 1966, p. 4). In the USA, it was the so-called "New Criticism" (or "close reading") that strove to regard "poetry" as a subject in and of itself. A text (above all a narrative) has to be assessed as an entity without any relation to the intentions of the author or to the real world (the realm of science), simply as a piece of art. Sometimes – not always – it is also regarded in its context.

Hans Frei's work *The Eclipse of Biblical Narrative* (Frei, 1974) shows the impact of the new hermeneutics on biblical exegesis (cf. Poland, 1985; Kermode, 1990, pp. 29–48). Frei fascinated his readers with his proposal to read the Bible as a collection of realistic novels without regarding ideas from the outside about revelation or ontology. Lindbeck (1984, pp. 32–41) formulates a "cultural-linguistic alternative" to the usual model of religion oriented on experience and expression. The movement goes at least partially in the opposite direction: human religious experience can be gained and formulated in confrontation with the symbolic system of a religious tradition, which is expressed in poetry, music, art and ritual. Narratives are a central medium of such a tradition.

Frye offers important additional hermeneutical considerations (Frye, 1982),
as does Ricoeur in numerous works on language, myth and metaphor (for a
short introduction, cf. Wallace, 1995 [1990], pp. 17–50, 55–7; Wallace, 1999.
More detailed is Clark, 1990, esp. pp. 152–98; Fodor, 1995, esp. pp. 183–225).
Ricoeur constructs a three-step hermeneutical arch (or threefold *mimesis*): (1)
an initial naïve pre-understanding of reality; (2) its restructuring and configuration by the text; (3) the final intersection between the world configured by the
text and the world of the reader (Ricoeur, 1984–8, vol. 1, pp. 52–87). There
are numerous examples of narrative exegesis of Old Testament texts (e.g., Licht,
1978, and the works of Fokkelman) that cover the entire Bible (Alter and
Kermode, 1987). For a textbook containing analyses of biblical stories and
literature in the wake of the Bible, cf. Ackerman and Warshaw, 1995). Auerbach
in his work *Mimesis* (Auerbach, 1968) was the first to describe the realistic style
of biblical tales. We have to distinguish between fables or parables (in the Old
Testament just 2 Sam 12: 1–4), myths, and "historical" narratives. Narrative
criticism (cf. Powell, Gray, and Curtis, 1992) mostly interpreted the last genre.
It uses methods of secular literary criticism, structuralism, and rhetorical criticism. Wolfgang Richter (Richter, 1971) wrote a basic methodology on poetics
and narrative, see Berlin, 1983. Alter (1981) offers a well-known exposition of
the literary analysis of biblical stories. Methodologically Alter follows the viewpoints of "close reading." Not unconscious of the useful results of historical
biblical scholarship, he focuses on the final form of the text. He is convinced
"that the religious vision of the Bible is given depth and subtlety precisely by
being conveyed through the most sophisticated resources of prose fiction"
(p. 22). In the second chapter, Alter discusses the problems for using the
methods of secular literary analysis on the Hebrew Bible perceived as sacred history. Are we allowed to apply categories adapted to prose fiction to narratives
intending to exhibit the revelation of God's will and to relate historical reality?
Alter agrees that, in fact, there *is* a difference between mere poetic fiction and
modern historiography. But biblical narrative is different. Granting that history is more similar to fiction than normally supposed, the definition of biblical
narrative as "*historicized* prose fiction" (p. 24) allows the use of critical categories for exploring their form and content. For example, in the stories about David,
although broadly based on obvious historical facts, the details of interior monologues which he formulated show the freedom of the writer to describe the
characters of the acting persons. History, in this way, is turned into fiction, and
the masterly writing that formed them fascinates us when reading these stories.
Speaking about the literary project of the biblical narratives, Alter repeats
that they actually intend "to reveal the enactment of God's purpose in historical
events" (p. 33). But he sees in these reports "a tension between the divine plan
and the disorderly character of actual historical events . . . between the divine
promise and its ostensible failure to be fulfilled . . . A double dialectic between
design and disorder, providence and freedom" (ibid.).
This is just a hint at what might be regarded as the main theological topic in
the biblical stories. In a later work (Alter, 1992) Alter takes the larger contexts

in the Bible into view. A special new-gained interest is directed to the cross-allusions in the Bible (pp. 107–30). But the (Jewish) author does not intend to write a Biblical Theology! So we gain the impression that the narrative approach can at best be enlisted among the "overtures" to Biblical Theology. "Story is not theology, but is the 'raw material' of theology" (Barr, 1999, p. 354). A theology of the Bible closely connected with the text needs other means of reflection, construction, argumentation. Even Ricoeur (1995, p. 247) fully supports the "conceptual duty of theology" (with D. Ritschl). However, for a positive answer on the problem "How can a narrative theology be justified?" see Goldberg, 1981: esp. pp. 194ff. The issue is more a question of hermeneutics. It regards the ways in which readers and believers appropriate the stories of the Bible in the life of the church and in their own lives (cf. Stroup, 1981). For several aspects see also Sternberg, 1985.

Liberation Theology and Feminist Approaches

Liberation Theology and Feminist Theology, which partly have a different sociological background, typically have similar presuppositions. They both start from current conditions of life. They look back to the Bible, seeking support for actual political demands or defending themselves against biblical arguments contra their claims. Their maxims derive from the ideals of the French Revolution (rooted in typically American traditions): "liberty," "equality," and "brotherhood" – by the feminists changed into "sisterhood." Another impact comes from Marxism, which regards the economic conditions as fundamental for the structures of human society and ideological super-structures.

Liberation theology (cf. Turner, 1994) originated in Latin America in its modern form in the 1960s in consequence of political and economic developments (oppression and pauperization of the masses) that had – after Vatican II – an impact also on Christians and the church. The Bible – formerly prohibited to Roman Catholic laypeople by the church authorities – was applied because it had much to say to the actual situation.

Biblical interpretations in Latin America and other countries in similar sociological and economic situations take place on two levels. One is the popular reading of the Bible in the grassroots communities – partly supported by Bible courses, meetings organized by the church, and trained visitors helping and motivating such endeavors. The communication is mostly oral, the standard simple. Poor and suppressed people detect their situation in the Bible, especially in the Old Testament, and also see encouraging examples of the hoped-for liberation. The exodus event becomes the symbol for the mighty deeds of a God who liberates his chosen people *now* from the hands of the oppressor. The prophetic witness (especially Jer 22: 13–16) is taken as a direct call to doing justice and intervening on behalf of the oppressed. In this and other adaptations of the history of biblical Israel to the Latin American reality of today, a naïve actualization of the Bible is practiced: the poor peasants, e.g., of Brazil, identify themselves with the ancient people of God. Similar movements arose in other countries of the Third World. (For a short overview and literature cf. Schmeller, 1999.)

A scholarly exegesis of a higher standard developed in Latin America and elsewhere comparatively late and is still partly in its beginnings. It partakes in the same themes as the popular Bible reading. Cf., e.g., Miranda, 1977; Croatto, 1981; Lohfink, 1987; Gottwald and Horsley, 1993.

Feminist theology has its roots in the secular women's liberation movement. Usually, Betty Friedan's *The Feminist Mystique* (Friedan, 1963) is regarded as the starting signal for the modern reopening of the feminist discussion. Feminist biblical studies as an academic discipline originated first in the 1970s in the USA and spread from there to other western countries. (For a survey and comprehensive bibliography see Phillips, 1999.) Ruether (1983, pp. 41–5, 216–32) distinguishes between three directions of feminist theology: (1) a liberal direction, mostly carried by upper-class white women believing in progress and a reformable society, postulating "women's rights" and equality with their male competitors; (2) a socialist or Marxist direction, fighting for the ideals of building up a just egalitarian society, full integration of women in the working class and common property in the means of production; and (3) romantic feminism glorifying the feminine qualities of sensitivity, creativity, etc., stressing the difference from the male world which represses women by upholding patriarchal domination. Either it regards the male world as reformable, or, in a more radical direction, it proclaims a total separation from the male world as the only way to preserve a genuine female lifestyle. Ruether herself considers it possible to unite the best elements of all three directions: fighting for human development and the emancipation of women, building a just society, and developing sensitivity for the deeper feminine human values.

Theological feminism partakes in these general directions in its own special way. The situation in which women find themselves in Christian communities normally is the starting point for turning to the Bible. Feeling suppressed by male dominance, they can first of all reject the Bible once for all, despairing that this book representing a patriarchal order could be used at all for the emancipation of women. This is the solution of Mary Daly who left the church totally behind, fighting for a post-Christian faith free of patriarchalism and representing female spirituality (Daly, 1973; 1979; 1992). Initiatives like the revival of the cult of the Great Goddess (cf. Starhawk, 1979) belong in this direction, or women can be loyal to the Bible as God's Word. Principally, these feminists assert that the divine plan cannot contain suppression of human beings, but must be directed toward the happiness of all believers, and mutual love. The obvious texts in the Bible presupposing a patriarchal society and postulating the submission of women under their husbands can be counterbalanced by other texts showing that the position of women was sometimes much better than a first look seems to suggest. Understandably enough, the majority of these studies are dedicated to the New Testament, allegedly more directly important for a Christian lifestyle. However, there are also exegetical treatments of Old Testament themes and passages. These include studies on the status of women in Israelite society, often combined with criticism of the patriarchal order reigning in the Old Testament period, which in feminist opinion resulted in a sometimes cruel suppression of women (cf. esp. Trible, 1984). However, there are voices indicating that women in Ancient Israel may have had a more important social position than often presumed, especially if compared with other ancient and modern oriental societies (cf., e.g., Camp, 1983). They also include selecting the stories about brave and courageous women frequently passed by in the usual treatments by male authors (cf., e.g., Brenner, 1985; Meyers, 1988) and a critical examination of God-talk in the Bible and in modern language. Feminists used to criticize the social world and especially theological language as male-dominated. They ask for an "inclusive" language comprising male and female aspects. In the Old Testament they check the metaphors used for God, especially those that use female images (God as mother, divine love and compassion [*rehm* = womb]; cf., e.g., Trible, 1978). Meanwhile, the insight has grown that we can speak about God only in metaphors and that the deity is neither male nor female. Especially debated is the Old Testament metaphor of God as king. Feminists declare that this picture obfuscates the maternal attributes of God just mentioned. For a feminist exegesis of the Old Testament, see, e.g., Russell, 1985; Newsom and Ringe, 1992; Brenner, 1993–7, pp. 1998ff; Schottroff and Wacker, 1998. Thus, there is no complete feminist Old Testament theology. Trible (1989) sketches what it could look like. In locating feminist biblical theology in reference to the classical discipline, she stresses that it could not be descriptive, but should be "primarily constructive and hermeneutical" (p. 289). But it "belongs to diverse communities, including academy, synagogue, church, and world. It is neither essentially nor necessarily Christian" (a point still to be debated). Basic for such a theology and the first step is exegesis. Essentials for it are: (a) it should start with Genesis 1–3, creation and the "image of God male and female" (p. 293); (b) it would "explore the presence and absence of female in Scripture" (ibid.); (c) it would reflect folk religion (e.g., the worship of the "Queen of Heaven" [Jer 7:16–20; 44:15–28]) and its effect upon the character of faith; (d) it would expose (androcentric) idolatry in the use of imagery; (e) it would "wrestle" with patriarchal language; and (f) for the authority of the Bible, it favors the model of interaction between text and reader, whose choice between alternative understandings might alter the meaning of the text. But beware of an exegesis that is self-pleasing! (against Trible, 1995).

A complete feminist Old Testament Theology is not yet written. The discussion is in full progress in this field.

Sociological and Materialistic Approaches

The use of methods and results of the social sciences has had an important impact also on the interpretation of the Old Testament (cf. Mayes, 1989; Carter and Meyers, 1996). Especially significant for an Old Testament Theology is the neo-Marxist ("materialistic") approach, using the conflict model for society. A prominent adherent of a revolution theory for the conquest of Canaan and a conflict model for the society of tribal Israel in the premonarchical period is Gottwald (cf. Gottwald, 1979, 1985). Lower-class, marginal Canaanites, according to this theory, revolted against their feudal rulers and (secondarily) formed tribes that united as a confederation. Early Israelite society, in Gottwald's eyes, was an example of an egalitarian system, in which the access to the resources of economic production was open to every adult member of the tribes, and power was equally distributed in the absence of any central authority. As regards religion, Gottwald proposed that "mono-Yahwism was the function of sociopolitical egalitarianism in premonarchic Israel" (Gottwald, 1979, p. 611). According to the Marxist model of ideology as superstructure, "religion is the function of social relations rooted in cultural-material conditions of life" (Gottwald, 1979, p. 701). Mono-Yahwism "typifies the explicitly religious symbol and action sub-system, or the cultic-ideological dimension or plane, of general Israelite society" (Gottwald, 1979, p. 614). But inherent in early Israel's religious symbolism was also the power for a total change of the existing social conditions, realizing " 'the impossible impossibility' of free communal life in hierarchic Canaan" (ibid.). The change to monarchy brought an end to the system, inducing also a new form of religious ideology in the form of the selection of Zion and the covenant with David (2 Sam 7). Gottwald reproaches the usual biblical theologies asserting Israel's religious uniqueness with "religious idealism" in failing "to root the religious organization and ideology of early Israel in its distinctive social-constitutional framework" (Gottwald, 1979, p. 692).

Gottwald's theory on early Israel's tribal organization as well as his theological assumptions have been fiercely debated (cf. Perdue, 1994a, pp. 99–109). His thesis has strong ideological premises, reducing biblical religion to a small sector. Whether transcendence keeps a place, remains unsolved. But the Bible can also be taken as motivating social initiatives (cf. Stegemann and Schottroff, 1984; Clévenot, 1985; Thomas and Visick, 1991).

Jewish Approaches

"Why Jews Are Not Interested in Biblical Theology" is the title of an essay by Levenson (Neusner, 1987, pp. 281–307 = Levenson, 1993, pp. 33–61). He points to a remarkable fact: the Jewish way of intercourse with the Bible for a long time seemed to exclude a Jewish Biblical Theology. The whole enterprise usually was regarded as typically Christian, especially if called Old Testament Theology. However, some recent authors demand a Jewish Biblical Theology, which might have other themes, but similar methods and a similar structure as the Christian counterpart. Moshe H. Goshen-Gottstein, as one of the first, saw the need for a Jewish Biblical Theology, which in some way should be developed in analogy to the Christian enterprise (cf., e.g., Goshen-Gottstein, 1987). He even left an uncompleted manuscript of a Biblical Theology after his death (cf. also Sweeney, 1997; Kalimi, 1997. For a critical report cf. Barr, 1999, pp. 286–311).

Biblical Theology

The older models of constructing a relationship between the testaments, as ongoing salvation history, typology, promise and fulfillment (cf. Reventlow, 1986, pp. 12–54), recently are often regarded as old-fashioned. Notwithstanding such reserve, in a way they keep their traditional place (cf. Görg, 1991, p. 23). However, recent approaches frequently leave the traditional paths. The insight among Christian scholars has grown that a Biblical Theology comprising both testaments is needed for theological reasons and for the use of the Bible in the church.

One way of connecting both testaments is to seek for a term or theological motif that has a prominent place in both testaments (for the different proposals cf. Reventlow, 1986, pp. 154–60). Of course, it is impossible to find a center that will be approved by everybody. One general proposal seems to find much consent (cf. Reventlow, 1986, p. 160f): a positive answer to O. Eissfeldt's question, "Is the God of the Old Testament also the God of the New?" (Eissfeldt, 1947, pp. 37–54). This identity seems to be the basic condition for Christians to preserve the unity of both testaments as Holy Scripture.

A special answer was given by H.-H. Schmid (Schmid, 1974, pp. 9–30) and U. Luck (Luck, 1976). Both worked together and declared that the world order (Schmid) or the experience of the world (Luck), i.e., creation faith, is the connecting link between the testaments. Seebass is the author of one of the first newer theologies comprising the whole Bible (Seebass, 1982). The book is presented as a first attempt at outlining how such a work should look and is destined for a broader public. The starting point and "center" is Paul's utterance (2 Cor 5:19): "God was in Christ" (2:34–57) and the program is "Biblical theology as the way to the knowledge of God" (ch. 8, pp. 212–18). Finding the one God in both testaments is the opinion of many scholars. But this was the first work built upon this presupposition. The most important publication in the field is Childs' *Biblical Theology of the Old and New Testaments* (Childs, 1993). He sees his program including both testaments in "the church's ongoing *search* for the Christian Bible" (p. 67). In the frame of the canon, the "movement from the outer parameters of tradition to the inner parameters of Word is constitutive of the theological task" (p. 68). In a Barthian tradition, it is the "hearing of God's Word" according to "the church's christological rule of faith" (p. 67) that is the guiding measure for developing a Biblical Theology. The "subject matter" of the whole Bible is Jesus Christ. Neither the use of the Old Testament in the New (Hübner, 1990), nor a simple traditio-historical continuation of the Old Testament in the New (Gese, 1977) is a basis. Neither is it possible to regard the

234 HENNING GRAF REVENTLOW

Old Testament as the negative background to the New (Bultmann and his school). The Old Testament must be heard according to its own witness. But this is also a witness to Jesus Christ.

For structuring a Biblical Theology of the Old Testament, Childs follows essentially von Rad's method: "to describe the theological functions of the great revelatory events in Israel's history and their subsequent appropriation by the tradition" (p. 92), in which the witness of God's historical encounters with Israel was preserved. But, contrary to von Rad, not the streams of tradition as reconstructed by scholarly research, but the canonical literature itself should be the basis.

Part 3 (pp. 95–207) contains an exegetical exposition following the order of biblical chronology, surprisingly beginning with creation. Childs does not seem to see a problem here: "Indeed the beginning of the world and the beginning of history fall together" (p. 107). However, originally the exodus event stood at the beginning of Israel's belief, and creation-faith was added later (p. 110; cf. von Rad). Topics not fitting in the chronological order ensue at the end of this part: prophecy, apocalyptic, wisdom and psalms (chs. XI–XIV). The treatment of the New Testament (part 4) follows at first unconnected. Part 6 (pp. 349–716) is a new start: here Childs uses a systematic structure and subsumes Old and New Testament materials under theological topics.

The structural dualism indicates an unsolved problem. The combination of a traditio-historical with a systematic approach remains a halfway decision as long as a complete amalgamation of the testaments in Biblical Theology is not attempted. How this could be done without completely destroying the peculiarity of each testament is not easy to decide.

Also Childs' student, Seitz (Seitz, 1998) follows the canonical model, with practical intentions. In the first chapter (pp. 3–12), which furnishes the title to the book, he asks for a Biblical Theology searching the Scriptures after a witness about God in Israel and in Christ. We should no longer ask after Israel's, the New Testament's and our own thinking about self and God, but: "How does the God we confess and raised Jesus from the dead think about Israel and the world?" (p. 8). A Christian hearing from the beginning (p. 22) follows a "rule of faith" (p. 11). "This book was written to the glory of God" (p. xi). The aim is for "biblical studies to be more theological and theological studies to be more biblical" (p. 25).

Another attempt to integrate the testaments is the work of Beauchamp (Beauchamp, 1976, 1990). Combining a detailed knowledge of French linguistics with Catholic exegetical tradition (Beauchamp, 1976, pp. 15–38), Beauchamp follows the program of "re-lecture" (André Gelin). A similar difference as between the three main parts of the Old Testament itself – law, prophets, and wisdom – exists between the testaments, but also an inner unity. Law and salvation history are related by the "covenant formula." Whereas the law has a tendency to become torpid, prophecy breaks through with the lively word of proclamation. Wisdom – in its early form without a relation to history – remains independent for a long period. Beauchamp stresses the importance of apocalyptic (1976, pp. 200–28) as combining elements of the three main traditions and, directing the view to the eschaton, enabling the Christian community to see the Old Testament as one book. Already the earlier parts of the Old Testament look forward to a new order (1976, pp. 229–74). Beauchamp sketches an all-comprising panorama of the whole Bible. The reader is encouraged to read it in the light of modern exegetical methods and insights, though from New Testament presuppositions (1976, pp. 275–98).

Vol. 2 (Beauchamp, 1990) contains the re-lecture of different parts of the Old Testament. Without negating the results of historical criticism, this re-lecture detects a second, spiritual level in the Holy Scripture. Here Beauchamp relies on old and new rhetorical observations about metaphor, figures, allegorical sense, narrative, word (*parole*), and writing (cf. Beauchamp, 1990, pp. 21–112), and interspersed among the exegetical passages in the main part are re-readings of Gen 2–3, the patriarchal stories and the exodus-narrative, which bear the heading "Fulfill the Scriptures." For Beauchamp, such fulfillment, aiming at the "end of ends" Jesus Christ (pp. 411–27), is hidden behind the literal sense. The texts have an anthropological as well as a theological relevance. Beauchamp's exegetical procedure can be seen in his treatment of the Song of Songs (pp. 159–95). Against the traditional understanding of church and synagogue, but with critical exegesis he states "that the text surely expresses the experience of love between humans of different sex" (p. 185). But he continues: "It teaches us that this love is spiritual." The next step is, that this love recognizes its origin from God, and detects the allegorical sense: human love reflects the love of God, for: "the matters of man signify the matters of God" (p. 186). With this hermeneutical key the whole Scripture can be unlocked and spiritual insights can be won.

Bibliography

Ackerman, J. and T. Warshaw, *The Bible as/in Literature* (Glenview, IL: Scott Foresman [HarperCollins], 2nd edn., 1995).

Albertz, R., *Weltschöpfung und Menschenschöpfung* (Stuttgart: Calwer Verlag, 1974).

——, *A History of Israelite Religion in the Old Testament Period*, 2 vols. (Louisville: Westminster/John Knox, 1992, 1994).

Alter, R., *The Art of Biblical Narrative* (New York: Basic Books, 1981).

——, *The World of Biblical Literature* (New York: Basic Books, 1992).

Alter, R. and F. Kermode, eds., *The Literary Guide to the Bible* (Cambridge, MA: Harvard Belknap Press, 1987).

Anderson, Bernhard W., ed., *Creation in the Old Testament* (Philadelphia: Fortress, 1984).

Auerbach, E., *Mimesis* (Princeton: Princeton University Press, 1968).

Barr, J., *Biblical Faith and Natural Theology* (Oxford: Oxford University Press, 1991).

——, *The Concept of Biblical Theology: An Old Testament Perspective* (London: SCM Press, 1999).

Bauer, G., *Biblische Theologie des Alten und Neuen Testaments* (Leipzig: Weygand, 1797).

Beauchamp, P., *L'un et l'autre Testament*, 2 vols. (Paris: Editions du Seuil, 1976, 1990).

Berlin, Adele, *Poetics and Interpretation* (Sheffield: Sheffield University Press, 1983).

Bornemann, R., "Toward a Biblical Theology," in P. Reumann, *The Promise and Practice of Biblical Theology* (Minneapolis: Fortress Press, 1991), 117–28.

Brenner, Athalya, *The Israelite Women* (Sheffield: JSOT Press, 1985).

——, *The Feminist Companion to the Bible* (Sheffield: Sheffield Academic Press, 1993–7), 2nd series, 1998f.

Brett, M., *Biblical Theology in Crisis?* (Cambridge: Cambridge University Press, 1991).

Brueggemann, Walter, *In Man We Trust* (Atlanta: John Knox Press, 1972).

——, *Old Testament Theology. Essays on Structure, Theme, and Text*, ed. P. D. Miller (Minneapolis: Fortress Press, 1992).

——, *Theology of the Old Testament: Testimony, Dispute, Advocacy* (Minneapolis: Fortress Press, 1997).

Burnham, F., ed., *Postmodern Theology: Christian Faith in a Pluralist World* (New York: Harper & Row, 1989).

Camp, C., "Female Voice, Written Word: Women and Authority in Hebrew Scripture," in *Embodied Love: Sensuality and Relationship as Feminist Values* (San Francisco: Harper & Row, 1983), 97–113.

Carter, C. and C. Meyers, eds., *Community, Identity, and Ideology: Social Science Approaches to the Hebrew Bible* (Winona Lake, IN: Eisenbrauns, 1996).

Childs, B., *Introduction to the Old Testament as Scripture* (Philadelphia: Fortress, 1979).

——, *Old Testament Theology in a Canonical Context* (Philadelphia: Fortress, 1985).

——, *Biblical Theology of the Old and New Testaments* (Minneapolis: Fortress, 1993).

Clark, S., *Paul Ricoeur* (London and New York: Routledge, 1990).

Clements, R., *Wisdom in Theology* (Grand Rapids: Eerdmans, 1992).

Clévenot, M., *Materialist Approaches to the Bible* (Maryknoll: Orbis, 1985).

Cooey, Paula M., Sharon A. Farmer, Mary Ellen Ross, eds., *Embodied Love: Sensuality and Relationship as Feminist Values* (San Francisco: Harper & Row, 1987).

Croatto, S., *Exodus: A Hermeneutics of Freedom* (Maryknoll: Orbis, 1981).

Daly, M., *Beyond God the Father* (Boston: Beacon, 1973).

——, *Gyn/Ecology* (Boston: Beacon, 1979).

——, *Outercourse: The Dazzling Voyage* (autobiography) (San Francisco: Harper, 1992).

Davidson, A., *The Theology of the Old Testament*, 2nd edn. (New York: Scribners, 1910).

Day, John, et al., eds., *Wisdom in Ancient Israel: Essays in Honor of J. A. Emerton* (Cambridge: Cambridge University Press, 1995).

Doll, P., *Menschenschöpfung und Weltschöpfung in der alttestamentlichen Weisheit* (Stuttgart: Katholisches Bibelwerk, 1985).

Eichrodt, W., *Theology of the Old Testament* (Philadelphia: Westminster, 1961–7).

Eissfeldt, Otto, *Geschichtliches und Übergeschichtliches im Alten Testament*, ThStKr 109 (Berlin: Evangelische Verlagsanstalt, 1947).

Fodor, J., *Christian Hermeneutics: Paul Ricoeur and the Refiguring of Theology* (Oxford: Clarendon Press, 1995).

Fokkelman, J., *Narrative Art in Genesis* (Assen: Van Gorcum, 1978).

——, *Narrative Art and Poetry in the Books of Samuel*, 4 vols. (Assen: Van Gorcum, 1981–93).

Frei, H., *The Eclipse of Biblical Narrative: A Study in Eighteenth and Nineteenth Century Biblical Narrative* (New Haven: Yale University Press, 1974).

Friedan, B., *The Feminist Mystique* (New York: W. W. Norton, 1963).

Frye, N., *The Great Code: The Bible and Literature* (London: Routledge & Kegan Paul, 1982).

Gabler, Johann Philipp, 1787, *Oratio de justo discrimine theologiae biblicae et dogmaticae regundisque recte utriusque finibus* ("Lecture on the right distinction between biblical and dogmatic theology and the correct definition of the boundaries between them"). ET in B. Ollenburger, E. Martens and G. Hasel, *The Flowering of Biblical Theology* (Winona Lake, IN, 1992), 489–502.

Gese, Hartmut, "Tradition and Biblical Theology," in D. Knight, ed., *Tradition and Theology* (Philadelphia: Fortress, 1977), 301–26.

——, *Essays on Biblical Theology* (Minneapolis: Fortress 1981 (German original 1977).

Goldberg, M., *Theology and Narrative. A Critical Introduction* (Nashville: Abingdon, 1981).

Görg, M., "Christentum und Altes Testament," in *Jahrbuch für Biblische Theologie* 6, *Altes Testament und christlicher Glaube* (Neukirchen-Vluyn: Neukirchen Verlag, 1991), 5–31.

Goshen-Gottstein, M., "Tanakh Theology: The Religion of the Old Testament and the Place of Jewish Biblical Theology," in P. Miller, P. Hanson and D. McBride, eds., *Ancient Israelite Religion* (Philadelphia: Fortress Press, 1987), 617–44.

Gottwald, N., *The Tribes of Yahweh: A Sociology of the Religion of Liberated Israel, 1250–1050 B.C.E.* (Maryknoll: Orbis, 1979).

——, *The Hebrew Bible: A Socio-Literary Introduction* (Philadelphia: Fortress, 1985).

Gottwald, N., K. Horsley, A. Richard, eds., *The Bible and Liberation: Political and Social Hermeneutics* (Maryknoll: Orbis/London: SPCK, 1993).

Gunneweg, A., *Biblische Theologie des Alten Testaments. Eine Religionsgeschichte Israels in biblisch-theologischer Sicht* (Stuttgart: Kohlhammer, 1993).

Hasel, G., "The Problem of the Center of the Old Testament," *ZAW* 86 (1974), 65–82.

——, *Old Testament Theology: Basic Issues in the Current Debate*, 4th edn. (Grand Rapids: Eerdmans, 1991).

Hauerwas, S., *Unleashing the Scripture: Freeing the Bible from Captivity to America* (Nashville: Abingdon, 1993).

Hayes, J., ed., *Dictionary of Biblical Interpretation*, 2 vols. (Nashville: Abingdon, 1999).

Hübner, H., *Biblische Theologie des Neuen Testaments*, vol. 1, Prolegomena (Göttingen: Vandenhoeck & Ruprecht, 1990).

Kaiser, O., *Der Gott des Alten Testaments. Wesen und Wirken*, 2 vols. (Göttingen: Vandenhoeck & Ruprecht, 1993, 1998).

Kalimi, I., "History of Israelite Religion or Old Testament Theology? Jewish Interest in Biblical Theology," *JSOT* 11 (1997), 100–23.

Kermode, F., *Poetry, Narrative, History* (Oxford: Basil Blackwell, 1990).

Knierim, R., *The Task of Old Testament Theology* (Grand Rapids: Eerdmans, 1995a).

——, "On Gabler," *The Task of Old Testament Theology* (Grand Rapids: Eerdmans, 1995b), 495–556.

Knight, D., ed., *Tradition and Theology* (Philadelphia: Fortress, 1977).

Knight, D. and G. Tucker, eds., *The Hebrew Bible and Its Modern Interpreters* (Chico, CA: Scholars Press, 1985).

Koehler, L., *Theology of the Old Testament* (London: Lutterworth Press, 1957).

Levenson, Jon D., *Creation and the Persistence of Evil* (San Francisco: Harper & Row, 1988).

——, *The Hebrew Bible, the Old Testament, and Historical Criticism* (Louisville: Westminster/John Knox, 1993).

Licht, J., *Storytelling in the Bible* (Jerusalem: Magnes, 1978).

Lindbeck, G., *The Nature of Doctrine: Religion and Theology in a Postliberal Age* (Philadelphia: Westminster, 1984).

Lohfink, N., *Option for the Poor. The Basic Principle of Liberation Theology in the Light of the Bible* (Berkeley, CA: BIBAL Press, 1987).

Luck, U., *Welterfahrung und Glaube als Grundproblem biblischer Theologie* (Munich: Kaiser, 1976).

Mayes, A., *The Old Testament in Sociological Perspective* (London: Marshall Morgan and Scott, 1989).

Meyers, C., *Discovering Eve: Ancient Israelite Women in Context* (New York: Oxford University Press, 1988).

Miller, Patrick D., "Israelite Religion," in D. Knight and G. Tucker, eds., *The Hebrew Bible and Its Modern Interpreters* (Chico, CA: Scholars Press, 1985), 201–37.

Miller, P., P. Hanson, D. McBride, and S. Dean, eds., *Ancient Israelite Religion*. FS F. M. Cross (Philadelphia: Fortress Press, 1987).

Miranda, José P., *A Critique of the Philosophy of Oppression* (Maryknoll: Orbis, 1977).

Neusner, J., et al., eds., *Judaic Perspectives on Ancient Israel* (Philadelphia: Fortress, 1987).

Newsom, C. and S. Ringe, eds., *The Women's Bible Commentary*, vol. 1 (Louisville: Westminster/John Knox, 1992).

Ollenburger, B., E. Martens and G. Hasel, eds., *The Flowering of Old Testament Theology* (Winona Lake: Eisenbrauns, 1992).

Perdue, L., *The Collapse of History* (Minneapolis: Fortress Press, 1994a).

——, *Wisdom and Creation* (Nashville: Abingdon, 1994b).

Phillips, V., "Feminist Interpretation," in *Dictionary of Biblical Interpretation*, vol. 1 (1999), 388–98.

Poland, L., *Literary Criticism and Biblical Hermeneutics: A Critique of Formalist Approaches* (Chico, CA: Scholars Press, 1985).

Powell, M., C. Gray, and M. Curtis, *The Bible and Modern Literary Criticism: A Critical Assessment and Annotated Bibliography* (New York: Greenwood, 1992).

Preuss, H., *Old Testament Theology*, vols. 1 and 2 (Louisville: Westminster/John Knox, 1995–6).

Procksch, Otto, *Theologie des Alten Testaments* (Gütersloh: Bertelsmann, 1950).

Rendtorff, R., *Theologie des Alten Testaments. Ein kanonischer Entwurf*, vol. 1. *Kanonische Grundlegung* (Neukirchen-Vluyn: Neukirchener Verlag, 1999).

Reumann, John, ed., *The Promise and Practice of Biblical Theology* (Minneapolis: Fortress Press, 1991).

Reventlow, H. Graf, *Problems of Old Testament Theology in the Twentieth Century* (London: SCM Press, 1985).

——, *Problems of Biblical Theology in the Twentieth Century* (London: SCM Press, 1986).

Richter, Wolfgang, *Exegese als Literaturwissenschaft* (Göttingen: Vandenhoeck & Ruprecht, 1971).

Ricoeur, Paul, *Time and Narrative*, 3 vols. (Chicago: University of Chicago Press, 1984–7).

——, "Toward a Narrative Theology" (1982), in M. Wallace, ed., *Figuring the Sacred: Religion, Narrative, and Evil*, trans. D. Pellauer (Minneapolis: Fortress Press, 1995), 236–48.

Ruether, R., *Sexism and God-Talk: Toward a Feminist Theology* (Boston: Beacon, 1983).

Russell, L., *Feminist Interpretation of the Bible* (Philadelphia: Westminster, 1985).

Sanders, J., *Torah and Canon*, 2nd edn. (Philadelphia: Fortress Press, 1972).

——, *Canon and Community. A Guide to Canonical Criticism* (Philadelphia: Fortress Press, 1987a).

——, *From Sacred Story to Sacred Text* (Philadelphia: Fortress Press, 1987b).

Schmeller, Thomas, "Liberation Theologies," in *Dictionary of Biblical Interpretation* 2 (1999), 66–74.

Schmid, H.-H., *Gerechtigkeit als Weltordnung* (Tübingen: Mohr-Siebeck, 1968).

——, *Altorientalische Welt in der alttestamentlichen Theologie* (Zurich: Theologischer Verlag, 1974).

Scholes, R. and R. Kellogg, *The Nature of Narrative* (New York: Oxford University Press, 1966).

Schottroff, L. and M.-T. Wacker, *Kompendium Feministische Bibelauslegung* (Gütersloh: Kaiser/Gütersloher Verlagshaus, 1998).

Seebass, H., *Der Gott der ganzan Bibel* (Freiburg: Herder, 1982).

Seitz, C., *Word Without End. The Old Testament as Abiding Theological Witness* (Grand Rapids: Eerdmans, 1998).

Smend, Rudolf, *Die Mitte des Alten Testaments* (Munich: Kaiser, 1986).

Smith, Huston, "Postmodernism's Impact on the Study of Religion," *JAAR* 68 (1990), 653–70.

Smith, R., *Old Testament Theology. Its History, Method, and Message* (Nashville: Broadman & Holman, 1993).

Starhawk, M., *The Spiritual Dance: The Rebirth of the Ancient Religion of the Great Goddess* (San Francisco: Harper & Row, 1979).

Stegemann, W. and W. Schottroff, eds., *God of the Lowly: Socio-Historical Interpretation of the Bible* (Maryknoll: Orbis, 1984).

Stendahl, Krister, "Biblical Theology, Contemporary," *IDB* 1 (1962), 418–32.

——, *Meanings: The Bible as Document and as Guide* (Philadelphia: Fortress Press, 1984).

Sternberg, M., *The Poetics of Biblical Narrative. Ideological Literature and the Drama of Reading* (Bloomington: Indiana University Press, 1985).

Stroup, George W., *The Promise of Narrative Theology. Recovering the Gospel in the Church* (Atlanta: John Knox, 1981).

Sun, H. and K. Eades, eds., *Problems in Biblical Theology: Essays in Honor of Rolf Knierim* (Grand Rapids: Eerdmans, 1997).

Sweeney, M., "Tanak versus Old Testament: Concerning the Foundation for a Jewish Theology of the Bible," in H. Sun and K. Eades, *Problems in Biblical Theology: Essays in Honor of Rolf Knierim* (1997), 353–72.

Taylor, M., *Erring. A Postmodern A/theology* (Chicago: University of Chicago Press, 1984).

Thomas, J. and V. Visick, eds., *God and Capitalism. A Prophetic Critique of Market Economy* (Madison, WI: A-R Editions, 1991).

Trible, P., *God and the Rhetoric of Sexuality* (Philadelphia: Fortress, 1978).

——, *Texts of Terror: Literary-Feminist Readings of Biblical Narratives* (Philadelphia: Fortress Press, 1984).

——, "Five Loaves and Two Fishes: Feminist Hermeneutics and Biblical Theology," *Theological Studies* 50 (1989): 279–95.

——, "Exegesis for Storytellers and Other Strangers," *JBL* 114 (1995), 3–19.

Turner, J. David, *An Introduction to Liberation Theology* (Lanham: University Press of America, 1994).

Von Rad, Gerhard, *Genesis* (London: SCM Press, 1961).

——, *Old Testament Theology*, vols. 1 and 2 (New York: Harper & Row, 1962, 1965).

Vriezen, T., *An Outline of Old Testament Theology*, 2nd edn. (Wageningen: Veernman & Zonen, 1970).

Wallace, M., *The Second Naivité. Barth, Ricoeur, and the New Yale Theology*, 2nd edn. (Macon, GA: Mercer, 1995 [1990]).

——, "Ricoeur, Paul," *Dictionary of Biblical Interpretation* 2 (1999), 403–5.

Watson, F., *Text, Church and World* (Grand Rapids: Eerdmans, 1994).

——, *Text and Truth: Redefining Biblical Theology* (Grand Rapids: Eerdmans, 1997).

Wellek, R. and A. Warren, *Theory of Literature* (New York: Harcourt, Brace and World, 1942).

Westermann, C., *Blessing in the Bible and the Life of the Church* (Philadelphia: Fortress, 1978).

——, *Elements of Old Testament Theology* (Atlanta: John Knox, 1982).

Wright, G., *God Who Acts: Biblical Theology as Recital* (London: SCM Press, 1952).

Zimmerli, W., *Das Alte Testament als Anrede* (Munich: Kaiser, 1956).

——, Review of G. von Rad's "Theology," in *Vetus Testamentum* 13 (1963), 100–11.

——, *Old Testament Theology in Outline* (Atlanta: John Knox, 1978).

CHAPTER 14
Symmetry and Extremity in the Images of YHWH

Walter Brueggemann

The corpus of the Hebrew Bible that scripts YHWH, the God of Israel, is profoundly complicated and variegated. The development of the literature covers a very long period, in which the community of faith was in and responded to a variety of circumstances in a variety of modes of faith. This community and its God, moreover, participated in the richness of Ancient Near Eastern culture and its several forms and modes of religion. It is for these reasons, that the articulation of God in the Hebrew Bible is complex and variegated, admitting of no single or simplistic characterization. Interpretive issues concerning this God tend to be on a spectrum, moving between the religious context and modes of *faith in that ancient culture* on the one hand, and on the other, faith that moves toward a *settled normative, canonical shape* that comes to be expressed in the faith of emerging Judaism – and derivatively – the more settled, canonical formulations of Christianity. There is no easy, durable, or obvious settlement of this deep tension. Because this essay is under the rubric of "Old Testament Theology," our attention will be toward the more "normative, canonical" theological claims of the text; attention to the more complex, diverse traditions behind the canonical are well considered in other parts of this volume (Edelman, 1996).

(i) The God of Hebrew Scriptures is most characteristically presented in *political metaphor* as king, judge, and warrior (Wright, 1969, pp. 70–150; Miller, 1986; and Brueggemann, 1997). The imagery makes YHWH in important ways parallel to the great "High Gods" of the great imperial religions of the Near East who in turn are linked to their earthly counterparts with their immense power and prestige. As an awesome political force in the world, YHWH's characteristic work is to *govern*, for YHWH's own proper realm, the world, is understood as YHWH's "creation." The creation is willed, authorized, and ordered as an enactment of YHWH's intention for the life of the world and for life in the world.

Through the way in which YHWH's governance is understood, YHWH is said to be "incomparable"; there is no other God like YHWH (Labuschagne, 1966; and Brueggemann, 1997, pp. 139–44). It is apparent that this incomparability consists in two important aspects in the confession of Israel. First, there is no other god with comparable *power*. Second, there is no other God so willingly *in solidarity* with subjects, and especially subjects who are poor, needy, or marginated. It is this twofold marking of power and solidarity that gives YHWH a peculiar identity in a world much peopled by a variety of gods.

The governance of YHWH has two recurring, characteristic features. First, YHWH as governor *generates and maintains the ordering of the world* (in classical theology, "creation"). It is insisted in Israel YHWH has bestowed vitality upon the formless mass of chaos, so that creation is ordered life that is sustained as a prosperous, abundant, peaceable, secure order (Levenson, 1987; and Clifford and Collins, 1992). It is this defining activity of YHWH that is "scripted" in the liturgy of Gen 1:1–2:4a, celebrated in the great doxologies (Psalms 104, 145), and assumed in the pedagogy of Proverbs that counts on the reliability of the creation (Boström, 1990).

Second, YHWH as governor *rehabilitates the ordering of the world* when that order is lost, distorted, or subverted (in classical theological categories, "redemption"). The Scriptures are not precise about the ways in which creation may be distorted, perhaps by willful sin as a violation of YHWH's willed order, or by the recalcitrance of chaos not yet tamed by YHWH. Conventional theology is much more likely to credit chaos to willful sin, but this is opposed by Lindström (1994). In either case, the well-being of YHWH's realm of creation is endlessly under assault and in jeopardy. For that reason, YHWH must regularly and often and decisively undertake "rescue missions" that restore, rehabilitate, and bring the world back to its proper function and shape.

It is evident that in both aspects of governance, *ordering and rehabilitating*, YHWH is seen to be an active, intervening agent who can decisively impinge upon, effect, and transform the character of the world as creation. YHWH's work in ordering may be only the *hidden, sustaining guarantee* of order upon which the world may count, expressed, for example, in Gen 8:22:

> As long as the earth endures,
> seedtime and harvest, cold and heat,
> summer and winter, day and night,
> shall not cease.

YHWH's work of rehabilitation, however, is more likely to be *active, concrete, and transformative*, so that in speaking of this rehabilitative work, Israel's doxological lyrics regularly use decisive and powerful verbs of rescue, healing, and liberation, of which YHWH is the singular subject. Claus Westermann was among the first in recent times to link ordering and rehabilitation (Westermann, 1971, pp. 11–38; and Brueggemann, 1997, pp. 145–212).

Thus YHWH's characteristic work is to exercise full governance (see Brueggemann, 1997, pp. 233–50):

As king, YHWH is an imperial potentate who decrees the future of the world, decrees that may be implemented by a panoply of attentive, subordinate gods and that may be connected to earthly reality through prophetic messengers and mediators (see Psalms 96–99).

As judge, YHWH is a "judicial activist," who not only pronounces verdicts from the bench, but actively intervenes in particular cases, most often as advocate for the weak against the strong. This aspect of YHWH brings to Hebrew Scripture a powerful and sustained interest in distributive social justice, so that YHWH is on many occasions (as in the Exodus narrative) the great Equalizer between haves and have-nots (e.g., Weinfeld, 1995). The litigious quality of much of Hebrew Scriptures is especially evident in prophetic law-suits; in earlier texts these speeches feature YHWH versus Israel, in later texts they tend to be YHWH versus other gods (Westermann, 1967).

As warrior, YHWH may forcibly and violently intervene in order to effect the decrees of kingship and to implement the verdicts of the divine court (Miller, 1973). YHWH's role as warrior is the enactment of concrete sanctions against those who violate YHWH's intention for the realm (Mendenhall, 1973; and from the human side, Zenger, 1996). It is at the same time true, consequently, that this portrayal of YHWH caused much of the religious tradition of Israel to be permeated with violence. Thus YHWH's need to restore full authority against every challenge and every recalcitrant subject evokes harshness, some of which is appropriate to YHWH's purposes and some of which appears to be a convenient ideological appendage on the part of Israel.

(ii) YHWH is "He who must be obeyed." YHWH is given in Israel's text as a force and agent of unrivaled power. The texts thus yield a virile figure who is unembarrassed about the most direct machismo activity in establishing and maintaining a monopoly of authority and control. Out of Israel's great doxologies, one is struck by the *immense power* of YHWH's life in the world. Having said that, we may immediately notice two important qualifiers that situate YHWH's unrivaled, machismo power in a more qualified and nuanced way.

The first qualifier is that YHWH's massive power and authority – enacted as king, judge, and warrior – is in the service of a righteous will that is marked by acute ethical resolve. The God of Israel is not simply massive force; rather this God intends cosmic wholeness, peaceableness, fruitfulness, and well-being, all those qualities subsumed in the term *shalom*. It is this long-term resolve for *shalom* that is YHWH's characteristic marking, of which power is a function and a subset. Thus the theological pivot of the Hebrew Scriptures is the capacity to hold together and affirm at the same time the sheer *overwhelming holiness* of YHWH and the steady resolve for *righteousness in the world* (see Gammie, 1989).

This *resolve for righteousness*, taken in largest scope, is already signaled in the opening liturgy of Gen 1:1–2:4a, wherein God decrees that when the world is fully fruitful and abundant, it fulfills its purpose and is "very good" (Gen 1:31). This same resolve for generosity that makes well-being possible is expressed in two creation hymns in verses that traditionally have functioned among the faithful as table prayers:

These all look to you
to give them their food in due season;
when you give it to them, they gather it up;
when you open your hand,
they are filled with good things.

(Ps 104:27–28)

The eyes of all look to you,
and you give them their food in due season.
You open your hand, satisfying the desire of every living thing.

(Ps 145:15–16)

It is intended that the world should generate sustenance, prosperity, and the joy of all its creatures.

This will for *šālōm* is intrinsic to the very structure and shape of creation as YHWH has ordered and ordained it. Thus in largest scope it is right to say that something like a "natural law" pertains, an elemental ordering that cannot be violated without cost (Barton, 1979; and Barr, 1993). This hidden, uncompromising requirement for a life of well-being is operative in the teaching of the Book of Proverbs, wherein benefit or punishment is not the direct gift of YHWH, but arises out of choices made that hold inescapable consequences (Koch, 1983). This same hidden but firm resolve is evident in the way in which foreign nations are held accountable by the prophets for the elemental practice of justice and mercy, and are castigated for practices of brutality that violate the very fabric of YHWH's creation (Barton, 1980).

The righteous intention of YHWH, however, is not simply known in cosmic overview. The Scriptures are able, in what we may regard as a pre-scientific way, to engage in systematic social analysis. For example, Wilson addresses the social location and awareness of the prophets (1980), while Miranda gives a more intentional consideration of social analysis in the Old Testament (1974). Thus YHWH's righteous intentionality concerns the ways in which social power, social goods, and social access are administered and denied to some. While Israel's doxologies think very large about YHWH's purposes, Israel also knows that the socially marginalized – widows, orphans, aliens – come to be litmus tests for well-being in the community. Hiebert addresses the category of widows (1989), while Spina examines the sojourners (1983). A parallel discussion of "orphan" is not known to me. There is in covenantal–prophetic literature a constant insistence that the practice of public power must always be critiqued and reorganized in order that social systems may be reflective of and faithful to YHWH's intention. The ethical insistence of the Old Testament cannot be overstated in its capacity to hold together *large cosmic intention* and *immediate concrete social practice*:

For the Lord your God is God of gods and Lord of lords, the great God, mighty and awesome, who is not partial and takes no bribe, who executes justice for the orphan and the widow, and who loves the stranger, providing them food and clothing. (Deut 10:17–18)

The capacity to put YHWH's *holiness* in the service of YHWH's *righteousness* means that the God of Israel is an insistent ethical force in the world who has endlessly insisted that all social power must be deployed in the service of communal well-being. Where that well-being is violated and YHWH is thereby mocked or trivialized, death and disorder are sure to come.

(**iii**) YHWH's sheer power is first qualified by righteous will that is cosmic and often hidden insistence. The second qualification of YHWH's sheer power that I shall mention is *the peculiar and defining presence of Israel* in the life of YHWH. YHWH is indeed "God of gods and Lord of lords" who holds universal sway and presides over a pantheon of lesser gods. In that regard, YHWH is not unlike every other great God in the Ancient Near East. That large claim for YHWH, however, is held in deep tension in the Hebrew Scriptures with YHWH's odd and decisive resolve to grant Israel peculiar status in the future of the world:

> Now therefore, if you obey my voice and keep my covenant, you shall be my treasured possession out of all the peoples. Indeed, the whole earth is mine, but you shall be for me a priestly kingdom and a holy nation. (Ex 19:6)

> When the Most High apportioned the nations,
> when he divided humankind,
> he fixed the boundaries of the peoples
> according to the number of the gods;
> the Lord's own portion was his people,
> Jacob his allotted share.
>
> (Deut 32:8–9)

The historical origins of Israel as an identifiable community are obscure and difficult, and need not concern us here. It is enough that from the outset of the sojourn of Abraham and Sarah (Gen 12:1–3) and from the stunning emancipation from Egypt (Ex 15:1–18), Israel understands and presents itself as a defining feature of YHWH, causing YHWH to be inescapably a God *in relation to* it, that is, never alone, never in splendid isolation. Concerning the self-understanding of Israel as suggested in the texts, as distinct from belated critical understanding, the distinction between etic and emic approaches is important (see Gottwald, 1979). For that reason, much of what we are able to say about YHWH we are able to say only in and through and with reference to the life and testimony of Israel. Elsewhere I have proposed that YHWH lives by the speech of Israel who bears witness (1997). Without in any way detracting from or qualifying the more cosmic aspects of YHWH's character, we are able to see that what is decisive for YHWH's character is refracted through Israel's life. We may identify three aspects of this testimony that discloses what comes to be defining about YHWH's own life.

(**a**) Israel testifies that YHWH has performed a series of *dramatic transformations* in Israel's own life, of a very public kind, transformations so astonishing and yet so evident and undeniable that they have the quality of "miracle" (Buber, 1988, p. 75; and Brueggemann, 1991). Israel developed a fairly stable recital of these "miracles," a recital that has become the normative assertion of who YHWH is and what YHWH does (G. von Rad, 1966, pp. 1–78; see Brueggemann, 1997, pp. 117–313).

YHWH has *made and kept promises* to the ancestors against every odds (Genesis 12–36). The long-term promise is for a land of well-being. But the immediate crisis, time after time, is that the family should have a son and heir who can carry the promise of land into the next generation. Israel attests that in every barren generation, YHWH at the last minute inexplicably grants a son to keep the promise intact (Gen 21:1–7; 25:22–26; 30:22–24).

YHWH has powerfully and decisively *ended Pharonic oppression* for Israel, has made "a way out of no way" for Israel to move from the grief of slavery to the joy of emancipation. This defining narrative is governed by powerful verbs, "redeem, liberate, save, deliver, bring out," YHWH's most characteristic verbs (Exodus 1–15). YHWH has the capacity and will to break open systems of power and abuse that have precluded human community of šālōm. Fretheim has persuasively shown how the "historical narrative" of the Exodus serves an interest in ecology as a mode of creation theology (1991, pp. 385–96). Israel endlessly retells the wonder of that emancipation that belatedly becomes a model through which Israel notices and receives many subsequent emancipations, each of which shows YHWH acting against circumstance to create a new social possibility.

YHWH *led emancipated Israel* in the wilderness for a generation. The wilderness is a context without visible life-support systems, so that Israel's life is deeply at risk. In that context, however, YHWH generously and inexplicably supplies life supports of water, bread, and meat, thus transforming wilderness into a place of viable human community. In all three of these defining moments, Israel attests that YHWH is able and willing, on behalf of Israel, to establish a rule of šālōm in a most recalcitrant circumstance.

(**b**) YHWH met Israel at Sinai for an extended rendezvous that issued in a new relation of covenant (Exodus 19–24). It is impossible to overstate the cruciality of this hour for the redefinition of Israel, just as YHWH in this hour becomes decisively the God of Israel (Buber, 1988; Muilenburg, 1961, pp. 44–74; *passim*). The upshot of this meeting is a covenant of mutual commitment and fidelity. But the primal substance of the meeting is YHWH's declaration of YHWH's will for Israel (and the world) in the form of Torah (Crüsemann, 1996). In the first instant, the Ten Commandments are declared directly out of YHWH's own mouth (Ex 20:1–17). In the second instant, in several derivative offers, Moses, as YHWH's mediator, announces statutes and ordinances that explicate and detail the "policy" of the Decalogue. The intention of the whole is to bring every aspect of life – public and personal – under the direct rule of YHWH. As YHWH is governor of the entire creation, so YHWH will be the orderer and supervisor of every detail of the life of Israel.

The body of commandments, teaching, and instruction is "Torah," a term that may refer in different ways to different materials. In all such cases, however, YHWH is now *The God of Torah*, the one who has clearly enunciated a public will and purpose for the world through Israel. Frank Crüsemann has proposed that

Sinai functions theologically in Israel's Scripture as the "utopian place . . . outside state authority" that gives both YHWH and Israel covenantal identity (1996, p. 57). The Torah provides a way to bring YHWH's holiness and Israel's life in the world together around a quite particular social vision. It is proposed, moreover, that Torah contains all future possibilities, so that keeping or rejecting Torah determines life or death:

> See, I have set before you today life and prosperity, death and adversity. If you obey the commandments of the Lord your God that I am commanding you today, by loving the Lord your God, walking in his ways, and observing his commandments, decrees, and ordinances, then you shall live and become numerous, and the Lord your God will bless you in the land that you are entering to possess. But if your heart turns away and you do not hear, but are led astray to bow down to other gods and serve them, I declare to you today that you shall perish . . . Choose life so that you and your descendants may live . . . (Deut 30:15–19)

At its most intense, the Sinai materials – extrapolated in the traditions of Deuteronomy – offer a God–people relation completely defined by obedience.

(c) As Israel leaves Sinai, it is en route to *the new land* of well-being already promised to Abraham and Sarah, already anticipated in the departure from Egypt. The long-term anticipation of a land of promise is both a primal gift of YHWH and a deep problematic for Israel.

YHWH is a land-giving God who wills a safe, placed existence for Israel. Because Israel trusts in YHWH, it lives, always in its precariousness, toward "placed well-being." Indeed the land of promise, so well voiced in the Genesis narratives, continues to receive subsequent lyrical affirmation in prophetic imagery, so that the God of Genesis is seen to be a God who is endlessly creating new, good futures in the world.

The buoyant quality of such concrete anticipation, however, is deeply sobered by the recognition that the land-seizing narratives of Joshua and Judges are deeply saturated with social conflict and violence. The problem of course is that the land promised turns out to be land occupied by others who assume it is properly their land. Thus violence was intrinsic to the land traditions (Schwartz, 1997). It may well be that the land promises are in fact shot through with ideological edge, so that the promise in YHWH's mouth is in fact a way to legitimate otherwise risky land claims. However the ideological component is assessed, it is clear that YHWH is deeply implicated in the problematic of granting futures to Israel where none is easily available. This deep problematic is one of the most powerful and awkward legacies of the Bible in subsequent history. Davies discusses the crucuality and problematic of land (1974; 1982; see O'Brien, 1988, for a broader perspective that moves beyond Israel).

YHWH is now known, through the testimony of Israel, as the God who does *transformative miracles*, who enunciates *sovereign commands through Torah*, and who generates new future *possibilities for life in the world*. This is a God who is doing something new in the world, refusing to accept old circumstance or to yield to old orders of legitimacy. By observing this collage of evidence, YHWH emerges as a God of newness who is always subverting what has been for the sake of what will yet be. It is likely that the enigmatic announcement of the divine name in Ex 3:14 is indicative of a subversive newness in the very identity of the God of Israel.

(iv) YAHWEH is a governor who will be obeyed as king, judge, and warrior. That is a base line of conviction in the Bible. The defining attachment of YHWH to Israel, however, raises important issues about the single claim of governance, and evokes other nuances in the character of YHWH more immediately pertinent to life with Israel. Israel's life with YHWH turned out not to be a simple one of trust and obedience. The covenantal relationship between the two became much more complex, complicated, and dense, requiring a thickness in YHWH's personality beyond simple governance. In short, the images of governance are impinged upon by other images of YHWH, especially those of familial intimacy that bespeak complexity and ambiguity.

As Israel stood at Mt. Sinai, gazed upon YHWH, and made deep covenant oaths, the relationship seemed clear (Ex 24:9–11). As the tradition has it, however, the direct move from agreement in Ex 24 to conflict in Ex 32 opens the way for the profound enhancement of YHWH's character. This is a God who commands complete fidelity but who must live in a determined relationship marked by profound infidelity (Ex 32:7–10, 19–23). That profound infidelity on Israel's part evokes enraged hostility on the part of YHWH (Ex 32:33). In the end, however, it is not profound infidelity that marks YHWH; rather it is YHWH's resolve for a durable relationship that now matters decisively for YHWH and, derivatively, matters decisively for Israel. After the violation and rage of Exodus 32, after the negotiations with Moses in Exodus 33, comes YHWH's definitive self-announcement in Ex 34:6–7:

> The Lord, the Lord,
> A God merciful and gracious,
> slow to anger,
> and abounding in steadfast love and faithfulness,
> keeping steadfast love for the thousandth generation,
> forgiving iniquity and transgression and sin,
> yet by no means clearing the guilty,
> but visiting the iniquity of the parents
> upon the children and the children's children,
> to the third and fourth generation.

This assertion, commonly taken as pivotal for biblical theology, constitutes YHWH's resolve to move beyond rage to a sustained relationship (see Brueggemann, 1997, pp. 213–24). The statement fully characterizes YHWH's intention for life with Israel in the future – and we may extrapolate – YHWH's intention for life with the world as creation into the future. Notice that images of governance are now powerfully supplemented or even redefined by images of fidelity, in which YHWH's way with Israel concerns passionate commitment and not simply legitimate power.

The first part of this self-announcement permits the range of terms that most centrally characterize YHWH (vv. 6–7a). YHWH is an agent of fidelity, reliability, and compassion (Brueggemann, 1994). YHWH is deeply committed to Israel and can be counted upon to stand by, even into the unknown future. More than that, YHWH is a God who generously forgives in order to sustain the relationship. This is not the God of hard-nosed ethical, covenantal symmetry (as suggested by Deut 30:15–20) but a God who moves beyond symmetry into generosity.

> He does not deal with us according to our sins,
> nor repay us according to our iniquities.
> For as the heavens are high above the earth,
> so great is his steadfast love toward those who fear him;
> As far as the east is from the west,
> so far he removes our transgressions from us.
> As a father has compassion for his children,
> so the lord has compassion for those who fear him.
> For he knows how we were made;
> he remembers that we are dust.
>
> (Ps 103:10–14)

YHWH invests YHWH's own life fully, generously, unreservedly into the life of Israel for the future well-being of Israel.

We are ill-prepared for the reversal of tone in Ex 34:7b, beginning with "yet." We do not know if there are limits to YHWH's fidelity and generosity, or if this is simply a counter-theme that sobers the rhetoric. In any case, this latter half-verse indicates that YHWH has YHWH's own life to live, for YHWH takes the role of ruler seriously. YHWH will not be mocked or trivialized by a covenant partner who is guilty and unresponsive. Thus taken by itself, v. 7b is not remarkable, for it serves to assert the primal claims of king, judge, and warrior who will always "visit iniquities" upon perpetrators. What makes the statement remarkable, however, is its juxtaposition to vv. 6–7a, which sets up a telling tension if not contradiction. It is evident that YHWH's *life for Israel* and YHWH's *life for YHWH's self* are both important, both asserted here, but left in an unarticulated tension that receives no resolution and perhaps cannot receive resolution. For the tension itself is in the very character of the relationship.

(v) The dominant images of king, judge, and warrior bespeak a formal relationship of command and obedience that can be spelled out with clarity. In Israel's attestation to YHWH, however, it is clear that the YHWH–Israel relationship is no simple, formal one, precisely because interpersonal dimensions of fidelity and infidelity are seen to be at work underneath formal relationships. Thus Israel knows something of the complex, internal life of YHWH upon which a faith of depth depends, and this complex interior life in turn depends upon daring, imaginative poets to go beyond formal relationships. The poetry adequate to YHWH's full life is given us in the Psalter and especially in prophetic utterance, most notably Isaiah, Jeremiah, Ezekiel, and Hosea. These prophets are well informed by normative Torah traditions, but are required by their lived sense of the tensive quality of Israel's life to move beyond and underneath these more formal characterizations. The prophetic poets thus are evoked by the sense of "underneathness" in YHWH to utilize a rich variety of daring images and metaphors, in order to bring to speech what is nearly unsayable about the Holy One of Israel. The saying of the unsayable means that images are not stable or precise, but they are traces and teases and probes that invite us underneath formal theological claims to the dangerous, threatening intimacy of a God who is near, in self-giving and in dread.

While these poetic figures employ a range of images, it is especially familial images of father–son and husband–wife that carry us beyond the more stable king, judge, and warrior. The familial images of relatedness give voice to delicate ambiguities, contradictions, and incongruities that mark every intimate relationship and that, so they insist, mark this rich and overwhelming relationship. I suggest that these poets must account for *two surpluses* in the life of YHWH that spill over beyond the formal relationships of governance.

(**vi**) The first "spill-over" concerning YHWH beyond the symmetry of command–obedience under the metaphors of king, judge, and warrior is that YHWH exhibits profound *pathos* toward Israel, a pathos that violates and redefines YHWH's sovereignty (Heschel, 1962; Robinson, 1955). In both founding narratives of the ancestors (Gen 12–36) and the Exodus (Exodus 1–15), YHWH had enacted peculiar commitment toward and solidarity with Israel. It was not until the threat and reality of exile, however, that YHWH's commitment toward and solidarity with Israel came to be expressed as suffering with and suffering for Israel. It is as though originary covenantal commitments have so bound YHWH to Israel that when historical circumstance causes Israel to suffer, YHWH is prepared to suffer in the suffering of Israel, so great is YHWH's passion and compassion toward Israel.

This dimension of YHWH's character is voiced especially in the most daring and most imaginative poets, whose words bring to speech the hurt and dismay that envelops both Israel and YHWH. Hosea, in anticipation of the failure of the Northern Kingdom, offers a poem (ch. 11) that voices YHWH's founding graciousness toward Israel (vv. 1–3), but that moves to indignation and rejection (vv. 5–7). In characteristic prophetic speech we might expect the prophetic utterance to end at that point. Most remarkably, however, this poem continues with the most unexpected verses:

> How can I give you up, Ephraim?
> How can I hand you over, O Israel?
> How can I make you like Adman?
> How can I treat you like Zeboiim?
> My heart recoils within me;
> my compassion grows warm and tender.

> I will not execute my fierce anger;
> I will not again destroy Ephraim;
> for I am God and no mortal,
> the Holy One in your midst,
> and I will not come in wrath.

In these verses, YHWH asserts that Israel cannot be "given up" (handed over) to wrath and punishment as vv. 5–7 might indicate. The reason is that Israel is not like Sodom and Gomorrah, so easily rejected and given over to punishment. YHWH's own attachment to Israel makes this impossible. Indeed, YHWH's own heart must "quake" ("recoil") with the quaking of Sodom and Gomorrah (see Gen 19:25 where the same term occurs). That is, YHWH internalizes the devastation of Israel, a devastation contained in YHWH's own life. The imagery of father–son in vv. 1–3 suggests a parent willing to endure the suffering deserved by the child, in order to shield the child. The final assertion of v. 9 shows YHWH breaking all old patterns of wrath. This "Holy One of Israel" violates all the conventional categories of divine wrath in radical commitment to Israel, a commitment most costly to YHWH.

A century later with reference to the failure of Judah, Jeremiah, perhaps especially informed by and derived from Hosea, utilizes the parent–child imagery in parallel fashion:

> Is Ephraim my dear son?
> Is he the child I delight in?
> As often as I speak against him,
> I still remember him.
> Therefore I am deeply moved for him;
> I will surely have mercy on him, says the Lord.
> (Jer 31:20) (Kitamori, 1965)

YHWH would "speak against" Judah in characteristic prophetic rejection and denunciation. In doing so, however, YHWH finds that such a mood and tone of rejection do not prevail, for in the very midst of such negation, YHWH still *remembers* Israel, still recalls old commitments, still knows that Israel is "precious" and a cause of "delight." The verb "remember" is stated with an infinitive absolute, thus giving it heavy accent. The powerful metaphor of parent–child witnesses to the way in which parental devotion operates in and through rejection. The will to "speak against" is overcome. The last lines draw the inescapable conclusion: "Therefore" . . . as a consequence . . . As a result of old, deep connections, YHWH's own innards are stirred in parental ways; YHWH will have mercy, mercy for the very child who merits rejection. The term "have mercy" is again an infinitive absolute, matching the accent on "remember." It is as though YHWH acts in this way in spite of YHWH's own inclination to wrath and rejection. It is as though YHWH cannot "help himself," but finds himself drawn in by positive emotions of a most elemental kind. Clearly the poet offers a scenario of wrenching emotional inclination that overrides justified rejection.

The articulation of "mercy" in Jer 31:20 points to Isa 49:15, a text situated later in the exile. In 49:14, the poet quotes a liturgical lament from exilic Judah, perhaps a quote from the grief of Lamentations 5:20. In 49:15, YHWH responds to the complaint of v. 14:

> Can a woman forget her nursing child,
> or show no compassion for the child of her womb?
> Even these may forget,
> yet I will not forget you.

The imagery now is of a nursing mother; thus the metaphor becomes more intimate and more elemental. It is clear that the connection between nursing mother and nursing child is a most intimate one (see Isa 66:10–13). This poet must seek the most compelling imagery available from primary familial relations to make the point. The mother, YHWH, cannot and will not forget the nursing child, perhaps out of deep affection, perhaps because the nursing mother must be relieved by the suckling child. In any case, the bond between the two is deep; but YHWH's bond to Israel is yet deeper and beyond forfeiture.

It is clear that this trajectory of poets strains to bring to speech the relational crisis evoked in the failure of exile. The poets are more than adequate to the crisis by probing the most intimate imagery available, and therefore moving underneath all formal, juridical language to the non-negotiable connections that attest to YHWH's fidelity. Because YHWH cannot get free of Israel, YHWH is destined as well to submit to the loss, risk, and rejection of exile. Moltmann has seen how this same motif operates in Christian theology so that the Father suffers as much on Friday as does the Son: "The Fatherlessness of the Son is matched by the Sonlessness of the Father . . ." (Moltmann, 1974, p. 243). This is not God immune to danger. The dangers arise from intimate commitment.

(**vii**) The second "spill-over" in the character of YHWH that moves beyond the symmetry of command–obedience is in the opposite direction, from pathos into *deeply emotive rage* of hysterical proportion. While it moves in the opposite direction, it seems clear that this sensibility on the part of YHWH arises from the same emotional depth as does pathos, that is a deep covenant commitment that lives below formal relationships.

The clearest evidence for what appears to be a "loss of control" is in the text of Ezekiel. These texts witness to the very depth of exile and the full estrangement of YHWH from Israel. The prophet, moreover, strives for the most extreme rhetoric available to match the extremity of the case. In the three long historical recitals of chapters 16, 20, and 23, the story of Israel with YHWH is taken as an act of originary grace on YHWH's part, but then alienation and judgment. The imagery of chapter 16 begins in the pity and gentleness of a parent toward an abandoned child, a parent who showers the needy child with every kind of generosity. But then the imagery shades over from parent–child toward something like husband–wife, wherein the wife is accused:

Adulterous wife, who receives strangers instead of her husband! Gifts are given to all whores; but you gave your gifts to all your lovers, bribing them to come to you from all around for your whorings. So you were different from the women in your whorings; no one solicited you to play the whore; and you gave payment, while no payment was given to you; you were different. (16:32–34)

The juxtaposition of the two sets of images may raise questions about the relationship that is offered by the poet that may even hint of incest. What interests us, however, is that the double image offers a relationship of generosity whereby the beneficiary of the relationship acts in rejecting ways, thereby shaming and humiliating the father–husband YHWH. The emotive power of YHWH's response to the humiliation and shame is that of a betrayed lover who is filled with deep rage over the social shame of the skewed relationship (Weems, 1995). In deep indignation, this betrayed lover threatens:

Therefore I will gather all your lovers with whom you took pleasure, all those you loved and all those you hated; I will gather them against you from all around, and will uncover your nakedness to them, so that they may see all nakedness. I will judge you as women who commit adultery and shed blood are judged, and bring blood upon you in wrath and jealousy . . . so I will satisfy my fury on you, and my jealousy shall turn away from you; I will be calm, and will be angry no longer. (vv. 37–42; see 20:8, 13, 21)

The emotional, uncontrolled response of YHWH is clear:

Thus I will put an end to lewdness in the land, so that all women may take warning and not commit lewdness as you have done. They shall repay you for your lewdness, and you shall bear the penalty for your sinful idolatry; and you shall know that I am the lord your God. (23:48–49; see 39:21–24)

It is clear that YHWH's response is not that of a reasoning judge who exacts appropriate penalty for affront. The emotional overload of these verses indicates that the force of indignation is that of woundedness of a most primal kind. It is clear, moreover, that what YHWH, the betrayed lover, cares most about is "his" reputation, for he has been shamed and embarrassed in a patriarchal society, shamed by a partner he is unable to control. I am here using masculine pronouns for YHWH as required by the metaphor. Clearly I intend such usage only *inside* the metaphor. And therefore YHWH's responding wrath is to clear his reputation, "sanctifying his name," restoring his place of honor in the community:

But I acted for the sake of my name, that it should not be profaned in the sight of the nations among whom they lived . . . But I withheld my hand, and acted for the sake of my name, so that it should not be profaned in the sight of the nations, in whose sight I had brought them out. (20:9, 20)

It is not for your sake, O house of Israel, that I am about to act, but for the sake of my holy name which you have profaned among the nations to which you came.

> I will sanctify my great name, which has been profaned among the nations and which you have profaned among them. (36:22–23)

> Now I will restore the fortunes of Jacob, and have mercy on the whole house of Israel and I will be jealous for my holy name. (39:25)

Both punishment and restoration are enacted in order to enhance the name of YHWH.

It is astonishing that this characterization of YHWH should be offered in Israel's Scripture. We should, moreover, make no mistake. This is not equitable, symmetrical punishment for the violation of Torah. This is rather "out of control" candidness. That it has such emotional power suggests that the *spill-over of deep anger* is profoundly connected to the *spill-over of pathos*, for it is deep emotional engagement that leads to both pathos and rage. It is willingness to suffer that results in the pathos. It is unguarded vulnerability that has created a situation of shame. In both directions, YHWH is exhibited *in extremis*, that most characterizes YHWH but that is not entertained in more conventional, symmetrical images.

(**viii**) It is to be noticed that the texts that give us both pathos and rage are from Israel's most daring poets in Israel's most vulnerable situation of exile. These participants *in extremis* are not the primary clues for YHWH, for the primary clues are voiced in Deuteronomic texts that are much more symmetrical and reliably committed to ethical coherence and stability. But the ethical coherence and stability of the main claims should not cause us to miss the extremity to which YHWH is pushed by Israel's circumstance. YHWH is given in the text as one who both *causes* the extremity of Israel (so rage) and who *enters into* it with Israel (so pathos); YHWH shares much with other gods in that ancient environment and the covenantal symmetry of divine character is reasonably stable. It is the extremity, however, that most distinguishes YHWH and that most exhibits Israel's courage on the lips of its risk-taking poets.

YHWH, the God of Israel, will not be fully discerned until attention is paid to the extremity. YHWH is available to Israel in odd ways, precisely in the disjunctions where more settled theological claims fail. Thus one can trace through Israel's self-presentation the original *chaos* of "pre-creation" (Gen 1:2), the repeated *barrenness* of Israel's mothers (Gen 11:30; 25:21; and 29:31), the *bondage* of Israel in slavery, and the risk of exposure in *the wilderness*; these are the places where YHWH is known by Israel. This entire recital culminates in or is under the aegis of the *exile*, Israel's extreme defining moment, of which chaos, barrenness, slavery, and wilderness are all subsets and witnesses. Exile is the great disjunction in Israel's faith, and it is in this disjunction that YHWH is known as the one present in absence and absent in presence (Brueggemann, 1995, pp. 169–82). The God of Israel is not easily available but a God *in extremis*, suited to Israel's life *in extremis*. It is this extremity that compels faith. In Christian extrapolation, it is this God given in the Friday of crucifixion. In subsequent Jewish experience, it is this God yet to be parleyed in the unutterable dread of holocaust. It is in all such disjunctions that Israel must face the holiness of YHWH, a holiness that shatters all conventional theological categories, and promises a more elemental ground for life, a holiness that in Hos 11:8–9 curbs destruction, a holiness that in Ezek 36:22–23 makes new life possible. Johnson speaks of the holiness that keeps all our interpretive categories from being final (1997).

(**ix**) It is because of these extremities of pathos and rage given in disjunction that the more settled claims of symmetry are endlessly open and unstable in the faith of Israel. I do not suggest that these extremities constitute the whole claim of Israel's faith, but they do endlessly haunt Israel and counter Israel's embrace of easier claims. It is the realm of ordered faith in Judaism and Christianity that produces "orthodoxies" that are "canonical" and more or less reliable and manageable. There is indeed enough material to fashion such settled, reliable formulations. Such formulations, moreover, are indispensable for ongoing canonical life and for the maintenance and sustenance of institutional claims. The temptation is obviously more acute for Christianity than for Judaism. Indeed, it is a hallmark of Western Christianity, now coming back to haunt churches with authoritarian habits but with loss of hegemony, to give the final word (see the critique of Kort, 1996, and his accent upon "centripetal" reading).

It is to be noticed in the end, however, that the production of normative, canonical characterizations of YHWH must live uneasily with those extremities of pathos and rage that endlessly unsettle more settled claims. When these extremities are excluded from purview and when these texts go unnoticed, theological reflection draws very close to idolatry, the production of a manageable God. The Psalmist characterizes such a "safe" God:

> Their idols are silver and gold,
> the work of human hands.
> They have mouths, but do not speak;
> eyes, but do not see.
> They have ears, but do not hear;
> noses, but do not smell.
> They have hands, but do not feel;
> feet, but do not walk;
> they make no sound in their throats.
> (Ps 115:4–7)

The characterization of the idols, however, is simply a foil for the true God:

> Our God is in the heavens;
> he does whatever he pleases.
> (v. 3)

The holiness of YHWH escapes stable formulation but becomes in Israel the ground for trust and hope. The "Holy One of Israel" is open to a limitless range of postures. Faith in this God is costly and not easy. But faith in this God has been found, over many times and circumstances, to be a viable way midst the vagaries of history that characteristically defy either security or meaning.

Bibliography

Barr, J., *Biblical Faith and Natural Theology: The Gifford Lectures for 1991* (Oxford: Clarendon Press, 1993).

Barton, J., "Natural Law and Poetic Justice in the Old Testament," *JTS* 30 (1979), 1–14.

——, *Amos's Oracles Against the Nations: A Study of Amos 1:3–2:5* (Cambridge: Cambridge University Press, 1980).

Boström, L., *The God of the Sages: The Portrayal of God in the Book of Proverbs*, Coniectanea Biblica Old Testament Series 29 (Stockholm: Almqvist & Wiksell International, 1990).

Brueggemann Walter, *Abiding Astonishment: Psalms, Modernity, and the Making of History*, Literary Currents in Biblical Interpretation (Louisville: Westminster/John Knox Press, 1991).

——, "Crisis-Evoked, Crisis-Resolving Speech," *BTB* 24 (1994), 95–105.

——, "A Shattered Transcendence? Exile and Restoration," in S. Kraftchick, et al., eds., *Biblical Theology: Problems and Perspectives. In Honor of J. Christiaan Beker* (Nashville: Abingdon Press, 1995), 169–82.

——, *Theology of the Old Testament: Testimony, Dispute, Advocacy* (Minneapolis: Fortress Press, 1997).

Buber, M., "Holy Event (Exodus 9–27)," *On the Bible: Eighteen Studies* (New York: Schocken Books, 1969).

——, *Moses: The Revelation and the Covenant* (Atlantic Highlands, NJ: Humanities Press International, Inc., 1946, 1988).

Clifford, R. J. and J. J. Collins, eds., *Creation in the Biblical Traditions*, The Catholic Biblical Quarterly Monograph Series 24 (Washington: The Catholic Biblical Association of America, 1992).

Crüsemann, F., *The Torah: Theology and Social History of Old Testament Law* (Edinburgh: T & T Clark, 1996).

Davies, W. D., *The Gospel and the Land: Early Christianity and Jewish Territorial Doctrine* (Berkeley: University of California Press, 1974),

——, *The Territorial Dimension of Judaism* (Berkeley: University of California Press, 1982).

Edelman, D. A., *The Triumph of Elohim: From Yahwisms to Judaisms* (Grand Rapids: Eerdmans, 1996).

Fretheim, T., "The Plagues as Ecological Signs of Historical Disaster," *JBL* 110 (1991), 385–96.

Gammie, J. G., *Holiness in Israel*, OBT (Minneapolis: Fortress Press, 1989).

Gottwald, N. K., *The Tribes of Yahweh: A Sociology of the Religion of Liberated Israel, 1250–1050 B.C.* (Maryknoll, NY: Orbis Books, 1979).

Heschel, A., *The Prophets* (New York: Harper & Row, 1962).

Hiebert, P. S., " 'Whence Shall Help Come to Me?' The Biblical Widow," in P. Day, ed., *Gender and Difference in Ancient Israel* (Minneapolis: Fortress Press, 1989), 125–41.

Johnson, W. S., *The Mystery of God: Karl Barth and the Postmodern Foundations of Theology*, Columbia Series in Reformed Theology (Louisville: Westminster/John Knox Press, 1997).

Kitamori, K., *Theology of the Pain of God* (Richmond: John Knox Press, 1965).

Koch, K., "Is There a Doctrine of Retribution in the Old Testament?" in J. Crenshaw, ed., *Theodicy in the Old Testament*, Issues in Religion and Theology 4 (Philadelphia: Fortress Press, 1983), 57–87.

Kort, W., *"Take, Read": Scripture, Textuality, and Cultural Practice* (University Park, PA: Pennsylvania State University Press, 1996).

Labuschagne, C., *The Incomparability of Yahweh in the Old Testament* (Leiden: E. J. Brill, 1966).

Levenson, J., *Creation and the Persistence of Evil: The Jewish Drama of Divine Omnipotence* (San Francisco: Harper & Row, 1987).

Lindström, F., *Suffering and Sin: Interpretations of Illness in the Individual Complaint Psalms*, Coniectanea Biblica Old Testament Series 37 (Stockholm: Almqvist & Wiksell International, 1994).

Mendenhall, G., "The 'Vengeance' of Yahweh," *The Tenth Generation: The Origins of the Biblical Tradition* (Baltimore: Johns Hopkins University Press, 1973).

Miller, Jr., P., *The Divine Warrior in Early Israel*, Harvard Semitic Monographs 5 (Cambridge: Harvard University Press, 1973).

——, "The Sovereignty of God," in D. Miller, ed., *The Hermeneutical Quest: Essays in Honor of James Luther Mays on his Sixty-Fifth Birthday* (Allison Park, PA: Pickwick Publications, 1986), 129–44.

Miranda, J., *Marx and the Bible: A Critique of the Philosophy of Oppression* (Maryknoll, NY: Orbis Books, 1974).

Moltmann, J., *The Crucified God: The Cross of Christ as the Foundation and Criticism of Christian Theology* (New York: Harper & Row, 1974).

Mullenburg, J., *The Way of Israel: Biblical Faith and Ethics*, Religious Perspectives (New York: Harper and Brothers, 1961), 44–74.

O'Brien, C., *God Land: Reflections on Religion and Nationalism* (Cambridge: Harvard University Press, 1988).

Rad, G. von, "The Form-Critical Problem of the Hexateuch," *The Problem of the Hexateuch and Other Essays* (New York: McGrawHill, 1966), 1–78.

Robinson, H., *The Cross in the Old Testament* (Philadelphia: Westminster Press, 1955).

Schwartz, R., *The Curse of Cain: The Violent Legacy of Monotheism* (Chicago: University of Chicago Press, 1997).

Spina, F. A., "Israelites as *gērîm*, 'Sojourners,' in Social and Historical Context," in C. Meyers and M. O'Connor, eds., *The Word of the Lord Shall Go Forth: Essays in Honor of David Noel Freedman in Celebration of his Sixtieth Birthday* (Winona Lake: Eisenbrauns, 1983), 321–35.

Weems, R., *Battered Love: Marriage, Sex, and Violence in the Hebrew Prophets*, OBT (Minneapolis: Fortress Press, 1995).

Weinfeld, M., *Social Justice in Ancient Israel and in the Ancient Near East* (Minneapolis: Fortress Press, 1995).

Westermann, C., *Basic Forms of Prophetic Speech* (Philadelphia: Westminster Press, 1967).

——, Creation and History in the Old Testament," in V. Vajta, ed., *The Gospel and Human Destiny* (Minneapolis: Augsburg Publishing House, 1971), 11–38.

Wilson, R., *Prophecy and Society in Ancient Israel* (Philadelphia: Fortress Press, 1980).

Wright, G., *The Old Testament and Theology* (New York: Harper & Row, 1969).

Zenger, E., *A God of Vengeance? Understanding the Psalms of Divine Wrath* (Louisville: Westminster/John Knox Press, 1996).

CHAPTER 15

Theological Anthropology in the Hebrew Bible

Phyllis A. Bird

Theological anthropology in both Jewish and Christian tradition has looked to Gen 1:26–27 as a foundational text. Here, in the Bible's first reference to human-kind, humans are described in their "original" or "essential" nature as created "in the image of God." This striking correlation of the human with the divine is unique, and isolated, within the Hebrew scriptures, but it generated a history of speculation that has continued unabated since the first centuries BCE.[1] A critical factor in this history is the distinctive interpretation given to the text in early Christian writings, which combined it with Genesis 2–3 in speculation on the problem of sin and the effect of the "fall" on the image. In New Testament writings of the Pauline school, Christ was identified with the image (Rom 8:29; 1 Cor 11:7; 15:49; 2 Cor 3:18; 4:4; Col 1:15; 3:10; Heb 1:3), and cast as a "second Adam" (Rom 5:12–21). Continuing speculation in the early church produced a doctrine of the *imago Dei* in which the Genesis text was read through the eyes of Paul – as interpreted by Augustine and other church "fathers."[2] As a consequence of this Christian dogmatic appropriation of the text, the theo-logical anthropology of the Hebrew Bible has long been subordinated to a biblical anthropology in which the Old Testament[3] witness was selected, and distorted, to fit the needs of a Pauline trajectory.

Although the concept of the divine image had an important place in Jewish theology – and ethics – it did not dominate Jewish anthropology in the same way as the *imago* symbol in Christian theology.[4] And while modern biblical scholarship attempted to free itself from dogmatic constraints, it has nevertheless been shaped in large measure by Christian (and post-Christian) agendas. The legacy of Christian theological speculation still weighs heavily on contemporary biblical interpretation – in the disproportionate attention devoted to the "*imago*" text and in the focus of the exegesis, which has been directed especially to questions of gender and dominion, and debate concerning the content of the "image." It has also penetrated deeply into western culture, fueling contemporary debates over such issues as evolution, the role of women, environmental ethics, population control, and sexual orientation.

This essay is shaped by awareness of these contemporary debates, but its primary aim is to present the testimony of the Hebrew Bible as the testimony of ancient Israel and explore the meaning of its statements in and for their own time(s). As a work of descriptive theology, it adopts the perspective and tools of historical criticism. In attempting to articulate the theology of the ancient authors in their own historical settings, it recognizes multiple and conflicting voices and perspectives. But it also recognizes a canonical context, or contexts, in which these voices are brought into dialogue with one another and with external traditions. Different canonical boundaries establish different arenas of discourse, and different reading communities give differing weight to the various sources. Thus Christian interpreters will set the theological anthropology of the Old Testament in relation to that of the New Testament, while Jewish interpreters will relate the same textual evidence to the ongoing tradition of rabbinic interpretation.

Genesis 1:26–28 in its Historical and Canonical Context

Genesis 1:26–28, with its concept of the ṣelem 'elōhîm ("image of God"), is too narrow a base upon which to construct a full theological anthropology of the Hebrew Bible, but it is a fitting starting point in its canonical position as the Bible's first word about the nature of humankind. It commands particular attention for its attempt to position humans within the created order, through explicit terms of relationship to other creatures and to the divine. But it is the claim of God-likeness, expressed in the language of divine image, that is most arresting. The history of interpretation of the passage has been dominated by attempts to specify the content of this "likeness" or "image." Proposals range from physical interpretations that equate the image with upright stature or some other aspect of bodily nature or appearance, to psychosocial or spiritual interpretations that identify the image with such attributes as language, mental capacity, or ability to communicate with God. Attempts have also been made to understand the image in terms of the divine plurals of v. 26 or the gender dualism in v. 27. But the text, viewed in its larger literary context and according to the normal rules of Hebrew grammar, excludes all of these interpretations. To understand the meaning of its theological affirmations as an expression of Israelite theology it must be considered in its primary exegetical context, the Priestly account of creation.[5]

Genesis 1:26–28 within the Priestly Account of Creation

The account of creation that opens the Hebrew scriptures moves in a six-day progression from formless void to ordered universe, capped by a seventh day of rest for the Creator (Gen 1:1–2:4a). Through a series of solemn proclamations, God summons into being all of the elements of the ancient cosmos and all forms of life, both animal and vegetable. Compared with the creation myths known from the ancient Near East, it is an exceedingly spare account, and devoid of drama, resembling liturgy more than story. Modern scholarship has attributed it to a Priestly author or "school," whose distinctive style and theology can be traced through the first four books of the Bible. Thus it forms the first chapter of a distinct literary work, or edition of the Pentateuch, as well as an introduction to the scriptures as a whole. This same literary source or stratum continues in the genealogies that punctuate the book of Genesis and in the Flood story, which contain the only other references to the divine image, or likeness, in the Hebrew Bible.

Within this opening account of origins, the creation of humankind (*'ādām*) is presented as the final and climactic act: *'ādām* is the crown of creation.[6] This message of human exaltation is conveyed not only by the sequence of acts, which represents a hierarchy of being, but also by changes of diction, elaboration and expansion of basic themes, and explicit statements of divine likeness and earthly dominion.

> (26)   And God said:
> "Let us make *'ādām* in our image, according to our likeness, And let them have dominion over the fish of the sea and the birds of the air and the cattle and all the earth and everything that creeps upon the earth."
>
> (27)   And God created *'ādām* in his image, in the image of God he created him; Male and female he created them.
>
> (28)   And God blessed them, and God said to them:
> "Be fruitful and multiply and fill the earth and subdue it, And have dominion over the fish of the sea and the birds of the air and every living creature that creeps upon the earth."

Despite the elaborations and distinctions in this account of the final act of creation, it shares a common literary structure with the other reported acts and incorporates themes belonging to the larger composition. The account as a whole is dominated by an interest in stability and order; each element or class has its place, and its nature and function are determined at creation. Thus the firmament is to separate the cosmic waters; the heavenly bodies are to mark times and seasons and govern day and night; and humans are to rule over the realm of living creatures. This ruling function of the human species is specified in the opening announcement that introduces the final act of creation. And it is in relation to this specification that the divine image must be understood, for it is the precondition of that rule. Humans are to be God's vice-gerents on earth.

The Hebrew phrase *ṣelem 'elōhîm* ("image of God") is the exact counterpart of the Akkadian expression (*ṣalam* [God's name]: "image of Enlil [Marduk, etc.]"), which appears as an epithet of Mesopotamian kings. The king in ancient Babylonia and Assyria was understood to be a special representative of the god or gods, possessing a divine mandate to rule, and hence divine authority; but he was not himself divine. The epithet "image of the god" served to emphasize his divinely sanctioned authority and god-like dignity.

The Hebrew term ṣelem, like Akkadian ṣalmu, is used elsewhere to designate a statue or picture, a representation (of a god, animal, or other thing) that brings to mind, or stands in for, the thing it depicts or represents. Its biblical uses are mostly concrete, and mostly negative – describing foreign deities (Num 33:52; 2 Kgs 11:18; 2 Chr 23:17; Ezek 7:20, 16:17; Amos 5:26), golden images of mice and tumors (1 Sam 6:5, 11), and painted pictures of Babylonians (Ezek 23:14). It could also be used figuratively, to describe the insubstantial nature of life (Ps 39:6 [Heb 39:7]) or a dream image (Ps 73:20). It is a term of wholistic representation based on form. Thus when the expression "image of God" is applied to human beings, it suggests a notion of physical resemblance. Its meaning, however, is determined by its context of use – and its use here has no parallel within the Hebrew Bible. That is why the ancient Near Eastern parallels are critical; they evidence the identical phrase *and* similar associations.

"Image" and "Likeness"

The Priestly author has made use of a Mesopotamian royal epithet, but he has qualified or elaborated it in two ways. He has coupled it with the abstract noun, *demût*, meaning "likeness,"[7] and employed both terms in adverbial constructions that describe the activity of the creator, rather than the nature of the creature. Thus, according to Gen 1:26, 27, humans are not the image of God, nor do they possess it; rather they are created "in" or "according to"[8] the divine image and/or likeness.

Despite these qualifications, however, the basic sense of the characterization remains one of form or appearance; the one who is modeled on the divine, must be understood as modeling the divine in the world of creatures. And although the noun *demût* is used figuratively (Ezek 1:5, 26; 8:2; 10:1; cf. Isa 13:4), it is also used to describe a model of an altar (2 Kgs 16:10) and the "likeness" of oxen holding up the molten sea (2 Chr 4:3). Thus the two nouns are essentially synonymous, as suggested also by their interchange in Genesis 5:1, 3. It would appear then that a God who elsewhere prohibits the making of any image as a representation of the divine (Ex 20:4) here accords this function and dignity to the whole of humankind; and a God to whom nothing can be likened (Isa 40:25; 46:5, 9) creates humankind in his own likeness. Such comparisons move outside the Priestly writer's own thought, as do the speculations about the meaning of the two terms that preoccupied Jewish and Christian interpreters through the ages. The latter require brief mention because of their influence in past exegesis.

Jewish interpretation generally recognized the two nouns as equivalent in meaning and accepted the corporeal nature of the image, resulting in speculation about the nature of the divine body and the "original" body of "Adam." In contrast, Christian interpretation associated both nouns with spiritual and/or mental faculties,[9] making a further distinction between a "natural" and a "supernatural" likeness. According to Irenaeus, the "image" (Latin *imago*) represented the human nature that was unaffected by the Fall – identified as rationality and freedom – while the "likeness" (Latin *simultudo*) represented the original relationship with God – which was lost in the Fall and restored through Christ. Both Jewish and Christian interpretation focused on the distinguishing and enduring qualities of the original creation, and both assumed some degree of diminution or loss of the image as they sought, in different ways, to reconcile the claim of God-likeness with the realities of sin and death[10] (see below). Both abstracted and absolutized the idea of the divine image, or likeness, removing it from its literary context.

It is context, however, that determines meaning in historical–critical interpretation. Thus while the notion of corporeal resemblance appears to stand behind the Priestly writer's use of the language of "image" and "likeness" in his account of origins (especially in Gen 5:1), it plays no role in the understanding of human nature or duty in the rest of the Priestly writings, and it has no echo or parallel elsewhere in the Hebrew scriptures. Its theological significance is in the place it gives to humans within the created order, not in any physical or moral attribute of the species, in either its present or "original" state.

Ancient Near Eastern Context

According to Gen 1:26, humans are in some unspecified but essential way "like" God, and this is related to their position or function within the created order, as exercising dominion over their fellow creatures. In adopting this metaphor of ruler, couched in the language of ancient Near Eastern kingship, the author has constructed a portrait of human dignity and responsibility in creation that counters the picture presented by the creation myths of surrounding cultures. In those traditions, human beings were created to be slaves of the gods. They were to do the hard labor needed to maintain the functioning of the universe; they were to relieve the gods from their toil.[11]

The Priestly account of creation is a "counter-myth" that redefines the nature of both God and humankind in its alternative view of the cosmos. God in the Priestly creation account is not only the sole actor and designer of the universe, who accomplishes everything that he proposes and recognizes it as good. The God of Genesis 1 has also designed a universe that does not require subsequent divine intervention or human petition to maintain its stability and course. It is not in danger of disintegrating or dying; it does not need to be revived or recreated in an annual New Year's ritual. Its orders are fixed and unchanging, and each form of life, both plant and animal, is endowed with the means of reproducing its kind. Plants are constituted with seed-bearing organs for "automatic" reproduction, while living creatures are designed as sexual pairs (implied by the blessing) and enjoined to "be fruitful and multiply and fill the earth" (vv. 22, 28). This word of blessing and command applies to humans as well as other creatures. Like them, but unlike God, humans are sexual beings. That is the meaning of the statement that is added in v. 27 to the report of the final act of creation; *'ādām* is created in the image of God, but *also* male and female.

Male and female

Humans are understood as a distinct order of creature with a unique resemblance to God; but they are not divine. Like all other creatures they share the capacity and the duty to perpetuate their kind. But while sexual differentiation could be assumed of the other creatures and did not need to be specified, it could not be assumed of humans; for they have been defined only by their resemblance to God (v. 26) – and God for the Priestly author possessed no gender or sexuality.[12] The specification of creation as male and female is the necessary prerequisite to the blessing pronounced in v. 28.[13] The terms used here are identical to those used for the animal species in 6:19 and 7:9: *zākār* ("male") and *neqēbâ* ("female"). They are biological terms, not social terms – in contrast to the "man" and "woman" of Genesis 2–3.

Some interpreters have sought to explain the divine image through correlation of the "male-and-female" of v. 27 with the plural references to God in v. 26. Such correlation ignores the structure of the account, with its double theme of order and reproduction and its progressive articulation of the two. It also misinterprets the Priestly theology. The divine plurals of v. 26 ("Let us make *'ādām* in our image") are no unreflective remnant of an earlier polytheism encompassing male and female deities, but a rhetorical device of the author to emphasize the solemnity and deliberative nature of this final act of creation. The author draws on the mythic notion of the divine council, in which the voices of the heavenly court join that of the Deity without revealing their identity or compromising the authority of the sole God (cf. Isa 6:8). Analogous to the familiar "royal 'we,'" it claims universal authority and assent for its proclamation. But the word of Gen 1:26 does more. For the first time in the series of creation decrees, the form of the divine announcement shifts from indirect command ("Let there be X" or "Let Y bring forth X") to first-person speech. "Let us make" replaces the decrees of a distant monarch. The creature who will bear a divine resemblance cannot be conceived apart from divine self-involvement.

The divine plural indicates divine deliberation that sets this creature apart from all others, but it also serves to guard the boundary between *'ādām* and God. For the image that likens the human to God is the image of *'elōhîm*, a plural noun. Israel distinguished its God from the gods of the nations, not only by the name YHWH, but also by using the plural of the common noun for "god." As *the* God, *'elōhîm* incorporated the powers and attributes of all the gods of the nations, representing the entire pantheon in one. The image of such a God cannot be identified with any known representation. The plural guards the one within the many, so that the human representation cannot simply be "read back" to reveal the divine prototype.

The concept of the divine image is unique to the Priestly source in Genesis and finds no further theological elaboration within the Hebrew scriptures. But it does appear in two other texts belonging to the Priestly account of origins. In Gen 5:1–3 and 9:6 allusions are made to the original creation account, in which attention is drawn to the continuing significance of the divine likeness as a mark of the species.

Image and likeness of God in Gen 5:1–3 and Gen 9:6

Genesis 5 is a genealogical table, in which the species *'ādām* is personified in an individual, "Adam." But the tension between the class term of Genesis 1 and the individual of Genesis 5 is preserved in the author's attempt to connect them. The chapter begins with an introductory title, "This is the book of the generations of *'ādām*." Here *'ādām* may be read either as a name or as a collective noun (Hebrew writing does not distinguish names from common nouns). This is followed by a recapitulation of Gen 1:26–28 before the line of descent begins:

> In the day that God created *'ādām*, he made him in the likeness (*demût*) of God. Male and female he created them and he blessed them and called their name *'ādām* in the day when they were created. (Gen 5:1–2)

Here the idea of the divine likeness is conveyed through the single term *demût* ("likeness"). The collective understanding of *'ādām* is preserved by the plural pronouns and the explicit identification of the name with the plural representation: "and he called *their* name *'ādām*." This passage leaves no doubt about the gender inclusiveness of the term in Genesis 1; both male and female are named *'ādām*.

In the following sentence, however, the name describes an individual: "When *'ādām* had lived a hundred and thirty years he became the father of a son in his own likeness (*demût*), after his own image (*ṣelem*)" (v. 3). The compound expression for likeness reappears, with the terms in reversed order – not, however, with God as the point of reference, but Adam. The notion of physical resemblance seems unavoidable, but the meaning is to be found in the preceding words (vv. 1b–2). What this notice asserts is that the divine image identified with humankind at creation also characterizes successive generations. This distinguishing feature of the species is not lost or diminished, nor can it be won; it is a birthright. That it is immutable is brought out in Gen 9:1–7.

Here, following the Deluge, the blessing of procreation is repeated,[14] and the theme of human dominion is restated – now, however, with new provisions and new consequences. Dominion after the flood includes the use of animals for food, and hence killing, thereby altering the relationship between ruler and ruled. The language of holy war replaces the language of governance: "fear" and "dread" will fall upon all creatures, who are "delivered into the hand" of humans (vv. 2–3). But the new order that is announced to Noah and his sons is accompanied by restrictions: while humans may eat the flesh of other creatures, they may not eat the "life" (*nepeš*), identified here with the blood, which belongs to God (v. 4).

Verse 5 shifts attention to the human as victim, and the divine speech shifts to first person as God declares that he will demand the life of any creature, beast or "brother," who takes a human life. The principle of retribution is then stated in poetic form, and grounded in the notion of the divine image:

> Whoever sheds the blood of the human (*hā'ādām*),
>   by the human (*bā'ādām*) shall his blood be shed,
>   for in the image of God [God] made the human (*hā'ādām*).
>
> (v. 6)

Here is the basis for the notion of the sacred worth of every human being and the prohibition of taking a human life. If the Priestly writer envisioned circumstances in which God might permit or demand the taking of human life (as here in retribution), it is as a socially and historically conditioned response to a violation of the divine in the human. In this pronouncement, the terms of creation (ontology) are confronted by the circumstances of history, bringing anthropology into the realm of ethics and law.

Exaltation and dominion in Psalm 8

The view that the human is creature yet elevated above all other creatures is associated in Genesis 1 (and 9) with the unique concept of the divine image, but the same idea is also found in Psalm 8. There the psalmist, contemplating the heavenly bodies as testimony to God's handiwork, asks, "What is the human (*'enôš*) that you are mindful of him/a 'son of humanity' (*ben 'ādām*)[15] that you take note of him?" His answer, like Gen 1:26, involves a comparison with God and employs a royal metaphor.

> You have made him little less than God (or divine beings, *'elōhîm*),
>   And crowned him with glory and honor.
> You have made him rule (*mšl* hiphil) over the works of your hands,
>   Put all [creatures] under his feet.
>
> (vv. 6–7)

Rule here is spelled out as subjugation through the image of the conquering suzerain placing his foot on the neck of the conquered (v. 7). The sense is close to that conveyed by the verb *rdh* ("have dominion") in Gen 1:26, 28 – a verb that describes the exercise of authority or power over an individual, group, or territory, often in contexts that specify harsh or illegitimate rule. When used of kings, *rdh* is usually to describe their subjugation of other nations or peoples, or rule over their own people as though they were foreigners (1 Kgs 4:24 [Heb 5:4]; Ps 110:2; 72:8; Isa 14:2, 6; Ezek 34:4; Lev 25:43, 46, 53). Thus both Genesis 1 and Psalm 8 view humans within the created order primarily in terms of superiority and control over other creatures. In a hierarchy of being, humans stand next to God, to whom they are likened.

This exalted view of humans as the God-like among creatures and as rulers of the inhabited earth was, for its ancient author, a declaration of faith in the wisdom and power of God – not a claim of special entitlement, nor a theological justification for human exploitation of the environment. The commands given to humans at the conclusion of the Creator's work are initiating commands that envision a newly formed earth empty of human inhabitants and not yet brought under cultivation. Thus it must be filled ("be fruitful and multiply and fill the earth"), made livable ("subdue the earth"), and ordered ("have dominion over . . . every living creature"). The terms of the commands reflect Israel's world as a world of peasant farmers, attempting to secure a precarious existence from a hostile land. For the earth to support life in this region of marginal rainfall it had to be "subdued," which entailed a constant battle. A recurring theme in the Hebrew Bible is the threat of land returning to "wilderness," where only thorns and briars grow, and inhabited only by wild animals (e.g., Isa 32:13).[16]

Gen 1:26–28 in canonical context

The image of God that defines humans in Genesis 1 serves there as a royal metaphor, but the image itself has no content. Although it appears to originate in anthropomorphic conceptions of deity, it does not reveal the shape or character of the One it images. As a term for likeness it is concrete, formal, wholistic – and empty; it cannot be identified with any organ, attribute, or capacity – however distinctive or desirable. But because it expresses a notion of correlation or correspondence, it is open to continued reinterpretation in relation to changing understandings of God and humankind.

One early line of interpretation combined elements of the Bible's two creation accounts, identifying the image of Genesis 1 with the man of Genesis 2–3. Emphasizing the secondary nature of the woman, as possessing the image only in a derived manner, it identified the "fall" of Genesis 3 with a loss of the image, for which it held the woman responsible. It is this interpretation that provided the background for NT and patristic speculation and underlies views of women's nature and place in the "order of creation" that are still current today.[17] But this manner of combining the texts violates the terms of both OT accounts, in which the image is not lost or effaced and the man and the woman are held equally accountable for their disobedience to the divine command.

The Yahwist's Account of Creation (Gen 2:4b–3:24)

The account that begins in Gen 2:4b is the older of the Bible's two creation stories, known as the "Yahwist's" account for the author's use of the divine name YHWH (pronounced "Yahweh"). Like the Priestly account, it introduces a larger composition that spans the first four books of the Bible. In its present form it is composite, presenting a story imbedded within a larger story and moving in successive episodes from creation to "fall" and finally to "history." The frame story, which appears in 2:4b–8 and 3:23–24, tells of a human being (*hāʾādām* "the human") who is formed from the dust of the ground (*ʾadāmâ*) and placed in a garden; at the end he is driven from the garden to till the ground from which he was taken. The opening and closing scenes have only two actors: God YHWH and "the human." This story is a story of a lost paradise and a lost opportunity for immortality (3:22), told as the story of the first human. It is a story that explains the terms of human existence at the point where "history" begins, that is, the conditions under which we (author and readers) live.

The author has personified humankind in a single representative, to whom he has given the name of the species; and as in Genesis 1, his model is male – here a peasant farmer. In place of the solemn declarations and liturgical cadences of the Priestly composition, the Yahwist's account exhibits the features and form of a folktale, describing a time "when the world was very young," when God walked the earth and animals could speak. It makes the same essential points about human nature as Genesis 1, but it does so through narrated actions, rather than declarations. Here the human is formed from dust like the animals, enlivened by divine breath, given the plant world for food, and set over all other creatures, who are brought to him to name. The theme of sexual differentiation is here too, but the way in which it is introduced gives unique attention to the relationship between the sexes – in the "original" order and in the "fallen" state that describes life as we know it, "outside the garden."

The story begins with a solitary human, bearing the name of the species. But there is something defective about this representation; as God YHWH observes, "It is not good that the human should be alone." What he needs is a "help suitable (or 'fit') for him" (2:18).[18] God then proceeds to create each of the animal species, from the same ground as his first creation, and present them to "the human." But none proves to be a "suitable help." Only one of his own kind can meet that test. And so God extracts a rib from "the human," which he "builds up" into a woman. On seeing her, "the human" exclaims:

> This one at last is bone of my bone and flesh of my flesh;
> She shall be called 'iššâ ("woman"),
>   because she was taken from 'îš ("man").
>
> (2:23)

In his recognition of the woman as his own kind, he is revealed as "man." The woman who confronts him is not a separate creation, formed from the ground like the animal species, but of the very same substance. The "help suitable for him" has been found, but in the moment of recognition she is no longer identified as a "help." Rather she is presented as one to whom the man is drawn, so that he leaves even father and mother to be united to her.

The author clearly intends to speak of the sexual drive and the institution of marriage (v. 24), as the means by which the species will be perpetuated. The message is essentially the same as Genesis 1. But the story has introduced new elements into the portrait of human existence that are not simply requirements of the story form; they belong to the essence of being human. Human life, in this account, is characterized by interactions – with other creatures, with others of the same species, and with God (elaborated as the story continues). Humans are relational beings in their fundamental nature. And these relationships have both social and psychological dimensions. Social institutions, represented here by the primary family unit, are essential to human survival and the fulfillment of human needs, and the relationship of the sexes is not simply physical but psychological. Being alone is "not good"; finding the one who will satisfy the need for a "suitable help" elicits an exclamation of recognition; a man will henceforth leave father and mother to "cleave" to his wife (2:24); and the woman's "desire" will be for her husband (3:16). Social terms ("man" and "woman") replace the biological terms ("male" and "female") of Genesis 1.

The story is told from the man's point of view, reflecting the male-centered society in which it arose; but the message is one of mutuality, of man and woman made for each other and bound together, in joy and (in the next episode) in pain. There is no time in this account, unlike the Priestly narrative, and sequence has no ontological meaning – either in creation or fall. Only when the man and woman appear onstage together is the creation complete, and the drama of life may begin. In the following episode the man and the woman are united in sin and bear equal shares of punishment. There, however, the woman has the lead role in the opening scene, speaking for the pair.

Sin and its Consequences (Genesis 3)

The terms for the action in Genesis 3 have been set in the preceding chapter, in a prohibition announced when God placed "the human" in the garden (2:15–17). The prohibition carries the message that human life is limited; it has boundaries that may not be transgressed, and these are both physical and moral in nature. Although the boundaries change in chapter 3, the notion of limits does not. Humans are finite and bounded creatures, and the boundaries are set by God. In Genesis 2, the boundary is marked by a divine command: one tree of all the trees in the garden may not be eaten, on penalty of death. The prohibition assumes the freedom to disobey and the capacity for moral discrimination – to know right from wrong and to weigh the consequences of actions. Thus the "knowledge of good and bad (evil)"[19] represented by the forbidden tree is not the ability to distinguish between good and evil, but the ability to know all things, both good and bad – a divine attribute according to 3:22. The prohibition is presented as a test – and the outcome is known, for a prohibition in a story will always be violated. The story presented in Genesis 3 is an etiology; it seeks to explain why life as we know it is not as it was intended, or might have been.

Genesis 3 is a complex account, exhibiting internal tensions and interwoven with themes and characters from ancient Near Eastern myth and legend: a tree of life, a serpent, and a woman who imparts knowledge. But the Israelite author has used these traditions to create an entirely new story, with a new theological message. Israel's ancestors and neighbors had also speculated about the limits of human life and the qualities that distinguished humans from gods and other

creatures. Their accounts focused on knowledge and death. The gods were characterized by superior wisdom and immortality; and while humans possessed a
degree of knowledge that distinguished them from the animals, immortality
eluded them. Ancient Near Eastern myth accounted for human mortality either
as tragic loss or divine withholding.[20] Gen 3:22–23 contains an echo of the latter
tradition.[21] In the final form of the account, however, interest in immortality has
been eclipsed by another concern, which focuses on the tree of knowledge, not the
tree of life. For the Yahwist, the primary problem of human existence is not death,
but disobedience – here associated with the desire to obtain God-like wisdom.

Whence arises the impulse to disobey the divine command and question its
motive? The author of Gen 3:1–7 is unwilling to lodge it within the human
creation, and so he finds an instigator among the other creatures God has made:
the snake, whom ancient lore endowed with quasi-divine powers. A symbol of
immortality in its ability to rejuvenate itself by shedding its skin, it was also
ascribed special wisdom and associated with magic and the healing arts (Joines,
1975). The Yahwist has tamed him; here he is only the "most crafty"[22] of the
creatures God had made (3:1), and his power is only the power of suggestion.
While this displacement of the impulse to disobedience does not absolve the
human pair nor solve the problem of the origins of sin within a divinely ordered
creation, it does suggest that sin is not a defect of creation, but arises in the
exercise of God-given powers.[23] It arises in interactions involving external partners and internal conversations in which alternatives are envisioned and
weighed. The snake plants the question that initiates the conversation and then
claims to know God's mind: "God knows that when you eat of it your eyes will
be opened, and you will be like God, knowing good and bad" (3:5).

The snake's words are addressed to the pair (the second-person verbs are
plural in Hebrew), but it is the woman who weighs the arguments and the
evidence. Observing that the fruit of the forbidden tree was good for food, pleas-
ant to look at, and desirable to make one wise, and heeding the snake's assurance that they will not die, she eats – and gives to her husband, who also eats.
Although the woman speaks and reasons, both man and woman eat, in knowing disobedience. And the divine sentences that follow draw no consequence
from either the order of disobedience or the rationale offered. Neither reasoned
reflection nor unreflective trust excuse the pair, who have each chosen to heed
the voice of another in place of the voice of God. That is the common crime
addressed in the following judgment scene.

But divine judgment is not the first consequence of disobedience. Shame, not
death, follows this act of human self-assertion, the pained recognition of altered
conditions of life. It appears that the snake was right, at least on two counts: the
violators of the prohibition do not die, and their eyes are opened. But their
opened eyes do not give them the omniscience they desire, only acute self-
consciousness of their own vulnerability. Now they know themselves to be
naked, before one another and God. The nakedness of their created state has
become cause for shame; God's good gift of sexuality is transformed by human
self-interest into a source of pain and exploitation. With this act of disobedience

the "original" state of trusting relationships is broken; the couple now cover themselves and attempt to hide from God.

The judgment scene that concludes the story spells out the consequences of the broken relationship to God in every other relationship. As etiologies, the terms of the punishment are formulated in relation to the terms of creation – not the terms of the crime – and they are presented in close parallelism for the woman and the man. For the man, estrangement from God brings painful and incessant toil – in estrangement from the ground, from which he was taken; it no longer yields fruit freely but brings forth only thorns (3:17–19). For the woman, estrangement from God brings painful and repeated labor in childbirth – in estrangement from the man, from whom she was taken; he no longer yields freely to her desire, but instead rules over her (3:16).

One of the most remarkable features of this account is its view of the male domination that characterized the world of ancient Israel. For the Yahwist, this "given" order is the primary sign of disordered relationships in a creation estranged from God. Such was not the intended relationship of the sexes, he insists, but a tragic consequence of human rebellion. If he could envision no alternative under the prevailing social and economic conditions of his day, he could still identify this order as a distortion of the Creator's original design. In his story of origins it serves as the root expression of estrangement within the human community, which will soon extend to the relationship between brothers – and occupational groups (Genesis 4), father and son – and competing ethnic groups (Gen 9:20–27), and finally nations and peoples (Gen 11:1–9).

The Priestly and Yahwistic Accounts Combined and Compared

The Yahwist's story of creation complements the Priestly account by focusing on the social and psychological aspects of human nature and the human condition and by giving an essential role to the mind and the will. But it also stands in tension with the Priestly view, for it envisions a different world. The world of the Priestly writer is an ordered world in which history proceeds according to divine plan, and neither human ignorance nor arrogance can keep it from its intended course. In successive covenants with Noah and Abraham, God's purposes for the world are focused in a single people, who at Sinai are given the means in cult and law to maintain their identity and calling as a holy people.

The Yahwist's world is not so ordered. It is a world of human striving and failing, a world of violence that grieves the heart of its Maker (6:5–6). But it is also a world in which a righteous man can affect the Creator's decision to destroy (6:9; 18:16–33). And it is a world in which divine punishment is always followed by divine grace – beginning with the act of clothing the naked couple. For the Yahwist, a "fallen" human creation survives only through the grace of God – and by its wits. For the knowledge obtained from the forbidden fruit is essential to life outside the garden. The Yahwist, like the Priestly writer, knows that humans share some attribute of the divine, but he identifies this with the superior knowledge that sets humans apart from animals. The wisdom possessed by humankind is indeed a God-like quality (3:22), but under the conditions of human existence it is not an unmixed blessing. It is susceptible to distortion and manipulation, and it can hurt as well as heal.

The Problem of Gendered Existence

The creation accounts of Genesis 1–3 present two Israelite attempts to describe human beings in their essential nature. As accounts of origins, they attempt to look behind the features of history and culture and individual variation, while betraying these very particularities in their composition. Both accounts give pointed attention to sexual differentiation as an essential feature of human existence, but neither spells out the implications of this bifurcated nature for the common nature that both sexes share. In Genesis 1 this common nature is symbolized by the divine image. Although the model is male, the grammar makes clear that it characterizes the species as a whole. But gendered existence under historical conditions of life means gender-differentiated roles, values, and authority. In the male-oriented systems of authority and honor that characterized ancient Israel and the early Church, the male was taken not only as the model of the human, but as the norm. The female was legally and conceptually subordinate – or "other" – so that even in her most elevated image, as mother, she could not represent the species in the same way as the male.

Thus despite wider and more positive employment of female models and metaphors than is commonly recognized, the Hebrew Bible draws most of its generalizing statements about human nature and destiny from male experience. Tension between attempts to discern the meaning of human existence common to all members of the species, and recognition of biological and cultural differences (including age, race, gender, and class) as equally characteristic of the species, pervades the biblical writings and challenges contemporary theologians. But it went largely unrecognized until recent times. As a consequence, the theological anthropology in the Hebrew Bible and the theological anthropology derived from the Hebrew Bible both perpetuated a view of humans in the image of God as explicitly or implicitly male.

Creation in Context: The Witness of History, Prophets, Wisdom, and Psalms

The two creation accounts each served to introduce a history that placed Israel's origins in a global context. In their combined and augmented form (the

Pentateuch), these sources offer a rich and varied portrait of life as divine–human interaction, in which human freedom and responsibility is always exercised within the guiding, chastening, and renewing providence of God. In this history, God not only acts, but speaks. Thus large blocks of the Pentateuch consist of instructions, presented as divine speech, mediated by Moses (Deuteronomy, Leviticus, and portions of Exodus and Numbers). The corpus of prophetic writings further attests to Israel's belief in the continued speaking of God in its history and the need to attend to that word. To be human, according to the Hebrew scriptures, is to know oneself addressed by God; to be a member of the covenant people is to know the name and history of that God and the meaning of the address.

The creation accounts do not exhaust Israel's theological reflection on the nature of the human being or the meaning of human existence, but they do identify key elements that are assumed by other writings. The Yahwist's account of events in the garden assumes that humans are created with the capacity and freedom to make moral judgments. This capacity is also assumed by the Deuteronomist, who pleads with Israel to choose life and good – by obeying the commandments (Deut 30:15–19) – and by the prophets, who condemn evildoers and exhort to acts of justice and mercy. Although neither creation account spells out the content of the God-likeness shared by humans, both authors assume, with other biblical writers, that humans are capable of exhibiting God-like qualities and are most true to their own nature when they exercise these capacities. Thus Israel is exhorted to be holy as God is holy (Lev 19:2); to do justice and act mercifully, as God is just and merciful; to love God and neighbor, as God has loved them. It is in showing such divine qualities that humans reflect the nature of their maker and distinguish themselves from other orders of creation. Thus the limited focus of each creation text on a particular point of correlation between the human and the divine serves to alert readers to broader areas of correspondence assumed by other texts and writers.

If the creation texts point to a correspondence between the human and the divine, they also recognize an absolute distinction, emphasized in the Yahwist's account: "Dust you are and to dust you shall return" (Gen 3:19).[24] This too correlates with testimony found elsewhere in the Hebrew Bible (cf. Gen 18:27; Ps 22:29 [Heb 22:30]; Job 10:9). Humans are frail as well as sinful. Their days are limited,[25] and full of sorrow. They strive for what they cannot attain. Their work finds no reward. These themes come to the fore in the Wisdom literature.[26]

The creation texts introduce us to normative, or at least dominant, currents of thought within ancient Israel, but there were dissenting voices and alternative views. Within the Wisdom writings (including the books of Proverbs, Ecclesiastes, Job, and certain psalms), we encounter skeptics who believed that the ways of God are unknowable and that humans are cut off from God, left to make their way unaided in a hostile or indifferent universe. Possessing both knowledge and moral instinct, they find no confirmation or reward in the exercise of these capacities; injustice prevails and ignorance is rewarded. Moral discernment reveals an unjust world. This skepticism confronts another view of the human cultivated in Wisdom circles, one that correlates right action with success and views wisdom as the key that unlocks the secrets of the divine.[27] Thus correlation between the human and the divine is exaggerated in this literature, both in its affirmations and in its denials.

Finally, there is the testimony of the heart, as it reveals the human condition in its ecstasy and its despair. The Psalms portray the human being in conversation with God – in every condition of life, and in individual and collective voice. Expectation of a hearing and a sense of absolute dependence on God are revealed here as fundamental to Israel's understanding of human existence. For the psalmist, divine silence only heightened the demand for a response. The thirst for God was implanted in the soul. The heart seeks refuge and rest in God – and finding it, rejoices. Humans are created for praise of their creator. That is their primary vocation.

The Bible's first word about human beings sets forth the presupposition of all subsequent words by defining them in relation to God. But the content and consequences of that defining relationship are the subject of never-ending theological reflection and debate.

Notes

1 For a survey of interpretations, see Westermann, 1984, pp. 147–55.
2 For a brief history of interpretation in Christian theology, see Hall, 1986, pp. 76–112. More detailed treatments may be found in Cairns, 1953, and Berkouwer, 1962.
3 The term "Hebrew Bible" is adopted in this essay as a non-confessional designation for the Christian "Old Testament." There is, however, no common term or conception for this literature when considered from the perspectives of the several religious communities that continue to regard it as sacred scripture.
4 For an introduction to Jewish theological anthropology by a modern Jewish philosopher and biblical scholar, see Heschel, 1966.
5 The following analysis draws on the author's more detailed studies in Bird, 1997, pp. 123–54; 174–93, and Børresen, 1995, pp. 5–28. Cf. Jónsson, 1988, and commentaries.
6 Hebrew *ʾādām* is a collective noun (grammatically singular). It designates the species as a class, parallel to the other classes of life identified in Genesis 1 – all collective nouns in Hebrew, generally translated as English plurals ("plants," "trees," "swarms," "birds," "beasts," etc.). See Bird, 1997, pp. 141, n. 45; 161–2, 168–73. It is sometimes used for an individual to emphasize the species identification over every other distinguishing feature, such as gender or nationality.
7 The noun, like the related verb *dmh* ("to liken"), emphasizes comparison, and hence similarity in difference.
8 The two prepositions should be understood as having the same meaning, namely "according to," "like" (or "as"). Cf. Gen 5:1, 3; 9:6 and the LXX.
9 Jónsson, 1988, pp. 12–13, 175–7; Cairns, 1953, pp. 73–83. There were, to be sure, Jewish interpreters who found a spiritual meaning in the image.
10 See Heschel, 1996, pp. 154, 159–69. For Judaism, the cure for human corruption is Sinai and the covenant; for Christians, it is Christ. Both Christian and Jewish

theologians encounter difficulties when they attempt to make the divine image *the* foundational concept for anthropology. As a non-moral category it stands in inevitable tension with efforts to define the human in moral terms.

11 See, e.g., *Enuma Elish* 6.34–35 (*ANET*, 68) and *Atrahasis* 1. 194–97 (W. Lambert and A. Millard, *Atra-hasis* [Oxford: Clarendon, 1969], pp. 56–7).

12 Although the Priestly writer uses exclusively male terms to refer to God, they are to be understood metaphorically. Popular religion may have given YHWH a consort in ancient Israel, but the biblical writings consistently oppose any notion of sexuality for Israel's God.

13 A similar need to specify male and female lies behind the Priestly description of the animal pairs who enter the ark (Gen 6:19; 7:9). What may be assumed elsewhere must be spelled out there; the pairs that are to preserve their kind from the flood must be reproductive pairs.

14 The command to be fruitful is addressed here to Noah and his sons (9:1), not Noah and his wife, revealing the author's focus on the male characters in narratives as well as genealogies.

15 Here the common Semitic *'enôš* (a human, or humanity) parallels the specifically Hebrew *'ādām*. The expression "son/daughter of" is used to describe an individual member of a class.

16 The modern notion of dominion as stewardship (e.g., Hall, 1986) is a creative interpretation in a changed environment, but it introduces a sense of vocation that is lacking in the Priestly author's notion of image and dominion. See Hiebert, 1996, pp. 20–1.

17 See Bird, 1997, p. 175.

18 The Hebrew expression *kenegdô* means "like his opposite (or 'counterpart'/'vis-à-vis')." See Bird, 1997, pp. 181–3.

19 The Hebrew term (*ra'*) describes aesthetic as well as moral judgments and also misfortune and displeasure.

20 See Bird, 1997, pp. 184–6.

21 See Barr, 1993.

22 The Hebrew term (*'ārûm*) is chosen for the word play it creates with the word for "naked" (*'arûmmîm*) in the preceding verse (Gen 2:25).

23 Terminology for sin is lacking in this passage, appearing for the first time in Gen 4:7, in relation to murder. What the garden story seeks to explain is the disposition toward sin, which is not "original" with creation, but nevertheless characterizes every individual who goes forth from the garden or the womb. See Bird, 1997, pp. 191–3, and Westermann, 1984, pp. 275–8.

24 Notions of resurrection that find expression in later writings of the Hebrew Bible do not imply a more elevated view of human nature, but derive from eschatological reflection that emphasizes God's continuing providence and creative power.

25 Ps 144:3–4 answers the question "What is *'ādām*?" with the statement: "They are like a breath (*hebel*); their days are like a passing shadow."

26 On the anthropology of the Wisdom traditions, see Perdue, 1994, pp. 19–48, 333–6 and *passim*.

27 Skepticism becomes open revolt in Job as traditional theological affirmations are challenged and turned on their head. Thus Job parodies Psalm 8 with the complaint that God makes too much of lowly humankind. Humans are not the exalted rulers of creation but slaves, born to divine service (Job 7:1–2, 17–21). See Perdue, 1994, pp. 140–4, 335–6.

Bibliography

Barr, J., *The Garden of Eden and the Hope of Immortality* (Minneapolis: Fortress Press, 1993).

Bird, P., *Missing Persons and Mistaken Identities: Women and Gender in Ancient Israel* (Minneapolis: Fortress Press, 1997).

Berkouwer, G., *Man: The Image of God*, trans. D. Jellema (Grand Rapids: Eerdmans, 1962).

Børresen, K., ed., *The Image of God: Gender Models in Judaeo-Christian Tradition* (Minneapolis: Fortress Press, 1995).

Cairns, D., *The Image of God in Man* (London: SCM, 1953).

Curtis, E., "Image of God (OT)," *Anchor Bible Dictionary*, vol. 3 (New York, 1992), 389–91.

Hall, D., *Imaging God: Dominion as Stewardship* (Grand Rapids: Eerdmans, 1986).

Hiebert, T., "Rethinking Dominion Theology," *Direction* 25 (1996), 16–25.

Heschel, A., "The Concept of Man in Jewish Thought," in S. Radhahkrishnan and P. Raju, eds., *The Concept of Man: A Study in Comparative Philosophy* (London: Allen & Unwin, 1966), 122–71.

Joines, Karen Randolph, *Serpent Symbolism in the Old Testament: a linguistic, archaeological, and literary study* (Haddonfield, NJ: Haddonfield Home, 1975).

Jónsson, G., *The Image of God: Genesis 1:26–28 in a Century of Old Testament Research* (Lund: Almquist & Wiksell, 1988).

Perdue, L., *Wisdom and Creation: The Theology of Wisdom Literature* (Nashville: Abingdon, 1994).

Westermann, C., *Genesis 1–11. A Commentary*, translated by John J. Scullion (Minneapolis: Augsburg, 1984).

CHAPTER 16

The Community of God in the Hebrew Bible

R. E. Clements

The Hebrew Bible exists both as the canon of Holy Scripture for Judaism and, in a modified canonical structure, as the Old Testament of the Christian Church. In these socioreligious contexts it is inseparably related to a community of faith each of which maintains the belief that it constitutes a uniquely chosen and privileged community of God. Both communities claim to enjoy a unique tradition of knowledge of the one and only God and a belief in God's call to serve in a special way as divine servants and advocates on earth. But who does, or may, belong to these believing communities; what demands does doing so impose and what form should such communities take? Knowledge of God and membership of a community are closely interrelated so that there exists a very close relationship between possession and use of the Hebrew Bible as a canon of Holy Scripture and the social structure, worship and activities of each of these communities (cf. J. A. Sanders: 1984, *passim*; 1986, pp. 145–57). Dialogue between Jews and Christians has consequently focused heavily, not simply on matters of doctrine, but on questions concerning the nature and origin of the biblical communities. The roots of the concepts of both "Church" and "Synagogue" reach back into the very heart of the formation of the scriptural canon (Rost, 1938, *passim*).

The Hebrew Bible in Jewish and Christian Life

How then do Jews and Christians differ? How far do they share a common heritage? How far can we discern, with the aid of a modern critical understanding of the growth of the Hebrew Bible, the origins of both communities, and the vital turning-points in their development (Dahl, 1963 [1941], pp. 144–74)? Seeking the answers to these questions carries us into central areas of biblical theology and to an examination of the nature of community conveyed by the name Israel. Seen from a Christian perspective the Old Testament is a collection which witnesses to the origin and form of the Christian Church (Hanson, 1987, pp. 382–426). From a Jewish point of view these writings answer the question, "Who is a Jew?" and show how the modern historical experience of Jews, settled in many lands, but sharing a common faith and heritage, originated. For each of these communities there is an issue of continuity and a sense of a shared spiritual identity with the communities of the Hebrew Bible. Undoubtedly it is vital, if the natures of both Judaism and Christianity are to be understood, that post-biblical developments are fully taken into account, yet even these developments require to be interpreted against the background of the canon of the Hebrew Bible which establishes their central reference point.

In historical perspective it becomes evident that the Old Testament does not bear witness to one single form of community in what it reveals about the people who are called variously "Israel" and "Judah" (Hanson, 1987, pp. 87–176). So the reason why these titles carry an implication regarding a relationship to God needs to be explored in regard to what these titles actually meant historically. To do this necessarily carries us back to reexamine the historical origins of Israel and the connection between this nation and the God YHWH. It is this situation which testifies to a process of interactive self-definition in which the title of the nation became synonymous with "The people of YHWH" and the identity of the God YHWH became that of "The God of Israel." Such a mutual relationship between a nation and its deity stands at the beginning of the biblical understanding of community. Further questions lie behind this concerning the origin of the nation and why worship of the God YHWH was such an important factor in its emergence.

After the fall of Jerusalem in 587 BCE the surviving kingdom of Judah underwent a change from being a nation to becoming a multiplicity of scattered communities residing among many nations. These changes necessarily brought with them related changes in the understanding of God which such survivors carried to their new places of domicile (Smith-Christopher, 1997, pp. 7–36). From being the patron deity of one nation, YHWH came to be recognized as the one sole God – the Sovereign Creator of the Universe.

So there is a wide-ranging ideological and sociopolitical history which can be traced in the Hebrew Bible. From the perspective of both biblical theology and biblical ethics the close relationship between ideas of community and ideas of God provides a major feature. Yet it has brought problems as well as provided valuable insights. In the latter category such a relationship has encouraged a deep humanizing and moralizing of doctrine, since the understanding of God has been directly embedded in human experience and human social concerns. It is, in the best sense, a human, liberating, theology.

Yet among the problems that have arisen we must certainly include the fact that ideas of divine election, and of divinely privileged human communities, have led to attitudes of prejudice and exclusion – even at times to demands for campaigns of genocide (cf. Deut 7:2)! These result from claims to ethnic and national superiority which have proved damaging and strongly reprehensible

(Deist, 1994, pp. 13–29). By gaining a better understanding of the biblical context to ideas of "a community of God," we may hope to give clearer focus to a number of contemporary questions which note the dangers, as well as the visionary insights, which belong to such a conjunction of ideas.

It is also important for us to note that the relationship between biblical language about God and the structures of human communities have loomed prominently in attempts to present a "theology of the Old Testament." Most celebrated here has been the pioneering work of W. Eichrodt (1961–7) who used the idea of covenant to establish a central, coordinating, principle by which the variety of theological ideas could be organized into a system. The weaknesses of this have become apparent, yet, in some measure, all other comparable attempts to construct an Old Testament theology have had to face the same issues. If God is made known through the pages of the Hebrew Bible, then this revelation has been mediated through the people called Israel (Kaiser, 1998, pp. 29–87).

The Historical Forms of the Biblical Community

Who or what is Israel? We have seen that the question can initially be answered historically by recognizing that Israel was a kingdom which emerged in the eastern Mediterranean sometime about the turn of the millennium in 1000 BCE. As a single nation-state it lasted only very briefly before it split into what were effectively the two sister kingdoms of Israel and Judah. These sister kingdoms maintained an uneasy relationship with each other, sharing many features in common besides their religion, but divided over the issue of allegiance to the dynastic claims of the royal house of the family of David from the tribe of Judah. When the larger of the two kingdoms fell victim to the Assyrians in the final quarter of the 8th century BCE then only the smaller kingdom of Judah remained until it too collapsed in futile endeavors to rebel against Babylonian imperial control (598 and 587 BCE). After these disasters Israel no longer formed a single national entity and expectations of this were transferred to the realm of future hopes and ideals. Not until the Hellenistic and Roman times were these ideals given even a partial fulfillment, by which time a far wider spread of Jewish communities had become well established.

Yet Israel did not disappear after the disasters of 598 and 587 BCE. During the years 520–516 BCE a small temple community was reestablished in Jerusalem, providing a restored focal point for religious aspiration and leadership. However, after 598 and 587 BCE Israel increasingly took on new forms in which scattered remnants of the former kingdom of Judah established themselves in a variety of lands. They marked the beginning of the Jewish Diaspora, forming small immigrant communities which quickly developed viable social and religious lifestyles of their own. These retained a deep commitment to their past national heritage but remained flexible enough to adapt to the new social and political world in which they found themselves. A significant factor in their growth, survival, and sense of identity was their continued relationship to the worship and authority of the Jerusalem temple (Porteous, 1967; Clements, 1996, pp. 57–69).

It was during this period, and in this environment, that the religion which we have come to know as Judaism took shape. The rise of these scattered communities provides a significant hidden background to the growth and formation of the biblical canon whose writings chiefly focus on the developments in Jerusalem. Nevertheless, the fact of the existence of these more diverse communities has contributed extensively to the shape, structure, and theology of the Hebrew Bible. The notion of "exile," with all its political, social, and religious overtones, became a formative assumption which colors Jewish religious and social ideals (Neusner, 1997, pp. 221–38). Accordingly, awareness of the existence of this Jewish world of "exile" pervades the writings of the New Testament (Evans, 1997, pp. 299–328). Not only has it contributed hugely to the historical shape of Judaism, but it has provided a biblical background for the Christian ideal of the Church. Paradoxically such a state of exile was readily accepted as a semi-permanent one. Historically the social structures of Church and Synagogue belong to Hellenistic antiquity, yet their nomenclature derives from Greek terminology employed to translate central Hebrew biblical concepts. These had originally been employed to describe Israel as a community of God's people at a time when the national dimension had been relegated to play only a secondary, idealized, role.

Israel as a Community of Tribes

In the biblical tradition of the book of Genesis, Israel is the divinely given name of the nation's ancestor (Gen 32:28) from whom it passed to become the name of the community of tribes which sprang from him (Gen 49:2–28). These were twelve in number who shared this common bond of kinship. So we are pointed to Israel's earliest form of existence as a group of tribes in which the bonds of kinship and genealogical affiliation provide the controlling force. As the most common, and most self-evidently natural, form for a primitive society to adopt, it identifies a community as effectively one large extended family. Nothing could then appear to be more natural than that such a tribal group should direct its worship to "the God of my/your father" (cf. Gen 31:5; 49:25; 50:17), or more broadly to "the God of your fathers (ancestors)" (cf. Ex 3:13–15). The biblical tradition attests the use of such a title in early Israel and, in the story of the revelation of God to Moses out of a thornbush, explicitly links the title "the God of the Fathers" with the revelation of the new divine name yhwh (Ex 3:15). So the link between God and community in the Israelite patriarchal tradition is shown to be mediated through the traditions of tribal ancestry which formed the primary bond within the larger group (Rogerson and Davies, 1989, pp. 45–62; Albertz, 1994 [1992], pp. 25–39). The god who had protected and blessed the ancestor of the tribal community was naturally trusted to continue to uphold his descendants. Where a number of tribes were grouped together then this necessarily required a recognition that it had been the same god who had been worshipped by each of them.

Closer investigation into the relevant evidence, however, shows the situation to have been more complex than this. The most direct testimony to the existence of worship in which the deity was regarded as related to the tribe through a kin relationship lies in the widespread popularity of names which affirm that the god was father or brother to the name-bearer (Albertz, 1994, pp. 29–34, 250–1). The widespread popularity, well into the historical period, of such theophorous names as Abraham, Abimelech, and the like attest this belief. The relationship between the god and the individual is portrayed on the analogy of the kind of kin-relationship which was formative of society more broadly. God was, in effect, "one of the family."

However, closer examination of the evidence of Israel's patriarchal traditions indicates that, even if this was once the prevalent understanding, the situation had developed into something more complex. The retention of such traditional proper names may well have become a conservative archaising convention as the understanding which had generated such names became progressively obsolete. The bonds of kin-relationships were being modified and idealized as other features brought substantial changes into the tribe's social and religious life.

The names of the gods worshipped by Israel's ancestors are recorded as forms of the major divine name El. Thus El-Bethel (Gen 31:13; 35:7), El-Elyon (Gen 14:19,22), El-'Olam (Gen 21:33), and El-Shaddai (Gen 17:1; 28:3, etc.) are all attested. Other more distinctive names, such as Pahad-Yishaq (Gen 31:53), Abbir (Mighty One) Ya'aqob (Gen 49:24), also appear. These must have been titles of gods worshipped at local altars and sanctuaries, apparently as forms of the high god El. The most striking feature is the absence of names compounded with the divine title Baal (cf. Ex 14:2 for Baal-Zephon) but even this could be accounted for as the consequence of later scribal censorship. The very purpose of recalling that Israel's ancestors offered such worship, and were blessed for doing so, was to ensure that their entitlement to retain use of the land, to farm it and to utilize it for pasture, remained unprejudiced. Religion itself included an element of territorial claim.

In this light it becomes clear that it was not simply the sense of belonging to an extended family, or kin-group, which gave shape and content to the tribe's worship, but a recognition that the land on which the tribe had settled, and on the productivity of which it depended, belonged to God. Such rural sanctuaries and altars had undoubtedly been in existence long before the time of the Israelite tribe's arrival. Incoming settlers were bound to establish a positive relationship with the divine "lords" of the region. The bonds of kinship were then not the only bonds which bound the community to God. Territory, with all its life-giving promise, was a major factor which incurred a religious obligation.

Even the narrative report of the revelation of YAHWEH to Moses in Ex 3:1–22 has been designed to serve an apologetic purpose by showing that all the various titles by which God had earlier been known to Israel's ancestors were collectively to be fully identified with the new name YHWH. From henceforth this was the name by which God was to be invoked. So, in accordance with the same principle, the stories of the tribal ancestors preserved in Genesis which show that they had called upon God by many and various names are systematized under the unifying authority of the name YHWH. In a surprisingly extensive way this retention of ancient tradition within the framework of later national religious development reveals how the "gods of the land" came to be regarded as earlier revelations of the national deity YHWH. Tribal tradition with all its kinship affiliations, and national ambition with its territorial claims, became joined together under a religious claim which provided a major stimulus in the direction of a national, quasi-monotheistic, faith. The very foundations of Israel's nationhood were religious in their coloring.

In such a light it may be strongly insisted that the earliest evidence for the idea of a "community of God," as attested in the stories of Genesis, indicates that it possessed a necessary triangularity (cf. Block, 1988, p. 5). As a community of tribes Israel could not exist without territory. In consequence its structure as a "community of God" required to be affirmed, not simply through its tribal ethnicity but through its claim to land on which it depended for its survival. The very patterns and goals of worship were aimed at securing the good will and protection of those deities whose ownership and blessing of the land was increasingly regarded as of paramount importance.

Israel On the Way to Becoming a Nation-State

Stories of Israel's forebears point us to a period prior to the introduction of a monarchy in which Israel is nevertheless described as a unified entity. The tradition that it was composed of a group of twelve tribes is evidently built around a recognition that the number twelve was important (de Geus, 1976; Anderson, 1970, pp. 135–51). Although most of the preserved stories of deeds and personalities which shaped the history of each of the tribes are peculiar to that one individual tribe, there is nonetheless an awareness that membership of the larger group calling itself "Israel" distinguished these tribes from others who lay outside their boundaries. The earliest extra-biblical attestation of the name Israel (ca. 1230 BCE) confirms its existence at a very substantial interval before the rise of the Davidic state approximately two centuries later.

In spite of careful historical investigation, it is not surprising that many aspects of the organization, character and responsibilities which pertained to ancient Israel in this formative period remain shrouded in uncertainty. Of greatest importance to a study of the idea of a "community of God" is the recognition that cultic activities and the mythic ideologies of prayer were a primary factor in defining, preserving, and promoting the sense of unity which bound the tribes of Israel together (Albertz, 1994 [1992], pp. 67–94). There are good reasons for concluding that, well before the formation of the first Israelite kingdom, the divine name YHWH had become linked with the worship of the tribes known as Israel. There is a degree of historical anomaly in this, since the very name Israel is built up from the widely used divine title El.

How the divine names YHWH and El came to be identified has therefore long been a subject of critical speculation. Questions regarding the tribal and regional developments which led to the establishing of these connections must therefore be left unresolved in the present context. Whether these had occurred independently, or whether they were themselves directly linked to the inner pressures which led to the introduction of a monarchy into Israel cannot be determined here. Part of the reason for this uncertainty results from the fact that all the ancient traditions concerning this early formative period of Israel's existence have been set within a literary framework which imbued them with a dominating conviction that Israel had become "one nation" under YHWH its God. The story of how this occurred has consequently been remembered in such a way as to show that it resulted from the providential outworking of a divine plan.

Fortunately the early Israelite tribal traditions have retained a number of features which help towards understanding the nature of the obligations and duties which were attendant upon Israel's self-understanding as a "community of God." These are most forcibly to be found in the claim that the commitment to YHWH involved a commitment to warfare on behalf of any, or all, of those tribes of Israel which were threatened from outside (Niditch, 1993, pp. 28–55). Conflicts between tribes from within the Israelite group posed different problems from these external threats and required to be dealt with in a different fashion (cf. Judg 20:12–48). YHWH was envisaged as a Warrior-god who could be called upon to defend the tribes of Israel from threats by other external groups.

Belonging to Israel incurred duties to bear arms in any cause which was understood to threaten member tribes of Israel and also, by implication, to threaten the name and holiness of YHWH as God. It is not hard to see how the ultimacy of a religious sanction served to promote the concern for united action in support of threatened tribes. The appeal to divine authority required all adult males to support military action. So Israel's wars became "the wars of YHWH" (cf. Num 21:14; 1 Sam 18:17; 25:28) and the major religious symbol venerated by Israel as a larger community of tribes was the Ark of YHWH Sebaoth, which appears to have been a war palladium (cf. Num 10:35–6).

According to the biblical tradition the primary factor which contributed to the introduction of a monarchy into Israel was the necessity for strong military leadership (cf. 1 Sam 11:1–15). Since the Israelite tribes encountered a serious territorial threat from the Philistine Pentapolis in the coastal region, the military significance of the worship of YHWH contributed strongly toward the demand for greater unity between them. Kingship, in the guise of strong military leadership, was an evident solution which the worship of YHWH could foster.

So the biblical tradition perceived the need for strong military leadership as a primary factor in Israel's transition to nationhood. Analogous developments indicate that a wide variety of factors must historically have led to such a step, partly economic and partly geographical (cf. Finkelstein, 1989, pp. 43–74). Nevertheless, the biblical perception serves to highlight the prominence of military necessity in Israel's developing sense of national identity and statehood. National territory pointed to a divine Lord and Owner. Israel's occupation of the land was conceived in a feudalistic manner in which the nation were regarded as the beneficiaries of a divine grant.

The introduction of this view of the nation-state as essentially a divine creation brought with it fundamental shifts in the legal and political administration of the region. It brought into existence an Israelite monarchy which in turn called for a far-reaching apologetic of the nature, privileges and responsibilities of this institution. So necessarily the national God YHWH is presented in biblical tradition as the divine Initiator and Authoriser who willed this change. Saul's brief reign was the first step in such a development, which foundered when Saul failed both to remove the Philistine threat and to establish a royal dynasty from among his sons. The fact that Saul introduced kingship to Israel without a supporting dynastic royal line was subsequently to call for apologetic explanation when the claims for a Davidic royal dynasty were challenged (cf. 1 Sam 19:1–10).

Israel as a Nation-State

Clearly there are many historical questions which require to be answered in order to understand the internal historical processes and developments which led to Israel's becoming a nation-state. Our present concern, however, lies not with these historical issues, but rather with the need to note the ideological and theological shifts which this transition incurred. Territoriality now took on an added significance and, with it, new anxieties concerning the ownership, development, and protection of the land. Loss of the land implied divine anger and abandonment. So now the interaction between warfare and religion was placed in a wider ideological context, and this has undoubtedly contributed to the manner in which the formation of the state was celebrated and remembered. In turn the later break-up and dismemberment of the state was to have far-reaching theological repercussions. When the nation-state of ancient Israel came into being around 1000 BCE, this development could be celebrated and ascribed to the will and purpose of the God YHWH. In like fashion, when that state broke apart and collapsed, the conclusion was inescapable that this too had to be ascribed to the will and purpose of the national deity.

The religious ideology of the state required that there should be shown to exist a continuity with the past ancestral religion of the nation's forebears. Against such a background it becomes evident that even the story of the revelation of the name YHWH through Moses (Exodus 3) has, in the formation of the tradition, been drawn into this national state ideology of the post-Davidic period.

The consequences of this elevation of the God YHWH to be the supreme God of Israel were many and various. Seen negatively it is possible to brand such a development as one of "syncretism," combining traditions which had at one time been separate and independent. Yet this is an unduly negative assessment of a process of integration which, in a more positive vein, must be regarded as a monotheizing process. Order and sovereignty had to be seen to prevail in the divine sphere, just as they did on earth under the rule of a powerful monarch. Whatever the personal religious aspirations of King David may have been, then, certainly the group which his triumph brought to power, ascribed his success to YHWH's will and divine support. The claim that he had been chosen and marked out by YHWH, from earliest years, for such high office is well attested by the preservation of a narrative tradition to this effect (1 Sam 16:1–23).

The episode of David's divine election from being a rustic youth to become designated the nation's ruler forms one element in the more extended literary composition, which we have come to know as the Story of David's Rise (1 Sam 15:1–2 Sam 5:10*; Grønbaek, 1971, passim). It tells how YHWH mysteriously planned and directed the supplanting of the Saulide royal family by David, denying a dynasty to the former but guaranteeing it in perpetuity to the latter. It is through and through an apology for the Davidic royal house. The same is true of what has come to be described as The Succession Narrative (2 Samuel 9–20; Rost, [1926] 1982, passim), which defends the legitimacy of Solomon's succession to the throne in Jerusalem after David.

The divine election of the dynasty founder was a formula of divine authority and blessing for the state since the nation itself was regarded as embodied in the person of its kingly head. Divine approval of the royal successor was also then an inescapable aspect of this relationship between God, nation, and monarch. Although ostensibly formulated as a bilateral covenant between YHWH and David, in reality the whole concept of such a covenant formed part of the theopolitical basis of the state. So the introduction of a dynastic monarchy was itself an indispensable feature of the changed nature of Israel's self-understanding which the transition to nationhood entailed. The person of the king had become the primary focal point for establishing the divine dimension of Israel's life among the nations.

If the kingship of the royal house of David was the institution in which the divine element of Israel's existence as a nation was embodied, then the temple of Jerusalem was the external symbol which demonstrated this belief (Clements, 1965, pp. 55–6). Since the site on which the temple was built had undoubtedly been a holy place before the city was made David's administrative center, the installation of the holy ark there marked a further step in reminting old traditions to fulfill new purposes.

That it was David's controversial successor Solomon who had actually built the temple in Jerusalem called for special explanation, as did the related fact that Solomon's entitlement to succeed David was under serious, and probably justified, suspicion. So Israel's tradition declared that it had been the desire of King David to build a temple. The founder of the dynasty was rightly expected to build a "house" for the deity who had chosen him to rule the nation.

The age of David and Solomon has been variously judged as one of great cultural "enlightenment," yet also as one of widespread "religious syncretism."

To some extent both claims must be upheld, but they must each be seen in light of the concern to integrate and unify Israel as a nation-state which stood under the authority and blessing of YHWH. Under David Israel had entered the world of nations, and so its life as a "community of God" required it to adopt both the administrative trappings of nationhood and also the political mythology which gave it status and honor among the great imperial powers (cf. especially Ps 2:8–9).

In the course of adopting these changes it was inevitable that the wide diversity of local and regional traditions of the varied tribal members of the nation should be brought into relationship with each other and with the central authority. So not only was faith in YHWH a major factor in the formative history of the nation Israel, but that faith was inevitably subtly, but permanently, changed thereby.

Against such a background, claims for the supremacy of YHWH over other gods (cf. Ps 96:4–5) take on a new significance, since there was a necessary "monotheizing" tendency intrinsic to the concept of nationhood when this was given a religious interpretation. One nation required one monarchic head, which in turn demanded one divine Ruler in heaven. Local and regional traditions of worship, no matter how ancient and venerable, required to be immersed in the new spirit of nationhood. At times the active suppression of older cultic traditions may have been implemented. More often, however, it appears that these local traditions were simply recast in a new mold which took nothing away from the overall supremacy of YHWH as God.

The fact that, after Solomon's death (ca. 922 BCE), the United Kingdom of Israel split into two over the issue of adherence to the dynastic rule of the Davidic royal house shows this to have been an event which had far-reaching religious implications. It is in such a light that the biblical historian has recalled the consequences of the event, and, in a rather awkward fashion, endeavored to continue the story of the nation as though it had remained one nation in the eyes of God.

The Deuteronomistic Theology of Israel

The story of how Israel became a nation is recorded for us in what is unquestionably the most remarkable historical writing of the Hebrew Bible, known traditionally as The Former Prophets. It is more usually described in modern critical perspective as "The Deuteronomistic History" (Joshua – Judges – 1 & 2 Samuel – 1 & 2 Kings) on account of its close, though not uniform, relationship to the book of Deuteronomy. Overall this lawbook, followed by the history, and supplemented yet further by the Deuteronomistic edition of Jeremiah's prophecies, present us with the fullest theological presentation of Israel as a divinely protected nation-state (Mayes, 1996, pp. 477–508). Whereas the Deuteronomic lawbook sets out the polity of Israel as the community of YHWH, the History tells of its rise and fall as a nation among the nations of earth. The Deuteronomistic edition of the prophecies of Jeremiah supplements the account of the nation's downfall by showing how the prophet Jeremiah foretold and justified its occurrence (Stulman, 1998, pp. 23–55). More strikingly it looks beyond this downfall to unfold a picture of the future in which an interval period of Israel's chastisement among the nations must pass, before a return to the land will lead to the rebuilding of the nation. So all three of the "Deuteronomistic" compositions take as their central theme the conviction that Israel is the people of YHWH.

This trilogy of Deuteronomistic writings is, par excellence, the biblical literature which expounds a thoroughgoing theology of nationhood, introducing the fundamental concepts of election, covenant and national unity in a remarkable way. A prominent aspect of the Deuteronomic theology of Israel's status as a community of God is the introduction of the concept of a "covenant" (Deut 5:3) made on Mount Horeb in which God had bound Israel to observe the law given there to Moses. Yet even this "theology of covenant" has been introduced into the Deuteronomic thinking at an advanced stage (Perlitt, 1969, pp. 47–8; Nicholson, 1986, pp. 68–78). It anticipates the possibility of disaster, if not its actual occurrence, by introducing a note of uncertainty and conditionality into the very heart of the belief that Israel was the privileged recipient of YHWH's protection and blessing. No longer could the visible symbols of kingship and temple declare to the nations of the earth that Israel was YHWH's people. Instead only Israel's obedience to the law could ultimately ensure that this privileged status remained valid.

It is also in the lawbook of Deuteronomy that we uncover the more dangerous and destructive aspects of Israel's revised consciousness of its divinely elect status among the nations of the world with a frenetic call for the extermination of religious rivals and enemies. The disasters of 587 BCE had provided a terrible warning, so that this somber guilt-consciousness that Israel had, in the past, proved disobedient to God is now turned in vindictive fury against those peoples whose misguided religious loyalties had led Israel astray. Even defectors within Israel are threatened with relentless lack of compassion, if they step outside the circle of obedience which YHWH's law has drawn. Let the unwary offender beware, for God's choice is seen, not only as a privilege filled with unbounded promise, but also as a responsibility fraught with the direst penalties for those who placed themselves outside its boundaries.

So the Deuteronomistic theology of divine election passed a major turning-point by turning to contemplate the uncertainties of the people's future. In the eyes of these Deuteronomistic authors who narrated the history of Judah's painful misadventures among the nations, Israel had suffered a deserved fate by forfeiting its land, temple, and kingship. Yet it had not, in their eyes, forfeited its privileged status as the people of YHWH. There was still a future! God's covenant allowed room for repentance and opportunity for renewal of commitment. What had happened was that Israel now had to face a different future from that envisaged by the triumphalist pro-Davidic, pro-monarchist, circle who had inherited the mantle of Israelite ambition in Josiah's reign. The ultimate outcome of this hope for the rebirth of the nation remained clouded in uncertainty.

What was now called for was a much amended theology of community which took account of the new political situation in which Israel found itself. It had to take note of the fact that remnants of the nation were now dispersed into many lands. It had to make room for awareness that the worship of YHWH could no longer remain meaningful if it was confined to the rituals of a ruined Jerusalem. Yet it would forfeit its integrity altogether if Jerusalem lost its authority as the controlling center of faith and practice. The Deuteronomic ideals had to counter the temptations facing every former citizen of Judah who could look back on the Davidic–Zion theology as a discredited failure. Not surprisingly many such persons were ready to return to the old, but not wholly forgotten, household deities, or to the strange gods of the homeland.

There are major issues concerning the literary origin and growth of all three of the Deuteronomistic writings which have a significant bearing on their interpretation. That they represent the productions of a Deuteronomic movement, or "school," which was active over a period of approximately a century appears highly probable. This becomes most evident in the fundamental shift of perspective that they reveal, which became inevitable after the disasters of the early 6th century BCE had overtaken Judah. The necessity for accommodating this shift of outlook explains the ambivalent Deuteronomistic outlook towards the role of the Davidic dynasty and the role of the centralized Jerusalem cultus. The most striking of these unexpected shifts is to be seen in the History, which was evidently originally structured around the institution of a divine covenant between YHWH and the Davidic dynasty (2 Sam 7:1–17). Once the future of the Davidic dynasty had become clouded in doubt and uncertainty (2 Kgs 25:27–30) the question whether the kingship would be restored became problematic. The Deuteronomic "law of the king" (Deut 17:14–20) presents this fundamental institution as no more than an option for Israel. In any case the scattered Israel of the future had to learn to live under the authority of foreign rulers whose power could not be challenged.

A similar ambivalence is displayed in the presentation of the divine choice of Jerusalem as the place to which Israel's offerings were to be brought and of the threat of idolatry posed to Israel by worship at other historic sanctuaries of Israel's past. The Deuteronomic demands both elevate Jerusalem to an unparalleled eminence, and yet, in doing so, reduce its daily impact on the lives of Israel's citizens. The presence of such incongruities shows that the Deuteronomistic theology was originally built up around a pro-monarchic, pro-Davidic, view of Israel as a nation-state with its capital in Jerusalem and with a high belief in the role of this sanctuary as a guarantee of YHWH's protection. Yet, in the wake of the disasters of 587 BCE, it had proved essential to accommodate this royalist theology to the lessons and consequences of the disasters that had overtaken the nation.

In its attitude to the concepts and practices of cultic worship the Deuteronomistic legislation and History has begun to come to terms with the scattering of Israel among the nations. This was a process which, from this time onwards, was to shape the life and thought of Judaism. The Deuteronomistic theology of

Israel as a "community of God" displays its close links with the collapse of the last organized part of the nation in Judah by a new book-centered theology of Torah. Out of the ruins of the kingdom of Judah the beginnings of a more international, universally oriented, theology of a world-embracing community of God began to take shape. In this the ideology of a nation-state has been modified to take account of what had happened when the central institutions of that state had been destroyed.

More far-reaching attempts to present a "theology of exile" are made in the Deuteronomistic edition, or more accurately editions, of Jeremiah's prophecies. Here we find ample evidence of extensive Deuteronomistic editing and supplementation which take account of Jerusalem's downfall and the political hopelessness of the community that remained in Judah after 587 BCE. Here we have set out some of the basic theological foundations for Israel's future in a "theology of exile" (cf. Stulman, 1998). This theology is succinctly summarized in Jeremiah's letter of Jer 29:4–14.

Exile and Beyond

So far as the belief in a "community of God" is concerned the events of the years 598 and 587 BCE changed everything. In its broad structure and presentation the canonical form of the Old Testament is the product of this post-national period of Israel's existence. This does not mean that it does not contain valid and informative traditions which took their origin before these calamitous events had occurred. On the contrary it strongly indicates that such traditions as had survived acquired added importance precisely because of the catastrophes which had humiliated the nation. Yet all of these traditions are remembered in light of the disruption and new demands that these disasters brought. The shadow of the events of 598 and 587 BCE is cast over the entire collection of writings known as the Torah and Prophets so that the Old Testament looks back in order to look forward. It does so necessarily because such a backward look provides knowledge of the form, and more especially the religious content, of what it means to live as the people of God. In broad outline it may be claimed that the historical recollection of Israel as a once powerful national entity provides a framework for a community ideal, but the content and inner faith constituents of this ideal are presented on the recognition that Israel is a people living in "exile."

We may note three primary ways in which this modified presentation of Israel as the "community of God" is set out in the Hebrew Bible.

The Torah

The first, and most striking, way of rethinking the nature of Israel is to be found in the compilation and production of a written Torah, which, in every respect, remains the heart of the biblical canon. Most of the essential constituents of Torah, with its claims for an origin with Moses, its structure as a covenant document, and its primary function in Jewish education and worship are to be found in the Deuteronomic lawbook. Yet the final form of the Torah is only partially Deuteronomistic in its character, since this older material has been extensively modified and supplemented by the grafting in of traditions and rulings which are usually critically described as Priestly (P-Document) in their character. Even after the combining together of Deuteronomic and Priestly material a significant work of further supplementation took place in order to provide a comprehensive guidebook which every heir of Abraham could learn and use. Both those living in the land and those living among the nations (cf. Dan 9:7) were to be subject to this overarching rule of life.

The Former and Latter Prophets

The second division of the Hebrew biblical canon is of an altogether different cast from the Torah, and contains both the Former Prophets (the "Deuteronomistic History") and the Latter Prophets. We have already encountered the importance of the former work as the highly informative story of how Israel rose as a nation and how it fell through disobedience to the law of YHWH. Not surprisingly, since it focuses on Israel as a nation, its central theme is that of the land, setting out the story of how this land was won, under Joshua's leadership, and how it was lost through disobedience which the rulers of the Davidic dynasty did not prevent, and most actually fostered. For the readers of this work, many of whom were clearly now assumed to be scattered among the nations, there had taken place a "return to the beginning." For the regaining of the land Israel had now to look to a future return which God would bring about at some unspecified time. By learning the lessons of past failure the motives for repentance and future restoration were established.

The second part of the prophetic division of the canon consists of four great collections of written prophecy, which in reality contain the words, judgments and promises, of many prophets. Beginning in the 8th century BCE, when internal strife between Israel and Judah led to the increasing intervention of the Mesopotamian empires in Israel's politics, the story of Israel's downfall is unfolded. The reasons for this are shown to have arisen, not because militarily Israel was too weak to fend off these superpowers, but because the nation had a heart for disobedience and disloyalty. So accusations are leveled against Israel and Judah, and especially their respective rulers. Hope for the future is focused on the power of God to intervene on behalf of a law-abiding community that is faithful to him. Meanwhile Israel's actual contemporary state of existence, as small scattered communities enduring a punitive period of waiting for God among the nations, is explained (Ezek 36:16–21). The nation was living in "exile," which is interpreted as an interim period in which accommodations had to be made on many fronts. Worship had to be maintained, but modified in order to take account of the circumstances in which Jews found themselves and to avoid idolatry. In politics Israel had to learn to live under the jurisdiction of foreign rulers and authorities, which at times could become threatening and oppressive. Above all, each individual had to shape his, or her, life and conduct in accordance with the spiritual and moral demands of God's covenants made with Abraham and Moses.

The Central Authority of Jerusalem

The idea of a "community of God," which is not a nation, possesses no single territory of its own, and has no single king to administer its affairs, points to a new kind of religio-political society. In the Hebrew Torah it is defined as a "community" (Heb. *ʿēdâ*), or "congregation" (KJV), which the Greek translators variously translated as "assembly" (Gr. *ekklesía* = "church," or "synagogué" (Gr. *sunagoge*). It may well be that such terminology reaches back to the very earliest stages of Israel, before the formation of the nation-state (cf. Anderson, 1970, p. 142). However, it has clearly been the desire generated by the post-587 BCE experience of Israel that has given rise to the portrayal of such assemblies of people acting under the leadership and authority of Moses. They are the pre-cursers of the post-national, Torah-centered communities of worshippers whose lack of any one single badge of national identity has been filled by a new religious identity as members of "a community of God." Clearly those later communities which followed this example could find in their obedience to the Torah which Moses had bequeathed them the sufficient grounds of assurance to fulfill this requirement. Yet, even so, these communities could not be autonomous and a more centralized authority was needed, both in the formulation of a written Torah and in establishing the main features of its interpretation. In this respect we can recognize the great importance of the restoration and rebuilding of the Jerusalem temple in the years 520–516 BCE. This provided a central point of focus and of religious authority to which even the most dispersed and impoverished of Judah's survivors could look (cf. Daniel in Dan 6:10). The role of a restored and newly glorified Jerusalem as the focal point to which the scattered remnants of the nation could eventually return was also a central feature of this new order of life for the Jewish community of God. Hope itself became a community-building virtue.

Against such a background we find that the biblical portrait of an ideal community of God is set in an uneasy tension with the experienced historical reality in which Jews found themselves living. In social and political terms problems abounded so that the realization of the idealized future in which these problems were to be overcome had to be left in the hands of God. Hope held together the stresses imposed by these tensions, making the present acceptable, even though the sometimes inordinately idealized future remained unattainable. Such hope, however, was not the clinging to an illusion, but constantly remained a practical incentive to remold the present in accordance with the future that was yet to come. By not forgetting the past Israel maintained a powerful reason for constantly adapting and reshaping a far from ideal present.

Bibliography

Albertz, Rainer, *A History of Israelite Religion in the Old Testament Period 1*, OTL (Louisville: Westminster/John Knox, 1994).

Alt, A., "The God of the Fathers," *Essays on Old Testament History and Religion*; trans. S. Rudman from German of 1930 (Oxford: B. H. Blackwell, 1966), pp. 3–77.

Anderson, G., "Israel: Amphictyony: 'AM; KAHAL; EDAH,'" in H. Frank and W. Reed, eds., *Translating and Understanding the Old Testament, Essays in Honor of H. G. May* (Nashville: Abingdon Press, 1970), 135–51.

Block, Daniel Isaac, *The Gods of the Nations. Studies in Ancient Near Eastern National Theology* (Jackson: Evangelical Theological Society, 1988).

Carr, D., "Canonization in the Context of Community," in R. Weis and D. Carr, eds., *A Gift of God in Due Season. Essays on Scripture and Community in Honor of James A. Sanders*, JSOTSup 225 (Sheffield: Sheffield Academic Press, 1996), 22–64.

Clements, R., *God and Temple: The Idea of the Divine Presence in Ancient Israel* (Oxford: B. H. Blackwell, 1965).

——, "A Light to the Nations: A Central Theme of the Book of Isaiah," in J. W. Watts, and P. R. House, eds., *Forming Prophetic Literature. Essays on Isaiah and the Twelve in Honor of J. D. W. Watts*, JSOTSup 235 (Sheffield: Sheffield Academic Press, 1996), 57–69.

——, "Zion as Symbol and Political Reality," in J. Van Ruiten, et al., eds., *Studies in the Book of Isaiah*, FS W. A. M. Beuken, BETL CXXXII (Leuven: Peeters, 1997), 3–17.

Dahl, N. A., *Das Volk Gottes. Eine Untersuchung zum Kirchenbewusstsein des Urchristentum* (Darmstadt: Wissenschaftliche Buchgesellschaft, rep. from Oslo, 1941, 1963).

Deist, Ferdinand, "The Dangers of Deuteronomy. A Page from the Reception History of the Book," in F. Garcia Martinez et al., eds., *Studies in Honour of C.J. Labuschagne on the Occasion of his 65th Birthday* (Leiden: E. J. Brill, 1994), pp. 13–29.

Eichrodt, W., *Theology of the Old Testament*, 2 vols., Eng. trans. J. A. Baker (London: SCM Press, 1967/69).

Evans, C. A., "Aspects of Exile and Restoration in the Proclamation of Jesus and the Gospels," in J. Scott, ed., *Exile: Old Testament, Jewish and Christian Conceptions*, JSJSup 56 (Leiden, New York, Köln: E. J. Brill, 1997), 299–328.

Finkelstein, I., "The Emergence of the Monarchy in Israel. The Environmental and Socio-economic Aspects," *JSOT* 44 (1989), 43–74.

Grønbaek, J. H., *Die Geschichte vom Aufstieg Davids (1 Sam. 15–2, Sam 5). Tradition und Komposition*, ATHD 10 (Kopenhagen: G. E. C. Gad, 1971).

Hanson, Jr., P., *The People Called. The Growth of Community in the Bible* (San Francisco: Harper & Row, 1987).

Kaiser, O., *Der Gott des Alten Testaments. Wesen und Wirken Theologie des AT*, vol. 2 (Göttingen: Vandenhoeck & Ruprecht, 1998).

Kraus, H.-J., *The People of God in the Old Testament*, World Christian Books 22 (London: Lutterworth Press, 1958).

Mayes, A. D. H., *The Story of Israel between Settlement and Exile: A Redactional Study of the Deuteronomistic History* (London: SCM Press, 1983).

——, *The Old Testament in Sociological Perspective* (London: Marshall Pickering, 1989).

——, "De l'idéologie deutéronomiste à la Théologie de l'Ancien Testament," in A. de Pury, et al., eds., *Israël construit son histoire. L'historiographie deutéronomiste à la lumière des recherches récentes*. Le monde de la Bible No. 34 (Geneva: Labor et Fides, 1996), 477–508.

Neusner, J., "Exile and Return as the History of Judaism," in J. Scott, ed., *Exile: Old Testament, Jewish and Christian Conceptions*, JSOTSup 56 (Leiden, New York, Köln: E. J. Brill, 1997), 7–37.

Nicholson, E., *God and His People: Covenant and Theology in the Old Testament* (Oxford: Oxford University Press, 1986).

Niditch, S., *War in the Hebrew Bible: A Study in the Ethics of Violence* (New York: Oxford University Press, 1993).

Noth, M., *Die israelitischen Personennamen im Rahmen der gemeinsemitischen Namengebung*, BWANT 3 (Stuttgart: J. C. B. Mohr, 1930).

Perlitt, L., *Bundestheologie im Alten Testament*, WMANT 36 (Neukirchen-Vluyn: Neukirchener Verlag, 1969).

Porteous, N. W., "Jerusalem–Zion: The Growth of a Symbol," in *Living the Mystery: Collected Essays* (Oxford: B. H. Blackwell, 1967).

Rogerson, J. W. and Philip Davies, *The Old Testament World* (Cambridge: Cambridge University Press, 1989).

Rost, L., *Die Vorstufen von Kirche und Synagoge im Alten Testament*, BWANT IV:24 (Stuttgart: J. C. B. Mohr, 1938).

——, *The Succession to the Throne of David*, trans. M. D. Rutter and D. M. Gunn from the original German edition of 1926 (Sheffield: Almond Press, 1982).

Sanders, J. A., *Canon and Community: A Guide to Canonical Criticism* (Philadelphia: Fortress Press, 1984).

——, "The Bible and the Believing Communities," in D. Miller, ed., *The Hermeneutical Quest. Essays in Honor of James L. Mays* (Pittsburgh: Pickwick Press, 1986), 145–57.

——, "The Exile and Canon Formation," in J. Scott, ed., *Exile: Old Testament, Jewish and Christian Conceptions*, JSTSupp 56 (Leiden, New York, Köln: E. J. Brill, 1997), 7–37.

Smith-Christopher, D., "Re-assessing the Historical and Sociological Impact of the Babylonian Exile (597/587–539 BCE)," in J., Scott, ed., *Exile: Old Testament, Jewish and Christian Conceptions*, JSJSup 56 (Leiden: New York, Köln: E. J. Brill, 1997), 7–37.

Stulman, L. *Order and Chaos: Jeremiah as Symbolic Tapestry*, The Biblical Seminar 57 (Sheffield: Sheffield Academic Press, 1998).

CHAPTER 17

Old Testament Ethics

Bruce C. Birch

Only a decade ago it was still commonplace for scholars to decry the lack of attention given to the subject of ethics in relation to the Hebrew Bible. However, by 1990 this situation of neglect had already begun to change with the publication of a number of significant studies on OT ethics, and at the writing of this essay, there has been a further decade of considerable scholarly activity exploring a variety of issues concerning ethics and the Hebrew Bible. It is the intention of this essay to draw on the fruits of this renewed interest and to describe some of the key issues, methodological approaches, and insights emerging in the area of OT ethics.

The Meaning of Old Testament Ethics

There are several different ways in which the enterprise of OT ethics can be construed. Some of the literature on ethics and the Hebrew Bible suffers from a confusion of these different enterprises.

The subject of OT ethics has sometimes been taken as the investigation of the *morality of ancient Israel*. This is, of course, a complex undertaking since the literature of the Hebrew Bible is the product of different individuals and groups within ancient Israel scattered over a period of time that is a millennium or more in duration.

It is the work of Johannes Hempel in the middle of the 20th century that is most closely associated with this approach to OT ethics (Hempel, 1964 [1938]). He properly saw the roots of morality in ancient Israel as the product of differing social contexts (peasants, pastoralists, urban dwellers) and differing historical contexts with their attendant social conditions (semi-nomadic tribal society, agrarian tribal federation, urbanizing early monarchy, defeated and scattered exiles, rebuilding provincial outpost).

Unfortunately Hempel, and others following his approach, still sought to find and describe in this complexity a coherent, developmental Israelite morality often described as "the ethics of the Old Testament." The problem, of course, is that we do not have in the Hebrew Bible the evidence for the morality of all social groupings in all periods of Israel's history. Some texts may represent popular perspectives held by most Israelites in a particular time, while other texts may represent dissident voices not at all characteristic of the general populace. Some texts originate in privileged court circles while others are associated with the life of common peasants. John Barton, an effective critic of efforts that confidently describe the morality of ancient Israel, writes:

> The Old Testament is evidence for, not coterminus with, the life and thought of ancient Israel; Old Testament writers may at times state or imply positions which were the common currency of ancient Israelites, but they may also propound novel, or controversial, or minority positions. . . . The mistake is . . . to assume that *extant* evidence is also *typical* or *complete* evidence. (Barton, 1978, pp. 46, 49)

More recently, the application of social scientific methods to the study of the Hebrew Bible has led to a renewed interest in the ethics of particular groups or particular periods in the life of ancient Israel. Such studies can only be undertaken where texts allow us an adequate view of ancient moral practices. Scholars like Douglas A. Knight (1994) and Robert R. Wilson (1988, 1994) have advocated and put forward such studies while resisting the synthesizing efforts of Hempel. Such studies are descriptive of the ethics of particular times and contexts in ancient Israel and add to the richness of our understanding of the ancient communities that produced the Hebrew Bible. They allow us to acknowledge the moral dimensions of life in ancient Israel while recognizing that we do not have access to a typical or complete history of ancient Israelite ethics.

The enterprise of OT ethics might also refer to the *ethical dimensions of the Hebrew canon.* The collection of texts that Christians call the Hebrew Bible and Jews refer to as Tanach was never intended to be a systematic treatment of Israel's history, theology, or ethics. It is a collection of witnesses to Israel's experience of relationship to God drawn from different times in Israel's life and from different social and theological perspectives. Nevertheless, these texts have gone through a complex process in ancient Israel to collect them together as somehow authoritative for the ongoing life of the community of faith. We shall say more below about the significance of this canonization process and its community context.

The study of OT ethics can be understood as the study of the ethical dimensions of this canonical collection. As such one can properly describe and reflect critically on the ethics of particular biblical books and the voices contained therein. Further, one may legitimately study the convergences and the tensions that arise from the differing ethical perspectives that are now a part of a single authoritative collection. Such study may reflect on the effect of redactors' work in placing texts and their attendant moral perspectives in various relationships to one another.

For example, what is the effect on our moral perspective as readers of the canon that we should read of God's universal intention to create all humans in the image of God before reading the story of God's particular relationship to the descendants of Abraham? Or what is the ethical effect of reading both Ezra–Nehemiah and Jonah within the same canon? The study of OT ethics focused on the Hebrew canon can find an enduring voice granted to one who might have been a despised minority in his own time (Jeremiah) while finding no voice at all for popular and respected figures (Hananiah?), whose contributions are not judged worthy for preservation by the ongoing community. Within the canon ethical perspectives may be dialogic, even adversarial (Proverbs and Job), or complemenatry and continuous (Isaiah and Deutero-Isaiah). Studies of Old Testament ethics focused on the varied ethical perspectives of the canon and not on recovery of ancient Israelite morality have become more common in the last twenty years (Birch, 1991; Barton, 1998a; Clements, 1992; Wright, 1983; and Kaiser, 1983).

Closely allied with the study of Old Testament ethics focused on the Hebrew canon is the study of the *Hebrew Bible as a moral resource for ongoing communities of faith to the present*. The canon is not just an ancient document. This collection helped define and guide the life of both ongoing Jewish and later Christian communities. The ethical perspectives of canonical texts have played an authoritative role in the ethical reflections of Jewish and Christian communities historically and are regarded as centrally important moral resources in the present. These communities regard the Hebrew canon as scripture, and OT ethics can properly focus on the ethical implications that flow from this confessional stance as well as the methodologies associated with relating scripture to contemporary ethical issues and discussions (see Birch and Rasmussen, 1989; Ogletree, 1983; Kaiser, 1983; and Janzen, 1994).

If contemporary communities use the Hebrew Bible as a moral resource to reflect on who God wishes us to be and what God wishes us to do this does not require the recovery of the actual moral practices of ancient Israel. It is, of course, enriching and illuminating to discover as much as possible about the social, historical, and theological contexts out of which ancient texts arise. But such efforts will not uncover a consistent, developed ethic of ancient Israel with which contemporary communities simply align themselves. The moral witness of a given text may be the product of an individual visionary considered a fringe element in his own time (Jeremiah) or it may be the collective witness of a particular social and theological perspective (Proverbs). In either case, the presence of such divergent texts in the canon represents the judgment of the ongoing community that the witness of these texts was worthy of ongoing theological and ethical reflection. The reconstruction of ancient Israelite morality will never be more than partially possible. But the value of the Hebrew canon for Jewish and Christian ethics is not dependent on such a reconstruction (although it can be enriched by such efforts). Rather, its value comes from a continuous discussion through generations of these texts as scripture and therefore, as a necessary foundation for ethics as understood within the Judeo-Christian tradition.

Problematic Issues

There are inherent barriers to our modern understanding of the ethical dimensions of the Hebrew Bible let alone our use of those texts as a positive ethical resource for contemporary faith communities.

One of those barriers is to be seen in the tension between the *recognition of diversity* in the ethical perspectives reflected in the texts of the Hebrew Bible and the *desire to find some degree of unity* in the moral stance of the Hebrew Bible as a whole. Biblical scholars and ethicists alike have recognized that the Hebrew canon is a complex collection of witnesses from a variety of social contexts and over a thousand years of history. No one could reasonably expect consistency and homogeneity of moral perspective in such a collection. But this can be confusing to the modern reader. How can a reader reconcile the attitude toward foreigners reflected in the quiet pride in the Moabite woman, Ruth, as an ancestor of David on the one hand, over against the exclusivist reforms of Ezra and Nehemiah that forced Israelite men to divorce and send away their foreign wives, on the other hand? Or what of the fierce, often violent, nationalism that seems approved in texts such as Joshua 1–11 contrasted with the condemnation of the self-serving nationalism of many Israelite kings by prophets such as Jeremiah? How is the reader to reconcile the moral passion and radical ethics of Moses or Amos with the reasoned, pragmatic perspective of the sages speaking in the Book of Proverbs? The Hebrew Bible is both a diverse and a complex collection of ethical witnesses and perspectives.

The *diversity of moral voices in the Hebrew Bible* can be affirmed as an enrichment of available testimony to the experience of ancient Israel in relation to its God, but there is a danger to be avoided here. The danger is that the study of OT ethics could settle for the atomistic description of differing ethical perspectives as ends in themselves. But the collection, preservation, and handing on of these texts in the Hebrew canon implies a recognition that these texts are valued as part of a moral dialogue within the ancient Israelite community in testimony to its experience with God. The God of the Hebrew Bible is one God even if experienced in a variety of ways and affirmed through a multiplicity of images. Thus, the existence of multiple witnesses to God in the same canon collected and handed on to new generations invites moral reflection on those witnesses in relation to one another. Because the texts of the Hebrew Bible relate to a common God and to the community of God's people their moral perspectives are not mutually exclusive or standing in intolerable tension. One might suggest that the Hebrew Bible reflects a diversity of ethical approaches and perspectives similar to what we experience in the church and society of our own time. Hence, the moral dialogue of diverse perspectives within the Hebrew canon might teach the contemporary faith community something about moral dialogue in the complexities of our own time.

There is also a danger in the opposite direction. The dialogue between the diverse moral voices of the Hebrew Bible can also be obscured or diminished by an artificial imposition of *patterns of unity* claimed for OT ethics. Two of the most famous are the pattern of evolutionary development from primitive to more sophisticated morality discerned by Hempel, and the relation of all Israelite ethics to a central pattern of covenant morality by Eichrodt. Both of these approaches are insightful in details but artificial in their attempt to find a unifying schema. The result is a blunting of the sharpness of moral dialogue within the canon between texts of diverse perspective. The existence of differing perspectives within the canon invites dialogue over the moral issues raised and should not be obscured by a false unity imposed on the texts of the Hebrew Bible.

A second barrier to our modern regard for the ethical dimension of the Hebrew Bible is to be found in our experience of the world of Israel as a *totally alien world reflecting social locations utterly unlike our own.* Any treatment of the Hebrew Bible with regard to ethics, especially as an ethical resource to contemporary communities, must acknowledge the impediment created by the simple fact that these texts are rooted in a cultural context utterly unlike our own, with moral presuppositions and categories that are alien and in some cases repugnant to our modern sensibilities.

A part of the issue here is the vast cultural difference between the ancient world and our own. Matters taken for granted in that ancient world, such as systems of ritual purity and defilement, are incomprehensible to us. Many biblical texts reflect a world that accepts practices that are morally unacceptable to most modern religious communities: polygamy, holy war, kingship, patriarchal structures that reduce women to property, and slavery, to name but a few.

Some of these issues can be better understood against their own social context and such studies are important for understanding Israel's own morality. However, the use of the Hebrew Bible as a canon of scripture for historic communities and a moral resource for contemporary faith communities requires an understanding that biblical texts do not simply model normative behavior intended for unquestioning emulation. The moral function of the canon is more complex than that. "Some stories reflect Israel's unexamined participation in widespread social practice (e.g., subordination of women); other stories are stories of Israel's sin (e.g., the excesses of nationalism and idolatry); still other stories reflect Israel's incomplete understanding of God's will (e.g., the request for a king) [Birch, 1991, p. 43]."

These differences between the world of the Hebrew Bible and our own are not to be simply explained away or ignored. They must be faced honestly and confronted in all their difficulty. Israel is not the perfect embodiment of the moral life that God intended, and the moral witness of the Hebrew Bible to modern communities that claim these texts as scripture must at times be reclaimed from ancient contexts that would limit or distort that witness. The Hebrew Bible does not provide a unified, systematic statement of moral principles or a detailed ethical program. It is a collection of stories and cultural artifacts (e.g., hymns, archives, lawcodes, teaching collections) preserved by ancient faith communities for the purpose of testimony to succeeding generations of the faith community. The enduring use of the canon through generations to the present

298 BRUCE C. BIRCH

is itself testimony to moral resources that have been found meaningful in spite of the alien world of Hebrew Bible times and the sometimes objectionable moral perspectives that are reflected in the texts of the Hebrew Bible. After acknowledging the impediments to our use of the Hebrew Bible in relation to ethics we can turn to a discussion of constructive elements in Old Testament ethics that seem to transcend the impediments.

The Community Foundation of Old Testament Ethics

Recent work in biblical studies and in ethics has stressed the importance of community as the context for the development of moral character and the practice of moral deliberation and action. The result has been a new interest in OT ethics as both rooted in the ancient communities that produced the texts of the Hebrew Bible and passed on by the historic and contemporary communities that appropriated those texts in various ways as a resource for their own moral life (Birch and Rasmussen; Hauerwas, 1983; Cahill; Fowl and Jones). It is the experience of community that provides the context for understanding OT ethics.

The text of the Hebrew Bible is produced in community context

It is uniformly understood in biblical studies today that every text must be, as much as possible, understood in the social context from which it originated. Ethical perspectives found in Hebrew Bible texts are not the product of individual witnesses in isolation from community. Neither do they emerge as abstract principles or timeless norms for moral behavior. "There is no private morality which is not also in its varying commitments, a public morality. The Old Testament knows nothing of the notion that morality could be a purely private and individual affair" (Clements, 1992, p. 13).

Early form criticism already recognized the importance of *Sitz im Leben* ("setting in life") as a part of textual analysis. Modern biblical research methods have made extensive employment of social scientific tools to build on this concern for the social context out of which texts arise. Use of these methods has made possible a much more complex and sophisticated portrait of the ethics of ancient Israel. In spite of the limitations described earlier much important work has been done on the phenomenological description of various aspects of ancient Israelite morality. This includes important work on the historical development of legal and ethical rules (Otto, 1994), investigation of the background for particular texts and issues (e.g., the adultery laws, McKeating, 1979), the morality of particular subgroups in Israel and their literature (e.g. Deuteronomistic ethics, Wilson, 1988), and the morality reflected in structures of political power in monarchic Israel (Knight, 1994). These and other studies are descriptive of various aspects of ancient Israelite morality and enrich our understanding of the complex interrelations of social subgroups, historical contexts, institutions of influence, and leadership roles that contributed to the collection of texts we call the Hebrew Bible.

Exploration of the community context which gave rise to various biblical texts can enrich our understanding, but cannot provide the basis for ethics in subsequent communities that look to these texts as scripture. The sum total of such studies by themselves would only constitute a growing description of Israel's ethics in various times and places.

The text of the Hebrew Bible is intended to form community

"The contribution of the Bible to ethics is at the level of community-formation, not primarily at that of rules or principles" (Cahill, 1990, p. 395). It is clear from the texts of the Hebrew Bible that the intention is not just witness to a historical time or place but formation of an ongoing community in relation to the God witnessed in the texts. Testimony from voices within the originating communities throughout Israel's history is preserved in these texts as a resource for the faith and ethics of future generations of the people of God.

Although the Hebrew Bible contains a wide variety of materials, it is the framing of those materials in a story that is most formative of community through ongoing generations. It is the work of Stanley Hauerwas (1975, 1981, 1983) that has most influenced discussions in Christian ethics on this point. Because communities are shaped by the stories they tell of themselves, he gives biblical narrative material priority as the most formative element in shaping community character and identity. The narrative character of human existence itself has been widely recognized. Individual moral character is itself shaped by moral communities and their stories (e.g., families, nations, religious groups). These stories may or may not correspond to historical events; they undergo corporate revision and development over time; they may be critically examined and more deeply understood; they may encompass and give meaning to various non-narrative data about persons, subgroups, time periods, or geographic locations.

It is the narrative traditions of the Hebrew Bible that enable the generations of Israel to remember and reinterpret their own past, and in so doing to be ethically shaped as a community of character (Hauerwas, 1983, p. 39). In turn, the early church saw the story of Jesus as a continuation of Israel's story, and the acceptance of the Hebrew Bible as Christian scripture shaped subsequent generations of the church through Israel's story remembered and reclaimed.

The Hebrew Bible, of course, contains many genres of material other than the narrative texts, but we would argue that these are all made accessible to the remembrance and reappropriation of subsequent generations by their incorporation into Israel's narrative story. Lawcodes, liturgical collections, archival material, apocalyptic visions, and prophetic utterances all become available to later generations in Israel, synagogue and church by their incorporation into Israel's basic story. That story begins with promise to the ancestors and proceeds through Egyptian bondage and Exodus deliverance, covenant at Sinai, settlement in the land, establishment and experience with kingship and kingdoms, Babylonian exile, and returned community. All elements of this story are told in terms of Israel's relationship to God acting in and through these episodes of Israel's story. Beyond Israel's own experience as a people the story is expanded to include stories of God as Creator of all things, and the brokenness of that creation which God seeks to restore. Even the sapiential literature, the most remote from Israel's narrative traditions, uses the name of Israel's God and invokes the role of God as Creator, and eventually in the Book of Sirach relates wisdom to Torah.

To argue that narrative is primary for the function of Hebrew Bible texts in shaping moral community is not an argument of historicity for these narratives nor is it an argument for priority of narrative texts in the chronological development of Hebrew Bible texts. Indeed, Otto has made an excellent case that lawcodes developed prior to the narratives of covenant at Sinai in which these lawcodes are now imbedded (Otto, 1994, pp. 162–6). Our argument is that these lawcodes would not have survived to help shape subsequent generations in Israel except that they became part of a story that carried the memory of Israel as a covenant people and the law as an expression of that identity shaping relationship between God and Israel. Covenant relationship was established (in the terms of the story) as an intentional act of divine initiative and even elements within the lawcodes themselves refer to the stories of Exodus, wilderness, and Sinai as clues to the wider meaning of the law (e.g., Exod 22:20 [Engl. 22:21]; 23:9; Lev 19:34).

Israel's story, as reflected in the narrative traditions, is not without its tensions. There is no single, consistent, official version of Israel's story by which moral community is formed. The texts and the story appropriated through the texts represent a dynamic process in which memory is both appropriated and constantly reshaped in the process. Exodus 1–15 not only tells the Exodus story but through literary analysis and traditio-historical methods can be seen as evidence of the liturgical and literary reshaping of Exodus memory. For example, Exodus 6, with its recurrent formula emphasizing the identity and person of YHWH ("I am YHWH."), is widely regarded as shaped by the importance of divine identity to a generation in Babylonian exile. That way of priestly, exilic remembering and reclaiming of the Exodus story now becomes incorporated into the story itself. The fixing of that text in canon may end that process in the text but not in the interpretation and appropriation of those texts by subsequent generations of the faith community. Old Testament ethics, thus, refers to the moral character and actions of ongoing communities shaped by critical engagement with and appropriation of Israel's story and the materials embedded and carried forward by that story (e.g., the Decalogue).

It is the canon that makes the text of the Hebrew Bible available for community formation

The existence of the canon of the Hebrew Bible is itself a witness to the redirection of those texts beyond their own originating social location. Texts are preserved and canon formed in order to form and influence the theology and ethics of future generations of the faith community that receives and values the canon as scripture. Much has been written on the canon and its role in biblical theology and ethics. Emphasis on the importance of the canonical collection we call the Hebrew Bible does not exclude attention to historical and sociological realities discernible within and behind the texts. These insights enrich our understanding of the text. But the intention of the canonical collection is not historical or sociological in character. The texts of the canon will have varying correspondence to discoverable historical realities and come from a diverse and inconsistent variety of social locations. The purpose of the canon and its arrangement is to make Israel's story as presently shaped by the canon and its collectors available for a role in shaping future generations of community. The canon as a whole is a theological construct, which does not correspond to any one time, place, or group in the experience of historical Israel.

> In the Hebrew canonical corpus, what was experienced as vertical encounter with God in crucial historical moments (e.g., deliverance and commandment) is horizontally redirected . . . through texts to subsequent generations of the community, e.g., "Remember you were a slave . . ." (Deut 15:15); "Not with our ancestors . . . but with us, who are all of us here alive today" (Deut 5:3). This horizontal redirection may create new juxtapositions (the creation stories at the start of Genesis), blur or redirect original historical contexts (Amos), or apply specific witnesses to new contexts (the redirecting of Isaiah's eighth-century witness to new contexts by the addition of chaps. 40–55 and 56–66). (Birch, 1994, p. 28)

The texts of the Hebrew Bible function in and of themselves only as a partial description of the ethics of ancient Israel. As a moral resource the Hebrew Bible gives us no timeless rules and principles or independent systems of philosophical ethics. The Hebrew Bible only functions as a moral resource to the degree that communities past and present have found their story reflected in and shaped by Israel's story. It is the passing on of the canon of the Hebrew Bible that makes the ongoing dynamics of this reappropriation of Israel's theological and ethical witness possible.

Divine Reality and the Bases of Old Testament Ethics

For the Old Testament ethics cannot be separated from theology. Israel's story per se does not shape subsequent generations of community. It is the belief that Israel's story witnesses to the reality of a God encountered by Israel who is still available in relationship to subsequent generations of faith community that is crucial (see Childs' criticism of Hauerwas on this point (1993, p. 665). Neither the text itself nor the community that produced the text nor the story of Israel told in the text would provide a sufficient basis for Old Testament ethics as a shaping influence beyond its originating context. God is the reality behind all bases of ethics in the Hebrew Bible. All moral responses are understood as responses to the reality of experience in relation to the character and activity of God. It is the ability of story, community, and text to point to God and give testimony to the reality of God at work in the world that is decisive.

The knowledge of God – divine initiative, character and conduct – is the precondition for Old Testament ethics

Although sociohistorical investigation might paint a different picture of Israel's origins, the biblical story itself understands Israel's life and identity as shaped in response to divine initiative. Israel is called into being by God. "You have seen what I did to the Egyptians, and how I bore you on eagle's wings and brought you to myself." In response to this divine saving initiative Israel now becomes God's "treasured possession out of all the peoples . . . a priestly kingdom . . . a holy nation" (Ex 19:4–6). Israel's life is not self-initiated; Israel is God's "firstborn son" and Pharaoh is commanded to "let my son go" (Ex 4:22–23). From the viewpoint of the Hebrew Bible, Israelite community is not a human achievement, and the moral character of that community is not an autonomous possession. "Rather than viewing ethics as a cultural phenomenon, the Old Testament judges human behavior consistently in relation to God and his creation. Human conduct is therefore evaluated in terms of response, and measured by its conformity to the divine will which is continually making itself known in the world" (Childs, 1993, p. 684).

The knowledge of God, who God is and what God has done, is, therefore, the precondition to Old Testament ethics. "My people are destroyed for lack of knowledge" (Hosea 4:6a). "Did not your father eat and drink and do justice and righteousness? . . . He judged the cause of the poor and needy; then it was well. Is not this to know me? says the Lord" (Jer 22:15–16). The reality of God consists not only in what God does (or commands) but in who God is experienced to be. It is the character of God that is given expression in the conduct of God. For example, the mighty act of deliverance from bondage in Egypt, narrated and celebrated in Ex 14–15, is preceded by important accounts of divine self-revelation in Ex 3–4 and 6, and the contest with Pharaoh through the plagues sent upon Egypt is described as taking place so that both Israel and Pharaoh will "know" YHWH. Exodus 6, in particular, with its constant affirmation "I am YHWH," connects the very identity and character of God with Israelite suffering in Egypt (and also exilic suffering since this chapter receives its final shape at that time). When it comes, God's deliverance is not an isolated action, but an expression of God's very identity. Such divine consistency of character becomes the hope for saving action in future generations that hear this story or read this text. Divine moral character finds expression in divine moral action. Commenting on Exodus 6, Brueggemann writes, "As much as any text in the Exodus tradition, this one invites reflection upon the character of the God of Israel . . . God's very character is to make relationships, bring emancipation, and establish covenants . . . Israel is now always Yahweh-connected, but . . . Yahweh is always Israel-connected, and will not again be peopleless . . . The God of Israel is defined by that relatedness" (1994, pp. 736–7).

Moral norms in the Hebrew Bible arise not only from discerning God's will but from imitating God's character and conduct and from acknowledging all life as a part of God's creation

Although God is at the center of all understandings of the basis of Old Testament ethics, the reality of God is experienced and given witness in a variety of modes. We wish to discuss the bases of OT ethics as imitation of God, obedience to divine will, and life lived as creatures of God's creation (perhaps a form of natural law) (see Barton, 1994, 1998a).

Imitation of God (imitatio dei).   It has been traditional in discussions of Old Testament ethics to regard obedience to the revealed divine will as the primary basis for ethics, whether in ancient Israel or in contemporary communities reading these texts as scripture. Moral norms were seen primarily as arising from commandment, law, materials intended to instruct, or prophetic moral admonition. Recent analysis of Hebrew Bible materials by ethicists have seen commandment as the primary source of moral norms in Israel and thus treated OT ethics as almost entirely deontological and as addressed almost entirely to moral conduct (e.g., Ogletree). Such views contribute to the caricature of the entire Hebrew Bible as "law" contrasted unfavorably with the New Testament as "gospel."

   Although obedience to divine will is an important element of OT ethics there has been increasing recognition that divine command has little meaning apart from the community's prior experience of divine character and conduct. Before God commands moral conduct as obedience, God has modeled the moral life in God's own identity and action. Thus, we suggest that the moral life as imitation of God deserves discussion prior to discussion of commandment and divine will.

   The importance of the imitation of God as a basis for OT ethics has received increasing attention in recent scholarship (Barton, 1978, 1994, 1998a, 1998b; Nasuti; Hanson; Kaiser; Birch 1991, 1994, 1995). God's own actions provide a model for Israel's moral behavior. Even the legal codes appeal at times to this imitation of God as justification. "[God] executes justice for the orphan and the widow and . . . loves the strangers, providing them with food and clothing. You shall also love the stranger, for you were strangers in the land of Egypt" (Deut 10:18–19). The implication is that God has committed the divine character to patterns of moral character and behavior that serve to commit the community who enters covenant partnership with God. Consider the conclusion of Micah's great covenant law-suit passage, "He has shown you, O mortal, what is good; and what does the Lord require of you but to do justice, and to love kindness, and to walk humbly with your God?" (Mic 6:8). Coming after God's prior speech detailing divine graciousness and salvation the implication is that God has demonstrated the qualities of moral behavior that God now requires of Israel.

This, of course, suggests that the moral community not only imitates God's actions but is shaped by qualities of God's character. "You shall be holy, for I the Lord your God am holy" (Lev 19:2). Qualities such as justice, righteousness, compassion, and love are not just commanded, they are characteristic of Israel's experience of God and the community is called to know and be like God in these same qualities (Lev 19:18; Deut 7:8; Jer 22:16). The development in Israel of the notion of Torah as instruction rather than law suggests that ethics is not simply obedience to an external code of behavior but an entering into a way of life that is in effect an entering into the life of God. "The purpose of the Old Testament is not primarily to give information about morality . . . but to provide materials which, when pondered and absorbed into the mind, will suggest the pattern or shape of a way of life lived in the presence of God . . . Ethics is not so much a system of obligations as a way of communion with God" (Barton, 1998a, pp. 128, 130).

Obedience to Divine Will.   Out of experiences that establish relationship in which yhwh has made the divine self known to Israel do come strong demands for obedience to the divine will. Covenant obligation for Israel is spelled out in commandments and lawcode, in priestly requirement and prophetic admonition. Obedience to divinely revealed will for Israel and subsequent faith communities is not, however, a matter of blind obedience. It is obedience rooted in trust that the God who commands is also the God who has acted in compassion and justice. It is significant that the Decalogue, the most fundamental expression of commandment to the community of God's people, opens with a reminder of prior relationship, "I am the Lord your God who brought you out of the land of Egypt, out of the house of slavery . . ." (Ex 20:2). Obedience is not to an arbitrary power but to God who has already demonstrated the divine moral character which serves as a basis for community moral identity and obedience to divine moral command. Such obedience is more than submission to the divine ought and the deontological (duty oriented) ethics that implies. Obedience in Old Testament ethics is directed to the end of life lived in the presence and purposes of God, and might be understood as teleological (purpose or end oriented) as well.

Natural Law.   Barton (1994, 1998a, 1998b) has argued convincingly that there is a third basis for ethics in the Hebrew Bible that does not depend on imitation of God or obedience to revealed divine will. It is instead based on "fitting one's life to the orders and patterns observable in the world that is God's creation" (1998a, p. 120), which is akin to natural law. This term is used with some reservations because it does not imply the highly developed philosophy of natural law that developed in western thought. It is simply to suggest that the Hebrew Bible knows of a morality that is not dependent on the experience with Israel's God or the revealed will of that God. Wisdom literature, with its well-known international character, seems to draw on a tradition of ethics that knows or acknowledges little from the specific religious experiences of Israel with YHWH. Patterns of behavior that make for a "good person" are seen, for example, in Job 31 and seem to reflect an appeal to commonly held standards of morality that do not require knowledge of Israel's God in any way. Likewise, oracles against the nations (as in Amos 1–2) suggest standards of ethics that arise out of the common experience of being human. Even those who do not "know YHWH" can be held accountable against these ethical norms.

Of course, Israel theologized even this notion of a universal, non-revealed basis for ethics by encompassing all peoples, times and places in God's creation. God is yet the source in all bases for ethics in the Hebrew Bible for God created all things. In the present arrangement of the canon we encounter God's creation of an orderly universe as the first witness of the canon (Gen 1). Further, humanity created in the image of God is thus to be "like God" in responsibility for a "good" creation. God as Creator provides the basis for all ethics, all moral frameworks, whether the specific God of Israel's story has become known or not. Thus, ethics based even in so-called natural law is ultimately understood in the Old Testament tradition as originating in the same God known in Exodus and Sinai.

Trajectories of Old Testament Ethics

This final word must acknowledge that this treatment of OT ethics is written from a Christian perspective as the very use of the term "Old Testament" implies. The Hebrew canon is a part of the Christian canon and is regarded by the Christian churches as scripture alongside the New Testament. The perspectives on ethics reflected in the Hebrew Bible do not end there. Through the intertestamental period and into the New Testament these perspectives continue, develop, and are given response in the ongoing communities of the early church. This, of course, is not the only trajectory for these perspectives because they are likewise carried forward, developed and given response in the communities of early Judaism. Both Jews and Christians have continued to regard these same texts as scripture through subsequent generations of tradition down to the present. Only the study of the ethics of ancient Israel can limit itself to the texts of the Hebrew canon itself. Any concern for ethics in those ancient Israelite witnesses that continue to speak with meaning and authority for subsequent generations must take seriously the ongoing conversations with these texts in Jewish and Christian histories of interpretation and response. It is desirable that these two trajectories of meaning for the ethics reflected in the Hebrew canon know something of each other, enter in dialogue, and strive for mutual enrichment of moral reflection on these texts. This happens now to some degree, but if the ethics of ancient Israel are to be more than a historical curiosity then the long and rich conversations of Jewish and Christian ethics with their commonly held foundations in the Hebrew canon must take place more often together.

Bibliography

Barton, John, "Understanding Old Testament Ethics," *JSOT* 9 (1978), 44–64.

——, "The Basics of Ethics in the Hebrew Bible," *Ethics and Politics in the Hebrew Bible, Semeia* 66 (1994), 11–22.

——, "Approaches to Ethics in the Old Testament," in J. Rogerson, ed., *Beginning Old Testament Study*, 2nd edn (London: SPCK/ St. Louis: Chalice Press, 1998a), 114–31.

——, *Ethics and the Old Testament* (Harrisburg: Trinity Press International), 1998b.

Birch, Bruce C., *Let Justice Roll Down: The Old Testament, Ethics, and Christian Life* (Louisville: Westminster/John Knox, 1991).

——, "Moral Agency, Community, and the Character of God in the Hebrew Bible," *Ethics and Politics in the Hebrew Bible, Semeia* 66 (1994), 23–41.

——, "Divine Character and the Formation of Moral Community in the Book of Exodus," in J. Rogerson, M. Davies, M. D. Carroll R, eds., *The Bible in Ethics*, The Second Sheffield Colloquium (Sheffield: Sheffield Academic Press, 1995).

Birch, Bruce C. and Larry L. Rasmussen, *Bible and Ethics in the Christian Life*, revised and expanded edn. (Minneapolis: Augsburg, 1989).

Bondi, Richard, "The Elements of Character," *JRE* 12 (1984), 201–18.

Brueggemann, Walter, "The Book of Exodus: Introduction, Commentary, and Reflections," in L. Keck, et al., *The New Interpreter's Bible*, vol. 1 (Nashville: Abingdon, 1994), 677–981.

Cahill, Lisa Sowle, "The New Testament and Ethics: Communities of Social Change," *Interpretation* 44 (1990), 383–95.

Childs, Brevard S., *Old Testament Theology in a Canonical Context* (Philadelphia: Fortress Press, 1985).

——, *Biblical Theology of the Old and New Testaments: Theological Reflection on the Christian Bible* (Minneapolis: Fortress Press, 1993).

Clements, Ronald E., *Loving One's Neighbor: Old Testament Ethics in Context* (London: University of London Press, 1992).

Eichrodt, Walther, "The Effect of Piety on Conduct (Old Testament Morality)," *Theology of the Old Testament*, vol. 2, OTL (Philadelphia: Westminster, 1967). German original, 5th edn., 1964.

Fowl, Stephen E. and L. Gregory Jones, *Reading in Communion: Scripture and Ethics in Christian Life* (Grand Rapids: Eerdmans, 1991).

Hanson, Paul D., *The People Called: The Growth of Community in the Bible* (San Francisco: Harper & Row, 1986).

Hauerwas, Stanley, *Character and the Christian Life* (San Antonio: Trinity University Press, 1975).

——, *A Community of Character: Toward a Constructive Christian Social Ethic* (South Bend: University of Notre Dame Press, 1981).

——, *The Peaceable Kingdom: A Primer in Christian Ethics* (South Bend: University of Notre Dame Press, 1983).

Hempel, Johannes, *Das Ethos des Alten Testaments*, BZAW 67, 2nd edn. (Berlin: Alfred Topelmann, 1964 [1938]).

Janzen, Waldemar, *Toward Old Testament Ethics* (Grand Rapids: Academic Books, Zondervan, 1994).

Kaiser, Walter C., Jr., *Toward Old Testament Ethics* (Grand Rapids: Academic Books, Zondervan, 1983).

Knight, Douglas A., "Political Rights and Powers in Monarchic Israel," *Ethics and Politics in the Hebrew Bible, Semeia* 66 (1994), 93–118.

McKeating, Henry, "Sanctions Against Adultery in Ancient Israelite Society, with Some Reflections on Methodology in the Study of Old Testament Ethics," *JSOT* 11 (1979), 57–72.

Nasuti, Harry P., "Identity, Identification, and Imitation: The Narrative Hermeneutics of Biblical Law," *Journal of Law and Religion* 4 (1986), 9–23.

Ogletree, Thomas W., *The Use of the Bible in Christian Ethics* (Philadelphia: Fortress, 1983).

Otto, Eckart, *Theologische Ethik des Alten Testaments* (Stuttgart, Berlin, Köln: W. Kohlhammer, 1994).

Wilson, Robert R., "Approaches to Old Testament Ethics," in G. Tucker, D. Petersen and R. Wilson, eds., *Canon, Theology, and Old Testament Interpretation: Essays in Honor of Brevard S. Childs* (Philadelphia: Fortress, 1988), 62–74.

——, "Sources and Methods in the Study of Ancient Israelite Ethics," *Ethics and Politics in the Hebrew Bible, Semeia* 66 (1994), 55–63.

Wright, Christopher J. H., *An Eye for an Eye: The Place of Old Testament Ethics Today* (Downers Grove: InterVarsity Press, 1983).

PART VI
The Torah

CHAPTER 18

Creation and Redemption in the Torah

Rolf Rendtorff

The first five books of the Bible, the "Torah" or the "Pentateuch," could be understood as the foundation document of Israel. Before the life of the people in its own land begins, which is recorded in the books beginning with Joshua (the "Former Prophets"), the basic elements of its belief and the basic norms and regulations for its life are laid down here. In the center of these foundational texts stands the dramatic record of the giving of the Torah on Mount Sinai (Ex 19–Lev 27) from where the whole collection of these five books received its name.

But Israel's story does not begin with the reception of the Torah. In the text of the Pentateuch there are several sections recording very important events before Israel's arriving at Mount Sinai. Stepping backward from the Sinai events we enter the dramatic story of Israel's redemption from slavery in Egypt (Ex 1–15), usually called the "exodus" (which is now also the name of the second book of the Torah). This is the first event that happens to Israel as a people or nation, and therefore it is also of fundamental importance for Israel's self-consciousness. The next step backwards brings us to the pre-history of the people of Israel in the life of its ancestors, the patriarchs Abraham, Isaac and Jacob. These traditions build the bridge to the exodus events because it was the sons of Jacob from whom the people emerged.

But from where did the patriarchs come? In a geographical sense the answer could be: from Ur of the Chaldeans (Gen 11:31, cf. 15:7). But this answer is not really important for the reader of the Torah. The main answer is: God called Abraham (Gen 12:1–3). This is the moment where Israel's history actually begins, when God the first time spoke to the first of Israel's ancestors. But even this event did not happen without a prehistory recorded in the Torah. The calling of Abraham was a divine act of electing one specific person out of the whole worldwide humankind. According to the biblical texts the human beings had already a long and dramatic history behind them which is recorded in the first eleven chapters of the Book of Genesis (which means "origin"), the so-called primeval history. At the beginning of all that there is the first sentence of the Bible: "In the beginning God created heaven and earth."

Where shall we now begin to explain the history of Israel as told in the Bible? There has been a very interesting proposal by Gerhard von Rad. He realized that there are a number of texts in the Hebrew Bible formulated in a credo-like manner (Deut 26:5b–9; 6:20–24; Josh 24:2b–13; etc.). Their central point is the confession: "The LORD brought us out of Egypt." Von Rad developed the thesis that this kind of a "historical creed" was the nucleus of Israel's understanding of its own history. In this view Israel's history actually began in Egypt. Accordingly von Rad saw the story of exodus and *Landnahme* as the basic elements of the "Hexateuch," i.e. the first six books of the Bible including the Book of Joshua with its records of the settlement of the Israelites in Canaan. Later the story had been developed stepwise by (a) incorporation of the Sinai tradition that did not appear in the formulations of the credo, (b) expansion of the patriarchal tradition that only appeared rudimentarily in some of the credo formulations (e.g., Deut 26:5: "A wandering Aramean was my ancestor"), and (c) putting the primeval history in front of the whole.[1] In the present context it is not my point to ask whether the text of the Pentateuch really developed that way. But von Rad showed two things very clearly: On the one hand the basic thematic difference between the main sections of the pentateuchal traditions, and on the other hand their close interrelation with each other in the given context.

When von Rad later published his *Old Testament Theology*[2] one might have expected that he would structure it according to his credo concept beginning with the exodus. Surprisingly this was not the case: The Old Testament Theology begins with creation. What was the reason for this apparent change of the concept? It was von Rad's conviction that the theological interpreter of the Old Testament should not follow any historical or traditio-historical scholarly insights but should let himself or herself be guided by the order of events as Israel's faith did see it.

The Biblical Concept of Creation

Let us follow this advice and begin with some reflections on the biblical concept of creation. First of all, we should take the fact very seriously that creation is the first topic the authors of the Hebrew Bible wanted to present to the reader. There are good reasons to assume that creation was not the most ancient element in the development of Israel's faith. But reading the Bible does not mean to reconstruct the history of its individual traditions but to listen carefully to the message of its final authors or editors. Speaking about God does first of all mean to speak about the *one* and only God who is the creator of everything that exists. Whatever else can be said and has to be said about this God, it has to be viewed under this basic precondition.

The first word of the Torah is "In the beginning" – in Hebrew just one word, *běrēsît*. It is a beginning in an absolute sense. As the psalmist says: "Before the mountains were brought forth, or ever you had formed the earth and the world, from everlasting to everlasting you are God" (Ps 90:2). Before the "beginning" there was nothing but God. The second word in Genesis is also of particular relevance: "To create" (*bārāʾ*) is one of the very few verbs in the Hebrew Bible that is only used with God as subject. Nothing happens at this beginning except God's creative actions.

But the next verse seems to contradict the absoluteness of this beginning: The earth did already exist. Yet it was still *tōhû wābōhû* "formless and void," a chaos dominated by waters and darkness. This shows that the author of the creation story in Genesis was not the first one to think and to speak about the beginning of the world. There existed many traditions in other countries and cultures of the ancient world about the origins of the world, some of whom were obviously known in Israel. In particular the Babylonian tradition tells us about an original chaos that had to be beaten by a creator god in order to establish the habitable world. The Hebrew word for the chaotic waters, *těhôm*, echoes the name of *Tiamat*, the chaotic monster in the Babylonian mythology.

Yet the relationship between these two traditions shows at the same time their fundamental difference. The Babylonian creator god, Marduk, had to go through a hard and dangerous fight against the chaotic monster. But the god of Genesis does not fight. He just speaks. It is one of the basic wordings in the biblical creation story: God spoke – and it happened. To quote again a psalmist: "For he spoke, and it came to be; he commanded, and it stood firm" (Ps 33:9). Yet the Hebrew Bible contains also certain echoes of the mythological tradition of a primeval fight of the creator god against chaotic powers. For example, in the Book of Isaiah: "Awake, awake, put on strength, O arm of the LORD! Awake as in days of old, the generations of long ago! Was it not you who cut Rahab in pieces, who pierced the dragon?" (Isa 51:9). Similar reminiscences are to be found in Ps 74:13–17; 89:9–10; Job 26:12–13f.

It might have been a long way of religious experience and reflection in Israel to transform the idea of a deity fighting against chaotic powers into the image of the sovereign God whose only "weapon" is his word. But we can observe analogous developments in other fields of biblical faith. Many elements of divergent cultural and religious backgrounds have been brought together, and finally all of them have been incorporated into a wide and complex image of the one sovereign God.

That the creator God had no longer to fight does not at all mean that he became a *deus otiosus*, an inactive, idle one. On the contrary: The first chapter of the Bible shows us the well-planned and successful creative activity by which God structures and organizes the world and the creatures living therein. It is of particular importance how God incorporates the "chaotic" elements. First the darkness: With his first creative word God creates the light (Gen 1:3) and then incorporates the darkness as the counter-element into the basic structure of day and night. As a specific act of sovereignty he gives the darkness its name:

"Night" (v. 5), by which it is now an element of creation. The same with the chaotic waters: God builds something new, a dome or firmament, which he calls "Sky" and by which he separates the waters into those under the dome and those above it. By that also the waters become an element within the divinely structured creation. Even more so when God restricts the waters under the dome to certain areas and calls them "Seas" (vv. 6–10). Darkness and flood, the chaotic elements, are now integral parts of God's creation.

A similar de-mythologization happens with the celestial bodies, sun, moon, and stars. God creates them and assigns to them clear and limited functions: "to give light upon the earth, to rule over the day and over the night, and to separate the light from the darkness" (vv. 17–18). Surprisingly, the names of these celestial bodies are not mentioned. They are just called "lamps" (*mā'ōr*; cf., e.g., Ex 25:6). Of course, sun and moon played an important role in many religions in the Ancient Near East, and the Hebrew Bible is fully aware of that. Deuteronomy declares the worship of sun, moon, and stars as allotted by God to all the other peoples – but strictly forbidden for Israel (Deut 4:19–20). But time and again such an illegitimate worship did take place in Israel itself (cf. 2 Kgs 23:5,11; Jer 8:2; Ezek 8:16). Yet in the creation story these celestial elements are simply taken as creatures like any others.

Creation of Humanity

On the sixth and last day of his creative work God creates a pair of human beings, male and female (vv. 26–30). This is one of the most important passages in the Hebrew Bible, but it includes certain difficult questions. First: God decides to create *'ādām*. From the context it is obvious that it means "humankind," because it continues speaking about "their" obligations (v. 26) and that they are "male and female" (v. 27). (In chapter 2 the word *'ādām* with an article means only the first created man.) The first thing that characterizes these new creatures is the fact that they are made "in the image of God." But why does God say "in *our* image, according to *our* likeness"? Is it in order to keep a certain distance between God himself and his most highly valued creatures? Psalm 8 comes quite close to that, saying: "You made him (or: them) a little lower than God" (v. 6, Engl. v. 5). The Septuagint, the Greek version of the Old Testament, reads: "a little lower than angels." What was it that God had in mind by saying "in our image"? Many scholars have tried to solve these problems, but there is no generally accepted answer. So we have to leave this question undecided.

But what exactly does it mean that the human beings are made "in the image of God"? In the following chapters this wording is repeated twice. In Gen 5:3 it is said that Adam begot a son "in his likeness, according to his image." This is the one aspect: Adam continues God's creative work in fulfilling his task to "be fruitful and multiply" (1:28), and thereby he transmits his share in the image of God to the next generation. Later, after the great flood, God forbids the shedding of human blood, "for in his own image God made humankind" (9:6). This is the other aspect: To be created in the image of God gives such a high value to every human being that "whoever kills a human being for him it is counted as if he had damaged the image of God," as Rabbi Akiba declared.[3] To know that human beings are created in the image of God imposes on everyone a responsibility for the life and well-being of his or her fellow-beings.

Then God gives the human beings the advice: "Fill the earth and master it" (1:28). What exactly does this mean? It is often said that this actually would be an excuse for exploiting the earth, so that the Bible could be made responsible for the destruction of our world. But this is a basic misunderstanding. At this point we have to continue to read into the second chapter of Genesis. Here we have another version of the biblical creation story (beginning in v. 4). It is obvious that it is written by a different author looking from a different point of view and transmitting a different set of traditions. But it is not the task of theological interpretation to re-separate these chapters from each other but to try to understand their common message. In Genesis 2 it is told that God plants a garden and then puts the man in the garden "to till it and keep it" (v. 15). Instead of "to keep it" we could translate "to tend it" – or even better: "to guard it," which is the basic meaning of the Hebrew word šāmār. Looking back from here, "to master" in chapter 1 may mean not "to subdue" or "to rule" but rather to work carefully and to guard. It seems to me obvious that the author of the given text understood the common message of the now united creation story that way. God did not create humans to be the authoritarian rulers over the rest of the world but to be responsible stewards of God's creation.

Rest on the Seventh Day

When God in six days had finished his creative work he saw that everything was "very good" (Gen 1:31). And he rested on the seventh day and he blessed and hallowed it (2:2–3). This divine rest is reflected on when God on Mount Sinai gives the Israelites the Ten Commandments. Here it is mentioned as the reason for Israel to keep the Sabbath (Ex 20:8–11). But when the Ten Commandments are repeated in Deuteronomy still another reason is brought in: "Remember that you were a slave in the land of Egypt, and the LORD your God brought you out from there with a mighty hand and an outstretched arm; therefore the LORD your God commanded you to keep the sabbath day" (Deut 5:15). Here the Sabbath is looked at from the view of the exodus, i.e., from Israel's own history. Creation and exodus are the two basic events not only by which God demonstrated his overwhelming power but by which he also laid the foundations of the life of humankind as well as of Israel as a people. The same immediate connection between creation and exodus is shown, e.g., in Psalm 136, which begins with the praise of God's creative work (vv. 4–9) with wordings quite similar to Genesis 1, and then jumps to the dramatic events of the exodus using the same words as Deut 5: "with a mighty hand and an outstretched arm" (Ps 136:10–12).

Now we are back to exodus. These examples show us that it is not a question of "either-or" where to begin with the story Israel has transmitted to us in its Holy Scriptures. There are different aspects from which to look at this wide-spanned collection of faith traditions. Two of the most important viewpoints are, of course, creation and exodus. In some cases they are closely connected and even interlinked. The above quoted verse from Isa 51:9 about God's primeval fight against the chaos monsters continues: "Was it not you who dried up the sea, the waters of the great deep (těhôm); who made the depth of the sea a way for the redeemed to cross over?" (v. 10). In the words of the prophet the chaotic waters of the earliest times, the těhom has changed into the waters of the Sea of Reeds which God dried up before the Israelites when they fled from Egypt. The latter was another act of creation to open a way for God's elected people into a secure future. Also in the great hymn that Moses and the Israelites sang after crossing the sea (Ex 15:1–18) the waters are called těhōmôt (v. 5, 8).

Redemption from Egypt

The exodus of the Israelites from Egypt is echoed in the Pentateuch and in the Hebrew Bible as a whole in different ways. First it is recorded in one of the most extended stories in the Pentateuch (Ex 1–15). As mentioned before, only here does the history of Israel as a people begin. As the deuteronomic version of the Decalogue has it: they were slaves in Egypt (Deut 5:15). The reader of the Bible knows about the former history of Israel's patriarchs and about God's very intimate relation to them. But at the beginning of the Book of Exodus one gets the impression that the Israelites in Egypt had no memory of all that. Therefore the story has to build up a new relation between God and the people.

The mediator for this new beginning is Moses. God reveals himself to Moses, presents himself as the "God of the fathers," and identifies this description with his explicit name YHWH (Ex 3:1–15). This is one of the fascinating stories in the Bible where the reader knows more than the acting persons, and then becomes witness of their successive realization of what is going on. God tells Moses that he has seen the sufferings of the Israelites and has decided "to deliver them from the Egyptians, and to bring them up out of that land to a good and broad land, a land flowing with milk and honey" (vv. 7–10). The reader is aware of the promises God had given to the patriarchs to give them the land they already lived in as foreigners (Gen 12:7 a.o.), and also of the announcement to Abraham that there will be a long time of suffering for his descendants in a foreign country until they finally will come back to the promised land (Gen 15:13–16). But this prehistory is not mentioned when God begins to speak to Moses. Only later in a theological summary is the whole concept unfolded: God's self-revelation to the patriarchs, the establishment of a covenant between God and the people, the promise to give them the land of Canaan – and now God's decision to bring them out of the Egyptian slavery (Ex 6:2–8).

The following story one can read on different levels. One level is the reaction of the Israelites to the new epoch in their lives Moses announces to them. Moses expects that they would be skeptical (Ex 4:1), but God vests him with the ability to perform some "signs" that demonstrate his divine mission. When he finally tells the people what shall happen and performs the signs before them, "the people believed" (v. 31). In the following chapters the people do not play an independent role in the struggle between Moses and the Pharaoh. But finally when everything has happened and the people have seen God's "mighty hand" it is said again: "the people believed," this time "in the LORD and in his servant Moses" (14:31). This is very remarkable because later it is recorded again and again that the Israelites did not believe but complained against Moses and Aaron in the wilderness (Ex 15:24; 16:2; 17:3 a.o.). Yet the biblical author wants to state that at the beginning of this history the people believed.

The main struggle happens between Moses and the Pharaoh. But actually it is a struggle between Pharaoh and the God of Israel. Already in the first encounter between Moses and the Pharaoh the latter declared: "Who is YHWH? I do not know YHWH!" (5:2). What follows is YHWH's progressively heightened attempt to convince the Pharaoh that he is mightier than the Gods of Egypt. The "plagues" God brought upon the Egyptians (chs. 7–11; 12:29–30) are to be understood from that point of view. This is the first time that God demonstrates his "mighty hand" in the history of his people. Thereby he shows that he is not only the creator of the world but also the redeemer of his people Israel.

But before the beginning of the last and most terrible plague, the slaying of the firstborn, suddenly the narration slows down. Broad and detailed prescriptions for a cultic ceremony are given: the Passover (Ex 12–13). This interruption shows the interweavement of two main aspects in the biblical text: the telling of the story of Israel's redemption and the continuous remembering of this fundamental event by the people of Israel. The decisive day is mentioned twice, from these two points of view: "That very day the LORD brought the Israelites out of the land of Egypt" (12:51), and: "This day shall be a day of remembrance for you. You shall celebrate it as a festival to the LORD; throughout your generations you shall observe it as a perpetual ordinance" (12:14). What Israel shall remember is, of course, not the terrible plague God inflicted on the Egyptians, but that God "passed over the houses of the Israelites" (12:27). On that day Israel was saved in a double sense: by protection before the stroke that hit the Egyptian houses, and by the chance to get out of the slavery in the land of Egypt. The Passover shall keep alive both aspects, but with a clear accent on the more personal side: the protection of the Israelite families.

The public side, so to speak, became one of the most frequent characterizations of God throughout the whole Hebrew Bible. At one of the most central points, at the giving of his commandments to Israel, God introduces himself saying: "I am the LORD your God, who brought you out of the land of Egypt, out of the house of slavery" (Ex 20:2; Deut 5:6). Usually this event is called "exodus," but actually it was not Israel's walking out of the land of Egypt but God's bringing out his people from slavery to freedom. It is often quoted as a self-presentation of God, as in the Decalogue: "I brought you/them out of Egypt." Already before it happened God had ordered Moses to say to the Israelites: "You shall know that I am the LORD your God, who brought you out from under the burdens of the Egyptians" (Ex 6:7). But the redemption from the Egyptian slavery is not an end in itself. It establishes God's specific relation to his people: "I am the LORD who brought you up from the land of Egypt, to be your God" (Lev 11:45). One of the goals of this divine action is expressed like this: "And they shall know that I am the LORD their God, who brought them out of the land of Egypt that I might dwell among them" (Ex 29:46). From now on God will be the God of Israel and will dwell among them. The prophet Hosea expresses it very briefly: "I am the LORD your God from the land of Egypt" (or: "ever since the land of Egypt," Hos 12:10 [Engl. v. 9]; 13:4).[4]

Creation and Redemption in the Hebrew Bible

The redemption from the slavery in Egypt is, in a sense, the foundation event of Israel's history as a people. But redemption is for Israel a topic not only of the past but also of the present and of the future. Of course, there have been certain periods when Israel lived in its country in more or less peaceful and quiet circumstances. But again and again the people were disturbed by all kinds of trouble from external powers which often included the danger of being expelled or exiled from the land. Therefore the situation of living under bad circumstances in a foreign country and longing for redemption and return was always a possibility to be imagined.

It is important to see that already in the books of the Torah those imaginations are visible. At the end of the giving of the commandments including all the cultic regulations there is a kind of summary (Lev 26). It is a long divine speech looking ahead from the situation at Mount Sinai to Israel's future life in its country. The leading point of view is Israel's keeping and observing of God's statutes and commandments (v. 3). First there is a depiction of the good life Israel will have in its country if they follow God's commandments. At the end of this section there is one of the typical reminders of God's bringing out Israel from the Egyptian slavery (v. 13). This first section began with the word "if" (v. 3), but then follows the next one, beginning by "if not": "But if you will not obey me, and do not observe all the commandments" (v. 14). This much longer section includes a sometimes terrible description of all kinds of inner and outer troubles Israel will suffer as a consequence of its disobedience towards the divine commandments. The peak of all that will be the people being scattered among the nations and the land lying desolate (v. 33). "But if they confess their iniquity and the iniquity of their ancestors" (v. 40), "I will remember in their favor the covenant with their ancestors whom I brought out of the land of Egypt in the sight of the nations, to be their God: I am the LORD" (v. 45). Here the memory of the redemption at the beginning of Israel's history is at the same time a consolation for the despairing people, giving hope for a new redemption out of the present misery.

This is even more explicit in a similar summary at the end of Deuteronomy. In Deut 28 we find a description of Israel's fate depending on its obedience or disobedience toward God's commandments, quite similar to Lev 26. But then in Deut 30 it is clearly said that if Israel will return to the LORD (*šûb*), he will gather them and bring them back "into the land that your ancestors possessed, and you will possess it" (v. 1–5). Here at the end of the Torah a new redemption is envisaged in a foresight to coming epochs of Israel's history.

Of course, these words were written at a time when Israel had already had such experiences in one way or the other. They are echoing the words of some of the prophets who are explicitly dealing with Israel's fate in exile and with the hope of return. It would go beyond the scope of this essay to deal with those utterances of prophets in detail; but I want to give some examples. The first will link the two topics of this essay, creation and redemption, in a specific way. Above I have quoted Isa 51:9–11 twice; now it has to be quoted a third time. The prophet speaks about God's fight with the chaos monsters, and then about the exodus, thereby changing the chaotic waters into the Sea of Reeds. But while speaking about the exodus, the "redeemed" from Egypt are turning into the "ransomed" that return from the exile and come to Zion with singing (v. 11). Creation, exodus from Egypt, and return from the exile are here seen together as the great deeds of the mighty arm of the LORD. Another aspect is the use of the term *gālâ* "to redeem." In Ex 6:6 and also in the hymn Ex 15:13 it is used for God's redeeming Israel from the Egyptian slavery, while in Isa 40–55 (the so-called "Deutero-Isaiah") it frequently refers to God's present actions during the times of the Babylonian exile and even for his future actions; here God is often called *gō'ēl* "redeemer." In 44:24–27 God calls himself "redeemer," speaking about his work as creator, then about his superiority over the different kinds of wise men, while the words of his prophets will become true: Jerusalem will be inhabited again. The creator is the redeemer who is going to bring his people back to Jerusalem.

Jeremiah speaks about the exodus from Egypt several times. In our context the prayer in Jer 32:17–25 would be of particular interest. It begins with creation (v. 17), and continues with the exodus from Egypt and the giving of the land (vv. 20–22), up to the present situation with the Chaldeans laying siege to Jerusalem (v. 24). But then the following divine word goes the next step, announcing that God will gather the people from the exile and bring them back to Jerusalem (vv. 36–37). Here we have again the connection of these three important deeds of God: creation, exodus and return. In another place Jeremiah says that one day it shall no longer be spoken about the LORD "who brought the people of Israel up out of the land of Egypt," but "out of the lands where he had driven them. For I will bring them back to their own land that I gave to their ancestors" (16:14–15 = 23:5–6). It seems as if here the redemption from exile is taken as more important than the exodus from Egypt.

This essay has tried to explain briefly two of the most important themes of the Torah, the first five books of the Bible, that are at the same time among the most important themes of the Bible as a whole. It is obvious that the redemption from the slavery in the land of Egypt stood in the center of Israel's consciousness as a kind of foundation event of its identity as a people. But it is also clearly visible that the authors of the book of Torah had very good reasons to place the message of God's creation of the world and of humankind first in the whole collection of Israel's Holy Scriptures. Everything that later had to be said about God and his part in the history of his people Israel had its basis in the belief that the God who redeemed Israel from the Egyptian slavery was the *one* and only God who created the world and who was mightier than any other power in the world. And therefore the remembrance of the redemption from Egypt was not only a subject of the past, but it was also the basis of hope for a future redemption from other countries where members of the people of Israel lived scattered in the diaspora. The Bible tells about some return. But up to this day, every year members of the Jewish people all over the world, when celebrating the Passover, pray: "This year here, next year in the land of Israel."

Notes

1   G. von Rad, *The Problem of the Hexateuch and Other Essays*, trans. E. W. Trueman (New York: McGraw-Hill, 1966), 1–78.
2   G. von Rad, *Old Testament Theology*, 2 vols. (Philadelphia: Westminster, 1962 [1965]).
3   Midrash Bereshit Rabba, 34, 14.
4   See R. Rendtorff, "Die Herausführungsformel in ihrem literarischen und theologischen Kontext," in M. Vervenne and J. Lust, eds., *Deuteronomy and Deuteronomic Literature*. BETHL 133 (Louvain: Louvain University Press, 1997), 501–27.

Bibliography

Rad, G. von, *The Problem of the Hexateuch and Other Essays* (Edinburgh: Oliver and Boyd, 1966).
——, *Old Testament Theology*, 2 vols. (New York: Harper and Row, 1965 [1962]).
Rendtorff, R., "Die Herausführungsformel in ihrem literarischen und theologischen Kontext," in M. Vervenne and J. Lust, eds., *Deuteronomy and Deuteronomic Literature*, BEThL 133 (Louvain: Louvain University Press, 1997), 501–27.

Further Reading

Anderson, B., ed., *Creation in the Old Testament* (Philadelphia: Fortress Press, 1984).
Levenson, J., *Creation and the Persistence of Evil: The Jewish Drama of Divine Omnipotence* (Princeton: Princeton University Press, 1997).
Rendtorff, R., *Canon and Theology*, OBT (Minneapolis: Fortress Press, 1993).

CHAPTER 19

Law and Narrative in the Pentateuch

Calum Carmichael

Until recently scholars examined the legal material in the Pentateuch separate from the narrative histories in which it is embedded. A longstanding consensus was that even though the narratives read as an integrated whole a critical eye could detect originally separate sources behind them. The laws, however, presented no such blend (Kaufmann, 1960, p. 166). That view has undergone a radical change and much recent research focuses especially on how each genre might relate to the other.

The change is a timely one. In a multicultural society different groups possess their own communal narratives that incorporate myths, histories, stories, textual traditions, and bodies of law special to each. Legal scholars, particularly in the United States, claim that these various narratives should be taken into account when deciding legal issues, especially constitutional ones. A group's commitment to its story generates a set of moral ideals and its distinctive voice should be heard, for example, in the Supreme Court, which itself is an institution that possesses its own special narrative history and ideals. An inspiration for this contemporary view of law tied to narrative is the enduring influence of the Bible. It presents a body of law inseparably attached to a narrative history that has a profound impact on some of these groups – African American, Amish, Jewish, and Southern Baptist, for instance (Cover, 1983, pp. 4–68).

The Connection between Law and Narrative:
Initial Perceptions

A new way of considering how law and story came together in the Pentateuch arose from the claim that the world of international politics of the Ancient Near East of the second and first millennium BCE gave rise to the biblical notion of covenant. Hittite and Assyrian treaties between a stronger power and a weaker one in need of its protection or following the weaker power's defeat in war, spell out the obligations that each has to the other. Among other matters, the text of an agreement between the two parties recounts the history of events pertinent to the agreement, what obligations follow, and what desirable consequences would come from observing them, or undesirable ones from not observing them.

Biblical scholars saw in these suzerainty treaties, and in comparable treaties concerning royal grants of land to a party in return for its loyalty, parallels to how God's relationship to Israel seemed to play out. The narrative portions of the Pentateuch that are so taken up with the history of God's deeds in the international arena on behalf of Israel appeared to parallel the secular sovereign's presentation of his benevolent actions on behalf of his vassal. The Pentateuchal lawcodes, in turn, seemed to be the equivalent of the duties that the suzerain imposes on the vassal. To be sure, in light of the supposed parallel, because God does not defeat the Israelites in battle but is their sovereign who defeats other groups, the latter should really constitute the vassals.

While insightful, the parallels between the Near Eastern types of document and the biblical material that meshes law and narrative have proved elusive. So much so that Ernest Nicholson (1986, p. 81) concluded: "the attempt to relate the Old Testament covenant to suzerainty treaties may be said to represent a dead-end in the social/functional approach." One problem is that the term "covenant" in English does not satisfactorily convey the ancient sense of an agreement or pact. Nor does the term lend itself to such a ready comparison with a suzerainty treaty because in the Bible there are so many different types of covenants. There are covenants between equals, between a ruler and his subject, between gods and men, and between God and men. A covenant may bind both parties, or it may bind one only (God in Gen 9:8, the people in 2 Kgs 23:3). A suzerainty treaty, by contrast, is between a powerful party and a less powerful one, and there are mutual obligations. Another problem is the extent of the link. Language about God, reflecting the cultural settings in which it is coined, always draws on the world of human experience and ways of communicating. One should not go so far, however, as to claim that biblical covenants are direct transfers from the Near Eastern world of international treaty-making. On any inspection, the contents of the Near Eastern treaties do not illumine the rich, idiosyncratic features of the biblical material. The merging of narrative and law in the Bible is not a replica of the linkage of historical prologue and stipulations of the suzerainty treaties or the royal grants of land. We cannot compare the diverse situations in the Bible that use the language of covenant with the quite specific Near Eastern ones. Lacking in addition is any illumination of the substance of the biblical laws and how each may relate to the contents of the biblical narratives.

A seminal work in looking at biblical law and narrative together is David Daube's *Studies in Biblical Law* (1947). Daube examined the narratives in the Pentateuch for insights into legal subtleties in them. For example, the story of how Jacob cheats his brother out of his birthright shows how sophisticated the ancient writers and readers were. Alert to the clash between the letter of the law and its spirit, they saw how by keeping the law to the letter Jacob could cleverly proceed to break it.

Daube further showed how the story of the exodus could not be properly understood without appreciation of its legal underpinnings. Whoever wrote about the deliverance of the Israelites from enslavement in Egypt did so from the perspective of ancient laws pertaining to the release of slaves. In biblical antiquity a relative was duty bound to act on behalf of his enslaved kin and, should they be enslaved abroad, to send an emissary to invoke social rules considered to be of universal application. Thus in the exodus story God is father to his firstborn son Israel and he sends Moses to Egypt to appeal to the pharaoh to act in the spirit of such rules. An independence movement of enormous significance in later western history has to be understood in light of these rules. Down through the centuries the exodus of the children of Israel from Egypt became the dominant model for groups of all kinds seeking deliverance from oppression. Daube postulated a development in three stages. There were social laws similar to but existing before those found in the Pentateuch. The earlier laws, although not available in written form, influenced the way in which the exodus was understood and described. The story exerted, in turn, its influence on the social laws about the institution of slavery, the result being the rules about slavery in the Pentateuch.

Daube's insight concerning the intertwining of law and narrative was a major step forward in perceiving that there was indeed a very interesting relationship between one genre and the other. One consequence is that an increasing number of scholars pay close attention to the following questions. Why does a body of rules appear at a particular point in the overall narration of Pentateuchal events (Chirichigno, 1987, pp. 457–79)? From a perspective inspired by the contemporary study of law and economics, do the narratives about Jacob's dealings with Esau themselves constitute examples of contracts that enjoyed a degree of legal force despite the manifest cheating in the transactions (Miller, 1993, pp. 15–45)? If the ancient art of rhetoric inserted lists of things into narrative structures to highlight their significance, do the individual rules in the Pentateuch derive their persuasive force from the encompassing story (Watts, 1999, pp. 37–9)?

Fundamental Connection between Law and Narrative

The relationship between laws in the Pentateuch and the accompanying stories is in fact a quite fundamental and fascinating one, yielding insights well beyond the confines of biblical scholarship. Its obviousness, once seen, immediately indicates its importance, because what emerges is a remarkable picture of laws inextricably linked up with issues that appear in the narratives. A casual reader of the Bible can see that there is a continuous story line from the opening of the Book of Genesis through, for example, to the death of Moses at the point in time when the Israelites are about to enter the land of Canaan. The reader can also readily observe that bodies of rules now and again interrupt this story line. It will be far from clear, however, why such legal material should find a place in an ongoing narrative and, even more so, why it contains certain rules and not others.

The clue comes from noting the character of the narratives themselves. Their aim is to recount origins: for example, the origin of the structure of the universe, of distinctions between humankind, the gods, and animals, and of language. Histories of the first families ever of the Israelites follow (Abraham's, Isaac's, Jacob's), accounts of the beginnings of the nation Israel (the coming together of Jacob, Joseph, and his brothers in Egypt), and explanations of how the nation acquired institutions (the Passover ceremony), a judicature (from Moses' father-in-law Jethro), and fundamental norms (the Decalogue). As we follow the format-ive experiences that created the identity of the Israelites, we find that the ancient writers were struck by the fact that what happens in one generation tends to repeat itself in another. If one family has a problem with its firstborn son (Abraham's Ishmael), the next family does also (Isaac's Esau, and then Jacob's Reuben). If a member of one generation experiences oppression in foreign parts (Jacob under Laban), so does a member of the next (Joseph as a slave in Egypt), and members of the next again (each Israelite under the pharaoh).

The pattern of problems repeating themselves down through the generations is precisely what the laws picked up on. In the persons of God (the Decalogue) and Moses (laws in Exodus 21–23, Deuteronomy 12–26, Leviticus), they looked back to these very problems in the history and prehistory of the nation. They particularly focused on the first time that a problem arises but also concerned themselves with the recurrence of it in succeeding generations. Each doing the same thing in their own ways, lawgivers and narrators complement each other in producing an edifice that conveys the nation's history and identity.

To be sure, later recipients of the laws are not told in so many words about just how integrated is the structure of their foundational document. Rather they are to appreciate how one part relates to another by immersing themselves in the traditions recounted in it. By doing so, they come to see that Moses deserved his reputation as their great national lawgiver because his laws express from the inside the spirit of the stories, especially the voice of the deity as it communicates itself in the various narratives. Writing about great teachers of the past, the Greek philosopher Heraclitus claimed that they "neither told, nor concealed, but indicated" (Plutarch, 21.404 Df.). Such was, it would appear, the intended way in which readers of the laws were to be initiated into their significance.

Actually, the narratives themselves bring out this quality of indirect com-munication. "It is half the art of storytelling to keep a story free from explana-tion as one reproduces it" (Benjamin, 1968, p. 89). It is for the reader to read between the lines that Jacob receives retribution after he cheats Esau out of his birthright when, in effect, the younger son becomes the elder one. In time, Laban cheats Jacob, when the latter is about to acquire a wife, and substitutes in the wedding tent his older daughter Leah, whom Jacob does not want, for the younger one Rachel, whom he does want – the elder becomes the younger to Jacob's discomfort. Much else the reader can and is intended to pick up without being openly told to do so. Jacob finds that as a father he too faces a problem with his firstborn son. Reuben is Jacob's firstborn, produced from a somewhat irregular union with Leah. Reuben later causes his father to take away his birthright when he has an irregular union with one of his father's wives. In such indirect ways through a series of interrelated stories the narrator explores aspects of justice in the various situations described. The reader has indications of heaven's inscrutable justice at work but is not told directly that such is the interpretation to be placed on events.

The laws, in turn, explored issues that arise in the narratives; but there is no direct communication that the narratives are their focus – with the exception of events that occur during Moses' lifetime (for example, Miriam's leprosy, in the rule on the topic in Deut 24:8, 9). Moses speaks out of his own experience; such is the impression deliberately conveyed. His laws are authoritative because they come from the formative period of the nation's history. Their aptness derives from his intimate knowledge not just of the events and developments that led to the nation's birth after the exodus from Egypt, but also of those in the period of time leading up to it (and those long after he died; for example, Solomon's excesses, in the rule about kingship in Deut 17:14–20). In regard to the patriarchal and pre-patriarchal age, the laws' recipients learn about problems then by immersing themselves in the pertinent narratives. Having done so, they perceive that Moses recorded his judgments on these problems too. One result is, presumably, that their respect for Moses deepens.

The problem during the lifetime of the father of the nation, Jacob/Israel, as to who should bear the right of the firstborn son illustrates how and why a law links up with a story. His son Reuben deserves to lose his right of primogeniture seemingly because, in his father's own words, he "defiled my bed" (Gen 49:4). A son is the "firstfruits" of a father's virility and for him to misuse it by lying with a wife of his father (Gen 35:22) is cause enough to deny him the honor of being the one who primarily perpetuates the family line. But Jacob does not then confer the right upon the next son in line, upon Simeon or Levi. Instead he confers it upon the late born Joseph. This is unjust and Moses perceived the problem. Jacob chooses to give his son by his loved wife Rachel the right of primogeniture and ignores the more rightful claim of a son by the hated wife Leah.

One of the laws Moses laid down concerns the narrow circumstances where a man has two wives, one hated and the other loved, the firstborn son is by the hated wife, and the father inclines to bestow on a son by the loved wife the right of primogeniture (Deut 21:15–17). The judgment is that if a firstborn son comes from the hated wife he must be given the right attaching to a firstborn. The issue that the law drew from the traditions is not an obvious one because Reuben's reprehensible conduct obscures it. The problem the lawgiver nonetheless noticed is that even if Reuben had not offended, his father might still have awarded the right in question to Joseph because Jacob favors Joseph's mother Rachel. It is this kind of "seeing" that the laws invite so that the wisdom of Moses comes into view, and the reader also acquires it (Deut 4:6, 34:9).

The Decalogue

The Decalogue and the stories that determine the sequence and substance of its contents, plus the narrative in which it is embedded, serve to indicate just how profound is the integration of law and narrative in the Bible. Consider the rule against murder in the Decalogue. The lawgiver seeks out the first occurrence ever of such a crime and he finds it in the myth about the history of the first human family. Cain kills his brother Abel. The lawgiver and the narrator share in common a desire to ponder such an incident and each does so in terms of the deity's response to murder. Cain, a tiller of the soil, is denied the capacity to produce crops, because his brother's blood cries out from the ground. As a consequence he becomes a fugitive and a wanderer on the earth. Cain protests that in such an unprotected state he faces the prospect of being murdered himself. The deity regards the punishment of banishment from the soil as sufficient, and he puts a protective mark on Cain to prevent his murder. The presentation of the prohibition against murder in the Decalogue has this sophisticated review of Cain's deed in the background.

One feature of the story's attitude to murder is that the punishment should match the misdeed. In this regard, because Cain has defiled the very earth by spilling Abel's blood upon it, Cain's punishment is to be denied access to that earth for the purpose of growing food. At all times and places, in both secular or religious societies, there exists a notion that, when a fearful crime has been committed, the punishment should reflect some aspect of it. Again, when the deity moves to protect Cain from a violent end his use of a protective mark reflects an ancient practice that corresponds to our notion of the due process of law that guarantees that justice is carried out in an orderly proceeding. Someone who is implicated in a misdeed seeks shelter at a sanctuary because there may be factors to be taken into account that merit such protection. In Cain's situation there is a judgment that his banishment from the soil is sufficient punishment. There is also the judgment that a stranger, however suspicious his presence in a place, deserves protection from gratuitous attack. In the absence of institutionalized law enforcement agencies the role of a sanctuary, depending as it does on reverence deriving from a consciousness of higher powers, serves an important judicial function.

The lawgiver's method of exploring an epic with a view to setting down norms explains the puzzling sequence in the Decalogue: the honor of parents, murder, and adultery. The puzzle exercised writers as far back as the translators of the Septuagint, Philo, the authors of the New Testament and the scribe of the Nash Papyrus, all of whom chose to dispose of it by rearranging the rules so that the rule about adultery followed the one about parents. A better solution might be to note that each of the commandments reaches into the life of Cain. With his brother Abel Cain is the product of sexual union between his parents, Adam and Eve. The author of the Genesis myth links to the deity's prior creation of all life these unions for the purpose of producing children. Human procreation perpetuates the initial process of divine creation. To destroy a life is a deed that dishonors parents in a fundamental way. It is Cain's action against his parents' child that prompts the lawgiver to promote the positive injunction to honor them. One honors parents precisely because, in line with the original creation, they gave one life.

Evidence that this line of reasoning underlies the formulation of the injunction in the Decalogue comes from noting the curious motivation that the lawgiver attached to it. Honoring parents is, the addressed son in the Decalogue is told, to continue long "upon the ground [in the original Hebrew, not land]" that God has given to him. In focus is the situation that Cain finds himself in: he could not continue tilling the ground because he destroyed what his parents had produced. If he had held his parents in honor he would have held back from murdering his brother. The unexpected juxtaposition of a rule about murder with one about honoring parents is rendered more explicable by a reflection on Cain's biography. The issue of honoring parents is but implicit in Genesis 4, just as the issue of a firstborn losing his inheritance right because of a father's dis-crimination against an unloved wife is not explicitly brought out in Genesis 48. It is for the reader to see what Moses or the deity responds to in his judgment.

The prohibition against adultery likewise comes from Cain's biography and, again, the key is the shared attempt by the lawgiver and the storyteller to specu-late about human origins. Following his offense and its consequences, Cain imitates his father and takes a wife. That the narration is mythical in nature is shown by the unconcern of the author to take account of the impossibility of the situation: no wife can possibly be available to Cain. The author, however, is not dwelling on historical realities but is intent on probing origins. When he states in language identical to that used for Cain's parents before him, "Cain knew his wife, and she conceived and bore Enoch" (Gen 4:17, cp. 4:1), the author links Cain's life-cycle to Adam's – one generation to the previous one. In this way, the way of mythical storytelling, focus falls not on a real-life human relationship from a particular time and place, but on maleness and femaleness and the origin of the institution of marriage.

To express the mystery of sexual union the Genesis author traces it to Eve's origination from Adam's body. When a man and a woman unite they recreate the original union of male and female at Eve's creation. That is why the text states that "a man leaves his father and mother and cleaves to his wife and they become one flesh" (Gen 2:24). The first man ever to do so is not Adam but his son Cain. Reflecting on the origin of marriage, the lawgiver noted that the act of cleaving to a wife and becoming one flesh with her carries with it, as the Talmudic sages saw (*Babylonian Sanhedrin* 58a), the implicit norm against interference with such a union, the prohibition against adultery. The issue is not an obvious one in the narrative, but is nonetheless implicit in its description of marital union.

There are two parts of the Decalogue. From a myth about the beginnings of life the compiler of the Decalogue derived the second part of it (the second tablet): from the command to honor parents to the prohibition against coveting. The first part (the first tablet), from the affirmation about God's bringing the Israelites out of enslavement in Egypt to the command to observe a Sabbath day in his honor, he derived from a legend in Exodus 32 (Carmichael, 1996, pp. 86–92). It is the incident of the golden calf when, for the first time in the history of the nation, its members commit idolatry. The compiler of the Decalogue viewed the fracturing of the relationship between the Israelites and their god as a fundamental matter, and the event attracted his attention precisely because, like the story of Adam, Eve and Cain and Abel, it is about beginnings – in this instance, national beginnings. The mythical character of the Decalogue is highlighted by the fact that God knows, in advance, the detailed wrongdoing that will occur in the incident of the golden calf (taking place, as it does, some days after the giving of the Decalogue). It is also revealed by the fact that in the incident itself, the people, quite astonishingly, make a graven image, use God's name for it, and set aside a special day to honor this man-made god, thereby breaking the very prohibitions that had supposedly just been imparted to them in such awesome circumstances. The convention of the prophets, including God and Moses when they communicate laws, to speak after the event as though they were speaking before it applies.

The compiler of the Decalogue set out laws fundamental to the nation's well-being, initially by responding to the first ever occurrence of rebellion against divine authority in the nation's history (the making of the golden calf). He then turned his attention to the occasion when human beings first encountered this higher authority (in the Garden of Eden). Jewish tradition similarly linked the offense of the golden calf to Adam's offense. In writing up the event at Sinai its narrator suggests that the voice that utters the Decalogue is not the usual voice that gives the nation's laws – that of Moses, or, in the quite specific context of Exodus 18 and 19, Moses' father-in-law, Jethro. At Sinai it is the voice of the deity that speaks, representing the same voice that spoke at the beginning of time. Any story contains within it implicit rules. The story of Adam, Eve and Cain and Abel is that of the deity's first ever interaction with human beings and it presupposes the existence of his moral and legal code for them. The Decalogue articulated this code and the voice that enunciated it echoed the "voice" that is behind the moral and legal rules implicit in the story of the first human family.

Integration of law and narrative goes even further. The extraordinary presentation of the Decalogue in Exodus 19, a supernatural event breaking into the history of Israel, reveals the mutually dependent roles of law and storytelling. The story serves needs that characterize law and lawmaking at all times. In his study of the history of the Common Law, J. G. A. Pocock (1957) focuses on conflicting views in European nations of the 16th and 17th centuries about the origin of their laws. The anti-monarchist Sir Edward Coke, for example, took the position that English laws were without origin, not just ancient but immemorial and unmade. Affirming the royal prerogative, others opposed this stance with the claim that English laws, like those of other European nations, had a more recent history, going back to the Middle Ages and to national origins. The clash of views reflected opposing political ideologies, but central to each side's attempt to bolster its position was a focus on beginnings. Similar appeals to beginnings for political purposes show up in most legal systems at one time or another.

The same features – a focus on beginnings and a background of political tension – are revealed when we probe the significance of the giving of the Decalogue. However, rather than a clash, as in the history of the Common Law, between the notion of the law having its origin in the beginnings of the nation as against the idea that it is unmade and from time immemorial, the two perceptions are combined. The nation experiences, at its very inception, a communication that demonstrates that its laws come from the beginning of time. In a way, the view expressed in Rabbinic sources that the creation of the world was conditional on Israel's acceptance of the Law at Sinai makes this point (*Babylonian Shabbath* 88a; *Deuteronomy Rabba* 8:5).

The event at Mount Sinai is the formal beginning of nationhood, but its write-up communicates the notion that the nation's beginning is also a return to the origin of the world. Deut 4:32, 33 explicitly link the Decalogue's delivery to the creation. Recalling the event at Sinai, Moses addresses the nation: "For ask now of the days that are past, which were before thee, since the day that God created man upon the earth, and ask from the one side of heaven unto the other, whether there hath been any such thing as this great thing, or hath been heard like it? Did ever people hear the voice of God speaking out of the midst of the fire, as thou hast heard, and live?" In his praise of creation Ben Sira has the Decalogue delivered to the first humans (Sir 17:1, 11–13). Differently, but along similar lines, Sophocles well expresses the notion that law transcends time and place: "They are not of yesterday, or to-day, but everlasting, Though where they came from, none of us can tell" (*Antigone*, lines 445–446).

A number of features suggest that the aim of the author who describes events when God delivers the Decalogue is indeed to create an atmosphere that evokes the origin of the world (Exodus 19). There is the explicit point that the deity chooses Israel as his special possession out of all the nations of the earth. The curious role of the trumpet in the story seems to point to the significance associated with the instrument in those texts that describe matters to do with the whole earth and the created order. Thus Isa 18:3, "All you inhabitants of the world, you who dwell on the earth, when a signal is raised on the mountains, look! When a trumpet is blown, hear," and Jer 51:27, "Set up a standard on the earth, blow the trumpet among the nations." Trumpets and other instruments played by the inhabitants of the entire earth join nature itself in testifying to God's capacity to judge the peoples of the earth in a just manner (Psalms 98). In Exodus 19 elements of nature – thunder, lightning, and thick cloud – merge with the sound of the trumpet to contribute to the awesome character of the occasion.

The deity descends onto a mountain in order to communicate his pronouncements on the same day, the third, that the dry land and hence the mountains first came into existence (Gen 1:10). Whereas ordinarily it is Moses who communicates God's commands, in the Pentateuch there are three exceptions: the creation of the world, the renewal of the creation after the Flood, and the giving of the Decalogue. In each of these instances God communicates them directly. The tractate of the Mishnah, *Pirke Aboth* 5:1 (pre-200 CE), pointed out that there are ten pronouncements in the Decalogue and that there are also ten at the creation of the world.

Less certain, but tantalizing, are some curious features of Exodus 19 that may specifically point back to origins as depicted in the Genesis account of them. The people have to wash their clothes and also refrain from sexual commerce. The action of washing clothes may be to counter the negative implication of the clothing of the first couple. Adam and Eve acquire clothes because their state becomes such that human beings are pitted against the gods on account of knowledge of which the gods claim they alone are the proprietors. Washing them – not removing them permanently, which is out of the question – serves as a ritualistic reminder of that first clash between humankind and divinity. The injunction that the males should not approach their wives may be similarly motivated. When the first couple acquired knowledge they became sexually aware, and this awareness meant that human beings had "become like one of us [the gods], knowing good and evil" (Gen 3:22).

While the professed aim of the two requirements about clothing and sexual conduct in Exodus 19 is to separate the people from the divine activity on the mountain, they may also serve symbolically to undo the first, unwanted encroachment of the first humans into the divine realm. In Exodus 19 both humans and animals must not touch the sacred mountain. In Genesis 2–4 the serpent, as well as Adam and Eve, offends God by encroaching on the forbidden tree.

What the narrator of Exodus 19 does within the compass of the single occasion when Israel becomes a nation, the compiler of all the events in the Pentateuch does on a grand scale. Its compiler links Israel's formation as a nation, which occurs after the exodus from Egypt (Exodus 1–19), to the preceding history (Genesis 12–50) of the fathers of the nation (Joseph, Jacob, Isaac, and Abraham), and, in turn, to primeval history and the beginnings of life itself (Genesis 1–11).

The supernatural aura surrounding the giving of the Decalogue is patently an attempt to lend authority to its contents. Every system of law involves such an augmentation of its rules. The word authority comes from the Latin term *auctoritas*, which in turn is from a verb *augere* meaning, "to increase," "to wax." The suggestion is of the strength that is added behind the scene. The delivery of the Decalogue is a good example. We have the typical reaching out to higher forces by those with power in order to sanction control over those they rule.

Caution and exactitude appear to be prominent in such attempts to harness the higher powers. Uzzah, a servant of King David, reaches out with his hand to prevent the sacred Ark of the Covenant from falling from the cart in which it is being transported. He dies on the spot, much to David's anger (2 Sam 6:6, 7). Because the holy order has been disturbed, whoever records the story chooses not to recognize the distinction between intentional and unintentional action. The view is that even an accidental breach of custom has to prove fatal. The weight of divine authority is brought to bear on other legal situations by the use of ordeals (Num 5:11–31), oaths (Ex 22:11), and other magical acts (1 Sam 14:41). The situations are typically those where the machinery of earthly justice is powerless to cope, for example, when adultery has been committed in secret or when a human court cannot resolve a dispute.

A background of political tension is also a likely feature of the promulgation of the Decalogue. Its first part is a defense of a particular religious ideology. The setting up of golden calves in the shrines in the Northern Kingdom of Israel threatens the authority of the Jerusalem-based Southern Kingdom (1 Kgs 12:25–33). In any discussion of the story of the golden calf, critics turn to the struggle between the Judean authorities in Jerusalem and the breakaway tribes of the Northern Kingdom under Jeroboam. The Judeans, the triumphant party, seek to preserve the hegemony of worship at the temple in Jerusalem against the northern threat of the newly established shrines at Bethel and Dan, each with its golden calf as an iconic reminder of the god YHWH. The dramatic presentation of the Decalogue has as one of its aims an attempt to bolster the Jerusalemite ideological stance.

Additional Observations

Modern scholars who see much of the biblical material, especially the legal, as haphazardly set out and extensively edited are misreading the sophisticated relationship between the laws and the narratives. To be sure, the way in which the two genres are stitched together is indeed puzzling. In examining the laws the standard approach has been to ask what the here and now, practical impact of the laws would have been. The result is that scholars commonly view the laws as incorporating amendments and additions that reflect changing societal conditions in Ancient Israel. In searching for such changes over time they go to the narratives and treat them as sources from which they can glean historical information.

The idea that laws may develop in comparative isolation from social and economic factors is one that runs counter to the powerful tendency to treat law as a social phenomenon inextricably bound up with pressures and forces in society as a whole. What we forget, and this is especially true of biblical law, is that reflection on the past can have as its aim the creation of a myth about a nation's identity. It is the biblical lawgivers themselves who quarry the narratives for their historical content. Their aim, however, is not that of modern inquirers.

Like the narratives, the laws are marvelously wrought literary constructions. It is difficult for us to appreciate just how much time the biblical lawgivers gave to what from our perspective is a very limited amount of material, the narratives in Genesis–2 Kings that recount national origins. But time they did give. So much so that their familiarity with the legends would have been on a par with those who enjoyed the most popular form of literature until some 300 years ago, the Cento, a type of composition that used the texts of Homer or Virgil. By taking a half line here and a half line there, the composer stitched together (hence Cento, patchwork) the new composition; for example, a Life of Christ. The pleasure for the recipients was that not only did they find stimulation in the novelty of the composition, but also they knew exactly where the half line from Homer or Virgil came from and its original context.

Intense intellectual effort is characteristic, then, of the ancient biblical lawgivers and narrators. The anthropologist Lévi-Strauss recognized that the so-called primitives were just as "scientific" as we are today when he discovered that their myths reveal profound attempts at categorization. It can hardly be surprising that biblical material reveals similar qualities of intellect. Although we have a higher regard for the intellectual rigors of Greek philosophy and thought than for biblical thinking, what the Greeks do philosophically the ancient Hebrews do through their laws and stories.

When God accuses Adam of stealing the fruit from the garden, Adam's defense, one of indirect causation, is: "The woman whom you gave to be with me, she gave me of the tree and I ate." Adam took nothing from that tree, he just accepted its fruit from Eve. She, not he, is the person to cross-examine. There is even more to his defense. He describes her as "the woman you gave to be with me." So it was really God himself who handed him the fruit. The repetition of the verb "to give" in Adam's statement, "The woman you gave . . . she gave" is far from inelegant. In fact, it is necessary because it draws out the connection. "It is the first donation from the creator that led to the second from his creature: surely – so runs the argument – it would not do for the very initiator of the offer to take it out on the recipient" (Daube, 2000, p. 17). Adam's defense exceeds in ingenuity most of what the Greek orators could deliver centuries later.

A directness of expression, a naturalness of language, and an instinctive grasp of issues characterize the biblical authors, and testify to formidable powers of reasoning. Comparable powers might be found among later Talmudic sages and medieval canonists, but often they come concealed in extraordinarily convoluted writings. There are many reasons for the difference. One is that the biblical writers are free of having to acknowledge authorities that these later worthies have to bow to, for example, to the canon of Scripture itself or to the requirements of hermeneutic norms. Despite the restraints on later interpreters of the Bible, the capacity of the biblical texts to inspire continued unabated.

Thus the medieval canonists traced to the story of Adam and Eve certain rules that we consider fundamental for any system of criminal law. (In the 1st century BCE the Jewish philosopher Philo was in some respects a precursor.) They saw in the story general rules for how human justice should proceed if it was to properly convict a person for an offense (Helmholz, 1995, pp. 1557–81). From God's commandment to Adam, "Of the tree of the knowledge of good and evil, thou shalt not eat" (Gen 2:17), the canonists derived a rule that no one may be punished for an action that the criminal law has not previously defined and prohibited. The passage in Gen 3:9, "And the Lord God called unto Adam, and said unto him, Where art thou?" pointed to a requirement that in criminal procedure a defendant must be summoned before he can be lawfully punished. When God says to Adam: "Hast thou eaten of the tree whereof I commanded thee that thou shouldest not eat?" (Gen 3:11), the question indicated that a defendant must be told the precise nature of the crime he has been charged with. When Adam replies to God ("And the man said"), some of the canonists saw this development in the story as pointing to the origin of pleading. A defendant must be permitted to reply to any charge laid against him, even if it was certain that he was guilty of the offense. After all, he may be able to proffer, as up to a point Adam did, mitigating circumstances that would reduce the penalty appropriate to the offense. There was too the matter of the sentencing of the criminal. God pronounces his sentences on each of the culprits in the story, and also gives reasons for his judgments. A human judge must likewise speak his sentence aloud to the defendant and the court; and he must also give a reason for it.

Certain principles of justice and rules of judicial procedure would have been known to the canonists in some form or another when they read the Adam and Eve story. Unfortunately, we have little evidence of the make-up of existing procedural norms. The canonists turned to the Genesis narrative both to give clearer expression to any such norms and, presumably, to lend further authority to them by anchoring them as far back in time as possible and to the highest authority possible. In this instance they traced them to the pre-past, so to speak – a feature that turns out to be characteristic of rules in the Decalogue itself. It would be an error to think that the canonists were in any way naïve when they linked legal norms to the Genesis narrative. What they did is what the biblical lawgivers had done before them – I am not suggesting that the canonists in any way knew how their ancient forerunners proceeded – even if the aims of both might have differed in many respects. The biblical lawgivers also worked with rules known to them, but alas, not to us unless a case can be made out that they were familiar with, for example, the laws of Hammurabi (Westbrook, 1988 pp. 1–8). They too chose to relate existing rules to stories that were part of their cultural heritage.

Bibliography

Benjamin, W., *Illuminations, Essays and Reflections* (New York: Harcourt, Brace, and World, 1968).
Carmichael, C., *The Spirit of Biblical Law* (Athens, GA: University of Georgia Press, 1996).
Chirichigno, G., "The Narrative Structure of Exod 19–24," *Biblica* 68 (1987), 457–79.
Cover, R., "Foreword: Nomos and Narrative," *Harvard Law Review* 97 (1983), 4–68.
Daube, D., *Studies in Biblical Law* (Cambridge: Cambridge University Press, 1947).
——, "Word Formation in Indo-European and Semitic," in M. Hoeflich, ed., *Lex et Romanitas: Essays for Alan Watson* (Berkeley: Robbins Collection, 2000).

Helmholz, R., "The Bible in the Service of the Canon Law," *Chicago–Kent Law Review* 70 (1995), 1557–81.

Kaufmann, Y., *The Religion of Israel*, trans. Moshe Greenberg (New York: Schocken, 1960).

Miller, G., "Contracts of Genesis," *Journal of Legal Studies* 22 (1993), 15–45.

Nicholson, E., *God and His People: Covenant and Theology in the Old Testament* (Oxford: Blackwell, 1986).

Pocock, J. G. A., *The Ancient Constitution and the Feudal Law* (Cambridge: Cambridge University Press, 1957).

Watts, J., *Reading Law* (Sheffield: Sheffield Academic Press, 1999).

Westbrook, R., *Studies in Biblical and Cuneiform Law* (Paris: Gabaldi, 1988).

PART VII
The Prophets

Part III
The Prophets

CHAPTER 20

Former Prophets: The Deuteronomistic History

Hermann Spieckermann
Translated by Leo G. Perdue

The name "Former Prophets" derives from Jewish tradition and serves in the Hebrew Bible as the designation for the Books of Joshua, Judges, 1–2 Samuel, and 1–2 Kings. The designation is significant. It refers to the prophetic narratives in the Books of Kings and to others which fit the image of the prophets of Jewish tradition. Subsequently, the prophets are interpreters of the Torah who admonish the people to be obedient to the law. They also pronounce the unquestionably verifiable word of judgment when the people refuse to repent. The prominent figures Joshua, Samuel, Elijah, and Elisha meet the features of this image. The question as to the authors of these books also is explained in this sense. As the "Prophet Moses" (Deut 18:15; 34:10) has written the Torah, so, according to the information of the Babylonian Talmud (Baba Batra 14b.15a), Joshua and Samuel wrote the books that bear their names. Accordingly, Samuel is also presented as the author of Judges and Ruth, while Jeremiah is said to have written the Book of Kings. In the Hebrew Bible, the "Latter Prophets" follow. The writing prophets Isaiah, Jeremiah, Ezekiel, and the Twelve Minor Prophets are understood as belonging to this category. According to Jewish tradition, the oldest biblical sources of the history of Israel are entirely due to the spirit of prophecy.

In the Septuagint, upon which the Vulgate and consequently all Christian translations of the Old Testament are dependent, the Books of Joshua through Kings come to be understood as existing in permanent proximity to the Torah and to be clearly disassociated from the writing prophets. These latter texts are sometimes even placed at the end of the canon and judged to be eschatological. By contrast, the perception of the Books of Joshua through Kings increasingly come to be understood as an authoritative description of history. This becomes evident in different ways. The most important way is the unified designation of the Books of Samuel through Kings as the βασιλειῶν "(Books of) Kingdoms," or in the Vulgate as Regum "([Books of] Kings." The four books which are sequentially numbered and grouped together in this way are perceived as a whole as the history of the monarchy in Israel. Numbering these writings as four distinct books was not at home in the Hebrew tradition. It has been appropriated for the first time in the 15th and 16th century. During this time, Samuel and Kings are divided into two separate books each. In order to bring together and complete the history of Israel, the Septuagint, and occasionally also the Hebraic tradition, has added the Book of Ruth (cf. the genealogy of David, Ruth 4:17–22) and caused to follow the literature of Chronicles as well as Esther, Judith, Tobit, and the Books of Maccabees. In this manner, a tradition complex has originated for the history of Israel in the Septuagint and its dependent translations. The theological profile for this tradition complex clearly is to distinguish it from the "Former Prophets" of the Hebrew Bible.

The designation "Deuteronomistic History" is a scientific term which Martin Noth has coined in his influential book *Überlieferungsgeschichtliche Studien* (1943). He determined that the Deuteronomistic History ran from Deuteronomy through 2 Kings in the arrangement of the Hebrew Bible. In designating these texts in this way, he took over the adjective "Deuteronomic" that already existed in the criticism of the 19th century. This adjective was used to characterize the works infused by the theological spirit of Deuteronomy in the Pentateuch and the "Former Prophets." However, the idea of a systematic work to the aforementioned extent had still not been grasped. The designation "Deuteronomic History," which has an identical meaning, is to be found in most of the older English language literature. Today, if "Deuteronomic" and "Deuteronomistic" are distinguished, then the first mentioned adjective refers to the contents of Deuteronomy while the latter adjective refers to the contents of the historical work. However, this distinction is problematic, since both Deuteronomy and the attached historical books have grown simultaneously over a long period of time and are literarily linked closely together. Accordingly, the distinction of "Deuteronomic" and "Deuteronomistic" does not make sense any longer. Beyond the various individual differences in recent research, the designation "Deuteronomistic History" is commonly used for the Old Testament work that is introduced and infused by the theology of Deuteronomy and contains the Books of the "Former Prophets," which present the oldest description of the history of Israel.

The following remarks are divided into three parts. First of all, on the basis of the biblical books themselves, the effort is undertaken to determine what evidence exists for such a work of history. Then follow, secondly, insights into both the history of criticism and the present situation. Thirdly, and finally, on the basis of what has been learnt so far, the literary history of the Deuteronomistic History and its theological profile are traced.

The Biblical Data: Unity and Multiplicity

The Books of Deuteronomy through Kings are connected to each other by means of both a characteristic style and a well organized theological profile. They may be read as a continuing narrative of history so that it is not incorrect to think that a literary unity resides at its basis. This presumed unity comprises a multiplicity of different thematic features. Thus, a critical survey has to take into consideration both the unity and multiplicity of the Deuteronomistic History.

As the literary beginning of the entire History, Deuteronomy, which provides the name of this work of history, already presents a problem. Namely, one is able to understand only with some difficulty the whole of Deuteronomy as a historical narrative. In its final form, Deuteronomy is shaped as a testamentary speech of Moses shortly before his death in the land of East Jordan. Only Deuteronomy 1–3 are to be easily read, as an historical narrative that looks back to the guidance by God during the period of the wilderness and the entrance into the land east of Jordan. Following this, Deuteronomy 4 introduces a literary complex that considers Israel's future in the promised land in persuasive, admonitional, and threatening speeches (Deuteronomy 4–11) and in laws (Deuteronomy 12–26). These speeches and laws are to establish Israel's identity as YHWH's own people (Deut 7:6; 14:2; and 26:18). Curse and blessing, the sealing of the covenant in the land of Moab, and the last instructions and concluding words (Deuteronomy 27–33) give added weight to the speeches and laws. Subsequently, after this powerful activity, Moses finally may die seeing, but not entering, the promised land (Deuteronomy 34).

The reasons why Moses may not enter the promised land are unclear and sketchy (cf. Num 20:12; Deut 1:34–39; 3:23–28; 4:21; 32:50–51; and 34:4). The connection of guilt and punishment obviously is at work here in only a marginal way. Instead, central is the differentiation between Israel's primeval and historical time. This is clearly confirmed in Deut 34:10: "And there has not arisen a prophet since in Israel like Moses, whom the LORD knew face to face" (RSV). Although according to Jewish tradition Moses is bound with the following authors of the history of Israel: Joshua, Samuel, and Jeremiah, by means of the prophetic spirit, the decisive distinction of the primeval time consists in the characteristic access to God. In this respect, the death of Moses marks a break. The prophetic spirit is active further in figures which accompany the people of Israel, by means of the indirect presence of God in the law of Moses recording the history of Israel's obedience or disobedience to the law. If in this way the close connection between Deuteronomy and the following narrative of history therefore is evident, still it can be no wonder that the Jewish tradition soon, probably in the 5th century BCE, distances Deuteronomy from the narrative of history and adds the tradition of the primeval time. It is in this way that the Pentateuchal Torah was shaped. Deuteronomy also has had the power to shape the Torah, although in another way. Under Deuteronomy's influence, above all through the occurrences of "torah" in sections of the framework (Deut 4:8, 44; 17:11, 18; 27:3, 8, 26; 28:58, 61; 29:20, 28; 30:10; 31:12, 24, 26 and 32:46), the perception of the entire Pentateuch as Torah has progressed.

If one refrains from looking at the final Jewish subdivision of the Bible into Torah, Nebiim, and Kethubim, one is able to understand how Deuteronomy wishes to present its framing sections: as a narration of Moses' instructions before his death which then finds its seamless continuation in the Book of Joshua with the conquest of the promised land. In addition, Joshua at the same time is shown to be the successor of Moses. Before he takes a step in the promised land, he delivers a speech (Joshua 1) in which he, in the spirit of Moses, admonishes the people to be obedient to the law. The formulations in Josh 7–8 would not be thinkable without the Torah theology of the framing parts of Deuteronomy and without the linguistic borrowing from Ps 1:2–3. The continuity of the narrative and the literary clamping together of the final blocks of tradition of the Hebrew Bible come into view in this way.

In looking at the continuity of the narrative between Deuteronomy and Joshua, one should recognize that the tribes of Reuben, Gad, and half of Manasseh, which had already settled in the land of East Jordan, are expected to participate in the conquest of the land of West Jordan (Josh 1:10–18). The unity of Israel confirmed by oath in Deuteronomy indeed should be demonstrated immediately. If one reads the conquest narratives in Joshua 2–12 with the twelve tribes as its background, the call for the unity of Israel becomes understandable. What is narrated with an anecdotal and etiological point concerns only a very few cities in the sphere of the tribe of Benjamin: Jericho (Joshua 2; 6), Ai (7–8), and Gibeon (9). Israel's army was bivouacked in Gilgal and did not appear especially anxious to advance further their position in the land. Interest in cultic matters is just as great as the interest in the conquest. This includes the religiously significant crossing of the Jordan River (Joshua 3–4) and the events associated with it (5). At the end of Joshua 9, the inclusion of the entire land of West Jordan still seems a long way off. However, this changes very quickly in Joshua 10–11. In two battles the coalitions of the kings of the Canaanite cities of the South and the North are defeated. Immediately, the West Jordan area is included, something that should be confirmed by the concluding list in Joshua 12. Although the narrated course of events is strange from a strategic perspective, the inner logic of the narrative cannot be denied. The narratives dealing with Jericho, Ai, and Gibeon cause the inhabitants of the land of Canaan to realize that the common efforts of defense are the dictates of the hour. The missing outcome is grounded in YHWH's promise that the entire land of Canaan will be given into the hands of the Israelites. Any strategy is powerless in the face of the miracle of the word of God and the divine act that follows it.

It is remarkable how the conquest proceeds directly to the division of the land among the Israelite tribes. The division of the land is determined by means of the casting of lots. It is grounded in God's decision and thus removes any human manipulation. Accordingly, each tribe receives its domain according to a divine decision (Joshua 13–19). The establishment of asylum and designated Levitical cities (Joshua 20–21) is just as carefully considered as the building of the altar in the region near the Jordan (Joshua 22). This attests to Israel's belonging together on both sides of the Jordan. The lengthy list of places in the division of the land varies considerably from the vivid narratives of the conquest. A complete picture of the taking of the land results only when both the conquest narratives and the lists of places conquered and distributed among the tribes are taken together. This is the message included in the final shape of the text. That Joshua takes up the word twice again before his death, as reported in Josh 24:29–31, appears to be appropriate in establishing the meaning of the conquest. However, it can only be a matter of amazement that Israel according to Joshua 23 still is exposed to religious peril at the hands of the nations remaining in the land (cf. also Josh 13:1–13). And it is a matter of amazement as well that according to Joshua 24 the exclusive worship of YHWH is not yet finally established. Here the authors obviously know more about the state of affairs than they could be able to know according to the description of the conquest in the Book of Joshua.

What these authors have in view is to be read in the Book of Judges. The entire book is determined by the view that Israel must defend its existence against the threatening attacks of other nations. Now and then in the readings, the impression is made that the conquest, which is narrated in the Book of Joshua, could not have taken place in such a way. The speech in Joshua 23 with its warning about the nations remaining in the land appears to be entirely confirmed. The Canaanites, according to Judges 1, are found to be present everywhere in the land. Many of the tribes must first conquer their area of dwelling, while for many tribes important parts of their areas have remained in Canaanite hands (see the so-called negative list of areas in Judg 1:19, 21, 27–35). This state of affairs is not only to be explained by reference to Joshua 23. It needs a more thorough grounding. In reference to Joshua's period as the leader of Israel, and in the literary incorporation of the report of his death (cf. Judg 2:6–10 with Josh 24:29–31), there is recognized in the programmatic speech in 2:11–3:6 the reason for the continuing threat by the nations, and that is Israel's flourishing worship of foreign gods. This is the reason why the jealous God YHWH delivers Israel to its enemies and yet continues to raise up judges who liberate them out of the distress. The worship of YHWH never continued uninterrupted beyond the lifetime of a judge. After his death, the circle of apostasy, the jealousy of God, the distress caused by the enemy, and the rousing of a judge continued. The systematic presentation of the history set forth in the speech is illustrated by the following narratives of the judges in Judg 3:7–16:31.

Schematic and anecdotal notes about less significant judges are interwoven with complex texts about impressive figures: Deborah and Barak (Judges 4–5), Gideon/Jerubbaal (6–8) as well as his son, the usurper Abimelech (9), Jephthah (10–12), and Samson (13–16). If one learns one thing from the stereotypical reproach of apostasy, it is above all that the continuing threat to Israel is so impressive that one asks what chance this nation had of surviving without any political and military stability. The Philistines are the most dangerous of the political nations, as is shown by the Samson narratives and the ensuing Samuel and Saul narratives in 1 Samuel. The Israelites had already offered the crown to Gideon, who had been victorious over the Midianites. This represents, therefore, in a disguised form nothing other than the monarchy, something that is refused, however, with pious words. These words judge each monarchy in the light of apostasy (Judg 8:22–23). Accordingly, Abimelech's effort to erect a kingdom out of the Canaanite city-state of Shechem is judged in a negative way (Judges 9). The two narrative supplements in Judges 17–18 and 19–21 represent by contrast a different view. "In those days there was no king in Israel; every man did what was right in his own eyes" (17:6; cf. 18:1; 19:1; and 21:25). Indeed, both narratives handle internal Israelite affairs. Still, in looking back at Judges as a whole and forward to 1 Samuel it becomes clear that there was given no alternative to the monarchy in Israel as a guarantor of the self-defense of the nation.

1 Samuel 1–15 narrates the climax of the period of the judges, represented in the form of Samuel, and at the same time its end, represented by Saul. Both figures incorporate rival systems: judgeship and monarchy. The narrative in 1 Samuel reaches its intensity and tension primarily in the polarity of Samuel and Saul and then in Saul and David. The compositional arcs are constructed in a criss-crossing fashion. The fall of the judgeship interweaves with the first effort to establish the monarchy, i.e., the fall of Saul with the rise of David. World literature has been written in 1 and 2 Samuel. Their narrative culture reaches another plateau than that in Joshua and Judges.

The compositional arc in 1 Samuel 1–7 delivers the impression that the sovereignty of the Philistines indeed brings Israel into utmost peril. However, in Samuel God has chosen a judge who may turn around this misfortune. Accordingly, Samuel's victory over the Philistines in 1 Samuel 7 is to be read as proceeding from a decisive weakness of the enemy. The origin of Saul's monarchy, narrated in 1 Samuel 8–15, freely transmits another impression. Saul, victorious against the Ammonites (11), is made king by the Israelites, because he is capable of subduing the oppressive Philistine rule. In these chapters, positive and negative voices about kingship are solidly situated alongside each other. Again, the impression is unavoidable that the critics of the monarchy know more than they could know at the time of Saul.

The downfall of Saul, who not without reason loses his life against the Philistines (31), is artistically interwoven with the rise of David (1 Samuel 16–2 Samuel 6). His kingship over Israel in the North and in the South as well as over Jerusalem is valid at the moment when the Philistines are definitely conquered. The theological assessment of David's kingship appreciates his military and political success. In 2 Samuel 7, the Prophet Nathan utters a dynastic promise in which David and his successors are to participate. The accompanying composition pushes the question of succession to the center. It ends with the enthronement of Solomon (1 Kings 2) where the aged King David already has been a manipulative figure of intrigue at court. Even before this, the narrative does not dismiss the indications of guilt, weakness, and failures of David. The greatness and tragedy of the king are narrated masterfully in 2 Samuel 7–1 Kings 2.

A description of considerable proportion is also dedicated to the successor, Solomon. This description is certainly of another kind than that of David. After the rigorous consolidation of rule in 1 Kings 2, which allows to be recognized the power of resolve that is missing in the aging David, Solomon is presented in 1 Kings 3–5 as the wise ruler. In addition, his powers of administration, including the organization of servant labor, are seen in light of his wisdom. Everything stands in service to the decisive act, the building of the temple reported in 1 Kings 6–9. The perfection of Solomon's wisdom and the greatness of his wealth are again praised in the visit of the Queen of Sheba narrated in 1 Kings 10. In contrast to this, the reports found in 1 Kings 11 concerning Solomon's questionable religious associations with foreign wives as well as movements of rebellion provide the impression of an addendum to the famous, sapiential portrait of Solomon. The modification of this portrait is certainly of decisive significance for the separation between the Northern and the Southern Kingdoms that is introduced after Solomon's death.

The following synchronic description of the history of Israel (Northern Kingdom) and Judah (Southern Kingdom) in 1 Kings 14–2 Kings 17 consists of a schematic, basic outline. The various elements in the description of the kings of the Northern Kingdom include: the date of the enthronement in correspondence to the regnal year of the present king in Judah, the length of the regnal period, a generally negative judgment of the kingship according to the standard of the imageless worship of YHWH only, the optional notices of the results of the regnal period, the indication of the obligatory recording in the "Book of the History of the Kings of Israel," the death of the king, the place of burial, and his successor. Among the Kings of Judah the corresponding dates of the Kings of the Northern Kingdom are used for the dating of the enthronement. In addition, the name of the Queen Mother is imparted as quite naturally the notice to the parallel reference work, the "Book of the History of the Kings of Judah." While the judgments also against the Judahite Kings turn out bad in most cases, there are still noteworthy exceptions. In addition to the idealized founder of the dynasty, David, there are three others who are fairly pleasing. These are Asa (1 Kgs 15:9–24), Hezekiah (2 Kings 18–20), and Josiah (2 Kings 22–23). All three are reformers of the cult, although of a different status.

The last two mentioned kings are the most important representatives of the Judahite monarchy in the period following the liquidation of the Northern Kingdom by the Assyrians in the year 722/720, an event that receives intensive reflection in 2 Kings 17 considering Israel's and Judah's fate as well. The subsequent description of the remaining Judahite monarchy follows in 2 Kings 18–25. The fiasco of the religious and national restoration under Josiah is coupled with the report about the events in the year 587/586. These events bring the nation to an end and include the conquest of Jerusalem, the destruction of the temple and palace, and the deportation. The final report to be sure pertains to the good will shown to the Judahite King Jehoiachin who was interned in Babylon (2 Kgs 25:2–30). This act must have been understood as a sign of hope. It does not matter how small or how great the act may have been thought to be.

The history of the Northern and Southern Kingdoms would be limited to rather dry lists of stereotypical annals reshaped by religious judgments, if it were not for the formation of great arcs of composition through prophetic threats and notices of fulfillment as well as through comprehensive and sometimes tense narrations of prophets and men of God. Among those that are especially impressive are the Elijah Cycle (1 Kings 17–19; 21; 2 Kings 1) and the Elisha Cycle (2 Kings 2–8; 23:14–21). Additional prophetic figures are represented through notices and narratives, among whom only Isaiah is a true prophet, well known by his book, and only Isaiah is represented as a writing prophet (2 Kings 9–20). In this way the history of Israel in the Books of Kings becomes a witness to God's leadership through the prophetic word. To be sure, it remains at the same time clear that this theology of the prophets has not been the kernel of the historical work. This work consists much more of the reports of the palace and the temple archives, which have now been reworked secondarily into a transmitted description of history with predominantly negative theological judgment. Thus, similar observations can be made in the description of the period of the kings as in the preceding epochs. Different traditions have flowed into a large description which seeks to present in explanatory fashion both the success and failure of the history of Israel from the conquest until the end of political independence. The destruction of Jerusalem (587/586) and the gracious treatment of Jehoiachin must be presupposed as the terminus a quo. These two events are understood as bringing the work to an end, since they are the last reported events. Scholarly criticism debates the type of older literary forms the work may have had and the time from which they originated. The most important positions of critical inquiry are described in what follows.

The History of Criticism and the Position of Current Criticism

The person who discovered the Deuteronomistic History is Martin Noth, who has sought to demonstrate that both the Books of Deuteronomy through 2 Kings (the Deuteronomistic History) as well as the sequence 1–2 Chronicles, Ezra, and Nehemiah (the so-called Chronicler's History) are each a planned work and written by one author respectively. Noth's publication of this evidence under the title *Überlieferungsgeschichtliche Studien* (1943) corresponded to the position of exegetical understanding at that time. Traditions become valid as the result of a long, oral process which are more or less only ratified by their being written down. The combination of such traditions into comprehensive works under a uniform theological perspective surely leads back to a specific, literary, creative will. According to Noth, the writer of the Deuteronomistic History found the greatest part of the traditions he used previously existing in a literary form and incorporated them into a single work. He stamped it with his theological view of the history of Israel through biased additions, schematic judgments of the kings, and explanatory speeches at key points. During Noth's time the idea of redaction was in use only for marginal elements of organization. Therefore, Noth laid emphasis on designating his Deuteronomist as a writer and not as a redactor. The theological intention that Noth recognized in his exilic work was the account of God's just judgment of Israel and Judah. The catastrophes of 722/720 and 587/586 are the results of the guilt of kings and nation. Whether, and which, consequences were to be drawn from the evidence of guilt were not the object of explicit reflection by the writer. The writing Deuteronomist soon after the gracious act shown to Jehoiachin (562) did not want, according to Noth, to move beyond the religious and national disaster, but rather to lead to insight into the nation's own guilt (cf. also O'Brien 1989).

The strength of Noth's analysis of the Deuteronomistic History resides in the working out of the dominating theological intention and the exegetical characteristics which could be made valid for a uniform plan of the entire work. According to Noth's reconstruction, the tensions within the work are caused by the traditions incorporated, which the Deuteronomist did not wish to improperly harmonize. To be sure, another explanation for the uneven features can be considered. They can go back to the work of different redactors who have brought to expression their own view of things in different and new editions which respect the presently existing literary condition of the work. Before Noth, even though published later, Alfred Jepsen (1953) sought to explain the tensions in the content in this way. According to him, three redactions have shaped the form of the work of history on the foundation of two separate sources from the pre-exilic period that deal with the Kings of Israel and of Judah. Jepsen's "prophetic redaction" significantly conforms with Noth's Deuteronomistic writer. Thus, further criticism was confronted with the problem of how the sources and redactions in the work of history are related to each other. The debate over this has not led to a consensus even until today. Certainly, it should not be overlooked that the general agreement with respect to the dominant Deuteronomistic formation of the work of history is great.

In the English-speaking sphere, the thesis of Frank Moore Cross (1973) has achieved continuing influence. He argued that a comprehensive work of history is to be attributed to a Deuteronomistic school which may have edited in the late pre-exilic time a Deuteronomistic work (Dtr^1) under the influence of the Josianic reform. This first edition may have been expanded in the exilic time to include the remnant history of Judah and texts that explained the catastrophe of 587/586 (Dtr^2). R. D. Nelson has further elaborated this thesis. In fact the different evaluation of the kingship and certain tensions in the description of Josiah as well as other observations could be explained by two Deuteronomistic levels of redaction from the pre-exilic and (post-)exilic time. It is informative that almost parallel German-language publications could establish a thesis which, inspired by an essay by Rudolf Smend (1971), has been further elaborated especially by Walter Dietrich (1972 and 1999) and Timo Veijola (1975 and 1977). This thesis is similar to that of Cross in arguing for the dominant influence of Deuteronomistic redactors in the work of history. It identifies three redactors, each of whom was active in the (post-)exilic period: the Deuteronomistic Historian (DtrH) who composed the fundamental outline of the work, a redaction (DtrP) oriented to the figures of the prophets and the fulfillment of the prophetic word, and a nomistic redaction (DtrN) which gave effect to the increasing importance of the Deuteronomic law. It certainly is not to be concluded that one of the named

levels of Deuteronomistic redaction would be thinkable without the Deuteronomic law. Notwithstanding the differences of the redactional profile, all levels
of redaction presuppose according to this thesis the catastrophe of 587/586.

Two complexes of problems bound together stand in the midpoint of the debate
that is still occurring to this day. The first complex is the controversy surrounding
the dating of the first composition of the Deuteronomistic History. Was there a
late pre-exilic composition of the Deuteronomistic History from the time of Josiah
that comprehended this period as the culminating point in the dynastic promise
to David? Or does the entire Deuteronomistic activity presuppose the catastrophe
of 587/586 so that the first draft of the historical work can stem at its earliest
from the exilic period? In this context, the assessment of the Josianic reform in
2 Kings 22–23 (and of the Book of Deuteronomy) plays an important role. Is
the reform the objective of a pre-exilic Deuteronomistic composition (Cross, 1973;
McKenzie, 1991; and Eynikel, 1996), or is it, on the basis of sources, a determinant in an exilic Deuteronomistic work (Spieckermann, 1982), or is it purely
a Deuteronomistic fiction together with the Book of Deuteronomy (Hoffmann,
1980; Van Seters, 1983)? For each of these options there is certain exegetical
evidence. The preference for the one or the other options hangs on the assessments to which one gives precedence, not finally on the question as to when
intolerant monotheism, which is presupposed in the Book of Deuteronomy, came
to be regarded as valid in Israel.

A second complex of problems pertains to the question of how the literary
growth of the Deuteronomistic History may be adequately envisaged. The so-
called block model (Cross, Nelson, etc.) and the so-called stratum model (Smend,
Dietrich, Veijola, etc.) can be clearly distinguished in theory. Either a literary
kernel has been expanded by new literary blocks at the beginning and end of
the work, or a first edition of the work has been superimposed by several
redactional layers. As a matter of fact, both models have been closely connected
in exegetical research so that the easily distinguishable theoretical ideas are no
longer of any practical use. In spite of all disagreements in the concrete analysis, a consensus prevails that neither in the block nor in the stratum models are
simple reconstructions of the work possible. Since a considerable number of
literary blocks has been added to the first edition of the work, redactional reworking pertaining to the whole has been necessary at the same time. Thus, the
block model needs finer distinction. And the stratum model can in no way be
limited to three identifiable redactional strata. Rather, a series of redaction strata
is bound together with block-like additions, certainly fewer at the end than at
the beginning to of the work. The proof that the block and strata models have
lost their value in exegetical practice may be indicated in such examples as the
works of H. Weippert (1972), I. W. Provan (1988), and B. Halpern and D. S.
Vanderhooft (1991) on the one side and E. Würthwein (1994) on the other. In
spite of considerable differences in analysis and dating, it is striking that today
both models are amazingly similar in intention. While Weippert, Provan, and
Halpern–Vanderhooft reconstruct in the Books of Kings and beyond the Pre-
deuteronomistic and Deuteronomistic forms of the work of history, Würthwein,

partially on the assumptions of G. Fohrer and G. von Rad, proceeds from a first Deuteronomistic edition of the Books of Kings, which has been progressively expanded by literary blocks including Saul and David in the Books of Samuel, the description of the period of the Judges, and finally the conquest of the land of Canaan in Joshua 1–11. The work, which has grown in this manner and has experienced in this way a thoroughgoing Deuteronomistic redaction, can point to no uniform theological tendency. Deuteronomy, which first originated in the exilic time, does not belong to the work of history. While Würthwein regards the Deuteronomistic theology as the basis of the presently existing Deuteronomistic History, Westermann (1994) denies this hypothesis, because he is not able to recognize any theological intentions that unite the different traditions of the relevant biblical Books in the sense of a comprehensive description of history. Westermann's voice may be understood as a parenthesis that utters the warning not to lose sight of the clearly identifiable character of Deuteronomistic theology in the biblical books referred to.

The History of Literature and Theology

In the present state of research, every reconstruction of the development of the Deuteronomistic History represents simply an educated effort. However, characteristic intentions of present scholarly criticism may be concentrated together into a common view, although the points of departure and methods are different. On the basis of language and theological conception, it appears that the Deuteronomistic Historian (DtrH) composed a first edition of the Deuteronomistic History. This initial edition has been largely expanded by a Deuteronomistic school through the addition of entire tradition blocks, through various redactions, and through individual modifications. The Deuteronomistic History shaped by the Deuteronomistic Historian probably contained as a basic component both the books of Samuel and of Kings. Perhaps the Septuagint, through putting together these books under one title, has preserved a memory of the original literary unity. The Greek designation "(Books of the) Kingdoms" at any rate reflects the content appropriately. The work deals with the history of the kingdoms of Israel and Judah from the very beginning to the end. Sources were available to DtrH covering the whole of this period of a good 400 years. Narratives about Samuel, Saul, and the ark, novelistic descriptions about David's rise and succession as well as works of annals from the Northern and Southern Kingdom were used by DtrH. While the sources evaluated in the Books of Samuel testify to a remarkable narrative culture, the annals cultivated in the Northern and Southern Kingdoms as elsewhere in the Ancient Near East have been taken up without any literary ambitions in the registration of dates, the use of important political and military data, and the remarks about building plans. That DtrH has taken up the annals only in part, shows that we have to be aware of a considerable loss of tradition.

The Deuteronomistic Historian shapes his text primarily with existing sources and is limited in his own formation to the clear evaluation of the kingdom in rather spare textual terms. According to his view, the history of the kingship started with the "kingmaker" Samuel (1 Samuel 1–3), chosen by God himself. The narratives of the ark which follow (1 Samuel 4–6) document Israel's oppression by the Philistines. Their lordship renders possible the kingship of Saul, which DtrH, through the traditions in 1 Samuel 9–11, puts in a positive light. How difficult it is for the ancient traditions and DtrH to reverse to a negative evaluation of Saul, can still be traced out in the texts in 1 Samuel 13–14. The turn is nevertheless necessary, because the consolidation of the kingship was not achieved until the victory over the Philistines by David. Except for a few interventions, DtrH renders here the already existing literary units of David's rise to power (1 Sam 16:14–2 Sam 5:25), of the bringing of the ark to Jerusalem (2 Samuel 6), and of the succession to the throne (2 Samuel 7–1 Kings 2). All disturbances and cataclysms in this history place the strongly redacted promise of Nathan (DtrH and additional Deuteronomistic editors) under the covenant of the eternal dynasty (2 Sam 7:16). This promise has been sinfully gambled away, above all by the kings. Condemned are Solomon, with some restraint, due to the building of the temple (1 Kgs 3:3; parts of 11:1–8), the kings of the Northern Kingdom on account of the sin of Jeroboam (1 Kgs 12:16–33; 15:26, 34; 16:19, 26, 31; etc.), and all the kings of the Southern Kingdom with the exception of the cult reformers Asa, Hezekiah, and Josiah (1 Kgs 15:11–15; 2Kgs 18:3–4; parts of 22–23). DtrH places his stamp on the judgments of the kings and on a few speeches which document God's devotion to (1 Kgs 8:14–21) and eventual turning away from Israel (2 Kgs 17:7–11, 21–23). These speeches contain stereotypical formulations over the doing of evil in the eyes of YHWH, and the accusation of abandoning the worship of the one God YHWH and the centralization of the cult. DtrH wishes to awaken insight into the guilt of the kings and of the nation. He brings his work to an end after the downfall of the Southern Kingdom, not with a speech to prove guilt, but with the report of the good deed shown to Jehoiachin at the court of the Babylonian king, Evil-Merodach (2 Kgs 25:27–30). This gives hope to the belief that the eternal dynasty (2 Sam 7:16) may still have another chance. However, primarily through confrontation with its history, Israel must gain insight into guilt.

Through further editings, the Deuteronomistic History has grown to approximately twice the size of the text of DtrH. The Deuteronomistic school is responsible for this considerable expansion. Its precursor in the 7th century has been a circle of Deuteronomic theologians from whom the basic outline of Deuteronomy has emerged. It still was not immediately incorporated with the literary historical work of DtrH originating around the middle of the 6th century. This first occurred in the following decades, in which an impressive Deuteronomistic activity of redaction was carried out by many hands. Since the numerous expansions cannot be identified using only a few scientific abbreviations, they are designated here in summary fashion as late Deuteronomistic additions. Although the number of the redactors is unclear, one can still identify the leading motives of the additions.

In the Books of Kings, there are above all the prophetic narratives and the entries of the fulfillment of prophetic threats, which have been integrated in several stages into the description of DtrH. Certain prophetic figures play an important part in the final composition of the work. While the narratives about the man of God, Elisha (2 Kgs 2:8; 13:14–21), focus on his miraculous activity and his role in the wars with Syria, Elijah is adapted in a later edition of the work to fit the Deuteronomistic prototype of the prophet of judgment. At the risk of his life, he defends the worship of YHWH alone against the rulers of his period (1 Kings 17–19; 2 Kings 1). Last of all, the prophetic books find their proper place mentioning Isaiah in the circle of the prophetic narratives (2 Kgs 18:17–19:37).

The prophets are YHWH's servants (2 Kgs 9:7; 17:13, 23; 21:10; 24:2). They bring forth a voice to be heard which accomplishes its powerful word. Therefore, late Deuteronomistic circles place value on the realization of the threatened catastrophe (1 Kgs 14:7–11 and 15:29–30; 16:1–4 and 16: 11–13; 1 Kgs 21:19b, 20b–27 and 2 Kgs 9:7–10a, 36–37; 10:17). Subsequently, Israel has never lacked the knowledge of the consequences of its activity, and therefore cannot avoid responsibility for its guilt.

The question of where the beginnings of this guilt resides, has driven the Deuteronomists to a close study of Israel's origins and led to a considerable increase in the introductory part of the work. The first step was the insertion of the Book of Judges at the beginning of the work. Using the traditions originating in the Northern Kingdom, which narrate the oppression and liberation of parts of Israel, late Deuteronomistic circles sketched a system of history that attributed the early guilt to the worship of foreign gods. This occasioned YHWH to bring ever again new salvation through the sending of judges. The idea of a period of judges, only hinted at in the tradition, was first composed by this stage of Deuteronomistic redaction. The programmatic view is set forth by the Deuteronomists in Judg 2:11–3:6. This shift in the accent of the work attributes responsibility for sin to the premonarchical period, thus involving not only the kings but the whole nation as it came into existence. The essentially positive view of kingship in the work of DtrH now receives a negative outline, because, according to the late Deuteronomistic view, kingship in Israel is perceived as an attack on YHWH's kingship over Israel. Consequently, Gideon rejects the kingship offered to him by the people (Judg 8:22–23), and Samuel, who now is understood as the last representative of the epoch of the judges, informs the people that the decision for an earthly monarch is identical with the rejection of YHWH (1 Sam 8:6–22a; 12). Saul, most closely connected with the origin of the monarchy, ultimately becomes a negative figure (1 Sam 15; 28:3–25), while David, Hezekiah, and Josiah by contrast are designated as positive representatives of a, strictly speaking, reprehensible institution (1 Samuel 16; parts of 2 Sam 7:5–11, 22–27; 2 Kgs 18:5–7a; and 23:21–27). Deuteronomy is no longer only an implicit section of the Deuteronomistic movement, but has now become the norm that expresses Israel's obligation to offer obedience to the law (1 Kgs 2:3–4; 2 Kgs 17:12–19; 18:5–7a; 21:8; and 23:25–27). The admonition to observe the law is always present. With this background, neither the kings nor the people can escape the pronouncement of guilt. Above all, the structure of the Book of Judges has made the Deuteronomistic History into an etiology of the guilt of the nation. The clear assignment of guilt implies at the same time the acquittal of God. His harsh judgment against his people is completely justified. He cannot be condemned for his actions as other texts from the exilic period do (Psalms 44; 74; 80; Lamentations 2; 5). The texts that are positively oriented in their view of kingship occur at the end of the Book of Judges (Judg 17–21; 17:6; 18:1; 19:1; and 21:25). They are very late and yet do not belong to the Deuteronomistic composition which is introduced by the Book of Judges comprising Judg 2:11–16:31.

This composition, however, was an intermediate stage as well. The negative beginning, with the period of the judges and its influence on the total purpose of the work, has necessitated a correction because it is in contradiction to traditions of the conquest of Israel that were equally cultivated by the Deuteronomistic school. These traditions are contained in the Book of Joshua. Originally belonging to a Deuteronomistic edition of the Tetrateuch which concluded the composition with materials about the conquest, the division of the land, and the assembly in Shechem (Joshua 24), these traditions of the Book of Joshua together with the Book of Deuteronomy have been placed at the beginning of the Deuteronomistic History. Through this considerable expansion, the profile of the Deuteronomistic History once again has been significantly altered. The beginning no longer depicts the etiology of Israel's downfall earlier in the founding phase of the period of the judges, but rather the "salvific time" of the lawgiver Moses and the conquest under his successor Joshua, reaching a high point in the people accepting the obligation only to serve the one God YHWH. The people, already lacking trust in God during the wilderness wandering, have experienced nevertheless the faithfulness of God through his guidance into the land flowing with milk and honey (Deut 6:3; 11:9; 26:9, 15; 27:3; 31:20, and Josh 5:6). The transition to Israel's predisposition to the worship of foreign gods in the period of the judges is therefore less understandable and receives even more of a harsh accusation. The abrupt encountering of the "salvific time" (Moses and Joshua) with the history of guilt starting with the period of the judges remains well recognizable as a literary seam although an even later edition of the work has inserted various texts to smooth out this inconsistency. Joshua 23 is among them. The report that a portion of the early population cannot be driven out does not conform at all to the Book of Joshua, but it does with the Book of Judges. The same intentions are pursued by the so-called negative catalogue in Judges 1 and the modified resumption of the report of the death of Joshua (24:29–31) in Judg 2:6–10.

As a final result the first history of Israel from Moses to the loss of the statehood of the Northern and Southern Kingdoms was created. Like all great literary works of the Ancient Near East and of the Old Testament the Deuteronomistic History has been elaborated over a long period of time. Its genesis could be traced here only in outline. If the different points of emphasis in the course of this growth cannot be ignored, the distinct theological profile from the first to the last edition has not been affected. Israel is a people who were chosen by YHWH and led by Moses and Joshua in spite of their disobedience to YHWH's requirement that he alone be worshiped. The history of salvation has become therefore a history of guilt, the consequences of which Israel has to bear. For the Northern Kingdom, the events that took place during 722/720 are irreversible. The continuation of the history of the people of God after the divine judgment of 587/586 of the Southern Kingdom is not the theme of the Deuteronomistic History. This continuation was no longer in question at the time of the final composition of the work, because the latest expansions parallel the developing Priestly document and the consolidation of the post-exilic temple community in Jerusalem. Nevertheless, Israel has preserved the first great outline of its history in the form of a history of guilt. The deep insight into the roots of collective guilt, which matured during the exile, in great suffering, should be documented forever.

Bibliography

Cross, F. M., "The Themes of the Book of Kings and the Structure of the Deuteronomistic History," in *Canaanite Myth and Hebrew Epic Essays in the History of the Religion of Israel* (Cambridge, MA: Harvard, 1973), 274–89.

Dietrich, W., *Prophetie und Geschichte. Eine redaktionsgeschichtliche Untersuchung zum deuteronomistischen Geschichtswerk*, FRLANT 108 (Göttingen: Vandenhoeck und Ruprecht, 1972).

———, "Niedergang und Neuavfang: Die Haltung der Schlussredaktion des deuteronomistischen Geschichtswerkes zu den wichtigsten Fragen ihrer Zeit," in *The Crisis of Israelite Religion*, ed. B. Becking and M. C. A. Korpel, OTS 42 (Leiden, 1999), 45–70.

Eynikel, E., *The Reform of King Josiah and the Composition of the Deuteronomistic History*, OTS 33 (Leiden: E. J. Brill, 1996).

Halpern, B. and D. Vanderhooft, "The Editions of Kings in the 7th–6th Centuries BCE," *HUCA* 62 (1991), 179–244.

Hoffmann, H.-D., *Reform und Reformen. Untersuchungen zu einem Grundthema der deuteronomistischen Geschichtsschreibung*, ATANT 66 (Zürich: Theologischer Verlag, 1980).

Jepsen, A., *Die Quellen des Königsbuches* (Halle: M. Niemeyer, 1953, 2nd edn. 1956).

Kratz, R. G., "Die Komposition der erzählenden Bücher des Alten Testaments," UTB 2157 (Göttingen: Vandenhoeck und Ruprecht, 2000).

McKenzie, S., *The Trouble with Kings. The Composition of the Book of Kings in the Deuteronomistic History*, VTSup 42 (Leiden: E. J. Brill, 1991).

Nelson, R. D., *The Double Redaction of the Deuteronomistic History*, JSOTSup 18 (Sheffield: JSOT Press, 1981).

Noth, M., The *Deuteronomistic History*, JSOTSup 15 (Sheffield: Sheffield Academic Press, 1981, 2nd edn. 1991; German: *Überlieferungsgeschichtliche Studien*, 1943).

O'Brien, M., *The Deuteronomistic History Hypothesis: A Reassessment*, OBO (Göttingen: Vandenhoeck und Ruprecht, 1989).

Pakkala, J., *Intolerant Monolatry in the Deuteronomistic History*, PFES 76 (Göttingen: Vandenhoeck und Ruprecht, 1999).

Provan, I., *Hezekiah and the Books of Kings: A Contribution to the Debate about the Composition of the Deuteronomistic History*, BZAW 172 (New York: de Gruyter, 1988).

Smend, R., "Das Gesetz und die Völker. Ein Beitrag zur deuteronomistischen Redaktionsgeschichte," in H. W. Wolff, ed., *Probleme biblischer Theologie. Festschrift G. von Rad* (Munich: C. Kaiser, 1971), 494–509.

Spieckermann, H., *Juda unter Assur in der Sargonidenzeit*, FRLANT 129 (Göttingen: Vandenhoeck und Ruprecht, 1982).

Van Seters, J., *In Search of History* (New Haven: Yale, 1983).

Veijola, T., *Die ewige Dynastie. David und die Entstehung seiner Dynastie nach der deuteronomistischen Darstellung*, AASFB 193 (Helsinki: Suomalainen Tideakatemia, 1975).

——, *Das Königtum in der Beurteilung der deuteronomistischen Historiographie*, AASFB 198 (Helsinki: Suomalainen Tideakatemia, 1977).

Weippert, H., "Die 'deuteronomistischen' Beurteilungen der Könige von Israel und Juda und das Problem der Redaktion der Königsbücher," *Bib* 53 (1972), 301–39.

Westermann, C., "Die Geschichtsbücher des Alten Testaments. Gab es ein deuteronomistisches Geschichtswerk?" TBü 87 (Gütersloh: Kaiser, 1994).

Würthwein, E., "Erwägungen zum Sog, deuteronomistischen Geschichtswerk. Eine Skizze," in *Studien zum Deuteronomistischen Geschichtswerk*, BZAW 227 (New York: de Gruyter, 1994), 1–11.

CHAPTER 21
Latter Prophets: The Major Prophets

Klaus Koch

Name and Literary Structure

The book of Isaiah is the longest of the Major Prophets but not a uniform one. Between Isaiah 1–39 and Isaiah 40ff a linguistic and conceptual break is obvious. In the first part, Isaiah, concerned with the conditions of Judah in the 8th century BCE, pronounces his message in the capital Jerusalem, criticizing the contemporary kings together with the social and cultic establishment, threatening the danger of an Assyrian invasion. From chapter 40 onward, however, the name of the prophet is never mentioned. The message is directed toward a community without a political leadership of its own, toward Israelites deported from their homeland and suffering under Babylonian, and no longer Assyrian, oppression. He speaks, not of the forthcoming decline of kingdom and nation, but of consolation and the promise of a miraculous return to Jerusalem and Zion. For 200 years, therefore, modern scholars have proposed an anonymous author of the 6th century BCE for the second part of the book, chapters 40–55, and given him the name Deutero-(Second) Isaiah. Although chapters (chs.) 56–66 are cognate in language to chs. 40–55, they refer to the poor conditions of post-exilic Palestine. Many exegetes suggest one or probably several disciples of Deutero-Isaiah, returned from the exile, as authors of Isa 56–66 (= Trito-[Third] Isaiah).

Compared with Proto-Isaiah, the books of Jeremiah and Ezekiel presumably display the same arrangement in three or four parts according to the main subjects: predictions of disaster for their own people Judah, oracles against foreign nations, promises of salvation for Judah–Israel (and eventually a biographical supplement). The threefold sequence is obvious in Ezekiel: I, chs. 1–24; II, chs. 25–32; and III, chs. 33–48. In Jeremiah the same construction appears in the Old Greek version, which seems to be original in this regard: I, chs. 1–25:14; II, chs. 26–32 (= MT 25, 15ff. + 46–51); III, chs. 33–42 (= MT 26–35), together with the biographical addition IV, chs. 43–51 (= MT 36–45). In Isaiah the pattern may be followed in I, chs. 1–12 (with intermingled promises); II, chs. 13–23 with the supplement of the so-called Isaiah–apocalypse chs. 24–27; and IV, the narratives chs. 36–39. The intermediate part III, chs. 28–35, however, brings predictions both of salvation and of damnation for Israel. Except perhaps Ezekiel, these arrangements probably did not originate with the prophets themselves but with later editors and their intention to stress the final salvation for their own people after the total decline of Israel's enemies.

Authenticity and Redactions

The prophetic literature of Israel was transmitted according to the usual manner of sacred literature in the Ancient Near East. In its civilizations, no ideas of literary originality, of plagiarism, or of mental theft were known. On the contrary, it was a matter of course that authoritative writings sometimes required actualization by supplementary remarks or even by verbal alterations in spite of a still remembered origin with a spiritual hero of the past.

Therefore, regarding the growth of the Major Prophets an intense debate has arisen in the last decades. Some scholars are inclined to trace back only a few passages, if any at all, to the historical Isaiah, Jeremiah, and Ezekiel or even to deny any authenticity; whereas others are convinced that most of the predictions are rightly ascribed to those figures, because the severe critique of the social and cultic circumstances in Jerusalem and Judah corresponds much better to the pre-exilic structures of society than the post-exilic ones; the description of the power of the Assyrians in Proto-Isaiah and of Nebuchadrezzar in Jeremiah convincingly mirrors the political situation of just those epochs.

Originally a prophet proclaimed his words orally. The speech to the audience is as a rule introduced and legitimated by the messenger- or proclamation-formula: Thus said "YHWH." In the mouth of a prophet, it expresses the self-confidence to have heard the voice of God personally, even if its exact articulation in Hebrew may have been formulated by the receiver himself. In the prophetic books, that formula is often repeated before new passages (in Amos some fourteen times), and probably has as its reason the recourse to independent oral borrowings.

It is told that the prophets wrote down their message when an appearance in public was forbidden to them (Jeremiah 36), or it seemed useless because of the foreseen refusal of the audience (Isa 8:16–18). So books developed as collections of separate units, not as an outline of a preceding literary concept. During the exile, the situation apparently altered with Ezekiel; he probably already had knowledge of prophetic books and felt the impetus to write down his intuitive experience from the very beginning (Ezekiel 2).

One genre especially was used in combination with the messenger-formula in speaking to the public. It was the two-piece prophecy, consisting of an indication of the (evil) situation of the present society and its representatives in the eyes of God (the diatribe), and continuing with a prediction of coming disaster (seldom of rescue and salvation) by a sudden divine intervention often executed by heavenly powers or human agents (cf., e.g., Isa 1:21–23 with vv. 24–27). In such small units, a stringent logic may be recognized. First the human depravity is announced. Then comes the inevitable divine reaction to cleanse the earthly realm. The structure of that genre is instructive for the prophet's understanding of his mission. He does not act like a mere soothsayer. His prediction is based on an extrapolation out of the observation of developments in the past and the present; his God does not arbitrarily intervene.

When a prophet began to write down his message, he took over many of his oral sayings uttered at different occasions to serve as a witness in future times for the truth of his prophecy. This intention explains the loose coherence in the longer units, changes from the present to the future and vice versa.

None of the prophetic books is preserved in an edition of the original author. Generally, the redactional intention placed less emphasis on a further critique of past and present conditions of the society and more on the motivation of repentance and in the outlook to the future, which became more and more an eschatological one (eschatology = doctrine of the change of history and world to a fundamental new kind of event, first catastrophic and then salvific, which had never happened in such a manner in history before).

Modern scholarship disagrees widely over how large the redactional portion may be. The following comments presuppose that around half of the texts are assumed to be authentic, at least regarding Isaiah and Jeremiah.

Proto-Isaiah

The above-mentioned division of Isaiah 1–39 into four thematic sections is based on several older collections of sayings which perhaps Isaiah himself had initiated (cf. 8:16–18; 30:8). In addition, narratives about the prophet were integrated, such as chs. 7 and 20, which were presumably transmitted by his adherents, and chs. 36–39, taken over probably from 2 Kgs 18–20.

The period of social critique

The first we hear from Isaiah's biography is the account of a vision he had in the year of the death of King Uzziah (ch. 6; 742 BCE?). He became aware of the sudden appearance of God enthroned above the temple on Mt. Zion, who sent him to harden the mind of his people so that they no longer are able to obtain insight and convert themselves, but are irrevocably delivered to ruin. Modern exegetes used to take the chapter as the documentation of the initial vocation of Isaiah. They connected it closely with chs. 7 and 8 and postulated an original prophetic memory from the time of the Syro-Ephraimitic war. But 7:1–17 is a narrative about the prophet in the third person with a new historical

introduction taken from 2 Kgs 16:5–9. Chapter 6 stands at the right place
behind chs. 1–5, which received the harsh social critique of the earliest period
of the prophet. Not the first inspiration but a decisive change in the prophetic
mission is narrated. Now in God's eyes the point of no return has been reached.

What in chs. 1–6 is preserved of his sayings presumably mirrors the first
phase of his activity. During it the prophet uttered a harsh social critique of the
conditions in Judah and Jerusalem which recalls the message of Amos and may
have been influenced by him. The economic development in the second half
of the 8th century BCE seems to have raised a social crisis in Judah similar to
that in Northern Israel. Like Amos Isaiah attacked the increasing but illegitimate expropriation of peasant-farmers and their ground-property (5:8; 3:14f),
which belonged to the Promised Land attributed by YHWH to Israel. Beyond
Amos he also criticized the discrimination against widows and orphans (1:17,
23; 10:2), the common practice of bribery (1:23; 5:20–23), and cases of juridical murder (1:21; 5:7). As in Amos a critique of the cult is combined with the
social one. The Judahites were supposed to believe that the holy temple delivers
a magic protection against greater evils and outward enemies and that the lack
of communal solidarity can easily be compensated by an intensified cultic activity with sacrifices and processions. According to Isaiah, this was a dangerous
deception. He is sure that God had turned away from the worship of this generation; even prayers he will never more accept (1:10–17). (Former interpreters had supposed that the critical prophets denied the use of cultic worship at
all. But Isaiah was, like his fellow countrymen, convinced that the temple is the
only place where YHWH appears to his people in a paramount way. However, he
will not come near to *these* people graciously.)

The prophet is convinced of an indissoluble connection between human behavior and a corresponding destiny, between misdeeds and disaster. Therefore,
the decline of the ruling class, together with that of the whole city of Jerusalem
and the devastation of Judah, seems unavoidable (3:9–11; 5:24). The anger of
the Lord will quicken and encourage this process of abolishing the sphere of evil
from the earth.

Moreover, according to the obdurancy vision (ch. 6), YHWH will henceforth
harden the heart of the people, which has become unclean, so that it will be no
more able to become aware of important events occuring around them or to
understand the real meaning of the prophetic message until the coming general
catastrophy. Already in the first phase Isaiah had seen the future of his people
determined by a devastating foreign invasion (5:26ff; 6:11–13), although the
enemy remained anonymous.

Isaiah's later phases and his fundamental critique of Israel's politics

From the reign of King Ahaz until that of Hezekiah (725–700 BCE?), the treatment of political and military affairs of the Judean government came to the fore
in the prophetic predictions. Now the Assyrian superpower had spread to the

Mediterranean and threatened Judah. Isaiah stalwartly insisted on the avoidance of any alliance with foreign nations, because it would include a tie with
alien deities and a betrayal of the exclusive connection with God on Mt. Zion.
This YHWH is able to repulse every inimical army as strong as it may be, but he
is also willing to call one, if Israel refuses obedience.

A first clash with the official strategy took place when the Aramaen king of
Damascus and the king of Northern Israel were advancing toward Jerusalem to
replace Ahaz and to compel Judah to join an anti-Assyrian coalition. To make the
country fit for defense, Ahaz was going to strengthen the military installations
at Jerusalem and, according to 2 Kgs 16:5–9, called Assyria for help. Isaiah,
however, opposed this alliance, predicted the defeat of Aram and Northern Israel,
and confronted his king with the famous warning: "If you will not believe,
surely you shall not be established" (7:9). In Hebrew, belief means the trust in
divine promises concerning institutions which were created in the course of
Israel's salvation history. The king refused to stop his endeavors; therefore, Isaiah
predicted the coming of the Assyrians, not to help, but to destroy (8:1–8).
Although YHWH is king over the world, he is no longer only active in favor of
Israel and Judah! Perhaps in this connection the messianic prophecy of a future
savior king was uttered (9:1–6).

In the following decades no Assyrian invasion of Judah occurred. At the right
moment, Ahaz submitted to the mighty Tiglath-pileser (2 Kgs 16:8–18). Nevertheless, Isaiah did not retract his predictions. But he altered his view regarding
the Assyrians. In the meantime, their army had conquered and devastated
nearby countries in a cruel manner. The announcements of their great kings
had expressed an extreme haughtiness and a contempt for all the other nations.
This arrogance must have been abominable in the eyes of the God of Israel as
much as the behavior of the ruling class of Judah in former times. Therefore,
now Isaiah had to announce that YHWH would punish the superpower of the
East in the future too: "Ah Assyria, the rod of my anger, the staff of my fury!
Against a godless nation I send him . . . But it is in his mind to destroy and to
cut off nations not a few . . . Therefore the Sovereign, the Lord of the hosts, will
send wasting sickness among his stout warriors, and under his glory a burning
will be kindled" (10:5–19; cf. 14:24–27; 37:21–29). The prophet recommended
that Judah once more should patiently wait for YHWH's hour and the turn of
domination on the earth.

In spite of Isaiah's continued warnings, Hezekiah started a war with the
Assyrian king with the effect that in 701 BCE the Assyrian army invaded Judah,
conquered the country, and besieged Jerusalem. According to the narratives in
Isaiah 36–39 the prophet would have altered his convictions again, now neglect-
ing the burden of sin of his people and an unavoidable decline of kingdom
and capital, and would have promised the complete rescue of Judah and the
unsuccessful return of the Assyrian king: "I (YHWH) will put my hook in your
nose . . . I will turn you back on the way by which you came" (37:29). Most
exegetes doubt whether these narratives deliver the true content of the prophetic
message in his last phase.

According to a supplementary tale in chapter 39, indeed, Isaiah predicted the deportation of the royal treasures and the princes of Jerusalem by the Babylonians – not the Assyrians – in the far future; but this conclusion of the Proto-Isaiah composition, which says nothing about Judah's guilt as the reason for that disaster, was probably added around 150 years later.

In spite of certain alterations of the prophetic evaluation of the present and of the developments in the future in the course of some 40 years, the special predictions always emerged from the Isaianic conviction of an all-embracing metahistorical horizon of the unity of YHWH's work (5:19; 28:21) and his steadfast counsel (5:19; 28:29; 30:1), which are realized by his word again and again. This word will not only communicate information but also act as a dynamic force on earth (9:7), because it conforms to the substance of the Holy One of Israel.

Certainly Isaiah had to predict an irrevocable doom because of the excess of guilt in the history of his people. But did he think that YHWH would get rid of Israel now and forever? Many exegetes maintain this conclusion and attribute every positive allusion in the texts to later redactors. Did, however, such a decision not emerge from a rather Western desire for strictly logical consequence? Could any ancient Israelite imagine a God who thoroughly annihilates the community of his devotees forever?

Nowhere in Isaiah 1–39 is the destruction of the temple announced. Of course, the dynasty will perish, the cities will be burned, and the capital, the daughter Zion, will remain like a booth in a vineyard (1:8; 29:1–4). The sanctuary however, where Isaiah had his important vision, which is filled with God's holiness and is the footstool of his throne (ch. 6), remains the one point of hope in view of the coming catastrophe (8:17f; 28:16–18). Moreover, in the end it will be the place where Israel's enemies will be destroyed by a divine theophany (14:32; 30:27–33; 31:4–9).

More difficult to answer is the question of whether the prophet accounted for a revitalization of the kingdom after the decline of the present one. The two most famous messianic prophecies of the Hebrew Bible (although the term Messiah is not used) are found in Isa 9:1–6 and 11:1–9. They display an image of a future king, arising from the clan of David through his father Jesse, not from the sinful Jerusalem branch but from the uncorrupted collateral line (at Bethlehem). Although a human being and not of supranatural origin, the king will during his rule always be directed by the spirit of YHWH resting on him, will unite North and South Israel, and establish justice and peace in the country forever (cf. also 32:1–5). Both passages are not formulated in the usual style of the other prophecies. So the Isaianic origin is not certain. The new David is no warrior, he will arise after God's destroying stroke against the power from the East.

Whether the Immanuel sign (7:14) had a messianic significance remains uncertain. During the encounter with King Ahaz, Isaiah had predicted the birth of a son with this symbolic name, born to a woman who apparently was already pregnant. Did he think of a child of his own wife? Or of the queen? Or of an anonymous woman?

Even more crucial seems the decision about the mentioning of a remnant of Israel which will survive and constitute the kernel of a new nation (4:3; 11:11–16; 28:5). The name of one of the sons of Isaiah is Shear-jashub, "a remnant shall return (from the battlefield)" or "shall convert" (7:3), which is of symbolic relevance. If the second translation is right, the prophet accounted for such a little remnant rather early in his message.

Subsequent Redactions

In many chapters, adaptions to the conditions of later times were added, but it is difficult to detect thoroughgoing reworkings. Often the final salvation of Israel after the great catastrophe is put in more concrete forms. In chapter 35 the return of the exiles to Zion with everlasting joy upon their head is announced in a language similar to Deutero-Isaiah.

The Isaianic prophecies about foreign nations were extended to other peoples in the surrounding areas. Some of them predict total destruction, the wiping out even of the remnant of Babel (13:22) or Moab (15:9). Others, however, promise final salvation either to Egypt and Assyria (18:7; 19:18–25) or to all nations, and the end of war by a Torah going forth from Zion (2:2–4).

Jeremiah

More than 100 years later, Jeremiah started his prophetic mission at Jerusalem in 626 BCE, according to the superscription Jer 1:1. The latest utterance transmitted from him was pronounced in Egypt (ch. 44) around 585 BCE.

In the first part (chs. 1–25) short poetic sayings in the I-style of the prophet alternate with comprehensive prosaic sermons whose language recalls that of the Deuteronomistic History; they presumably grew up with a (post-?) exilic reworking of oral Jeremiah traditions (e.g., chs. 7, 11, 25). This deuteronomistic redaction has given the book its final structure.

The oracles against foreign nations, originally in 25:13ff (thus LXX; in MT this is transferred to the end of the book in order to stress the downfall of Babylonia, chs. 50f), are formulated in a poetic manner although only few of them will be authentic.

As in Isaiah the book was finished (chs. 43–51, LXX = 36–45 MT) with biographical narratives, in which the chapters about the future salvation (chs. 30–35 MT) are enclosed. What is told about Jeremiah's destiny seems to be the remembrance of an eye-witness; many scholars suppose Baruch, Jeremiah's secretary and friend (cf. chs. 36, 45), to be the author (ch. 52 was later taken over from 2 Kgs 24f).

The beginnings under Josiah

Jeremiah 2–6 seem to have belonged to the reign of King Josiah between 626 and 622. At this time the Assyrian empire was declining. So the Judahites were highly inspired by the hope that the glorious day of final salvation would soon begin. Jeremiah, however, had realized that the religious and social conditions in Judah were still bad and had not really changed since the times of Isaiah and other critical prophets. Therefore, he prophesied the coming attack of another foreign army, of a mysterious enemy from the North (chs. 2–6). During this initial period of his prophesy, the prophetic critique centered around a veneration of Baal together with that of holy trees and stones, in which even priests and prophets were intensely engaged (2:8, 27; 5:31). Jeremiah's judgment recalls that of Hosea more than 100 years before. The country, indeed, had not converted to the old Canaanite deity of fertility; but in a syncretistic manner ceremonies belonging to this cult for the regeneration of earth, vegetation and humankind, even with rites of sexual intercourse, had been incorporated into the worship of YHWH. In that way, according to Jeremiah, the real essence of the God of Israel's history and the kind of diverse relation to this people is darkened. Israel has neglected the indirect manner in which YHWH creates rain and harvest by laws of nature (5:24) without needing magic support.

Jeremiah announced that God will react, bringing their ways and their doings upon them. The people will earn what they have prepared. YHWH allowed to emerge an anonymous enemy, more terrible than the Assyrians, just from the north, where the Canaanite Baal had his residence. The abuses which the God of the prophet was condemning were (partially) abandoned by Josiah's reform in 622/21, probably on the basis of the now officially introduced laws of Deuteronomy. Surprisingly, any certain indication is lacking as to how Jeremiah reacted. There are no sayings which can be attributed to the time following the reform until the death of Josiah in 609, except perhaps some admonitions to heed the words of the covenant (11:1–8).

Four years under Jehoiakim: The beginning of persecution

Josiah's son was appointed by the Egyptian Pharaoh Necho who had vanquished Assyria, but must submit to the mightier Babylonian King Nebuchadrezzar four years later (605). Shortly after his enthronement Jeremiah pronounced his anti-temple speech condemning the common trust in a magical protection because of a traditional faith in YHWH's indissoluble connection with Mt. Zion. The prophet declared the present temple was a den of robbers because of the social injustice around him, and predicted: "This house shall be like Shiloh, and this city shall be desolate, without inhabitants" (7:4, 11, 14; 26:9). The message stood in clear contrast to the (Deuteronomistic? and) Isaianic conviction of an inassailable Zion (2 Kgs 8, esp. v. 48; Isa 28:16). The speech raised an enormous anger among the audience. People, priests and prophets tried to lynch him, and only the intervention of some higher officials saved his life.

Jeremiah continued to condemn the mingling of the devotion to YHWH with rites of Baal. This deity, however, is more and more depicted by him as a heavenly power determining the celestial bodies and by them the course of events on earth. The conception of such a master of the astral realm had become dominant since neo-Assyrian times in Mesopotamia and Syria and was apparently spreading out to include Judah as well. To make contact with the host of heaven, offerings were made on the roofs of Jerusalem and the abominable Mōlēk-sacrifice in the valley Ben Hinnom outside the wall, where probably children were let go (mōlēk), i.e., burnt on a special altar for ascending as smoke into heaven. According to the prophetic message this crime will evoke a terrible end when the whole people will be slaughtered in that valley (7:30–8:3; 19).

The king became a resolute adversary of this prophet. One day he forbad him to enter the temple and to speak there. So Jeremiah was to write down his words on a scroll, an assignment he gave to Baruch who read it to the public on a fast day. Then the scroll was confiscated and burnt by the king himself who thereafter commanded Jeremiah and his secretary be arrested. The prophet went into the underground for several years and wrote the scroll again (ch. 36).

Probably in that time the famous confessions of Jeremiah originated. Five songs are incorporated in the present book and are composed in the genre of individual psalms of lament. These, in turn, are mostly answered by a subsequent oracle of assurance (11:18–12:6; 15:10–20; 17:14–18; 18:18–23; 20:7–18). The author is cast out by his relatives at Anathoth and the remaining people of the land. A divine vocation had suddenly overcome him, for he did not personally strive to obtain such a mission. He must alter his life-style since that day, and he had to suffer contempt and persecution. The divine answers predicted further hardship instead of consolation. The final composition had presumably referred these songs to the nation and its exile. But originally they certainly expressed the voice and feeling of a real individual, most likely Jeremiah himself. They reveal a deep discord between the private person and the charge which is forced upon him. It is the first time in world history that the feeling of an individual was so expressively formulated.

Acknowledging the Babylonian supremacy during the reign of Zedekiah

Jehoiakim had started a rebellion against Nebuchadrezzar which ended after his death with the conquest of Jerusalem by the Babylonians and the first deportation. For the redactor of 25:9, the enemies from the North had really been led by the Babylonian king. But that surely was not the opinion of Jeremiah. No burning of city and temple had occurred, no deportation of all of Judah (13:19; 20:4f). Doubtless he was waiting for a more severe disaster in the future. For the time after 597, no writing of the prophet himself is preserved, only the cycle of narratives about him. In this part the failures and persecutions of Jeremiah came to the fore as an exemplary fate of prophets in Israel.

After the defeat of Judah, Nebuchadrezzar had installed Zedekiah as a vassal king there, a man of a wavering character. Sometimes he clandestinely sought the advice of Jeremiah, who appeared anew in the public, otherwise he heard to the war-party at his court, which claimed for death penalty over the prophet.

Jeremiah was inspired with the conviction that the Neo-Babylonian empire was not only an instrument of wrath in the hand of YHWH but was determined by the creator to be a universal monarchy for an epoch of seventy years (25:11f; 29:10). That was an outrageous message never before heard in Israel. Jeremiah's colleagues at Jerusalem and some prophets in the exile pronounced just the contrary, the coming rescue from Babylonian oppression. But Jeremiah got right by the course of history.

Apparently with Jeremiah the rise of the monotheistic idea in Israel proceeded one step further. In the time before the belief in the uniqueness of God was closely connected with the political sovereignty and power of Israel, if not with the expectation of her future global rulership (Ps 2; Mic 5:4f). Now the concept of the creation of the human race was extended. The idea of an alternation of universal rulership emerged. Babylon will also become guilty and prepare herself for decline which will be fullfilled by people from the North (50:9, 41; 51:27).

In alliance with Egypt, Zedekiah rose up against Babylonia in 590. Since that year Jeremiah again and again recommended desertion in the name of his God to king and people, but in vain (21:8f; 38:2, 17).

After the catastrophic fall of Jerusalem in 587/86, Jeremiah supported the governor Gedaliah who was appointed by the Babylonians. But the nationalistic Judeans killed Gedaliah and compelled Jeremiah to flee with themselves to Egypt. His last words announced the coming conquest of Egypt too by Nebuchadrezzar and the perishing of the Judean refugees who continued to worship a queen of heaven instead of YHWH also in the foreign country (Jer 42–44).

Promises of a final renewal

Although the predicted catastrophy should be terrible and became so in 586, Jeremiah expected a subsequent positive change of destiny. His picture of future salvation was limited to a restoration of former more fortunate days. The exiles will return to their homeland (50:4). Possession and buying of houses and fields will begin there again (32:15, 43f). Whether some short remarks about a new just King David were formulated by the prophet or later redactors remains unsure (23:5f; 33:15f). The authenticy of the famous prediction of God's making a new covenant is also questionable (31:31–34). That YHWH's covenant with Israel is really broken (also 11:10) was never expressed before. The predicted new one will still be a covenant with Israel and Judah (otherwise the universal idea of the New Testament), perhaps inaugurated on the holy mountain (31:23–

30; 50:4f; 32:36–41) but with a fundamental change in the conciousness, so that knowledge of God will no more be lacking among the members of the community. The burden of collective guilt will never emerge again.

The so-called Deuteronomistic redaction

Their redaction did enlarge and alternate Jeremiah's message. Whereas Jeremiah saw no more possibility for repentance for a generation whose sin was inscribed in the heart (cf. 13:23), that opportunity is presupposed now for all times (7:3–7; 25:5f; 35:15). Thus many of the unconditional predictions were changed into alternative admonitions for younger generations.

Ezekiel

This younger contemporary, was, like Jeremiah, of priestly origin, but much more indebted to the traditions of Mt. Zion. After Nebuchadrezzar had conquered Jerusalem for the first time in 598/97, Ezekiel was deported with other members of the upper class to a settlement of Judean exiles in Mesopotamia. His first inspiration is dated in 593 BCE, his last in 571. The accounts of his visions and symbolic actions reveal a curious psychic constitution. Sometimes he behaved in such an ecstatic manner that the neighbors bound him (3:14f, 22–26). One time by the inner voice he is commanded to lie on his left side for 190 years, then on the right side for 40 days to symbolize the years of Israel's and Judah's apostasy (ch. 4). He also experienced the divine *ruah*, which means wind as well as spirit, that took him by the lock of his head and lifted him between heaven and earth and to and from Mesopotamia and Jerusalem (8:3; 11:1–24; 37:1; 40:1f). Many scholars have diagnosed a psychic illness in him.

The only direct biographical remark refers to the death of his wife who died just at the time when the news arrived that Jerusalem had fallen a second and final time (24:15–27; 33:21f). It marked a fundamental change in his mission. Before that date he had always pronounced disaster over his people. From now on he predicts the turn to salvation for Israel.

Some chapters are probably reworked or composed from a later hand (e.g. the Gog-Magog events in ch. 38f). To discern between the prophetic original and the additions of his school, however, is much more difficult than in the case of Isaiah or Jeremiah.

Ezekiel is well informed about the conditions in Jerusalem and the behavior of prominent persons there. So some scholars maintain an alternation of his stay between Jerusalem and Babylonia. Although Ezekiel was attacking the behavior of his fellow deportees, his main critique between 593 and the fall of Jerusalem in 587 concerned the conditions in the homeland. His audience had to become aware that the decreed disaster over Judah had not yet reached the equivalence of her sin and therefore their exile in Babylonia will endure. The deportees are the kernel of the future renewed Israel; not the people who remained in Palestine who demonstrated no sign of repentance.

For the priestly prophet ritual and moral transgressions belong on the same level. The crimes of Jerusalem are not only blood-guilt, oppression of widows and orphans, and taking bribes, but also the profanation of the Sabbath, intercourse with menstruating women, and sexual perversions (22:1–12). The temple is defiled by rites which perhaps were called forth by a syncretistic identification of YHWH with the astral causalities of time and fate venerated in the whole Near East in that epoch. Ezekiel had seen in one of the gateways of the temple the image of jealously, presumably of the heavenly goddess Asherah, and in other parts of the sanctuary incense offerings to the symbols of animals, women weeping for Tammuz, and men prostrating to the sun (ch. 8). So Mt. Zion is no more a suitable place for the true God. His glory (kâbōd) had already left the temple on a throne chariot towards the East (9:3; 10; 11:22f). One year before it had on the same vehicle twice appeared in Babylonia before the prophet's eyes (1; 3:12–15, 22–26). At the end of the book (ch. 43), however, it is announced that the glory of God will return to Zion from the East after the great eschatological turn. (These passages became the root of Jewish Merkabah-mysticism.)

Ezekiel concentrates his indications of Israel's situation before God on the transgressions of the contemporary society. But more than Isaiah or Jeremiah he traced back the beginnings of the false behavior to the remote past. Sometimes in a metaphoric survey he overviews the metahistory of his nation as a history of increasing apostasy during which the people liked to play the whore instead of remaining as YHWH's faithful wife (chs. 16, 23 cf. 20). Already the forefathers in Egypt had preferred to venerate alien deities as objects of their lust (20:8; 23:8). Later on Israel eagerly made love with foreign powers. So it will be inescapable that these lovers soon come upon her with torture (20:35–43; 23:22–31).

A new subject in Ezekiel's teaching is the reference to a stubborn disobedience of his people toward the statues and commandments which YHWH had given (5:7–10 et seq.). With Isaiah and Jeremiah the divine law did not receive any significant role; their criterion was the practising of ṣĕdāqâ, i.e., the will to sustain the life-giving institutions or the covenant community with Israel's God. With Ezekiel (likewise in the Deuteronomistic redaction of Jeremiah) divine ordinances came to the fore, enlightening the alternative of life and death as an authorative interpretation of ṣĕdāqâ. Connected with this was a second issue, the alteration of the traditional conception of the indissoluble connection between between human act and destiny. Hitherto everybody had been convinced that it functioned in a collective way extended over the generations. Concerning this tradition the exiles around Ezekiel used to lament: "The parents have eaten sour grapes, and the children's teeth are set on edge." The God of the prophet rejected the proverb decisively. Every human life stands in an immediate relation to the creator, so only the person who sins shall die (18:1–3; cf. 14:13–20; 33:10–20). That meant a radical reduction of the conception to individual responsibility. (In other passages the prophet presupposed the participation of the individual in the common destiny and saw especially himself in such a position, cf. chs. 4–5.)

These divergencies from the traditional faith have probably grown up under the conditions of the exile. The deportation had torn the Judahites out of the connections with the inherited forms of community and interaction. A new, authoritative determination was needed.

Concerning the turn to an era of salvation Ezekiel predicted the destruction of Israel's enemies, a gathering and unification of the dispersed parts of Israel, a returning David, who is called only prince and no more king, and the making of a new covenant. All that will happen for the sake of YHWH's name in order that Israel as well as the other nations "shall know that I am YHWH"; thus the often used formula. Contrary to Jeremiah's view the old covenant is not broken, but will be revitalised by God as an everlasting covenant (16:60–63; 34:25–31; 37:26–28). Because of the hitherto in ability to sustain righteousness Ezekiel imagined a divine transplantation of heart: "I will remove from your body the heart of stone and give you a heart of flesh. I will put my spirit within you" (36:26f; 11:17–20).

A draft constitution of the future Israel is added in chs. 40–48. Around the temple which is built anew the land is distributed; every tribe will receive the like portion. Water will spring from beneath the Temple and make even the Dead Sea in to fresh water. For cult and administration a separation of power will function between the prince, the priests, and the Levites.

Deutero- and Trito-Isaiah

The turn of the exile

An unrestricted message of hope comes to the fore in Isaiah 40–55. As mentioned above, these chapters assume an origin in the Babylonian exile rather than in Palestine. The fall of the Judean kingdom and cult is presupposed, and the Babylonian rule has become a matter of course. The language differs largely from that of the Proto-Isaiah corpus. Most sayings of this complex have presumably grown up among the deportees between 550 and 540 BCE. Among the exilic community there is no longer any hope of a return to the homeland, but a deep resignation was prevalent, a lament over human transcience: "All people are grass, their constancy is like the flower of the field." Against that the prophet had to protest: "But the word of our God will stand for ever," and this word is now predicting comfort and salvation (40:6–8). The time of catastrophy has finally gone, the great turn of fate is already in preparation. YHWH takes care for a second exodus of his imprisoned people; he will establish a marvelous highway through a fertilized desert from Babylonia to Jerusalem under the guidance of divine glory (cf. Ezekiel 43). After a successful return, Jerusalem will be rebuilt with indestructible walls of previous stones. A free Israel will emerge. Deutero-Isaiah did not know any limitation to a pious remnant; the whole of Israel will be endowed with a new and steadfast ability to righteous behavior and solidarity (45:8). Then the apex will be the self-enthronement of YHWH, the final salvation will be announced by the call: "Your God reigns" (52:7). And not only Israel is concerned. All nations will recognise the paramount intervention of the mightiest God: "Every tongue will affirm: Only in YHWH is there for me righteousness and strength," one will say (45:23–24).

Surprisingly the divine agent on earth shall be a foreign ruler, the Persian prince Cyrus. He will be victorious as YHWH's Messiah, his Anointed, and will rebuild Jerusalem and the temple (44:28–45:7). Deutero-Isaiah was even expecting that Cyrus will know that it is I, YHWH, who called you by your name. Historically, some years later Cyrus conquered Babylonia and afterwards permitted the liberation of the exiles and a rebuilding of the temple at Jerusalem. Deutero-Isaiah promised that the salvation of the coming age will surpass every analogy of past history (51:9–11; 52:11f). Even the first things done by God in favor of Israel like primeval creation or the exodus from Egypt will no more be remembered (43:16–21). Thus the prophet fomulated eschatology, but also the monotheistic idea in a stricter sense than ever before. His God is proclaiming: "Before me no god was formed nor shall there be any after me" (43:10f; cf. 45:5, 18). Deutero-Isaiah as did Proto-Isaiah could call the unique God, The Holy One of Israel, but with an opposite perspective: the title no longer referred to the supreme eminence which consumes every unclean being (Isa 6), but to the merciful redeemer (41:14; 43:14; 47:4).

After the conviction of the Prophet every decisive metahistorical event in the past was preestablished by divine predictions. This is still more valid regarding the imminent great events.

The songs of the servant of the Lord

Most scholars used to separate Isa 42:1ff; 49:1ff; 50:4ff and 52:13–53:12 from the remaining chapters. In these four passages someone is addressed as his servant or, in the mouth of God as my servant to whom a decisive mission is entrusted concerning the imminent turn of fate. Whereas in other sayings this title refers to the forefather Jacob or to the nation embodied in him (41:8f etc.), in Deutero-Isaiah the servant is depicted in a very individual way and received the task of reestablishing the lost Israel. Regarding his identity, Jewish exegesis as a rule argued for a personification of the empirical (or the ideal) Israel, and Christian scholars are inclined to join this interpretation still today. But his mission to Israel speaks against that. (The collective interpretation was possibly already accepted by the redactors who placed the passages between other sayings regarding the nation.)

Each of the songs is composed as a liturgy. In 42:1–4 God presents my servant to the public, God has endowed him with his spirit to spread his world-order all over the earth; thereafter in vv. 5–9 God turns to him personally with an oracle of assurance. In 49:1–6 the servant himself proclaims his mission first to his own people, then to the nations; again a supporting speech of God follows (vv. 7–9). Verses 52:13–53:12 presuppose that in the meantime the violent death of the servant has happened, as a substitute for the guilt of the Many. The unit starts with a divine promise of the (future) elevation of the servant over nations and kings (52:13–15). Then his adherents lament that they had held him in contempt because of his lack of beauty and that the enemies (the Babylonians?) rejected and killed him (53:1–9). The text closes with a second promise probably alluding to his resurrection (vv. 10–12).

Most scholars add to this sequence 50:4–11, where a prophetic person deplores his difficult duty and the enduring rejection by his hearers; but he does not call himself servant. The title is given to a third person (v. 10; perhaps in a later addition); so the inclusion of this passage in the cycle remains doubtful. Today many scholars, nevertheless, take 50:4ff as an important proof that all these songs are autobiographical and mirror the experience of Deutero-Isaiah himself (cf. Acts 8:34: Does the prophet say this about himself?).

Except for 50:4ff, however, the royal attributes of the servant, who will be elevated above kings at the end, stand out much more prominently than prophetic ones. Therefore, the Targum and hereafter Christian exegesis identified the figure with the Messiah, i.e., with Christ. If the close relation to the conditions of the exile is taken into consideration, perhaps a Davidic prince living among the community and killed by the Babylonians might have been meant (cf. the blind servant, Meshullam, in 42:19 and 1 Chr 3:19).

The Trito-Isaiah Appendix

Isaiah 56–66 depend on Isaiah 40–55 in varying degrees, but both originate with different authors. Trito-Isaiah's sayings refer to the terrible moral and economic conditions in post-exilic Judah. Judean groups had returned from Babylonia, but without any eschatological dramatics, without a turn to abundant salvation. The reason for the delay lies in a new unfaithfullness of the Judeans: they oppress the needy and value the cultus over social activity (chs. 58f). The monotheistic idea goes one step further: Mt. Zion remains God's anchor on earth, but he does not seem to like their bloody offerings (66:3).

A temple building is superfluous (66:1); moreover, the place should be open to foreigners and eunuchs: My house shall be called a house of prayer for all peoples (56:7). Nevertheless, the present unsatisfactory status will soon disappear, when the theophany of the divine glory will occur and a new heaven and new earth will be created (60–62; 66:22).

Bibliography

Barton, J., "Postexilic Hebrew Prophecy," *Anchor Bible Dictionary* 5 (1992), 489–95.
Blenkinsopp, J., *A History of Prophecy in Israel*, 2nd edn. (Louisville: Westminster/John Knox, 1996).

Boadt, L., "Ezekiel," *Anchor Bible Dictionary* 2 (1992), 711–22.

Koch, K., "Propheten/Prophetie, II: in Israel und seiner Umwelt," *Theologische Realenzyklopaedie* 27 (1997), 473–99.

——, *The Prophets*, 2 vols. (Philadelphia: Westminster, 1983–4).

Lundblom, J., "Jeremiah, Book of," *Anchor Bible Dictionary* 3 (1992), 706–21.

Mowinckel, S., *Prophecy and Tradition* (Oslo: J. Dybwad, 1946).

Schmitt J., "Preexilic Hebrew Prophecy," *Anchor Bible Dictionary* 5 (1992), 482–9.

Seitz, C., W. Millar, and R. Clifford, "Isaiah, Book of," *Anchor Bible Dictionary* 3 (1992), 711–22.

Westermann, C., Basic *Forms of Prophetic Speech* (Philadelphia: Westminister, 1967).

CHAPTER 22
Latter Prophets: The Minor Prophets

James L. Crenshaw

In the Hebrew Bible twelve short prophetic compositions follow the three longer books of Isaiah, Jeremiah, and Ezekiel. The earliest reference to the twelve as a unit occurs in Sir 49:10 ("May the bones of the Twelve Prophets send forth new life from where they lie, for they comforted the people of Jacob and delivered them with confident hope"), an allusion to the devotional legend in 2 Kings 13:20–21 associated with Elisha's bones. Whereas each of the other three prophetic books filled a separate scroll, the Twelve occupied an additional one, making four complete scrolls of Latter Prophets. Their final form seems designed to complete the number twelve, and evidence of earlier groupings has been adduced.

The twelve Minor Prophets – the adjective refers to length, not substance – are Hosea, Joel, Amos, Obadiah, Jonah, Micah, Nahum, Habakkuk, Zephaniah, Haggai, Zechariah, and Malachi. Both Hosea and Amos prophesied to the northern kingdom in the 8th century when the Assyrian empire flourished; Micah appeared in Judah roughly contemporaneously. Nahum, Habakkuk, and Zephaniah proclaimed their messages against the backdrop of Assyria's collapse near the end of the 7th century. Haggai and Zechariah spurred on the rebuilding of the temple in Jerusalem. They were active from 521 to 520, if their chronological observations are accurate. The dates of Obadiah, Joel, and Malachi are less certain, and the very existence of a prophet named Malachi is doubtful, the reference in 1:1 deriving from the promise of a coming messenger in 3:1 (Malachi means "my messenger").

Although the other eleven books have been associated with prophetic figures, as putative "authors" (except for the book of Jonah, which is a story about a prophet), their content bears evidence of later redaction to a greater or lesser extent. Large portions of the books of Micah and Zechariah are generally considered secondary, and several other books have been edited in the light of later interests. The resulting inconsistency rules out a unitary interpretation of the text, despite the occurrence of certain themes in both old and new units. Even a single prophet seems to pronounce words of weal and woe for the same people, and different understandings of prophecy underlie such individuals as Nahum, who announces Nineveh's destruction, Amos, whose word of doom is directed at Israel, and Micah, who predicts Jerusalem's downfall.

Some books combine oracles and visions, while others restrict their prophetic message to oracles. One book, Jonah, limits its oracular content to five words in Hebrew ("Yet forty days and Nineveh will be overturned," 3:4), the final word carrying a double sense of destroyed/converted. The book of Malachi resembles a discussion between competing groups of priests and laity. In length, the books range from a single chapter of twenty-one verses in Obadiah to fourteen chapters in Hosea and Zechariah. Most books combine poetry and prose, but occasionally one will restrict itself to prose (Malachi) or poetry (Nahum and Zephaniah), if modern interpreters rightly recognize Hebrew verse.

A few books within the collection bear the marks of efforts to form a macro-structure, as if an editor wanted to promote the reading of a larger unit than any single book. For example, Amos 9:12 alludes to a prediction in Obadiah 21 that the saved will rule over the Edomites, and the utopian vision in Amos 9:13 resembles Joel 4:18 [3:18]. Similarly, the opening utterance in Amos 1:2 ("The Lord roars from Zion, and utters his voice from Jerusalem") is identical with the first part of Joel 4:16 [3:16]. Moreover, both Joel 2:13 and Jonah 4:2 cite a portion of the credo in Ex 34:6–7. Whether or not one of these prophets influenced the other in this respect cannot be ascertained. Thematic links among various books also occur, and these connections indicate common traditions as ubiquitous as Zion's special status and as rare as a book of remembrance containing "the names of those who revered the Lord and thought on his name" (Mal 3:16).

How can modern readers make sense of such diversity? That task becomes formidable when one considers the competing voices clamoring for recognition in the interpretive marketplace. The traditional near-consensus about a hermeneutical principle has given way to a contemporary Tower of Babel, in one sense enriching the discussion but in another sense relativizing all approaches and privileging everything and therefore nothing. The earlier striving for objectivity, never fully achieved, has given way to celebrated subjectivity, and open advocacy rules the day. In some camps a definite shift in paradigm has occurred, history succumbing to a literary model. In other circles, emphasis falls on the way sociology informs and shapes all knowledge.

In such an intellectual climate, the sky is the limit. The possibilities can be illustrated by means of broad strokes, easily filled in by the informed reader. Heuristically, the 20th century has witnessed a sequence of interpretive givens, beginning with an assumption of prophetic oracles as *ipsissima verba dei*, exact words of God. By exhaustive philological and stylistic arguments, scholars endeavored to separate the wheat from the chaff, divine oracles from secondary human additions. In due time this pursuit of the revelatory word gave way to efforts to appreciate editorial additions in their own right as a living tradition in dialogue with earlier traditions. This search for competing value systems gave birth to form and redaction criticism, and to further refinements that virtually eclipsed the presence of editors. The multiple voices in the ancient world were soon matched by modern multivocality, a competition to be heard over issues of gender, ethnicity, sexual preference, marginalization of all sorts. Thus Hosea has been viewed as a wife-beater, Zephaniah as a person of color, and Amos as a champion of the poor. Clearly, the old questions of authorship, date, and historical setting have been replaced by entirely different queries mostly aimed at legitimating modern segments of the population.

Chronologically, the Book of the Twelve begins with courageous prophets announcing the destruction of an entire kingdom because it understood election as privilege rather than responsibility (Amos 3:2) or because it adulterated the cult and abandoned its Lord (Hosea). Almost concomitantly, another brave individual announced that the holy city Jerusalem would be plowed like a field because of the atrocities of the rich against the poor (Micah). A remarkable change has occurred by the time the book of Malachi poses questions about ritual and ethical purity, in a sense justifying the observation that the Minor Prophets begin with a bang and end with a whimper. Eighth century prophets proclaim words that they believed originated with the deity; prophets from the post-exilic period begin to interpret earlier revelatory words in the light of their own day. In large part, prophecy changes from mediation of a divine message to its explication. Prophetic intermediation with the deity on behalf of a vulnerable nation (Amos 7:2, 5) vanishes and the conversation moves more freely on the human plane than vertically (Malachi).

Canonically, the opening book tells a story of an ill-fated marriage, and the last book condemns individuals who divorce the wives of their youth. In the first instance marriage functions as a metaphor for the relationship between God and Israel; in the second, it designates a bond between two humans. Another metaphor stands alongside that of marriage in the initial prophetic book, the equally powerful notion of parent. The concluding book also uses this metaphor, while accusing the people of failing to honor YHWH as father. Both Hosea and Malachi attribute strong passion to the deity; alongside love there is hate, in the first instance for wayward Israel, in the second, for Esau.

Politically, the Minor Prophets open on the scene of world history, with Israel at the mercy of the Assyrian empire. Amos' prophetic activity comes just prior to the wakening giant, Israelites waxing jubilant over minor victories in local skirmishes. In a few years, as Hosea experiences firsthand, the Assyrian forces enter a land torn by regicide, leaving ruin in their wake. This conqueror finally meets its match in the Babylonians, jubilantly described in the book of Nahum, and a new power emerges as the scourge of Judah. Micah predicts the destruction of Jerusalem and Habakkuk struggles to understand the rationale for violence as a response to sin, especially when the agent of punishment has no claim to moral superiority. Obadiah ponders the circumstances accompanying Jerusalem's collapse, the unexpected betrayal of fleeing Judeans by a kinship group, the Edomites. Haggai and Zechariah encourage a small remnant of returning exiles to rebuild a religious center, in accord with Persian administrative policy. Such temples served as a financial institution, an administrative locus for collecting taxes, and an executive branch of local government. The nation no longer has political autonomy, and tiny Yehud (the Aramaic word for Judah) may even lack its own governor. The few hundred inhabitants of Jerusalem must look to rival Samaria for political leadership. Monarchic rule in Israel and Judah has vanished except in hope, which crops up now and again within prophetic anticipations of future restoration (Amos 9:11; Mic 5:1–4 [5:2–5]). Others envision the crowning of a priestly leader (Zech 6:9–15), complain about worthless shepherds (Zech 13:7), and discard human rule in favor of divine leadership (Mic 4:1–4).

Economically, the Book of the Twelve is largely restricted to local real estate, although Amos predicts a mass departure into exile and the prophet Jonah embarks on a journey to a foreign capital, Nineveh. The prosperous times of the 8th century, documented in part by the ivories discovered at the site of ancient Samaria, occasioned the emergence of an affluent group who used their newly-acquired influence to impoverish the weak. While the former basked in the comfort of summer and winter homes, enjoyed lavish feasts, and paraded their piety, the latter suffered the loss of land, livelihood, and freedom. Economic cannibalism characterized existence in 8th century Judah, according to Micah, and poverty threatened the survival of late 6th century Yehud, as earned wages vanished through holes in the common purse. The growing centrality of the temple in Jerusalem was accompanied by heirocratic authority, with priestly interests being foisted on the general populace. Over the centuries an agrarian economy suffered from excessive taxation to fill the royal treasury, inclement weather (drought) or infestations of locusts, and invading armies in need of supplies.

Theologically, the Minor Prophets begin with a passionate plea for the purging of the cult of all syncretistic features (Hosea) and a reminder that the election of Israel implied responsibility, specifically the implementation of justice in all aspects of life (Amos). They conclude with a rational discussion aimed at convincing listeners to purify their lives and their sacrificial offerings, along with a promise that God can be trusted to act justly in spite of evidence to the contrary. A pervasive issue from start to finish – the scope of divine patience – evokes different responses. At first Amos intercedes for Israel, counting on divine compassion, only to abandon this endeavor on the assumption that forgiveness has run its course. For him, the virgin Israel had fallen, to rise no more, for the end had come after repeated discipline by YHWH. Hosea, too, envisioned a deity devoid of compassion, although later editors softened his harsh message. That tendency to discover a warm spot in the deity's heart resulted from the conviction that God's people had suffered enough for their sins and that YHWH's mercy triumphed over justice. The desire for vengeance on foreign enemies was given theological legitimacy by emphasizing YHWH's sovereignty and the choice of Israel as a covenant partner. Increasingly, the prophets spoke of an eschaton, envisioned as YHWH's day, and of the elevation of Zion as an international religious center. Perhaps the most vexing theological issue, that of theodicy, was also the most creative. The ruminations of Habakkuk and the poignant object lesson at the end of the book of Jonah indicate the profundity of prophetic thinking about divine justice, and the ubiquity of the problem can be gauged by its frequency of appearance in the discussions within Malachi.

Stylistically, the Book of the Twelve moves from above to below, from theological proclamation understood as divine revelation to human discussion as the dominant mode of discourse. The earlier prophetic works employ poetry almost exclusively, whereas the later authors Haggai and Zechariah prefer prose, and one book, Jonah, takes the form of narration, except for the embedded psalm in chapter 2. A move from clear imagery and precise metaphors in pre-exilic prophecy to dark visions that require explanation in post-exilic prophecy suggests that the phenomenon has become more cerebral, possibly with a more limited clientele because prophecy itself has fallen under suspicion (Zech 13:1–6).

Redactionally, a shift occurs from orality to literacy. Original oracles and visions, circulated orally by survivors who treasured the message that had passed the Deuteronomistic test of accuracy, evoked alternative readings of divine intention (Amos 9:8b–10; Hos 2:1–4 [1:10–2:1], 2:16–23). Messages of doom were superseded by promises of hope (Micah 1–3 and 4–7), at times yielding perfect symmetry (Joel 1:1–2:17; 2:17–4:21). A proper prayer (Jonah 2) and a hymn (Hab 3) render the story of a wayward prophet and Habakkuk's doubt more palatable, and complex visions extend the metaphorical reach of Zechariah (9–14). Editorial revisions reflect geographical affinities (Amos 2:4–5; Hos 4:15a), ideological concerns (Hos 14:9), priestly self-interest (Zech 6:11; Mal 3:8–12), and theological agendas (Amos 9:11–15).

Pedagogically, the Minor Prophets start with divine invective against Israel and Judah, extend that curse to foreign nations, then offer solace to a small enclave of faithful – or lucky – survivors. The divine punishment comes with appropriate rationale and spectacular fanfare, particularly visions and theophanies. Liturgical examples reinforce the heavy message, while reminders of YHWH's compassionate nature emphasize the gravity of human offense. Appeals to deep emotions and lasting ties of affection, both divine and human, pervade the literature. Utopian dreams compete with stark reality, national ruin with the hope of an emerging devout remnant. Rhetoric of persuasion runs the gamut from pathos (appeal to emotions) in Hosea, ethos (appeal to character) in Jonah, to logos (appeal to reason) in Habakkuk.

This brief foray into alternative ways of approaching the Minor Prophets could be expanded, but the preceding discussion indicates the complexity of any analysis of such diverse texts. Other interpreters would undoubtedly stress different things, but that only reinforces the point. Can one sift through the competing concepts and expose sufficient commonalities to justify treating the twelve books as a single corpus? That question will remain in the background as we look more closely at the social role of the prophets in their historical contexts and their religious views.

Social Roles

Israelite prophecy was part of a larger phenomenon within the Ancient Near East, beginning as early as the 18th century in Mari. At least four types of prophets are mentioned in the literature from the kingdom of Zimri Lim; these include the ecstatic, diviner, cultic functionary, and independent messenger of the deity. The prophets communicated divine words, frequently introducing them with oracular formulae such as "The God Adad has sent me," "Thus shall you say," and "Fear not." They concentrated their attention on the royal figure, promoting at one and the same time the welfare of the state and its primary deity. They also posed a danger to the ruler, introducing critical remarks that could easily stir up conspiracy and intrigue. For this reason, the palace sought to regulate prophetic activity, holding individuals responsible for their views.

Prophecy in 7th century Neo-Assyrian records suggests remarkable stability in the phenomenon over more than a millennium. The texts derive exclusively from the reign of Esarhaddon (680–669) and Assurbanipal (668–627), kings who consulted diviners of all kinds and entered prophetic oracles into the royal archives. During the reign of these two kings, prophetic activity is mentioned in letters, inscriptions, and documents. The records imply that diviners used inductive means to determine the deity's will, hence belonged to a learned class, whereas prophets received the divine word through non-inductive means. In essence, prophets conveyed the deity's word to the king, a message they usually received in a dream or vision.

In Neo-Assyrian texts the terminology for prophecy is *maḫḫû* (ecstatic), *raggimu* (proclaimer); the related terms *šabrû* and *šā'ilu* designate visionaries and interpreters of dreams. Although the latter two terms indicate human means of inquiry, not the deity's mouthpiece as in the two earlier ones, the line of demarcation is slippery, as in biblical *nābî'*, *ḥōzeh*, and *rō'eh* (1 Sam 9:9). For example, in one text three terms occur alongside one another as follows: "from the mouth of a prophet (*raggimi*), an ecstatic (*maḫḫû*), an inquirer of oracles (*ša'ili*). The goddess who commissioned the Neo-Assyrian prophets was Ishtar of Arbela.

In the sixteen prophetic texts consulted by Martti Nissinen, King Esarhaddon refers to frequent messages from the goddess that encouraged his heart and strengthened his sacerdotal throne. A prophet named Baya assured him that he was chosen by the deity from childhood, and a certain Sinqiša-amur promised deliverance from enemies. Other prophets claim that the royal throne belongs to the exiled king and that his enemies will be annihilated. Similarly, Assurbanipal refers to unanimity in prophetic messages from Šamaš and Adad with regard to the restoration of a temple, protection from the goddess Ishtar in accord with her promises, and divine presence in war as communicated by prophets and omens.

One divine oracle concerning Elamites uses a numerical formula ("He said [this] five, six times . . ."), and a list of military personnel includes Ququ, prophet. In an account of a substitute king, prophetesses offer instruction about royal clothes and insignia. A report by Urad-Gula indicates that people other than kings also consulted prophets for good omens, a letter from Bel-ušezib complains that the king consulted prophets and prophetesses although Bel-ušezib had already divulged the truth to him, and a treaty warns against concealing information about possibly seditious prophets.

To sum up, Neo-Assyrian prophecy aided the imperium in its propaganda, provided instruction for the king and his subjects, and strengthened the royal cult. Because of its potential for conspiracy, prophecy became subject to empirical control. Prophetic figures viewed certain kings as favorites of the deities, identified their battles as waged on behalf of a particular deity and its cultic apparatus, and provided theological support for certain human rulers.

In some respects, the Minor Prophets resemble Neo-Assyrian prophets. They offered their support to the effort at restoring the temple in Jerusalem, promised the revitalization of the Davidic dynasty, proclaimed oracles against YHWH's enemies and those of the Judean state, instructed kings and their subjects, and kept alive hopes for better days. They used oracular formulas to distinguish divine from human words, and they sometimes concerned themselves with matters pertaining to the cult. Nevertheless, many of the prophets in the Book of the Twelve lived after the collapse of the monarchy, and their predecessors directed sharp criticism at royal figures. In one instance, the forces of the state endeavored to silence a prophet, with the priest Amaziah boldly asserting that the temple belonged to King Jeroboam, not to YHWH (Amos 7:13). The several attempts to overthrow the government in Israel furnished Hosea ample opportunity to cast his lot with one or other incumbent, but he identified kingship itself with rebellion against God (8:4). The closest a member of the Twelve came to endorsing a ruler was Zechariah, who thinks in terms of hierocracy (6:9–14). A certain democratization of prophecy, and in Habakkuk's case a pronounced individualism, is evident in the Minor Prophets.

The close relationship between prophecy and priestly divination, evident in Neo-Assyrian records, occurs in the Minor Prophets also. Amos seems to put on priestly apparel and to adopt the language of an alien office in the invitation to come to the local sanctuaries in order to sin (4:4–5), Micah and Hosea employ priestly liturgies, Haggai and Malachi take extraordinary interest in determining what is clean and unclean. When Amos uses a numerical formula, he combines it with one of divine irrevocability, and his understanding of vocation carries a strong sense of coercion (3:8; 7:14–15).

The impression that 8th century prophets urged society to repent of evil and escape punishment has meager support in the text. Amos' invitation to seek the Lord and live stands alongside considerable qualification (perhaps, a remnant), just as the prophet's initial intercession gives way to resignation in the face of a sure thing. For Joel, the invitation to turn to YHWH in genuine contrition rests under a similar umbrella ("Who knows," 2:14), even when grounded in ancient confessional language (Ex 34:6). Such attempts to guard divine freedom contrast mightily with Deuteronomic promises based on the logic of deed and consequence and a merciful deity, as well as those fueled by a belief that a covenantal relationship assured the safety of YHWH's people.

Some Minor Prophets are often called reformers, but the term more appropriately applies to royalty, especially Hezekiah and Josiah. Prophets lacked the authority to institute genuine reform, whereas these kings are remembered as instigators of reforms aimed at purifying Yahwism of alien features and bringing

376 JAMES L. CRENSHAW

it in line with divine revelation as reflected in Deuteronomy. Prophets did, however, call the people back to traditional values, whether the Decalogue (Hos 4:2), legal injunctions protecting the poor (Amos 2:6–8), or remembered experience (Hab 3). The situation remained the same in the restored community of Yehud, for the actual reformers were administrative appointees, Nehemiah the political authority (governor?) and Ezra the priest. The role of Haggai and Zechariah was that of catalyst in the reconstruction of the temple.

One function, often attributed to cultic prophets on the basis of 1 Kings 22, is that of providing divine support for national politics. Initially, Amos' oracles against foreign nations appear to fall into this category, but they quickly disabuse one of that notion. The prophets Nahum and Obadiah may be understood as supporters of national politics, but they come closer to the sentiment expressed in the latter part of the book of Joel. Here the inner logic of Yahwism has led to a conviction that justice will prevail on an international scale, so that YHWH will be recognized far and wide as present and active on behalf of a covenanted people.

Enacted prophecy seems to have been a feature of the cult, but it existed much more widely. Hosea chose to embody his message in the most personal manner possible, marriage; he was followed in this regard by Isaiah, Ezekiel, and Jeremiah. Micah announces that he will walk about naked, lamenting like jackals and ostriches (1:8), but he is no more a professional lamenter than Habakkuk is a sentinel when reporting that he will watch for the vision, or a courier when reading the contents of that divine disclosure, or Hosea is a baker because he describes Ephraim as a partially baked cake. Prophetic mediation, that is, made use of various rhetorical strategies to communicate what they believed was a divine word for the populace.

Religious Views

The theological teachings of the Minor Prophets are not easily perceived, partly because they reflect an alien worldview from the modern understanding of reality and partly because they come largely in poetic dress. Even when one succeeds in distinguishing what is presented as a divine word from the prophet's own view, no easy task because of the frequent transition from one to the other, the dense language makes such free use of metaphor and symbolism that the essence escapes detection. How much of the language falls into the category of rhetoric, chosen either for its shock value or to demonstrate YAHWEH's grandeur? Answering this question would seem to be mandatory before proceeding to distill the religious views of the Minor Prophets, but no key has been found to unlock the mystery. Therefore, the reader should remain attentive to the polyvalency of the text, its capacity for multiple meanings. That includes irony, so easily overlooked. Two examples suffice. In Hosea's poignant characterization of YHWH as utterly different from mortals, human emotions fill the description of the deity to the breaking point (Hos 11:1–9). While resisting a Baalistic religion based on nature's cycles, Hosea clothes his message in naturalistic imagery (Hos 14:5–7).

The dominant theological interests of the Minor Prophets were justice, the purity of worship, the character of the deity, the identity of the community of YHWH, and its future. Eighth century prophets focused on social justice (Amos and Micah) and the purging of worship to get rid of Baalistic practices (Hosea). The crisis following the fall of Jerusalem to the Babylonians brought the divine character to the forefront, particularly the issue of theodicy (Habakkuk, Nahum, Obadiah, and Jonah). The struggle to restore Yehud introduced the vexing problem of determining the precise constituency of the religious community. In addition, the difficulties encountered at this time – social, economic, political, religious – called forth utopian descriptions of the future, promises attributed to the deity that provided encouragement for hard times. Adjustments to earlier oracles of judgment (Amos 9:11–15; Hos 2:1–5 [1:10–11]; 2:16–23; Mic 4:1–4) gave voice to the conviction that YHWH's final word of blessing cancelled the earlier sentence of doom.

The principle of justice as understood by Amos implied social solidarity, a commitment to fairness and equity at all levels of society. His oracles against foreign nations held Israel's immediate neighbors accountable before YHWH. Their offenses – genocide, fratricide, violation of appropriate burial, slaughtering non-combatants – fall in the realm of universal norms governing warfare similar to the Geneva Convention regulating the conduct of modern military conflict. Israel's own violations differed in that they involved local citizens, either sexual abuse or enslavement by economic oppression. Amos denounced the powerful who adopted a luxurious lifestyle, often at the expense of the poor, and he mocked the people's presumption with regard to YHWH, which produced overzealous religious activity devoid of compassion for the needy. The prophet acknowledged Israel's special place in the divine scheme of things, although extending YHWH's salvific activity to include parallel exodi of Syrians and Philistines. In his view, YHWH's long history of disciplinary chastening (4:6–11) had failed, leaving no choice but to destroy sacred place and people (9:1–4). This horrific vision of YHWH standing on top of the altar poised to demolish the temple and chase down every survivor, the last of five visions becoming progressively more dire, recalls the warning in 4:12 to prepare to meet the Lord in battle.

Whereas Amos was a southerner who felt constrained to denounce the northern kingdom, leaving open the possibility of cultural bias, Micah delivered a similar word to his own people. Curiously, interpreters have often accused him of applying rural standards to urbanites. Like Amos, he concentrated on breaches of social justice, but Micah's language graphically underlines the excesses. The harshest charge, cannibalism, functions as a metaphor for land-grabbing, perversion of justice by means of bribes, and similar behavior conjured up in nocturnal preoccupation. Grounded in the ancient theophanic tradition, his oracles expanded this concept to include Zion's total destruction and YHWH's silence, leaving prophets with no divine revelation. Like Amos, he encountered resistance among the people whom he stoutly rebuffed with a boast that he possessed authority, justice, and the spirit. Possibly secondary material, attributed to Micah, raises the issue of idols (5:13–14), employs fertility curses (6:14–15), accuses the entire population of untrustworthiness (7:1–6), sums up the divine imperative as doing justice, loving mercy, and walking humbly with YHWH (6:6–8), and echoes the credo in Ex 34:6–7 (7:18–20).

The social unrest during Hosea's activity notwithstanding, his sharpest criticism fell on the rituals at the high places and sanctuaries, especially those associated with sacred bulls. Such syncretism, which he likened to adultery, was accompanied by wholesale breaking of the Decalogue. Hosea faced the problem of persuading Israelites that YHWH, not Baal, was the true source of agrarian success. In Hosea's view, Israel had a moment of innocence, but that vanished with the orgy at Baal-Peor. History was important to him, especially the ancestral traditions about Jacob, but also those concerning Moses. These memories contrast earlier leaders with those in his own day, whose rapacious conduct prompts Hosea to counter with bestial images for YHWH. The divine love has turned to hate, and the deity confronts Israel as a vulture, a lion, a bear, and a leopard. Hosea has the deity declare that compassion is hidden from his eyes. Underneath the emphasis on cultic offenses the careful reader notices another theme, the absence of knowledge. An editor highlights this idea in the final verse of the book.

The understanding of history in these three prophets, reinforced by Isaiah, Ezekiel, and Jeremiah, generated a monumental problem for their successors. If YHWH used the powerful nations of Assyria and Babylonia to punish Israel and Judah, should they not exemplify more virtue than the people they punish? In the end, YHWH's character becomes an issue. Can one expect justice from the deity? Habakkuk recognizes the problem with extraordinary clarity and puts his question before YHWH, who postpones an answer. The prophet must wait for decisive demonstration that the deity is acting justly on the international scene. If any comfort can be found, it is the confidence that the just person will live by faithfulness. A theophany provides a doxological conclusion, a remarkable "nevertheless" of faith. The prophet Jonah does not reach this high point of resolve to trust YHWH in the face of evidence to the contrary, although he exposes the theodic problem in his very person. A recipient of YHWH's mercy, Jonah refuses to grant the deity the right to extend similar compassion to the inhabitants of Nineveh. The confession in Ex 34:6–7 has become for him an offense precisely because divine forgiveness lets oppressive nations get away with unthinkable cruelty. The story closes with an angry Jonah, stunned by YHWH's question directing his attention to vulnerable people and animals, toward whom the prophet has shown no compassion.

The prophets Nahum and Obadiah wanted no part of Habakkuk's patient waiting or Jonah's sulking. Instead, they reaffirmed the traditional Deuteronomic formulation. In short, the nations who act wickedly will be punished for their conduct. Nahum bases his prophecy about Nineveh's downfall on the divine character as proclaimed in Ex 34:6–7, but he emphasizes the judgmental side rather than the compassionate one. With exquisite poetry, Nahum describes the fall of Nineveh and the desperate actions of its citizens. The prophet Obadiah applies the Deuteronomic "measure for measure" to the Edomites, who are accused of aiding the Babylonians on the occasion of the fall of Jerusalem. A single refrain echoes through the brief book: "you should not have . . ."

This emphasis on justice, which inevitably led to examination of the divine character, focused the spotlight on the ones calling for fairness in the world. Could the tiny community pass inspection? The desire to present a good face to the deity resulted in considerable soul-searching with regard to membership. The temple assumes a central place, and with it priestly authority over daily conduct. Haggai, Zechariah, and Malachi concentrate on proper ritual, believing that the deity demands purity, fasts, sacrifice, and tithes. Holiness thus becomes a tangible reality, one that extends to every dimension of life. Ezekiel would have been proud of his successors.

The prophet Joel also emphasizes ritual as a means of escaping a devastating plague of locusts, reinforcing the external activity with a call for inner contrition. For him, priestly ministry at the temple was vital to the well-being of the people. His belief in perfect justice finds expression in the concept of lex talionis, an exact retribution for wrongs committed. He joins Jonah in reciting part of the credal statement in Ex 34:6–7, although Joel applies YHWH's mercy to an endangered Zion.

Increasingly, the tiny community despaired of its present circumstances and looked to a future rectification. That hope took multiple forms: an ideal king, a transformed Zion, the outpouring of the divine spirit, and a new era. A decisive day of the Lord would usher in a radical transformation after returning earth to primordial chaos (cf. Jer 4:23–26). A liturgy in Hos 6:1–13 tantalizingly broaches the possibility of life beyond the grave, but the reference seems metaphorical, like a similar text in Ezekiel 37, with reference to national restoration. Belief in personal resurrection, and this only in extreme cases, does not find clear expression until the Maccabean period (Dan 12:2).

Anticipation of an ideal ruler, who inaugurates an era of peace and prosperity, had a long history in Judah, as various psalms indicate (2, 89, 110). The birth of a messiah (Mic 4:14–5:4 [5:1–5]) and the restoration of the Davidic dynasty, called a fallen booth in Amos 9:11, will mean that foreign nations, particularly a greatly diminished Edom, will pay homage to Judah. Jerusalem will be transformed into a center of administrative and economic activity, and the surrounding mountains and hills will overflow with agricultural products (Amos 9:11–15; Joel 4:18 [3:18]). The outpouring of the divine vital force (spirit) on the Yehudites irrespective of age, gender, or social status will result in widespread prophetic activity (Joel 3:1–2 [4:1–2]). Terrifying signs and portents will announce YHWH's day of judgment on the nations, and Yehud will once again take up weapons forged from agricultural implements (Joel 3:3–5 [2:30–32]). As the apocalypse unfolds, Zion will enjoy YHWH's favor, and light will dispel darkness (Zech 14:1–6). Another scenario has Elijah reappear before the dawning of that awful day (Mal 3:23 [4:5]), a virtual outpouring of divine wrath, the inspiration for the medieval hymn *Dies Irae* (Zephaniah).

The hardships of the moment suggested to some that they were standing at the threshold of a new era (Zechariah 1–9). The deity was prepared to forgive unfaithful conduct and to whisper sweet nothings once more (Hos 2:16–25 [2:14–23]). In this idyllic setting, a mutuality will ensure a full response by the deity to every expressed wish. From YHWH's mouth will come the words "my people," and they will acknowledge YHWH similarly, "my God."

The extraordinary richness and diversity of these prophets, together with Isaiah, Jeremiah, and Ezekiel, presented a major dilemma for society at large. When prophets with conflicting viewpoints claimed that their oracles originated with the deity, who spoke the truth? In short, how could anyone distinguish between an authentic prophet and false prophets? Individual prophets, especially Jeremiah, Ezekiel, and Micah, struggled with this issue, either by labeling opponents liars, thieves, adulterers, and crowd-pleasers or by aggressively maintaining their own integrity. Various attempts to develop adequate criteria for distinguishing true from false prophecy, above all Deuteronomy's principle of fulfillment and Jeremiah's insistence that only a message of destruction derived from YHWH, failed in the end. The first criterion, fulfillment, required the perspective of time, often over several generations, and the second did not take into account changing historical circumstances as well as divine compassion.

It seems that this dilemma rendered prophecy virtually powerless in some circles, to judge from the remarkable comments in Zechariah 13. Even if the injunction laid on parents to murder a son who claimed the prophetic vocation pertained only to illegitimate prophecy, the near silence of the prophetic voice during the next five centuries, together with the emergence of an idealized hope that a prophet like Moses would appear or that Elijah would return, suggest that prophecy entered a period of decline.

Just as kingship lost its luster as a result of actual rulers in Israel and Judah, prophecy also surrendered something significant when consciousness of inspiration shifted to interpreting human words rather than proclaiming divine oracles. This shift paralleled the rise of extraordinary sages, professional teachers who transmitted the learning of past generations to their students and thus to posterity. In this way a human voice soon vied with the record of a divine communication through prophetic intermediation.

The phenomenon of prophecy owes its origin to the necessity for mediation of the divine will to humans. For some unknown reason, prophecy in Israel largely coincides with the monarchy, the exceptions being notable for their interest in a holy place and its sacerdotal leadership. As in ancient Mari and later Assyria and Babylon, Israelite prophets lent their support to kings, but they also energetically criticized them. Taking for granted a covenantal relationship between the deity and king, prophets held royal figures to the demands of this special relationship. In doing so, they risked life and limb.

These courageous individuals contended for justice in society and for authentic worship. Although not of one mind with respect to the scope of divine compassion, the nature of YHWH's plan for the elect people, the place of an anointed ruler, and the extent of the deity's wrath, these prophets were constrained to bear witness to a transcendent reality whom they understood to be not merely the judge of all humankind but also the source of life and well-being. In their own way the prophets immortalized in the Book of the Twelve lent their voice to this majestic but otherwise silent One.

Bibliography

Barton, J., *Oracles of God: Perceptions of Ancient Prophecy in Israel After the Exile* (Oxford: Oxford University Press, 1986).

Blenkinsopp, J., *A History of Prophecy in Israel* (Philadelphia: Westminster Press, 1983).

Brenner, A., ed., *A Feminist Companion to the Latter Prophets* (Sheffield: Academic Press, 1995).

Clements, R., *Prophecy and Tradition* (Atlanta: John Knox Press, 1975).

Crenshaw, J., *Prophetic Conflict: Its Effect upon Israelite Religion*, BZAW 124 (Berlin and New York: Walter de Gruyter, 1971).

Gitai, J., ed., *Prophecy and Prophets: The Diversity of Contemporary Issues in Scholarship*, SBLSS (Atlanta: Scholars Press, 1997).

Gowan, D., *Theology of the Prophetic Books: The Death and Resurrection of Israel* (Louisville: Westminster/John Knox Press, 1998).

Heschel, A., *The Prophets* (New York: Harper & Row, 1962).

Koch, K., *The Prophets*, vols. 1–2 (Philadelphia: Fortress Press, 1983–4).

Lindblom, J., *Prophecy in Ancient Israel* (Philadelphia: Muhlenberg Press, 1962).

Mays, J. and P. Achtemeier, eds., *Interpreting the Prophets* (Philadelphia: Fortress Press, 1987).

Nissinen, M., *References to Prophecy in Neo-Assyrian Sources*, SAA VII (Helsinki: Helsinki University Press, 1998).

Overholt, T., *Channels of Prophecy: The Social Dynamics of Prophetic Activity* (Minneapolis: Fortress Press, 1989).

Parpola, S., *Assyrian Prophecies*, SAS IX (Helsinki: Helsinki University Press, 1997).

Petersen, D., *The Roles of Israel's Prophets*, JSOTS 17 (Sheffield: Academic Press, 1981).

Wilson, R., *Prophecy and Society in Ancient Israel* (Philadelphia: Westminster Press, 1980).

PART VIII
The Writings

CHAPTER 23

Narrative Texts: Chronicles, Ezra, and Nehemiah

Ralph W. Klein

Chronicles, Ezra, and Nehemiah are the final works in the Hebrew canon, but they appear there in the order of Ezra, Nehemiah, and 1 and 2 Chronicles. The Books of Chronicles tell the story of Israel from the death of Saul, the first king of Israel (1 Chronicles 10), to the announcement of the rise of Cyrus, King of Persia, who authorized the Jews who had been exiled in Babylon to return to Jerusalem and rebuild the temple (2 Chr 36:22–23). The first nine chapters of 1 Chronicles are genealogies of the tribes of Israel.

The book of Ezra begins by repeating the final verses of Chronicles and then reports the return of the exiles, their rebuilding of the temple (chs. 1–6), and the first part of the mission of Ezra, who had been sent by Artaxerxes to make inquiries about Judah and Jerusalem according to the law of God (chs. 7–10). The book of Nehemiah tells the story of Nehemiah, who was also sent by Artaxerxes to Jerusalem to rebuild the walls, but it also describes Ezra's reading of the law and the subsequent confession of the people and their covenant-making (chs. 8–10), and a number of corrective measures initiated by Nehemiah (13:4–31). In addition to the narrative texts, all three books contain numerous lists of names and genealogies, which will not be discussed in any detail in this chapter.

For the better part of the last two centuries, the majority of scholars believed that these books formed a unity known as the Chronicler's History, beginning with Chronicles and concluding with Ezra and Nehemiah. While some scholars still advocate that today (e.g. Blenkinsopp, 1988, pp. 47–54), it seems likely, for both linguistic and theological reasons, that Chronicles and Ezra–Nehemiah had separate origins. Two prominent themes in Chronicles, for example, immediate retribution and prophecy, are virtually absent from Ezra–Nehemiah, and Chronicles has a much more favorable view of the northern tribes and an inclusive view of Israel, whereas Israel in Ezra–Nehemiah is limited to Judah and Benjamin. Even if these books had separate authorship, they deal with common themes – Jerusalem, its temple, its clergy, and its worship – and all of them were written during the post-exilic or Persian period (539 BCE – 330 BCE). We will give primary attention in this chapter to reading the narratives in Chronicles, but we will also provide some orientation to the narratives in Ezra–Nehemiah.

Narratives in Chronicles

Methods used to read narratives elsewhere in the Bible also apply to Chronicles (see Miscall, 1998, pp. 539–52), but Chronicles also provides a unique challenge and opportunity, since the author (hereafter: the Chronicler) drew upon and recast Israel's history as it had been recounted in 1 and 2 Samuel and 1 and 2 Kings. Hence readers can compare Chronicles with its major source, using a synopsis that lists parallel passages side by side (see the English synopsis by Endres, Millar, and Burns, and the more technical Hebrew–Greek synopsis by Vannutelli). In such study, interpreters note what has been added by the Chronicler, what has been omitted, where the order of passages has been rearranged, and where individual words have been changed. Among additions made by the Chronicler are materials from the Psalms and other canonical writings. The genealogies and lists, not to be considered here, were drawn both from Genesis and other canonical writings and from archival sources that are no longer available.

We propose to consider the Chronicler's treatment of David in 1 Chronicles 10–29 in order to understand the emphases of this book and to illustrate one common method of reading this book. Using a synopsis, readers will then be able to investigate the Chronicler's message and literary method in 2 Chronicles 1–36 as well.

The Chronicler's Story of David

1 Chronicles 10–29 and their Canonical Parallels

Passage	1 Chronicles	1 and 2 Samuel
1	10:1–12 death of Saul	1 Sam 31:1–13
2	10:13–14 evaluation of Saul	
3		2 Sam 1:1–4:12 interregnum
4	11:1–3 anointing of David	5:1–3
5		5:4–5 chronology of David
6	11:4–9 David and all Israel capture Jerusalem	5:6–10
7	11:10 chiefs supporting David	

8	11:11–41a David's warriors	23:8–39
9	11:41b–47 more warriors	
10	12:1–22 leaders rallied to David at Ziklag	
11	12:23–40 armed troops rallying to David at Hebron	
12	13:1–4 invitation to bring ark to Jerusalem	
13	13:5–7 the ark's journey begins	6:1–3
14		6:4 brief note about Ahio
15	13:8–14 Uzzah killed for touching the ark	6:5–11
16	14:1–2 Hiram's support; David's kingdom established	5:11–12
17	14:3–7 David's wives and children in Jerusalem	5:13–16
18	14:8–16 Philistines defeated	5:17–25
19	14:17 David's fame	
20	15:1–3 preparations for moving the ark	
21	15:4–10 six Levite chiefs	
22	15:11–15 clergy ordered to carry the ark	
23	15:16–24 installation of Levitical musicians	
24		6:12a house of Obed-Edom blessed
25	15:25–16:3 ark brought to Jerusalem	6:12b–19a
26	16:4–7 David appoints Levites to thank and praise	
27	16:8–22 Israel's praise	Ps 105:1–15
28	16:23–33 international and cosmic praise	Ps 96:1b–13a
29	16:34–36 thanksgiving and petition	Ps 106:1b, 47–48
30	16:37–42 regular worship established	
31	16:43 David's blessing	2 Sam 6:19b–20a
32		6:20b–23 David rebuked by Michal
33	17:1–15 oracle of Nathan	7:1–17
34	17:16–27 prayer of David	7:18–29
35	18:1–13 defeat of the Philistines	8:1–14
36	18:14–17 officers of David	8:15–18

37		9:1–13 story of Mephibosheth
38	19:1–19 defeat of Ammonites and Arameans	10:1–19
39	20:1a spring as time of war	11:1a
40		11:1b–12:25 David and Bathsheba
41	20:1b Joab attacked Rabbah of the Ammonites	12:26
42		12:27–29 David summoned to Rabbah of the Ammonites
43	20:2–3 David seized Ammonite crown and returned to Jerusalem	12:30–31
44		13:1–20:26 rape of Tamar and murder of Amnon; revolt and death of Absalom; negotiations for David's restoration to the throne; rebellion of Sheba, and a listing of the officers of David
45		21:1–17 dismemberment of Saul's descendants; exploits of David's warriors
46	20:4–8 Elhanan killed Lahmi the brother of Goliath	21:18–22
47		22:1–51 = Psalm 18:1–50
48		23:1–7 last words of David
49	21:1–4a David incited to take census	24:1–4a
50		24:4b–7 Joab's census
51	21:4b–15 report of census	24:8–16
52	21:16 angel with drawn sword	
53	21:17–27 purchase of threshing floor of Ornan and altar to YHWH erected	24:17–25
54	21:28–22:1 tabernacle of Moses and altar of burnt offering were at Gibeon	
55	22:2–5 David provides materials for the temple	

56	22:6–16 David's private speech to Solomon	
57	22:17–19 leaders commanded to build	
58	23:1–2 Solomon made king by David	
59	23:3–32 families of Levites and their functions	
60	24:1–31 twenty-four priestly houses; more Levites	
61	25:1–31 Levitical singers	
62	26:1–32 gatekeepers; other Levites	
63	27:1–34 commanders of the monthly divisions; tribal leaders; David's administrators	
64	28:1–10 David's public speech to Solomon	
65	28:11–21 instructions for building temple	
66	29:1–9 David's contributions to the temple	
67	29:10–22a David's praise of God; sacrifices by assembly	
68	29:22b–25 anointing of Solomon	
69	29:26 summary of David's reign	
70	29:28 death of David	1 Kgs 1:1–2:10 David warmed by Abishag on his deathbed; revolt of Adonijah; intervention by Bathsheba; anointing of Solomon; death of David
71	29:27 length of David's reign	2:11
72		2:12 Solomon's kingdom established
73	29:29–30 sources: words of Samuel, Nathan, and Gad	

The Chronicler strongly encourages his readers to support the temple in Jerusalem and maintains that it, its priesthood, and its worship patterns were established by the kings of the United Monarchy, David and Solomon. In 1 Chronicles 10–29 he tells the story of David as a model monarch who made Jerusalem and its worship life his chief priorities. To make these points the Chronicler drastically reworked the story of David that had been told in 1 Samuel 16–1

Kings 2 and that had been included in the Deuteronomistic History, which was probably completed in the mid-sixth century BCE, roughly two centuries before the Chronicler wrote.

Additions in Chronicles

It is in his additions to the text of Samuel–Kings that we expect to find some of the clearest statements of the Chronicler's theology and the reasons that led him to write his lengthy literary document. In the Old Testament, Chronicles, Isaiah, and Jeremiah are all virtually of the same length; only Psalms is longer. Among the more significant additions of the Chronicler are the following:

- In passage 2, the Chronicler accuses Saul of unfaithfulness (one of his frequent accusations that led finally to the exile of both Northern and Southern Kingdoms), and he notes that YHWH took responsibility for Saul's death – even though Saul was a suicide – and turned the kingdom over to David. Thus the Chronicler affirms the legitimacy of David's kingship and omits almost all of the so-called History of David's Rise (1 Sam 16:14–2 Sam 5:10), which records the protracted struggle between David and Saul and a number of questionable acts involving David: his demand for support from Nabal and his subsequent marrying of Nabal's widow Abigail (1 Samuel 25); his alliance with Achish, the Philistine (1 Samuel 27–30); and the murders of Abner and Ishbaal (passage 3), from which David had vehemently – and somewhat defensively – distanced himself (2 Sam 3:28–29; 4:9–12).
- In passage 10, leaders of Saul's own tribe of Benjamin, of the TransJordanian tribe of Gad, of the tribe of Judah, and of the northern tribe of Manasseh rallied to David's cause when he was still at Ziklag, that is, before Saul's death. The Chronicler attributes his stay at Ziklag to his conflict with Saul. The Chronicler also adds passage 11 (1 Chr 12:23–40), which notes that the size of the armies that rallied to David at Hebron from the southern tribes was relatively small, but the troops from the north are quite large, as are the volunteers from Transjordan.
- Before David's attempting to move the ark to Jerusalem, the Chronicler adds passage 12 (1 Chr 13:1–4) that has David consulting with the whole assembly of Israel to get their agreement on this important first step in creating Jerusalem as the cult center.
- The Chronicler moved passages 16–18 (2 Sam 5:11–25) to a position *after* the death of Uzzah, who was killed by YHWH for touching the ark. He also added at this point passages 19–23 (1 Chr 14:17–15:24). By repositioning the passage from 2 Samuel he made David's efforts to move the ark to Jerusalem follow immediately upon his capture of Jerusalem, showing the high priority he gave to worship there. In their new context, these passages show how David was blessed for his efforts to bring the ark to Jerusalem – by the gifts of

Hiram, his acquisition of wives and children, and his defeat of the Philistines. The new passages (19–23) indicate that David used this period to make sure that it was Levites who carried the ark and to install the Levites permanently as musicians. Throughout his book the Chronicler is a constant advocate for the Levites. All told, the Chronicler added forty-one verses at this point, which has the effect of signifying the passage of three months' time between the first and the second attempts to bring the ark to Jerusalem.

- The Chronicler also inserts thirty-nine verses (passages 26–30) after the ark has safely arrived in Jerusalem. These passages emphasize the significance of the day on which the ark arrived at its final resting place. The bulk of this addition consists of an amalgam of three canonical Psalms that call for Israel's praise ("Remember . . . the covenant that he made with Abraham, his sworn promise to Isaac, which he confirmed to Jacob . . . to Israel as an everlasting covenant" [16:15–17 = Ps 105:8–10]), international praise ("Declare his glory among the nations" [16:24 = Ps 96:3]), and even cosmic praise ("Let the heavens be glad, and let the earth rejoice" [16:31 = Ps 96:11]). While the Chronicler in general seems content with the political status quo in the Persian Empire, his inclusion of v. 35 expresses a guarded hope for a greater Israel: "Gather and rescue us from among the nations" (16:35 = Ps 106:47). Ezra–Nehemiah also supports the Persian authorities. Only in Neh 9:37 does the writer seriously complain: "[The kings whom you have set over us] have power also over our bodies and over our livestock at their pleasure, and we are in great distress."

- The longest addition is in passages 54–69, 1 Chr 21:28–29:26. Many scholars believe that some of these sections may have been added at various times after the original composition of Chronicles although in recent years more and more sections are attributed to the Chronicler himself (for details see the commentaries).

    - The addition in passage 54 (21:28–22:1) affirms that the tabernacle of YHWH and the altar of burnt offering were in Gibeon at the time of David, thereby explaining why Solomon could have his great revelation at this "high place" (1 Kgs 3:4–5; cf. 2 Chr 1:3–6). By locating the tabernacle and the altar at Gibeon, the Chronicler removed the heterodox character of that site.

    - Passage 55 (1 Chr 22:2–5) reports that David gathered stones, iron, bronze, and cedar logs for the temple so that it could be magnificent. David's efforts to acquire building materials were necessary because his son Solomon was young and inexperienced.

    - In passage 56 (1 Chr 22:6–16) David delivers a private speech to Solomon informing him that he should build the temple since David himself was prevented from this by his shedding of blood (perhaps a reference to the seventy thousand people who had died in 1 Chr 21:14 because of David's sin) and the waging of many wars (an idea found also in 1 Kgs 5:3 where the emphasis is more on David's preoccupation with foreign enemies than on the violence of the wars themselves). Solomon on the other hand was a man of peace. David provided 3,750 tons of gold and 37,500 tons of silver for the temple. David's words of encouragement to Solomon in v. 13 echo those of Moses to Joshua in Deut 31:7–8.

- David followed this speech with additional instructions to the Israelite leaders (passage 57, 1 Chr 22:17–19) to encourage them to help Solomon in his temple-building.

- Passage 58 (1 Chr 23:1–2) reports that David in his old age made Solomon king. Chronicles tells nothing of the struggles within David's family in the latter part of his reign, let alone the attempted coup by Adonijah when he was on his deathbed (2 Samuel 9–20; 1 Kings 1–2). See also passage 68 (1 Chr 29:22b–25) below, where the whole assembly makes Solomon king.

- In passage 59 (1 Chr 23:2–32) the Chronicler notes how David assigned 38,000 Levites to four specific tasks, and he lists the father's houses of the Levites and contrasts their duties with those of the priests. The responsibilities and rights of the Levites in the Chronicler's day are thus grounded in decisions by David.

- Passage 60 (1 Chr 24:1–31) notes that the twenty-four priestly courses were set up by David though many scholars today believe this arrangement did not develop historically before the mid-fourth century BCE at the earliest. The passage concludes with a supplementary list of Levites.

- In passage 61 (1 Chr 25:1–31) David is credited with setting apart several groups of Levitical singers, who also had prophetic powers. This chapter divides the Levites, like the priests, into twenty-four courses.

- Additional passage 62 (1 Chr 26:1–32) reports on the gatekeepers who were appointed by David.

- In passage 63 (1 Chr 27:1–34) the era of David is described as a time of perfect order, with the people providing a contingent of 24,000 royal workers each month under twelve commanders. The addition of a list of tribal leaders in vv. 16–24 may be an attempt to lessen the criticism focused on David for the census taken in chapter 21. Instead it provides a list of those who were responsible for the census in each tribe. The chapter concludes with lists of administrators and advisers.

- After the descriptions of the Davidic appointments in passages 59–63, the Chronicler adds a public speech by David to Solomon (passage 64, 1 Chr 28:1–10). This speech and the private speech given by David in passage 56 form bookends around the passages dealing with Davidic appointments. David observes that God had chosen both Solomon and himself and that Solomon would build the temple for which David had made preparations.

- In passage 65 (1 Chr 28:11–21) David hands over to Solomon the plan for the temple, which he had received by divine inspiration (v. 19). The passage ends with admonition and encouragement for Solomon.

- Passage 66 (1 Chr 29:1–9) returns to the theme of David's donations to the temple, and reports how the other leaders also give generously. The amounts are enormous: 187.5 tons of gold, 375 tons of silver, 675 tons of bronze, and 3,750 tons of iron. In v. 7 the Chronicler mentions "darics," a Persian coin, which of course is anachronistic for the time of David.

- David's praise of God and the people's offering of sacrifices in response to this praise comprise the content of passage 67 (1 Chr 29:10–22a). Verse 11 is the source of the concluding doxology for the Lord's Prayer. The large number of sacrifices demonstrates the importance of this day.
- In passage 68 (1 Chr 29:22b–25) the people endorse Solomon's kingship by anointing him (cf. David's making him king in 1 Chr 23:1). Various leaders pledged their loyalty to him and YHWH highly exalted him. Solomon, therefore, is fully authorized to implement the temple and its worship for which David had made such lavish preparations.
- Passage 69 (1 Chr 29:26) notes explicitly that David was king over all Israel.

• The Chronicler claims prophetic authority for his account of David in additional passage 73 (1 Chr 29:29) by stating that the sources for his information about David are written in the records of the seer Samuel (who of course died before David became king), in the records of the prophet Nathan, and in the records of the seer Gad.

Omissions in Chronicles

The Chronicler omitted much of the "History of David's Rise" (1 Sam 16:14–2 Sam 5:10) by choosing to begin his account with the death of Saul (cf. 1 Samuel 31). But he also omitted other major passages from Samuel, most of which contained deeds that are harmful to the reputation of David and therefore would diminish his credibility as the founder of the temple, the priesthood, and the cult.

- Passage 3 (2 Sam 1:1–4:12), discussed briefly in connection with passage 2 under additions, narrates a number of questionable acts of David and his associates and the relative weakness of his kingship until the death of Abner and the capitulation of the North. The Chronicler insisted, on the contrary, that YHWH had turned over the kingdom to David immediately after the death of Saul (passage 2).
- The basic chronological content of passage 5 (2 Sam 5:4–5) is repeated in passage 71 (1 Chr 29:27 = 1 Kgs 2:11) and this could be considered the reason for its omission here. But by removing this passage the Chronicler also made the account of David's conquest of Jerusalem come immediately after his anointing.
- The Chronicler omits passage 24, 2 Sam 6:12a, which tells how YHWH blessed the house of Obed-Edom, where the ark stayed for three months after the death of Uzzah. Its inclusion might have implied that David was being

opportunistic in taking the ark from Obed-Edom's house. This thought is actually expressed by David in a reading in the Lucianic LXX and the Old Latin text of Samuel: "I will bring this blessing to my own home." This sentence may in fact be part of the original text of Samuel.

- While the Chronicler retained the notice about David leaping and dancing during the procession of the ark and about his wife Michal despising him for it (passage 25, 1 Chr 15:29), he omitted passage 32 (2 Sam 6:20b–23), where Michal castigated him for his dancing and where David vowed to make himself even more contemptible. In the context in 2 Samuel, David's return to bless his household introduced the angry scene with Michal. Now it forms an *incluso* with 1 Chr 16:2, where David blessed the people, and with 1 Chr 13:14, where YHWH blessed the house of Obed-Edom.

- Because of the unsavory character of the stories and because of the instability of the Davidic rule, the Chronicler omitted almost all of the Succession Narrative (2 Samuel 9–20; 1 Kings 1–2), including the story of David's adultery with Bathsheba and his murder of Uriah (passage 40, 2 Sam 11:1b–12:25). Also omitted, and for similar reasons, are Amnon's rape of Tamar, David's half-hearted response to this violation, Amnon's subsequent murder by Absalom, Absalom's usurpation of the throne, Shimei's cursing of David, Absalom's death at the hand of Joab, the protracted negotiations to restore David to the throne, and the subsequent revolt and execution of Sheba (passage 44, 2 Sam 13:1–20:26). His omission of passage 37, 2 Sam 9:1–13, resulted from his general silence about the house of Saul after the king's death, except for the story about Michal. A study of the parallels in 2 Samuel to 1 Chronicles 20 indicates the great extent of the Chronicler's omissions from this section of 2 Samuel:
  Passage 39: 1 Chr 20:1a = 2 Sam 11:1a
  Passage 41: 1 Chr 20:1b = 2 Sam 12:26
  Passage 43: 1 Chr 20:2–3 = 2 Sam 12:30–31
  Passage 46: 1 Chr 20:4–8 = 2 Sam 21:18–22.
  Thus the Chronicler retains only eleven verses out of some eleven chapters. His omission of the final part of the Succession Narrative, passage 70 (1 Kgs 1:1–2:10), probably came about because of its news about the attempted rebellion by Adonijah while David was on his deathbed and, perhaps, because of the somewhat compromising ministrations of Abishag.

- The general lack of attention to Saul and the violence done to Saul's descendants by the Gibeonites, to whom David had handed over these descendants, account for the omission of passage 45 (2 Sam 21:1–17).

- The Chronicler does not repeat the geographical data from Samuel about the area covered by the census (passage 50, 2 Sam 24:4b–7), either because he found it unimportant or perhaps because he did not completely understand the itinerary. The Chronicler gives the extent of the land as "from Beersheba to Dan" (passage 49, 1 Chr 21:3), reversing the order of city names in this common biblical cliché (cf. 1 Chr 13:5; 2 Chr 19:4; 30:5).

Representative Changes in Chronicles of Texts Taken from Samuel–Kings

In this essay we can only review a few representative changes introduced by the Chronicler. A full study would require an examination line by line in a synopsis.

- Because the Chronicler omitted 2 Samuel 1–4, his report that "all Israel" gathered to David at Hebron and anointed him king (passage 4, 1 Chr 11:1–3) now refers to all twelve tribes whereas "all the tribes of Israel" in 2 Sam 5:1 refers only to the ten northern tribes. David is only anointed once in Chronicles whereas 1 and 2 Samuel also have him anointed two additional times, by Samuel (1 Sam 16:1–13) and by the tribe of Judah (2 Sam 2:4).
- According to passage 6 (1 Chr 11:4–9) *David and all Israel* captured Jerusalem whereas in 2 Sam 5:6 the conquest was made by David's personal army ("David and his men"). This change is part of the Chronicler's overall strategy to give highest credence to Jerusalem and its worship center and to relate its validity to the whole nation.
- We note three significant changes introduced by the Chronicler in the oracle of Nathan (passage 33, 1 Sam 17:1–15). First, in v. 1, he deletes the following clause that is contained in 2 Sam 7:1: "YHWH had given him [David] rest from all his enemies around him." The Chronicler apparently felt this clause contradicted the following three chapters (passages 35–46, 1 Chr 18:1–20:8), which tell of David's numerous wars. In a later oracle reported in Chronicles, God names Solomon as a man of peace whereas David had shed much blood and waged great wars (1 Chr 22:8–9). Second, in v. 13, the Chronicler deletes a sentence found in 2 Sam 7:14 that threatens an errant Solomon with punishment: "When he commits iniquity, I will punish him with a rod such as mortals use, with blows inflicted by human beings." Since the Chronicler largely omits the sins of David and Solomon, such a warning was unnecessary. Third, in v. 14, the Chronicler quotes YHWH as follows: "I will confirm him in my house and in my kingdom forever," but 2 Sam 7:16 reads: "Your [David's] house and your kingdom shall be made sure forever before me." The promise in Chronicles applies to Solomon rather than to David. This accords with the nearly equal standing the Chronicler ascribes to Solomon. "House" in this verse in Chronicles refers to the temple whereas the same word in Samuel refers to the dynasty.
- The Chronicler credits Abishai, the nephew of David, rather than David himself, with the killing of 18,000 Edomites (passage 35, 1 Chr 18:12–2 Sam 8:13). This change may reflect variant traditions or a text-critical problem. Consult the commentaries.
- The Chronicler states that David's sons were the chief officials in the service of the king (passage 36, 1 Chr 18:17), while his source in 2 Sam 8:18 read

"and David's sons were priests." The Chronicler could not allow that Judahites who were not descendants of Aaron were able to serve as priests.

- In passage 49, 1 Chr 21:1, the Chronicler states that Satan (or "an adversary") incited David to number the people while his source in 2 Sam 24:1 attributed this incitement to YHWH. Whether this change refers to Satan (one of three references to this figure in the Old Testament) or to an unidentified foe (as recently argued by Japhet, 1993, pp. 373–5), the Chronicler is trying to remove the difficulty of YHWH being the cause of David's sin.
- In the miscellaneous materials of chapters 21–24, 2 Samuel noted that Elhanan, the Bethlehemite, killed Goliath the Gittite (passage 46, 2 Sam 21:19). Some scholars have argued that Elhanan was an alternate name for David while others have claimed that a deed of an otherwise unknown Elhanan was attributed to David in 1 Samuel 17. In either case, the Chronicler seems to be harmonizing when he states that Elhanan killed Lahmi, the brother of Goliath (passage 46, 1 Chr 20:5). The name "Lahmi" is made up of the last two syllables of the Hebrew word "Bethlehemite."

Changes in Chronicles based on an alternate form of the Text of Samuel

Readers of Chronicles and Samuel–Kings in a synopsis, whether in Hebrew or in English, probably begin with the assumption that the Chronicler used a text of Samuel–Kings that was much like the one we now have in our Hebrew and English Bibles. Scholars have long known, however, that the Hebrew and Greek texts (the Septuagint or LXX) of Samuel often differ considerably from one another and in many cases the ancient Greek translation seems to preserve a superior version of the text. That conclusion was reinforced with the discovery of the Dead Sea Scrolls, and especially of three copies of Samuel from Cave 4, called 4QSam[a], 4QSam[b], 4QSam[c]. In some cases, including in the Chronicler's story of David, it is possible to show that where Chronicles differs from the present text of Samuel–Kings it is because the Chronicler used a different version of Samuel or Kings. Hence the change was not introduced by the Chronicler himself, but had already been introduced into the text of Samuel and Kings by the time the Chronicler wrote. Students who can use the Hebrew–Greek synopsis of Vannutelli need to be on the constant lookout for such readings. Here are a few examples.

- Consider these two readings from passage 18:
  2 Sam 5:21, "The Philistines abandoned their idols there, and David and his men carried them away."
  1 Chr 14:12, "They abandoned their gods there, and at David's command they were burned."
  The person who introduced this change made David's actions conform to the letter of the law in Deut 7:5: "But this is how you must deal with them:

break down their altars . . . and burn their idols with fire." It would not be surprising to find the Chronicler making such a change, but a careful study of the Septuagint of Samuel, in this case the Lucianic family of LXX manuscripts, shows that this change had already been made in some texts of Samuel: "They abandoned their gods there, and David and the men who were with him took them, and David ordered to burn them with fire." In this case the reading in the Lucianic text is conflate, that is, it contains both a clause about David taking away the gods and a clause about his burning them. The change, in any case, was not introduced by the Chronicler, but it had been inserted in his Hebrew copy of Samuel, and the Lucianic LXX preserves a translation of this divergent Hebrew text in Greek.

• To understand the next example (passage 52, 1 Chr 21:16), we need to begin with the last sentence of the preceding verse and continue with the first words of the following verse:

1 Chr 21:15b, "And the angel of YHWH was standing by the threshing floor of Ornan the Jebusite." 1 Chr 21:16, "And David lifted up his eyes and saw the angel of YHWH standing between earth and between heaven. And there was a drawn sword in his hand stretched out against Jerusalem. And David and the elders, covering themselves in sackcloth, fell down on their faces." 1 Chr 21:17, "And David said to . . ."

2 Sam 24:16, "And the Angel of YHWH was by the threshing floor of Araunah the Jebusite." 2 Sam 24:17, "And David said to . . ."

The present Hebrew text of Samuel (the Masoretic Text or MT) lacks an equivalent for 1 Chr 21:16, which could easily lead to the conclusion that the Chronicler added this verse because of the greater emphasis on angels in his day. But this verse does appear at this place in Samuel in 4QSam^a. We believe this verse was accidentally omitted in the MT because the words "and David lifted up" and "and David said" are similar in Hebrew and a scribe's eyes skipped inadvertently from the first to the second verb.

• In our third example, from passage 8, the variant, shorter text of Chronicles is not supported by the LXX, the Lucianic recension of the LXX or the Dead Sea Scrolls of Samuel. Nevertheless the omission in Chronicles can be explained by standard text-critical tools.

1 Chr 11:13, "He [Eleazar] was with David at Pas-dammim, when the Philistines were gathered there for battle. There was a plot of ground full of barley."

2 Sam 23:9b, "He [Eleazar] was with David when they defied the Philistines who were gathered there for battle. *The Israelites withdrew, but he stood his ground. He struck down the Philistines until his arm grew weary, though his hand clung to the sword. The LORD brought about a great victory that day. Then the people came back to him – but only to strip the dead. Next to him was Shammah son of Agree, the Hararite. The Philistines gathered together at Lehi, where there was a plot of ground full of lentils.*" The materials printed in italics are not attested in the text of Chronicles, but this is not because the Chronicler deleted them. Rather, a scribe's eye had shifted from the end of the words "the Philistines were gathered there for battle" (2 Sam 23:9 = 1 Chr 11–13) to

the end of the words "the Philistines gathered together at Lehi" (at the end of 2 Sam 23:11a) and left out everything in between. So the difference between Samuel and Chronicles in this case is due to an accident of textual transmission which may have occurred in some manuscript of Samuel or even in the transmission of the book of Chronicles itself. While the Chronicler omitted all of passage 14, 2 Sam 6:4, a major portion of that verse ("new [cart]. And they brought it out of the house of Abinadab, which was on the hill") in a duplicate writing (dittography) of words in 2 Sam 6:3 is omitted by the LXX and 4QSam[a] in 2 Samuel. It is unclear why the Chronicler omitted the rest of the verse.

- In another example, from passage 35, the remarkably high numbers in Chronicles for the chariots and the cavalry that were taken from Hadadezer would seem at first to reflect the Chronicler's general tendency to inflate numbers:

1 Chr 18:4, "David took from him one thousand chariots, seven thousand cavalry, and twenty thousand foot soldiers."

2 Sam 8:4, "David took from him one thousand seven hundred cavalry and twenty thousand foot soldiers."

Remarkably, the LXX of Samuel has the same numbers as the Chronicler. The large numbers, therefore, were already in the text of Samuel read by the Chronicler and they were not inflated by his own editorial hand.

- An additional clause in this same passage 35 (1 Chr 18:8b), without parallel in 2 Samuel 8, explains what Solomon did with the great quantities of bronze David had taken from the cities of Hadadezer: "With them he made the bronze sea, the pillars, and the vessels of bronze for the temple." This extra sentence is, however, attested in the LXX of Samuel. It was either accidentally lost in the Masoretic Text of Samuel or it was added to the Hebrew text of Samuel used by the translators of the LXX and the Chronicler.

Changed Order of Passages in Chronicles

In addition to his movement of passages 16–18 (1 Chr 14:1–16 = 2 Sam 5:11–25) to a position between the two journeys of the ark (see the discussion above), the Chronicler also repositioned passage 8, 2 Sam 23:8–39, the list of David's warriors, in order to express the widespread support of David shortly after he became king.

Narratives in Ezra and Nehemiah

The books of Ezra and Nehemiah bristle with historical and literary problems that have often diverted readers from the present shape of the text. Scholars have debated whether Ezra in fact came to Palestine in 458 BCE and Nehemiah in 445 BCE, during the reign of Artaxerxes I, as an initial reading of the book would suggest, or whether Ezra may have come after Nehemiah, in 398 BCE, in the time of Artaxerxes II. If Ezra were sent to establish the place of the law in the Jewish community, it seems strange that he would wait thirteen years after his initial activity (Ezra 7–10) to read the law to the people (Nehemiah 8). Some scholars have proposed transferring Nehemiah 8 to a position between Ezra 8 and 9 or to a position after Ezra 10:44. While the historical questions remain as baffling as ever, Neh 7:73b–10:39 forms a very coherent unit consisting of Ezra's reading of the law (Nehemiah 8), the people's subsequent confession of their sin (Nehemiah 9), and their entering a firm agreement to keep the law (Nehemiah 10). This unit shows that those people whom Nehemiah transferred to Jerusalem (Neh 7:4–5; 11:1–2) had in fact dedicated themselves to the law. Hence, whatever the correct reconstruction of the chronology of the historical Ezra and Nehemiah might turn out to be, the Books of Ezra and Nehemiah need to be read in their present arrangement. To understand Ezra–Nehemiah as a literary and theological document, it is best to read it in its canonical order (Eskenazi, *passim*).

Ezra–Nehemiah is not a reworking of an earlier canonical document in the way that the author of 1 and 2 Chronicles had reworked the books of Samuel and Kings. Nevertheless, the following list indicates some of the sources which were incorporated into Ezra 1–6. 1:2–4, a Hebrew copy of the decree of Cyrus; 1:9–11, an inventory of temple vessels; 2:1–67, a list of those who returned from the exile (this list is repeated, with small changes in Neh 7:6–69); 4:6–7, summaries of letters from Jewish adversaries in the time of Xerxes and Artaxerxes; 4:8–16, a letter in Aramaic from Rehum to Artaxerxes; 4:17–22, Artaxerxes' reply, in Aramaic; 5:6–17, a letter from Tattenai, in Aramaic, to Darius; 6:3–12, Darius' reply, in Aramaic, including an Aramaic copy of the decree of Cyrus. All of Ezra 4:18–6:18 is written in Aramaic, but we believe the editor of the book used that language when he wrote the narrative framework that now incorporates the Aramaic letters into his document. We do not believe he incorporated a preexisting Aramaic Chronicle consisting of 4:18–6:18.

Other probable source documents, in addition to lists, include Ezra 7:12–26, an Aramaic document giving the Persian king's commission of Ezra, and the Ezra Memoir, consisting of first-person (Ezra 7:27–8:34; 9:1–15) and third-person (Ezra 7:1–11; 8:35–36; 10:1–44) accounts of Ezra. Finally, the book of Nehemiah is dominated by a first-person account by Nehemiah called the Nehemiah Memoir (Neh 1:1–7:73a; 12:27–43; 13:4–31) in which Nehemiah defends and promotes his own activities. One of its most striking character-istics is Nehemiah's appeal to God: "Remember for my good, O my God, all that I have done for this people" (Neh 5:19; cf. Neh 13:14, 22, 31).

Here are some of the emphases articulated in Ezra–Nehemiah: YHWH brought about the return of the exiles and the rebuilding of the temple through favorable actions of the Persian kings toward Israel. The community in Jerusalem is made up of those who returned from the exile, who constitute the true Israel. The celebration of the Feast of Tabernacles after the completion of the altar (Ezra 3:4–5) anticipates the joyful dedication of the temple (Ezra 6:16–18) and the equally joyous observation of the Passover a few months thereafter (Ezra 6:19–22). The delay in the completion of the temple is blamed on the actions of the "people of the land," who opposed the work in Jerusalem and disheartened the returned exiles. (Ezra 1–6; Haggai blamed the delay on the people's neglect of the temple [1:4–6].)

Some fifty-eight years after the dedication of the temple, Ezra led a group of exiles home under authorization by Artaxerxes (chs. 7–8). When the problem of mixed marriages arose, Ezra offered a prayer that indicated that the community was not yet the complete embodiment of YAHWEH's will since it was still under bondage to Persian power (9:7). Within a year of Ezra's departure from Babylon, a purified community was created in Jerusalem. Ezra's actions included a forced divorce of 110 or 111 men who had intermarried with foreign women (Ezra 10:9–44).

Nehemiah also led a group of exiles home and his work, despite the opposition of Sanballat, was successful. The purified community of Ezra 7–10 completed the building of the walls (Neh 6:15) around the holy city (Ezra 1–6). Nehemiah also corrected abuses in the making of loans and the charging of interest (Neh 5:1–13) and generously provided for others at his table without drawing on the taxes enjoyed by former governors (Neh 5:14–19). Nehemiah decided to remedy the low population in the city by selecting people for relocation whose genealogy could be correlated with the list of those who had returned with Zerubbabel (Neh 7:73a).

Before the repopulation of Jerusalem had begun, the people requested that Ezra read the law to them (Neh 8:1). The people resolved to study the law (Neh 8:13) and they held a unique celebration of the Feast of Tabernacles unparalleled since the days of Joshua (Neh 8:17). The people's confession in chapter 9 concludes with an acknowledgment that the present Persian rulership leaves the community in a desperate situation: "We are slaves this day . . . and we are in great distress" (Neh 9:36–37). The community then entered into a covenant to walk in God's law and keep all the commandments (Nehemiah 10).

The perfected community relocated one of every ten persons from the local towns to Jerusalem. Subsequent lists identify those who lived in Jerusalem and in the villages and provide the names of priests, Levites, and high priests at various times during the restoration period. The final chapter of the book consists of specific corrections of abuses during Nehemiah's second term in Jerusalem. The plea "Remember me, O my God, for good" calls attention to the virtue of Nehemiah, the wall builder and reformer of the community. Nehemiah 13 also reminds the reader that even the best intentions of the perfect community (Nehemiah 8–10) can fail and the people can lapse into sin. The final chapter of Nehemiah concedes that the behavior of the restored community was never fully perfected and often was in need of reform. The real circumstances in which people live – still under Persian rulership and in imperfection – set limits to the salvation that God gives in fulfillment of promises.

Conclusion

The style of writing in Chronicles, Ezra, and Nehemiah, replete with lists and genealogies, is not, at first glance, inviting, but the writers of these works were making a profound effort to forge community identity and unity at a time when the options for political independence were humanly out of the question. The Chronicler sought to support and promote the community worshipping at the temple in Jerusalem by grounding all aspects of this institution in the decisions and actions of an idealized David and Solomon. Lying behind the religious work of Ezra and Nehemiah may lie another political phenomenon: the law (Penta-teuch) brought by Ezra, according to Ezra 7:11–28, and to which the community obligated itself in Nehemiah 8–10, may also have been simultaneously recognized by the Persians as the legitimate Persian law of the land (Klein, 1999: p. 722).

Further Reading

Special Studies

Eskenazi, T., *In an Age of Prose: A Literary Approach to Ezra–Nehemiah*, SBLMS 36 (Atlanta: Scholars Press, 1988).
Klein, R., "Chronicles, Book of 1–2," *ABD* 1 (1992), 992–1002.
——, "Ezra–Nehemiah, Books of," *ABD* 2 (1992), 731–42.
Miscall, P., "Introduction to Narrative Literature," in L. E. Keck, ed., *New Interpreter's Bible*, vol. 2 (Nashville: Abingdon, 1998), 539–52.

Synopses

Endres, J., W. Millar, and J. Burns, eds., *Chronicles and its Synoptic Parallels in Samuel, Kings, and Related Texts* (Collegeville: MN: The Liturgical Press, 1995).
Vannutelli, P., *Libri Synoptici Veteris Testamenti*, 2 vols. (Rome: Pontifical Biblical Institute, 1931).

Commentaries

Allen, L., "The First and Second Books of Chronicles," in L. Keck, ed., *New Interpreter's Bible*, vol. 3 (Nashville: Abingdon, 1999), 297–659.
Blenkinsopp, J., *Ezra–Nehemiah*, The Old Testament Library (Philadelphia: Westminster, 1988).
Braun, R., *I Chronicles*, Word Biblical Commentary, vol. 14 (Waco, TX: Word, 1986).
Dillard, R., *2 Chronicles*, Word Biblical Commentary, vol. 15 (Waco, TX: Word, 1987).
Japhet, S., *I & II Chronicles*, The Old Testament Library (Louisville: Westminster/John Knox, 1993).
Klein, R., "The Books of Ezra & Nehemiah," in L. E. Keck, ed., *New Interpreter's Bible* 3 (Nashville: Abingdon, 1999), 661–851.
Williamson, H., *1 and 2 Chronicles*, The New Century Bible Commentary (Grand Rapids: Eerdmans, 1982).

CHAPTER 24
The Psalter

Erhard S. Gerstenberger

Towards the 20th Century

The Old Testament Book of Psalms in Jewish and Christian tradition has always been of very high liturgical, doctrinal, and ethical value for the congregations using it in manifold ways. Small wonder, therefore, that exegetical approaches and methods have varied over the centuries and that, in fact, Psalm-interpretation (as any other branch of biblical exegesis) has followed, by and large, the winding movements of cultural and ecclesiastic developments. Thus, until the liberating effects of the Renaissance and the Reformation could imprint themselves on psalm-reading, Christians usually had interpreted a good many psalms in the light of the life, death, and resurrection of Jesus Christ (cf. e.g. Aurelius Augustinus, *Ennarationes in psalmos*). Jews normally understood the prayers and hymns for the most part as Davidic in origin and thus serving as prototypes for individual and congregational prayer (cf. Yair Zakovitch, "David's Birth and Childhood," in Zenger, 1998, pp. 185–98). Post-Reformation readings discovered ever more contemporary and contextual metaphors, meanings, and ancient intercultural connections. Protestant scholars especially, however, losing sight of the strictly cultic roots of psalmic texts, usually tried to attribute the psalms to gifted poets, or authors in the modern individualistic and personalistic sense. They would apply their own ideas in regard to literary creativity to the old texts, like Bernhard Duhm and Rudolph Kittel in the 20th or Ernst Wilhelm Hengstenberg, Heinrich Ewald, and others in the 19th century. In principle, even more cautious and more romantic investigators of the matter, considering the psalms rather as anonymous poems of mostly popular or liturgical origin (cf. Robert Lowth; Johann Gottfried Herder; Wilhem M. L. de Wette), would, in the last analysis, stick to that idea of a necessarily literary origin and growth of the psalms.

Genres and their Settings

As is well known in scholarship, form-critical research connected with the names of Hermann Gunkel of Giessen and Halle (1862–1932) and Sigmund Mowinckel of Oslo (1884–1965) to a considerable degree abandoned the concept of strict literary authorship. The psalms were primarily seen in their communicative or liturgical settings, which were, at the same time, made at least equally responsible for their very origin. Even though H. Gunkel considered present-day texts within the Psalter as "pious secondary poetry" (cf. *Einleitung*, p. 28) he was firm in believing that these works of individual writers had been modeled according to older cultic songs and prayers comparable to anonymous folk-poetry in our own cultures (cf. *Einleitung*, p. 27). His first criterion for identifying a genre of psalms, therefore, is a definite and recurring "opportunity in worship" (*Einleitung*, p. 22; cf. p. 10). Secondly, he calls attention to a "common treasure of concepts and moods" (p. 22), another collective and nonliterary idea. Only in the third place does he mention "linguistic forms" (p. 23), but again without driving towards personal authorship. Societal origin and collective use for H. Gunkel have been the essential and formative forces in the shaping of the psalms. Later form-critical investigations quite often turned this list of criteria upside down, dwelling predominantly on formal registration of linguistic phenomena and reinstating more and more personal authorship. Sigmund Mowinckel, of course, in his overall "cultic-historical" approach, for the most part did consider the older psalms as genuine liturgical pieces. Only in regard to late, sapiential poetry did he admit learned and individual authorship (cf. Mowinckel, 1962, vol. 2, pp. 104–5). In his evaluation of the role of individual psalmists he favors collective influences: "The content, the formal language and the thoughts are determined by purpose and custom. To write poetry was, one may say, to put together the details, thoughts, and phrases which were presented by tradition . . ." (p. 126). Small wonder, as he sees it, because personal feeling was deeply imbedded in "common experience" (p. 126). Suffice it to say that in form- and cult-critical interpretation of the first decades of the 20th century the immense importance of life-settings for our understanding of the psalms was discovered, paving the way for later socio-historical interpretations of psalmic texts. The "context" of any given psalm in form criticism means insertion in life and mood, not in "book" or "literature," and there seems to be an important truth in this vision. After all, every human utterance, to be decoded correctly and serve as a means of communication, proves to be dependent on specific germinal situations of origin and use. There is no word coming from anybody's lips or flowing from anybody's pen really lacking the meat and bones of situational matrices (cf. e.g. Brian Blount).

Beyond Form Criticism – Whither?

Psalm-interpretation at the beginning of the 21st century is all but uniform. The reasons for the present-day diversity of approaches are multiplex, too. For one, we are living in truly pluralistic societies, at least as far as western cultures are concerned. Diverse standpoints of exegetes quite naturally produce different visions of the matters to be interpreted. Secondly, the psalms in themselves because of their richness in settings, genres, moods, and articulations demand flexible handling and calling on variable modern experiences. Thirdly – and unfortunately – the modern (or western) hypocrisy of "knowing better" than anybody else in the history of humankind often leads to deeply diverging exclusivist claims, instead of inclusive cooperation and comparison between different methods and stances. As much as possible we should strive for a "joining of forces" in Psalm-interpretation.

We hardly need to comment on *linguistic concerns* in Psalm-research. Exploration of grammar, vocabulary, tenses, and topics of the Psalter and ancient Hebrew "Lyrical Literature" have been going on since the Renaissance with ever increasing awareness of cognate ancient idioms. What makes a language poetic and liturgical? How does one determine the characteristics of ancient Hebrew psalmody in comparison with, e.g., the sacred songs of Ugarit, Mesopotamia or Egypt? Be it the statistics of consonants per line (colometry), of determined article or prepositions in the Psalter, the questions of meter and verse-structure, rhythm and rhyme – all such features have found gifted and dedicated linguists to work on them. One may name only a very few representing a much larger group: Luis Alonso Schökel, Wilfred G. E. Watts, and Oswald Loretz. Strangely enough, there is – to my knowledge – no outright dictionary of poetic usages so far, and the new Hebrew lexica (*Gesenius-*; *Köhler-Baumgartner-Stamm*; *Sheffield Hebrew Dictionary*) place little emphasis on differentiated layers of language, the *Diccionario Bíblico Hebreo-Español*, 1995 (L. Alonso Schökel, ed.) being somewhat of an exception.

Traditional *literary criticism* is much alive in psalm-interpretation today. The presupposition of individual authors or poets working on their own right may be questionable, but there is a certain justification in applying literary-critical yardsticks to the Psalter, because the texts have been written down and transmitted as literature at some point. Thus, investigations of individual psalms as well as of their collections and compositions may look for and certainly find traces of elementary "literary" handling, that is, of being written down in the course of transmission (most scholars apply literary-critical analysis without making it an end in itself, cf. W. Beyerlin, C. Levin, K. Seybold, P. W. Flint, et al.). Early authors, however, presumably used the art of writing with a variety of intentions, from a mere technique of preserving words, to the artistic molding of finest poetry. To encounter traces of writing and rewriting in the psalm-texts does betray, in the first place, the existence of different uses of these texts, most probably in communal acts of communication. Literary criticism, therefore, is quite valuable for our discipline as one tool of scrutiny. From my perspective, it reveals not so much authorial idiosyncrasies as collective needs and concepts.

New literary theories (constructuralist, destructionist, postmodern, reader-response, etc.) abound in modern literary studies. They are being applied to biblical texts in general and the Book of Psalms in particular. The psalms are looked at as independent, autonomous entities with a voice of their own, which may be analyzed in regard to our own involvement in reading and interpreting. A universal interconnection of life-patterns is at the bottom of this perspective. The results are portraits of psalms and compilations of psalms as literary creations, with all the inclusions, correspondences, etc. (cf. Meir Weiss, L. Alonso Schökel, H. Irsigler, P. Auffret, et al.). Sometimes scholars focus on their different outlook as against the older form-critical and historical-critical methods. Thus Meir Weiss blames them for looking for meaning "behind" and "beside" the text itself, and secondly for fragmenting it, ignoring the "whole" of the text's appearance (in P. Neumann, 1976, pp. 402f). The poem, of and for itself, is power and truth; describing its structure and essence for many experts is the only legitimate interpretive task. A one-dimensional concentration on textual shape and literary organization like this has yielded many new insights, indeed. The inner texture of many individual psalms, its vibrations and deep connotations, its protagonists and villains, and speech-acts and hearer-responses have come to the fore, all to the benefit of our common understanding of the ancient prayers. If we do not forget that psalms have been used in biblical times by people of flesh and blood like ourselves, the new literary analyses are quite helpful. Other areas of questioning which are exercising some influence on psalm-research are, e.g., psychological, dramaturgic, musical, and pedagogic concerns. They do lend themselves as paradigmatic tools because the texts under scrutiny are very dynamic and esthetic. Thus, O. Keel in a study of 1969 investigated the psychological concept of "enemies and godless" in the Psalter; I. Baldermann, 1990, adapted the psalmic web of interpersonal relations to be reenacted in school classes.

And, of course, there are numerous *itemized studies* on the Psalms as a whole, on groupings and collections, as well as on individual texts and topics. The bibliographical array of relevant books and articles is so immense (cf. T. Wittstruck, 1994; also: surveys like the ones by W. Thiel, 1986; D. M. Howard, in J. C. McCann, 1993, pp. 52–70; M. Oeming, 1995; K. Seybold, 1998, pp. 46–74 [reprint from *Theologische Rundschau* 61, 1996, 247–74]) that no individual person can remain knowledgeable in depth and breadth. Even the commentaries written in a period of the last ten or fifteen years provoke already lengthy reviews, let alone the rest of scholarly endeavors. Many subjects beyond those already mentioned deserve thorough discussion: metaphors, the nature of prayer and enemies, circumstances of petition and thanksgivings, feasts, calendars, linkage to historical writings, the role of kingship, Levites, wisdom teachers, lay Psalm-composition. There are probings into theological outlooks on creation and salvation, exodus and sapiential values, sin and forgiveness, temple-cult and – in short, dozens and hundreds of interesting details to be discussed in the Psalter, which proves to be an immensely rich source of knowledge concerning ancient faith and inspiration for present-day God-seekers. A few outstanding pieces of research – of very different approaches and outlooks – from my vantage point are P. Casetti on Ps 49 (Is life worth living?), T. Veijola on Ps 89 (defeat and hope in exilic times), and C. Barth (salvation from death and the netherworld).

A very special kind of pursuit is followed by such colleagues, who take seriously that intimate affinity between Israel's psalms and those of the neighboring people and cultures. *Ancient Near Eastern psalmody* has to enter the picture if we want to understand the Old Testament materials. There are available editions of sacred poetry, principally from Ancient Egypt (cf. J. Assmann; E. Hornung) and Mesopotamia (E. Ebeling; E. Reiner; R. J. Caplice; W. W. Hallo; M.-J. Seux; M. E. Cohen, 1981; J. C. Moyer, in W. W. Hallo 1983, pp. 19–38; Th. Jacobson, 1987; and S. Maul, 1994). Very many of these texts equal Old Testament psalms, be it on the side of complaint and petition or on the side of hymns. Structure, outlook, vocabulary, mood, theological concepts, quest for world-order, justice, and equity often are very much comparable to those found in the Old Testament. The ritualistic environment of performed prayers and intoned hymns is much more obvious especially in Mesopotamian incantations. There always has been some attention paid to these parallels (G. Widengren; W. Mayer, 1976; and E. S. Gerstenberger, 1980), but not enough, considering the wealth of materials, which will increase with future publications (many texts are still slumbering in museums). Furthermore, Ancient Near Eastern examples of ritual give us some idea about original psalm-uses and do promote our inquiry into Old Testament cultic situations. Direct and descriptive references to worship, feasts, and rituals are relatively scarce in the Old Testament (cf. Psalm headings). Only Ps 102:1 dimly suggests a ritual for suffering individuals. Somewhat strange is a hesitance to include prayers and songs of other cultures into psalm-research. Friedrich Heiler of Marburg once did exactly this (*Prayer*, [2]1958). But the predominant mood is not yet too favourable to including sacred literature of other religions, perhaps for fear of syncretism (see below.)

Highlighting Some Special Areas

Looking at present-day endeavors to understand more fully the form and contents of the psalmic literature, I recognize the following fields of study as the most promising ones (cf. also E. Gerstenberger, 1985):

Socio-liturgical research

To my mind texts are always intrinsically tied to life-situations or communicative actions; in the case of psalmic texts we may from the very beginning think of religious communication, i.e., some kind of worship. In ancient times, presupposing a great deal of illiteracy and quite high prices for any kind of written document as far as ordinary people in Syria and Palestine are concerned, private use of manuscripts very probably was an exception, not a general rule. At best, we have evidence of private reading and libraries from Hellenistic times onward, among well-to-do people or else in school-situations. In the Christian era personal reading habits began to develop and monastic orders started to produce books and use them extensively in their spiritual life. The majority of the people until the beginning of the industrial age stayed more or less illiterate but did participate in the advanced culture by listening to masses and plays, and by oral repetition and transmission. In regard to life-settings, therefore, we are led to assume that oral texts obviously are rooted in societal exchanges. But even written documents – even if less obviously so – are embedded in real communicative events. They demand an audience, a group of users, and procedures of reception and perpetuation. All this essentially is of communitarian concern. Any text, on the other hand, not used and reused, copied, and commented upon is dead like a clay tablet buried in a tell or a book forgotten in a library. So we should abandon the idea of texts lacking "life-settings." What may take place, of course, in transmission is a change of such settings, as a given text moves on from its first matrix to different groups of people and varying communicative situations.

The psalms collected in the Psalter, no one contests this affirmation, had their original, and recognizably so, diversified life-settings. Most scholars accept the form-critical hypothesis that these settings were cultic in character including the gamut of cultic rituals present in Israel and the Ancient Near East (house-cults; local shrines; victory celebrations; temple-feasts; synagogal gatherings . . . to name but a few. Limitation of the Psalms to the Jerusalem cult is unwarranted. To declare the exilic and post-exilic assembly as "non cultic" in essence [thus F. Stolz] seems to be a rather Calvinistic prejudice). Few people would think of some academic or entirely private situation as giving birth to our extant OT psalms – individualistic privacy is an invention of the industrial age.

Granted so much it would be the first task of psalm-exegesis to investigate as far as possible the liturgical/cultic procedures which gave rise to the psalmic text. Some recurring ceremonial patterns can be detected in OT texts (cf. e.g. the prayers of Hannah, Hezekiah or Jonah) as well as in countless Mesopotamian clay tablets or, for that matter, in tribal societies to this very day. No healing rituals are identical with old Jewish petitionary prayers, but they do have something in common with them. To say the least, they can alert us to the exigencies and mysteries of ritualistic healing. Hymn-singing is likely to occur as a group-event in many cultures given determined situations of victory or surprising acts of grace. The liturgical conditions of early Jewish communities, which collected, adapted, and created psalms and eventually the Psalter, have to be taken into account as an ultimate stage of the texts and a specific setting. Nehemiah 8 tells us, for example, in an archetypal way about a Torah worship gathering, and the Chronicles are full of tales about psalm-singing and praying at different turns of life (cf. 1 Chr 16; 2 Chr 32:20, 24; 33:12; 35:25, etc.). Not very much has been done by Psalms-experts to elucidate the ritual parameters behind these references, understanding them as reflections of contemporary Jewish practices. This means to say, the life-situations accompanying the transmission of psalm-texts in Israel from early forms of worship to the latest stage – gathering around

Torah and at the Jerusalem temple in the Babylonian, Persian, perhaps even Hellenistic epochs – should be considered an essential background of extant psalms. To a certain extent we may also consider school-situations as a possible matrix in later times. A criterion to be used in determining this eventuality could be the degree of learned reflection visible in a given text (cf., e.g., Psalm 49 and P. Casetti). The text of our psalms would have to be interpreted in the light of the different uses it has received in the course of transmission and not so much according to the assumption of one determined author and subsequent literary redactors who modeled the prayer (or song, meditation, homily, etc.). Much more so than in our own time (where this rule still has vigorous support, however), the shape and contents of a liturgical text are molded by the needs of the community staging a sacred ceremony. Any possible single author would yield to these communal and liturgical necessities. Even though each psalm in the Psalter does have a special profile, none being just an exact copy of another (this also applies to Pss 14 and 53, and other chance duplications), linguistic smoothness and persistent anonymity of the texts betray liturgical use. For this reason, the social and liturgical situations should be kept in mind in psalm-exegesis (cf. P. Miller).

Feminist interpretation

Comparatively little energy, so far, has been spent on the psalms by feminist exegetes. Yet the lost traces of women's participation in Israel's worship need to be recovered, after all. Ulrike Bail (in L. Schottroff, ed., 1998, pp. 180–91) is among the few women who dedicate themselves to the issues of prayer and cult in relation to female members of a community. The basic question is simply: "Where is the voice of women in the Psalter and Israelite cult?" While the image of the praying Hannah (1 Samuel 1–2) is a strong indication of women's participation in local cults, the Psalter barely mentions them at all. On the other hand, prayers of the individual, recited in the common first-person singular, logically would serve both genders. Also the first-person plural, a communitarian mode of speech, certainly includes men and women, as is stressed exactly in late writings (cf. Deut 29:9f; Neh 8:2, etc.). So, if we take seriously some sociological data and the explicit statements just mentioned, there need not be any doubt about women participating in the worshiping community in Ancient Israel (cf. Phyllis Bird). Old Testament writers do not have any problems with this state of affairs. They make a point of counting women and children, besides adult males, in the congregation of YHWH. If this be so, there is no real point of proving that, e.g., Psalm 55 reflects the experiences of violence of a female citizen in Israel. Liturgical prayers were texts to be spoken by generations of participants expressing their own experiences. Liturgical language is capable of being both general and at the same time specific so that both opportunities are present (cf. A. Brenner and C. Fontaine, 1997).

Ancient Near Eastern texts and iconography

Many experts in Psalm-research are fully aware of Israel's interconnection with surrounding Ancient Near Eastern cultures, especially in the field of worship. Ever since textual and other archaeological evidence has come to light in Israel, Syria, Mesopotamia, Egypt, and other countries, revealing common features in sacred architecture (altars, shrines, temples) and implements, sacrificial as well as other rites and liturgical texts, interest in comparative studies has been keen. It did result in scattered special studies as far as the psalmic texts and festive rituals are concerned. Geo Widengren very early (1937) compared complaints and lamentations, to be followed by others. Joachim Begrich investigated expressions of confidence in Babylonia and Israel. Sigmund Mowinckel and his pupils made a point of elaborating a large New Year's festival common to Ancient Near Eastern religions, and a significant part of the Israelite psalms in their opinion fitted very neatly into this yearly enactment of creation by destroying chaos powers, of ritual death and resurrection of the king, of sacred marriage, and of determining destinies for the following year. Ugaritic and Hittite findings also permitted reconstructions of related rituals. Othmar Keel (Engl. 1978) took a fresh look at the iconography of the Ancient Near East in relation to psalmic metaphors and visions, creating a marvelous commentary and lively picture-book to bring to our minds and eyes such concepts as "guardian spirits," "demonic powers," "holy trees," "high places," "royal armour," "capturing nets," "besieged cities," "overpowered enemies," etc. Taking into account, however, the sheer amount of Ancient Near Eastern witnesses to the psalms and their accompanying ritual, and the differentiation clearly recognizable in the materials between various layers and opportunities of cultic performance, we still are very far from giving due recognition to this important field of psalm-study. With the exception of a few scholars (cf. P. Miller, 1994, pp. 5–31) the final interpretation of our psalms is kept free of "alien" influences or analogies. There seems to have occurred a withdrawal from too much "foreign" contact in the psalms (in spite of undeniable affinities!).

What we surely are able to learn today is this: our Old Testament songs and prayers are part and parcel of Ancient Near Eastern sacred literature. If we enter the third millennium and study the psalms in the new set-up of world affairs (free competition among the fittest and deadly exploitation of the majority of humans in that part of the world), we do have to take into account the prayers of "other" cultural and religious groups, and we find the same quite often surprisingly close to our own. In the case of Ancient Near Eastern psalmody, sometimes hidden away in magical and incantation-rituals, research has both to use the "Treasures of Darkness" (T. Jacobsen), in our case the many texts already published, and to promote, as far as possible, publication of the many found but still unpublished ones (it is a cultural disgrace, that relatively few resources of our wealthy world are being spent to recover the earliest literature of humankind). Experts in Near Eastern studies are increasingly paying attention to sacred texts. If they keep putting out accessible editions of relevant texts they will greatly enhance the awareness of teachers, students, and general readers in this respect (cf. J. Pritchard, ed., *ANET* and *ANEP*; M. Seux; O. Kaiser, ed., *TUAT*, vol. 2). With the material at hand and hopefully more to come, we may place Old Testament psalms into intercultural contexts, elaborating the common roots and the specific traits of each psalmody. There certainly is no easy and full-scale identification of Israelite and Ancient Near Eastern psalmodies, but a comprehensive, thorough juxtaposition and comparison does illuminate the profiles of each of them.

Anthropological studies

The tendency to open up psalm-studies instead of closing it down in a type of cultural narcissism may be followed up by admitting more comparative material from anthropological research (studies in "primitive" song and ritual: cf. F. Heiler, 1923; V. Turner, 1969; L. Wyman, 1975). As is the case with Near Eastern texts we cannot expect to reconstruct Old Testament worship and prayer by quoting Navajo, Dinka, or Eskimo songs and rituals. But given comparable occasions and purposes for staging a prayer service in different times and cultures we get a better idea of what people were after in their performances before God, and how they have been reciting prayer through the ages. Purification from uncleannesses has produced similar reactions in different societies down to our own time (cf. M. Douglas). Healing or mourning rites touch on basic human sentiments and do produce comparable ritual results. Happiness and thanks-givings, victory or escape from grave dangers, enthronement of leaders, and expulsion from office and society are definite occasions for ritualistic practice and opportune texts along the psalmic lines. Why not recognize these ongoing efforts of humankind to communicate with the divine in very special kinds of situations?

The work of many scholars can be helpful for psalm-research. In fact, there is a vast quantity of publications, especially in the field of social anthropology, which takes note of religious beliefs and practices. E. E. Evans-Pritchard was one of the pioneers in field-studies of religious behavior in Europe. Earlier American cultural anthropologists had already given some attention to religious beliefs in tribal societies (cf. R. Fortune), thereafter notably Gladys A. Reichard (1944) and Ruth Underhill. Also, in French ethnological circles, religion and ritual played an important role (cf. E. Durkheim; C. Lévi-Strauss) in exploring the archaic or primitive pre-stages of civilized mentality or organized faith (cf. also B. Malinowski). Subsequent generations of anthropologists in Europe and the USA seem to deal more pragmatically with religion, ritual and prayers. Journals and lexica in the field (cf. *The Encyclopedia of Religion*, ed. M. Eliade) provide texts and insights more than any psalm-scholar will be able to digest. To my mind, all this amazing wealth of information concerning psalms and psalm-recitation may bring to our attention the importance of our subject, and it reminds us that this treasure has hardly been tapped yet by modern exegetes. Interestingly, there is an awareness of how deeply Old Testament psalms have influenced our own cultures: literature, music, piety, liturgy, etc. (cf., e.g., P. Kurz, 1978, 1997). Latin-American hymn-singing has been greatly inspired by the psalms (cf. E. Gerstenberger, 1985b).

Redactional criticism

During the past twenty years or so critics of historical and form criticism have raised the issue of what kind of text we are really dealing with in the Psalter. Individual textual units, they claim, need not be the sole objects of analyses. All kinds of collecting and redactional processes of the early centuries of transmission need to be taken into account. The texts, as they stand now, are not representing original life-situations. They have been molded according to a long social, "ecclesiastic," and theological development within the emerging Jewish communities from the 6th until at least the 2nd centuries BCE – if the last date should mark the final point of Psalm canonization. (Some of the evidence from Qumran would speak for a later date, perhaps even the 1st century AD, cf. P. Flint, 1997.)

The issues surrounding the importance of redactional work need to be discussed, and they do result in new interpretative perspectives. Even a staunch form critic like myself has to concede that they have been neglected too long. Subcollections of psalms and the construction of the Psalter itself nicely prove the existence of a good deal of compository work. But exactly what message did these redactors, composers, and collectors impress on the final text? And for which audience or readership? There are various answers given in the extant literature, rapidly increasing in the USA and Europe. First, they left slight imprints of their own congregational and personal conditions, outlooks, and theological dispositions modifying inherited texts a little here and there, adding some. That means, the Psalter became either a prayer-book for the early Jewish congregation, or a scroll for private edification by meditating on the Word of YHWH. The original meanings of separate psalms have been partly painted over, e.g., by a royalist or messianic interpretation or typical Torah piety. Psalms with a "David" designation were waiting for a new David to come and rescue his people Israel (cf. J. Becker, 1967; J. McCann, 1993; P. Miller, 1994, et al.). Torah texts like Psalms 1, 19, and 119 gained an important position within the whole book. In this perspective, the collection of psalms in groups and finally in the Psalter are but steps of interpretation, which do not exclude either the original meaning or the continuity of using individual texts in appropriate liturgical set-ups (healing services; communal hymn-singing; instruction, etc.). Second, a more sophisticated discovery was that of significant lines of theological meaning permeating collections and the Psalter as a whole. These messages seem to be tied to the written composition only, presupposing a reading community dedicated to the larger rhythm of groups of adjacent psalms or, for that matter, counting on the present-day interpreter who is studying blocks of literature. In this sense scholars speak of clusters and compositions of Psalms, of overarching theological messages and trajectories of motives and faith. Individual texts now acquire a new meaning by being arranged around a central Psalm, e.g., Psalm 19, a hymn to creation and Torah, inserted between Psalms 15–18 and 20–24. Some psalms are considered pillars and cornerstones of pre-canonic collections or the whole intricate edifice of the Psalter, e.g., Psalms 72, 89, 119; 1 and 150, etc. The finished work seems to start out mainly from laments of the afflicted (concentration in Psalms 3–41; 42–71), to move towards an ever more jubilant praise for YHWH by those saved and rehabilitated (Psalms 103–150). Trajectories of eschatological hope and the momentum of God's grace in history are being pointed out. One may mention summarily a few protagonists in this scholarly debate: C. Westermann, 1984; G. Wilson, 1985; W. Brueggemann, 1995; M. Millard, 1994; F.-L. Hossfeld and E. Zenger, 1993; E. Zenger, 1998, etc.). Third, some exegetes are trying to recover a real Christian theology from OT psalms by reading psalms in the light of others, thus disposing of irritating affirmations like revengeful wishes in Ps 109 or violent submission of enemies like in Ps 18 or 137 or too exclusive a fixation on the people of Israel. Tied in with neighboring psalms of confidence, forgiveness, and praise, the sting of "unchristian" harshness, they believe, can be taken out of biblical texts, and the full message of God's saving acts for all nations can be inserted (cf. partially N. Lohfink, 1992; N. Flüglister; opposing: R. Whybray, 1996; E. Gerstenberger, 1998).

The methods of analysis applied in these new interpretative endeavors are manifold. Assuming that the redactors of old successively joined psalmic texts with a clear intention to create new meaning, one still has to ask for the means and opportunities to do so. Much depends on clear recognition of the redactors modifying and amplifying of textual interventions. Some will be easily discernible, like superscriptions to the individual psalms or the famous "book-dividers" after Psalms 41, 72, 89, 106. The prooemium and postludium of the Psalter (Psalms 1–2; 150) probably are accretions, too, and possibly so some reinterpretations of older texts (cf. Pss 22:28–32; 51:20–21; 102:14–17; 139:19–22, etc.). What else can we claim to be undebatable vestiges of late redaction? And can we be sure that all the alterations and additions to older texts are the result of one determined theological mind or the planned editing of generations of users? When we leave the area of undeniable redactional activity, we enter realms of lesser certitude. Scholars adduce topical affinities between neighboring or clustering psalms, structural likeness, progress of thought, dramatizations, liturgical connections, cross-word references, and similar phenomena to prove coherence, and eventually tight and firm theological planning. Some of the interconnecting devices surely belong to the armory of modern interpreters, because the features to be explained hardly were on the minds of intermittent redactors. What we have to be careful about is the distinction of our own purposes and those of the ancient redactors. We certainly are allowed to read old texts freshly, in the light of our own times. This is the usual way of interpetation. But the intentions and dimensions of today's exegetical projections should not remain subconsciously in scholarly discourse. Critical exegetes have constantly to check their own standpoints admitting their own contextuality and motivations, and draw a line, as much as possible, between unavoidable "eisegesis" and proper "exegesis" of the texts at hand (on that matter cf. S. Croatto, *Hermeneutics of Freedom*, Maryknoll: Orbis, 1978).

In search of theology

Much of psalm-research today is – and rightly so – motivated by theological concerns. This is true for large parts of the form-critical, structuralist, semiotic, feminist, and new literary studies referred to above. In particular, however, the new mode of looking at the Psalter as a coherent, integral, canonical text, a book composed for the main purpose of private reading and meditation, deserves to be discussed here separately. The new perspective is linked to a general holistic or canonical reading of the Bible (cf. B. Childs; J. Sanders et al.). In regard to the Psalter it is based on the conviction, that transmitters and final composers of the Book of Psalms are to be credited with far more theological influence on the final text than has been admitted so far.

The purpose of psalm analysis in general is to achieve a better understanding – in terms of historical and poetic knowledge – of Old Testament psalmody. But theological queries for truth and orientation are legitimate concerns of churches and synagogues or anybody seeking answers on questions of faith. What kinds of beliefs are expressing themselves in the Psalter? Are we able to enter into a meaningful dialogue with the ancient testimonies? (cf. P. Miller, W. Brueggemann). To begin with, according to the accumulated facts and interpretations about the Hebrew Psalter, we have to expect a plurality of theological articulations in the many types of texts and compositions, by no means a uniform system. The Psalter, it may be maintained on the basis of two centuries of penetrating research, definitely is not a theological handbook, neatly organized according to systematic topics (H.-J. Kraus, R. Tournay, H. Spieckermann, et al. may leave that wrong impression!).

But what can be found in the Psalter to guide us theologically? First of all, basic human conditions, expectations, needs, fears over against the Holy Ones, the Powerful and Benevolent Ones, and the Holy One, YHWH, are articulated over a long span of time, perhaps a thousand years, and clothed in the specific garments of succeeding cultures in the Near Middle East. The Psalter is full of vivid experiences of divine and demonic powers (cf. only Palms 22, 29, 82), and Israel is seen struggling with their relation to the supreme God, whose benevolence very often is unrecognizable in daily life and history (cf. Psalms 9/10, 44, 73, etc.). In a historical perspective, the congregations of exilic–post-exilic times – this is increasingly recognized by many scholars – did heavily imprint their religious stamp on the psalms, but without extinguishing traces of preceding faiths and theologies (cf. only those amazingly interreligious psalms Psalms 29 and 104!). Thus, we do have, on the level of personal experience, very strong witnesses of individual faith in a supreme God who nevertheless is available for his client in a very intimate, personal way, a theology inherited from millennia of family beliefs in a personal God (cf. K. van der Toorn, 1995; E. Gerstenberger, 1996). Age-old patterns of complaint, petition, expressing confidence, reprimanding the deity for neglect, confessing innocence and guilt, performing ablutions and sacrifices in connection with personal distress, receiving words of grace and remission of sins, turning into exuberant private ceremonies of thanksgiving and praise after being heard and healed (cf. Psalm 22!) – all this is beautifully preserved within the Psalter. And H. Gunkel was right in noting that this individual, familiar aspect of religion is predominant in the Psalter. Those complaints and thanksgivings of the individual indeed are the very core of prayer extending to our own time. And we should be extremely grateful to have received in the Old Testament Psalter (with ramifications in OT narratives, inter-testamental and New Testament literature and a huge entourage of secondary psalmic poetry reaching into our own period) such a lively treasure of explosive testimony of faith and hope for our spiritual life. It is exactly that close interconnection of textual articulations and real-life situations (or, let us say, authentic worship, meaningful ritual) within the psalms which makes Old Testament prayer so powerful even today, soliciting as it were "new songs" all the time (cf. Ps 33:3; 96:1; Isa 42:10) in sorrow and bliss. What these old examples of personal encounter with God can teach us is simply this: in spite of all scientific and bureaucratic anonymity prevailing in mass societies at large, human life is fully dependent on small group existence, with its characteristic solidarity and love, in which God is prepared to participate, in all ups and downs, shadows and lights, and joy and distress.

The other level of theological thinking and existence prominent in the Psalter is that of local parishes as they organized themselves among the Jewish people in the 6th and 5th centuries BCE. From all we know there have been some overarching ties, and a good amount of conflict, between those dispersed communities in Palestine, Babylonia, Egypt, and possibly some other countries. Temple and Torah were the common grounds for all those who adhered to YHWH, but with significant emphases on local autonomy, as the texts of Elephantine, the Jewish colony in southern Egypt, demonstrate. The Psalter reveals some centrism on Zion and much liberty to sing praises and teach Torah all around the world. Faith and ethics on this community level betray deep sensitivity for the unity of the political world and its social structures, and the need to ward off pressures of imperial religions. Therefore, we find ample polemics against other gods and emphasis on the supreme power of YHWH, the exclusive creator of heaven and earth, ruler over all nations. But in substance, much of the psalmodic theology of the communitarian type is inner-directed, particular, and exclusivistic (cf. Psalms 2, 99, 100, 115, 137, etc.). Only a few texts, mostly of the Wisdom type, are open to human beings in general, still propagating their belief – so it seems – to pious members of the Israelite fold. What we hardly can expect, but sometimes do encounter (cf. Psalm 104 except for v. 35; Psalm 139 except for vv. 19–22), are prayers of true ecumenical dimensions or, for that matter, orientations for the pluralist society at large as found already in the Babylonian and Persian Empires. Messianic strands within the Psalter (cf. at least Psalms 2, 110, but probably also Psalms 20, 21, 45, 72, etc.) are facing the question of a just world government, but they do so with the burning question of why injustice is being done to Israel.

This means to say that we are hearing in the Psalter wonderful testimonies of our forefathers and foremothers in the faith. They are discernible according to their ancient layering of society and their particular situations of life. Turning back to our own times – a move which exegesis and theology have to perform – we must not underestimate the different social structures and cultural habits we experience today. But understanding the analogies of our "modern" situations, and knowing about our responsibilities towards God and humankind today, we are asked to accept the inspiration and challenge of the old prayers and take on the task of articulating present-day experiences with God, fragmented as they are in contextual situations of many kinds. Global existence today demands – on its uppermost, artificial level of social existence – global answers ventured by precariously limited communities. Doing research in our own restricted world of traditions and interests we reach out to listen to those authentic voices of prayer. We peruse them in our spiritual lives, adapting the texts to present-day circumstances, and in doing so are encouraged to sing our own songs of faith and hope in this endangered world of ours.

Bibliography

Allen, L., *Psalms*, WBC 21 (Waco, TX: Word Books, 1983).

Alonso, Schökel, L., *Manual de poética Hebrea* (Madrid: Cristendad, 1987).

Assmann, J., *Ägyptische Hymnen und Gebete* (Zürich: Artemis, 1975).

Auffret, P., *Hymnes d'Egypte et d'Israel* (Fribourg: University Press, 1983).

Baldermann, I., *Ich werde nicht sterben, sondern leben* (Neukirchen-Vluyn: Neukirchener Verlag, 1990).

Barth, C., *Die Errettung vom Tode in den individuellen Klage- und Dankliedern des AT* (reprint; Zürich: Theol. Verlag, 1987).

Becker, J., *Israel deutet seine Psalmen*, 2nd edn., SBS 18 (Stuttgart: Katholisches Bibelwerk, 1967).

Beyerlin, W., *Im Licht der Traditionen, Psalm LXVII und CXV. Ein Entwicklungszusammenhang*, VTSup 45 (Leiden: E. J. Brill Publishers, 1992).

Bird, P., *Missing Persons and Mistaken Identities* (Minneapolis: Fortress Press, 1997).

Blount, B., *Cultural Interpretation* (Minneapolis: Fortress Press, 1995).

Brenner, A. and Fontaine, C., *A Feminist Companion to Reading the Bible* (Sheffield: Academic Press, 1997).

Brueggemann, W., *The Psalms and the Life of Faith*, ed. P. Miller (Minneapolis: Fortress Press, 1995).

Casetti, P., *Gibt es ein Leben vor dem Tod?* OBO 44 (Fribourg: Universitätsverlag, 1982).

Cohen, M., *Sumerian Hymnology*, HUCA Sup. 2 (Cincinnati: Hebrew Union College, 1981).

Craigie, P., *Psalms*, WBC 19 (Waco, TX: Word Books, 1983).

Crüsemann, F., *Studien zur Formgeschichte von Hymnus und Danklied in Israel*, WMANT 32 (Neukirchen-Vluyn: Neukirchener Verlag, 1969).

Culley, R., *Oral Formulaic Language in the Psalms* (Toronto: University Press, 1967).

Evans-Pritchard, E. E., *Nuer Religion* (Oxford: University Press, 1956).

Falkenstein, A. and W. von Soden, *Sumerische und Akkadische Hymnen und Gebete* (Zürich: Artemis Verlag, 1953).

Flint, P., *The Dead Sea Psalms Scroll and the Book of Psalms* (Leiden: E. J. Brill Publishers, 1997).

Gerstenberger, E., *Der bittende Mensch*, WMANT 51 (Neukirchen-Vluyn: Neukirchener Verlag, 1980).

——, "The Lyrical Literature," in D. Knight, et al. eds., *The Hebrew Bible and Its Modern Interpreters* (Philadelphia/Chico: Fortress Press/Scholars Press, 1985 (1985a), 409–44.

——, "Singing a New Song," *Word and World* 5 (1985b), 155–67.

——, *Yahweh, the Patriarch* (Minneapolis: Fortress Press, 1996).

——, *The Psalms*, FOTL XIV/1 (Grand Rapids: Eerdmans, 1988; 2nd vol. FOTL XV, 2001).

——, "Christliche Psalmenlektüre?" in E. Wengst, et al., eds., *Ja und Nein. Christliche Theologie im Angesicht Israels* (Neukirchen-Vluyn: Neukirchener Verlag, 1998), pp. 43–54.

Goulder, M, *The Psalms of the Return*, JSOTSup 258 (Sheffield: Academic Press, 1998).

Gunkel, H. and J. Begrich, *Einleitung in die Psalmen* (Göttingen: Vandenhoeck, 1932).

Hallo, W., J. Moyer, L. Perdue, eds., *Scripture in Context* 12 (Winona Lake: Eisenbrauns, 1983).

Heiler, F., *Das Gebet*, 5th edn. (München/Basel: Reinhardt Verlag, 1923); English: *Prayer*, 2nd edn. (Oxford: University Press, 1958).

Hornung, E., *Gesänge vom Nil* (Zürich: Artemis Verlag, 1990).

Hossfeld, F.-L. and E. Zenger, *Psalm 1–50*, Neue Echter Bibel (Würzburg: Echter Verlag, 1993).

——, *Psalmen 51–100*, Freiburg: Herder, 2000.

Irsigler, H., *Ps 73 – Monolog eines Weisen*, ATSAT (St. Ottilien: EOS–Verlag, 1984).

Janowski, B., *Rettungsgewißheit und Epiphanie des Heils*, WMANT 59 (Neukirchen-Vluyn: Neukirchener Verlag, 1989).

Jacobsen, Th., *The Harp that once . . .* (New Haven: Yale University Press, 1987).

Jeremias, J., *Das Königtum Gottes in den Psalmen* (Göttingen: Vandenhoeck, 1987).

Keel, O., *Feinde und Gottesleugner* (Stuttgart: Katholisches Bibelwerk, 1969).

——, *Die Welt der altorientalischen Bildsymbolik* (Neukirchen-Vluyn: Neukirchener Verlag, 1972); = *The Symbolism of the Biblical World* (New York: Seabury Press, 1978).

Kraus, H.-J., *Theologie der Psalmen*, BKAT XV/3 (Neukirchen-Vluyn: Neukirchener Verlag, 1979).

Kurz, Paul W., *Psalmen vom Expressionismus bis zur Gegenwart* (Freiburg: Herder Verlag, 1978).

——, "Höre, Gott," *Psalmen des Jahrendats* (Fünch/Düsseldorf: Patmos 1997).

Levin, C., "Das Gebetbuch der Gerechten," *ZTK* 90 (1993), 355–81.

Lohfink, N., "Der Psalter und die christliche Meditation," *BiKi* 4 (1992), 195–200.

Loretz, O. and I. Kottsieper, *Colometry in Ugaritic and Biblical Poetry* (Soest: CIS-Verlag, 1987).

Maul, S., *Zukunftsbewältigung* (Mainz: Philipp von Zabern, 1994).

Mayer, W., *Untersuchungen zur Formensprache der babylonischen "Gebetsbeschwörungen,"* (Rome: Pontifical Biblical Institute, 1976).

McCann, Jr., J., ed., *The Shape and Shaping of the Psalter*, JSOT 159 (Sheffield: Academic Press, 1993).

Millard, M., *Die Komposition des Psalters*, FAT 9 (Tübingen: Mohr, 1994).

Miller, P., *They Cried to the Lord. The Form and Theology of Biblical Prayer* (Minneapolis: Fortress Press, 1994).

Mitchell, D., *The Message of the Psalms*, JSOTSup 252 (Sheffield: Academic Press, 1997).

Mowinckel, S., *The Psalms in Israel's Worship*, 2 vols. (Nashville: Abingdon, 1962).

Neumann, P., ed., *Zur neueren Psalmenforschung*, WdF 192 (Darmstadt: Wissenschaftliche Buchgesellschaft, 1976).

Oeming, M., "Die Psalmen in Forschung und Verkündigung," *VuF* 40 (1995), 28–50.

Reichard, G., *Prayer: The Compulsive Word*, Monographs of the American Ethnological Society 7 (Washington: Smithsonian Institute, 1944).

Schottroff, L. and M.-T. Wacker, *Kompendium feministischer Bibelauslegung* (Gütersloh: Gütersloher Verlagshaus, 1998).

Seux, M.-J., *Hymnes et prières aux dieux de Babylonie et d'Assyrie* (Paris: Éditions du Cerf, 1976).

Seybold, K., *Die Psalmen*, HAT I, 15 (Tübingen: Mohr, 1996).

——, *Studien zur Psalmenauslegung* (Stuttgart: Kohlhammer Verlag, 1998).

Seybold, K. et al., eds., *Neue Wege der Psalmenforschung*, HBS 1 (Freiburg: Herder Verlag, 1994; 2nd edn., 1995).

Spieckermann, H., *Heilsgegenwart: Eine Theologie der Psalmen*, FRLANT 148 (Stuttgart: Kohlhammer, 1989).

Stolz, F., *Psalmen im nachkultischen Raum*, ThSt(B) 129 (Zürich: Theol. Verlag, 1983).

Tate, M., *Psalms*, WBC 20 (Waco, TX: Word Books, 1990).

Texte aus der Umwelt des Alten Testaments, TUAT, ed. O. Kaiser, vol. 2 (Gütersloh: Gütersloher Verlag, 1989–91). (W. Römer, W. Farber, et al., "Rituale," 163–452; W. H. Ph. Römer, K. Hecker, et al., "Lieder und Gebete," 645–936).

Thiel, W., "Literaturbericht: Gottesdienst – Altorientalische und israelitisch-jüdische Religion," *JLH* 30 (1986), 133–56.

Toorn, K. van der., *Family Religion* (Leiden: E. J. Brill, 1995).

Tournay, R., *Seeing and Hearing God with the Psalms*, JSOTSup 118 (Sheffield: Academic Press, 1991).

Turner, V., *The Ritual Process* (Chicago: The University of Chicago Press, 1969).

Veijola, T., *Verheißung in der Krise* (Helsinki: Suomalainen Tiedeakatemia, 1982).

Watson, W., *Classical Hebrew Poetry* (Sheffield: University Press, 1984).

Westermann, C., *Praise and Lament in the Psalter* (Louisville: Westminster/John Knox Press, 1984).

Whybray, R., *Reading the Psalms as a Book*, JSOTSup 222 (Sheffield: Academic Press, 1996).

Widengren, G., *The Accadian and Hebrew Psalms of Lamentation* (Stockholm, 1937).

Wilson, G., *The Editing of the Hebrew Psalter*, SBLDS 76 (Chico: Scholars Press, 1985).

Wittstruck, T., *The Book of Psalms: An Annotated Bibliography*, 2 vols. (New York: Garland, 1994).

Wyman, L., *The Mountainway of the Navajo* (Tucson: University Press, 1975).

Zenger, E., *Mit meinem Gott überspringe ich Mauern* (Freiburg: Herder Verlag, 1987).

——, ed., *Der Psalter in Judentum und Christentum*, HBS 18 (Freiburg: Herder, 1998).

CHAPTER 25
Wisdom Literature

Katharine J. Dell

In this essay, I will be considering Proverbs, Job and Ecclesiastes, generally regarded as the three mainstream works of Wisdom literature in the Hebrew Bible. While there is much that unites these three books with regard to theological ideas, literary forms and social context, it will become clear how different from each other these three books of wisdom actually are. They represent a considerable development within the Israelite Wisdom enterprise: notably, in the theological sphere, a change from a confident worldview to a questioning one and ultimately to a resigned, even pessimistic one. In literary forms and in the social sphere, there is most strikingly a change from simple sentences and collections of sayings that may have had an oral origin to the production of great works of literature among groups of intellectuals.

The Theologies of the Books

The thought-world of Proverbs is that of "the act–consequence relationship" (von Rad, 1972), that is, the principle that good and bad deeds have consequences that can be known through the study of patterns of human behavior. This principle and various other insights into human characteristics are summed up in pithy proverbial sayings, the fruit of the experiences of many generations. The wise person needs to learn to walk along the smooth path, as opposed to the one covered in thorns – "Thorns and snares are in the way of the perverse; the cautious will keep far from them" (Prov 22:5). The image of the path and of walking along it is often used, e.g., Prov 12:28. "In the path of righteousness there is life, in walking its path there is no death." This righteous path can be trodden by careful attention to certain behavioral patterns such as hard work, carefulness with money, sparing words and so on, themselves the fruit of experience. The righteous and the wicked are often contrasted, e.g. Prov 12:26, "The righteous gives good advice to friends, but the way of the wicked leads astray." This is a system of ethics concerned with the development of moral character (Brown, 1996) that teaches one to beware of the loquacious fool, the liar, the cheat and the sluggard, e.g., Prov 12:24, "The hand of the diligent will rule, while the lazy will be put to forced labor." It is also a compendium of insights into human nature, e.g., Prov 12:25, "Anxiety weighs down the human heart, but a good word cheers it up." There is a pragmatism about this worldview – it promotes "interested righteousness," i.e., righteous behavior with one's own interests in mind, in relation both to others and to God. The acquisition of wealth, for example, is seen as a security – e.g., Prov 18:11, "The wealth of the rich is their strong city; in their imagination it is like a high wall" – and the accumulation of it, albeit slowly and surely and not to excess, is recommended (Whybray, 1990). There is a just and individual accounting system in relation to God too – he rewards righteousness and punishes wickedness. It is as simple as that. There are occasional hints that the wicked might appear to prosper, but this is generally regarded as fleeting. There are moments of contradiction in the proverbial collection, but it is regarded as a healthy ambiguity about life rather than as a problem that might threaten this neat system of justice and reward. Rewards are to be enjoyed in this life, they bring prosperity, longevity, and many offspring. The pattern of good and evil is linked to a world order in which YHWH is the controller of an order that is essentially orientated towards the good.

In Job this pattern of act and consequence goes horribly wrong. Job is a just man who did everything according to the pattern recommended in Proverbs and he suffers calamity after calamity, culminating in an illness that brings him close to death. How is the Wisdom tradition to cope with this? The prologue to the book airs the issue of disinterested righteousness. The self-interest of the Wisdom tradition comes under scrutiny. A debate between God and the Satan introduces the idea of Job's motives for doing good deeds. Are Job's motives truly altruistic or are they simply done for personal reward? This is to introduce a profundity to the debate that leads on to a more overtly theological level. It is not that serving God was absent from the proverbial pattern, but here God moves more center-stage – a system of ethics is nothing unless it is grounded in real faith. The "just deserts" theory also comes under fire. What happens when a man does all that is right and then still suffers? This issue is raised in the dialogue section to the book in which three friends come to "comfort" Job and put forward traditional arguments about suffering as a result of sin. There is no innocent suffering, rather Job must have sinned in some way. As Eliphaz, the first friend, exclaims, "Who that was innocent ever perished?" (Job 4:7), and he proceeds to give examples of God's punishment of the wicked. Thus there is no other way to understand this sudden change in fortune, according to the friends, except to see it as punishment for sin in a rational manner (Albertz, 1990). Job angrily counters their arguments, proclaiming his innocence and protesting at this unfair treatment from God. Although his speeches are directed at the friends, and he enjoys mocking them at times and accusing them of "windy words," it becomes increasingly clear that his real debate is with God and he gradually leaves the arguments of the friends behind.

In Ecclesiastes we find a different picture again. Here there is a resigned airing of ideas that often contradict. One might say that the author is not concerned with interested or disinterested righteousness, he is just disinterested. Contradictory ideas are juxtaposed with the idea of throwing up the inconsistencies between them (see Loader who argues for polar structures in the book, which he describes as "patterns of tension created by the counterposition of two elements to one another," p. 1) and so traditional proverbs are aligned with commentary that throws previous certainties into question, e.g., 5:2–7; 9:3–7. The theory of just deserts is again questioned, but not in a loud, protesting manner, rather with a quiet air of resignation. All is relativized in the light of death, the great equalizer. "How can the wise die just like fools?" she asks (Eccl 2:16) – there is no enduring remembrance of either – "So I hated life, because what is done under the sun was grievous to me; for all is vanity and a chasing after wind" (2:17). One might try to do good deeds, one might work hard, one might try to attain status and position. But everyone is equal in death, all pomp and show is fleeting and what is the point of working hard and accumulating money when it will simply pass on to those who come after you (2:21)? Here the pointlessness of endless striving comes across, punctuated, however, with moments of joy (Whybray, 1982) in which the author recommends the good life and enjoying the present moment (Eccl 2:24), confirms the just deserts theory (2:26) and sees life as God's gift (3:13), standing in awe of Him (3:14). It is hard to know what the author's true sentiments are because he often cites an optimistic saying, such as in 2:26, but then relativizes it in the next verse by appeal to the "vanity" of everything. This is where the contradiction and tension in his thought lies.

In Proverbs there is a basic theology of God as creator and orderer. Zimmerli made the oft-quoted statement that "Wisdom thinks resolutely within the framework of a theology of creation" (1964, p. 148). Studies by Hermisson (1978), Murphy (1978), and most recently Perdue (1994) have explored the place of the theology of creation in Wisdom. Perdue finds a dialectic between cosmology and anthropology to characterize the creation motif in Wisdom. The connection with creation is perhaps made most clear in the personification of Wisdom in Prov 8:22f, in which Wisdom is created before all things and delights in God and in his inhabited world: "The Lord created me at the beginning of his work, the first of his acts of long ago . . . When he established the heavens, I was there . . . then I was beside him, like a master worker; and I was daily his delight, rejoicing before him always, rejoicing in his inhabited world and delighting in the human race" (Prov 8:22, 27a, 30, 31). In this image we can find this tension between cosmology and anthropology in that Wisdom is created like human beings but is a part of the creative process and is the mediator of wisdom between God and humanity. There is also a more overt theological content to Proverbs 1–9, notably in the concept of the "fear of the Lord" being the beginning of wisdom, which has led scholars to see the section as a later development from a more anthropological starting point in other parts of Proverbs. However, God is present in a number of proverbs in other sections, notably in chapter 16, which is part of the earliest section of Proverbs 10:1–22:16, and the "fear of the Lord" idea comes in elsewhere (as seen in Prov 19:13, for example). Scholars debate the direction of the development – was it from a more human-centered, even "secular" kind of wisdom to a more overtly theological one as found in Proverbs 1–9 (von Rad, 1972) or did the development happen the other way around – from a basic theological concern to a hardening into a moralistic framework (Schmid, 1966)? God is often seen to be at the limits of the quest for wisdom – when human understanding reaches its limits there is God. God directs the steps of humans even though they may attempt to plan their way (Prov 16:1) – maybe in this there is the recognition that individual lives do not always work out in expected ways (cf. Job). In Proverbs 8, however, this thought moves onto a higher plane – not only is God at the limits of the quest for knowledge and understanding, he is offering these qualities and more, through the wisdom quest itself. Wisdom personified as a woman offers them to young men who are learning the paths of wisdom, thus the wisdom quest gains a kind of divine legitimation which is a development away from its starting point in human observation and experience. There is some debate as to the origins of the Wisdom image – is it the vestige of a Goddess-myth, an early idea coming from a time when YHWH had a consort (Lang, 1975), or is the idea related to the Egyptian concept of ma'at, order, which resembles in many ways this Wisdom figure? Whatever its origins, this image is a central one in that it combines concepts of human and divine wisdom – wisdom is a practical quest and yet it has the highest legitimation from God.

It is this more divine dimension to the Wisdom debate that is explored in the book of Job, in which it becomes clear that the real argument is not between Job and his friends but between Job and God. Job struggles to understand his fate and begins to realize that it is none other than God himself who can provide the answers to his questions. He calls for a mediator to judge between himself and God, because he realizes that God holds all the cards in being both chief prosecutor and judge, a sentiment that comes to a head in Job 19:25–27 in a rare moment of affirmation. Eventually God does appear in the book, although seemingly not to answer Job's questions directly. There is an unparalleled picture here of God as creator. The description includes God's creation of the animals, including the Behemoth and Leviathan, and the inference is that God does wonderful things in nature of which human beings have but limited understanding. The question is raised: why do human beings try to limit God and think that he works by strict rules that they seek to impose on him? There is a sense of the order of the world and of creation and yet also a breaking outside that order to state a profundity about the nature of the Godhead. In Ecclesiastes there is a hymnic section in chapter 3 which appears to glorify the order that is in the world in the recognition that there is a time for all things – "A time to be born and a time to die . . ." (Eccl 3:1). However, it soon becomes clear that while God knows the times of things, such things are beyond human understanding and human beings cannot predict or know when events are likely to happen. Therefore, trying to understand such things is pointless. God is the creator and orderer of all and for that commands respect and praise – and we find a note of joy in creation as God's gift. However, human life is just as mysterious as ever. So in Job and Ecclesiastes we get a sense of the limits of the attempt to order the world, which is the keynote of the wisdom quest. The emphasis on God that was relatively slight in Proverbs becomes central in these more developed and more theological books. In all three there is a preoccupation with the God–human relationship – in Proverbs it springs from the human side, primarily from human experience, while in Job the relationship itself is more at the forefront, again the product of experience – this time more individual experience – aired in particular in the God speeches and in Job's response. In Ecclesiastes the ambivalence in the relationship is drawn out – the relationship is there, but God holds the keys and human beings are left with limited understanding. Again the experience is expressed in individual terms, although in this case it has a clear wider reference to humankind in general.

In Proverbs there is an optimistic tone that is not shared by the other two books. There is a delight in human relationships with each other, with God and indeed with the created world. The possibility of getting the most out of life is stressed – e.g. with a religious tone in Prov 19:3, "The fear of the Lord is life indeed; filled with it one rests secure and suffers no harm" – it is all on offer for the one who would be wise. There is occasional ambiguity – for example, the silent person is generally the one who is tactful and discerning but sometimes a fool keeps quiet too (e.g., Prov 17:27–8). The wise person has to steer a path that avoids the pitfalls, but ultimately confidence in the wisdom quest is high. In Job the ambiguities of life come center stage and, although the doctrine of retribution seems to be upheld in the book's "happy ending" in which Job is restored, there is much questioning of established conclusions along the way. For Job, God's formerly protective hedge around him has become a choking and restrictive one (Job 3:23 echoing Satan's accusing words to God in Job 1:10, "Have you not put a fence around him . . . ?"); the God in whom Job took delight has become terrible and unpredictable (e.g., Job 16:6–17). The idea of life as good has become turned on its head for Job as he sits on his dung heap scratching his itchy skin. He at once longs for death and then fears it when he realizes that death will cut him off from his conversation with God. He formerly did all that was required of him and more – he even offered sacrifices on behalf of his children in case they had sinned (Job 1:5) – and yet this did not prevent calamity from striking. Job is unaware that this is a test of his motivation – for him God has turned nasty and all his previous certainties have been shattered. The book airs traditional Wisdom positions in the viewpoints of the friends, but the overall atmosphere of the book is one in which confidence in the wisdom quest is seriously under question.

In Ecclesiastes life is seen as a mixture of good and bad – there is full recognition of the ambiguity of life. Various tests are made of pleasure, notably wealth (Bickerman, 1967) and fulfillment, but ultimately each is proved worthless and yet there is a sense of the need to enjoy life without expecting too much. It is clear that there are limits to the human mastery of life. There are notes of pessimism, even despair, in the preoccupation with death and the perception of life as "vanity," a phrase repeated thirty-eight times in the book (Fredericks, 1993). Confidence in the wisdom quest seems to have been definitively undermined – and yet the use of traditional proverbs juxtaposed with fresh insights suggests that it is not defunct. M. Fox (1989) argues that the author is not attacking the Wisdom tradition, rather he is expressing disappointment in the non-realization of its ideas. In this context, Murphy writes of the author of Ecclesiastes, "His own wisdom consisted in seeing deeper and further than the traditional wisdom, in purifying it, even to such an extent that it did not appear to be viable. But in style he remained faithful to the tradition of the sages" (1990, p. 271).

The Forms of the Literature

The Wisdom literature is easily recognizable by the use of certain forms, most notably the proverb, which lies at the heart of the Wisdom enterprise. In Proverbs itself we find the largest number of proverbs, notably in Proverbs 10:1–22:16. They appear in this section to be in no special order and to relate to a number of different issues such as wealth and poverty, communication, work, pride, and so on. There are some that mention God although the majority do not. There are also quite a number that make use of imagery from the animal world, e.g. Proverbs 6:6–8: "Go to the ant, you lazybones; consider its ways, and be wise. Without having any chief or officer or ruler, it prepares its food in summer and gathers its sustenance in harvest." They also take a number of different forms – some are basic statements and others have a more complex formulation. This led some scholars to posit a development from the one-limbed to the multi-limbed saying (McKane), although this is not widely supported. Rather it looks likely that different formulations grew up alongside and independently and that at some stage these collections came together as a kind of compendium. Proverbs include statements of fact, commands, similes, and metaphors which make up a rich and multifaceted tradition. We also have in Proverbs the instruction form, in which a father and mother give their instruction to a son, probably in a teaching context (Whybray, 1994). We find these in Proverbs 1–9 and 22:17–24:22 and they are known to us from Egyptian circles. We also find in Proverbs numerical sayings, short sections of autobiographical narrative, such as the description of the loose woman looking out from her window in Proverbs 7:6–9, and we find hymnic description of personified wisdom in Proverbs 8.

The book of Job is rather different in style with a prose story surrounding a poetic dialogue. The dialogue form is known to us from ancient Mesopotamia. We also find isolated proverbs, a hymnic chapter in chapter 28 and a good deal of poetry as well as the use of genres from a wider thought-world, such as the lament and the lawsuit. It looks therefore as if the author of Job draws on a broader number of types to make up his work. In Ecclesiastes we find a number of proverbs, but often with an accompanying interpretation that relativizes the saying. We find hymns and poetic sections too. Generally, however, the finding is that this book is more mainstream wisdom in regard to the forms used, than is Job.

Questions of Social and Historical Context

Those who produced the Wisdom literature are often characterized as wise men or sages (see Blenkinsopp, 1995). Questions such as who these sages were, whether they existed as a group, whether they were primarily located at the king's court or whether they had a connection to some kind of school have been raised by scholars. In this section we will look at each of the books under consideration in the light of these questions and then pursue the more historical question of the relative dating of the books.

An important distinction needs to be made between the process of writing down this material and the origins of the material. In the case of Job we generally speak of an author writing the book. Despite various theories as to stages of redaction after the main text was written, theories that have largely fallen from favor in recent scholarship (Habel, 1985; Clines, 1989), the main dialogue section is seen as a unified composition, written by an author who may have had personal experience of suffering and who certainly wished to use the test case of Job to make some profound theological judgments about the relationship between God and human beings. The folktale-like prologue and epilogue opens up a more complex question of whether this existed in some kind of written form before being taken over by the main author of Job and used for fresh purposes or whether it was a tale that only existed in oral form and was simply adapted by our author. The style of the prologue and epilogue suggests a different hand and has a traditional setting in patriarchal times, but then there would be nothing to stop a later author imitating such a style. The way the book, as we have it, is structured throws up some interesting counterpoints (Zuckerman, 1991) between Job the patient of the prologue and Job the impatient of the dialogue; between Job the silent and between Job the verbose, and so on. This may be a deliberate technique by the author, who used this juxtaposition to parody traditional tales as represented by the prologue/epilogue. The author also parodies literary forms, in particular from the psalms, in the speeches of Job in the dialogue (Dell, 1991) so that Job says the opposite of traditional sentiments – a way of underlining his protest. On a literary level we find a work that makes use of literary genres from a whole range of Israelite material – from the psalms and from legal quarters, which suggests a broader intellectual milieu than a narrowly Wisdom one. Scholars have made various suggestions for an overall genre for Job but each suggestion has had its shortcomings, including Whedbee's suggestion of Job as a "comedy" (1977). What kind of sage is this author, we might ask?

My answer would be a renegade one, standing at the edge of the Wisdom tradition, well-versed in it, but wishing to point out its limitations and weaknesses.

When we turn to Ecclesiastes we can also speak of a main author, Qoheleth, mentioned in the first verse of the book. We are also given an indication of a teaching milieu. There is a curious alignment with the persona of Solomon in the book – the author describes himself as "son of David in Jerusalem" and later in chapter 1 the attempt to find meaning in life by pursuing fame, wealth, and so on gives the further impression of a king speaking. This is often seen as a clever technique by the author, deliberately recalling the "father" of wisdom, Solomon (see recently Christianson, 1998, who sees the Solomonic fiction as pervading the whole book). Exactly who this sage was is intriguing – why the taking on of another persona, and why the curious juxtaposition of traditional ideas with his own? Luther suggested that the book showed Solomon in dialogue with his political associates and the idea of a dialogue is an interesting one. It has been suggested that this author was a teacher in a wisdom school and that the book represents debates had with his pupils. However, this is perhaps stretching the evidence too far. The author could be employing a technique of quotation of traditional ideas in order to refute them (Gordis, 1939–40) or he could even have formulated the more traditional sentiments himself for the purpose of contradicting the ideas contained in them. The book is generally considered a literary whole, apart from a short epilogue in 12:7f and possibly one or two small additions. There has been considerable interest in trying to find an overall structure for the book, but no one model leads to scholarly agreement. In fact Fox has recently argued that it is the epilogist who is the real author of the book, citing Qoheleth for his own purposes (1977). The epilogue adds the injunction to fear God and keep his commandments and seems therefore to be aligning the book more closely with a more legal emphasis, and it also bewails the endless production of books! Sheppard stresses the importance of the epilogue to Ecclesiastes for understanding the way in which wisdom was to develop later on, in the apocryphal Wisdom books of Ecclesiasticus and the Wisdom of Solomon (1977). This links up with the legal emphasis, found which anticipates the alignment of Wisdom and Torah in Jewish thought that we find in Ecclesiasticus. Both Job and Ecclesiastes must have been written by highly educated men and both suggest a broader intellectual milieu than a narrow Wisdom one. In fact Ecclesiastes is more dominated by the use of Wisdom forms and in that sense is more mainstream Wisdom than Job. It seems likely that sages are their "authors" although in precisely what context is unknown. Ecclesiastes may have been formulated in an instructional context and Job itself offers instruction, although perhaps not in a teaching context. Are we to see "instruction" as the keynote of wisdom as Collins argues when he states that the context of "instruction is more definitive of what constitutes wisdom literature than a study of literary forms, content or worldview? – if so, Job slightly falls outside its bounds.

Clearly with the book of Proverbs we need also to speak of educated authors who wrote down the material at some stage. Yet with Proverbs the situation is much more complex. The book has the nature of a number of "collections" so that in fact it is more appropriate to speak of a number of books within a book. Thus the book divides into sections such as Proverbs 1–9, the more theological section of the book and one that includes a number of "instructions"; Proverbs 10:1–22:16, the major and probably earliest section, made up of a seemingly disparate and very diverse selection of proverbs on a wide range of subjects, including some that concern the king; Proverbs 22:17–24:22, a section that closely parallels the Egyptian Instruction of Amenemope in form and subject matter; Proverbs 25–29, which is attributed to the "men of Hezekiah" and consists of proverbial material, and Proverbs 30 and 31, separate sections with their own attributions dealing with one or two themes, such as the benefits of a good wife (Proverbs 31:10). These different sections may well have been written down at different times. Furthermore the material that makes up these collections may well have been gathered together over a period of time. The proverbs in particular have the nature of a collection of traditional material which probably existed orally before they were written down. However, those that concern the king pose more of a problem – they may indicate a court context, although this is a debated question (Dell, 1998). Thus it was the work of the intellectuals – the sages – to write the material down but we should not limit the context of this material by reference only to this.

It is likely that much of the proverbial material circulated orally in the family or tribe. Proverbs 30 emphasizes the role of a mother in imparting wisdom to her son and Proverbs 1–9 speaks of the instruction of father and mother. This was a process that did not stop when Wisdom literature was written down in a more formal sense – it went on throughout the Old Testament period (Clements, 1992). There is also evidence of traditional Wisdom sayings in older material (Fontaine, 1982) and of Wisdom influence in the Psalter (Perdue, 1977) and prophets (Morgan, 1981). This suggests that the Wisdom tradition is an old one and that the roots of this wisdom may be tribal and nomadic, familial and educational (Westermann, 1995). The question is then raised as to when the sages adopted this material as their own. One very influential theory of the last few decades is that there was a kind of enlightenment at the time of Solomon in which wisdom gained a new status and became a form of expression for administrators, courtiers, and scribes. Wisdom on this model was seen as a basic training for young men on how to succeed in life, and court schools were posited in which those destined for high position were trained (Heaton, 1974). It was thought to be a period in which literature flourished among intellectuals, not merely the Wisdom literature but other pieces of writing showing influence from the Wisdom thought-world, such as the Yahwistic document of the Pentateuch, the Joseph story (a particular favorite among would-be administrators) and the Succession Narrative. This theory also strengthened the connection between wisdom and its patron Solomon, providing extra evidence beyond the account in 1 Kings 4, 10 of his legendary association with the Wisdom enterprise. The problem had been noted that the kind of wisdom in which Solomon seems to be versed is primarily nature wisdom in 1 Kings 4 (Alt, 1976) and that the transition is found in the Wisdom literature from this to a more humanistic wisdom. The "Solomonic enlightenment" theory has come under question in recent years, scholars citing the lack of evidence for such a period of enlightenment and wondering whether the administrative structure under Solomon would have been large enough to support such sophisticated intellectual activity and whether in fact there was such a developed administrative structure at all. The model was thought to have been based largely on Egyptian parallels which may not have been so close as was once thought (Weeks, 1994). One of the problems is that we do not know when the move from oral to literary took place – it may have been a very gradual process with pockets of literary activity emerging from time to time, some under Solomon perhaps (possibly the oldest collection in Proverbs 10:1–22:16 came together at this time) but some material may have been drawn together under the reign of Hezekiah (Scott, 1955) who was later regarded as a second Solomon (Chronicles) and who is mentioned in Prov 25:1. The idea of schools has received widespread support from some quarters, e.g. Lemaire (1981) who believes that there were schools around Israel for educational purposes (also Oliver). There may have been schools attached only specifically to temple (Doll, 1985) or court (Heaton, 1974). The archaeological evidence for schools is very weak and again the comparison is often made on the grounds of ancient Near Eastern parallels. We know from ancient Sumer and Egypt that use in schools was a major function of their wisdom works; but the enterprise seems to be broader than just that and to speak only of a school context is probably to limit wisdom. We know from Egypt that the Instruction of Amenemope was a school text that was copied over and over down the centuries. The similarity of Proverbs 22:17–24:22 to this Instruction suggests that there is some borrowing in Proverbs, but it does not necessitate a parallel school context. Sages may well have been aware of material from the Ancient Near East and been inspired by its contents – we suspect this to have been the case in reference to Babylonian literature in which we can find particular parallels with the book of Job.

So the question of the role of the sages is a vexed one – whether they were even an entirely separate group from other parts of society is a related question. The influence of wisdom on prophecy, worship, and on books such as Deuteronomy (Weinfeld, 1972) suggest that wisdom was not restricted to a highly literate group but may have influenced the formulation of material in its oral stages. Its influence pervaded other areas of Israelite life and thought, a process that happened increasingly as time went on so that the Wisdom literature itself becomes less and less distinct from other genres of literature by the time of the production of the apocryphal Wisdom books in the 2nd to 1st centuries BCE. Whybray speaks of "an intellectual tradition" rather than specific groups of prophets, sages, and so on, especially in the later period (1974). He also stresses the different intellectual and social world inhabited by the sages. The role of the sage is thus probably much broader than just being confined to the Wisdom literature itself (see Gammie and Perdue, 1990).

I have emphasized the uncertainty of knowing the context of this material – can we attempt to assign it to specific periods in the history of Israel? Proverbs tends to be dated to the 9th–8th century BCE, at least in its main central section, but as we have seen there are probably oral antecedents to the written material. The instruction texts of Amenemope might well have influenced Proverbs 22:17–24:22 at an early stage. However, the section Proverbs 1–9, which also contains evidence of instruction texts, is often dated considerably later on theological grounds. I wonder whether in fact the antiquity of the genres used in this section militate against too late a dating. It may be that the Proverbs 1–9 was connected to the rest of the book at a later period – possibly at the same time as Proverbs 25–29, which is connected to the reign of Hezekiah in the 7th century BCE (Proverbs 25:1). It could be then that the whole of Proverbs had essentially come together before the time of the Exile in the 6th century BCE. It is likely to be a Judean production rather than one formulated in Exile, but there are no indicators as to the place of writing.

Job then would be most likely to have come from the period after the Exile, notably when the question of suffering being a result of sin came up in reference to the whole nation. The Wisdom literature with its more individualistic cast may have chosen to deal with this question on a more individual level. Interestingly there is a reference to Job in Ezekiel 14:14 and 20, in which he is described as a righteous man alongside Noah and Daniel. This may indicate the antiquity of the tradition about a man called Job and may also indicate the thrust of the traditional folktale about him – he was a righteous man who bore suffering in a steadfast manner. The references to "the Satan" in the prologue often lead scholars to date the book to the 4th to 3rd century BCE, since this may be a Persian idea. However, many scholars believe that the prologue/epilogue section was earlier than the dialogue section, possibly even pre-exilic before the adding of a post-exilic dialogue section. In this case, the reference to "the Satan," which is unlikely to be pre-Persian, could be seen as a later addition to the whole (Batten, 1933). If this was the case and we were to remove the Satan passage to see what is left, we would find a story that resembles Ezekiel more closely – that of a righteous man on whom suffering was inflicted by God. This would make sense in relation to the dialogue, where "the Satan" is never mentioned – rather God is the one to whom at all times Job makes his complaints. It would also explain the fact that "the Satan" is not mentioned in connection with the restoration of Job's fortunes. Other possible later additions are the hymn to wisdom in chapter 28 and the Elihu speeches (see Gordis who thinks that they are by the same author but added at a later stage of his life, 1963) and possibly the second YHWH speech, although that is a more contested point. As to place of writing – Edom is often suggested on grounds of the possible location of the land of Uz and the homelands of the three friends (see Day, 1994).

Dating questions also emerge in reference to Ecclesiastes, which is generally dated slightly later than Job, to around the third century BCE but has also been placed in the 5th century BCE (recently Seow, 1997; also Kugel, 1989) on socioeconomic grounds. The question of Greek influence comes in here – is there evidence that the author thought in Greek categories? The evidence suggests in fact that this is a very Hebrew production (Forman, 1958) and that the author did not espouse any of the traditional Greek philosophical positions (although this is held by some, e.g., Gammie sees Ecclesiastes as deliberately anti-Stoic, 1985). Ranston (1925) agrees but finds the influence of Theognis on his thought. There is also influence in Ecclesiastes from other Old Testament texts (notably Genesis 1–11; Forman, 1960), a feature of a number of later texts and also evidence of later dating, and the linguistic evidence that suggests a post-exilic date. We have no clue in this book as to the place of writing.

This dating scheme for the three books would support the progression of thought between the three books, from optimism, to protest, to resignation, which we mentioned at the beginning of this essay (cf. Priest, 1968, who posited a development between the three books from humanism, to skepticism, to pessimism). However, we must be aware of the danger of positing a neat line of theological development from one to another and then imposing a dating scheme around this. There is no doubt though that the Wisdom tradition itself changed over a relatively short period of time and that the tradition is represented by three very different books.

A final key point is that the Wisdom tradition influenced the Old Testament at all stages of its development – Proverbs represents that earlier stage within the Wisdom literature in which the Wisdom enterprise is mainly represented by proverbs and instructions, but we can also find Wisdom providing a formative influence in the thought of psalmist and prophet. It also has its place in a redactive role, the editors of the Old Testament may well have been versed in the literary styles and theological concerns of Wisdom. And yet, the curiosity of Wisdom is that it retains its distinctiveness as a genre, perhaps because of its distinctive forms and content but perhaps too because of its lack of mention of the historical dimension of Israel's faith. Wisdom does not include great heroes of Israel's history until we arrive at Ecclesiasticus. Wisdom has a separateness in its concerns that makes it easy to discern as an influence upon other books. It is a separate tradition from the more historical traditions of the Old Testament, one that has a different starting point in human experience and knowledge of God as creator and orderer. It shares much with the Ancient Near Eastern context around it and yet is given a distinctive shape under the influence of the sages of Israel. Wisdom is thus to be regarded as a distinctive tradition rather than simply a set of Wisdom books themselves and this Wisdom tradition, although in a sense defined by the Wisdom books, is broader than just these in its wider influence on the Old Testament. This tradition, however, was not static and as it matured and began to question itself and in turn became more literary; it went on to produce, in the post-exilic period, works that are generally regarded as great literature, most notably the book of Job.

Bibliography

Albertz, R., "The Sage and Pious Wisdom in the Book of Job: The Friends' Perspective," in J. Gammie and L. Perdue, eds., *The Sage in Israel and the Ancient Near East* (Winona Lake, IN: Eisenbrauns, 1990), 231–61.

Alt, A., "Die Weisheit Salomos," *Theologische Literaturzeitung* 76 (1951), 139–44 = "Solomonic Wisdom," in J. Crenshaw, ed., *Studies in Ancient Israelite Wisdom* (New York: KTAV, 1976), 102–12.

Batten, L., "The Epilogue to the Book of Job," *ATR* 15 (1933), 125–8.

Bickerman, E., "Koheleth (Ecclesiastes) or The Philosophy of an Acquisitive Society," *Four Strange Books of the Bible* (New York: Schocken, 1967), 139–67.

Blenkinsopp, J., *Sage, Priest and Prophet: Religious and Intellectual Leadership in Ancient Israel* (Louisville: Westminster/John Knox Press, 1995).

Brown, W., *Character in Crisis: A Fresh Approach to the Wisdom Literature of the Old Testament* (Grand Rapids: Eerdmans, 1996).

Christianson, E., *A Time to Tell: Narrative Strategies in Ecclesiastes*, JSOTSup 280 (Sheffield: Sheffield Academic Press, 1998).

Clements, R., *Wisdom in Theology* (Carlisle: Paternoster Press, 1992).

Clines, D., *Job 1–20*, Word Biblical Commentary 17 (Waco, TX: Word Books, 1989).

Collins, J., *Jewish Wisdom in the Hellenistic Age*, Old Testament Library (Louisville, KY: Westminster/John Knox Press, 1997).

Day, J., "How Could Job Be an Edomite?" in W. Beuken, ed., *The Book of Job* (Leuven: Leuven University Press, 1994), 392–9.

Dell, K. J., *The Book of Job as Sceptical Literature*, BZAW 197 (Berlin: Walter de Gruyter, 1991.

——, "The King in the Wisdom Literature," in J. Day, ed., *King and Messiah in Israel and the Ancient Near East*, JSOTS 270 (Sheffield: Sheffield Academic Press, 1998), 163–86.

Doll, P., *Menschenschöpfung und Weltschöpfung in der alttestamentlichen Weisheit*, SBS 117 (Stuttgart: Katholisches Bibelwork, 1985).

Fontaine, C., "The Sage in Family and Tribe," in J. Gammie and L. Perdue, eds., *The Sage in Israel and the Ancient Near East* (Winona Lake, IN: Eisenbrauns, 1990), 155–64.

——, *Traditional Sayings in the Old Testament* (Sheffield: Almond Press, 1982).

Forman, C., "The Pessimism of Ecclesiastes," *JSS* 3 (1958), 336–43.

——, "Koheleth's Use of Genesis," *JSS* 5 (1960), 256–65.

Fox, M., *Qoheleth and His Contradictions*, JSOTS 18 (Sheffield: Almond Press, 1989).

——, "Frame Narrative and Composition in the Book of Quoleth," *HUCA* 48 (1977), 83–106.

Fredericks, D., *Coping with Transience: Ecclesiastes on Brevity in Life* (Sheffield: JSOT, 1993).

Gammie, J., "Stoicism and Anti-Stoicism in Qoheleth," *HAR* 9 (1985), 169–87.

Gammiè, J. and L. Perdue, eds., *The Sage in Israel and the Ancient Near East* (Winona Lake, IN: Eisenbrauns, 1990).

Gordis, R., "Quotations in Wisdom Literature," *JQR* 30 (1939–40), 123–47; reprinted in J. L. Crenshaw, ed., *Studies in Ancient Israelite Wisdom* (New York: KTAV, 1976), 220–44.

——, "Elihu the Intruder: A Study of the Authenticity of Job (Chapters 32–33)," in A. Altman, ed., *Biblical and Other Studies* (Cambridge, MA: Harvard University Press, 1963), 60–78.

Habel, N., *The Book of Job*, Old Testament Library (London: SCM Press, 1985).

Heaton, E. W., *Solomon's New Men* (London: Pica Press, 1974).

Hermisson, H-J., "Observations on the Creation Theology in Wisdom," in J. Gammie, et al., eds., *Israelite Wisdom: Theological and Literary Essays in Honor of Samuel Terrien* (Missoula: Scholars Press, 1978), 43–57.

Kugel, J., "Qohelet and Money," *CBQ* 51 (1989), 32–49.

Lang, B., *Frau Weisheit, Deutung einer biblischen Gestalt* (Düsseldorf: Patmos-Verlag, 1975).

Lemaire, A., *Les écoles et la formation de la Bible dans l'ancien Israël*, OBO 39 (Göttingen: Vandenhoeck & Ruprecht, 1981).

Loader, J., *Polar Structures in the Book of Qoheleth*, BZAW 152 (Berlin and New York: Walter de Gruyter, 1979).

McCane, W., *Proverbs. A New Approach*, Old Testament Library (London: SCM Press, 1970).

Morgan, D., *Wisdom in the Old Testament Traditions* (Atlanta: John Knox Press, 1981).

Murphy, R., "Wisdom – Theses and Hypotheses," in J. Gammie, et al., eds., *Israelite Wisdom: Theological and Literary Essays in Honor of Samuel Terrien* (Missoula: Scholars Press, 1978), 35–42.

——, "The Sage in Ecclesiastes and Qoheleth the Sage," in J. Gammie and L. Perdue, eds., *The Sage in Israel and the Ancient Near East* (Winona Lake, IN: Eisenbrauns, 1990), 263–71.

Oliver, J., "Schools and Wisdom Literature," *JNSL* 4 (1975), 49–60.

Perdue, L., *Wisdom and Creation: The Theology of Wisdom Literature* (Nashville: Abingdon Press, 1994).

——, *Wisdom and Cult*, SBLDS 30 (Missoula, MT: Scholars Press, 1977).

Priest, J. F., "Humanism, Skepticism, and Pessimism in Israel," *JAAR* 36 (1968), 311–26.

Ranston, H., *Ecclesiastes and Early Greek Wisdom Literature* (London: Epworth Press, 1925).

Schmid, H., *Wesen und Geschichte der Weisheit*, BZAW 101 (Berlin: Töpelmann, 1966).

Scott, R., "Solomon and the Beginnings of Wisdom in Israel," *SVT* 3 (Leiden: E. J. Brill, 1955), 262–79.

Seow, C., *Ecclesiastes* (New York: Doubleday, 1997).

Sheppard, G., "The Epilogue to Qohelet as Theological Commentary," *CBQ* 39 (1977), 182–9.

von Rad, G., *Wisdom in Israel* (London: SCM Press, 1972).

——, *Old Testament Theology*, vol. 1 (Edinburgh: Oliver and Boyd, 1975).

Weeks, S., *Early Israelite Wisdom* (Oxford: Oxford University Press, 1994).

Weinfeld, M., *Deuteronomy and the Deuteronomic School* (Oxford: Oxford University Press, 1972).

Westermann, C., *Roots of Wisdom* (Edinburgh: T & T Clark, 1995).

Whedbee, J., "The Comedy of Job," in R. Polzin and D. Robertson, eds., *Studies in the Book of Job*, Semeia 7 (Missoula: Scholars Press, 1977), 1–39.

Whybray, R. N., *Wealth and Poverty in the Book of Proverbs* (Sheffield: *JSOT* Press, 1990).

——, "Qoheleth, Preacher of Joy?" *JSOT* 23 (1982), 87–98.

——, *Proverbs*, New Century Bible Commentary (London: Marshall Pickering, 1994).

——, *The Intellectual Tradition in the Old Testament*, BZAW 135 (Berlin: Walter de Gruyter, 1974).

Zimmerli, W., "The Place and Limit of Wisdom in the Framework of Old Testament Theology," *SJT* 17 (1964), 146–58; reprinted in J. L. Crenshaw, ed., *Studies in Ancient Israelite Wisdom* (New York: KTAV, 1976), 314–26.

Zuckerman, B., *Job the Silent: A Study of Historical Counterpoint* (Oxford: Oxford University Press, 1991).

CHAPTER 26
Apocalyptic Literature

John J. Collins

A Brief Description of Apocalyptic Literature

Apocalyptic literature takes its name from the Apocalypse, or Book of Revelation, the last book of the New Testament. The word means simply revelation, but it has come to be used for a specific kind of revelation, which is concerned either with heavenly mysteries or with eschatological events. It is closely related to other kinds of revelatory literature, especially prophecy, and indeed the Book of Revelation refers to "the words of the prophecy of this book" (Rev 22:10, 18). Apocalyptic literature is often regarded as a transformation of biblical prophecy, but it emerged as a genre in its own right in the Hellenistic period, some three centuries before the Book of Revelation was written. It is represented in the Hebrew Bible only by the Book of Daniel, but there was a flourishing Jewish apocalyptic literature that was not included in the canon. Much of this literature purported to describe revelations received by the ante-diluvian patriarch Enoch, but there were also apocalypses in the names of other ancient worthies, such as Abraham, Ezra and Baruch.

In contrast to the biblical prophets, the apocalyptic writers do not speak directly in the name of the Lord. In all the Jewish apocalypses, the author's identity is concealed and the revelation is ascribed to an ancient figure such as Enoch or Daniel. (The Christian Book of Revelation abandons this convention, but later Christian apocalypses revert to it.) Moreover, the revelation is typically given indirectly. Daniel, for example, has visions that are expressed in dream-like images, and have to be interpreted for him by an angel. A different kind of revelation is found in the early Enoch literature, where the visionary is taken up to heaven and given a guided tour. The content of the revelation contains much less direct exhortation than is usual in biblical prophecy. Instead we typically find descriptive narratives. One kind of apocalypse, typified by Daniel, presents an extensive overview of history, which is often divided into periods (four kingdoms, seventy weeks of years, etc.). This overview is in the form of a prophecy, given in the time of the Babylonian exile in the case of Daniel, and before the Flood in the case of Enoch. In fact, however, most of these prophecies are written after the fact, except for the final, eschatological events that they predict. So Daniel is able to give a detailed account of Hellenistic history down to the time of the Maccabean revolt, but concludes with an erroneous prediction of the death of Antiochus Epiphanes and the resurrection of the dead. Another kind of apocalypse, represented by the Book of the Watchers in 1 Enoch 1–36, has a spatial rather than a temporal focus. Enoch is taken on a tour of the ends of the earth and shown such places as the abodes of the dead and the scene of the future judgment. All apocalypses, however, include a final judgment of the world by God. This motif may be viewed as a development of the prophetic expectation of a "Day of the Lord." The apocalyptic judgment, however, differs from that of the prophets by including a judgment of the dead, resulting in eternal reward or punishment for individuals. The first such judgment scene in the Hebrew Bible is found in Daniel 12, although the language of resurrection is used metaphorically in several prophetic texts, such as Ezekiel 37 and Isa 26:19.

The genre apocalypse is constituted by the combination of mediated revelation (symbolic vision or otherworldly journey) and eschatological content, including the judgment of the dead (Collins, 1979). By this criterion it is possible to identify a corpus of Jewish apocalypses. Daniel, and the cluster of writings contained in 1 Enoch, date from the 2nd century BCE (except for the Similitudes of Enoch, 1 Enoch 37–71, which probably date from the first century CE). Another cluster of apocalypses (4 Ezra, 2 and 3 Baruch, Apocalypse of Abraham) can be dated around the end of the 1st century CE. There are also some fragmentary apocalypses in the Dead Sea Scrolls which come from the intervening period. But apocalyptic literature is not only a literary genre. It also embodies a worldview that was novel in the context of ancient Judaism (Collins, 1998a). This worldview was marked by a lively belief in the role of supernatural powers in shaping human destiny, and in reward or punishment for individuals after death. This worldview could also find expression in works that were not formally revelations. So, for example, the Instruction on the Two Spirits in the Community Rule from Qumran sees humanity shaped by the conflict between Light and Darkness, with eternal reward or punishment depending on the lot to which one belongs. The Qumran War Scroll describes the final conflict between those forces, on both the human and the superhuman level. Apocalypticism, as a worldview, was much more widespread than the literary genre apocalypse. It influenced the world of the early Christians to a far greater extent than might be inferred from the Book of Revelation, which is the only formal apocalypse in the New Testament.

The origins of this genre remain a matter of dispute (Hellholm, 1983; Collins, 1998b). Apocalypses such as Daniel and Revelation draw extensively on Ancient Near Eastern myths. These myths typically dealt with the beginnings rather than the end of history, but apocalyptic literature typically imagines the end in the likeness of the beginning. (Hence the well-known German formulation:

Endzeit gleicht Urzeit, the end-time is like the primeval time). The projection of creation motifs into the future can be found already in the Hebrew prophets, especially in the post-exilic books. After the collapse of the kingdoms of Israel and Judah, some prophets looked for a new creation (Isa 65:17) in which God would again defeat the sea-monster as in the old creation myths (Isa 27:1). There is a clear line of continuity from post-exilic prophecy to the Book of Daniel, which again evokes the old creation myths to describe a crisis in history (Daniel 7). The device of an angelic interpreter of symbolic visions is found already in the Book of Zechariah, and the heavenly tour is foreshadowed in Ezekiel's vision of the new Jerusalem (Ezekiel 40–48). Yet it is likely that other influences were also at work. Persian religion, Zoroastrianism, had its own native tradition of apocalypticism, and provides close parallels both to the Danielic type of symbolic vision (in the Bahman Yasht) and to otherworldly journeys (Arda Viraf). Some scholars argue that the genre originated in Persia (Cohn), and was appropriated by the Jews after the Babylonian exile. The Persian apocalyptic literature, however, is preserved in texts from the early Middle Ages, and it is difficult to determine how far it represents ideas that were current in the Achaemenid period. The motif of the heavenly journey was widespread in the Hellenistic world. Some of the later Jewish and Christian apocalypses were clearly influenced by motifs from this broader literature.

From a sociological point of view, apocalyptic literature is often viewed as crisis literature. It is certainly true that major outpourings of this literature are associated with the great crises of Jewish history, such as the Maccabean revolt and the destruction of Jerusalem by the Romans. (In the earlier case of the Babylonian literature we may speak of proto-apocalyptic motifs, in the prophecies of Ezekiel and Isaiah 56–66 and 24–27.) In these crises, visionaries were moved to dream of salvation beyond this world, in a realm no longer subject to the ravages of history. Yet it would be too simple to view apocalyptic literature only as a response to crises. The literature was taken up into the tradition, and was still read and studied when the crises had passed. Major elements of apocalyptic tradition, such as the belief in judgment after death, became standard in Judaism, and had a profound influence on the shape of Christian belief. While the Jewish apocalyptic literature receded into the background after the early 2nd century CE, perhaps because of disillusionment in the wake of the great revolts, Christian apocalyptic literature continued to flourish down through the Middle Ages (McGinn, 1998).

Modern Critiques of Apocalypticism

Some thirty years ago, the German Old Testament scholar Klaus Koch published a slim monograph with the title *Ratlos vor der Apokalyptik*. The book appeared in English a couple of years later, but with a significantly different title: *The Rediscovery of Apocalyptic*. The translator, or more likely the publisher, believed in positive thinking. The Rediscovery of something sounds like good news. But Koch's original title had a polemical edge. Modern scholarship, he suggested, and more generally the so-called mainline churches, were "clueless" as to what to do with a prominent part of the biblical heritage. He spoke of "Apocalyptic" as a disquieting motif, and documented at some length "the agonized attempt to save Jesus from Apocalyptic." Much ink has been spilled on the subject of apocalypticism in the intervening decades, and I would like to think that we have arrived at a much clearer understanding of the phenomenon. But the embarrassment indicated by Koch's title persists, and one need only conjure up the names of Robert Funk or Dominic Crossan to see that "the agonized attempt to save Jesus from apocalyptic" continues apace. Is that embarrassment justified? or is apocalypticism a valuable component of the biblical heritage?

The Causes of Embarrassment

First it may be well to consider the charges against the defendant. To a great degree liberal suspicion of the phenomenon is related to the popularity of apocalyptic texts in fundamentalist and very conservative circles. This is an issue that lies outside the competence of the biblical scholar as such, and I will touch on it only incidentally. Suffice it to say that the use that some people make of a body of literature does not necessarily exhaust its potential or value. But the charges are also rooted in perceptions of the literature itself. Four kinds of criticism of apocalyptic literature come to mind.

(1)   The books of Daniel and Revelation are somewhat exceptional in the biblical canon. Their closest analogues are to be found in the Pseudepigraphic literature of ancient Judaism and early Christianity, literature that is unfamiliar not only to the average layperson but also to many biblical scholars. The introductory essay in one recent collection of essays on "Apocalyptic and the New Testament" dismisses this extra-canonical literature as "abstruse and fantastic" (Sturm, 1989, p. 37). Even the canonical apocalypses are sometimes characterized as the products of what the late John A. T. Robinson called "a perfervid imagination."

(2)   Despite this recognition of the exuberance of apocalyptic symbolism, many people still think that it is supposed to be understood in a highly literalistic way – as interpreted, for example, by Hal Lindsey in *The Late Great Planet Earth*. The late Norman Perrin, in his presidential address to the Society of Biblical Literature in 1973, claimed that apocalyptic symbols were *steno-symbols*, that stood in a one-to-one relationship with their referents (Perrin, 1974). He buttressed this claim by referring to the interpretations given within some apocalyptic visions such as Daniel 7, where we are told that the four beasts from the sea represent four kings. Such interpretations were taken to reflect a deficient literary imagination.

(3)   Very often, apocalypticism is equated with an obsession about predicting the future, especially the end of the world. The books of Daniel and Revelation have indeed been used for this purpose throughout the history of Christianity (and in the case of Daniel, also of Judaism). The Millerite movement in 19th century America is perhaps the most prominent example of this kind of thinking (Boyer, 1992). Such predictions have been made repeatedly since antiquity, and have always proved unfounded. Consequently apocalypticism is viewed as a source of illusion and false hope, and there is reason to believe that some people in antiquity, such as the majority of the rabbinic sages, already saw it in this light.

(4)   Finally, perhaps the most weighty criticism of apocalyptic literature is that it exhibits and fosters a strong moral dualism. The world is divided between sons of light and sons of darkness. The opponents of the good are sons of Belial or Satan. This kind of thinking shows little appreciation for the shades of human behavior, and is rightly seen as simplistic. It encourages self-righteousness on the part of those who belong to the sons of light. Since apocalypses typically include judgment scenes, where the wicked are destroyed, often in a violent manner, there is also the fear that these texts may encourage violence by their readers, even if they do not explicitly condone it.

These criticisms of apocalyptic literature are not without foundation. This is indeed difficult and problematic literature. If we read the ancient texts in context, however, it is possible to arrive at a much more sympathetic assessment. This assessment will not amount to a blanket endorsement of apocalyptic values, but it will suggest that there is also much that is positive in the legacy of apocalypticism.

Apocalyptic Symbolism

First, the nature of the symbolism. Daniel's great vision of the beasts from the sea is introduced as a dream, visions in his head as he lay on his bed. We do not know whether any of the apocalyptic revelations that have come down to us actually originated in dreams. They are literary compositions, and the dreams are at least re-told and consciously shaped. Even if the dream is a literary construct, however, it governs the nature of the symbolism. Dreams are not coherent logical treatises. They are made up of scenes that may be quite disjointed and where meanings are displaced, and one thing may stand for another. We do not need to be psychiatrists to decipher these dreams, but we do need to know something about Ancient Near Eastern mythology. Anyone who knows the role of Sea in the Ugaritic myths of the second millennium, or indeed has paid attention to biblical allusions to "mighty waters" or "the dragon that is in the sea" (Isa 27:1) in the Hebrew Bible, will recognize an allusion here (Day, 1985). Equally, the "one like a son of man" riding on the clouds of heaven and the white-headed deity before whom he appears, recall the figures of Baal and El in the Ugaritic myths (Collins, 1993, pp. 286–94). Daniel's vision, in short, is not just a nightmare about strange animals. It is an evocation of an ancient myth that suggests that the forces of life and vitality ultimately triumph over those of chaos and disorder. Equally the great dragon that is cast down to earth in the Book of Revelation does not spring without precedent from the brain of John of Patmos, perfervid or otherwise. Rather it adapts imagery that had circulated for millennia in the combat myths in which Ancient Near Eastern religions had expressed some of their fundamental convictions about the world (Yarbro Collins, 1976). In short, to understand this literature at all one must know something of the traditions to which they allude, and while many of these traditions can be found in the Bible itself, some are drawn from the surrounding cultures of the Ancient Near East and Hellenistic world. Even when we are armed with this knowledge, however, we should not expect the apocalypses to take the form of rational discourses. These are works of imagination, highly symbolic and imagistic. They function, in the words of Clifford Geertz's famous definition of religion, to establish and shape the moods and motivations of the reader. One of the problems in the modern fundamentalist use of apocalyptic literature is that it lacks this contextual knowledge and this results in a flat literalistic interpretation, which is an impoverished view of the literature.

In view of the richly allusive character of apocalyptic visions, the argument that they are intended to be read as "steno-symbols," in Perrin's phrase, is clearly inadequate. It is true that the angel tells Daniel that the four great beasts are four kings that arise on the earth, but that interpretation does not begin to do justice to the vision. Even someone who fails to recognize the mythic allusions in the scene of beasts rising from the sea cannot fail to appreciate that the scene conveys a sense of turbulence and threat that is completely lacking in the interpretation. Moreover, the angel refrained from identifying the beasts specifically. Modern scholars identify them as Babylon, Media, Persia, and Greece, but in antiquity the fourth beast was usually identified as Rome. Later Christians would take it as Muslim Turks. In fact, it is the genius of apocalyptic symbols, like those of much prophetic literature, that they can be reinterpreted endlessly in the light of new circumstances. The fourth beast can be Hitler or Soviet Russia (Reagan's "evil empire"), or Saddam Hussein, or whoever is perceived as the villain of the hour. So far from being steno-symbols, restricted to a single referent, these symbols are essentially multivalent. The elusiveness of these symbols was recognized in antiquity. In a famous passage in 4 Ezra, written at the end of the 1st century CE, Ezra sees an eagle coming up from the sea and is told: "The eagle that you saw coming up from the sea is the fourth kingdom that appeared in a vision to your brother Daniel. But it was not explained to him as I now explain it to you" (4 Ezra 12:11–12). Even symbols whose meaning seems to be quite clear, like the whore of Babylon in Revelation, admit of reinterpretation. Because the referents are never identified explicitly in the texts, there is always what Paul Ricoeur has called "a surplus of meaning" (Ricoeur, 1969). The symbol is never exhausted by any one referent.

There is little substance then to the charge that ancient apocalypses show a defective literary imagination. Of course the literary quality of the apocalypses is uneven, but the best exemplars of the genre, such as Daniel, Revelation, or 4 Ezra, are works of considerable power. A significant part of their legacy is that they have furnished Jewish and Christian imaginations with symbols and images of exceptional evocative power, that have been rediscovered and re-employed through the centuries.

Apocalyptic Predictions

There is somewhat more substance to the charge that apocalypses inspire false hopes and lead to disillusionment. Attempts to predict specific events, or set a date for a definitive end, however, are remarkably rare. Daniel is the most notable exception in this regard. In Daniel 9, Jeremiah's prophecy that Jerusalem would be desolate for seventy years is reinterpreted to mean that the desolation would last seventy weeks of years, or 490 years. This passage was repeatedly taken as a key to the course of history, down into the Middle Ages. In its original context it pointed to a clearly specified time of fulfillment, three and a half years (half a week) after the disruption of the Jerusalem cult. But the numbers lent themselves easily to reinterpretation. After all, if seventy years could mean seventy weeks of years, why should the latter number too not have a symbolic meaning?

The most specific prediction of a date in all of ancient Jewish or Christian apocalyptic literature is found at the end of the Book of Daniel. There we are told: "From the time that the regular burnt offering is taken away and the abomination that desolates is set up, there shall be one thousand two hundred and ninety days. Happy are those who persevere and attain the thousand three hundred thirty five days." Two things about these statements are remarkable. First, we are given two different numbers of days, and second, we are not told what should happen at the end of them. Each of the numbers is a little more than three and a half years, the duration predicted at other points in the Book of Daniel. A slightly shorter figure was given in chapter 8, two thousand three hundred evenings and mornings, or 1,150 days. I think the conclusion is inescapable that attempts to specify the number of days were made when the three and a half years were thought to have expired. When the first number of days passed, the calculation was revised. This kind of recalculation is well known in the history of millennial movements. It was documented famously by Leon Festinger in his book *When Prophecy Fails* (Festinger et al., 1956). What is remarkable in the case of Daniel is that the outdated predictions were allowed to stand in the text. If three different numbers of days are given, too much weight cannot be placed on the literal accuracy of any one of them.

The first number of days in Daniel 8 is clearly related to the defilement of the Jerusalem temple: "For two thousand three hundred evenings and mornings; then the sanctuary shall be restored to its rightful state." According to 1

Maccabees the temple was restored exactly three years after it was desecrated (1 Macc 1:54; 4:54). At least the later predictions in Daniel must have been made after this had happened. At some point, the author or authors of Daniel no longer regarded the restoration of the temple as the "end" for which they looked, or at least they did not regard the Maccabean restoration as such a fulfillment. A clue to their understanding may be found in the last verse of the book where Daniel is told "go your way and rest; you shall rise for your reward at the end of days." The end was now conceived as the time of the resurrection, or what we might call the end of the world as we know it. But if this was the end in view, even the latest prediction in Daniel went unfulfilled, or at least has gone unfulfilled until now.

Daniel, then, would seem to be a paradigm case of the unreliability of apocalyptic predictions. Nonetheless the book was accepted as canonical scripture within a generation. Two hundred and fifty years later Josephus would say that Daniel was the greatest of the prophets, because he not only predicted what would happen, but said when it would happen. Josephus apparently failed to notice that Daniel's predictions had failed. We can only conclude that Daniel benefitted from the same kind of hermeneutic that he had applied to Jeremiah's prophecy of seventy years of desolation. The specific unambiguous numbers were treated as mysterious ciphers, just as surely as the beasts from the sea.

I do not deny that the author of Daniel tried to predict that something would happen on a specific date. There may be one or two other cases of such predictions in Jewish antiquity, but not many. (The Qumran sect seems to have expected an "end" forty years after the death of the Teacher.) But the failure of the calculation was not thought to invalidate the prediction as a whole. There was something else at issue in Daniel's prediction of the "end."

The Book of Daniel is the clearest case we have of an apocalypse written in the throes of persecution. Hence the urgency of the question, how long will these things be? People wanted to know how long their sufferings would last. But all the apocalypses that have come down to us envision a crisis of some sort. In the earliest Jewish apocalypse in the Book of Enoch, the crisis is a cultural one. The world was changed by the new mores of the Hellenistic age. The apocalypses of 4 Ezra and 2 Baruch look back on the crisis of the destruction of Jerusalem and its temple. There is no good evidence that the Book of Revelation was written in a time of persecution, but it nonetheless paints a picture of crisis. There was a perceived crisis, because the author regarded the pretensions of Rome to universal dominion as intolerable. All of these apocalypses portray their crises in cosmic terms. Beasts have arisen from the sea and threaten the order of creation. The dragon has been cast down from heaven and is loosing its fury on earth. But what is crucial to all of them is the sense of an ending, the assurance that closure is at hand. That sense of resolution is far more important than any specific date. Consequently, Josephus and indeed all of Jewish and Christian tradition could overlook the failure of Daniel's prediction in its original context. What mattered was the belief that sooner or later justice would be done. That belief does not admit of verification, short of eschatological verification at the end of history or in the hereafter, but it is fundamental to both Christianity and Judaism. Those who hold to that general faith should not be too quick to dismiss its concrete expression in the apocalyptic literature.

Moral Dualism

The idea of a final judgment, however, brings to the fore the problem of moral dualism, which touches, in my view, the most problematic aspect of apocalyptic literature. Apocalyptic literature typically divides the world into good and evil – sons of light and sons of darkness in the terminology of the Dead Sea Scrolls. The dualism admits of some modification. The Scrolls allow that people may have mixed natures, some parts light and some parts darkness. But in the end there is a clean separation. In Daniel some people rise to eternal life and some to shame and everlasting contempt. The Book of Revelation envisions the slaughter of all who follow the Beast. There is little appreciation for shades of gray. John of Patmos writes to the angel of the church in Laodicea: "I wish that you were either cold or hot. So because you are lukewarm and neither cold nor hot, I am about to spit you out of my mouth" (Rev 3:15–16).

The problem with this kind of mentality is shown by the one exceptional apocalyptic text that proves the rule. In the Testament of Abraham, the patriarch asks to see the whole inhabited world before he dies, and so he is taken on a chariot ride by the Archangel Michael (chapter 10). But the righteous Abraham is filled with indignation whenever he sees people sinning. So, for example, when he sees "a man and a woman engaging in sexual immorality with each other" he prays that the earth open and swallow them. And because of the efficacy of his prayer, the earth splits in two and swallows them up. After a few such incidents, however, a voice speaks from heaven to the Archangel: "Command the chariot to stop and turn Abraham away, lest he should see the entire inhabited world. For if he were to see all those who pass their lives in sin, he would destroy everything that exists. For behold, Abraham has not sinned and he has no mercy on sinners. But I made the world, and I do not want to destroy any one of them."

The Testament of Abraham has the form of an apocalypse, at least in part, but it is really a parody of the genre. The heroes of Daniel and Revelation may not be quite as sinless as Abraham, but they are unequivocally righteous, and their enemies are unequivocally wicked. Such a view of the world is surely too simplistic.

There are mitigating circumstances that may be adduced in defence of the moral dualism of the apocalypses. Most of them are written in times of crisis, that call for extreme rhetoric. Daniel depicts Antiochus Epiphanes, persecutor of the Jews, as a beast that should be thrown into the fire. Few people would object if the image were used with reference to Hitler. But while Hitler was not a unique phenomenon, he was certainly an extreme case. Crises are often in the eye of the beholder, and one person's beast may not seem so bad to someone else. Apocalyptic rhetoric should be used sparingly. The danger is that it may encourage polarization and discourage the kinds of compromises that make it possible for people to live together. It does not provide an ethic for all seasons, although it may be appropriate to some situations.

Positive Aspects of Apocalypticism

Thus far we have been considering the negative perceptions of apocalypticism that are often seen as a cause of embarrassment. Is there, however, a more positive case to be made? Are there ways in which apocalypticism has enriched the Jewish and Christian traditions?

The first and most obvious legacy of apocalypticism in this regard is the store of images that it has supplied to religious language. Think of the whore of Babylon or the four horsemen of the Apocalypse. As we have just noted, this imagery is a double-edged sword. It often lends itself to extreme and intolerant rhetoric. But its power and vividness cannot be denied. It is language that can shape one's view of the world for better or worse. Perhaps its greatest contribution in this regard is that it provides ways of naming evil that go beyond philosophical and theological abstractions and do justice to its concrete reality.

The Apocalyptic Worldview

Apocalyptic literature is a way of depicting reality. Unlike the prophetic or sapiential literature, it seldom resorts to direct exhortation. It is a visual medium, that constructs a view of the world. This view has implications for human behavior but these are not always spelled out. The goal of this literature is to transform the reader's understanding on a level prior to ethical decision making.

In speaking of an apocalyptic worldview I am obviously engaging in generalization, and abstracting from the specific nuances of individual apocalypses. The essential elements of this worldview are a lively belief in the role of supernatural forces in shaping human behavior and an equally lively belief in the certainty of a final definitive judgment which will not only set matters right on earth (if the earth is thought to endure) but also provide everlasting reward or punishment for individual behavior. Attempts to calculate the time of the "end" such as we have seen in Daniel are incidental to this worldview and not essential.

Does this worldview embody insights that we should accept as true or valid, that capture aspects of the human condition that are less adequately represented elsewhere? Three aspects of the literature seem to me to merit consideration in this regard: first, the sense that human life is subject to forces beyond human control; second, the sense of transience, that all human power is fading and that the world as we know it is passing away; and third the affirmation of transcendence, the faith that justice will prevail and that certain values demand our ultimate allegiance.

Apocalyptic determinism

First, the issue of supernatural forces. Apocalyptic literature is often viewed as deterministic and to some degree it is. History is typically measured out in set periods, and can supposedly be predicted centuries in advance. Many critics have drawn the inference that this determinism undermines human responsibility. Martin Buber wrote scathingly of the device of pseudepigraphy, which to his mind typified the difference between prophecy and "apocalyptic":

> The time the prophetic voice calls us to take part in is the time of the actual decision . . . In the world of the apocalyptic, this present historical-biographical hour hardly ever exists, precisely because a decision by men constituting a factor in the historical-suprahistorical decision is not in question here. The prophet addresses persons . . . to recognize their situation's demand for decision and to act accordingly. The apocalyptic writer has no audience turned towards him; he speaks into his notebook. (Buber, 1957, p. 200)

Again, with reference to 4 Ezra, Buber wrote, "Everything here is pre-determined, all human decisions are only sham struggles" (ibid., p. 201).

Buber, however, seems to have missed the point of most apocalyptic texts. In the book of Daniel, chapter 11, there is a long pseudo-prophecy of Hellenistic history, which serves to show that the persecution of the Jews by Antiochus Epiphanes falls in the penultimate stage of history, shortly before the final de-nouement. The point is not to relieve human beings of responsibility for decision making but to sharpen the context of the decision. In the time of persecution the "wise" are those who stand their ground, even though some of them lose their lives in the process. Their choice does not determine the course of events, but it directly determines their own destiny. (In some other apocalyptic texts, such as the Testament of Moses, human decisions seem to have a greater bearing on the course of events.) The message of Daniel is that one should act like these "wise" martyrs; the wisdom of their decision is confirmed by the resurrection in the following chapter. Moreover, apocalyptic visions usually presuppose a synergism between human and superhuman agents. In Daniel, the beasts that rise from the sea represent human kings or kingdoms, but they also suggest that they are embodiments of primordial chaos, the primeval sea that was sub-dued in the ancient myths. In Revelation 13, the dragon, or Satan, gives his power to the beast that rises from the sea and represents the Roman Empire. In each case the human ruler is still a responsible agent, but he is thought to tap into other greater forces as well. The same might be said of Hitler. In a modern secular analysis we might identify these forces as cultural, historical or economic, or even in some cases as the collective psychosis of a people. The idiom is different.

But the apocalyptic writers recognized that individuals who make decisions are often shaped by forces that they do not understand, and that those decisions often have effects that go far beyond anything that they intended. The same insight is expressed in a different way in Greek tragedy.

The sense of transience

A second insight of the apocalyptic literature that seems to me to have enduring significance is the sense that the form of this world is passing away. One popular motif that recurs in several apocalypses is the sequence of four kingdoms. Nebuchadrezzar may be the head of gold in Daniel's interpretation of the statue in the dream, but eventually he will crumble when the stone strikes the base of the statue. This motif was widespread in the ancient world. The Roman general Scipio is said to have wept at the destruction of Carthage, "realizing that all cities, nations and authorities must, like men, meet their doom, that this happened to Ilium, once a prosperous city, the empire of Assyria, Media and Persia, the greatest of their time, and to Macedonia itself, the brilliance of which was so recent, either deliberately or the verses escaping him, he said:

> A day will come when sacred Troy shall perish
> And Priam and his people shall be slain."

When Polybius asked him what he meant, he replied that when he reflected on the fate of all things human he also feared for Rome (Polybius 29.21; Cancik, 1998, pp. 108–9). Scipio, admittedly, was exceptional in following the idea through to its logical conclusion. More typically, the sequence is thought to culminate in an empire that is immune to decline. In the apocalyptic literature the sequence ends in a kingdom of God, which at least in some cases entails a Jewish kingdom on earth. There is nonetheless a powerful sense of the transience of all things human prior to the advent of that final kingdom.

A lasting kingdom

The hope for a lasting kingdom that will not pass away, whether in this world or in the next, is, however, an essential part of the apocalyptic worldview. This brings us to the question of transcendence, the belief in something over and above this transient world. In part this belief is born of the demand for justice, which so often is not seen to be done in this world. The belief in an ultimate judgment where things are set right provides the underpinning for decisions in the present. The Jewish martyrs in the Maccabean period could afford to risk or even lose their lives because they were convinced that they would shine like stars at the resurrection. In the Christian Book of Revelation those who had been beheaded for their testimony to Jesus are raised first to enjoy the thousand year reign before the general resurrection. "Over these the second death has no power" (Rev 20:6). It is the second death, and the prospect of the lake of fire, that is to be feared. The first death has lost its sting. Conversely, in the words of St. Paul, "if for this life only we have hoped . . . we are of all people most to be pitied" (1 Cor 15:19).

The need for de-mythologizing

The steadfastness of the martyrs, Jewish or Christian, in the face of death remains admirable two millennia later. But the faith on which that steadfastness was based presents more problems in the modern world. These problems have troubled Christians more than Jews, since in Judaism obedience to the law is central, rather than faith. Not surprisingly, the problems have surfaced especially in the study of the New Testament. Rudolf Bultmann saw the problem clearly:

> The whole conception of the world which is presupposed in the preaching of Jesus as in the New Testament generally is mythological; i.e. the conception of the world as being structured in three stories, heaven, earth and hell; the conception of the intervention of supernatural powers in the course of events; the conception of miracles, especially the conception of the intervention of supernatural powers in the inner life of the soul, the conception that men can be tempted and corrupted by the devil and possessed by evil spirits. This conception of the world we call mythological because it is different from the conception of the world which has been formed and developed by science since its inception in ancient Greece and which has been accepted by all modern men. (Bultmann, 1958, p. 15)

What Bultmann called the mythological worldview is essentially the worldview of apocalypticism. Bultmann fully accepted the arguments of Schweitzer and Weiss that Jesus was an apocalyptic prophet. He cannot then be accused of "the agonized attempt to save Jesus from apocalypticism." But he argued that the message of Jesus, and this would be true of all the apocalyptic writings, can only be appropriated in the modern world if it is de-mythologized. Bultmann did this by reinterpreting the text in terms of the existentialist philosophy of Heidegger. He did not simply discard the apocalyptic imagery, but understood it as the objectification of subjective feelings and convictions. The existentialist philosophy on which he relied now seems passé. In any case it was too individualistic to do justice to apocalyptic literature, with its central concerns for political and cosmic justice. But the process of de-mythologization, it seems to me, does not necessarily entail existentialist philosophy. Like most religious literature from antiquity, the apocalypses embody a view of the world based on assumptions about cosmology and history that are no longer tenable. Some kind of hermeneutic, or translation in light of modern assumptions, is necessary if these texts are to be meaningful at all.

One common way of dealing with this problem is to focus on the ethical aspects of the message and ignore the mythological wrappings in which it is presented. This strategy has been especially popular in connection with the figure of Jesus. Two hundred years ago, Thomas Jefferson offered a selection of those sayings of Jesus that he judged to be of enduring value. Much of the work associated with the Jesus Seminar seems to tend in the same direction, by attempting to distinguish between the enlightened and enduring teaching of Jesus and the apocalyptic trappings introduced, supposedly, by his followers. In some respects, such a distinction is easy enough to make. The Gospel of Matthew uses an apocalyptic judgment scene, where the Son of Man sits on his throne of glory, surrounded by his angels, to single out some essential features of Christian ethics. The judgment is based on what people have done to "the least of the brethern," on the grounds that it was done also to Christ. This ethical message is logically independent of the judgment scene. Similar teachings are presented elsewhere in the Gospels in other contexts. Much of them can already be found in the legal and sapiential traditions of Israel and the Ancient Near East. But many ethicists would dispute whether an ethical message can be separated so easily from the narrative and symbolic context in which it is embedded. Does not the judgment scene alter the message, if only by adding a sense of urgency that is not found in sapiential or legal texts? The meaning of the judgment scene in Matthew cannot be entirely reduced to the maxim that we should do unto others as we would have others do unto us. It also entails a claim that such an ethic will ultimately be vindicated by whatever means. It is, I think, impossible to argue that any apocalyptic judgment scene is a reliable prediction of the future in its details, if only because of the enormous variety we find in such scenes. But it is, I think, possible to de-mythologize such scenes so that they are still held to affirm some conviction about ultimate reality, even if it is only seen through a glass darkly and expressed in myths and symbols that attempt to articulate hopes and beliefs that lie beyond the clear grasp of knowledge.

Conclusion

The legacy of apocalypticism is a complex one. More than most of the biblical corpus, the apocalyptic texts present problems of intelligibility, because they are woven of allusions to ancient myths, some of which are only partly known to us. Sometimes they offer specific predictions that clearly failed. Even their more general hope for a comprehensive judgment and the coming of a just kingdom of God is by its nature unrealizable within the bounds of history as we know it. In every century since antiquity, such hopes have led some people astray. Worse, apocalypticism fosters a moral dualism that tends to demonize one's opponents and breed intolerance.

Nonetheless, this literature has also displayed extraordinary vitality through the ages. It has been largely immune to disconfirmation. Predicted "ends" have come and gone but apocalyptic hope persists. Persistence is no guarantee of truth, but it should give us pause if we are minded to relegate apocalypticism to a lunatic fringe of western society. Why is it that this literature continues to speak powerfully to some people? The reason, surely, is that it articulates in a powerful way a sense of dissatisfaction with this world and keeps alive the hope, however unrealistic it may seem, of a world free from sin and death. Inevitably, this literature appeals especially to those who are alienated in some way from the world around them, whether by poverty and oppression or by more subtle factors such as the sense that their values are not respected, even if they enjoy material comfort. The Heaven's Gate cult was no doubt an extreme example, but it was typically apocalyptic in some ways. One of the members explained the willingness of the group to end their lives in this world in the hope of being raised up to "the level higher than human", by the sad and simple statement: "there is nothing left for us here." Apocalypticism has always appealed most powerfully to such people, and much less so to "those who are at ease in Zion." But then the canon of scripture is not a single coherent theological document, but a collection of resources that may be helpful to different people on different occasions. As Qoheleth might have said, there is a time for rational wisdom and a time for apocalyptic fantasy. The canon would be poorer if it were limited to whatever is universally valid.

The example of Heaven's Gate, however, leads to a final reflection on the paradoxical nature of apocalyptic hope. As I have noted already, such hopes often seem immune to disconfirmation. Early Christians did not disband when the Second Coming was delayed indefinitely. Daniel was accepted as Scripture even though the end did not come within the three and a half years predicted. The Millerites survived their initial disappointment to give rise to a flourishing Adventist movement. In all these cases, apocalyptic hope continued to nourish people in the face of disappointment. Where these hopes lead to disaster is when people think that the time of fulfillment has come. The community at Qumran, which had long entertained dreams of a final battle of the Sons of Light against the Sons of Darkness, but preached pacifism until the "Day of Wrath" should come, seems to have perished at the hands of the Roman army. Rabbi Akiba prematurely hailed Bar Kochba as messiah, and was one of many who died at Roman hands in the following years. Numerous other examples can be cited, down to the native Americans at Wounded Knee and the recent suicides of the Heaven's Gate cult. Apocalyptic hopes can sustain life while they are anchored in the uncertain future. When they are thought to reflect present realities, they can be disastrous. Ultimately, such hopes must always be tempered by the realization that it is not given to mortals to know the day nor the hour.

Bibliography

Boyer, P., *When Time Shall Be No More: Prophecy Belief in Modern American Culture* (Cambridge, MA: Harvard University Press, 1992).

APOCALYPTIC LITERATURE   447

Boyer, P., "The Growth of Fundamentalist Apocalyptic in the United States," in S. Stein, ed., *The Encyclopedia of Apocalypticism, Vol. 3: Apocalypticism in the Modern Period and the Contemporary Age* (New York: Continuum, 1998), 140–78.

Buber, M., "Prophecy, Apocalyptic and the Historical Hour," in M. Friedman, trans. and ed., *Pointing the Way* (New York: Harper, 1957), 192–207.

Bultmann, R., *Jesus Christ and Mythology* (New York: Scribners, 1958).

Cancik, H., "The End of the World, of History and of the Individual in Greek and Roman Antiquity," in J. Collins, ed., *Encyclopedia of Apocalypticism* (New York: Continuum, 1998), 84–125.

Cohn, N., *Cosmos, Chaos and the World to Come* (New Haven: Yale, 1993).

Collins, J., ed., *Apocalypse: The Morphology of a Genre*, Semeia 14 (Missoula: Scholars Press, 1979).

——, *Daniel*, Hermeneia (Minneapolis: Fortress Press, 1993).

——, *The Apocalyptic Imagination*, revised edn. (Grand Rapids, MI: Eerdmans, 1998a).

——, ed., *The Encyclopedia of Apocalypticism, Vol. 1: The Origins of Apocalypticism in Judaism and Christianity* (New York: Continuum, 1998b).

Day, J., *God's Battle with the Dragon and the Sea* (Cambridge: Cambridge University Press, 1985).

Festinger, L., W. Riecken and S. Schachter, *When Prophecy Fails* (Minneapolis: University of Minnesota, 1956).

Hellholm, D., ed., *Apocalypticism in the Mediterranean World and the Near East* (Tübingen: Mohr, 1983).

Koch, K., *Ratlos vor der Apokalyptik* (Gütersloh: Mohn, 1970) = *The Rediscovery of Apocalyptic* (Naperville: Allenson, 1972).

Lindsey, H., *The Late Great Planet Earth* (New York: Bantam, 1973).

McGinn, B., ed., *The Encyclopedia of Apocalypticism, Vol. 3: Apocalypticism in Western History and Culture* (New York: Continuum, 1998).

Perrin, N., "Eschatology and Hermeneutics: Reflections on Method in the Interpretation of the New Testament," *Journal of Biblical Literature* 93 (1974), 3–14.

Ricoeur, P., *The Symbolism of Evil* (Boston: Beacon, 1969).

Sturm, R., "Defining the Word 'Apocalyptic': A Problem in Biblical Criticism," in J. Marcus and M. Soards, eds., *Apocalyptic and the New Testament* (Sheffield: JSOT, 1989), 17–48.

Yarbro Collins, A., *The Combat Myth in the Book of Revelation* (Missoula, MT: Scholar's Press, 1976).

Author Index

Scripture Index